# SPORT AND SOCIETY

*Series Editors*

Benjamin G. Rader
Randy Roberts

# Books in the Series Sport and Society

A Sporting Time: New York City and the Rise of Modern Athletics,
1820–70
*Melvin L. Adelman*

Sandlot Seasons: Sport in Black Pittsburgh
*Rob Ruck*

West Ham United: The Making of a Football Club
*Charles Korr*

Beyond the Ring: The Role of Boxing in American Society
*Jeffrey T. Sammons*

John L. Sullivan and His America
*Michael T. Isenberg*

*Reprint Editions*

The Nazi Olympics
*Richard D. Mandell*

# John L. Sullivan
## and
# His America

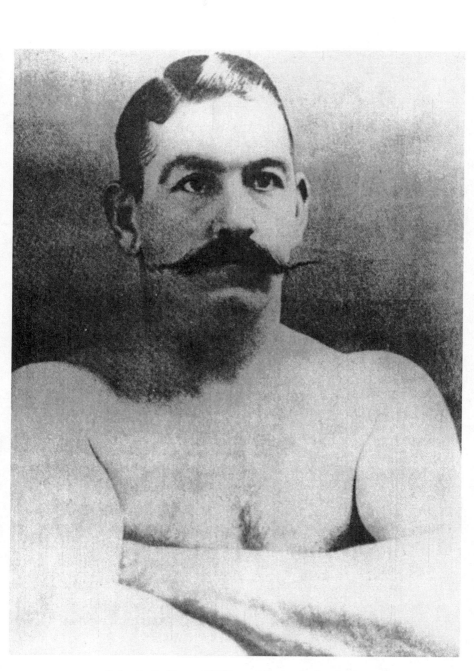

John L. Sullivan (William Schutte Collection)

# JOHN L. SULLIVAN
## AND
# HIS AMERICA

Michael T. Isenberg

UNIVERSITY OF ILLINOIS PRESS
Urbana and Chicago

Digitally reprinted from the first paperback printing

Illini Books edition, 1994
© 1988 by the Board of Trustees of the University of Illinois
Manufactured in the United States of America
2  3  4  5  C  P  5  4  3  2  1

*This book is printed on acid-free paper.*

Library of Congress Cataloging-in-Publication Data

Isenberg, Michael T.
 John L. Sullivan and His America

 (Sport and society)
 Bibliography: p.
 Includes index.
 ISBN 0-252-01381-6 (cl. : alk. paper). — ISBN 0-252-06434-8 (pb. :
alk. paper).
 1. Sullivan, John Lawrence, 1858–1918. 2. Boxers—United States—
Biography. 3. Boxing—United States—History. I. Title. II. Series.
GV1132.S95I84      1988          796.8'3'0924   [B]      87-16183

For my cousins,
as dear to me as brothers and sisters—

Janet Morgen Wettergren

Brian Harold Morgen

Glenda Meihak Somsen

Roberta Meihak Myers

Max Henry Meihak

# Contents

# List of Illustrations

# John L. Sullivan
## and
# His Times

# PROLOGUE

# Brawl on a Barge

May 1881: America was at peace, with the world and with itself. Sixteen years had passed since the Union began to heal at Appomattox. The nation's energies had turned inward, toward settling the West and peopling the rapidly expanding cities. By the census of 1880 New York had become the first American community to top one million. The typical American still lived in the countryside or in towns under twenty-five hundred, but the movement to the city was already clear and was accelerating.[1] So was the movement between cities. The leading literary figure of the day, Willam Dean Howells, had moved symbolically from Boston to Manhattan. "At the bottom of our wicked hearts we all like New York," he confessed to his friend Henry James.[2]

One colorful feature of this New York of 1881 was a social underclass, a collection of somewhat disparate groups whose activities were officially frowned on by the cultural elites, the "better sort." The underclass was bound together not so much by economic self-consciousness as by recreational activities. These groups provided outlets that, while clandestine, were much in demand. Prostitution, cheap saloons, gambling halls, and sleazy, smoke-filled sporting arenas abounded. These constituted "vice," absolutely necessary for any society, for only through these could "virtue" be determined.

The emerging mass culture tended to tie these two aspects of American life, the legitimate and the profane, more closely together. The profane might aspire to legitimacy or occasionally seek role models there, and legitimacy might occasionally need the delights sponsored by an officially outlawed activity. Thus a symbiotic relationship arose, made more concrete by communication and potential profit.

The underclass and other adherents of the sporting life had to snatch much of their recreation surreptitiously, outside the eyes of the law. Sometimes the law connived, sometimes it turned a blind eye, and sometimes it just did not know. Thus the thrill of the illicit often overlay the urge to enjoy a sporting contest and perhaps make a few wagers.

For those in the know on May 16, 1881, the news circulated swiftly. There was to be a prizefight, a boxing contest between two men for money, on which other money might be wagered. All this was illegal within the confines of New York and thus, for the sporting types, most desirable to attend. One of the participants was to be John Flood, a well-known bruiser from the New York streets.

# I

John Flood's lumpy ears bracketed a broad, square face surmounted by a pug nose. Born in New York in 1851 of Irish descent, he grew to just under six feet in height and 190 pounds. Flood had a local reputation as a fearsome brawler, or he never would have been matched that May evening. But he had never contested a real prizefight.[3]

Arrangements for Flood's match had been worked out in New York's most notorious night spot, Harry Hill's new dance house. Located on Houston Street a few doors west of Mulberry, Hill's establishment stood saucily in the shadow of police headquarters, marked by an enormous red and blue lantern at the front entrance. A private side door was provided for women, who, since they constituted the main attraction for male customers, were admitted free.

Harry Hill himself was a centerpiece of the city's sporting culture. Born about 1827, he had opened his business before the Civil War. A short, squat man with dark, wavy hair and saturnine countenance, he watched alertly over his trade with a shrewdness born of years of dealing with the urban underside of life. Of course he needed to "keep in touch" with the police and other municipal authorities, because he relied on the law in case of major trouble. Hill's proudest boast was that he kept a "respectable house." Some New Yorkers, particularly his business rivals, estimated his profits to be as high as fifty thousand dollars annually, in an age when a skilled artisan was lucky to take home two thousand. His new dance hall on Houston Street was expected to increase his take significantly.

All sorts of people frequented Harry Hill's. Prostitutes were found, of course; there was good trade to be had at Harry's, so long as you behaved. Some working women came, too, perhaps on the arm of a male friend, rarely in a group. All were handsomely dressed, for Hill's was not a "dive." Nevertheless, middle- and upper-class women would sooner have paraded down Broadway naked than have entered. As for the men, they constituted a perfect potpourri of city life: judges, lawyers, businessmen, bankers, army and navy officers, and newspaper editors rubbed shoulders with clerks, sailors, laborers, artisans, and even boys (you reached "drinking age" when you were tall enough to put your nickel on the bar). Most people, including the women, drank enormous quantities during the evening. The main idea was to carry on the age-old dance between the sexes. "The majority come here early in the evening alone, but few go away without company for the night."[4]

There was a darker side to Hill's, as well. A magnet for making and spending money, the place was an obvious target for robbers, pickpockets, and confidence men. Even the fair sex was involved; some women worked as decoys, and others ran confidence games with their pimps. Harry knew and liked some of these people; he would leave them alone as long as they behaved themselves, and he would even protect the intended victims if he felt they were too drunk to avoid disaster. But Hill and his bartenders could not control the drugging of drinks; occasionally a victim would be found in a nearby alley, roughed up and stripped of his valuables. And, perhaps, some of the nameless bodies found floating in the city harbor had begun their last night at Hill's.

John Flood may have worked as an enforcer around Harry Hill's; certainly he frequented the place and shared its delights with a wide variety of experienced pugilists, men such as Jem Mace, Joe Goss, and Joe Wormald. Not only the women and the drink drew the prizefighting crowd, however; Harry Hill was the premier prizefighting matchmaker in the city, probably in the East, and maybe nationwide. He was known to be scrupulously fair as a stakesholder and at times served as referee. Hill would travel anywhere, even abroad, to witness or officiate a fight between well-known antagonists. Matches like the one arranged for Flood were a common feature of the Houston Street dance house.

Flood was to face a twenty-two-year-old from Boston named Sullivan. The Bostonian had been to Hill's before and was well-known by the sporting crowd as an aspiring prizefighter. In November 1880 he appeared at a legal exhibition, or "benefit," for one Dooney Harris, sparring a few rounds with a man named Johnny Kenny in an improvised ring set up in the dance hall.[5] But no one knew what he could do in a real prizefight. Sullivan was rumored to be more than a bit of a braggart, and people observed that he did not come to Hill's for the male camaraderie alone. He obviously made friendships, or the Flood match would never have taken place. He knew Harry Hill, of course, probably knew Flood, and may already have met some of the bigger spenders on the New York scene, such as James Buchanan ("Diamond Jim") Brady, at twenty-five years old already gaining a reputation as a notorious profligate.[6]

The New York crowd learned a bit more about Sullivan in March 1881, when he visited the city a second time to receive a "testimonial benefit" at Hill's. There, on March 31, he suddenly offered fifty dollars to anyone in the room who could stay with him for four three-minute rounds. The amount was nothing to sneeze at in 1881; some families lived on as little as ten dollars a week. The offer was accepted by John McMahan, a boxer with political connections who fought under the name Steve Taylor and had once served as coroner of Jersey City, in addition to having a record as a spear-carrier in the now defunct organization of William Magear ("Boss") Tweed, Jr. Unlike Flood, who went by the colorful nickname of the Bull's Head Terror, Taylor was a veteran pugilist who had sparred with Joe Goss and helped train the present "American champion," Paddy Ryan. The small crowd at Hill's watched with growing interest as Sullivan, wearing padded gloves, forced Taylor to admit defeat after two rounds.[7] Sullivan generously gave the defeated boxer twenty-five dollars for his trouble.

The Taylor set-to was spontaneous; the police did not have an opportunity to intervene, but neither did the sporting crowd have time to assemble and place their bets. The Sullivan-Flood match would be different, a true prizefight. The men would fight with small gloves, under the London Prize Ring rules, which allowed some wrestling holds. Each round ended when one combatant went to one knee, and the contest lasted until one of the fighters could not come to "scratch," an arbitrary toe-to-toe line drawn in the center of the ring. Backers of the two men raised a purse of $1,000, easily half a year's wage for a laborer; the winner would get $750.

Sullivan prepared himself at Dan Sheehan's Sherman House in Natick, Massachusetts; Flood worked out at George Rooke's gym in New York. While the two men got ready, the New Yorker in charge of finding a suitable locale for the fight, William H. Borst, was having problems. The New York police already had the scent, and any spot in Manhattan that Borst might select would have the hounds as well as the hare present. Desperate, he arranged for a New York tug captain, John N. Starin, to tow a barge (the *Vanderbilt*) up the Hudson River along the west side of Manhattan and anchor it off the suburb of Yonkers. In this bizarre setting, afloat and hopefully beyond the clutches of the law, the fight would take place.[8]

The Bull's Head Terror, in spite of his inexperience and Sullivan's convincing victory over Taylor, had his supporters. His reputation as a brawler stemmed from a long career as a bullyboy in the Five Points area, located practically in the lap of City Hall. Five Points, called a "cesspool of crime" by one historian,[9] bred youth gangs, political bravos, and extortionists specializing in the pistol and the fist. The idealistic reformer Thomas Wentworth Higginson might be convinced that there was good in everyone, even the denizens of Five Points,[10] but he would have found few in New York of any social status to agree. Flood's backers hoped his undoubted size and strength would carry the day. Although he was not "the greatest heavyweight in Gotham at that time,"[11] he was considered by many to have the pluck to outlast his seemingly untested opponent. This view was prevalent; by the morning of May 16 the odds on the local favorite were 3 to 1.

## II

Sullivan and a small retinue arrived in the city around noon and at once boarded the barge at West Forty-third Street, there whiling away the time by playing cards until dusk. As darkness descended, boxing followers began to sneak aboard. They were carefully checked by Flood supporters at the gangway and paid the not inconsiderable sum of ten dollars apiece. At nine o'clock Captain Starin, with almost four hundred people in tow, nosed his tug into the turbid, oily Hudson. Within half an hour the entire *mise en scène* was anchored off Yonkers. Flaring, oil-soaked torches were lit to outline a "ring," their glare shielded from police boats by reflectors. In this eerie setting the two boxers stripped to the waist and, clad in ankle-length tights and leather shoes, prepared to fight.

News of the impending lawless act had indeed reached the authorities. Captain Killilea of the 22nd Precinct informed his superiors that a weird assemblage of sporting men and pugilists had left the West Forty-third Street pier and pushed slowly but steadily up the river, heavily laden with sandwiches and liquid refreshments. Inspector Thorne accordingly dispatched the Harbor Police and alerted the 30th, 31st, and 32nd precincts to be on the lookout for a suspicious barge.[12]

As the law's search proceeded, the crowd on the barge settled in to watch the fight, making their traditional last side bets on first blood and first knockdown. Paddy Ryan, in prominent attendance as champion, declared that he would not fight for less than five thousand dollars, implying that the present purse was chicken feed.[13] Each principal donned skintight leather coaching gloves, more to protect his own knuckles than the anatomy of his opponent. Thus stripped for action, each could take the measure of the other.

In the flickering torchlight, Flood saw a man weighing about 180 pounds and standing five feet eleven inches, in stature a slightly lighter replica of himself. Sullivan's close friends called him "John," although a few, striving to be familiar, knew him as "Jack"—a nickname he did not like. The Bostonian's hair was close-cropped, in the tradition of the London Prize Ring (long hair provided purchase for a throw-down hold). The most significant features of his face were jug ears, a sloping lantern jaw, and dark, beetling eyebrows. His eyes, even in the dim light, appeared a bright, staring black, concentrating totally on the task at hand. The crowd noted with approval the sloping shoulders, heavy forearms, and massive curled fists. The thickness of his trunk was matched by a sturdy pair of legs. The man from Boston had a "build," right enough, but could he stand before the Bull's Head Terror?

The stakesholder at these affairs occupied a position of honor, implying trust by both sides. Old Joe Elliot, for years the sporting editor of the *New York Herald*, was the chosen man, watching with one thousand dollars in cash in his pocket.[14] In Sullivan's corner were a handful of his Boston friends, led by Joe Goss and Billy Madden. Flood was seconded by Barney Aaron and Dooney Harris, the recipient of the November benefit. The odds favoring the Terror declined quickly as the crowd compared the physiques of the two men. The referee, Al Smith, a man well-known in local sporting circles for his straightforwardness, called the pair to scratch around ten o'clock. The spectators were restless but orderly and expectant as the pugilists faced each other at last.

Sullivan moved in with his right, and Flood responded by clinching. The New Yorker tried to get his opponent "in chancery" (a neckhold) but failed. The two sparred for a period until a sudden right sent Flood to the deck of the barge. The first round had taken three minutes. What followed was brutal, decisive, and, for Flood, total humiliation. Sullivan threw him in forty-five seconds to end the second round, knocked him into the thin strand of ropes connecting the torches with another right in the third, and threw him again in the fourth after Flood was late to scratch (thirty seconds was allowed), claiming a broken shoestring. Another fall ended the fifth, a knockdown the sixth, and a mutual fall the seventh, Sullivan ending up on top. Each of these "rounds" had been a matter of seconds, with Flood becoming so desperate that his legs windmilled wildly; he was even seen trying to bite his opponent.

By the start of the eighth round the Bull's Head Terror had to be partially coaxed to scratch by Aaron, Harris, and his desperate backers. He walked directly into yet another smashing right hand and fell senseless to the deck. Flood had to be carried to his corner, blood pouring from an ear and one side of his face badly swollen. His disgruntled followers offered the usual excuses: their man was not in trim, and his tactics of trying to clinch with a stronger fighter and move him against the ropes had been faulty. Once Flood had been revived, the victor promptly shook hands with the vanquished and, in the best tradition of the ring, started a subscription for his opponent with a small cash donation.[15]

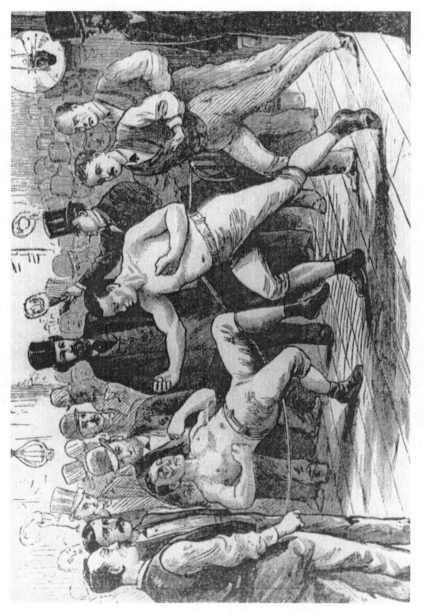

2. An artist's conception of the brawl on the barge (1881) (William Schutte Collection)

A *New York Herald* reporter on the barge was unimpressed. "Neither of them seemed to understand the first rudiments of self-defense. It was all pull and haul and hitting at close quarters." During the leisurely return trip to Forty-third Street (the Harbor Police still nowhere in sight), the spectators had the opportunity to discuss what they had just seen, while wolfing down the remaining sandwiches and liquor. The *Herald's* man was sure that "a more disgusted crowd never returned to New York,"[16] but not everyone on the barge agreed.

By the time the *Vanderbilt* docked in the wee hours of the morning, Sullivan's stock was rising. The *New York Clipper*, a sporting journal, had had its man on the barge, too, and he was impressed. Noting that Sullivan seemed "carefully prepared" by Billy Madden, he went on to describe the Bostonian as a "splendidly formed young fellow, with unusually fine shoulder development .... [He] is as fond of fighting as he is of the good things in life." The *Clipper's* somewhat inflated conclusion was that Sullivan had become the most promising boxer in America. Within two weeks the fighter was pictured in coat and tie in the widely-read *Clipper*, jutting jaw and jug ears subdivided by a small mustache, coal-black eyes staring straight at the camera.[17]

Flood, so far as is known, did not enter the prize ring again. As was the custom, he and Sullivan offered a sparring exhibition on June 13 at Clarendon Hall in New York. The exhibition was a device to gain money legally by attracting people who had heard of the illegal fight and wished to see the principals in action. Poor Flood, whose $250 had been split with several backers, was destitute. He was no longer the Bull's Head Terror, and his benefit was poorly attended; he and his conqueror sparred several desultory rounds. The only excitement of the evening was a brouhaha among the spectators over whether Sullivan was man enough to take on Paddy Ryan.[18]

Sullivan loudly and boisterously proclaimed his willingness to meet Ryan anywhere, fighting with gloves or bare fists, if the money was right. In the eyes of the cognoscenti, he was clearly the coming man. As for Paddy, the "champion," had he not been heard to say, that night on the barge, that "Sullivan is a clever young fellow?"[19]

## III

The muscular, glowering youngster who had made such an abrupt and dramatic entry on the New York sporting scene was, by state statute, municipal code, and popular opinion, an outlaw. Although he later paid a five-dollar fine for his role in the brawl on the barge, both the authorities and boxing men of all stripes knew that such wrist slaps were meaningless. Sullivan was simply the latest in a long line of prizefighters to dodge the law successfully. To most Americans, such open flouting of social and legal conventions could hardly be commendable. The social stigma against prizefighting ran broadly and deeply through American life. The critics, which is to say almost everyone in 1881, noted that most pugilists came from lower-class Irish backgrounds, were ill educated and worse mannered, and, after enjoying a brief moment of fistic publicity and notoriety, rapidly descended to the mire from which they had risen.

John Flood was indeed a typical Irish-American pugilist of the day, with a background involving bodyguard duty, getting out the vote in local elections, and dirty work in rent collecting and political gamesmanship. In short, he did not, could not make a living from prizefighting, nor could anyone else. The pug-dog face of this rugged bully from the notorious Five Points district seemed to suggest that he was little more than a simple-minded physical tool whose prime function was to entertain motley assemblages of sporting dandies, gamblers, lower-class ward heelers, and workingmen. Even the bizarre setting of the Sullivan-Flood fight was fully consonant with the tradition, almost dead by 1881, of two pugilists and their followers scurrying to a remote location at the last minute to conduct their business beyond the ken of the law.

America, when Sullivan and Flood fought, was not that far removed from a time when anti-Irish sentiment had fueled a major American political movement, the Know-Nothing party, in the 1850s. Throughout the urban Northeast, the Irish servant girl and the Irish navvy were already hardy stereotypes. Even though the American Irish were rising to positions of municipal political power, and would achieve it in Boston in the 1880s, their social burden, which included a particularly virulent strain of anti-Catholicism, remained heavy and enduring. As a group they remained largely stuck in the lower orders of society, doing the pick-and-shovel work that kept the urban world mushrooming. The avenues leading upward in politics, the church, and business were opening, to be sure—but slowly.

So here was Sullivan, a Catholic Irishman from an urban, working-class background, an outlaw in an outlaw sport. His name was known to only a few friends in Boston and those few members of the New York fight scene who frequented Harry Hill's or had paid their ten dollars to get on the barge. Practically everywhere in America, as its citizens looked forward, optimistically, to years of prosperity under their new president James A. Garfield, prizefighting was against the law, and prizefighters were considered the dregs of society.

A little more than a decade later this same Sullivan would fight indoors, in an arena fully illuminated with electricity, before a wildly screaming audience of ten thousand people. In attendance would be not only the familiar mixture of lower-class fight enthusiasts but also businessmen, professional people, and even "nice women." News of this contest, literally blow-by-blow, would be flashed by telegraph through an instantaneous web of communication to cities around the country, and within minutes broadsides would be pressed against windows of newspaper buildings so that eager crowds in the streets could be kept up to date on the fight's progress. The entire urban United States would be knit together by the tapping telegraph keys at ringside in New Orleans: Baltimore, Boston, Chicago; Cincinnati, Seattle, Minneapolis; New York, St. Louis, San Francisco—all, incidentally, cities in which Sullivan had by this time fought. Hundreds of thousands of dollars would change hands on the outcome. The purse itself would be twenty-five thousand dollars, winner take all, a sum an urban laborer would take at least twelve to fifteen years to accrue. And the name would be known nationwide: no longer John Sullivan of Boston, he had long since been instantly recognized as "John L."[20]

What had happened? Prizefighting certainly had not become socially acceptable; the backers of Jim Jeffries and Jack Johnson, working in a climate of intense racism, struggled to find a suitable fight location as late as 1910, and a particular odor of barbarism, violence, and corruption still clings to the sport today. Nor had the Catholic Irish suddenly transcended their social barriers and emerged as equal members of the American middle class; this process would take generations, perhaps culminating in the presidential victory of John F. Kennedy in 1960. No, the answers lie somewhere in what Sullivan did and what he symbolized for many Americans of his day.

For the young men in blue who had come home to their farms, towns, and cities in 1865, the traditional view of the heroic figure in American life was relatively fixed. The hero was known for deeds, not words, and those deeds were usually considered to be congruent with America's mission, as a beacon of democratic hope and purpose for humankind. Ur-figures, like Washington and Franklin, had a place in this pantheon. So, too, did the supposedly living symbols of the credo, such as Andrew Jackson. The Civil War had produced a multitude of new figures, led by the martyred Lincoln and, eventually, the regally noble Robert E. Lee. All of these individuals gained their fame through public lives connected with political or military leadership and achievement. Such was the traditional model.

But patterns of life for these veterans and their children were changing fundamentally. Immigration, industrialization, and urbanization were all accelerating. These interlinked processes ensured that the country would be in a state of flux and uncertainty about questions that had been of much less import to earlier generations, such as those concerning occupational status and mobility, economic success or failure, and choices concerning a "career" (in itself a novel idea in the

1880s). The later years of the nineteenth century, often seen as a placid, nostalgic template for the "good old days," were in fact a time of high social tension and conflict.

Against this backdrop John L. Sullivan emerged as the first significant mass cultural hero in American life. He was not merely a celebrity, a person known for being known. A celebrity he certainly was: his picture adorned countless barrooms from coast to coast, as did he himself with considerable frequency. His name was constantly before the public in newspapers and magazines, and even his handshake was famous. People would go to a theater simply to see him pose (his acting was another story). Sullivan was, like earlier heroic figures, famed for his deeds. But his deeds were controversial and conversational at the same time. People *talked about* John L. Sullivan in ways that they had not talked about, say, Lincoln.

No one would argue that Sullivan's fame, deserved or not, ranks him in the company of the Founding Fathers, Jackson, or the giants of the Civil War. But his America, the energetic, exuberant, enormously self-centered America of the late nineteenth century, was a place where organized recreation and sport made their first important impact and where sporting heroes became a prominent part of the emerging American mass culture. A changing world evoked unfamiliar models of heroism, achievement, and success.

In Sullivan many of the aspirations and fears of his time came to a sharp focus. Realistically, he was no more a "symbol for an age"[21] than Jackson had been, unless one wishes to consider a southern slave-holding aristocrat as the beau ideal of democracy. But Jackson represented the traditional American heroic model: a combination of democratic, military, political, and personal virtues. In contrast, it was a moot point for many Americans whether Sullivan and "his kind" had any virtue at all.

Borne on the active social currents of a volatile era in American history, Sullivan became a hero with two important differences. First, he deliberately sought to live his active adult life *in public*. As a public presence, he simply was unrivaled in his day. Second, since his flaws were at least as noteworthy as his achievements in the prize ring, Americans inevitably came to know him also as a drunkard, a wastrel, an adulterer, and a bully. The expanding media greedily consumed morsels of fact and fiction about him and regurgitated the resulting stew to a mass public increasingly accustomed to "news" about such figures. He moved in an environment of workingmen, gamblers, drunks, prostitutes, hustlers, and sporting types of all shades. These people formed an important part of the mosaic of Sullivan's America, one not usually discussed by historians concerned with immigrant groups such as the Irish, with the increasingly sharply drawn battle lines between capital and labor, or with the almost insoluble problems produced by the explosive growth of the cities.

But Sullivan's world included other figures as well. The brawny young man who had battered John Flood against the torchlit gloom of the Hudson River would come to the White House to shake the hand of one president and would routinely visit the home of another. He would appear before the Prince of Wales and receive a championship belt studded with valuable gems from adoring admirers. In the course of a lifetime he would earn from his various enterprises a sum probably in excess of one million dollars, a figure unheard of for one of his origins and occupation. And in the quiet twilight, after several bankruptcies, numerous public brawls, uncounted displays of drunkenness, and sexual peccadillos great and small, he would still be revered across the land as "heavyweight champion of the world." United in their penchant for following Sullivan would be not only the underside of society, not only the seamy and the profane. Sullivan's "fans" would include political leaders, middle-class professionals, literary figures, and even clergymen.

John L. Sullivan did not legitimize American boxing, any more than he legitimized the rise of the American Irish to positions of power and responsibility. For everyone who heralded the victorious Sullivan as a sign of Irish pride and social mobility, there was someone to vilify the drunken or brawling Sullivan as a clear indicator of barbarism. His sensational public career, coupled with the incredible excesses of his private life, does provide a fascinating window into America as it painfully emerged into the modern era. In the past lay the great cataclysm of Civil War. Ahead were promise and possibility. The newer forms that society was taking amid the bustle of industrial life were producing different values and different national standards. Not that older forms were now defunct; far from it. But with the increasingly money-oriented scramble for position and status and the rise of mass culture came public figures whom the generations of Washington, Jackson, and Lincoln could scarcely have imagined. Such was the emerging shape of the reconstituted Union, and such the pattern of Sullivan's America.

# PART I  IRISH AMERICAN

## CHAPTER ONE

# Heritage

## I

Irish immigration to the United States swelled to a flood in the middle of the nineteenth century. Unlike earlier English and German groups, which tended to migrate with both purpose and cohesion, the great new waves of Irish immigrants were simply fleeing, many with little plan or purpose beyond survival. Until about 1835 most of the American-bound Irish had come from the North, primarily Ulster and Tyrone, and most of these had been fairly well-to-do by Irish standards, chiefly farmers and out-of-work artisans. But now the poorest peasants were leaving southwestern Ireland, forced from their homes in Cork, Kerry, Galway, and Clare by fear and desperation, depending on someone else's generosity to get them, somehow, to a new land and a new start.[1] In 1847, for the first time, Irish arrivals topped 100,000, and they stayed above that level for eight years, peaking at 221,000 in 1851.

These dispossessed peasants of southwestern Ireland provided Boston's primary immigrant population at midcentury. Regardless of what they found in their new homes, their memories were clear about what they had left. In County Kerry two out of every three people lived in crude, single-room cabins. With luck they had a small plot of ground to cultivate, if the plentiful stones allowed.[2] Overdependence on one crop, the potato, had left them helpless against blight. Perhaps as much as half of Ireland's population of eight million in 1845 relied on the potato. The failure of the crop produced dire distress, followed by starvation. As a result, well over a million Irish were dead by 1850; a million more managed to migrate. They moved singly, in families, or in communal groups—and almost always they were destitute.

Where to go? England, while relying considerably on Irish laborers and Irish domestic help, offered no concerted plan to alleviate the problem. Besides, anti-Irish prejudice in England was strong and enduring. Language barriers and unfamiliar customs tended to foreclose the options east and south. But America—there were Irish already there, with enough wherewithal that it has been estimated the American Irish between 1848 and 1864 contributed over thirteen million British pounds to aid immigrants. By 1845, an agent of the Boston Census remarked on how exceedingly difficult it was "to trace the parentage and history of the foreign poor. There are so many John Sullivans, Jerry Daileys and William O'Briens, who are all made in the same mould."[3] In ten years this "mould" would expand to the perimeters of Boston and beyond.

One member of this massive influx of the poverty-stricken was a small, wiry man named Mike Sullivan, who landed in Boston sometime around 1850. He was about twenty-five, a native of Tralee in County Kerry. His town looked west, across the deep blue of Tralee Bay and past Rough Point, into the broad Atlantic. What he left behind by way of family, friends, or property is not known specifically, but the pressures driving him were those affecting hundreds of thousands of his countrymen. He probably traveled alone, indicating boldness, desperation, or both. Perhaps his diminutive stature (a shade over five feet two inches) had influenced his obvious pugnacity. He landed in the United States a fiery bantam who had probably had his share of scraps back in Tralee. And he was militantly "Irish." His eldest son remembered his saying later that there were a hundred men in Ireland who could have taken the measure of the great John L. Rumors of Mike Sullivan's flaming temper followed him all his life (he was once reported to have blackened the eye of a Boston politician), but he possessed little else that would improve his lot in the rough-and-ready underside of Boston. A laborer he became, and a laborer he remained. His death, at the height of his son's fame, was not even covered by the *Boston Pilot*, organ of the city's "lace-curtain Irish."[4]

A few years after his arrival Mike Sullivan met and courted Catherine Kelly, whose family had arrived in Boston in 1853. The Kellys were natives of Athlone, in the south of County Roscommon in central Ireland, where the majestic Shannon temporarily widens to become Lough Ree. Catherine was the second daughter of John and Bridget Kelly, who had farmed their small patch of ground with some success until driven under by the potato blight. She was born in 1834 and was thus well into her twenties when she and Mike Sullivan were married in Saint Patrick's Church on November 6, 1856. The bride was better educated than her husband, who may have been illiterate. A large girl for her age, she grew into an ample figure of a woman, weighing 180 pounds and practically dwarfing Mike.[5]

The newlyweds settled in the Roxbury district at 5 East Concord Street, boarding with a couple named Norton in the midst of many of the new Irish Americans. In this neighborhood they would live all their lives, rearing three children, two boys and a girl. All—John, Annie, and young Mike—grew to maturity, and they always remained close to their parents. As the children came along and the family circle expanded, Mike Sullivan moved from job to job as a common laborer on the edge of artisanship.[6] He dug trenches for sewers, smoothed roadbeds, laid bricks for a dollar and a half a day, and survived.

On October 12, 1858, as Lincoln and Stephen A. Douglas contested the senatorship in far-off Illinois with the eyes of a dividing nation on them, Catherine Kelly Sullivan gave birth in the East Concord home to a male child she and her husband named John Lawrence.[7] The family life she and Mike provided would form the steady shelter of the young boy's existence. Their home was stable; they left the Nortons in 1862 for a house of their own, in Amee Place, and there they stayed as John grew up, not moving again until he was past his tenth birthday. John always looked back on his youth with fondness and nostalgia. Clearly, parental nurture was there. "The love of the Irish parent is evident enough," wrote an outside observer, "but it is too often an impulsive, irrational, physical love."[8] Doubtless young John received cuffs on occasion from his temperamental father, and doubtless he was dominated at times by the sheer physical size of his imposing mother.

Looking back through the foggy prism of John's championship years, both parents would positively beam at the precocity of their older boy. His mother reflected that John had walked at ten months and "could talk" at fourteen months. And his strength! He supposedly blackened the eye of a visiting aunt when less than a year old and would struggle to be released from his mother's stout arms before he was weaned. "John was always a fighter. He was strong as a bear when a baby." But he was not quarrelsome, was not a bully, and grew to be fonder of baseball than fighting. As for his father, he appeared a bit mystified. In spite of the fact that his cousins back in Kerry were all six-footers and hard workers, none of them was much with his fists. John, full of fun and frolic as a boy, was "good at his books, but would rather play."[9]

As John grew, it became evident that his size and strength were that of his mother. (Little Mike, the youngest child, developed to be as slight and fair as his elder brother was muscular and dark.) John learned as he grew that his uncles and other of his father's relatives in Ireland were all large men, known throughout Tralee and County Kerry by a Celtic word roughly translated as "the Big Sullivans." Thus, he preferred to believe that the bulk of his genetic makeup, despite his father's lack of size, came from the male side.[10]

A surviving baby picture, featuring the usual pinafore, shows the level, black-eyed gaze and, already, an unusually large pair of hands.

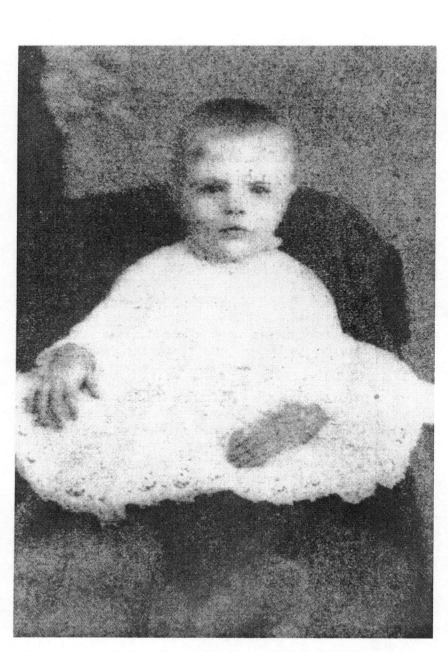

3. John Lawrence Sullivan, in pinafore (about 1860) (William Schutte Collection)

By the age of twelve, when John was posed with coat and loose-knotted bow tie, the gaze was still there, the large ears now prominent, the mouth full and downturned in an early semblance of the famous scowl.[11] The pictures betoken the pride of a close-knit family; both baby and boy are neatly dressed and carefully groomed. The parents were undeniably working class, but, typical of their immigrant generation, they had high hopes for their male progeny.

Catherine and Mike Sullivan's adoration would be returned in full. As their son progressed in the rough-and-tumble boxing game, they offered constant, if sometimes qualified, support. Mike, in particular, became a boxing aficionado, eagerly relating the merits of his elder boy to anyone who would listen and haunting newspaper offices, pestering the editors for news of John's latest fight. On John's part, he spent a significant amount of his prize money to provide for his parents. As early as 1883 they were heavily dependent on him for support, his mother declining into invalidism and his father unable (or unwilling) to keep a steady job. Following his first great victory, in 1882, he paid off their house and lot, at 8 Parnell Street in the Boston Highlands, valued at $5,000. From time to time he sent home considerable sums of money, $1,000 or even $2,000, true windfalls in the laboring-man's economy of the day. One observer believed that his parents had accumulated $8,000 in savings in this manner. In 1885 John bought them a second house, for $3,450, using his brother as agent. The parents used the second property, at 26 Sawyer Street in Boston, for rental income, remaining on Parnell Street until the end of her life and almost the end of his.[12]

John would travel far from this family circle, circulating with people wildly removed from the doting, proud parents he knew as a child. Yet his concern for their welfare was honest and open, and their regard for him grew with each victory while their concern deepened with reports of each drunken debauch. When he reached his quarters after one of his greatest triumphs, for example, there among the scores of telegrams littering the table of his room was one from his father in Boston, conveying his mother's love and admonishing John to "come home to us at once and don't drink any."[13]

## II

Born an American citizen, and a simple American patriot all his days, young John grew to maturity in an urban environment filled with anti-Irish prejudice. The American Irish had always constituted a "curiously unassimilable" lot; although their common language tended to ease their relations with their new countrymen, their brogue and their customs tended to keep them separate. They habitually clustered in the cities of the northeastern seaboard, stubbornly defiant of the Protestant social and cultural elites around them. While most Irish became ardent Jacksonian Democrats, culturally they were slow to "melt," and on questions of religion they did not melt at all. To old-line American families, particularly those of English descent, these unmannered "bog-trotters" were clearly beyond the pale.[14]

Irish behavior seemed made for stereotypical thinking. They were so *public* in their rude, boisterous conduct. Emotional, quick to anger and quick to cry, the Irish were perceived as unreserved, shallow, and quicksilver in intelligence and capacity to work. Olney's *Practical System of Modern Geography*, a popular schoolbook in its twenty-first edition by 1836, described the Irish as "quick of apprehension, active, brave and hospitable; but passionate, ignorant, vain, and superstitious." Thomas Colley Grattan, an Englishman of Irish descent, saw these qualities in the urban Irish of the 1850s. To him the Irish were "not by nature a cruel people, although revenge is one of their marked natural traits."[15] When observers such as Grattan talked of "natural traits," and the subjects were Irish, the connotations were almost always negative.

The Irish also dealt in stereotypes about themselves, but they tended to accentuate the positive: family loyalties, proper religious attitudes, an open, engaging friendliness, and steady habits. Jeremiah O'Donovan, a peripatetic bookseller who contacted hundreds of Irish families during his business journeys in the 1850s, described the "natural inheritance of a genuine Irish man" as good nature, good humor, and good manners. He viewed the Irishman's attributes as frankness, affability, unbounded generosity, and ready wit.[16]

Stereotypical thinking on all sides clearly inhibited the ability of the American Irish to assimilate. Social tension was the automatic result, since the spatial confines of urban life forced the Irish and old-line Americans to intermingle at the level of trade and in the streets, if not in social discourse. To proper Bostonians, the Irish seemed to be pouring in. In 1850 about thirty-five thousand Irish lived there, about one-quarter of the population. Only five years later, as a result of the immigrant wave that included Mike Sullivan and Catherine Kelly, there were more than fifty thousand—twice the entire population in 1800. In 1830 Boston's population had been approximately 95 percent native-born; by 1860, when John was two years old, this percentage had been more than halved. Even though land had been added to the city through expansion and reclamation from the sea, and even though numerous housing units had been built since that time, the crowded conditions into which the newcomers were forced changed the character of certain regions with devastating speed.[17]

Neighborhood friction inevitably develcped. Any social underclass is open to charges of shiftlessness and lack of ambition, but this was particularly true of Boston's Irish, including Mike Sullivan, who were forced into laboring or domestic jobs where servile behavior was expected and ambition, intelligence, and leadership traits were not. Old Boston, composed of classic Yankees produced by generations of public idealism and religious introspection, firmly believed in a vision of reform and progress, ending in ultimate perfection. The Irish, who seemed to them to live only for the present, were deemed alien to any notion of progress and hence hostile to the conception of Boston's elites of how the world moved. As a result, class distinctions in mid-century Boston were probably sharper than those of any other city in the country.[18]

The modern city of Mike Sullivan's day was growing increasingly complex, more and more requiring that its workers learn a trade or a special skill to make a decent living. Most of Boston's immigrant Irish were from poverty-stricken rural backgrounds, many with only a rudimentary education. The results might have been expected, but they were no less a social tragedy. The Massachusetts Sanitary Commission reported in 1850 that immigrants, the great bulk of them Irish, accounted for 58 percent of Boston's paupers, 90 percent of its truants, 75 percent of the prisoners in the county jail, and an astonishing 97 percent of the residents in the almshouse on Deer Island. Even at the end of the century, after a generation of Irish self-help and some marked social mobility, an impressionistic account could state that in Boston, "Ireland is far ahead of any other nationality in the number of its paupers."[19]

Mike and Catherine Sullivan may have skirted the edges of poverty at times, but Mike almost always worked, while Catherine managed the home. The Sullivans had their own house, and if their chances of upward mobility were minimal, neither were they destitute. They never sank, like so many unfortunates in their ethnic group, into the surrounding swamp of poverty or crime. Mike could provide, and this he did, but he and his countrymen could barely make a dent in the deep anti-Irish prejudice that surrounded them.

Ostensibly the Irish were in America to provide a cheap labor force for a rapidly industrializing society, but as a group they still had difficulty finding gainful employment. Had Catherine Sullivan chosen to try domestic work, as many Irish women both married and single did, she might have confronted classified ads such as this one from an 1853 newspaper: "WOMEN WANTED.—To do general housework. . . . English, Scotch, Welsh, German, or any other country or color except Irish." For Irish males, it was even worse. Many, like Mike, were forced to take the backbreaking menial jobs that everyone else disdained. And so the typical Boston Irishman, like his fellows throughout urban America, could be found (when he was working) as a ditchdigger, longshoreman, hod carrier, canal digger, railroad navvie, or marble quarry worker. Occupational mobility for Mike's generation and for that of his son was excruciatingly slow. And, as young John may have dimly grasped, the father's job level was a powerful determinant of the son's.[20]

The prejudices working against the Sullivans and "their kind" were both obvious and subtle. Bostonians had, from time to time, tried to ban foreigners from certain professions by law, but these attempts had been too blatant and had failed. Nevertheless, by 1845 job advertisements in Boston newspapers to the effect that "none need apply but Americans" had become familiar. Social distinctions were clear. One proper Bostonian lady remembered that in the Cambridge she knew as a girl, two horsecar lines ran parallel to each other. One took the Irish laborers to "work," and the other carried Boston gentlemen to their "offices."[21]

Perhaps the heaviest stigma borne by the Irish was their religion. To most American Protestants, in an age in which religious persuasion was taken with intense seriousness by the growing middle class, Catholicism was a political religion that sought to subvert the world by infiltration and coercion. Catholicism likewise was consistently pictured as cutting straight across the grain of American democracy. Catholics, it was believed, were held in thrall by the demanding hierarchy of the church; so bound in primary allegiance, they could make no contribution to a free society. The Catholic immigrant was often described as a person of inferior morals and obnoxious habits, an alien with an "un-American" religion who became, in the pale ugly light of pseudo-Darwinian social science, a racially inferior being as well.

Probably a minority of Americans really practiced their Protestantism, even in the nineteenth century. Clergymen amassed statistics to prove that the majority of the population was not being reached by the gospel. Boston, by 1890, had a ratio of one Protestant church organization to every 1,778 people, not as bad as the hellhole of Chicago (1 to 3,601) but a clear indication that there was a social gap between ideal and practice. Nevertheless, the unofficial credo of the country was heavily Protestant, and politicians ignored the profession of religious faith, like the proclaiming of love for hearth and home, at their peril.[22] When the loose, indistinct cocoon of Protestant benevolence and social justice seemed threatened, as in the 1850s, allegiance to the ideal, in the negative sense of anti-Catholicism, surfaced quickly and sometimes violently.

For the Irish, their church offered stability, a haven from the pressures of the outside world. Arriving lonely and dispossessed, they found that the religion they might have practiced so lackadaisically in the old country gave strength and refuge against the social prejudices of the new. In response, throughout the nation urban Catholics gave what they could, a penny here and a dollar there, as a generous and continuing offering that eventually produced the imposing cathedrals of their faith.[23] Mike and Catherine Sullivan's depth of religious feeling is unknown, but their elder son was pointed from birth toward the priesthood. The Catholic religion was a constant feature of the household.

In all the colonies there had been at most only fifty-six Roman Catholic churches, the great majority huddled in Maryland and Pennsylvania. In a new nation grown to over four million, they served perhaps twenty thousand people. By the Civil War, Catholicism had become the largest single communion in America, though considerably outnumbered by all the Protestant sects combined. The major reason for the dramatic shift was the Irish infusion; thus most of the country's Catholics were considered unacceptable and of inferior "racial stock." Throughout the first thirty years of John Sullivan's life, organized nativism was sparked by fundamentalist ministers, British Americans, and Protestant Irishmen, the latter advertising that they "knew" best of all the true nature of their enemy. Throughout the country, state aid was refused to Catholic charities, parochial schools were critically inspected by public officials, and state institutions were blessed by the presence of Protestant chaplains only. At the personal level the prejudice was often more vicious. Even a figure like John Boyle O'Reilly, admired by many Boston Protestants for both his literary and athletic powers and practically a saint to many of his fellow Catholics, could receive the following letter:

> John Boyle O'Reilly:—The following is a sentence that is as true as you are a mick: Rum, Romanism, and Rebellion. Eat it, swallow it, but it is going to live. Hoping the day is not far off when you and your broilers will be boiled in hell. Hurrah for the Queen. Damn the Irish.[24]

An even greater practical fear drove those who fulminated against the Irish: the "micks" could *vote*. In the emerging ward politics of the cities they proved ready fodder for politicians just learning how to organize and get out the vote at the grass-roots level. As early as the 1830s that great observer of the American scene, Alexis de Tocqueville, had perceived the Catholic Irish as instinctive democrats, arguing that below the priest, all were equal in their religion. As a minority, Tocqueville felt, the Irish thus had to support the principle of respecting the rights of everyone in order to ensure themselves the free exercise of their own privileges. "The Catholics of the United States are at the same time the most submissive believers and the most independent citizens."[25]

Tocqueville observed and wrote just before the genesis of great urban political machines, which quickly entered into a productive relationship with immigrant groups. In return for voting the right way they provided many of the social services unavailable from the municipalities by reason of either political doctrine or scarcity of funds. Most Irish became, and remained, ardent Democrats, true adherents of the Jacksonian persuasion. Boston's Irish elevated Hugh O'Brien to mayor in 1885, and by 1890 Irish politicians controlled the local governments of no less than sixty-eight Massachusetts cities and towns. The practical politics of Mike Sullivan are unknown, but since John later courted leading Boston Democrats for political office in the 1880s, and since Democratic political figures far outnumbered Republicans at his fights, a reasonable guess might be made that the Sullivan family was firmly within the Democratic party.

As young John Sullivan grew to adulthood, more and more of Boston's Irish were reaching middle-class status, although they were still in the minority compared with the Irish working class and urban poor. This minority, striving to "fit in" to middle-class patterns of morality and behavior, had arrived enough, in their own eyes at least, to look down on the Irish hod carrier and drayman. One of Sullivan's later biographers was assuredly correct when he asserted that some of these "lace-curtain Irish" were ashamed of the prizefighter and preferred not to meet or even talk about him.[26]

Boston's Irish world thus was no monolith of culture, social attitude, or even religion. In 1885 only a little more than one quarter of the Boston Irish could claim that both parents had been born in Massachusetts. Thus a predominant strain in John Sullivan's early life was that of a member of the "first-generation." He was part of a peer group that confronted problems of acculturation as it aspired to rise in the social scale. Older Irish-American families tended to regard the recent migrants not so much as fellow countrymen but rather as a crude, boisterous rabble to whom they were unfortunately attached by the stereotypical bonds of ethnic affinity.

The census of 1885 also listed the principal occupations of Boston's Irish. Most common among men were laborers (5,679), merchants and dealers (1,187), teamsters (1,129), masons (1,069), longshoremen (1,043), and railroad workers (1,026). Among women, housewives (21,635) predominated, followed by laundry workers (705), washerwomen (589), and hotel workers (449). Of the professions of the middle class, the Irish claimed a growing number of jobs in the national government service: the customs house (27), state government (25), and post office (16). They were making increasing inroads at the local level, in the police force (112), street department (59), water department (20), and fire department (17). But these jobs were, at best, on the lower margins of the middle class. Among the status-oriented professions the Boston Irish were scarcely represented. Among them were lawyers (13), physicians (18), surgeons (4), dentists (1), editors (4), professors (1), teachers (4), architects (3), chemists (4), and civil engineers (8).[27]

In young John's world, then, a "typical Irishman" worked with his hands, as Mike Sullivan did, and a "typical Irish woman" such as Catherine Sullivan stayed at home and kept house. True, more and more Irish were beginning to rise. In 1839 the tax records showed twenty-four Boston Irish who paid taxes on real estate and personal goods worth at least $100,000. Twenty-four—out of an Irish male population in excess of ninety thousand.[28] The road to status, which passed landmarks of property, rents, interest, and investment, was an exceedingly difficult one to travel for the Irish of John Sullivan's generation.

Anti-Irish prejudice would erode as John matured, but it would still provide a strong undercurrent in Boston life well past the end of the century. Although overt discrimination against the Irish declined, Boston's banks in the 1890s still refused to hire Irish clerks. Generous, daring, comradely, and good-natured the Irish might be, but they were still, somehow, "outside." "The Irishman fails to fit into the complex of our civilization," wrote a polished defender of the old order. "His talents are too little interwoven with the capacities which go to make up the modern successful man."[29]

A long row to hoe, then, for any Irish youth of John's generation. Centuries of Anglo-Irish strife had bitten deeply into American culture. Not everyone, to be sure, was as brutal as the pompous English historian Edward A. Freeman, who confidently asserted that the solution to America's social problems was for every Irishman to kill a Negro and then be hanged for it.[30] But John Sullivan faced an uphill struggle in life, measured by any index. Against him were aligned the powerful forces of social custom and prejudice. On his side he would have what he could make of his own Irish-American heritage.

## III

The Boston of John's youth retained, in spite of the upheaval of civil war, the quiet bustle of purposeful commercialism overlaid with an almost postcard serenity. Old Boston, picturesque and quaint, still survived, its streets a crazy quilt of angles and sudden corners, its small shops tilting crazily on unexpected slopes. To one observer, it was a "perfect chaos of disorder." But the city was bright and clean, the cleaner the more one moved toward the emerging suburbs. Inevitably, the closely knit small-town atmosphere of the eighteenth century had evaporated, leaving a series of small communities shaped by social background, ethnicity, and occupation. These urban regions generally flourished, for brotherly conflict was no bar to commercial advantage.

Even the Irish seemed to be better off. A visitor to the Hub in 1863 was struck by both their relative prosperity and the strict divisions of social class that lay just under the surface:

> The poorest cottages were always those of the . . . Irish emigrants, but there was still hardly one of them which was not a palace compared with the cottage of an ordinary English laborer, to say nothing of Ireland. It is curious, by the way, that there is a great deal of the old English prejudice against the Irish in New England. Intermarriages between the poor Irish and the poor New Englanders are almost unheard of, and it is a most unusual occurrence for an Irishman to be elected to any office in the State. However, the Irish make and what is more, save money; and for the most part lose both race and language and religion in the third generation.[31]

The visitor's observations on the relative prosperity of even the poorest Boston Irish, compared with the lack of possibilities in the land they had left, squares with the experience of the growing Sullivan family.

Roxbury, the community of John's youth, was located in Norfolk County. It was an overgrown village with a long lineage, having been incorporated by the Puritans on September 28, 1630. In 1790 the community had a population of little more than 2,000, a true New England town. Even as late as 1840 Roxbury still contained less than 10,000 people. But then came the influx: by 1860 the once-small town had swollen to a population of 25,000. It began to style itself a "city" in 1846 and fought a losing battle to prevent being swallowed up by Boston, adjusting its boundary lines twice in the next fifteen years.

The cause of the rapid growth was, of course, the Irish. By 1860 about three-quarters of the residents of Norfolk County had been born in Ireland. John grew up amid his own. Norfolk County was also heavily populated by working people; 4,342 told the census-takers in 1860 that their occupation was "laborer." There was still plenty of agricultural land in the county—over 2,800 still farmed—but the fields were being eaten away by the steadily advancing suburbs. The neat little houses sheltered carpenters, cabinet makers, blacksmiths, mill workers, and painters, but above all shoemakers. Almost 5,000 people in Norfolk county made their living in 1860 from the shoe industry, a harbinger of the developing industrial age.

In Roxbury laboring men such as Mike Sullivan predominated. Over twelve hundred of them lived in the community in 1860; it was a worker's town, not yet in thrall to the factory or the mill. Females outnumbered males, 13,288 to 11,789, although in John's age group (1–15) the ratio was somewhat less: 4,469 girls to 4,226 boys. Already the statisticians were noting that women were more numerous and tended to live longer. Only sixty blacks lived in Roxbury when John was a boy. He grew up with the standard antiblack prejudices of his generation. The former village could not long continue as an independent entity, however. Boston gobbled it whole in 1867, part of an expansion that included Dorchester two years later and Charlestown, Brighton, and West Roxbury in 1873.[32]

The Sullivans' Amee Place home, off Harrison Avenue, thus was one with its surroundings. The house was located practically opposite Boston College, and there the family lived until John was ten years old, when they moved to Parnell Street, located in a slight ripple of land optimistically nicknamed the Boston Highlands. Massachusetts, thanks to Horace Mann and other reformers, led the nation in the appreciation of the values of public education, and so there was little problem concerning the availability of learning, even for boys from working-class families. Either Catherine's dreams of the priesthood for her elder son, the classic wish of the nineteenth-century Irish-American mother, withered or money was lacking, for John was not educated in parochial schools. Instead, he was packed off to the primary school on Concord Street, where he was confronted by the formidable Miss Blanchard, a teacher who stuck in his mind as a disciplinarian but nevertheless good-hearted and as willing to instruct poorer children as she was those better off. Next came a sojourn at the Dwight Grammar School on Springfield Street, from which John graduated around 1872.[33] In all likelihood he was educated in Yankee Americanism in its purest and most undiluted form. His unabashed, flag-waving patriotism probably dated from his grammar school days.

By the few surviving accounts he was a lively boy, but no one, including himself, ever claimed any degree of academic excellence for him. He later asserted that he had taken better to mathematics than anything else, but his interest in strict scholarly activity was certainly marginal: "I was always on the lookout to avoid geography when it was geography day." He recalled being punished only once, when the Concord Street headmaster, James Page, applied a rattan cane for boisterous behavior in class:

> That was the only time I ever had to take the rattan, which I did like a little man. It was commonly taken for granted that if a boy cried he was a weak one. I guess I wanted to cry but I couldn't, although he gave me what I deserved; and I was quite a hero after that among the other boys.[34]

Most of his education came in the schoolyard, amid the games and scuffles of his peers. He had no regular chores to take up his time after school, and thus he was a steady and earnest competitor in marbles, spinning tops, and, above all, baseball, the boys' schoolyard game par excellence, which became his earliest passion and a lifelong love. At the Dwight School he established his first public reputation, as a strong and reliable baseball player. But he was also noticeably bigger and huskier than his friends, and his remarkable good humor masked an extremely aggressive personality. He had many schoolyard scraps and later bragged that he always came out on top. Adult oversight was minimal. Youngsters tended to run free in the Boston of his youth; the police force was small and completely unequipped to handle urban crime, much less rampaging gangs of boys.[35]

Indeed, with little interest in studies, John had no other avenue to satisfy his rapidly evolving ego than displays of his developing physical skills. His father was lost in a sea of Irish laborers; the family name was as common as the rows of whitewashed houses on Harrison Avenue. In the year of John's birth, 1858, there were 349 male Sullivans living in Boston, 21 of them laborers named Michael.[36] Whatever the young boy craved, it was not anonymity. As his body matured, his pride in his burgeoning physical power kept pace.

After his years at Dwight, John spent a few months at Comer's Commercial College (actually a small school specializing in training clerks) and put in some desultory hours attending night school at the old Bath House on Cabot Street, which was later turned into a polling booth. If Harvard was out of the question, there still remained the possibility of continuing education for Irish boys on the rise. This was Boston College, practically next door to John's boyhood home near Harrison Avenue. Holy Cross, established in Worcester in 1843, imposed fees of more than $150 a year, a forbidding barrier to most Irish laboring families. But when the Jesuits opened Boston College in 1843, the $30 annual charge was especially designed to attract poor Irish lads, who could further defray their expenses by living at home. The school, wedged between the City Hospital and a graveyard, was, as one wag put it, ideally situated in case of accident. Its principal business was educating candidates for the priesthood; of 352 graduates before 1898, 156 eventually were ordained. Critics might later scorn the little one-building institution as a "glorified high school," but for working-class Irish Americans it held aloft the lamp of promise.[37]

Sullivan always asserted that he had matriculated at Boston College, that his parents had sent him there to educate him for the priesthood. He remembered that he was sixteen or seventeen at the time. The plan was to go on to Holy Cross, followed by ordination. In interview after interview, culminating in his autobiography, he remembered that he had spent "two or three months" at the Jesuit school but had left because he could make his annual tuition in a week by playing semiprofessional baseball. So consistently did he make this claim that virtually every writer since has credited him with some college education, one even going so far as to call him the "only college man" among the heavyweight champions. This gave rise to much pretentious nonsense, put forth by Sullivan as well as others, that he was steeped in the classics and could quote the ancient Greeks as readily as he could deliver a right cross.[38]

The enrollment records at Boston College survive intact. The student registers list the names of everyone matriculating from September 1864 to June 1914, and that of John L. Sullivan is not among them.[39] His formal education probably ended around the age of fifteen, in boredom and dissatisfaction with the tedium of Comer's Commercial College and the Bath House night school. His surviving letters—notes, really, usually hasty scrawls across some piece of hotel stationery—indicate a fairly good command of spelling but a decided lack of grammatical structure. Sullivan received the modern-day equivalent of a junior high school education, which in his time was considered more than enough to fit him for the workaday life for which he seemed destined. His claim of college experience reflected his sneaking admiration for education and the educated man. He would often, and loudly, advertise the merits of being self-taught in the school of experience, but he always retained a grudging regard for the diploma.

Working-class teenagers fresh from school in Sullivan's time would customarily bind themselves to a trade as apprentices, many times to their own fathers. A written contract would seal the bargain; after being taught a skill, the boy was hoped to be on the road to becoming a master artisan or craftsman. But Mike Sullivan, after over twenty years in the land of promise, was still a laborer, with no skill to pass on to his son. So John bound himself to the plumbing trade with the firm of Moffat & Perry for four dollars a week because "I thought I would like plumbing." There he worked for six months as an apprentice. His most exciting adventure occurred when the water pipes froze in the old Williams Market at the corner of Dover and Washington streets. He and a journeyman (journeymen, the next step up from apprentice, could earn from three to six dollars a day), lugging a lighted torch and the pails of hot water necessary for thawing out frozen pipes, proceeded to the scene, where they devoted half a day to the tedious task, with apprentice Sullivan continually resupplying the pails of hot water. This day's work ended in a fistfight, the journeyman beating a retreat to the nearby shop of their employer.

Next came tinsmithing. Sullivan worked for eighteen months as an apprentice to the master tinsmith James Calvin, whose shop was located at the corner of Warren and Dudley streets. There he fought a running battle with a journeyman working at the same bench. They argued over everything: dogs (a lifelong Sullivan love), gamecocks, baseball, and sports in general. "His dogs were better than any I had ever seen; his gamecock was better than any I had; in fact, anything I had was no account, and his was number one." Again, finally, a challenge to fight, but the hated braggart backed down. Finally came two years in the mason's trade, at which Mike had at least worked in the past, so that he could teach his son a few tricks.

So passed his late teenage years, drifting as an apprentice from trade to trade, a replica of his father for all his education. The picture of young John Sullivan in the late 1870s is of a temperamental, rebellious youth, impatient, dissatisfied, and seeking. Unlike his father, however, he had an outlet valve: sports. Even as he moved aimlessly from job to job, Sullivan was playing baseball with a number of pickup teams in the Boston area. After starting as an amateur, he soon was earning up to twenty-five dollars a game, playing on Wednesdays and Saturdays for the Eglestons. Among his other clubs were the Tremonts, Etnas, and Our Boys. First base and left field were his slots, "although I could play in any position." He later claimed to have been good enough to have been offered thirteen hundred dollars to play in 1879 and 1880 for the famous Cincinnati Red Stockings, the team that had inaugurated professional baseball.

Baseball, however, was fading to second place in his sporting considerations. Already by the age of seventeen he scaled nearly 200 pounds, an enormous size for a youngster of his generation, and he displayed power to match. To impress his friends with his strength, he began to hoist kegs of nails or barrels of flour or beer over his head. Once he claimed to have righted a horsecar onto its tracks on Washington Street. Some of these feats are doubtless the apochrypha of the self-made physical specimen, but his neighborhood reputation as the Strong Boy (supposedly given him by a lightweight boxer named Fairbanks) was justly earned.[40]

The next step was obvious: a trial of strength in the boxing ring. Not a prizefight, certainly—Massachusetts law was death on fighting for money—but an "exhibition" of physical skill as part of an evening's entertainment was something else again. One night in 1878 John and a few friends went to the Dudley Street Opera House for an evening of variety entertainment honoring an old-time Boston sporting man, George Fogarty. There a youngster named Jack Scannell professed eagerness to meet a man of Sullivan's local reputation. John was working then at the tinsmith's trade; he had never been taught to box (and, indeed, never would be), although he had watched boxing exhibitions. He had no tights, shoes, or gloves, the uniform of the pugilist. Padded gloves were found. Sullivan simply shed his coat, rolled up his sleeves, entered the ring set up at center stage, and laced on the bulky leather mitts. The free-for-all that followed was short and decisive: Scannell cracked Sullivan on the back of the head and was quickly belted into a piano at the corner of the stage.[41]

Sullivan was on the way to local notoriety and fame. To be the center of attention of a circle of friends, to be admired for something, to have self-worth—here was a life that had been denied to his father. As John was taking his first amateurish steps into the prize ring, Mike was digging in the muck, one of hundreds of Irish laborers expanding the sewer system of Boston.[42] A choice between local fame in the ring and sweating through twelve-hour days in dank ditches was not hard to make, but the allure of boxing offered even more than baseball; it offered the chance to display individual merit in its most primal and masculine form.

Young John had developed many of what would later be the classic attributes of the professional boxer. On the surface an amiable, outgoing young man, he already had accumulated a history of arguments and disputes ending in brawls or challenges to fight. Although not impoverished himself, he could see a grim future in the model of his father, and he shied away from it in the direction of peer-group recognition. His friends, mostly Irish boys cut from the same cloth as himself, admired pugnacity as a key to manhood. Even after prizefighting became legal in many states, a considerable number of boxers would display uncertainty about the social and physical costs of a ring career, but not Sullivan. Once he heard the cheers, once he had a sense of his ability to so dominate other men, he never looked back. His own self-image, always egocentric regarding his strength, was leavened by his conviction that he himself was never aggressive or pugnacious, but responded only when forced to by circumstance.

Above all, boxing gave him what plumbing, tinsmithing, and masonry never could—a sense of upward social mobility, importance, and self-esteem. His early neighborhood scraps had differed little in origin from those of thousands of American boys and adolescents, but somewhere along the line his sense of inner worth had become wedded to the accomplishments of his physical being. The ability to fight (and win) gave him status among his peers, first in the schoolyard and then throughout the Highlands. With his strength he could become the final arbiter of disputes, the ultimate "judge." Unlike many boxers to follow, he was not influenced by a pugilist in the family or in the neighborhood; instead, he was driven from within to that staccato rhythm of preparation, release, and celebration that is the life cycle of the successful prizefighter.[43]

Of course, one devastating punch against an Irish lad like Jack Scannell, as green as himself, did not make Sullivan a prizefighter. "I didn't know the first thing about boxing then," he later confessed, "but I went at him for all I was worth and licked him quick." But the results had been eminently satisfying: "It wasn't much of a fight, and I done him up in about two minutes."[44] Nevertheless, he did not immediately become a staple of the "benefits" that punctuated the Boston sporting scene in the late 1870s. From month to month he attended with his friends. He watched men perform in exhibitions, fighters who actually had fought for prize money in some rural hideout far removed from the police.

There was, for example, the burly, gregarious Joe Goss, twice Sullivan's age but still willing to put up his fists for the right amount of money. Born in Northhampton, England, in 1838, Goss first fought in 1859, before John had passed his first birthday. Goss's early fights in England were endurance contests, one against a certain Bodger Crutchley lasting 120 rounds and reeling through three hours and twenty minutes. In his youth Goss had been quick and tough as nails, usually fighting with 150 pounds stretched over his 5-foot 8½-inch frame. He came to America in 1876 to fight his countryman Tom Allen; liking Boston, he became a fixture with the sporting crowd. He and Allen met on September 7, 1876, in a ring pitched in Kenton County, Kentucky, but the fighters and those in attendance were forced by the law to hurriedly move fifteen miles to Boone County, where they battled twenty-one rounds before the burly Allen, who had been beating Goss handily, smashed him in the face as Goss was kneeling on the turf— a foul even under the generous rules of the London Prize Ring. Goss was declared the winner and received a modicum of notoriety, though the spectators could easily see that both men were well past their pugilistic prime, overweight, and out of shape.[45]

Sullivan certainly knew of Goss by reputation and probably met him at one of the benefits, perhaps the one for a local saloon owner, Patsey Sheppard, at Beethoven Hall on October 15, 1878. Goss, loosely styled the "American champion" since his dubious victory over Allen two years before, was in attendance: he had not had a prizefight since the Allen match, though no one seemed to care much. Also present that evening was Patrick ("Paddy") Ryan, a much younger and larger man than Joe, whose once rawboned cheeks had fleshed out considerably and who now sported a prominent paunch. Ryan was born in 1853 in the town of Thurles in Tipperary. In the great wave of Irish immigration his family settled in Troy, New York, where Paddy grew to the commanding size of six feet one-half inch and 220 pounds. In 1878 Ryan was regarded, by those few who were interested, as the coming man in American prizefighting. The amazing thing about the Trojan Giant was that he had not one organized bout to his credit. Ryan had been matched to fight the New Yorker John Dwyer the previous summer, but the match fell through because neither man could agree to a stakesholder. In the interim Ryan had been involved in a street brawl in Brooklyn, during which he was knocked down, kicked in the face, and stabbed in the left side near the kidneys. Somewhat the worse for wear from this experience and missing two front teeth, he still made his appearances at the benefits and continued to be the subject of speculation.[46]

As the winter of 1878–79 wore on, Sullivan continued to attend the local exhibitions and met many of the men who made it their occasional business to be concerned with the outlaw sport. A November benefit for John Clark of Philadelphia attracted Goss and "Professor" John Laflin, along with local stalwarts Patsey Sheppard and Jack ("Patsy") Hogan. In December the recipient was John Dwyer; this marked the eleventh such sparring exhibition given in Boston that year. In January it was Patsy O'Hare's turn; his "night" at Webster's Hall featured amateur and juvenile fighters and even comic singing. The next month Goss himself was honored, and Paddy Ryan, recovered now from his injuries, sparred for two rounds with William Miller of Baltimore, this exhibition ending when the Trojan Giant began to pound the unfortunate Miller all over the stage, and police officers in attendance grew restless.[47]

In retrospect this winter was John's time of decision. Dissatisfied with every trade he had tried, he was being drawn more and more into the prizefighting crowd. He became particularly close to Goss, who dabbled in "training" fighters (he had had a hand in "preparing" Paddy Ryan for the John Dwyer fiasco) and who probably encouraged the young man from the Highlands to give boxing a try. Goss may have arranged Sullivan's spring exhibitions in 1879, which included sparring matches with Dan Dwyer, Tommy Chandler, and Patsy Hogan. Sullivan had the best of Dan Dwyer, who styled himself the "champion of Massachusetts," in a match in Revere Hall. Chandler was an oldster who gave Sullivan no problem, while Hogan proved to be a cipher. None of these matches, however, was reported in the sporting press or in the local papers. The name John Sullivan first reached print in March 1879 as a result of an exhibition with John ("Cockey") Woods at Dan Dwyer's benefit, which took place at the Alhambra on Hanover Street.

Friday, March 14, was a slow news day. The biggest sporting contest anywhere was a walking race in New York City, the latest event in a craze that was sweeping the eastern seaboard in the late 1870s. The *Boston Daily Globe*, the only local newspaper that bothered to cover the exhibitions, led off the next morning with the confusing headline that "Hempen Haters Encircle the Necks of Law's Victims." Inside, buried in the minuscule type so characteristic of newspapers before the tabloid revolution, was the revelation that John Sullivan, "the 'strong boy' of Boston Highlands," had given a sparring exhibition with Woods, a man at least ten years older than his opponent. The two men were part of a continuous parade of entertainment, a variety act among variety acts. Before and after them Walsh and King danced a clog and reel, the Kennigan Brothers sang "Lackawanna Spooners," the Boylston Quartet did a short medley, James Carroll performed some clog dances and sang, and William Dolan offered something called "Biddy, the Ballet Girl."

Woods was a large man but somewhat long in tooth. He was old enough to have once been thought of as a likely opponent for the almost legendary "Benicia Boy," John Carmel Heenan, who had died in 1873, but he had had relatively little ring experience. Sullivan, who had grown in confidence with the clear-cut exhibition victories over Scannell, Dan Dwyer, Chandler, and Hogan, pummeled him remorselessly. "I soon disposed of him," he would later say, with all the studied casualness of a man dropping a sack in the garbage can. "The encounter gave the spectators much pleasure," wrote the *Globe*'s reporter. One thing is certain from the Woods exhibition: Sullivan already had a considerable local reputation. He was the Strong Boy of the Boston Highlands, and his neighborhood following was much in evidence as he thrashed Woods. In spite of the other acts, he was the star of the evening.[48]

See him now, on the threshold of the 1880s, standing triumphant to the applause of friends and boxing devotees lining the wooden walls of the gaslit Alhambra. A raw-boned young man, almost twenty-one, remarkable for his strength and brute power, but a rough diamond if ever there was one, Sullivan had made the most important decision of his life. A winter spent associating with the fight crowd had produced in him a desire to become a prizefighter.

A prizefighter! He might as well register to be a professional criminal, according to the lights of the law. No one in American history—no one—had ever made a living as a prizefighter. Some of them owned or worked in saloons, like Joe Goss and Paddy Ryan. Others moved recklessly from odd job to odd job, like Mike McCoole or Joe Coburn. The worst indeed were little better than professional criminals, men of the stripe of James Ambrose ("Yankee Sullivan"). They inhabited the swampholes of society, emerging to protect political figures, serve as enforcers at the polling booth, and act as "collection agents" in various capacities. John Sullivan could not have been attracted to pugilism because it offered him a living.

Nor did the calling afford a chance to rise in the world. Most Americans did not even dignify prizefighting as a sport, considering it barbarous butchery for profit. There was no future in it. Prizefighters tended to end badly: vigilantes lynched Yankee Sullivan in San Francisco (1856); John Carmel Heenan died almost alone, entirely forgotten and destitute, at the remote Union Pacific outpost of Green River Station in Wyoming (1873); Joe Coburn spent most of the 1870s in

4. Joe Goss (about 1878) (William Schutte Collection)

prison for attempted murder; Mike McCoole killed another boxer in 1873 and spent the rest of his relatively brief life as a longshoreman on the Mississippi. In all the tawdry underground record of American prizefighting, only John Morrissey, once styled the "champion of America" before the Civil War, had ever beaten his origins, rising on the back of ward politics as an anti-Tweedite to gain election to the New York Senate in 1875. Morrissey proved to be a local politician of considerable skill, but he had died on May 1, 1878, at the age of forty-seven.[49]

Why, then, was it to be prizefighting? John Sullivan would work for a few more months in 1879 at the mason's trade, but his thoughts and ambitions were elsewhere. He had yet to make a dime directly on his nascent boxing skills; apart from side bets no money could legally change hands at the Boston exhibitions. Yet the lure of the ring drew him strongly—neither the idea of a "career" (that came much later) nor the notion that somehow he could make a living with his fists— but the social dimension that pugilism provided. As a boxer he saw himself with an identity, a reputation. As a victorious boxer he gained pride and social presence. And there were "prizes" to be won; not only the money, if the right locale and opponent could be found, but the "championship," whatever that might be.

> He, Hector like, although without a shield,
> Enters the ring and makes ambition yield;
> With matchless might he strikes the fearful blow,
> And wins the prize from his defeated foe.[50]

To be better than others, somehow; to best them in ways readily understood and as readily appreciated. Here was a way out. Religion, ethnicity, family could not be shed, nor did John care to do so. His trump card was his physical strength, and physical strength, it seemed, could be most directly exhibited in the prize ring, antiboxing statutes be damned. Above all, boxing could allow him to display "masculinity" in its most basic form; the fistic arena, which was destined to be his professional home, was, above all, a temple of manhood.

## CHAPTER TWO

# Sullivan's Boston:
# The Urban World and the Cult
# of Masculinity

The emerging modern city shaped John Sullivan's life. He grew up amid its pulsing dynamism and electric tensions. The rhythms and staccato patterns of excitement coursing through urban America left strong imprints on his habits and behavior as an adult. In the city he learned the difficult lot of many workingmen: the long, backbreaking hours, the difficulty in making ends meet, the constant struggle to keep one's head above water. He learned how tough it was to rise in the world and perhaps saw in his father, even given the love and respect due an Irish parent, a lesson to be avoided.

John was influenced by life in a workingman's neighborhood, not only the hard work but also the intimate, closely knit family life, the wider world of boyish play and games, and, above all, interaction with older neighborhood males. He perceived early on that the race was not always to the swift, for many seemed born with a head start. He learned to rely on male friendships to soften the obvious economic and social injustices that were becoming implicit in the urban experience. And he learned that gaining money was not only acceptable but also admired, and that spending it on himself and his friends could be immensely gratifying.

He learned to play, and in play and sport he found admiration from his peers and recognition from adults. By watching the behavior of the predominantly Irish males around him, he took on basic notions of what it meant to be a man and, conversely, what the proper roles for women should be. He learned, as a rite of passage, to drink and drink heavily, becoming a constant ornament of that important neighborhood center, the saloon. He drank so much and did it with such joyous abandon that by his early twenties he had become an alcoholic.

City life also taught John that, under certain conditions, power, force, and violent behavior could bring reward, not only in money but also, more importantly, in the respect and admiration of his male peers and of older and younger men as well. Such attention produced the self-satisfaction that would help raise him above the run of his fellows and bring him a public adulation that could never come to a plumber, a tinsmith, or a mason. To succeed in the eye of the city was to succeed in life, for the city seemed to be existence itself — he would live all his days in either Boston or New York, migrating from hotel to hotel on his many travels. Sullivan was a complete product of his time and place, a specific entity firmly rooted in the burgeoning urban world.

# I

The demographics of the Boston of John Sullivan's youth are suggestive of the formative patterns in his life. By 1880 the Hub ranked as the country's fourth largest population center, a position it would lose to western rivals such as Detroit, San Francisco, and Los Angeles in ensuing years. Sullivan's Boston was a classically urban setting, with more than a third of a million inhabitants packed within the city boundaries and another third of a million clustered in the surrounding suburbs, where John grew up. Between 1880 and 1890 the city's population grew by 24 percent; over three-quarters of this increase was due to immigration or relocation from the countryside. The Hub was a magnet for humanity, and this development was not new. In the three decades before John's birth, the population of Boston had nearly tripled, averaging an increase of over ten people a day.[1]

John lived in a relatively quiet, stable enclave amid this dynamism, where factors of occupation, religion, and residence tended to set the Irish apart and forced them to look within themselves and their ethnic group for social sustenance and social models. For them the road to the top barely existed, in practical terms. The way was always difficult. Sullivan's limited horizons might be contrasted with those of a Boston contemporary, Robert Bacon. Bacon was a member of Harvard's class of 1880, a group that contained no Boston Irish, no blacks, no Italians, no Swedes, no Latin Americans, no Jews. Indeed, there were no foreign students, no one whose name ended in *i* or *o*. Bacon was the most popular man in the class; he captained the football team, rowed number seven on the crew, was a sprint champion, and won laurels as a heavyweight boxer. *His* horizons seemed unlimited; the class of 1880 was ever after known as Bacon's class.[2]

Sullivan and Bacon were poles apart, even though living within the same urban scene. Their respective promise and potential might have been produced on two different planets. The melting pot was not melting; though both men boxed, the chances of their meeting in the ring were exactly zero. Boston was no longer a harmonious homogeneity of Protestantism and acquisitive Yankee shrewdness (if indeed it ever was)—by 1900 the total of newcomers outnumbered the old colonial stock two to one—but the bluebloods and longtime natives would not give ground voluntarily. Urban life around young Sullivan and Bacon was riddled with strain and strife as the Catholic Irish struggled at the ballot box, in the schools, in the police department, and in the job market for a share of power, prestige, and security.[3]

The Irish reinforced their urban insularity by their habit of looking down on newer immigrant groups. Men like Mike Sullivan knew of the strong biases against them (one of the coarsest of which was that Irishmen were simply "niggers turned inside out"), and they often passed on the custom of vicious disparagement. The Irish tended to move to more favored parts of the city, not only to escape residential crowding but also to place as much distance as possible between themselves and more recent immigrants from the Continent. The situation became so serious by the latter years of the century that both Irish churchmen and Irish ward politicians actively sought to prevent relocation of their parishioners and voters. John Sullivan came to maturity carrying a full cargo of ethnic prejudices gained from this cultural insularity, including a strong and enduring bias against blacks. This is not to say that Boston's Irish lived in a social and cultural ghetto, on the model of later black ghettos like Harlem. In fact, levels of residential segregation in Boston may have been lower in John's youth than they later became. Degrees of residential concentration are only secondary factors in developing ethnic consciousness, and "Irish" areas in Boston proved less enduring than later Italian and black neighborhoods. Irish communities in Boston failed to develop fully.[4]

Indeed, no element of Boston's working-class population was firmly rooted in the way advocates of the "ghetto hypothesis" suggest. Large numbers of every immigrant group, including the Irish, left Boston altogether within a relatively short time, and many of those who remained soon moved from inner-city neighborhoods toward the city's outskirts, as did Mike and Catherine Sullivan. Boston's Irish had fluid migratory patterns; they were not uniform in background and were not all impoverished or destitute.[5] They had spatial if not occupational mobility. Unfortunately for those who prefer the rags-to-riches myth, especially in the American sporting experience, John L. Sullivan did not battle his way to fame and fortune out of an urban slum.

Politics became the avenue by which the Irish could not only achieve local power but also demonstrate how "American" they actually were. Irish-American societies of all stripes generally were full-blown patriotic organizations, in addition to their other functions. The nativist nightmare of a horde of papists, in thrall to the Ould Sod or to His Eminence in Rome, undercutting true American values, never really materialized. The Irish assimilated politically to such a significant and successful degree that their victories at the ballot box were a continuous and ironic reminder of their difficulties in everyday life.

Thus the Boston Irish of Sullivan's day present the seeming paradox of growing success and achievement in one arena, accompanied by extremely limited mobility in another. Given the cultural barriers to their economic and social betterment, they drew in on themselves, blunting their frustration and hostility to the outside world by developing a sense of unity within their own cultural ranks. Most continued to value God, home, and community, and many honored Protestant-inspired homilies concerning the "cardinal virtues" of frugality, management, self-control, temperance, purpose, pluck, and persistence.[6] They generated their own symbols of hope and aspiration: the politician, the priest, and, eventually, the athlete. The lace-curtain Irish tended more toward arts and letters, favoring such flowers of Irish-American culture as John Boyle O'Reilly. But John Sullivan's Irish, and eventually his working-class compeers, preferred vivid and forceful symbols that were part of everyday life. These symbols encouraged some hope of individual social mobility, however circumscribed; of individual economic reward, however limited; and of some increase in status, particularly in the eyes of the group that counted most — one's own peers.

Drawn together by the forces of their urban environment, Boston's working-class Irish created an ethnic substratum in terms of communication, aspiration, and cultural symbolism. They engaged in endless combinations of social groupings, celebrating their heritage as they promoted the distant promise of American life. "The Hibernian is first, last and always a social being," wrote one observer, "and this instinct does not fail him even in his times of distress and bereavement."[7] Indeed, funerals and wakes were among the primary ceremonies through which Boston's Irish celebrated their culture.

And yet the inequities of urban life were hard to bear. The Irish were in constant conjunction with people at the upper end of the scale. They served the "better sort" in their well-appointed homes; they drove them on the clanking new street railway cars; they laid their sewer lines and cleaned their streets. The differences were painfully evident in daily life. An older generation of the elite had been sturdily convinced that God alone made the lot of the well-to-do superior to that of the deprived. Numerous Protestant ministers had advised those lower down on life's scale never to be dissatisfied with their calling. They must "choke that devilish envy," urged the evangelical liberal Horace Bushnell. Besides, too much work and concern with affairs brought strain and its own particular hardship. One made great sacrifices to get to the top, often at considerable cost. A foreign observer of the Boston of John's youth perceived with amazement that young businessmen were prematurely middle-aged. "The principal business of life seems to be to grow old as fast as possible."[8]

Many Americans, most of them urban, viewed the city as as a place of opportunity and progress, especially for the young. Municipalities of nineteenth-century America supposedly placed a premium on youthful energy and drive. Increasingly, the city grew more remote from the placid, stable agricultural world on which it depended. Older patterns of regularity and acceptance of things as they stood were giving way to ambition, acquisitiveness, and daring, the attributes of youth rather than advancing age. The problem for young Irish Americans like John Sullivan in this world of hustle, grab, and go was that they had trouble competing in the first place. Boston's Irish were almost distinguished in their inability to gain the kinds of employment that would offer financial rewards, security, and some sort of social status. Even though they were by far the largest of the city's immigrant groups, and even though they had seized political control in the wards by the late 1880s, the Irish faced considerable difficulty in translating their obvious political clout into meaningful economic and social terms.[9]

The city, in its nonintellectual dimensions, was becoming a far more materialist world then it had ever been before. After the Civil War a tendency arose to associate the wealth of the country with industrial wealth, which meant the city. Uncle Sam, the business figure, was now triumphant; Brother Jonathan, once the wise interlocutor of American folk wisdom, had metamorphosed into a clumsy hayseed. The new industrial state was coming to be connected with patriotism as well as individualism, and its material interests were often perceived as tantamount to moral values. This interaction of materialism and morality troubled many but in no way impeded the rise of the city as a beacon of opportunity. Reformers might believe that "society owed a man an environment sufficient to allow him to be moral without requiring him to be a hero."[10] But the materialist vision had powerful seductive force.

In truth, visitors to our shores had always noted the acquisitiveness and energy of Americans, particularly in the cities. Theoretically, every American had the inherent opportunity to define himself through the act of making money. Self-definition and identity could come through other routes, of course: a professional career, a calling, an education, inheritance, or public service. But essentially, young men in America (women did not count) had to resolve the question of how they would relate to money in their lives, in acquiring and spending it.[11] Modern success usually requires "expertise" of some sort, professionalism and special training. In John Sullivan's youth the roads to success were more broad and open, if one started with the right credentials. A few of the more prominent materialists in the public eye, men like Cornelius Vanderbilt, Andrew Carnegie, and John D. Rockefeller, had been burdened neither by weighty family lineage nor by much formal education as they amassed their fortunes. The practical rather than the professional man was the ideal of the era, the yardsticks of practicality being usefulness and profit. The inventor Thomas Edison was superior to Harvard's president, Charles Eliot, and his "five-foot shelf" of knowledge.

For cultural critics the pursuit of mammon was the virus of the age. Everything—economics, science, business—was "pursued in deadly earnest." Sullivan's contemporaries, particularly the middle classes, tended to take themselves with portentous seriousness, whether at work or at play. American society was generations away from evolving "safety nets" such as social security, unemployment insurance, and health benefits. To struggle for survival seemed an unavoidable condition of life. Reformers found easy targets in the ostentatious displays of the vulgar rich, venal politics, and chauvinistic spread-eagle orators. They offered much sympathy to and trenchant criticism of the plight of the slum dweller, the immigrant, and exploited blacks and women.[12] But their time, in spite of considerable labor strife and urban tension, had not yet come.

Most Americans could not, and would not, stand for such endless strain in their lives if it were, indeed, never-ending. More and more they were finding necessary psychological outlets in play and recreation, both as a release from the pressures of their urbanizing, industrializing society and as an analogue to it. In many ways they were beginning to define their culture through play and recreation as well as through occupation and social mobility. Play and recreation were rapidly developing fixed rules and a logical order all their own, partaking of the age of industrialism while avoiding the potentially permanent dangers of failure in the real industrial world. Indeed, the recreational experience offered a surcease from the cares of "real life" and a kind of freedom that could not be experienced in any other way.[13] John Sullivan, luckily for him, grew to manhood just as urban American society was organizing itself for play and competitive sport.

## II

Americans, even the much-maligned Puritans, had always been fond of their leisure time. In the colonial period, amid the more relaxed and bucolic patterns of an agricultural economy, play and purpose tended to be one, with recreations such as hunting and fishing supplying a most practical dimension to existence. The rural experience provided countless diversions throughout the nineteenth century, horse racing emerging as the favorite spectator sport. Andrew Jackson had a fair claim to being the nation's premier patron of the turf, and in his concerns and those of his followers can be found many of the preeminent sporting values of antebellum America.

The Jacksonians admired staying power, the willingness to stick with a task once started. To participate in the sporting life meant to take risks, to wager in some way on an outcome. Victory—at almost any cost—was vital, offering concrete proof of success and of the risk well-taken. Above all, the sporting contest, seen both as play and as a deadly serious game, was a school for life in which human conduct was most exposed. Sport was part of life's tissue, not something removed and remote.[14]

Here, then, was a cultural device that invited participation and stressed the implicit values of the contest. In the sporting arena the outsider could be brought inside, even if only for a little while. Most sport spoke in a universal language and tended to ameliorate some of the social and economic barriers raised by the industrial age. For example, Abraham Cahan's fictional Jewish immigrant, Jake, entertained his fellow sweatshop workers in New York City with tales of boxing champions, believing that he was improving his English and thus smoothing his acculturation into American society. Even an illiterate could comprehend sport.

The growth of the cities contributed directly to the developing fascination with all forms of sport. In a more and more regimented era, when people increasingly lived to the metronomic beat of the clock rather than the languid movement of the seasons, sports such as boxing encouraged defiance of convention, the urge to violate the established order of things. Urban life seemed in constant flux. The attendant uncertainty drove city dwellers to find outlets in recreation, both as participants and as spectators. People appeared to be in constant activity; urban culture spread from sensation to new sensation in an atmosphere where yesterday's news grew quickly stale and empty. European visitors, perhaps accustomed to more timeless patterns of culture and with an inbred suspicion of novelty, could only stand appalled. One of them noted on his American tour in 1876 that culture "lives in America from day to day."[15]

Some Americans also perceived the acceleration of pace. Changing patterns of work and play were accompanied by noticeable changes in family life, community, and sexual behavior. The problem was that industrialization and urbanization did not substitute a newer order of things for an older; in the late nineteenth century the industrial era had yet to find its cultural voice. "Despite many changes, the old ways had not yet generated a new religion, a new art, a new economics, or a new government which would be able to order up the vast scale of life in which the common people now lived."[16]

Nevertheless, the rhythms of the industrial workplace were penetrating the culture at all levels. An efficient businessman was naked without a fob watch to tell him when (precisely). By 1880 even the tiniest hamlet served by a railroad orbited around the railway timetable; to facilitate railroad scheduling the country dissected itself into "time zones." In the multiplying office warrens and in the factories the ubiquitous "time clock" made its appearance. Even the vaudeville house, purveyor of entertainment to the urban masses, scheduled its performances to coincide with the ebb and flow of people to and from work. Vaudevillians usually kept their performances brief, from seven to fifteen minutes, each transcendent sensation matching the pulse of urban life in the street outside. Nor was sport itself immune. Football, basketball (after 1891), and many other sports operated within a strict industrial time frame of minutes and seconds. Even baseball, the pastoral game par excellence, reflected the newer rhythms. A well-defined game of rules, it featured carefully regulated competition and the finest judgment on the part of the interpreters of the rules. Inside the ballpark, baseball fans could see order as well as experience a pastoral drama, a bifurcated vision that reflected the tensions of urban life even as it eased them.[17]

John Sullivan's Boston partook in these changes in the urban scene to the fullest measure. Schoolboy sports were always popular, and Sullivan's participation on several semipro neighborhood baseball teams was typical of athletically minded youngsters of his social and economic background. The city itself became involved in the 1880s, when it developed the first "local recreation ground" (the ancestor of today's all-weather, artificial-turfed monstrosities), replete with field houses, a running track, sports equipment, and trained attendants. Once community money and interest became involved, the older aristocratic tradition of track and field sports began to be shouldered aside. This tradition never gave way, and indeed newer sports like golf and tennis, as well as the older capital-intensive pursuits of polo and yachting, carried the aristocratic cachet well into the twentieth century.[18] But Americans in the industrial age demanded broader recreational outlets, and these opportunities grew dramatically in the latter years of the nineteenth century.

Recreation was practically an all-male preserve, a format for sexual segregation that faithfully reflected male attitudes in the wider society. The beautiful, athletic Gibson Girl was still a generation away. In Boston the Irish subculture carried sexual segregation and stereotyping of sexual roles to perhaps the furthest reaches in American life. Massachusetts had once been in the vanguard of feminist concerns, but that had been during the years before the Irish influx. Now, most males were intolerant of the notion of women voting, but Irish women were a special case. Oliver Wendell Holmes had refused to sign a petition against women's suffrage, but he could write a friend that "as our households are constituted, I do not care to see the basement arrayed in greater force against the drawing room (which it nearly governs already) by adding Bridget and Hanna to the list of votes." The Irish Democrats of Boston agreed; staunch tradition held that their wives and daughters had no place at the polls.[19]

Boston's Irish males saw the ideal woman as dutifully subordinate, submissive, and obedient to the natural authority of man. Indeed, Irish women never challenged male public hegemony. Men might be expected to rush into marriage, given such an opportunity for overlordship, but in fact Irish males were notoriously reluctant to marry, and since the good Irish colleen had to wait to be asked, Irish-American marriages tended to take place much later than those of other immigrant groups, such as the Germans and the Italians. Many Irish families numbered several bachelors between the ages of twenty and forty-five, most of whom lived at home (as did John Sullivan until the age of twenty-four). The Irish view of women was dramatically polarized, too, into the Madonna-whore duality. Most Irish girls were properly chaste, of course, but the growing numbers of Irish prostitutes on the streets of urban American betokened a vision that allowed for nothing between the angel and the fallen woman.[20]

Women were expected to moderate, if not govern, the tempestuous passions and sudden urges of the male. Their role was within the home; they were there to provide peace, tranquillity, and (unspoken) a legitimate sexual outlet for the dominant male. Sullivan, for example, would later claim that his "good little woman" could "keep him straight" and off the booze. Of course many women refused to live up to this smothering ideal in practical terms. Many feminists preached a sort of reverse stereotyping, seeing womanhood as implying harmony, love, purity, and altruistic thoughts. Manhood implied strength, unbridled sexual passion, and egoism. Male strength meant a dangerous, selfish individualism, and some women chose to resist. But not "good" Irish-American women. Rigidly trained from birth that their destiny was marriage, motherhood, and family, they could only wait submissively for the supposedly fulfilling proposal of wedlock that might never come. If it did, their sphere of dominance would be the home, not the workplace. If it did not, they would work where they could, as domestics, seamstresses, or, for the many who aggressively pursued an education, as schoolteachers. As in the Old Country, girls from poor families were permitted to select their own husbands, but even so, family wishes entered into the marital decision to a considerable degree. And these Irish women were encouraged to marry their own kind; between 1875 and 1879 the entire Boston Irish community averaged only fifty "mixed" marriages annually.[21]

It was natural, then, that Boston's young Irish males, searching for comradeship in their leisure time, would band together in masculine groups for recreation and self-support. They lived within an ethos of "gender hostility," with each sex possessing a rationale for the faults of the other. Marriage was a proposition to be deferred into the future, given economic and cultural constraints. In this the young men of Sullivan's generation mirrored the propensity of the growing middle class for all-male associations, both formal and informal. In these "privileged enclaves" such as clubs, colleges, and professional or ser-vice-oriented "brotherhoods," men could glory in their superiority and continue boyish behavior patterns well into middle age. Here they could perpetuate rather than abandon adolescent ties, and here they could leave the women to their natural "sphere," the home, while reserving to themselves the allegedly natural masculine prerogatives of thought and action. Sullivan rejoiced in this all-male world and, indeed, never left it until he was almost fifty. He would prove to be a classic "joiner," and he later proudly described himself as a worthy past president of New York Aerie Number 40, Fraternal Order of Eagles (he was also an Elk), "one of its most influential and active members."[22]

These all-male associations were a mix of bachelors and married men. Those with wives often participated in club or group activities all their lives. In the traditional Irish bachelor group, married men were often the leaders, chosen for their experiences in storytelling, fighting, and drinking.[23] For John Sullivan participation in the all-male world would bring enormous psychic rewards. He would prove to be a raconteur of considerable charm and dimension, the greatest fighter of his age, and, for most of his adult life, an alcoholic.

# III

This "cult of masculinity" into which Sullivan naturally and auto-matically entered as a young man was tied together by friendships, rough-and-ready camaraderie, tall tales, and masculine fantasies, but above all it was welded together by alcohol. Drinking had always been a part of the American scene, even among the Puritans, but as early as the Revolutionary period the practice had become public enough, and pernicious enough, to raise comment. The transplanted French-man Crèvecoeur noted that his fellow hunters divided their time "be-tween the toil of the chase, the idleness of repose, or the indulgence of inebriation." And he remarked of the Irish that they "do not prosper so well; they love to drink and quarrel—their wages are too low and their whiskey too cheap." The Irish were destined by their shortcomings to fail—out of twelve families of immigrants from each country, opined Crèvecoeur, seven Scotch families would succeed, nine German, and only four Irish. Thus, early in the American experience Irish foibles were connected with the use of alcohol.[24]

Amost everywhere, particularly in urban America, excessive drinking was a major social concern. As a boy on Long Island, Walt Whitman saw drunken behavior on every hand. He would reflect in old age that "it is very hard for the present generation . . . to understand the drinkingness of those years. . . . even little boys at, or under twelve years of age, go into stores, and tip off their drams!" Henry James, Jr., coming to maturity in an impeccably noteworthy Boston family, divided American society into three classes: "the busy, the tipsy, and Daniel Webster." The observant tourist Captain Frederick Marryat was lethally specific:

> Americans can fix nothing without a drink. If you meet, you drink; if you part, you drink; if you make acquaintance, you drink; if you close a bargain, you drink; they quarrel in their drink, and they make it up with a drink. They drink because it is hot; they drink because it is cold. If successful in elections, they drink and rejoice; if not they drink and swear; they begin to drink early in the morning, they leave off late at night; they commence it early in life, and they continue it, until they soon drop into the grave.[25]

Among John Sullivan's generation drink was no respecter of social class, despite middle-class pretensions to the contrary. For example, intemperance was rife at Harvard, particularly in the social clubs, even the vaunted Porcellian. Students drank whiskey (cheap and easy to get), French champagne, burgundy, beer and ale by the keg, and a deadly concoction of beer and ginger ale called shandygaff. The favorite grogshop of the class of 1880 was a pit called Carl's, situated below sidewalk level on Brighton Street. In spite of such obvious derelictions, some members of the middle class made the temperance cause their own and the wretched excesses of alcohol the property of their social inferiors. Henry Ward Beecher, the most admired preacher of his day (until sexual scandal intervened), was an ardent temperance man and a popular voice of middle class concerns, remembering that in his youth drinking had been all but universal. "The noisome odors of the bar polluted even the parsonage on the occasion of ordinations and other kindred ministerial gatherings."[26]

Protestant churchmen like Beecher were in the forefront of the crusade. They preached that whether a family lived in the city or on the frontier, a father's addiction to alcohol meant ruin for all. Many of them moved beyond temperance to the teetotal position of complete rejection of alcoholic drink. Eventually social reform campaigns came to mean not only a sympathetic effort to uplift the fallen but also a campaign of intolerance and hatred against the drinker. John Sullivan would come in time to feel the full force of this attitude. The reformer's view was that drink and its attendant vices sank the lower classes into a cycle of depravity, "inferior amusements degrading the people [and] degraded people enjoying inferior amusements." Intemperance had become so popular in Boston, fulminated Theodore Parker, that it was supported by the mayor and aldermen, had possession of the state's House of Representatives, and saturated the social and political climate. "Every thirty-fifth voter in Boston is a licensed seller of rum."[27]

Some Americans drank for company, and some, according to the more jaundiced critics, drank only to drink. The Irish appeared, especially in the eyes of the predominantly Protestant and middle-class reformers, to be a special case. They were given to reducing tension with strong drink, it was said. Their loud, boisterous drinking behavior was the least of it; within a few years the majority of these navvies, coal heavers, and canal diggers would drink themselves to death. A few reformers might recall the instructive tale of Sam Patch, a penniless Irishman who, in a fit of despair over his dismal life in the Land of Promise, threw himself into the seventy-foot deep at the Grand Falls of the Passaic River. He survived, to remember that a large crowd had gathered to watch him do himself in. Patch began to jump into rivers and gorges for money, until in 1829 near Rochester's Genessee Falls he climbed atop a platform, ceremoniously bowed to thousands of spectators, and thereupon plunged 122 feet to his death. He was dead drunk.[28]

Such salutary stories as that of poor Patch had no effect on the b'hoys in the barroom. In Boston they would have admired his pluck before mourning his stupidity. The cult of masculinity celebrated the deed before the disaster. But to outsiders used to dealing in the fundamental simplicities of ethnic stereotypes, "drunkenness . . . is the great sin of the Irish population." Statistics embellished the stereotypes. In all of Boston a total of twenty-two breweries opened before 1860. The German *Braumeisters* all located in the Roxbury section, where John Sullivan grew up, and helped establish it as the city's primary German neighborhood. Most of the employees lived near the breweries, which were notable facilities in a city lacking raw materials and significant heavy industry. Roxbury quickly became a regional center for the popular lager beer, and John matured amid its profitable manufacture and retailing.[29]

And not only beer. In 1846, 850 liquor dealers plied their trade in Boston; only three years later fully 1,200 outlets were engaged in the retail liquor business. A survey by the city marshal in 1851 indicated that a majority of these groggeries were operated by the Irish, almost half of them concentrated in the run-down North End and Fort Hill districts. Numerous Irish families traded in liquor without a license, many of them manufacturing gin of uncertain heritage and selling it as a sideline. Irish names riddled police blotters, their holders charged with insobriety and crimes committed under the influence. Other nationalities, particularly the Germans, partook of alcohol and beer, but owing to their more temperate habits they seldom drank to the excess displayed by some Irish males. The hypothesis has been advanced that the Irish tended to substitute drinking for eating as a consequence of guilt produced by the Catholic church's encouragement of fasting and remembrance of poverty and famine. In this view children were socialized into making drink the psychological equivalent of food.[30] The evidence from John Sullivan's youth speaks against this, suggesting strongly that, for the Irish male, drinking was a fundamental tool of socialization, the participation in which sealed one's entrance into the cult of masculinity. There was substance in the stereotype.

Most saloons in Boston managed some sort of propriety, and a few, like Harry Hill's in New York, had their pretensions to elegance. But some, like the worst Bowery dives in New York, purveyed nothing but drunkenness in its rawest form. In these dimly lit hutches drinks might be as little as three cents each, and no glasses or mugs were deemed necessary. Barrels of fiery alcohol, 100-proof or more, were aligned on shelves behind the bar, dispatching their contents through a slender rubber hose. The patron, having deposited his three cents on the bar, was entitled to place the end of the hose in his mouth and siphon off all he could without breathing. The supply would be turned off by the watchful bartender the moment he took another breath. A large lung capacity could bring complete inebriation for three pennies. Most saloons, however, featured some amenities. Seats were available in a few, though most had none. There was limited free space outside the bar, and indeed some of these establishments were nothing *but* bar, being mere holes-in-the-wall a little as ten feet wide. Loitering after drinking was not encouraged. As a concession to the forces of law and order some owners took down the screens over their windows so that the interior goings-on could be visible to passers-by. German-owned saloons tended to be better at providing tables, chairs, and the inducement of free sandwiches and pickles. The Irish preferred their drinking standing up, there sometimes being no room in these cribs for any other posture.[31]

The Irish pub filled several roles for the cult of masculinity. For recreation, relaxation, and participatory socialization it was practically the only meeting place available that was free of women and had the required ability to provide alcohol on demand. The pub developed into a centerpiece of ward politics, many publicans being themselves bastions of neighborhood political machines. Shop and union meetings were often held in saloons, and from time to time the military even sent in recruiters hoping to catch restless, rootless young males in a receptive mood. The saloon was often a commercial nexus as well, making change and, in a later era, cashing the checks of workingmen. It was, finally, a center of local communication, a gossip mart and forum for public opinion. With the alcoholic component sometimes temporarily removed, the saloon could (and did) serve as a dance hall, a locale for relief benefits, and a meeting place after that beloved Irish institution, the wake. The stereotype of the immigrant Irish publican, however, is groundless. Tradition held that "every other Celt wore a bar apron," but the census of 1880 showed that although the Irish were the largest immigrant group in Boston (23.3 percent of all the city's foreign-born), they made up only 22.3 percent of the employees in the retail liquor trade. Only 0.7 percent of the total Irish work force worked in the trade, exactly the same as the percentage among the native-born.[32]

Young John Sullivan probably never made a conscious decision to drink. The drinking man's environment was all around him, and he entered into it, with his peers, as naturally as slipping on an old pair of shoes. He was noticeably reticent about his drinking in his ghosted autobiography, and we do not know when he began to drink, where, or with whom. Perhaps he "ran the growler" for Mike, as so many lads did for their fathers. The growler, an ugly but highly functional tin pail, was universally found in immigrant neighborhoods. It was cheap and durable, a homemade inner lining often adding to its longevity. It could carry lunch, coffee, or a small bottle of whiskey to keep a worker going in the morning. But at noon the homely little pail would hold about half a gallon of beer. Every day dozens of boys would gather at factory gates and other workplaces to "rush the can" for their elders, some of them doubling up on a long pole to carry as many as twelve growlers per trip. The going wage for this service was a penny a person.[33] In the evening many fathers would send their sons out for more of the foaming brew.

John early became a member of an all-male environment in which masculine associations often were bonded (some would say pickled) in alcohol. In doing so he became part of a loosely knit web of masculine activity that comprised Boston's sporting establishments, gambling halls, billiard parlors, and houses of prostitution as well as saloons, for the cult of masculinity naturally ebbed and flowed around these enterprises, too. Such amusements were also steady, ingrained habits among Boston's males. In 1895 Boston patrolmen made a headcount indicating that daily patronage of the city's six hundred saloons amounted to almost half the entire urban population. Most noticeable in terms of their group cohesion amid this mass were the Irish. "In

Ireland drink was largely a sign of male identity; in America it was a symbol of Irish identity."[34]

Many of these young bachelors and married men away from home did not just drink, they drank *hard*. To consume, and overconsume, served several purposes. Masculine solidarity could be expressed at the same time that the assertion of male distinctiveness from the "female world" could be made. Males could establish and reaffirm their identities in the rituals of the bottle (treating, toasting, and so forth), both as individuals and as a group. Drinking served as a rite of passage as well, signifying the emergence of the youngster into the community of adult males. Finally, hard drinking was an avenue to status within the group. Ultimate prestige accrued to him who could drink often, drink long, and give little outward sign of intoxication; admiration centered on the man who "could hold his liquor."[35] (While he entered into this masculine world with gusto, John Sullivan always had a little trouble with the last part.)

Boys learned the rules early, surrounded as they were by adult male role models. At first shy of taking a drink, and perhaps disliking the taste, most of them responded to adult and peer pressure, and then initiated other youngsters in the same exercise. Hard drinking was held up to novices as a signature of group loyalty, personal status, and superiority. The treating ritual turned the saloon into a sanctuary of communal friendship and cozy insularity against the outside world; treating was a "symbol of group integration and an affirmation of male identity." John Sullivan soon learned that he must stand for drinks to belong and be respected. Such rituals could take place in any setting, from Carl's, the rat hole favored by the Harvard boys, to "the gilded saloon, with its welcoming warmth, its cheery light, and other enticements, where, for the price of two or three glasses of liquor, the poor man may pass an evening with boon companions."[36]

The saloon was never a completely all-male preserve. The public incidence of male drunkenness was far higher than that among women, but many people believed that women, particularly middle-class women, preferred to do their drinking in private because of the social pressures surrounding their "sphere." Except for the occasional daring renegades, women did not drink in large numbers in public until the invention of the "cocktail hour" and the speakeasy in the 1920s. Lower-class women in Sullivan's generation ran the growler just as children did, but they seldom stayed in the saloon with the men. Their fief was the home, but men sought surrogate homes and families: "Men left the home as much in search of a place to drink as of something to drink." Nevertheless, some women helped their husbands tend bar, particularly in the German-run saloons. Prostitutes were a common feature of the barroom scene, particularly in the lower dives, and on occasion a workingman and his wife would publicly drink together. But these rare female incursions did not dent the overwhelming force of the cult; saloons were an accurate reflection of the larger, male-dominated urban society.[37]

Public drinking fought a long and largely losing fight with the social values of sobriety and respectability. More precisely, the relaxed bonhomie of the saloon ran counter to the thrust of industrial society, which demanded regularity, discipline, and punctuality as well as productivity. In Boston the licensing process initiated in the 1880s was designed to make drinking as public as possible. In 1870 there had been as many as twenty-five hundred illegal bars in the Hub (one for every ninety-seven people); the License Board sought to limit the number of on-premises drinking places as well as the carry-home trade. By 1896, 79.3 percent of all liquor dealers in Boston were hotels or restaurants. The crippling blow to the saloon occurred in 1888, with the establishment of a legal ratio of one liquor license for every five hundred citizens. In 1899 the total number of Boston licenses was frozen at one thousand, no matter how much the city grew in the future.[38] In short, Sullivan's generation was the last to come of age in a Boston where the saloon-oriented and virtually all-male world reigned supreme. Although John, for most of his life, remained a classic model of the environment that had produced him, the surrounding urban scene was changing, and thus criticisms of his behavior, particularly from "respectable people," would double and redouble in volume.

Male drinking and bonding extended to the world of sport and recreation. In the colonial period taverns had tended to be individualized and rural. By the late nineteenth century many of the new professional athletes came from urban cults of masculinity, and they incorporated their drinking habits into their sporting life. Pugilists and their backers often used saloons as headquarters. The barroom was a center of neighborhood sporting gossip, and rare was the bartender who did not adorn his establishment with at least one portrait of a sporting hero of the day, even if he had four legs, like the famous trotter Dan Patch. Some bars offered a roped-off area in a back room where aspiring pugilists could spar or neighborhood enemies work out some of their antagonism.[39]

But these masculine drinking and bonding patterns carried an import beyond social custom and ethnic or class stereotyping. John Sullivan's youthful universe had a dark, nightmarish component of violence that was both disturbing and threatening to social order. Barrooms, booze, and exaggerated notions of masculinity formed a potent mix. The "model homicide" in nineteenth-century Philadelphia, and probably in the nineteenth-century American city, resulted from a saloon-originated brawl or quarrel that ended with death in the streets. Most killings occurred among the lower classes, and liquor was closely associated with both homicide and assault. In Boston violent, alcohol-related crimes were higher among the Irish than among all other ethnic groups, and the incidence of death from alchoholism among Boston's Irish in the 1880s was four times that of the next highest ethnic group.[40] John Sullivan, a temperamental young man contemplating a brutal trade, was part of a cult of masculinity that produced a considerable portion of the nation's criminal activity and violent behavior.

## IV

To modern psychoanalysts, aggressiveness is a psychologically determined drive that must be understood in light of the entire ego structure and personality. Claims that humans share the fighting instinct with lower orders of animals have been severely modified, and it is a matter of debate whether we lack inborn inhibitions against severely crippling, injuring, or killing our fellows.[41] Aggression that leads to violence may have deeply seated pyschological, physiological, or even biological causes, of course, but the *incidence* of violent behavior is predominantly an economic and social phenomenon.

Regional comparisons of violent behavior in post–Civil War America are instructive. The classic arena of violence, much beloved in song and story, was the Wild West. So firmly have the adventures of the cowboys, cattle punchers, miners, gamblers, and stern-jawed town marshals impressed themselves on our minds that it is almost inconceivable to perceive the region as anything other than a violent maelstrom of quick tempers and flashing guns. The cattle towns, in particular, live on in legend, outlined by endless confrontations on deserted, dusty streets. These booming conglomerations of hotels, brothels, and barrooms did indeed at one time harbor a veritable rogue's gallery of shady characters: John Wesley Hardin, Doc Holliday, Clay Allison, Ben Thompson. On the side of law and order, but with itchy trigger fingers, were such as Wild Bill Hickok, Wyatt Earp, and Bat Masterson.

With such a cast of gunmen, Abilene, Dodge City, Wichita, and the rest might be expected to have been bathed in flying lead during their heyday. They were not. Allison, Holliday, Thompson, and Masterson had clean records. Earp and another policeman may have mortally wounded one miscreant, and Hickok killed two men, one by mistake. John Wesley Hardin, a teenage thug, apparently fired through his hotel room wall one night while drunk and permanently silenced a guest who had been snoring too loudly next door. Not surprisingly, if this bunch could account for only three deaths and one possible, it is scarcely remarkable that the general incidence of homicide statistics in the cattle towns was not particularly high. The number of homicides never topped five in any cattle season year, reaching this number only in Ellsworth in 1873 and Dodge City in 1878. Overall, sixteen out of twenty-five cattle-town homicides can be attributed to law officers or citizens legitimately filling that role.[42]

The West yearned for stability and order. True badmen were rarely tolerated, and western towns were quick to build a bank, send for a schoolmarm, and appeal for the railroad to come their way. The OK Corral, Judge Roy Bean, and the Indian wars will always color our view, but, although solid statistics are lacking, it is fair to say that no determining evidence has yet been offered to show the West as America's most violent region in John Sullivan's youth. True, conflict was a major theme in the cattle towns as throughout the West, but the resolution of conflict by violence does not appear to have occurred more frequently there than anyplace else.

The South had its own particular strain of violence, scarcely taking a back seat to the West in this regard. Racial violence, a nationwide phenomenon, was at its most overt there. In addition, the South was the primary locale of that weird wedding of manners and violence, the duel. Mere feuds were deplored, particularly among the gentry, because they incited bad blood, initiated conflicts of loyalty among families, and generally disrupted community life. The duel, however, gave both structure and ritual to the South's vision of its manhood. Duels were refereed, supposed to be scrupulously fair, and theoretically a clear-cut indicator of masculine superiority. Although mostly confined to the social elite, dueling served the same social purpose as primal combat between specialists in the fine frontier art of eye gouging. Neither was dueling a sign of caste; those lower on the social scale could ape their betters with the ritual and even, at times, fight a social superior. The duel did have a certain social cachet: it was manly and honorable. The rough-and-tumble brawl, by contrast, was violence unrestrained and was much deprecated by the "better sort" across the South.[43]

Mere fighting had its place, however. Boyish battles often led to long-standing friendships and mutual admiration. Even adult scraps could end positively, as the rather incredible relationship between Thomas Hart Benton and Andrew Jackson might attest. Fighting gave experience in self-defense, endowed the winner with certain leadership traits (such as courage), and often served as a force in male bonding. At a different level altogether were the no-holds-barred donnybrooks of the southern frontier. Antagonists with spearlike fingernails honed to a razor's edge stalked each other with the express purpose of blinding or permanently maiming their opponents. The gouging match was truly barbaric, but it had its own rituals and pretenses to honor: "Eye gouging was the poor and middling whites' own version of an historical southern tendency to consider personal violence socially useful—indeed, ethically essential." As bloody and crude as they were, and they were beyond bestial since beasts do not fight to wound deliberately, these matches served as focal events in the lives of lower-class southern males, although even in this group they were obviously not everyone's cup of tea.[44]

The industrializing Northeast had never seen anything to approach the western cattle town, the duel, or the eye-gouging match. Violent behavior in the urban centers tended to be more family-centered than in the West and more closely allied to the saloon than in the South. There is every indication that industrialization produced a decline in violent and reckless conduct, simply because the industrial regimen of the factory, office, railroad, and schoolyard was highly intolerant of disruptive and deviant behavior. As John Sullivan came to manhood, the rates of major crimes in Boston, such as murders, rapes, robberies, burglaries, assaults, and larcenies, abruptly declined. Therefore, at the same time that industrialization and urbanization were increasing status uncertainties and creating tension-filled ambiguities in the patterns of daily life, the traditional outlets of sudden, violent behavior were being sealed off. The result, for some, might be tragic: disassociation, anomie, depression, and complete despair. Again, statistics are sparse, but it appears that urban America after the Civil War experienced an increasing rate of suicides, far higher than the rates in the West, with its seemingly infinite promise and appeal to youth, or those in the South, with its widespread network of supportive kinship systems and its recourse to structured violence.[45]

The Industrial Revolution had made personal firearms cheaper, more effective, and more readily available, and they were used as much in urban America as in the West for committing violent crime and wreaking other havoc. As urban society grew less tolerant of violent behavior (a bullet discharging on one of Boston's crowded thoroughfares had a much better chance of striking someone than a similar shot on the main street of Dodge City), people sought other outlets for the tensions of urban existence. The notion grew that violence could be accepted only if it were controlled and regulated, and if it resulted in an outcome not directly harmful to society. "Bloody violence," to many, was not "noble"; it was merely a return to primal urges, the unchaining of the human beast—a horrible reversal of Darwinian logic. What was required, it seemed, was not the cessation of aggressive urges; even in this pre-Freudian era most people considered that an impossibility. Instead, forms of surrogate violence, in which aggressive behavior could be acted out in a setting of rules and equity, became more and more popular.

Surrogate violence offered a strong appeal to the heroic dimensions in man. Honor could be fought for, and won; virtue could be upheld;

beauty, as in the masculine form, could be celebrated. Thus carefully closeted, violence need not overflow into every nook and cranny of urban life, destroying families, driving individuals to the hospital or the grave, and lowering the painfully erected standards of modern industrial civilization. The surrogate version allowed for necessary escape, but it fell short of admitting that cruelty and violence should be widely accepted as parts of everyday life, as they had been in England two centuries before. Then, men might pay twopence to go to Bedlam and jeer at the inmates; now they could jeer the referee at a football game. Then, devotees might spend a day at Tyburn, watching criminals slowly twist at the end of a rope; now they might attend a boxing match in hopes of seeing a detested fighter bloodied and beaten.[46]

Even surrogate violence, however, featured brutality as spectacle, and many of John Sullivan's contemporaries worried that the onlookers could be corrupted in a "bread-and-circuses" atmosphere, demanding more and more until the surrogate became the thing itself. The public execution, a guaranteed crowd pleaser in the preindustrial world, attracted much criticism in this regard, even as industrialized technology made the means of dispatch more efficient. New York abolished public executions as early as 1835, but in other states, particularly in the South and West, they were performed well into the twentieth century. Kentucky did not get around to making them illegal until 1938; only two years before, the state hanged a man before an audience estimated at twenty thousand.[47]

Any kind of regulated, surrogate violence involves learned behavior on the part of the spectator as well as the participant. It followed, then, that aggression and violence, to be subjugated to the wider interests of society, had to be environmentally controlled. In such a setting surrogate violence would take on the trappings of play, recreation, and sport. It must never be allowed to become serious; the things that mattered were for the world of Darwinian struggle, which supposedly encompassed business, politics, diplomacy, and war. In the ritual and order of surrogate violence lay stability and security. Here, in a competitive yet nonthreatening atmosphere, ferocity and toughness could have full play; violent sports could become a synonym for life itself, and one's own psychic tensions could be lost in or relieved by the spectacle.[48]

Here was a potential role for the prizefight. Pugilists were considered the dregs of sporting society, a cut below baseball players and completely out of the class of horse-racing fanciers. Yet they, among all the athletes who would crop up in the last twenty years of the century, possessed the best appeal in terms of surrogate violence. They were trained "to look a stranger in the face and strike or fell him without provocation or compunction," thus having for the common man "an intense, almost zoological fascination."[49] Urban America was moving in the direction of order, regularity, and control; most city dwellers (if they were lucky) would rarely encounter full-blown, face-to-face violence in their lives. Far safer and more satisfying to watch men battering themselves to smithereens in the prize ring.

The cult of masculinity celebrated the specialist in the applied use of force, because he provided a masculine model that resolved doubts and ambiguities; demonstrated all the old Jacksonian sporting virtues—pluck, grit, competitive risk taking, the relentless urge to ultimate victory; and allowed spectators to partake painlessly in the theater of surrogate violence. In an economic landscape where the road to the top was virtually impossible to negotiate and even the uphill climb tortuous and difficult, the surrogate could provide a pyschic outlet as well as a model of economic success. If competition was the way of the world, the brutal competition of the sporting arena struck deep chords of response in many, although certainly not all, males. The man who could defend himself, physically dominating others and forcing them to yield, was dealing in common and well-understand coin in the workshops, factories, and saloons strewn across urban America.

Fundamental forces in the marketplace, the neighborhood, and the lower orders of society, inchoate though they might be, were in existence and coalescing as John Sullivan restlessly plodded through his formative years. He emerged as a complete product of the cult of masculinity, dissatisfied with the limited job opportunities open to one of his ethnic background and education and at ease with the comforting and sustaining network of friendships, acquaintances, and admirers he found in the saloon. His chosen walk of life would offer ample demonstration of the values inherent in the urban milieu he came from and, indeed, never left. All his life Sullivan played to the environment which was his heritage and in which he had matured. But in 1880 no one could see if this chosen walk of life would produce anything more than facial scars, scrambled brains, and trouble with the law. For the "manly art" was neither profession nor calling nor career.

# CHAPTER THREE

# The "Manly Art" and the Bare-Knuckle Breed

The calling chosen by John Sullivan had a long and eminently disreputable heritage. The ancient world had fostered boxing and debased it as well. Then, for a thousand-year span, the sport was unknown in Western culture. After a millenium in desuetude, pugilism emerged again amid the roiling, roistering life of early modern England.[1]

The English gave the fight game a few rules, but despite this development pugilism was surrounded by an aura of savagery and barbarism that was fairly earned and justly criticized. Bare-knuckle fighting for money was brutal at best, seen by the respectable as on a par with the hideous cruelty of blood sports involving animals. Despite entrenched opposition, however, prizefighting found favor with the aristocracy and, with the backing of toffs, dandies, and even princes of the blood, generated a rude but evident popularity among both high and low in English society.[2]

Boxing's hold on American life, with such antecedents, was uncertain even though the country was beginning to celebrate recreation, play, and sport in many forms. The growing social and moral dominance of the American middle class during the nineteenth century ensured that prizefighting would be censured as a sport and completely outlawed as a commercial spectacle. The nascent sporting crowd being what it was, though, infrequent prizefights did take place, most often involving a brace of Irish Americans slugging each other before a motley assemblage sequestered at some remote site. Prizefighters were ranked among the dregs of society, the saloon and gambling hall their natural habitats. Their morals were considered suspect, their sexual practices promiscuous, their drinking habits Promethean, and their futures bleak and destitute.

There was support for boxing within America, but such praise as came its way was severely limited to the ethic of exercise and manly self-defense. On these grounds amateur sparring, as opposed to professional prizefighting, found backers even in the middle class and supporters among the politically and socially prominent. A friendly bout between gentlemen was one thing; the degrading spectacle of two brawny hoodlums mauling each other for a purse, quite another. The manly art, in its commercial guise, had few friends in America, and most of these were lumped together toward the bottom of the social heap. Sullivan could hardly have selected a more disgraceful way of life, and he could not have done so at a worse time.

# I

Americans, children of English patterns in recreation and sport as in so much else, developed a genteel tradition of athletic "manliness" in the early years of the nation. After the War of 1812 a galaxy of physicians, educators, and reformers developed a philosophical rationale concerning the physical, mental, and spiritual benefits gained from simple exercise, games, and competitive sports. They promoted athletic activity as against the sedentary habits of the city and the sheltered confinements of home and school. Almost never, however, was prizefighting included in any recipe for the cultivation of genteel manliness.[3]

The basic elements of modern American sport, though still inchoate, were coalescing in these years before the Civil War. Abstractly, they included an ethic of competition and some equity in competitive opportunity; a rationalization of the motives for competition, primarily deriving from the benefits of manly exercise; and an emerging popularity of play. As competitive sport evolved, it tended to establish forms of bureaucratic organization and regulation, and with this came a specialization of roles, both as to participation in a certain type of sport and within a sport itself, such as baseball. Finally, athletic feats began to be quantified, their histories were kept, and achievement came to be measured in the establishment of better norms, which were then "recorded" for posterity. Participants tended to be youthful rather than aged, educated more than uneducated, Protestants more than Catholics, and upwardly mobile rather than downwardly mobile.[4] Once again, except for the youth factor, the prizefighter—largely of limited education, predominantly Irish Catholic in the nineteenth century, and mired in a slough of economic despond—tended to be beyond the pale.

All sport, according to Thorstein Veblen's classic economic formulation, comprised exploits that were "manifestations of the predatory temperament." They were partly expressions of "emulative ferocity" and partly deliberate activities for gaining repute for prowess. Veblen swept up all sports, including prizefighting, in the wordy thicket of his broom, arguing that addiction to sports was an "archaic spiritual constitution" and concluding that "a strong proclivity to adventure-some exploit and to the infliction of damage is especially pronounced in those employments which are in colloquial usage specifically called sportsmanship."[5]

Beneath the sarcastic veneer of Veblen's turgid analysis lay a fundamental truth. Americans came to enjoy their sports as mock combat, a sometimes violent theater where reputations, and careers, could be made or broken. Those who guided youthful play recognized this tendency, and many reformers fought against it, preferring to instruct children and young adults in team play while stressing the values of cooperation and mutual support. Once again, the highly individualized and primal sport of boxing lay beyond orthodoxy. But the reformers were themselves swimming upstream against a powerful current in American life, the tendency to measure improvement and progress by the degree of individual independence available.[6]

John Sullivan came to manhood as social Darwinism, an illegitimate offspring of Darwin's biological theories, captured the imagination of a considerable portion of the educated public. Social Darwinism was ambivalent in its relation to American sport. On the one hand, the persuasive notion of "natural selection" suggested that the nation could progress through manly competition and the physical bettering of the breed. On the other hand, competition might produce decline and extinction through the creation of generations of "losers." Either way, sport came to be thought of as a device for shaping American institutions, from the grammar school to the board room. The urge to compete in sport and play was thought by some to be a basic human instinct, to be channeled for the betterment of society. Instinct theory is shaky scholarly ground, but many boxing analysts have argued that pugilism is a natural outgrowth of human combative nature. "Man is a fighting animal," wrote one. "The lure of the prize ring undoubtedly has its roots deep in this primal human instinct." From the time of the cave man this instinct had held true. "Fighting was necessary to life then, and from the day that the stone ax was invented love of battle grew in the human mind—there never yet has been a champion of the prize ring who was not born a fighter."[7]

Even some of the cultural lights of Sullivan's time adhered to this view. The historian James Parton, who hated pugilism, declared that he "had fallen into the habit of taking a Darwinian view of these things, and try to think that it is part of the system by which our Mother Nature preserves and improves our species." The aristocratic Josiah Quincy shared Parton's loathing for the sport, but he believed that "ancestral savagery" accounted for the popularity of boxing in both England and America. And even the stodgy and eminently respectable *North American Review* weighed in with the argument that the risk of pain and bodily harm improved the race. Besides, boxing made *men*. It was "distinctly a man's game—helping to stave off effeminacy that is one of the dangers of nations that grow old and soft and unwilling to endure hardships." "Has mawkish sentimentality become the shibboleth of the progress, civilization and refinement of this vaunted age?" shrieked one defender of the manly art. "If so, then in Heaven's name leave us a saving touch of honest, old-fashioned barbarism! that when we come to die, we shall die, leaving men behind us, and not a race of eminently respectable female saints."[8]

These arguments would reach their logical nadir later, in the hideous excesses of twentieth-century totalitarianism. Even social Darwinists assumed that social struggle must take place within some moral coda, or else anarchy would ensue. The shapers of the power state removed this brake. Mussolini as a boy was a hooligan and brawler, carrying this prediliction for violence into his adult life. He loved to watch boxing and used to boast fancifully that he liked to fight with his boxing instructor. Punching, pronounced Il Duce, "is an exquisitely fascist means of self-expression." Hitler also celebrated the sport as promoting the spirit of attack, training the body in steel dexterity, and demanding lightning decisions. "It is not the function of the folkish state to breed a colony of peaceful aesthetes and physical degenerates."[9]

Of course, boxing could hardly be blamed for Mussolini and Hitler, but after the Civil War it did emerge as a highly favored whipping boy for respectable American culture. It was, quite simply, unacceptable. Social Darwinism aside, sport rapidly settled into a key cultural role. The historian Frederick L. Paxson years ago advanced the controversial idea that the growing national penchant for athletic competition served as a "safety valve" for the new society. The frontier, à la the famous Turner thesis, was closed down; sport was a significant reason for continued bearable existence in the dynamic flux of the crowded industrial world. "And who shall say that . . . the quickened pulse, the healthy glow, the honest self-respect of honest sport have not served in part to steady and inspire a new Americanism for a new century?" Boxing was hardly "honest sport." The dominant culture of Sullivan's era praised hard work, sobriety, and punctuality, preached religious duty, and excoriated any form of licentiousness or overt sexual activity outside the marriage bond. The sporting fraternity of the prize ring, however, had one foot firmly planted in preindustrial and preurban patterns of life even as the other gropingly sought to establish a toehold on the slopes of the new sporting culture.[10]

Boxing was not completely without cultural allies. In addition to the possibility of promoting itself as the purest form of sporting social Darwinism, it advanced, in its prizefighting guise, a purely commercial pattern of behavior. True, while the powerful forces of organized Protestantism found room for mammon in the house of God, they were extremely reluctant before the twentieth century to look favorably on sport. Equally true, the cultural accent on team play and community made boxing a pariah sport among the bourgeoisie. But prizefighting had a long suit: since its modern origins in the seamy world of Englishmen such as James Figg and Jack Broughton, it had been a commercial spectacle. The sport had never been "owned" or initiated by its participants, in the sense that football and baseball began in the amateur dimension. Indeed, within a few short years after Sullivan's death, professional boxing would prove a commercial bonanza. Eighty thousand would pay $1.6 million to see Jack Dempsey take apart Georges Carpentier at Boyle's Thirty Acres in New Jersey, and million-dollar gates were repeated when Dempsey met Luis Firpo and Gene Tunney.[11]

The English had proved that even a subterranean sport such as boxing could produce cultural heroes among certain of the population. A prizefight, under favorable conditions, was sure to draw a paying and betting crowd. But appreciation of American boxing was split severely between canons of professionalism and amateur ideals. English social values, which had been so tolerant of the likes of Daniel Mendoza, "Gentleman" John Jackson, and Tom Cribb, found tough sledding in their translation to America. A majority of respectable Americans cultivated a strong distaste for the prizefight, not only for its propensity to commercial spectacle but also for its supposed immorality. No sport could ultimately succeed in the developing mass culture unless it could attain respectability among the middle and upper classes,[12] and boxing as prizefighting thus continued as an outlaw sport. But boxing as an athletic endeavor had its supporters in the United States, and indeed the amateur ideals connected with the sport cut across class and economic lines. It seemed that boxing per se might not be so bad; if one fought for money, however, public censure tended to be quick and loud.

## II

As boxing developed in Anglo-American culture, its advocates displayed a growing interest in "science." (So, too, would Sullivan, though he rarely practiced what he preached.) Indeed, some came to call the sport the "sweet science." Pugilists regarded knowledge of human anatomy as essential, and proponents of boxing argued its merits on rational, empirical grounds. The cardinal emphasis was on positioning and mechanics. Footwork, the angling of shoulders, arms, and chin, and the delivery of certain types of blows were all carefully analyzed. The art of parrying was essential, as the scientific approach emphasized defense rather than offense.[13] Boxing was about *mastery*, in two guises: the mastery of one's opponent, forcing him to submit physically, and the mastery of one's own body in self-defense. Respectable proponents of the manly art stressed the latter.

If each antagonist understood the mechanics, the science of boxing would provide both with the manly exercise of sparring and function as a school for character. "There are probably no circumstances in which a man's good and bad qualities are more clearly revealed than in a friendly boxing bout." Scientific boxing, then, was a sport for gentlemen. "We must . . . be as careful in selecting our companions in boxing as in social intercourse. . . . there is more honor among those whose opinions are worthy of consideration in losing like a gentleman than in winning like a blackguard." System was absolutely essential in the exercise of boxing, and "no one but a man who leads a moral, regular, and cleanly life, at some portions of his career, can expect to become a great boxer."[14]

Boxing was hardy exercise, perfectly suited to those with only moderate amounts of leisure time, such as the go-getting businessman. Indeed, if more people became skilled pugilists, "few weapons would be carried, and the mind of men would be developed more in the direction of the art of self-defence than in that of attack." To indulge in boxing on this plane was to partake in a ritual of social superiority, as well; the sport was "first among the chivalrous arts," and a gentleman "ought to be superior to a laborer physically as well as mentally."[15]

The manly art brought physical and mental gains. It taught self-reliance and resourcefulness, cultivating a useful regimen through training. The gentlemanly boxer confined his damage to the arena of friendly combat. Pugilistic exercise produced the following: coolness, bravery, endurance, steadiness, grace, muscularity, strength, forebearance, and mercy. These beliefs gained a wide following throughout the male bourgeoisie. John Boyle O'Reilly subscribed to them totally, and he even promoted Sullivan (at his best) as their exemplar. The physical benefits to be gained were endorsed by men like Congressman John E. Russell of Massachusetts, Mayor Hugh O'Brien of Boston, the city's health commissioner, William Taylor, and Mayor Abram Hewitt of New York. Numerous doctors, educators, editors, and athletes were on record as advocating the gentlemanly variant of the sport. George Wright, a baseball pioneer, believed that learning to box was a necessity, like learning to swim. Even a few clergymen, early apostles of muscular Christianity, extolled boxing's benefits. The bottom line was both social and civic; boxing developed wild young boys into trained, disciplined, and sturdy young men. It fitted youth to be "fair-minded, confident, courageous, peaceful and patriotic citizens." Boxing took the English stock and improved it.[16]

The genteel amateurs were greatly concerned over the "decline" of the manly art. John Sullivan, with his slugging and bull-like rushes, would be cited as a central cause of boxing's degeneration. To the gentility, form was everything, and the object of boxing as a gentlemanly exercise was *not* to knock your man out. Indeed, infighting "is not considered quite the thing when gentlemen are sparring for fun and pleasure." The effects of the knockout were minimized by some, who might argue that, "barring a broken bone or a dislocated shoulder, the well trained boxer does not feel much pain from blows in a contest. The knockout, which looks brutal, is not much harder to take than chloroform." Even Sullivan came to realize the power and logic of the gentlemanly advocates. He would propose to elevate the "science" by giving lectures supported by stereopticon views before an exhibition of actual sparring, which would demonstrate actual blows. He hoped in this way to attract women as well as male "gentlemen" to prizefights.[17]

Despite worries over the decline of pugilism, sporting and boxing metaphors permeated the genteel culture. Even that sedentary guardian of Protestant mores Henry Ward Beecher advocated athletic sports (for others), including fishing, hunting, riding, billiards, and bowling. It was common to celebrate pugnacity in the man of public affairs; scrappy qualities in politicians were often admired. "The Little Giant," Stephen A. Douglas, was often compared to a prizefighter, being described as plucky, quick, and strong, and as adroit in shifting positions, avoiding blows, and returning punches in unexpected places. Once, wrote the outraged John Quincy Adams, "in the midst of his roaring, to save himself from choking, he stripped off and cast away his cravat, unbuttoned his waistcoat, and had the air and aspect of a half-naked pugilist." Douglas's great foe, Lincoln, of course had made a local reputation as a young man in frontier Illinois through catch-as-catch-can wrestling. Metaphors from the political world, with models such as these, supported the idea that competition in all forms, including boxing, was vintage Americanism.[18]

Young men from the best families practiced the manly art. Richard Henry Dana noted young Harvard men working out at boxing as early as the 1820s, and students at Middlebury College at about the same time were treated to a lecture on the benefits of sparring. The famed historian Francis Parkman was instructed in self-defense at Harvard by one T. Belcher Kay in 1842, and even the puny and asthmatic Oliver Wendell Holmes followed the records of the prize ring. As the pontifical Autocrat, Holmes pronounced the best of sporting men as common idlers and the worst as very bad neighbors or denizens of a dark alley. Yet he supported boxing, for although it was rough play, it was not too rough for a hearty youngster. "Anything is better than this white-blooded degeneration to which we all tend." And, with just a hint of condescension: "It is a fine sight, that of a gentleman resolving himself into the primitive constituents of his humanity." Among numerous other gentlemen who so resolved themselves was the patrician William C. Whitney, who boxed at Yale. All these genteel young men practiced and admired the sport openly, unlike poor Pierre de Coubertin, founder of the modern Olympic movement, who had to practice boxing surreptitiously in France because it was considered English and reeked of lower-class associations.[19]

By far the most famous of the gentleman practitioners of the manly art, seen from the perspective of his later career, was John Sullivan's exact contemporary, Theodore Roosevelt. "Teedie" boxed as a lightweight at Harvard. In his junior year he fought for the university boxing cup against a senior, C. S. Hanks, and was "punished severely" according to the *New York Times*, which made it its business to cover the sporting activities of that hatchery of future political, economic, and social leaders. Young Roosevelt never distinguished himself athletically while wearing the crimson; he was not a natural and had little interest in organized sport. Nevertheless he possessed a flaming competitive urge that would help seal a bond of friendship with Sullivan in later life, as well as with other prizefighters such as Mike Donovan, Battling Nelson, and Bob Fitzsimmons. For years TR strongly supported either professional or amateur boxing as long as the sport was free of corruption, and as police commissioner of New York he heartily approved of an effort to get boxing clubs established in the city.[20]

Not only young men destined for prominent social roles practiced the sport. In its amateur variant middle-class gentlemen also found something to applaud. The military encouraged boxing, for obvious reasons. The U. S. Navy's fleet boxing championships were closely followed by admirals and swabbies alike, and the army consistently promoted matches, sometimes in the oddest places. After months of running Apaches to earth in the deserts of the Southwest, the future general Leonard Wood and his boss, General Nelson A. Miles (later TR's chief of staff), took time out to engage in boxing. The author Stephen Crane, who as a youngster had once sneaked away from a temperance lecture to watch a bare-knuckle prizefight in a barn, preferred boxing, beer drinking and other athletics to studying while at Lafayette. And G. Stanley Hall, one of the founding fathers of American academic psychology, analyzed himself as follows:

> I must confess ... to a trait of which even my intimates never knew the strength or manifold expressions, namely, a love for glimpsing at first hand the raw side of human life. I have never missed an opportunity to attend a prizefight if I could do so unknown and away from home, so that I have

seen most of the noted pugilists of my generation in action and felt the unique thrill at these encounters.[21]

Positive attitudes toward boxing thus were not foreign to any male segment of American society. Sullivan himself was not slow to note that many public men "recognized the fact that boxing is superior as an exercise for health to any other form of exercise known, including wrestling, running, rowing, and dumb-bell exercise." He applauded the efforts of political figures like Roscoe Conkling, Zack Chandler, and even James G. Blaine in taking up boxing for conditioning. Conkling and Chandler were even known to have judged boxing bouts. The preening Lord Roscoe had built himself up through boxing, and at six feet three inches was "the picture of conspicuous manhood," despised by Blaine for his "turkey-gobbler strut." The New York senator and Sullivan would become particularly close.[22]

All the gentry, and even those of somewhat more suspicious cast, such as Conkling, applauded boxing as a manly art as long as it was a game played by the *rules*. Over the years the few simple regulations designed by the Englishman Broughton had been developed into the London Prize Ring Rules, twenty-nine of them, which had been generally adopted by 1838 and were standard in both England and America. These prescribed a twenty-four-foot square ring on turf, seconds, two umpires, and a "scratch line" drawn in the center of the ring. A round ended when one or both combatants were down on at least one knee. They then had thirty seconds to "come to scratch" or lose the fight. Butting, gouging, striking a man when down, blows below the waist, and kicking were all declared fouls.[23] These rules were a clear improvement on Broughton's, at least in delineating what could and could not be done, but they did authorize bare-knuckle fighting, and this was where the gentility parted company.

By Sullivan's day there was an alternative, the rules authored by the Englishman Henry Sholto Douglas, eighth marquis of Queensberry. Queensberry was better known among his social peers as the father of Alfred Douglas, who carried on a notorious homosexual affair with Oscar Wilde, to the scandalized delight of late Victorian London. The marquis had boxed while "up at Oxford" in 1865, gaining through this exercise the inspiration for the rules he wrote the next year. The Queensberry Rules, originally twelve in number, outlawed all wrestling and grappling holds and established three-minute rounds with one minute of rest between. A man who was knocked down was allowed ten seconds to get to his feet or suffer loss by knockout. The timekeeper was thus elevated to a position of prime importance, consonant with the growing significance of time in the industrial age. Eventually, more than thirty-five nations adopted the marquis's rules, but the changeover from the London Rules was by no means immediate.

Most importantly, the Queensberry Rules prescribed gloved fights. Under the London Rules fights were to the finish, although exhausted fighters or their seconds might agree to a draw, as had happened in the famous international struggle between the American John Carmel Heenan (the "Benicia Boy") and the Englishman Tom Sayers. With Queensberry, fights were usually scheduled for a stated number of rounds, judges then declaring a winner if neither man had been knocked out or had failed to meet the bell summoning him for a new round. All these regulations, especially the use of gloves, were designed to refine and regularize the sport.[24]

Sullivan would fight under both sets of rules. He somewhat hypocritically objected to the London Rules as being illegal almost everywhere, attracting a rougher crowd, encouraging trickery, promoting brutality, and being contrary to public opinion. "I can win under any rules," he once bragged, but he favored Queensberry. The gloves established by Queensberry came in no particular size or style, but Sullivan preferred gloves, and he would eventually use all types. Gloves generally came in six regular sizes: skintight coaching gloves, padded gloves of two, four, six, or eight ounces, and fifteen-ounce pillows used for theatrical exhibitions. The eight-ounce glove became the most common, although Sullivan was weaned on the two-ounce mitts that were routinely worn in Boston club-room fights. The skintight coaching gloves were also popular and were usually donned only to give lip (or hand) service to the law. Usually these gloves were made of cured leather, made to fit the hand snugly, and were laced by long gauntlets, having about half of each finger cut to permit a natural fist. In operation, especially with sharp, glancing blows, the skintight gloves could slice like a razor.[25]

The gentry found these small articles as bad as bare knuckles, but they applauded the padded gloves—the more cushioning, the better. Such gloves seemed to go far in removing the barbarism and danger from the sport; as Sullivan's sidekick Billy Madden once said, "The worst that can be done with gloves is to knock a man 'silly' for a time." John Boyle O'Reilly praised Sullivan for fighting with gloves, believing that this aided in promoting boxing "science," and Sullivan himself tried many types before settling on a model by A. G. Spaulding that was marketed under his name as the "Sullivan Glove—California Style."[26]

Despite the obvious improvements of the Queensberry Rules over the brutality of the old bare-knuckle bouts, there remained a constant, vocal, and significant opposition to prizefighting. The amateur, after all, extolled the manly art for its own sake and for its intrinsic benefits. But there were those from similar walks of life who advanced what were, for them, telling arguments against the sport itself. For these critics boxing had no place in society, polite or otherwise.

## III

Idleness was suspect in the minds of many Americans. A strong, dutiful Calvinistic strain could still be found running through all social levels, particularly in the Northeast and Midwest, reaching at times the dimension of obsession. To while away time "frivolously" was to waste opportunity, and some who did so were driven to confess their excess to their diaries, as did Charles Francis Adams, son of John Quincy. After playing with his own sons for a few hours in 1843, Adams wrote that "perhaps this consumption of time is scarcely justifiable; but why not take some of life for simple enjoyments, provided that they interfere with no known duty?" *His* son, Charles Francis, Jr., would recall his own physical timidity as a boy and condemn his father's puritanical depreciation of sports, particularly outdoor games. Among the sterner sort there was a line between duty, hard work, and service, on the one hand, and frivolity, relaxation, and "time-wasting," on the other. At times these attitudes scaled the slopes of outright priggishness, as when that great liar, "Parson" Mason Locke Weems, had young George Washington upbraid his schoolmates for fighting. ("You shall never, boys, have my consent to a practice so shocking! Shocking even in slaves and dogs; then how utterly scandalous in little boys at school, who ought to look after one another as brothers.")[27]

Even though these spurious comments of the Father of His Country were stricken from later editions of the parson's best-selling farrago of lies, distortions, and half-truths, the moral argument was enduring. If man was made in God's image, then any attempt to defile this image through the pummeling of a prizefight was a sin, pure and simple. Further, prizefighting sinned by risking life or bodily integrity without sufficient reason; it was the only sport that aimed specifically at injuring an opponent; and to attempt to deprive a man of his consciousness was to remove that which made him special in the eyes of God. To a later Catholic priest, "Mortal sin would be committed by a man who adopts prizefighting as a career and who intends to advance in this career to the best of his ability."[28]

Beyond the basic moral argument lay more practical concerns. Prizefighting was badly tainted by its associations. Queensberry himself had been driven by 1894 to pronounce that "prizefighting has degenerated from a sport to a huge gambling machine. . . . I think the sport has had its day." The decline in boxing after 1863, according to one authority, was caused by those "barnacles of sport," professional gamblers. Some believed that in the palmy days of prizefighting, nostalgically celebrated by such as Thackeray and Conan Doyle, the sport had had the semblance of an honest contest despite its brutality. But now, "The man who confesses an interest in a prizefight is usually encouraging, not only brutality, but swindling and humbug." The association between prizefighting and gambling was close, perhaps even necessary. Some boxers, if they had the money, bet on themselves; some became specialists in "throwing" fights. Their "backers" were driven primarily by the profit motive, and some were none too scrupulous in the means they used to achieve these ends. The smell of corruption produced by gambling was consonant with the sport. Indeed, it was a fine question whether the prizefight existed for the gambler or vice versa.[29]

Moralists could flog the prizefighting world with little fear of reprisal. Horace Greeley, the self-appointed arbiter of national mores, might allow up to six columns in his *New York Daily Tribune* for boxing coverage and then deliver his viperish analysis on the editorial page: "The thing is whereby its natural gravity of baseness it stinks. It is in the grog-shops and the brothels and the low gaming hells." Greeley was enthusiastically joined by many other editors who sought to appeal to middle-class customs and manners, such as Henry Raymond of the *New York Times*. Henry Ward Beecher, that indefatigable guardian of public morality, ranked the news of prizefights with the disgusting and prurient details of divorce cases, the reports of police courts, and the recounting of salacious scandal and dissipation. The opinionated Greeley was not above slapping a political perspective on his views, fulminating that "every one who chooses to live by pugilism, or gambling, or harlotry, with nearly every keeper of a tippling house" was a Democrat. And even the Democracy's patron saint, Jefferson, had opined that every young American who went to England picked up the more disgusting peculiarities of English education, such as drinking, horse racing, and boxing.[30]

The new "science" of evolution was also brought into play, the arguments displaying the opposite side of the Darwinian coin from those stressing struggle, competition, victory, and cultural progress. Protestant theologians like Boston's George A. Gordon might censure prizefighting as athwart the path of progress, because "the historic movement is slowly but surely away from the brute." The Reverend Robert Collyer felt boxing evoked the bloody gladiatorial combat of the Roman arena. For the novelist George W. Cable, the sport had nothing to offer by way of human improvement; it suggested only the methods of force, cruelty, and violence. It was debasing and regressive; unfortunately, noted the popular orator George William Curtis, "the sewage is not wholly worked out of the blood." And the prince of bluenoses, Anthony Comstock, pontificated that boxing not only was brutalizing but also produced loss of self-respect. "I do not regard those who sneak into prize fights under the cover of night to witness these criminal proceedings as representing any decent element in society."[31]

Above all, the bare-knuckle brand of fighting seemed barbaric and degrading. "The prize fight with bare hands could only have been developed in England," declared the Anglophobic *Boston Pilot*. "It is fit only for brutalized men." News of bare-knuckle bouts was firmly within the "sewers and garbage-boxes of society," along with other tidbits for readers to whom life was a continuous panoply of rapes, suicides, murders, adulteries, swindles, forgeries, elopements, and parricides. Pugilists and the betting crowd that surrounded them displayed manners and morals that were a disgrace to civilization, and any interest in a prizefight was simply depraved. Even the *National Police Gazette*, which made a nice business of retailing the news from the sewers and garbage-boxes of society, could on occasion be shocked by brutal slugging exhibitions. Many observers felt that the sport was becoming more coarse as time went on, attracting only a "certain debased class of mind." The sporting crowd might deny that boxing was deadly and dangerous, but few believed them.[32]

Besides, bare-knuckle prizefights and most gloved fights, except for mere "exhibitions," were outside the law. The demoralizing effect boxing had on spectators made it a "doomed institution," unfit for modern social consumption. Sparring might be all right; prizefighting was not— its practitioners were barbarians, knowing no law but that of the fist. A bout for money was a crime, and spectators at such a match aided and abetted the breaking of the law. Not even gloves were the solution for hard-line critics: the "rushing style" of boxing featured by Irish Americans such as Sullivan was brutal just the same. "The vice of our race," observed one middle-class English magazine, "is our brutality."

> Are we going to allow this vice to be not only tolerated but positively encouraged and fostered? Judges have it in their power to put down the evil. The police is [sic] eager to give them the necessary opportunity. It is for the public to declare that it will not tolerate glove-fighting any more than prizefighting or bull-baiting, and the authorities may be trusted to do the rest.[33]

According to this legalistic critique, there was no legitimate place for prizefighting on either side of the Atlantic. In 1880, as John Sullivan was embarking on his chancy career, the *New York Times* editorialized that the most sincere and active supporters of prizefighting "are not only low scoundrels, but arrant cowards, equally ready to pick a pocket or stab an enemy in the dark." The end of prizefights seemed very near, because they were "essentially un-American." In 1880 prizefighting was illegal in all the thirty-eight states. Pennsylvania's statute, dating from 1867, was typical, citing participation in a prizefight as a misdemeanor punishable by a fine up to one thousand dollars and a prison sentence of up to two years. Among many cities with similar ordinances, New Orleans declared prizefighting unlawful in 1885, mildly fining violators twenty-five dollars or giving them thirty days in jail. Louisiana followed five years later by outlawing prizefighting but permitting "scientific" boxing in the salutary confines of athletic clubs, provided the club served no liquor, held no bouts on the Sabbath, donated fifty dollars per bout to charity, and posted a five-hundred-dollar bond for each event. This overprecise law proved useless, and soon Louisiana was described by the Reverend Clarence Greeley, who styled himself as the "General Agent" for something called the "International Law and Order League," as an "Africa" because of its supposed partiality to prizefighting. At the state level, authorities were extremely responsive to public pressure to uphold the law. From the end of the Civil War to 1906, governors summoned the National Guard 481 times to restore public order; in 3 of these instances prizefights were prevented from taking place.[34] Boxing acceptance in localities depended much more on the attitudes of city fathers, but these attitudes by 1880 had become almost totally censorious, as witness the many necessarily alfresco prizefights of the 1860s and 1870s.

Some critics took the further tack that commercialism was ruining the sport, a view often found among advocates of gentlemanly sparring. Dr. Dudley A. Sargent, director of the Hemenway gymnasium at Harvard and a man who would later do a detailed physical study of John Sullivan, argued that professional boxing should be discouraged, as it produced only dishonesty, corrupt gain, and demoralization. Even a sporting journal such as *Turf, Field and Farm* advertised that it denounced "pugilism, and all low, disgusting sports." And poor Queensberry, who supposedly was trying to *reform* the sport, was characterized by the *New York Daily Tribune* as "an English nobleman whose devotion to prizefighting was only equalled by his zeal for vice of every kind."[35]

Somehow it seemed especially base to pound away at someone *for money*. These "modern methods" had "debauched" boxing. Slugging was no substitute for science; any brutish lout could batter away at an opponent. "The fighter is 'born, not made,' but the opposite is true of the boxer." The appeal of a systematic approach to boxing would always be lost on the simple-minded man-brute who saw only a payday in the destruction of his opponent.[36]

A solid phalanx of opposition thus convoyed the sport on its ignominious passage through American life in the nineteenth century. On grounds of morality, evolution, legality, and commercialism, boxing, especially in its prizefighting variant, stood tried and condemned by every segment of middle- and upper-class opinion and by many in the lower orders as well. Philip Hone, relentless New York diarist and man-about-town, described it as "one of the fashionable abominations of our loafer-ridden city—the orderly citizens have wept for a shame which they could not prevent." In its early years, the later-to-be-notorious *National Police Gazette* could excoriate "another of these disgraceful scenes," in which two men brawled in Connecticut for two hundred dollars a side before sheriff and posse intervened. Indeed, under the editorial hand of the crusading journalist George Wilkes, the *Gazette* for years fired broadsides at those pet aversions—the underworld, immigrant crime, and pugilism—that were later, under decidedly different editorial direction, to bring it such profit.[37]

Sullivan would only exacerbate these antiboxing attitudes. They existed fully blown into the twentieth century, and indeed they exist today. Even Teddy Roosevelt, the former Harvard boxer, ultimately forsook the sport (but not the friends gained from it) after the Jack Johnson-James Jeffries title bout in 1910. Many Americans, like the historian Charles Beard, continued to be repelled by the commercial spectacle of the prize ring. Boxing always seemed to be ebbing in popularity, yet it lumbered on, amassing critics and complaints with each new generation. James Michener, storyteller par excellence for today's middle class, could have been writing a century ago when he avowed: "I cannot think of any legitimate grounds for recommending boxing to anyone."[38]

# IV

American boxing before Sullivan was part of the sporting world, in the sense that it was supposedly a contest and usually could draw a crowd, even if the spectators had to journey clandestinely miles off the beaten track. But it was part of a social underworld as well. In England this underworld had been sustained by an eccentric mix of aristocracy and "rabble," but in the United States, with its pretentions to classlessness and a line of old and socially prominent families that disdained the sport, the social underworld was largely a matrix of workingmen, saloon keepers, gamblers, criminals, and prostitutes. These people tended to be somewhat casual as regarded work habits; they were far more spontaneous and extravagant than their social betters, who preached those classic virtues so difficult to realize—hard work, temperance, frugality, and deferred gratification. Sport became one of the lynchpins of this social underworld in the nineteenth century, even as the joys of recreation, play, and competition in their "legitimate" forms were attracting the middle classes. The underworld favored professional footracing or walking races, the horse race in any guise, billiards, and the prizefight, although in a few despicable haunts a cock fight might occur or dog be set against dog for the pleasure of betting men.

Whereas the sports appealing more to the middle classes were moving toward regulation and bureaucratization by 1880, the underworld's sports lagged far behind; indeed, part of their appeal was their illegality or unvarnished brutality. Occasionally, the sporting fancy would become part of the action; betting arguments could disrupt a match, and it was common for fight fans to show up with something a little extra, such as brass knuckles, a knife, or a small pistol, just in case. Before Sullivan, professional pugilists maintained practically their entire following from their own social groupings. Nearly all prizefighters, right down to the present, have come from a low socioeconomic background and have sprung from urban America. They have usually been from minority groups, and it is possible to trace an ethnic succession of boxing dominance in cities like New York and Chicago: Irish, Jewish, Italian, black. Sullivan's contemporaries, like himself, came from blue-collar backgrounds or even lower. James Corbett was a modest exception, perched precariously in the lower middle class as a bank clerk. Sullivan, with his varied apprenticeships, was more typical. So was James Jeffries (a boilermaker), Bob Fitzsimmons (blacksmith), Gus Ruhlin (pressman), Peter Maher (cooper), Tom Sharkey (sailor), and Joe Choynski (candy maker). Other boxers of Sullivan's generation had backgrounds as farmers, miners, horseshoers, porters, plasterers, and teamsters.[39]

Life in the prize ring was hard and dangerous, and it was sometimes cut short by serious injury. True enough, legendary figures like Mendoza and Gentleman Jackson had lived past their allotted three score and ten, and Broughton, despite his savage pounding at the hands of a butcher named Jack Slack, had scaled eighty-five. But early death was the rule in America; both Yankee Sullivan and John Morrissey died in their mid-forties, and Heenan, the handsome Benicia Boy, was dead at thirty-eight. The average age of death of Anglo-American prizefighters from Broughton to Sullivan, based on loose calculation, was around forty-seven.[40] This figure does not depart dramatically from the demographics of lower-class nineteenth-century Anglo-American populations as a whole, but considering that these men were strong, healthy males at the outset of their careers, there can be little doubt that the sport contributed to physical debility and even early death.

A dangerous calling, then, but one in which most prizefighters took great satisfaction. American pugilists proudly traced their lineage back to Figg and Broughton, claiming a succession of "champions" much like the hereditary succession to a throne. Measured in this way, "the Trojan Giant," Paddy Ryan, was the forty-fourth lineal descendant of

Figg. The cognoscenti lovingly ticked off the bouts where the crown had passed from one hand to another.[41] In fact, however, the subterranean nature of the sport produced a profusion of claimants to "championships." Only in Sullivan's day did the division into weight classes take place, and "champions" were made and unmade in the press as often as in the ring. Essentially, a "champion" was he who won a noteworthy fight and kept winning, particularly over those who had styled themselves similarly.

Gentlemanly boxing had been popular around Chesapeake Bay as early as the 1730s, but actual prizefighting had been brought to the colonies by British sailors, who put on a few matches when the British occupied New York during the Revolutionary War. With independence the sport was made illegal immediately, not only for its violence but also because of its British associations. Nevertheless, bouts continued to take place "furtively, sporadically, and surreptitiously." No fighter made a living at the game, and some visiting English pugilists, after being scorned by the press up and down the eastern seaboard, abandoned the prize ring to establish "schools" for teaching the manly art, in the tradition of Figg and Broughton.

Another strain that contributed to American boxing was home grown, however, coming out of the rough-and-tumble scraps of the frontier. Whenever westerners gathered, the question of who was the "best man" was sure to arise. The casualties suffered in friendly wrestling matches, such as those in which Lincoln gained his reputation, were the usual cracked skulls, friction burns, and broken bones. Serious matches (those with "rules") featured biting, scratching, hair pulling, kicking, gouging, and, as a *fin de combat*, stamping on a downed man. Should the fight still continue, the experienced brawler might place his knees in the pit of the stomach of his prone opponent, apply thumbs to his victim's eyeballs, and, if word of surrender was not forthcoming, pop them out of their sockets. The colonial assembly in North Carolina had been forced to pass laws making it a felony "to cut out the tongue or pull out the eyes," as well as to slit, bite, or cut off noses. By 1786 South Carolina had made premeditated mayhem a capital offense, mayhem being defined as severing another's bodily parts.[42]

Small but growing American cities wanted no part of either the English brute or the uncouth backwoods lout. New England Calvinists were cool even to the moderate exercise of skating, hunting, or fishing. The Dutch influence in the Hudson River valley was a bit more liberal, and southern gentlemen were expected to be expert horsemen and fencers, but in general respectable urban Americans were opposed to boxing from the beginning. In the early nineteenth century numerous activities won widespread public approval—sailing, bowling, billiards, trotting, pedestrianism, and swimming (John Quincy Adams, as president, was fond of taking nude dips in the Potomac)—but not boxing.[43]

Outlawed, prizefighters nonetheless made their nefarious way. A black man named Bill Richmond (after his birth in Richmond, Staten Island) was taken back to England by the future duke of Northumberland in 1777 and won there a considerable reputation, fighting until at least the age of fifty. Richmond was practically a Britisher, but the following generation brought Tom Molyneaux, possibly born a Virginia slave, across the Atlantic to fight as an American. Molyneaux, under Richmond's tutelage, began to fight for money in July of 1810. His two fights with Tom Cribb, both losses, won him fame among the fancy, but little else. He was illiterate, and he skimped along by traveling with a circus, teaching boxing, and giving exhibitions. After a long, debilitating illness, Molyneaux died on August 4, 1818, in the quarters of the Seventy-seventh Regiment's band at Galway, Ireland.[44]

Richmond and Molyneaux were dimly seen black flashes before the dawn of American prizefighting. Interest in the sport was rekindled in the social underworld by the Irish influx and the appearance of several Irish-American pugilists, the first of whom was Tom Hyer, born in 1819 and a New Yorker most of his life. His father, Jacob, also had been a prizefighter, and young Tom gained fame as a "champion" with a victory over one George McCheester, alias "Country McCloskey," in a savage, 101-round contest at Caldwell's Landing, New York, in 1841. Hyer was inactive for almost a decade before he battered James Ambrose, better known as "Yankee Sullivan," into insensibility in eighteen minutes. Hyer then "retired" undefeated. He was a much-feared local tough in New York, conspicuous as a bullyboy in ward politics. Hyer favored the Know-Nothing cause in the 1850s and survived at least one attempt to assassinate him. In 1860 he reached the summit, shepherding several thousand professional applauders and marchers to the Republican national convention in Chicago. He died in 1864 at the age of forty-five.[45]

After Hyer left the prize ring, Yankee Sullivan unabashedly claimed the crown. A native of County Cork, Sullivan was six years older than Hyer and had much more fighting experience, participating in at least nine matches from the 1830s to 1853 in both England and America. Against Hyer, Sullivan was outweighed by thirty pounds. This bout between "undefeateds" was the first covered by the press as a sporting event. On February 7, 1849, the two pugilists and two hundred spectators set sail from Baltimore with a boatload of militia in pursuit. Eventually the miscreants outmaneuvered the waterborne posse and landed on a deserted section of Maryland's Eastern Shore. Stakes were quickly hewn from nearby woods, and ring ropes were slashed from the ship's rigging. A light covering of snow was brushed away, and the chilled spectators were then treated to a one-sided execution, Sullivan afterward being hauled away unconscious to a Baltimore hospital by his handlers. A dispatch from the scene read: "We hope never to have to record a similar case of brutality in this country."[46]

Sullivan's day in the sun was short. A spurius "champion," he did not fight for over four years after being mauled by Hyer. On October 12, 1853, he faced John Morrissey at a rural crossroads called Boston Corners, on the line between New York and Massachusetts. For ten rounds Sullivan was dominant, but Morrissey's youth and stamina prevailed; by the thirty-seventh round he was beating Sullivan terrifically. The round broke up with a brawl among the seconds and umpire, Sullivan enthusiastically joining in. Morrissey kept to his corner and the stakes were awarded to him. Outside the ring Sullivan distinguished himself as a petty thief and brawler. After the Morrissey fight he took his talents to the wide-open California gold fields, where they almost immediately earned him execution from a vigilance committee in 1856. Even a felon like Sullivan had his followers, though. Two years after the fighter's abrupt demise a Liverpool fan named James Malloy took the trouble to erect a tombstone over the unmarked California grave. "Remember not, O Lord, our offenses, nor those of our parents. Neither take thou vengeance of our sins. Thou shalt bring forth my soul out of tribulation, and in thy mercy thou shalt destroy mine enemies." With this pious appeal to revenge, the soul of the champion who beat no champions was ushered into eternity.[47]

Despite their decided lack of character, or perhaps because of it, men like Tom Hyer and Yankee Sullivan emerged as public figures. John Morrissey marked a slight step upward from the depths, as well as heralding a new generation of prizefighters. Born in Ireland in 1831, Morrissey was almost twenty years younger than Yankee Sullivan. He learned his trade brawling in New York barrooms. Seeking fast fortune in El Dorado, he fought his first prize match at Mare Island, California, in 1852, winning over Hyer's former trainer, George Thompson, on a foul after eleven rounds. Five years after his victory over Sullivan, Morrissey met John Carmel Heenan on an island in the Saint Lawrence River about eighty miles from Buffalo for the then incredible sum of twenty-five hundred dollars a side. Morrissey won in eleven bruising rounds and then, like Hyer, left the ring and went into politics, but at a much higher and more successful level.[48]

Heenan was an Irish American born in 1835 in Paddy Ryan's hometown, Troy, New York. He was trained in the machinist's trade at the Watervliet Arsenal, where his father had been chief of the ordinance department, but like Yankee Sullivan and John Morrissey migrated to California, where his work in the shops of the Pacific Mail Steamship Company north of San Francisco gained him the nickname of Benicia

Boy, after a town in California. Unlike the scowling, aggressive Morrissey, Heenan was a true naïf, easygong and amiable, preferring women to male companions. He would later carry on a tumultuous love affair with the seductive siren Adah Isaacs Menken. The Boy was well-muscled and received some training from professionals before he met Morrissey, but Morrissey's strength and brute force carried the day. Nevertheless, following Yankee Sullivan's precedent, Heenan claimed the "championship" on the retirement of his conqueror. The drawn bloodbath with Tom Sayers followed in 1860, but this was the high point for the Benicia Boy. He was beaten in England by Tom King in 1863, and only ten years later he lay dead in far-off Wyoming Territory, his Menken a memory and his pockets empty.[49]

While prizefighters from Hyer to Heenan were fighting in the most remote locales possible, boxing exhibitions in the urban North were increasing in popularity. The sport grew steadily in New York City in the 1840s and made rapid advances in the next decade. Bravos like Hyer and Morrissey were leading sports figures in the underworld, seen by some Irish-Americans as positive social examples. Before the Civil War, of the leading New York pugilists 56.3 percent were Irish and 15 percent more had at least one Irish parent, most of the rest being of English extraction. Eventually, little boxing clubs would spring from these ethnic roots, places where training could take place and even a prize bout occasionally sneaked past the prying eyes of the law. In New York from 1840 to 1870 the press gave boxing more coverage than any other sport except baseball. The thriving city also had other uses for pugilists—as bodyguards, political musclemen, and rent collectors. The Union Racetrack on Long Island, which attracted tens of thousands of fans, was so rowdy that professional fighters were hired to keep the peace.[50]

In Boston, boxing faced more severe social obstacles, but even in the eighteenth century an imported pugilist named James Sanford managed to win a following, and one G. L. Barrett offered instruction in the manly art. The Irish immigration produced an interest in boxing that seldom diminished, and the Boston Irish prizefighter was well on his way to becoming a stereotype by the Civil War. So popular did these Irish boxers become, especially after John Sullivan, that many Jewish lads adopted Irish *noms de ring* to further their careers. The Boston Irish never fully supported prizefighting, of course; many were embarrassed and denounced it as "human butchery." When in 1888 the popular John Boyle O'Reilly published his laudatory book, *Ethics of Boxing and Manly Sport*, he was vilified by the lace-curtain *Donahoe's Magazine* for endorsing such a barbarous pastime. Nevertheless, the Irish-American subculture was generally more tolerant of prizefighting than were other ethnic groups. The cult of masculinity, naturally, held the prizefighter in high esteem.[51]

Despite its urban popularity the illegality of the prizefight and the growing censure of states and muncipalities, plus the lackluster quality of the men who followed Morrissey and Heenan, pushed the sport to its nineteenth-century nadir in the twenty years following 1860. With Heenan overseas, a burly native of County Armagh named Joe Coburn claimed the title. Born in 1835, the untrained Coburn first fought in a marathon 160-round draw with Ned Price, later a New York lawyer and theatrical manager, at Spy Pond near Boston. He furthered his assertions by defeating the hulking Mike McCoole in 1863 in Cecil County, Maryland. A clutch of claimants—Bill Davis, Jim Dunn, Jim Elliott, McCoole himself, and the Englishmen Tom Allen and Jem Mace—followed in the next few years. By the 1870s the "championship" was almost completely discredited, even among the most hardy fight fans. When Joe Goss beat Allen on a foul in Kentucky in 1876, even the sporting press barely took notice. Paddy Ryan was the latest in this decidedly undistinguished line, having fought and won his first real prizefight in 1880 against the aging Goss.[52]

Even ardent defenders of the sport were placed on the defensive. "The poor pugilist . . . has been too long known to the public at large only by the false representations of his bigotedly legal or ignorantly illegal enemies," protested Robert Dewitt, who supplemented his pronouncements on prizefighting by publishing handbooks of games, songbooks, advice on how to tell fortunes by dreams, and something called *DeWitt's Complete American Farrier and Horse Doctor*. With friends like DeWitt the sport had no need of enemies—and it had plenty.

About the best American pugilism had to offer by the 1870s was the post-boxing career of John Morrissey. Immersed in ward politics and gambling dens, Morrissey in 1867 created a valhalla for high rollers and other assorted sports at Saratoga Springs. There he hobnobbed with the *nouveau riche* hurled to the top by the industrial age, men like old Cornelius Vanderbilt. His urban political connections brought fruit when the Tammany Hall machine in New York City got him elected in 1866 to Congress and repeated the feat two years later. He split from the corrupt Tweed operation in 1870, not so much over political ideals (there were very few of these in New York at the time) as over a share of the spoils. In 1875 he organized the "Irving Hall Democracy" and parlayed this base into election to the state Senate. He tried and failed to wrest control of Tammany from the unlamented Tweed's successor, John Kelly. These teapot political wars were at their height when Morrissey died in 1878. Even with his political clout he never became truly respectable, being labeled in one engaging social memoir of the period the "most conspicuous" of the "most prominent gamblers and crooks."[53]

By 1880, then, professional boxing in America was moribund. Many boxers were, indeed, no better than criminals. Hyer had routinely carried a gun and had occasionally used it; McCoole and numerous others were deadbeat drunks; some were lynched, like Yankee Sullivan, or murdered, like Bill Poole and Jim Elliott. Others, like Coburn, sported prison records. The best of them, Morrissey, began as a saloon brawler and ended as a high-stakes gambler and crooked politician.[54] Outlawed, excoriated, harangued from pulpit and press, the bare-knuckle breed as commercial spectacle found no home in American life. Such was the world young John Sullivan entered; his chances of fame and fortune seemed exactly nil.

# CHAPTER FOUR

# The Making of a Fighting Man
## (1880—1882)

## I

To learn the ropes of prizefighting, John Sullivan had to work at the fighter's trade. He trained on the job. Merely fighting here and there was not enough; he had to become known as an aspiring pugilist. And so, in November 1879 the following notice appeared in the *Boston Daily Globe*: "John Sullivan of Boston is desirous of meeting Jack Hogan of Providence for a hard-glove contest, for a purse of $250 a side, the contest to take place either in Providence or Boston."[1] It was John's first public challenge; after years of desultory, restless work as a tradesman, he was professing his new calling. Like most other public challenges of the day it went unaccepted, but with this humble beginning he was on his way.

During the winter of 1879–80 John continued his custom of attending Boston benefits, and he may have been at John Connelly's benefit in Horticultural Hall on November 14. In response to the *Daily Globe* challenge of two months before, it was announced that "Sullivan, the Highland novice," would fight Hogan January 5 at a benefit for a man named Marcellus Baker, but nothing came of it. Sullivan may have attended this show anyway, where about four hundred people witnessed "an average exhibition of the art of self-defence."[2]

Already his sights were set on the "championship." At the time that was a bone of contention between old Joe Goss and Paddy Ryan. Goss had been inactive since the Tom Allen fight in 1876, and Paddy was hardly a popular fighter. At a benefit for Goss held at Boston's Music Hall on February 3 before a throng of three thousand, Ryan was asked to leave the stage after two rounds of lazy sparring with William Miller of Baltimore. Now recovered from his knife wounds, the Troy native apologized for his poor showing, pleading that he was not a scientific boxer and was "given to getting excited." Nevertheless, Paddy had managed to arrange a championship match with Goss, and in June 1880 the two would meet shortly after daybreak in a bare-knuckle bout at Collier's Station, West Virginia. Eighty-seven rounds later, the unscientific Paddy was the new champion, trumpeted as such by a special edition of the *National Police Gazette*.[3] Sullivan would then have a target other than his hometown friend.

First, though, there was business. In February 1880 John appeared in an exhibition with his first experienced opponent, Mike Donovan of New York. Born in Chicago in 1847, Donovan had enlisted in a Union regiment in the Civil War and had marched with Sherman through Georgia as that unrepentant Roundhead cut his sixty-mile-wide swath to the sea. By 1880 Mike was a ring-wise veteran, an advocate of boxing science who taught the finer points of the manly art for most of his life. Eventually he became the much-loved boxing instructor at the New York Athletic Club and served as a sparring partner for none other than President Theodore Roosevelt. Originally Sullivan sought out the crafty New Yorker for a few pointers, but when the two met in a gloved fight at the Howard Street Athenaeum, it was the youngster who gave the lessons.

The cheering spectators were treated to two clashing styles. Donovan, who was outweighed by forty pounds, survived on ring wisdom alone; when he maneuvered the muscular Sullivan into a clinch to try some infighting, Sullivan "brought his sledgehammer right down on the back of my neck so hard I thought it was broken. As it was, I was knocked flat on the stage and my nose crushed." Donovan found that he was no match for Sullivan's strength and catlike quickness; he rapidly discovered he was in the ring with an aggressive, savage "natural." "Never in my life did I have to do such clever ducking and side-stepping." Sullivan missed more than he connected with his wild flailing, but the typhoon of punches rapidly sapped the more experienced man's energy. In the third round Donovan broke his right wrist, and his right thumb was disjointed. By the fourth and final round the Highland Strong Boy was using his right hand "as a blacksmith would use a sledge-hammer pounding a piece of iron into shape," pummeling the wounded Donovan on the head at will. While Donovan consoled himself that, in terms of the "science," he had had slightly the better of it, he left the exhibition knowing "I had just fought the coming champion of the prize-ring." When Donovan returned to his hotel, over fifty of Sullivan's cronies from the Highlands were eagerly awaiting his opinion on their boy. Donovan went home a convert, and he soon spread the word about the Boston *Wunderkind*.[4]

In the next month, March, Sullivan took his growing reputation for the first time to New York. There he boxed a brief exhibition with a local fighter named Jerry Murphy during a benefit for George Rooke at the Terrace Garden Theater. For the first time the name "J. Sullivan" appeared in a leading sporting organ of the city, the *New York Clipper*. Perhaps while in town he passed by Madison Square Garden, the scene of some of his memorable later fights. This edifice was the first of four bearing the name, having been rebaptized from Gilmore's Garden the previous year. It was a pseudo-Moorish horror on the outside, with porthole-like windows cut twelve feet above the street level to discourage gate crashers. The Garden was under the control of William Vanderbilt, son of the cantankerous old commodore, who had died in 1877. William reluctantly announced that he would continue the tradition of Patrick Sarsfield Gilmore, the popular bandmaster, in offering attractions such as revivals, dog shows, and the circus, but the new Garden would be an athletic center, a sporting showcase that would include boxing.[5] Slowly the city was preparing itself for more pugilistic "exhibitions."

Certainly Sullivan made acquaintance with some of the city's more notorious night spots on this trip. He may have dropped in at Owney Geoghegan's establishment, which occupied a two-story building in the Bowery. Each floor of Geoghegan's featured a twelve-foot-square prize ring. The rings were in constant use day and night, for Owney ran one of the local lures for that "swollen, gibbering and intoxicated legion," the fight crowd. Geoghegan's was a continuous show, packed to the walls with sweating, screaming fans urging on their favorites. The air was sullen with "villainous whiskey, stale beer, flat wines and decomposed breaths." Here John would have been among his own. The uptown swells would not be caught dead in such a place; as one early social muckraker observed, "The faces around us are worse than those seen in a bench show of pugnacious dogs, and instinct teaches us to have a care for our nickels, for our pockets are in imminent danger."[6]

Also popular with the fight crowd was Kit Burns's place, Sportsmen's Hall, which was a big, three-story frame house on Water Street. Burns ran an operation that made Owney Geoghegan look like the proprietor of the Ritz. A huge gilt sign hung over the entrance to the building, the lower half of which, for some reason, had been painted a bilious green. On the first floor was an amphitheater, and in the center of this was a ring enclosed by a solid three-foot-high wooden fence. This was Kit Burns's famous "pit," in which dogs would be set against huge rats, fresh caught on the nearby wharf, the object being to see how many rats a dog could kill in a stated period of time. On dull days starved rats might be pitted against each other for the entertainment of bettors. Bare-knuckle bouts, strictly illegal, were occasionally held in the pit; many of these featured a certain George Leese, otherwise known as "Snatchem." Snatchem, festooned with two revolvers in his belt and a knife stuck in his boot top, was the bouncer, but if one of the fighters began to bleed, he served a second office, sucking blood from the wound so the bout could continue. A final staple of Burns's entertainment offerings was his own son-in-law, known as Jack the Rat. For ten cents this individual would bite the head off a mouse, and for a quarter he would decapitate a rat.[7]

Sportsmen's Hall may have been too much even for Sullivan, but he probably sampled Geoghegan's and was generally much in evidence about town during his brief visit. He may also have met some members of the sporting press at this time, for within weeks his name was beginning to appear in print. In May 1880 the *National Police Gazette* published an overview of the newly coined "heavyweight" division (there were two other classes, middleweight and lightweight, loosely defined with a maximum weight in the vicinity of 160 and 130 pounds, respectively) as part of its buildup for the forthcoming Goss-Ryan match, and Sullivan was not mentioned. But in June the *Gazette* announced that "Sullivan, the great pugilist of Boston, would like to meet Jack Donaldson, the Chicago pugilist, with or without gloves for $500." It was John's first mention in that quarter. He was beginning to realize the value of being *known*. To this end, in the same month of June 1880, he announced that he would fight *anyone in America*, with or without gloves, for five hundred dollars.[8]

The spring of 1880, then, saw Sullivan promoting himself for the first time beyond Boston, beginning to establish himself with the New York sporting crowd, and making potentially important connections with the press. During this time, also, he met a colorful figure who would play a significant role in his life, William Muldoon. Muldoon's family had come from Galway ahead of the wave of famine-induced immigration and settled in a farming area of New York's Genessee Valley, where William was born in 1845. He grew into a tall, heavyset red-haired lad, working as a farmer and wood splitter during his youth. Even in rural America he became an avid boxing fan, eagerly following the news of the Sayers-Heenan match in 1860. Like Mike Donovan he went for the Union in the Civil War, serving with Company I in the Sixth New York Regiment. This was a hard-riding cavalry outfit, and teenaged William Muldoon was in the thick of it when Phil Sheridan's forces purged the Shenandoah Valley of Confederates in 1864.[9]

After the war, too restless and ambitious to return to farm life, the young Muldoon found his way to New York City. He lived from hand to mouth, working in a grocery warehouse, on the docks, and as a cart driver for twelve dollars a week. He developed into a stout six-footer with enormous arm and chest muscles. Having wrestled in friendly bouts in the army, he began to wrestle for a few dollars on the side, receiving all of seven dollars for his first match. His local fame grew; he went to work for Harry Hill, taking on all comers in wrestling matches. In the meantime his connections with the fight crowd became close, because he built rings for occasional clandestine bare-knuckle bouts around the city. Muldoon retained his love of boxing, traveling all the way to Bay Saint Louis, Mississippi, in 1871 to watch Jem Mace and Joe Coburn fight a three-hour, eleven-round draw. From 1876 to 1881 he was a member of the New York City Police Department.[10]

Muldoon resigned from the force to open a "saloon and reading room" at Tod's Stock Exchange. By this time he had gained more than local fame as a Greco-Roman wrestler, his enormous upper body strength making him a dominant figure in this rare and difficult variant of the sport. His most famous victory came over the German Thiebaud Bauer in January 1880. Along the way he had become an ardent physical culturalist, preaching the evils of tobacco and strong drink (he rapidly separated himself from the Stock Exchange operation). As an early apostle of physical fitness and a bit of a crank concerning diet, he was on the lookout for potential young torch bearers for the muscular, athletic life. He may have met Sullivan on a trip to Boston in early 1880; at any rate, the two men certainly knew each other by the end of Sullivan's first New York trip. There were rumors that Muldoon had given John's buddy, Billy Madden, one hundred dollars to bring the Strong Boy to New York. The older man rapidly took the Bostonian in tow. He dressed him in the most approved style of the fancy: Prince Albert cutaway, vest with braided piping, patent leather shoes, silk topper, and cane. A year later he would set up Sullivan's New York match with Steve Taylor. Sullivan had made an important ally, and Muldoon, at first, had high hopes for his protégé as an exemplar of American sporting manhood.[11]

Having dipped his toes in the rapidly swirling currents of New York's sporting scene, Sullivan returned to Boston, still intent on recognition. In April 1880, at a testimonial for Joe Goss in the old Music Hall, the "champion," looking ahead to his bout with Paddy Ryan in June, agreed to spar with his young friend in a three-round gloved exhibition. Eighteen hundred people were on hand, and for the first time in Boston a "fight" received front-page coverage, in the *Globe*. Everyone expected the ring-wise veteran to teach the brash youngster, who already had a reputation as a braggart, a few tricks. Sullivan was hell-bent on establishing himself. Instinctively, he never fought halfway, and exhibitions were no exception. He reached Goss's face easily in the first round, and in the second he pounded the aging champion to the floor with a succession of left-hand blows to the skull. Goss, staggered, was helped to his feet by the master of ceremonies, Thomas Earley, who, thinking Joe had only slipped, left him standing upright, at which point Goss "went reeling like a drunken man across the stage." He had to be assisted to his corner, barely surviving the light sparring of the third round. Throughout this surprising spectacle the crowd was in a frenzy; "cheer after cheer went up in honor of the Highland boy." Sullivan had made his local name. From this point forward, as far as the fight crowd was concerned, he was Boston's own.[12]

In June, after Goss had been defeated by Ryan, Sullivan met George Rooke at the Howard Athenaeum. It was no contest. Rooke was a boxer of some experience, but he was far outweighed by the 190-pound Sullivan. In addition, the interior of the old building was stifling in the summer heat; Rooke began the so-called "exhibition" badly debilitated and was knocked down three times in the initial round. Some in the crowd thought he was drunk. The authorities were on the alert; they had already stopped an earlier bout at the end of round one because it was too "realistic." Now they stepped in at the end of the third round and saved the hapless Rooke from further punishment. Sullivan's laurels were untarnished. Keen-eyed reporters noted that the Highland Boy (as he was still billed) had attracted not only the usual fight fans but also "some of our staid and first-class citizens."[13]

There followed months of idleness. Like most rising boxers clearly on the make, Sullivan had trouble arranging matches, but with his hometown repute secure, he was content to forge his way through a succession of Boston saloons loudly advertising his intent to dethrone Ryan. Not until November did he fight again, in the brief New York exhibition with Johnny Kenny. By then, however, it was time to get back to serious work, and a new opponent was on the horizon.

John Donaldson, from Cleveland, was a self-styled "Professor" of the manly art and had made a considerable reputation as a pugilist west of the Alleghenies despite his average size, 5 feet 10½ inches and 160 pounds. He and Sullivan agreed to give a four-round exhibition at Robertson's Opera House in Cincinnati, so for the first time the young Bostonian journeyed west. On December 20 they sparred for four rounds, Sullivan pounding his badly outweighed opponent all over the ring. Donaldson claimed afterward that he had been ill and demanded a real fight; the respective backers promptly got together and made the arrangements.

Cincinnati was a prime sporting town, proud of its famed Red Stockings baseball team and with a solid horse racing tradition that had drifted across the Ohio River from Kentucky. But city ordinances barred prizefighting, so the match was conducted in a conspiratorial cloud of rumors and false scents. On Friday, Christmas Eve, those few fans in the know began to congregate in the back of a condemned beer hall called the Pacific Garden, near the corner of Sixth and Vine streets. Only thirty people, in addition to the combatants, eventually made it, but the officers on the beat had no idea what was going on until it was over. Sullivan entered the Pacific Garden angry; he had not liked Donaldson's excuses. The men fought for a purse collected from the handful of people in the room. Sullivan contributed twenty-five dollars and the crowd chipped in fifty-three dollars more. Donaldson supplied the gloves, which were hard, small, and caked with blood from previous use. The crowd formed itself into a twenty-foot-square space, making a human ring, and several trunks were brought forward for the fighters and their seconds to sit on between rounds. Both men wore knit shirts and sparring shoes with rubber soles and canvas uppers, as well as the usual tights. Despite the gloves, London Prize Ring Rules governed.

The floor was swept of debris, and two circus lamps were ignited to provide a ghostly, flickering light. A canvas partition was hoisted to screen the doings from passers-by, and several men were paid to stand out on Vine Street at the front of the building, beating drums and blowing horns to drown the noise of the fight. The two men squared off at 10:30 P.M. Sullivan immediately charged "like a bull at a red rag" and knocked Donaldson to the floor. By round two Donaldson was bleeding. In the next round Sullivan pushed him into a pile of rubbish and knocked him over two trunks. Donaldson was also decked to end each of the next three rounds. By the seventh Sullivan's seconds, Johnny Moran and Tom Ryan, were arguing that Donaldson was not fighting, and indeed the westerner did not appear overly enthusiastic for further punishment, but his local supporters urged him to fight on. In the eighth Donaldson got in his one good punch of the fight, a left to the nose, but this served only to further enrage Sullivan, who again pounded the Professor over some trunks. By the ninth the Bostonian was slugging away at will; in the next round he forced Donaldson to the floor in twenty seconds.

Obviously, Donaldson had had enough. All present were satisfied, and Sullivan's festering rage ebbed as he and Donaldson shook hands. The crowd departed as furtively as they had come, meeting later for drinks at a nearby Vine Street saloon. A reporter who had witnessed the fray felt that "Sullivan is no boxer according to any standard rules," having fouled and kicked his opponent throughout. Most of the sparse crowd, however, had apparently departed impressed. Dozens more had scurried up and down Vine Street fruitlessly looking for the action, and they became automatic couriers of the gossip that contributed to Sullivan's growing reputation as a relentless fighting machine. News of the fight hit page one of the *New York Times*.[14]

On December 27 the two boxers were arraigned in Cincinnati, charged with engaging in a prizefight. No witnesses could be found to attest to the event, and two days later Sullivan and Donaldson were discharged. The defense lawyer, the judge, and the boxers promptly adjourned to a neighboring bar. One Boston supporter, elated at the broadening evidence of the Strong Boy's talents, offered to back Sullivan against "any man in the world" for $1,000 to $2,500 a side.[15] For nickels and dimes in the rear of a dimly lit, condemned saloon, John had added significantly to his prestige.

Back in Boston with the new year, Sullivan put on an exhibition with Joe Goss at the Music Hall, during which John beat up on Jack Stewart, styled the "champion of Canada," in two rounds. The friends split a hefty purse of thirteen hundred dollars between them and were encouraged to give a second exhibition later in the month. This was conducted for members of a few private clubs on Beacon Hill, about three hundred of the "better sort" turning out. Sullivan was widening his appeal. Now forty-two, Goss used his new-found money to open a saloon on LaGrange Street. Except for two more exhibitions with John, he decided, after years in and out of the fight game, to leave the ring as a contestant for good.[16]

Two months later, on March 21, Sullivan fought a second exhibition match with Mike Donovan during a benefit for Patsey Sheppard at the Music Hall. Donovan had learned his lesson from the first fight; for three rounds he dodged and weaved, avoiding Sullivan's rushing tactics and wild swings. The Strong Boy was far from a finished fighter, despite his string of triumphs, and Donovan got in a few good blows of his own. For the first time Sullivan was frustrated, and the sizable crowd vented its scorn at his inability to put Donovan away by prolonged hissing.[17] Sullivan may not have been unduly concerned. New York beckoned again, and the brawl on the barge with John Flood was just around the corner.

## II

New York City was the key to fame. Whereas Boston was regional, in 1881 New York already commanded national attention. The fight crowd might flock to the pleasure pits of Owney Geoghegan, Harry Hill, or even Kit Burns, but the real and growing power in the sporting culture lay with the press. Print was proving its power to make and unmake athletes. Prizefighting, in its subterranean American existence, was highly localized, with networks of friendships and acquaintances the wires along which fighting gossip was strung and fighting reputations were made. The neighborhood was still the heart of American boxing in 1881, but the means for changing this fragmented mosaic of sporting culture were already at hand.[18]

Following the Civil War increasing literacy and leisure time brought the American public to newsprint as never before. "The worlds before and after the Deluge were not more different than our republics of letters before and after the late war," wrote the New England poet Edmund Clarence Stedman in 1873 to a friend. "For ten years the new generation read nothing but newspapers." Those of greater education and wealth eagerly devoured "story" newspapers and magazines, but print was making its way steadily down the social scale as well. E. L. Godkin, an advocate of responsible journalism, sourly commented of the new "news" that "this stuff is greedily read by all classes."[19]

The sensationalistic urban press had its roots in antebellum America. The irrepressible James Gordon Bennett inaugurated the *New York Herald* in 1835, following a spate of penny newspapers in Boston, Philadelphia, and Baltimore. Bennett filled his sheet with salacious gossip, imaginative tales of events that never were, and lurid accounts of murder, suicide, adultery, and rape. He made money. Joyfully thumbing his nose at contemporary standards of etiquette and propriety, he sent fleets of "reporters" to cover court trials, executions, church meetings, and Wall Street. Along the way he pioneered the sports section, to appeal to the diverse interests of city life. Originally confined to horse racing, the *Herald's* sports reporting soon included prizefights, a move already anticipated by papers such as the *New York Transcript* and *Sun* and the *Philadelphia Public Ledger.*[20]

Bennett and the other barons of the penny press presented life in sections and subdivisions, which encouraged selective reading and the compartmentalization of urban life—something for everyone. The newspaper proved itself, for all its distortions and errors, as a true mirror of the city. In featuring events from the stage, the sports arena, and other areas of popular culture, the press gave leisure legitimate standing in the workaday world. Increasing complexities in the modern city made it impossible for personal experience and gossip to serve as adequate sources of information. The impact of the popular press thus exploded the tightly knit circle of neighborhood and family; now *everyone* began to own the "news." More and more, what was once ineluctably private became public, as the press scooped up practically every aspect of human existence in its greedy maw.[21]

At first the penny press appealed mainly to the middle class, but its effects were soon felt elsewhere. New immigrants speaking foreign languages cut their linguistic teeth on the popular newspaper, while each transient sensation had seemingly universal appeal. By the time of Fort Sumter, reporters were being hired on a regular basis by most metropolitan dailies instead of being employed piecemeal or by the assignment. They specialized in the "human interest story"—man bites dog—and turned urban America upside down for any tidbits that might enlighten readers and bring them back for more. The reporter as a social figure would come later, with flamboyant personalities such as Richard Harding Davis, but already in John Sullivan's youth those who "reported" had considerable leeway to make (and falsify) the news. During the Civil War the barons and their minions tentatively assayed interviews with public figures, and in time statesmen and politicians sensed the value of a newsprint channel to a mass public.[22]

The press was abetted by the technology of the industrial age. Most of the early prizefights, for example, were along rivers or waterways served by steamboats. The railroad made it even easier for reporters to get to the spot; the Morrissey-Heenan fight in 1858 had even been advertised by the Erie Railroad. When Mike McCoole fought Aaron Jones in 1867 at a pinprick on the Ohio map called Busenbark Station, tickets were sold openly for excursion trains to the fight and as eagerly gobbled up by eastern sportsmen. The telegraph made possible almost instant reportage, the first instance being wired dispatches from the scene of the Tom Hyer-Yankee Sullivan set-to in Maryland in 1849. In the 1880s the wire services would make the dissemination of news from remote sites even more rapid and universal.[23]

In Boston the press was divided in its notion of what was "proper news." The staid *Transcript* catered to the interests of the upper crust, its densely-packed, narrow columns chockablock with financial and shipping reports and the latest doings from Harvard, its back pages routinely devoted to unraveling the genealogical trees of Boston's "best families." It was the undiluted voice of Yankee Protestantism, and the likes of John Sullivan would never be seen within. The *Boston Herald* appealed to the middle class, and it (reluctantly) began to cover prizefighting in the 1880s. For the Irish, of course, there was John Boyle O'Reilly and the *Pilot*, but its coverage was too parochial to fully satisfy the inquiring urban reader. For these services Sullivan's contemporaries had to turn to the *Globe* or the *Post*. The *Globe's* publisher, Charles H. Taylor, made it an unabashed Democratic sheet, even supporting the odious Ben Butler for governor. The *Post* was a bit more balanced, going so far as to hire a few Harvard graduates as part of its reportorial staff.[24]

Taylor was Boston's answer to James Gordon Bennett. Here is the *Globe's* lead sentence, page one, on a local murder case circa 1879:

> The body of him who was sent out of this world by the hand of an assassin has been lain away in the earth, and these who sent him into the other world still defy the law, and tonight walk about unmolested, save by their conscience, which must be constantly holding up before their mental vision the picture of that struggle and death in the gloomy basement at number 13 Joy Street last Thursday night.

The *Globe* was later pleased to note that two Sicilians had been taken into custody. Under Taylor's management the paper continued its lively inventiveness, promoting sports coverage to a central concern.

At times sporting news even appeared on the front page. The *Herald* was a bit more dignified, but it swung fully behind Sullivan as he continued his climb.[25]

The *Globe* and *Herald*, along with a somewhat laggard *Post*, were in the mainstream of the new sporting journalism. Joseph Pulitzer's *New York World* staffed the first full-time sports section, giving "expert" accounts of athletic events aimed at those who took their diversions with increasing seriousness. Other metropolitan dailies soon followed. But the Everest of sports reporting in the late nineteenth century developed in New York in "the Big Three," all weeklies: the *Spirit of the Times*, the *New York Clipper*, and the *National Police Gazette*.[26]

The *Spirit of the Times* was created in 1831, brainchild of William Trotter Porter, a country journalist from Vermont. Porter added the *American Turf Register* to his stable in 1839 and dominated the sporting press at mid-century. By the 1850s the *Spirit* was routinely covering horse racing, angling, cricket, foot racing, rowing, yachting, and baseball, which Porter reportedly labeled the "national game." Porter accentuated the record; he was the great-grandfather of the present-day American obsession with sporting statistics. Through him the *Spirit* provided a source of authority and stability in rapidly changing times. The paper was in reality a brother act, but one by one the Porter brothers died, and in 1856 William struck out on his own with *Porter's Spirit of the Times*. He began to include news of prizefights. But in 1858 he, too, was dead; the two *Spirits* recombined in 1861, but in the next twenty years the readership dwindled. With Porter gone, some of the fire and dedication vanished as well.[27]

Frank Queen founded the *New York Clipper* in 1853 at the age of thirty. Queen was pure working class, having been a printer's devil and manager of a newspaper stand before he ventured out on his own. Buying out the interest of Harrison Trent, his early partner, Queen made the *Clipper* the sporting oracle of the 1860s and 1870s, symbolized by the erection of the *Clipper* building in 1869. Queen specialized in baseball coverage and employed the pioneer baseball writer and statistician Henry Chadwick, who did much to establish the modern rules of the game. The *Clipper* also defended prizefighting, which was once again barely covered by the badly limping *Spirit of the Times*. The *Clipper* published the first picture of John Sullivan in any paper anywhere, giving him a one-column head-and-shoulders view. Through Queen, *Clipper* readers began to form a visual image of the stern-eyed young man clad neatly in coat and tie, square-jawed, jug-eared, mustachioed—and looking straight at the camera.[28]

Then there was the *National Police Gazette*. George Wilkes and Enoch Camp had founded the original *Gazette* in 1845. Wilkes had previously published a four-page rag called the *Subterranean*, which specialized in exposing the sources of various political incomes. For his troubles along these lines, he was arrested no less than six times. Camp handled the business affairs of the *Gazette*, retiring wealthy after a few years. The early flavor of the paper, though, was provided by Wilkes. By its second month of publication the *Gazette* had a circulation of fifteen thousand. Wilkes responded to the obvious reader approval by serving it up raw: "We offer this week a most interesting record of horrid murders, outrageous robberies, bold forgeries, astounding burglaries, hideous rapes, vulgar seductions, and recent exploits of pickpockets and hotel thieves in various parts of the country."[29]

The early *Gazette* was aggressive and entrepreneurial, as well as outrageous. Wilkes established agents throughout the eastern United States in over forty towns and cities. These men, whether in New Orleans, Saint Louis, or Buffalo, were not reporters—they were promoters. Their business was to get the paper to the reader, and this they did by placing the sheet in the one bastion of masculinity where a man could sit at his ease and read: the barbershop. The daily shave and the regular haircut were common occurrences in the mid-nineteenth century, particularly for middle-class males. The local barbershop was a male social preserve, and Wilkes's agents showed a stroke of genius by targeting this institution. The agents also served as clearinghouses for "news" items, since most of the *Gazette's* reporters were its loyal readers.[30]

For twelve years the paper prospered. Then Wilkes was driven into debt in the flash financial panic of 1857. He was forced to sell the *Gazette* to George W. Matsell, once the New York City chief of police. Wilkes later made a comeback by buying Porter's *Spirit of the Times*, helping that paper enjoy a prolonged if stagnant career. Under Matsell's uninspiring direction the *Gazette* went rapidly downhill; by 1872 he himself was in debt and unloaded the property to two engravers to whom he owed money. They hired an Englishman named Herbert R. Mooney as editor, to no avail. By 1876 the once-flourishing *Gazette* appeared to be on its last legs. In that year it passed into the hands of Richard Kyle Fox.[31]

Fox was an Irish-American original. Born in Belfast in 1846 and experienced in the printer's trade, he emigrated in 1874 with less than five dollars in his pocket. Within two years, using his boundless hustle and nerve, he engineered an editorial takeover of the decaying *Gazette*. Fox's particular insight was the perception that a true journal for the masses needed to shock and titillate as much as inform. Using the old Wilkes network of agents, he set out to distribute his paper on a truly national scale. He did this so successfully that he outclassed them all.

Neither the Bennetts (father and son), Porter, Queen, nor Wilkes reached the *national* reading public on the mass scale that Fox achieved. By 1882 he was able to build a grand edifice, for the then-substantial sum of $250,000, to house his periodical. Over this empire of print he reigned as editor, owner, and "Proprietor."

The Proprietor's formula was simple: more of it, and keep it coming. Printed on pinked-tinted paper and priced at a nickel, the *Gazette* became "the most lurid journal ever published in the United States," an endless weekly panoply of buxom showgirls, crime, sex, and murder. Fox rapidly saw that the cult of masculinity eagerly responded to such fare, and he accordingly reduced the subscription rates to saloons, barbershops, and hotels. Many newsstands refused to sell the scandalous sheet, but no matter. By the 1880s Fox was able to maintain a steady circulation of 150,000 copies, funneled into every town and city in the country. Alongside the accounts of vice of all kinds resided wide coverage of sporting news. When sales of issues covering the Goss-Ryan fight temporarily topped 400,000 in 1880, Fox set out to make the *Gazette* the "leading prize ring authority in America." His sports editor, William E. Harding, quickly produced an interminable (and inaccurate) "History of the American Prize Ring."[32]

A staff of writers capable of the most purple prose fueled the assembly line of words. Fox hired them by the squad to write over the weekend; it was rumored that he would lock his crew in a room on Saturday afternoon, give them four bottles of whiskey for inspiration, and release them Monday morning. "Write! Write a lot!" he exhorted. "Write the stuff the dailies don't dare use! Be as truthful as possible, but a story's a story!" These besotted hacks were backed by a corps of artists who specialized in muscular pugilists and hefty females in spangled tights. "If they can't read, give them plenty of pictures," said Fox. It was a recipe for success. Eventually the *Gazette* was exported to twenty-six countries and made Fox a millionaire. While the paper would suffer a long, slow decline in the early years of the twentieth century, Fox at his death in 1922 left an estate of over $1.5 million, despite the fact that he had given away over $250,000 in medals, prize money, stakes, and promotional payments during the *Gazette's* golden age.[33]

Fox's weekly was not really a newspaper but a tabloid, a "trade organ of fast life." The editor himself was an excellent advertisement for the style of his paper; his inevitable Prince Albert and silk topper were known throughout the city. An inveterate party giver, he reached his apogee during the celebration of the opening of the Brooklyn Bridge in 1883. He gave a sweeping invitation to the sporting crowd to celebrate the great day at the *Gazette* offices. Over a thousand responded, consuming several hundred bottles of champagne and whiskey along

5. Richard Kyle Fox (about 1890) (William Schutte Collection)

with a barbecued ox. By the time the police arrived to clear the building, which was crammed to the rooftop, Fox's guests were busily engaged in smashing the furniture.[34]

The pride of the *Gazette* building was Fox's trophy room. The place
was a mecca for the sporting faithful, who trooped through daily to
see the artifacts of their heroes: ribbons and medals by the score, most
presented by Fox himself; ornate trophies, awarded for every achievement imaginable in walking, cycling, rowing, and countless other sports;
and huge oil paintings of the idols of the day, from Buffalo Bill Cody
to the unabashed Fox. Eventually a portrait of John Sullivan would
hang there, too. A uniformed attendant stood ready to explain the
collection to the curious.[35]

Of course, the established newspapers, journals, and magazines cursed
Fox and his villainous rag to high heaven. The editor cheekily welcomed all slings and arrows—it was good publicity. He blatantly touted
his product as "the leading illustrated paper in America, known alike
for its artistic taste, the beauty of its illustrations, and as being first in
its field in depicting accurately everything of importance." In pursuit
of these standards of excellence the *Gazette* displayed "George Bothner
of New York: The noted Eastern wrestler showing his famous Crotch
Hold on Nachad, the Turk." There were contests galore: "Tony Alemi,
the Italian human pin-cushion, offers to match himself to stick 2,000
needles, 20 awls, and two blades of a knife in his body without drawing
blood during the operation, against any man in America."

And Fox sought to reward his readers while entertaining them. He
ran a page-one series of biographies of "tonsorialists," bartenders, and
"leading hotel men," all of them inevitably described as first-rate. From
time to time, grateful for all his distribution outlets, he ran sketches
of news dealers and newsboys as well. Polite society was appalled by
all this, Theodore Roosevelt fuming that the *Gazette* was found in the
hands of every western ruffian. But all to no avail; one of Fox's treas-
ures was a scrawled note from Sempronius, Texas, dated December
20, 1879: "Please send me a copy of your paper (The Police Gazette),
and greatly oblige—Jesse James."[36]

Fox first met John Sullivan either in his office or at Harry Hill's
dance hall. On October 14, 1880, Hill opened his establishment on
Houston Street with a gala entertainment featuring boxers and wrestlers. The popular Harry was presented with a huge golden eagle, which
was prominently displayed between two lamps in the theater's cupola.
The new Hill's rapidly put Owney Geoghegan and Kit Burns in the
shade; it became *the* New York spot for the sporting crowd. In later
years Billy Madden told the boxing writer Nat Fleischer his story of
how Fox and Sullivan had met. According to Madden, the two were
introduced in the *Gazette* offices during Sullivan's spring visit in 1881

and disliked each other immediately. Sullivan considered Fox a toff, while Fox was used to prizefighters truckling to him for mention in the journal, and John displayed his usual independent, don't-give-a-damn attitude. Other accounts have the two meeting at Hill's at the same period, with Fox insulting Sullivan or vice versa. As Madden was an eyewitness, and the *New York Daily News* reported a meeting between the two at the *Gazette* offices in late March, the less colorful story is the more likely, even though the barroom episode has been repeated ever since. At any rate, Fox would promote Sullivan when it served the interests of circulation, but he would also assiduously seek a fighter who could take the Strong Boy down a peg. In this clash of two willful personalities, John had made his first important enemy in the sporting world. To Fox, Sullivan was nothing more than an "unreliable boaster," adept only at "backing and filling."[37]

Sullivan's fight against the Jersey City coroner, Steve Taylor, at Harry Hill's in March had served to place his name before the Big Three of the sporting press. The brawl on the barge with Flood, while not fully covered by reporters because of its bizarre circumstances, set him up as a man to watch in the heavyweight ranks. Fox had boosted the Flood fight by touting Flood as a "rough diamond"; as for Sullivan, "stripped he is a model for a sculptor." Fox did not join the crowd on the barge himself, but he sent his business manager, James Magowan. Before the fight began, Magowan flourished a blank check and shouted that Fox had authorized him to fill it out in an amount up to ten thousand dollars as the *Gazette*'s stake in a bout between Paddy Ryan and Sullivan. The Strong Boy, with other things on his mind at the moment, replied that his backers were in Boston; then he proceeded to dismantle Flood.[38]

John Sullivan had made a dramatic entry into the mainstream of sporting America. At a testimonial tendered him at Harry Hill's the night of the Taylor fight, he audaciously offered fifty dollars to any man who could stand against him for four rounds under the Queensberry Rules. This sort of brag infuriated Fox and many others, but as long as Sullivan kept winning, "it ain't braggin' if you can do it." And, for the first time, he was no longer "Sullivan," "John Sullivan," or "Jack Sullivan" in the press. Now the media, offering the respect due his triumphs, parted his name in the middle and began to call him "John L. Sullivan," which was quickly shortened to the appellation soon to be familiar throughout the country: John L.[39]

### III

Billy Madden first met John L. in Boston in early 1881. Madden remembered that his pal "had a most kindly disposition, and would do anything for a friend, but . . . could not bear to be crossed." Billy was a handsome, slender, well-proportioned man, with calm, widely spaced eyes surmounting a rather fleshy nose. Born in London of Irish parents in 1852, he was a full head shorter than Sullivan, but he had boxed as a teenager and, indeed, would remain around the fight game for most of his life as a trainer and manager. From time to time he and John L. would engage in some friendly sparring, Madden's speed and quickness allowing him to slip some punches in against the much bigger man. The two quickly became fast friends; in spite of many rifts, Madden would remain intensely loyal to Sullivan and fiercely proud of his friend's abilities in the ring.[40] It was natural that he accompany John L. on his first big New York trip, ostensibly to help with the training. A likable, open man, Madden provided many introductions, such as those to Muldoon and Fox.

Madden was much more than a mere factotum; he had the entepreneurial touch. Shortly after Sullivan returned to Boston in the spring of 1881, Billy conceived the idea of a tour that would showcase "the big fellow." The two men announced their intentions in early July, with Sullivan's fifty-dollar offer, four rounds under Queensberry rules, still in effect. "On each occasion Sullivan will be prepared to spar anybody." John L. was quoted as promising to meet all comers, "even if they weigh a ton." The enterprising Madden had rounded up one thousand dollars from Boston sporting men to fund the tour and serve as stakes.[41]

The idea of a tour was not new; "the Swedish Nightingale," Jenny Lind, had been a smashing success back in 1851, cleverly promoted as she was by P. T. Barnum. Public speakers routinely "toured," and vaudeville already had several "circuits." Nor was the idea of a tour new to athletics; the Cincinnati Red Stockings had been the first to barnstorm, back in 1869, and now the practice was accepted throughout the major leagues. But the idea of a single athlete touring, offering not only to defeat all comers in the ring but also to *knock them out*, and backing it up with fifty dollars—*that* was new. Advance men would rent the halls for the "exhibitions" and take care of advertising. Sullivan, "the Great Knocker-Out," was on the way!

First stop, Philadelphia. The contact there was Arthur Chambers, who ran a three-story saloon on Ridge Avenue. Chambers was from Boston and probably already knew John L. He was a veteran of over a dozen prizefights as a lightweight, including a victorious 136-round match with the Philadelphian John Clark in 1879. He had arranged a bout with the Englishman Fred Crossley, a rank and ungainly amateur whose only asset was his size: 6 feet 1 and 200 pounds. A perspiring, impatient crowd packed the third floor of Chambers's saloon on the evening of July 11 to see the fireworks. Crossley refused a preoffered

6. Billy Madden, Sullivan's first manager (about 1896) (William Schutte Collection

twenty-five dollars (the fifty dollars was temporarily forgotten) to step in the ring with Sullivan, saying good-humoredly that he would do it for nothing. He might better have taken the money; John L. quickly knocked him down, set his nose bleeding, and sent him fleeing to his corner. The crowd howled their disapproval when Crossley threw in the sponge, but Sullivan tried to save the evening by sparring a bit with Madden.[42]

Sullivan and Madden stayed in Philadelphia for a while, giving sparring exhibitions at John Clark's Olympic Boxing Academy and seeing the town. Ten days after the Crossley fiasco, a new victim was found, Dan McCarthy of Baltimore. Unlike the generous Crossley, McCarthy went in the ring for the fifty dollars. He was as quickly belted out, the finale a blow to the neck that sent him sprawling. McCarthy, who had been outweighed by twenty-five pounds, appeared later on stage with Sullivan to show that "his injuries were not serious." Sullivan's share of his light work in the City of Brotherly Love came to $150.[43] The tour passed on, through Buffalo, Pittsburgh, Cleveland, Cincinnati, and Louisville, but only Madden appeared in the ring with Sullivan.

Next stop, Chicago. At first, Sullivan and Madden did their sparring routine around town, attracting little attention. Chicago was booming, aggressively rebuilding from the disastrous conflagration of 1871, and seemed to have no time to spare for a couple of itinerant Boston pugilists. Finally, however, Sullivan's offer had its effect. On August 13, after John L. and Billy had sparred before a good crowd of three thousand people in McCormick Hall, James Dalton, the burly captain of a Lake Michigan tugboat called the *Ingram*, came forward and put on the gloves. Dalton was no ring novice. Among his victims were John Dwyer and Professor John Donaldson, Sullivan's Christmas Eve victim in Cincinnati. Dalton's strength carried him through the first two rounds, but by the third Sullivan was beating him steadily about the face. By the start of the fourth round, the crowd was fully involved: could the local man take the braggart's fifty dollars? No. Within an instant Sullivan "knocked him so stiff that when the allotted ten seconds had passed he was unable to put in an appearance." John L. gave his opponent twenty-five dollars for his trouble. The set-to had been the hit of a variety bill that included clog dancers, a song-and-dance team, and a burlesque skating act.[44]

The Bostonians remained in the Chicago area for the next two weeks, their show making money off the word-of-mouth of the Dalton fight. Sullivan also attracted the sponsorship of a local gambler named Charlie ("Parson") Davies. The Parson arranged for another McCormick Hall presentation on September 3. About two thousand people attended, hearing that the Strong Boy would face Jack Burns, the "champion of Michigan." Burns, who hailed from Jackson, was a hefty man well over six feet in height, but he must have declared himself the best man in the Wolverine state, rather than having fought for it. John L. went at his target with the usual savage rush and within twenty seconds had socked Burns under the chin and knocked him to the stage floor. Groggy, Burns staggered to his feet and assumed what he believed to be a boxing position, at which point Sullivan delivered a haymaker to the mouth that propelled the Michigan man flying off the south end of the stage and into the audience. Burns had had enough, so Sullivan and his new friend Dalton conducted a friendly sparring match before the crowd dispersed.[45]

The two Chicago fights attracted national attention from the sporting press. Parson Davies agreed to underwrite the rest of the tour. Another Chicago sportsman, Mike McDonald, offered to back Sullivan against Paddy Ryan, for five or ten thousand dollars a side. The *National Police Gazette* breathlessly reported that John L. was "creating a sensation throughout the west," admired the boldness of his challenge to all comers, and erroneously added that "he is never in want of a customer." In fact, such was the publicity from Chicago that for the rest of the tour no one would climb into the ring with Sullivan. In Kansas City, the next stop, Madden took up the slack, sparring with a former fighter named Jim King, followed by the usual routine between the two Boston men. From there, they returned to New York.[46]

Except for Dalton, Sullivan had met a string of novices. Nevertheless, the tour made him a national, as opposed to regional, reputation, and in today's jargon he had become the "number one contender" for Ryan's title. He and Madden attracted fairly substantial crowds in most locales. They were not harassed by the police, because they were promoting an "exhibition of the science of boxing." And they received good press coverage throughout the urban Northeast and Midwest. The entire tour probably gained Sullivan between six and seven thousand dollars, triple what a skilled laborer could make in a year. He had made great strides in winning a name for himself.[47]

The challenges now came to *him*. A variety of offers to fight the undefeated Strong Boy came cascading in to the *Gazette* offices (Fox eagerly served as middleman for these sorts of things), including one from grizzled Tom Allen, who had fought his first prizefight in 1861 and was now forty-one years old. Mike Donovan wanted another match. Sullivan agreed, providing "he stays and does not run away and lie down like he did on the two former occasions he sparred with me." In October, John L. received a benefit at the New York Aquarium, making his usual four-round offer; it went unaccepted. Instead, he sparred three tame rounds with Steve Taylor. The restless crowd gave three cheers for Paddy Ryan, and Sullivan angrily offered to fight any man in the house for $250. The spectators left grumbling.[48]

Ryan and Sullivan, Sullivan and Ryan—it was the obvious match in the minds of boxing fans everywhere.

## IV

John L. had been stalking Paddy for months, even before the start of the tour. As early as February he had offered to fight the champion for $1,000 a side. In June he sent a letter to Frank Queen at the *New York Clipper*, who like Fox occasionally served as a stakesholder and arranger of matches. Now Sullivan challenged Ryan for $2,500 a side, but Queen, possibly fearing legal reprisals, hurriedly returned $500 tendered in response by one of Ryan's backers and declared that the *Clipper* was out of the matchmaking business. On Ryan's part, he had authorized Fox to be his spokesman in May, declaring that he was ready to fight anyone, under the London Rules, for $2,500 to $5,000 a side and "the championship of the world" (the first known use of this phrase).[49]

Despite his claim Paddy was at heart a lethargic champion. Although fully recovered from his knifing over three years before, he was preoccupied with running his recently opened saloon in Albany. He wrote the *Gazette* that he did not intend to fight again. But the pressure on him to defend his title was growing; his patron, Fox, was eager to stage a Ryan-Sullivan bout, and he offered to back Paddy for five thousand dollars. Ryan responded in September that he had ballooned to 230 pounds and did not see how he could fight "at such short notice." Fox would have none of this; unlike Queen he rather enjoyed flouting the law and pressed ahead with his arrangements for the match.[50]

On September 24, 1881, a huge assemblage of sporting men, pugilists, merchants, turfmen, and interested fight fans gathered in the *Gazette* offices. The halls, corridors, and sidewalks outside were jammed, and rumors flew that the great match was to be made at last. Sullivan did not show up, being represented by Billy Madden and Parson Davies, who had come in from Chicago for the occasion. Ryan was there, proudly displayed by Fox as the "world's champion." Much negotiation followed, with William Harding, Fox's sports editor, insisting that the trusted Harry Hill hold the stakes. Mike McDonald, the Chicagoan who was underwriting Sullivan along with the Parson, wired his veto on Hill. Amid much self-conscious punctilio and gentlemanly negotiation over stakes, stakesholders, and fight location, the meeting broke up in confusion, everyone adjourning to Harry Hill's to continue the discussion. Everyone except Paddy; probably relieved, he returned home. Nevertheless, Fox was persistent. Both sets of backers and Sullivan wanted the match, and within two weeks it was announced. Ryan

7. Paddy Ryan (about 1882) (William Shutte Collection)

would meet Sullivan "within 100 miles of New Orleans" on February 7, 1882, under the London Rules.[51]

Fox began to beat the drums, and the reverberations were heard throughout the cult of masculinity. The "fistic gladiators" were profiled. Sullivan was "trained in condition" and had been a fighter since the age of sixteen (a patent falsehood), while Ryan was training hard. The *Gazette* vehemently denied rumors published in the *Boston Herald* that Ryan was "rapidly breaking up" from poor training. In mock-chivalrous fashion, the colors of the fighters were announced: Sullivan would sport a white silk handkerchief with a green border. The handkerchief would display American flags upper and lower left, and Irish flags upper and lower right, with an American eagle emblazoning the center. Ryan, not to be outdone, would feature a handkerchief with red, white, and blue borders. In the center an eagle stood on a blue, star-speckled globe, surmounting the inscription "Paddy Ryan, Champion of America [what had happened to "world"?], A.O.H. (Ancient Order of Hibernians)." The corners were decorated with an Irish harp, a sunburst, an American shield, and the word *Excelsior*, representing the seal of New York State.[52]

By November the publicity mill was in high gear. Despite McDonald's objections Harry Hill had been selected as stakesholder, and the backers were sending in their shares, eventually amounting to $2,500 a side. Sullivan contributed $500 of his own money, as did Madden, and $500 came from assorted Boston sporting men. The final $1,000 in Sullivan's corner was provided by James Keenan, a Boston gambler and owner of the famed trotting horse Emma B.

Ryan, really training for the first time in his life, was working under the tutelage of Johnny Roche and Charley McDonald at Lew Course's St. James Hotel in Rockaway Beach, eventually taking off thirty pounds of flab. Through Harding's pen, Paddy provided a sample of his regimen for *Gazette* readers:

> My first object will be to thoroughly purify my system, which will occupy probably a week. Then I will start in on schedule time. At 5:30 every morning I will arise, and after taking a little old sherry and a crust of stale bread I will saunter along the road for three miles just to get up an appetite. Breakfast will be found ready upon returning, the principle [*sic*] food being either muttonchops or beefsteak, medium cooked, with just enough salt upon it to make it palatable, in addition to dry toast and a cup of tea, with neither sugar nor milk. A rest is taken after breakfast for ¾ of an hour, then the hard work of the day commences. Encased in heavy flannels and with a heavy pair of walking shoes I start on a ten-mile tramp—five miles and return. The pace must be a severe one, and the last half mile of the distance is accomplished on a fast run. I then jump into bed with heavy coverings and remain there until perspiration ceases. I will then be subjected to a good hard rubbing by [Roche and McDonald], and afterward take a bath in luke-

warm water. Being rubbed perfectly dry I don a suit of light clothes and journey quietly around till dinner time, which is set down promptly at 12:30 p.m. The meal consists of roast beef, and sometimes boiled leg of mutton is allowed, vegetables once in a while are included, in addition to dry toast and a bottle of Bass' or Scotch ale. After dinner a row is indulged in for about ¾ hour, and then a set-to for ½ hour additional. Dumb-bells, weighing 2½ pounds each, are fondled with for some time. Particular care is taken to keep the limbs always in motion. Supper consists of a couple of boiled eggs, some toast and a cup of tea. A walk around is afterward taken until the time arrives for retiring, which is between 9 and 9:30 p.m. The last effort of the day is take up the dumb-bells, rattle them hard until you fairly drop into bed a very tired man.[53]

While Ryan was spending only half an hour a day sparring, along with drinking his ale, sauntering along the road, and fondling his dumbbells, Sullivan was getting into the best shape of his life up in Boston, practically the first time he had subordinated his fast-living habits to his new profession. Both men would enter the ring at around two hundred pounds, but Sullivan was paying much more attention to wind and speed. The betting was moving 5 to 4 in the direction of the challenger; Sullivan had been fighting actively for over a year, while Ryan had been inert. Some corners, like the *New York Daily News*, believed that Paddy could nevertheless prevail, since he was a bare-knuckler and Sullivan had heretofore fought only with gloves. "Fighting with pillows on the hands and contending with nature's weapons unadorned are two different things." For the first time in American sporting history, "informed" opinions came from all sides in advance of an illegal prizefight. Old Mike McCoole was uncertain that the Boston man could withstand bare-knuckle punishment. The correspondent for the *Albany Argus*, seeing Ryan entrain for the South, found it hard to believe that such a "specimen of male humanity," swankily attired in Prince Albert, silk topper, and kid gloves, could be beaten. Johnny Roche announced that his charge was trained to a fare-thee-well. Sullivan's supporters, including Mike McDonald, Keenan, Davies, and Joe Goss, noting that Paddy had only one real prizefight to his credit, were confident that their man would win easily.

In clubrooms, barrooms, barbershops, and theaters across America the fight was topic A. The vaudeville king Tony Pastor gave no opinion but said that if he favored Ryan he would never be able to play a good engagement in Boston. Henry Ward Beecher advised his congregation to bet no money on the result. Oscar Wilde, currently flitting about Philadelphia, announced that "I do not breathe my prejudices aloud, it would be too radical, the world is not ripe for that yet, [but] I'd go farther than New Orleans to see a good [fight] like that between Ryan and Sullivan is going to be."[54]

The state of Louisiana was less than pleased that an illegal prizefight had been announced for the vicinity of New Orleans. It promptly sought to beef up the city's antiboxing statutes. On January 17, 1882, a bill was introduced in the state legislature that its Judiciary Committee referred back with an amendment providing for the arrest and imprisonment of any parties found training for a prizefight, a goal somewhat difficult to achieve since the principals were training in the North. The amendment added that prizefighting was a felony, subject to a fine of not more than one thousand dollars and a possible prison sentence of up to five years. The seconds were to be guilty of a misdemeanor, and if a fighter should be killed in the ring, the offender was to be tried for murder. The fight's sponsors had originally selected a point on the New Orleans and Mobile Railroad, planning to run excursion trains to the site, but Governor Samuel D. McEnery got wind of the scheme and promised to run the entire gang out of the state.[55]

Sullivan and Madden arrived in New Orleans late in December with two other men who had helped in the training, Pete McCoy and Bob Farrell, the latter Joe Coburn's cousin. Sullivan had planned to conduct his final training near Bay Saint Louis, Mississippi, a spot hallowed by its association with the Mace-Coburn draw in 1871. But the Mississippi Legislature, like its Louisiana counterpart, began to show signs of restlessness, and the little band hurriedly relocated to the St. James Hotel in New Orleans. Sullivan established his training headquarters at Schroeder's Summer Garden in Carrolton, and Ryan was ensconced in the West End Hotel. By this time the city was awash with fight fanciers. Reporters from the Big Three of sports journalism rubbed shoulders with representatives of the *New York Herald*, the *New York Sun*, and the *Boston Globe* in the community's various watering holes. Both Boston and New York sent contingents in the hundreds, led by the stakesholder, Harry Hill. The famed pedestrian racer, Dan O'Leary, was in town, and so was the well-known actor Nat Goodwin. Reporters thought they had spotted the notorious bank robber Red O'Leary, and a few claimed to have glimpsed the James brothers, Frank and Jesse.[56]

Such a flood of riffraff enraged the "better sort." New Orleans ministers protested, from the pulpit and in public, that if city youths mingled with the fight crowd "the contact must soil them and leave a moral stain on their lives." The *New Orleans Picayune* regretted that there was "no legal remedy to avert the disgusting spectacle" (the antiboxing bill was stalled in the legislature). The best the city fathers could do was force the promoters to move the fight outside Orleans Parish. A quick meeting between the interested parties, which included representatives of the New Orleans and Mobile's rival railroad, the Louisville and Nashville, produced an agreement. The L & N would

8. Sullivan in 1882, about the time he challenged Paddy Ryan (William Schutte Collection)

run excursion trains to Mississippi City, Mississippi, famed for its Barnes Hotel and little else, on the announced date. The fighters would get a cut of the excursion fares. And the whole shebang would be back across the Louisiana state line before Mississippi authorities got wind of it.[57]

And so it came to pass. On February 6 scores of fight fans queued up at the railroad offices for tickets. The price was ten dollars, and the railroad filled a special train of twelve passenger cars to head for the site, about seventy miles from New Orleans. The engine left its Crescent City depot at 5 A.M. on the morning of the seventh, Sullivan, Ryan and their handlers riding along in the excited crowd of over two thousand people. The ring was pitched that morning immediately in front of the hotel, between the veranda and the gleaming waters of the Gulf of Mexico. The special train pulled in to Mississippi City a little after 10 A.M.; the fight would begin at high noon, with the late odds still favoring Sullivan at 5 to 4.[58]

## V

By 11:30 the seats on the porch of the hotel were going for high prices, and many ladies chose this shady spot. Other spectators lounged in the building's upper balconies, and a few shinnied up some nearby trees to get a better view. Sales of the colors of each fighter went briskly. Sullivan, his hair close-cropped, chatted with friends at the end of the long western extension of the veranda, waiting. Finally Joe Goss called out: "Your ring is ready." Goss and Madden served as his seconds, while Paddy chose Roche and Tom Kelly of Saint Louis. Each side had an "umpire," Sullivan selecting Arthur Chambers and Ryan picking James Shannon of New York. Two referees also were named: Alex Brewster of New Orleans and Jack Hardy of Vicksburg.[59]

A few in the excited crowd may have been aware of Mississippi Governor Robert Lowry's plan, calling on citizens to prevent the prize-fight, but no posse materialized. In the standing mass pressed close to the ring were judges, merchants, and bankers, as well as delegations from Cincinnati, Baltimore, Buffalo, Pittsburgh, Philadelphia, Washington, Richmond, and even San Francisco. Owney Geoghegan was there, along with a herd of gamblers, pugilists, restauranteurs, and ward politicians. Several pickpockets were noted trying to work the crowd.[60]

At 11:40 Sullivan literally threw his hat into the ring, an old prize-fighting tradition, and then waited fifteen minutes for Ryan to appear. Paddy finally emerged from the hotel, looking somewhat pale and with an overcoat draped over his shoulders. This he shed on climbing into the ring, and the throng could at last see the champion, garbed in a suit of white, knee-length drawers, flesh-colored stockings, white undershirt, and leather fighting shoes. Sullivan glowered on the other side of the ring. The toss for corners was won by Ryan, who placed Sullivan to the north, with his face to the noonday Gulf sunlight. The two referees and two umpires all took their places in the ring, as they were allowed to do. The seconds were also in the ring, stationed along the ropes.

The two fighters shook hands shortly after noon, toed the scratch line, and sparred lightly for a few seconds. Then Paddy was stunned by a quick left to the face. The men closed, grappling, with Sullivan getting in quick shots to the ribs and stomach. As they broke, Sullivan unleashed a terrific right against Ryan's jaw; the champion went to the grass like a shot. The first round had taken thirty seconds. Bob Farrell, the ring veteran who had helped train John L., said later that "I never saw such work as Sullivan did. He went at Ryan as you would chop a log of wood, and he broke him all up from the start." By the end of the third round Sullivan was simply pushing an exhausted and beaten Ryan all over the ring. The challenger concentrated on the head, slamming in blow after blow to drive the champion to the turf to end each round. Paddy tried to wrestle Sullivan but was unsuccessful. In the eighth, though, Ryan tagged his opponent with a blow to the neck; Sullivan, dazed, went into a clinch and shook it off. The round ended with the two wrestling each other to the ground.

The ninth was the end. Sullivan pummeled Ryan freely with rights to the face, and Paddy crumpled to the ground. His handlers were forced to throw in the sponge. The poleaxing had taken less than eleven minutes. Sullivan, elated, immediately hurdled over the ropes and ran back to the hotel, where he quickly stripped off his fighting togs, put on his street clothes, and hurried to the train. The crowd did likewise; the engine had kept steam up, and by 2 P.M. Mississippi City was slumbering once again under its winter-pale coastal sun.[61]

# VI

The disappointed Fox, who had held court in his *Gazette* office during the fight, was kind enough to offer to back Ryan again for five thousand dollars, and telegraphed: "Dear Paddy—am sorry you lost the fight. Can I do anything for you?" Anything but arrange another fight with Sullivan, Paddy might have replied. When John L. struck him, he said, "I thought a telegraph pole had been shoved against me endways." Fox was out several thousand dollars in stakes money and bets, but his sympathy and generosity were natural and unfeigned. Ryan, for his part, claimed that he had been bothered by a year-old ruptured hernia. He had pinned his hopes on his wrestling ability, but "any man that Sullivan can hit he can whip." Paddy disparaged his con-

9. The first known photograph of a prizefight, Sullivan versus Ryan in front of the Barnes Hotel (1882). The blurry figures of the boxers have been retouched. (William Schutte Collection.)

queror, though, as devoid of "science," a mere slugger, thus touching off a round of acrimonious mudslinging by the fighters that would be a companion piece to practically every later Sullivan prizefight.[62]

In Boston, Sullivan's friends had bet heavily on him. Crowds gathered early in the forenoon to watch the bulletins being posted on the newspaper windows. Travel in the city's narrow, twisting streets was obstructed. Washington street was clogged. When the news of victory came over the wires, three hearty cheers were given for the Irish boy, there in the heartland of Yankee Protestantism. In New York City it was estimated that $200,000 had changed hands as a result of the fight. Back in New Orleans, even the protesting *Picayune* was forced to devote over five columns to fight coverage to satisfy its readers. Across the land, from the Atlantic to the Mississippi River, newspaper offices were besieged for news. In saloons the fight was the only topic, and when Sullivan's victory was announced, Paddy Ryan's picture came down from behind the bar and a portrait of Sullivan in fighting togs replaced it. Paddy's wife, at their home in Troy, could not believe the news, nor could his mother-in-law, whom the press contrived to have say that "I could lick that man Sullivan meself."[63]

It had been a dark day for Paddy Ryan. The fight, following the custom of the London Rules, had been winner-take-all. Paddy expected at least six hundred dollars as part of his cut from the excursion money, but he eventually ended up with only eighty-five dollars, possibly bilked by his handlers. He arrived back in New York City on February 11, with bruises purpling the bridge of his nose and the left side of his neck, legacies of Sullivan's sledgehammer rights. Broke and beaten, Ryan retreated to his home, vowing never to fight again. In April he moved to Chicago and opened a saloon on State Street.[64]

In the meantime, Sullivan and his rollicking entourage left New Orleans by train for Chicago. John L. cleared forty-five hundred dollars on the fight, after expenses, and a considerable part of this was spent (in advance) as the merrymakers rolled north. In Chicago he received huge cheers in McCormick Hall, scene of his triumphs over Dalton and Burns the previous summer. He was lionized everywhere and, for the first time, was recognized in the streets and followed by crowds, by no means all of which were composed of adoring boys. "About half the leading saloons and billiard-rooms had signs out notifying the public that John L. Sullivan would visit them during certain hours of the evening."[65]

On to New York, via Cincinnati and Philadelphia, and more of the same. At Harry Hill's in early March he received his stakes money and then visited Vanderbilt's Madison Square Garden, where he was the sensation of the current pedestrian contest. Everywhere mobs of people trailed him, in and out of saloons and restaurants scattered throughout the city. Fox was sporting enough to concede that Sullivan had won the fight fairly, despite Paddy's disclaimers, and this concession added luster to the sheen of triumph. The *Gazette* editor quickly printed a picture of John L., a photograph taken in New Orleans. Now the sporting world saw a poised, confident young man, pencil mustache gone (it had been shaven for the fight), hair somewhat tousled, but neatly dressed in tie and bat-wing collar.[66]

Madden, who had sparred in an exhibition with his friend as they passed through Philadelphia on the way east, trumpeted that he would match Sullivan, with gloves, against any living man, without gloves. Almost every living man responded. Challenges poured in from Georgia, Virginia, Tennessee, Connecticut, even England. Thomas Richard Egan, "the Troy Terror," offered to avenge his fellow resident; when Madden aggressively took him up on the offer, the Terror refused, never to be heard from again. George Williams of Waxahachie, Texas, claimed he was suitable as an opponent; he weighed 240 pounds, and a man could sit astride his extended arm while he wrote his name on the wall. A woman informed the *Gazette* that she currently weighed 162, "but I think if I was trained down to about 96 lbs. that I could whip Sullivan myself and I would do it without trying to break his back or jawbone." And a certain John T. Erropin saw a way for Fox to get revenge for Sullivan's victory:

> I am prepared to jump from the top of the *Police Gazette* building with Sullivan, provided you agree to my terms.
>
> 1st—You must give me $2500 to be left to my family.
>
> 2nd—You shall print my picture on the front page of the *Gazette*, with the line "champion jumper of the world," beneath.
>
> 3rd—If I'm killed you will pay all funeral expenses, and see that my grave is kept green.[67]

The fact that the cranks were coming out of the woodwork was one sign of Sullivan's dramatically enhanced standing in the popular culture. There were more. His friends tendered him a reception in Boston on March 9, where he received the first of many gifts from admirers, a gold watch and chain valued at five hundred dollars. For the first time he was mentioned in the *Boston Pilot*, which credited him with supporting gloved bouts. On the 27th he was back in New York, at the American Institute, where he received another round of praise and sparred easily with Joe Douglass and Billy Madden. Some more serious challenges were coming in now, but they were either from fighters long in tooth, like Jim Elliott (who had first fought in 1861), or from men Sullivan had already beaten, like George Rooke. Steve Taylor added a refreshing twist to all the unrestrained pugnaciousness by offering to fight any man in America, *except Sullivan*, for one thousand dollars a side.[68]

Something new had taken place. John L. Sullivan, with his one-sided triumph over Paddy Ryan, had established himself as an individual sporting hero. He had made a name not only in the Big Three of sports journalism but also in the "respectable press." New York papers like the *Sun*, the *Daily Tribune,* and the *Times* and Boston papers like the *Herald* and the *Post* might not condone his occupation or his habits, but they reported what he did, because unlike the older prizefighters, Sullivan's exploits were attracting the attention of the middle class. Over at the *Nation*, E. L. Godkin sensed this, too. "Sullivan is doubtless of Irish origin," wrote Godkin, "but he has been exposed long enough to the agencies to which European philosophers like to describe the degeneracy of the American man, to make it clear that the degeneracy is easier to talk about than to prove." A Bostonian, after all, had beaten a Tipperary Irishman. Godkin hoped, in a tone of reluctant admiration linked with social concern, that Sullivan's sport would eventually vanish. In the meantime, prizefighting was popular because it was war on a small scale, and Godkin correctly noted that, with Sullivan, support for it no longer came wholly from the "coarse and uneducated and vicious class." Now, "it is fed by secret rills of sympathy which flow from higher sources." And an admirer of John L. only half-humorously penned the following bit of doggerel:

> Just fancy what mingled emotions
>   would fill the Puritan heart
> To learn what renown was won for his town
>   By means of the manly art!
> Imagine a Winthrop or Adams
>   In front of a bulletin board,
> Each flinging his hat at the statement that
>   The first blood was by Sullivan scored.
>
> Thy bards, henceforth, O Boston!
>   Of this triumph of triumphs will sing,
> For a muscular stroke has added a spoke
>   To the Hub, which will strengthen the ring!
> Now Lowell will speak of the "ruby,"
>   And Aldrich of "closing a match,"
> and Longfellow rhyme of "coming to time,"
>   of "bunches of fives," and "the scratch."[69]

He had reached the top of a gutter profession, flouting the law in the process. As a fighter he remained crude and unpolished, but to many his undiluted fury in the ring was the root of his appeal. From coast to coast his name was instantly recognized, his pugilistic triumphs heralded. His reputation as a "fighting man" was made; at last, he was *somebody*. Less than two years had elapsed since he chose the fighter's trade. And now, just past the age of twenty-three, John L. Sullivan was champion of the world.

# PART II CHAMPION

## CHAPTER FIVE

# Manufacturing "The Great John L." (1882—1883)

## I

The new champion rapidly learned that the demands placed upon him were significantly different now that he was wearing a "crown." Certainly, public admiration went with his victory over Paddy Ryan. The gold watch and splendid horseshoe of wax flowers set in a gilt frame that were given him by friends from the Highlands at his benefit in March 1882 presaged a practically continuous flood of gifts. But the growing legion of fight fans had been increasingly dissatisfied with Ryan's inactivity as champion. In return for the laurels and the praise, Sullivan was expected to *fight*.

John L. was wary of the legal repercussions of bare-knuckle prizefights. He also feared for his hands, and the three-minute rounds called for under the Queensberry Rules clearly favored his aggressive style. On March 23 he announced his willingness to be a fighting champion, on his own terms:

> There has been much newspaper talk from parties who state that they are desirous of meeting me in the ring that I am disgusted. Nevertheless, I am willing to fight any man in this country, in four weeks from signing articles, for five thousand dollars a side; or, any man ... for the same amount at two months from signing articles,—I to use gloves, and he, if he pleases, to fight with the bare knuckles. I will not fight again with the bare knuckles, as I do not wish to put myself in a position amenable to the law. My money is always ready, so I want these fellows to put up or shut up.
>
> John L. Sullivan[1]

Four days later he appeared at the American Institute on New York's Third Avenue, but his former opponent George Rooke refused to spar with him. To appease the crowd of four thousand, he waltzed through three rounds with an awkward novice, a blacksmith named Joseph

Douglass. This exhibition was followed by another with Billy Madden. The crowd left in a bitter mood because no one had been knocked out. Sullivan was learning some of the public difficulties of his trade.[2] John L. and his entourage returned to New England. On April 3 he and his "corps pugilistic"—Madden, Bob Farrell, and Pete McCoy—received a rousing reception at Hawes' Opera House in Bridgeport, Connecticut. Still, no volunteer could be found to challenge the champion.

Finally, almost three weeks later in Rochester, Sullivan "defended" his crown. He was scheduled to fight a local black barber named Johnson, but the barber, who had some fighting experience, failed to appear; whether John L. would have refused to fight after discovering the race of his opponent is unclear. Many locals were outraged by the mere presence of an admitted outlaw in their city. Sullivan did not help matters by promenading through the streets followed by "a rabble of small boys."[3] At the Grand Opera House an audience of eighteen hundred gathered to see Johnson's replacement, John McDermott, contest the champion for $100. McDermott was a fireman who showed more pluck than sense. He entered the ring at 147 pounds ("lightwaisted, small chested"), compared with Sullivan's 200. A complete amateur, the fireman appeared in blue flannel shirt, trousers, and ordinary street shoes. McDermott was lithe and quick, which saved him for a moment. Hostile fans in the crowd (and there were many) noted that Sullivan had to retire to the stage wings to catch his breath, but he carried McDermott for three rounds, striking him almost at will, until the fireman finally fell in the third round. John L.'s haul in Rochester was $852, which partially compensated for the booing, hissing, jeering crowd. Many in the audience were appalled at what appeared to them to be the champion's bullyboy tactics. When Sullivan attempted to address them from the stage after the fight, his words were drowned out by catcalls.[4] A new and deplorable part of his image was forming.

Returning disgusted to Boston, John L. quickly added to his negative reputation. When interviewed about his drinking habits by a *Chicago News* reporter the month before, he had claimed that he was no temperance man, "but I am not a hard drinker, either." He admitted he drank a little ale, even during training. "At other times I have a little fun sometimes, but never carry drinking to excess." He had a little fun in a saloon on Elliot Street on April 25, slugging a man named Charles Robbins and breaking his jaw. The next day he was charged with assault and battery, but an unnamed councilman made his bail bond of three hundred dollars. The case was never tried, because investigation indicated that Sullivan had been taunted and provoked.[5] Nevertheless, the sporting world was treated, not for the last time, to the spectacle of the champion of the world involved in a common saloon brawl.

While in Boston, Sullivan talked his friend Joe Goss, still the proprietor of the Saracen's Head on LaGrange Street, into another exhibition, which they duly gave before a crowd of seven hundred at Harry Hill's in New York. In Lynn, Massachusetts, he and Madden gave an exhibition when a one-hundred-dollar offer for four rounds produced no takers. But exhibitions did not satisfy the champion. He was eager for a real bout to remove the stigma of the McDermott mismatch and the Robbins affair.[6]

He found his opponent among the many prizefighting veterans of the 1860s. Jim Elliott had been born in County Athlone but grew up a scrappy kid on the streets of New York. His first prizefight took place in 1861, when Sullivan was two years old. Elliott had talents other than fighting; he was a convicted thief. He served two years in Trenton State Prison and was fined one thousand dollars for attempting to rob Hugh Dougherty, a Negro minstrel. While in prison he had an eye operation, and now, almost forty years old, he continued to have vision problems. Even sunshine bothered him. Elliott's last match had been in 1879, against John Dwyer of Brooklyn, a brother of Alderman William Dwyer. He lost this bout, which took place on an island in the Saint Lawrence River, in twelve rounds.[7]

Clearly over the hill, Elliott nonetheless needed a payday, and so he challenged Sullivan in April 1882, leaving $250 with Richard Kyle Fox at the *National Police Gazette* offices. Sullivan at first rejected this purse as too small. Elliott kept at it, and the two men bickered in the sporting press for months. In the meantime Elliott proved he was serious by knocking out "the Troy Terror," Thomas Richard Egan, in three rounds at New York's Irving Hall. Sullivan, still uninterested, accused Elliott of never winning a fight except "by jobbery." Finally the champion offered $500 to Elliott and $200 to any other man who could stand before him for four rounds at Brooklyn's Washington Park on the Fourth of July.[8] Supposedly, the match with Elliott was to be an "exhibition," but both men intended to wink at the law.

The rain poured down for hours on the holiday, but this did not dampen the spirits of thousands of picnickers and sports fans. By five o'clock, over five thousand people had gathered near a five-foot elevated ring on a wooden platform pitched in the center of the park. "Walk in and see your country's hero," the gatekeepers shouted, charging fifty cents to enter. A watchful squad of policemen patrolled the grounds. Elliott, the only man to take up Sullivan's offer, had chosen hard gloves for the fight. He entered the ring bare-chested, wearing white tights and stockings. A sharp shower fell. The boards of the stage were slippery and glistening when Sullivan appeared, brightly attired in a white sleeveless undershirt, green tights, and blue stockings. Dense crowds were gathered atop neighboring houses and prominent nearby rocks. Harry Hill and Owney Geoghegan were among the multitude, many of whom had been drinking for hours at the numerous bars scattered throughout the grounds. Johnny Roche, who had helped train Paddy Ryan for the championship fight, was seconding Elliott, while Madden was in John L.'s corner. Mike Cleary was the referee.

Sullivan forced the fighting in round one. Elliott was first staggered and then knocked down twice, the second time so hard that the ring ropes stripped skin from his back. In the second round, the champion pounded Elliott severely, causing a serious nosebleed. The older man, outweighed by ten pounds, slipped on the wet ring surface and, struggling to get to his feet, was clubbed down by a blow to the neck. He had to be helped to his chair. Between rounds Roche worked frantically, sucking blood from Elliott's nose and spitting it out on the platform. At the start of the third round Sullivan sprang from his corner and immediately delivered another crushing blow to the neck, which sent Elliott sprawling senseless. The fight had taken all of seven minutes, twenty seconds. Sullivan pressed a wad of bills into Elliott's limp hand—fifty dollars for his trouble.[9]

The decisive victory did much to restore Sullivan's sagging reputation, but Fox was still hunting for a man to dethrone the obnoxious John L. By the time of the Washington Park match, Fox thought he had found him in an Englishman named Joe Collins, who fought under the name Tug Wilson. In correspondence with his English counterpart, George W. Atkinson of *Sporting Life,* Fox set up a match for five hundred pounds a side, forwarding money to bring Wilson to the United States. Wilson was reported to be living "abstemiously" at his home in Leicester in preparation for the bout, a comment on his earlier habits. Urged on by Fox's promotion, fight fans across the country eagerly anticipated Sullivan's first international fight. Billy Madden, with bitter memories of the Louisiana authorities, announced that the champion would take on Wilson anywhere but in New Orleans.[10]

Wilson's reputation was built on one bout, a twenty-eight-round draw with a respected English boxer, Alf Greenfield. His first prizefight was in 1866, but he did not fight at all from 1868 to 1879. Undaunted by his inexperience, he left Liverpool on the *Lord Clive,* arriving in Philadelphia on June 21. There he was met by a delegation from the *Police Gazette;* champagne was served all around. *Gazette* readers learned that he "looks to be jovial and even-tempered and displayed good breeding." The challenger's great asset was announced to be his two-handed scientific skill. In actuality Wilson was a squat, five-foot-eight, badly aging fighter. He was poorly trained as well, his prominent jowls and double chin giving him the appearance of a slightly debauched elf. Fox, who greeted his charge on the latter's arrival in New York, wanted a match for $5,000, but Madden scaled that down during a meeting with Wilson and his backers at Harry Hill's on June 28. Sullivan, through Billy, agreed to give the Englishman $1,000 and half the gate if he stayed four rounds under the Queensberry Rules. Hill himself held the stakes for the fight, which was scheduled for Madison Square Garden on July 17.[11]

Over five thousand people, paying from one to five dollars a seat, waited for admission to the Garden that steamy Monday evening. All levels of New York's social scene were there, from the usual fight crowd to "the very highest and most intellectual classes," including Wall Street brokers and clerks. The sporting fraternity included lowlights: "It is safe to say that every man of the criminal classes within a hundred miles and more of City Hall was present, if he had no other engagement for the evening at the Tombs, or the Island, or at Sing Sing."

As the crowd sifted inside, betting was going on all over the building. The cocky little Madden laid $750 against $500 on his friend. The vast throng drove the already stifling temperature inside the Garden even higher. The police commissioner, several inspectors, and Captain Killilea (he who had alerted his superiors about the Flood fight) were on hand. By the time the two principals appeared on stage at 9:30, the arena was sweltering. Wilson, attired in white tights and pink stockings, was accompanied by a team of backers that included Arthur Chambers, who had recommended him to Fox. Tug immediately received a rubdown with a towel. Joe Goss and Madden did the same for Sullivan, who wore pink tights and green stockings. Both fighters donned two-ounce gloves and went to their respective corners. The throng began a prolonged uproar that continued throughout the bout.

John L. propelled himself out of his corner as usual, charging at Wilson and belting him all over the ring. The excited audience saw immediately what Wilson's tactics would be: Tug was not interested in fighting but in staying the distance. Accordingly, he backpedaled and skipped away from Sullivan's hay-makers throughout the first round. Even so, he was knocked down or intentionally fell down no less than nine times in three minutes. By the end of the round both men clearly were feeling the excessive heat, their bodies shedding rivulets of sweat.

The second round was more of the same, with John L. now "puffing and blowing like a grampus." He had done no special training for the fight, confident with his victory over Elliott. Wilson was knocked down three times. The third time Chambers fanned him "for ten seconds" before he got to his feet again. All told, Wilson went down eight times in the round. By now Sullivan realized his opponent's plan, and this only increased his rage. At the beginning of round three Wilson stayed in close, laughing as Sullivan tried to break to land a punch. Finally, the champion threw his tormentor to the floor, landing heavily on top of him. Once on his feet, Wilson intentionally slipped down and tried to pull Sullivan down by the leg with him. John L. punched him flat twice more as the round ended.

The farce concluded in the fourth round with more wrestling, running, and intentional falls by Wilson. Sullivan by now was badly winded, and his blows had lost much of their steam. Nevertheless, he managed two more knockdowns amid travesty. At the end Wilson was still on his feet, and a furious Sullivan had to watch the Englishman declared the winner. By any rules of boxing the champion had won, but under Sullivan's own ground rules Wilson had "lasted" the four rounds. John L. had been tricked. Fox, for his part, gloated. He said that Wilson had won "nearly $11,000" for his chicanery, a ridiculously inflated sum. Wilson and his *Police Gazette* crowd repaired to Harry Hill's, where they "opened wine like water."[12]

Sullivan was disgusted with his opponent's "floor-crawling and hugging" and embarrassed before the biggest audience of his career thus far. He knew he had been overconfident and careless, and he eagerly sought a second match with the Englishman. In the meantime he retreated to Centerville, Rhode Island, leaving the New York press to hash over the bizarre spectacle. The *Times* noted with surprise that not all the audience had been blackguards, loafers, and ruffians. The *Sun* suggested that the champion had tried to do too much and should henceforth stay within his bounds, like the Quakers. And the *Herald* was amazed at the ability of Wilson's head to absorb punishment. Fox crowed and crowed: "Sullivan would have been stopped by Tug Wilson if the contest had lasted another round." From Madden there were only excuses: "Sullivan failed to train as I asked him to." Boston was disconsolate.[13]

In early August a rematch was scheduled for the Garden on August 14. It never occurred. William C. Whitney, the erstwhile Yale boxer and the city's corporation counsel, decided that the first "exhibition" had been prizefighting within the meaning of the law and thus prohibited the proposed rematch. Fox, whose publicity mill had been once again in full gear, screamed that this action was "arrogant, arbitrary and unjust," but his hands were tied. Police Captain Alexander ("Clubber") Williams, notorious for his brutality and famed for baptizing the Tenderloin District ("I've had nothing but chuck steak for a long time, and now I'm going to get a little of the tenderloin"), was directed to apply for warrants for Sullivan and Wilson. Clubber understood his neighborhood; asked once why he did not close down the brothels in his precinct, he replied that "they were kind of fashionable at the time." The Garden was within Clubber's Twenty-ninth Precinct, and he was to arrest the fighters should they return to New York. Wilson had gone to Boston, where he received a good reception. A disgruntled Harry Hill returned the stakes: "I bow to the authorities, even when I think them wrong."[14]

On August 30 Wilson, who had split part of the hefty gate with Arthur Chambers, sailed for Liverpool on the *Indiana*, saying he would return with his wife and three children. He never did. Fox, who saw him off, rapidly became disenchanted, moaning that Wilson had "made a masterly but inglorious retreat, ungratefully leaving in the lurch those who had been his best friends." As for Tug, he failed to get a license as a publican, and opened a shoe store.[15]

Still the champion, Sullivan had been brought up short by a growing reputation as a bully and a decided disinclination to train for his profession. Still, his profits since the Ryan fight were in five figures. His numerous exhibitions, by the end of the summer of 1882, had netted him almost $10,000. The Elliott bout had been worth $2,600, and despite the embarrassment of the Wilson debacle John L. had made $10,000 from the huge Garden crowd. Almost overnight he had become a wealthy man. After returning home from New York, Sullivan paid off the Parnell Street house for his parents and tendered Mike and Catherine the deed.[16]

## II

Madden lost no time in setting up another tour. He quickly negotiated a contract for Sullivan and a boxing entourage to perform with a variety show in the fall of 1882. The show, managed by a variety veteran named Harry J. Sargent, would feature singers, jugglers, club swingers, wrestlers, and Sullivan, along with his pals Madden, Bob Farrell, and Pete McCoy. Sullivan and Madden were to spar six nights a week for twenty weeks, receiving the astronomical sum of $500 a night. John L., obviously, was the headliner. Madden made a standing offer for anyone who would be willing to take on the champion, from $500 to $5,000 a side.[17]

Chastened by his poor showing against Wilson, Sullivan threw himself into a more intense regimen, advised by Madden and Patsey Sheppard, who ran a saloon on Hayward Place in Boston. He revealed his routine, which did not include sparring, to *Police Gazette* readers:

During the first week I am passed through a course of physics by which the stomach is brought into a proper condition. During this time I get up every morning at 7 o'clock, walk a mile and breakfast at 8. My bill of fare throughout my training is a simple one. I avoid all greasy or heating food. My meats are cooked rare and I am prohibited from eating anything rich or sweet. The bread is either toasted or stale. In place of tea or coffee with every meal

I am allowed ale or porter. After breakfast I take a cold shower bath, followed by a brisk rubbing of every part of the body with coarse towels. After resting an hour I walk twelve miles, six out and six back, coming in on the last half mile on a brisk run. This is followed by knocking with dumb bells for about an hour. They weigh a pound and a half and the exercise affects the muscles of the arm. After dinner the exercises of the morning are repeated and supper is followed by another jaunt of twelve miles, more dumb bell knocking, a cold water sponge bath, a thorough rubbing and finally about 9 o'clock to bed. This is kept up every day until the day of the meeting. I will be relieved of about thirty pounds of superfluous flesh and ought to weigh 185 pounds when I step into the ring.[18]

On August 19 Sullivan sparred easily with Goss during a picnic at North Adams, Massachusetts. The tour kicked off in Newark on September 4, with Sullivan sparring against Madden. Then, in rapid succession, Sargent moved his show on to Philadelphia and the Pennsylvania towns of Scranton, Pittston, and Wilkes-Barre. In the latter city the manager rang the curtain down when the crowd began to yell for more action on the part of the fighters. For three weeks no challenger came forward, but finally in Buffalo an unknown named Henry Higgins appeared. Higgins was carried for two rounds before John L. polished him off in the third. The victim was unconscious for twenty minutes.[19]

The tour swept on, doing prosperous business. In the middle of October, Sullivan was challenged in Fort Wayne, Indiana, by a lanky hayseed, S. P. Stockton. By this time the champion was offering five hundred dollars to anyone who could stand against him for four rounds, and interest was intense. In the second round Stockton was blasted off his feet and "lay like a log on the stage." On regaining consciousness, S. P. wanted to know if he had fallen off a barn.[20]

Trouble followed. Receipts in Indiana fell off, and the boxers split with Sargent in Indianapolis. A few days later in Louisville, Sullivan and Madden quarreled. The *Clipper* hinted darkly that the trouble had been over a singer in the troupe, Annie Hart. Madden quit, leaving by rail for New York with Miss Hart and pronouncing that he held no grudges. Sullivan took on management of the boxing combination himself.

Madden promptly sailed for England, ostensibly to look for a challenger to take on his former pal. Billy was sincere in his regret at losing Sullivan's friendship, but he realized that there was money to be made if he could find a worthy opponent. He began to make the rounds of London sporting papers and saloons. To keep money coming in, Madden offered boxing lessons to the nobility at ten dollars a crack. Eventually he arranged for a series of matches for the "championship of England," which was won by Charlie Mitchell of Birmingham.[21]

Bereft of Madden's managerial talents, the small band of pugilists struggled onward, Sullivan sparring with either Farrell or McCoy. On a stormy night in Chicago, before a small audience in McCormick Hall, the champion was challenged by Charley O'Donnell of Cleveland. Another complete amateur, O'Donnell scrambled up on stage dressed in black pants and calico shirt, a cotton handkerchief tied around his waist for a belt. He was quickly knocked down five straight times, John L. using his left hand only.[22]

The tour wound down as it moved back eastward, Sullivan meeting one more opponent in Washington, D.C. A crowd of over two thousand was drawn to the Theater Comique by the news that a local railway hand would take on the champion. Some district commissioners occupied a private box. After a variety act left the stage, the crowd howled with approval at Sullivan's appearance. Mike Collins, the railway hand, failed to appear, but in his stead came a Georgetown blacksmith, P. J. Rentzler. Stepping to the front of the stage, Rentzler, attired in flushed tights and knit shirt, modestly announced that he had put on the gloves but once before. The theater was equipped with orchestra, and as Sullivan and Rentzler squared off, the violinist commenced a dirgelike squawk, the whole ensemble joining in. Rentzler assumed a pugilistic pose and was immediately driven to the floor. In all he was knocked down six times, helplessly holding his arms in front of him in an ineffectual attempt to ward off the blows. When Sullivan drew blood with a punch to the nose, the police at last intervened. At least part of the crowd was appalled and hissed John L. as he tried to explain that he had not used his full strength. "A more sickening spectacle of brutality was never witnessed here before," wrote a reporter for the *Washington Post*.[23]

The tour ended as Sullivan returned to Chicago to perform at Parson Davies's place, the Argyle. While there, the champion signed a contract with the Parson making the Chicagoan his manager for the next six months, with authority to arrange all his fights. Davies faced the basic problem of the law, however. There was talk of a match with the ancient Tom Allen, but nothing happened. John L.'s frustration was growing. He showed up at a sparring match between Allen and George Rooke in Madison Square Garden's Art Gallery. Before fifteen hundred people, including the observant Clubber Williams, Sullivan apologized for not fighting. To hisses and groans from the audience, he blamed the authorities: "They have stopped pugilists from knocking each other out in this city."[24]

Idling away his time, John L. sparred lackadaisically with Goss at Harry Hill's in December, "a very tame affair." It was the last time the two friends appeared in the ring together. In the meantime Davies signed a contract with Jim Elliott, John L.'s Fourth of July conquest, but a Chicago judge blocked the match. Elliott was near the end of his string anyway. On March 1, 1883, he was shot and killed by a gambler, Jere Dunn, during a brawl in Billy Langdon's Chicago saloon. Allen, another graybeard who had arrived in New York from England on October 28, was being heralded by Fox as the newest challenger, but fight fans noted that he was even older than Elliott, having been born in Birmingham in 1840. Fox invited Sullivan to Harry Hill's to arrange a match, but the champion did not bother to show, leaving the Proprietor frothing.[25]

Sullivan, restless for action, agreed to appear at Joe Coburn's benefit in the Garden during Christmas week. The sporting world felt sorry for Joe, who had first fought in 1856 at the age of twenty. Coburn had not been in the prize ring since 1870, because he had been committed to ten years in the Sing Sing penitentiary for assault with intent to kill a New York policeman, William Tobias. He had walked out of the prison gates, with time off for good behavior, on December 7, his early freedom a result of "faithful and meritorious services in aiding the promotion of prison discipline." Warden Bush sent him on his way by noting that "he was a perfect convict, a faithful worker, and we hate to lose him."[26]

Over three thousand showed up at the perfect convict's benefit. Sullivan, who knew that Coburn was destitute, was the big drawing card. The champion, "arrayed like a Wall Street broker . . . a fine silk hat [resting] easily on his shapely head," stood near the door, jovially greeting people. He then sparred a friendly three rounds with the balding veteran, interrupting the exhibition to tell the audience that "there will be no slugging here tonight. . . . I'll kill somebody for you people sometime." The crowd, which included bankers, physicians, lawyers, and merchants, responded with applause and laughter. The grateful Coburn, who had to fork over one thousand dollars of his proceeds for rental on the Garden, agreed to travel and give exhibitions with the champion.[27]

A newly relaxed Sullivan returned to Boston, where he sparred with Pete McCoy to begin the new year and received a striking gold scarf pin, shaped like the head of Taurus and with eyes of rubies, from his hometown admirers. Soon after, he made his first international trip, going through Buffalo and Rochester to Toronto. There he sparred with Coburn in Albert Hall before an audience packed to the doors. Two days later he beat up Harry Gilman, billed as the "champion light-weight of Canada," in three rounds. This little tour with Coburn was very successful, and with its conclusion the champion rested for a month.[28]

On March 1, continuing his generosity to the down-and-out, Sullivan gave an exhibition with John Laflin in Madison Square Garden for the benefit of western flood victims. "Professor" Laflin, also nick-named "the Society Adonis," had a number of supporters entrenched well up on the city's social ladder, and many of these turned out for the match. The noise was so loud that Gilmore's Band was forced to play the recently popular air "Hail to the Chief" to quiet the crowd. The three-round display was well-received, Sullivan clearly being superior to the slightly bigger Laflin.[29]

As the winter waned, John L.'s popularity and fame were on the rise again. He and Coburn had argued over remarks Joe made to a reporter in Auburn, New York, suggesting that the champion was deficient in boxing skills. But they had made up by mid-March, when they sparred at Billy Edwards's benefit in the Garden before five thousand people, including the inevitable Clubber Williams. John L. furbished his growing reputation for generosity by announcing that he would contribute one hundred dollars to a fund for the murdered Elliott's mother.[30] The money was coming in rapidly, but it was leaving just as fast.

A week later it was the champion's turn to be feted. On March 19 in Boston he was given another benefit, at which he boxed leisurely with Steve Taylor, Mike Cleary, and Coburn. Almost 15,000 people crammed the vast barn of the Mechanics' Association Exhibition Building, and almost 5,000 were turned away. Some said it was the largest crowd ever assembled in Boston, for anything. The affair was staged by wealthy members of the Cribb Club, a local sporting and social organization. It was a triumph. John Boyle O'Reilly, president of the club, presided. Next to him on the dais were city councilmen, aldermen, and Harvard graduates. More politicos and members of the swank Somerset Club were plumped in two-dollar seats reserved for them near the ring.

The three-hour extravaganza ran smoothly (a rarity for these shows), featuring eighteen bouts in all under the watchful eyes of no less than 153 police officers. Sullivan received a gold medal from the Commercial Athletic Club, laid in a box with crimson satin lining. The box was adorned in golden gilt letters "John L. Sullivan of Boston." The medal itself was a heavy gold bar, on which John L.'s name was engraved, followed by the legend "Champion of the World." Attached to this, by a golden chain, was a large medallion featuring an engraved likeness of the champion in his fighting jersey, beefy arms folded across his broad chest. Only a slight flaring of the building's new electric lights, quickly solved, marred the show. As Sullivan announced to the faithful, "I want no brutality shown at John L. Sullivan's exhibition." There was bonhomie all around. Buried in one account of the evening was the note that, in one of the bouts, "Mr. John Kilrain, of Somerville, then mildly knocked out Pete McCoy."[31]

Everyone had been on his best behavior, and all facets of Boston's sporting culture had rubbed elbows and celebrated their own. (One month later, as if to prove his capacity for recidivism, Mike Cleary was arrested in Philadelphia for assaulting a saloon keeper.) Sullivan and the event's sponsors netted over fifteen thousand dollars.[32] The champion's cup was full, but part of his life was soon to change. John L. Sullivan was getting married.

## III

Despite, or perhaps because of, the continuing applause, Sullivan's drinking was going from bad to worse. By now he was known in dozens of saloons throughout both New York and Boston, and only four days before the mass testimonial in the Hub he was observed in an "excited condition" at Harry Hill's. As the winter months passed, he had been increasingly careless of his health, boozing before, during, and after his busy schedule of exhibitions. On April 24, in Boston, his excesses caught up with him. His lungs hemorrhaged, and he began to cough up blood. He was unconscious for a day, and it was rumored that last rites had been performed. All told, it was said, he lost "about a quart of blood." His friends knew he had been on a prolonged binge since the celebration in the Mechanics' Building, leading the *New York Sun* to publish a cautionary editorial about alcohol being the Achilles heel for one so strong and famous.[33]

Billy Madden, back from England, and Patsey Sheppard, Sullivan's sometime "trainer," were among those deeply concerned. Sullivan lay in bed in his new home at 4 Lovering Place, hallucinating from time to time. A steady progression of friends passed through, bearing fruits and delicacies. His parents were on hand, and Catherine may have summoned a priest. In his lucid moments, Sullivan stoutly denied that drink had caused his illness, swearing that he had indulged in only four or five glasses of English ale a day. Get-well telegrams poured in, including one from Harry Hill. A twenty-four-hour alarm coursed through New York on reports that Sullivan had died. His physician recommended a mountain trip and absolute rest. The *New York Times*, gilding the lily only slightly, sermonized that "the fact that Sullivan has spent over $40,000 within a few years gives color to the statement that he has been living fast."[34]

Until 1882 John L. had lived with his parents on Parnell Street, paying them board as he made his way in the fight game. In early 1883, prosperous and craving spatial as well as personal independence, he bought the Lovering Place residence, proudly listing his occupation as "pugilist" in the 1883 City Directory. But there was another reason for the purchase of the house, a reason that many of his friends saw for the first time when they visited their ailing hero: Sullivan was living with a woman named Annie Bates Bailey.[35]

John L.'s early romantic life has been crudely falsified by myth-makers. The basic tale goes something like this: Sullivan's childhood sweetheart was Katherine Harkins, the daughter of a none-too-prosperous real estate agent in Sharon, Massachusetts. Katherine, with middle-class pretensions, tried and failed to wean John L. from his wicked ways. "They loved violently and quarreled with equal fervor." Sullivan proposed to her after the benefit in the Mechanics' Building; Katherine rejected him: "Goodby, John. My prayers will be with you till you come back to me. I will wait." Finally, John L. was stolen from her arms by Annie Bailey, the usurper. But this is a story with a happy ending: years later, mellow and placid at last, John L. and his sweetheart would marry and live happily ever after.[36]

Sullivan indeed may have known Katherine Harkins as a young man, but she was eighteen in 1883 and certainly much too sheltered to adapt to Sullivan's life style. In addition, the champion had kept steady company with Annie since shortly after the Ryan fight. He was almost completely silent in his autobiography on the subject of women, mentioning only his mother, and there is no way of knowing his sexual experience by the time he reached his early twenties. Certainly there had been the education of the streets and possibly the tender ministration of a prostitute here and there, which was common within the cult of masculinity. But Annie Bates Bailey was his first known romance.

By his own testimony, in April 1882 John L. was introduced to Annie at the corner of Hammond Street and Shawmut Avenue, at her request, by a hackman named Albert T. Stickney. The hackie knew them both, Annie for about ten years as "Mrs. Bailey," John L. because he customarily drove him home from saloons "five or six times a week." Annie was born in Natick, Rhode Island, and was probably a year older than Sullivan. As a teenager she contracted a marriage with a man named Bailey. He died, leaving her some Boston real estate and his name. She was a tall, prepossessing woman, scaling 180 pounds— almost the heft of Sullivan's mother, for those who believe in the Oedipus complex. Within three days of their meeting, Sullivan took her to the Hawthorne Hotel, a notorious trysting spot. "We were there about three hours, and she acted as my wife for the first time on that occasion."[37]

Annie traveled with Sullivan as his "wife" for months. Probably at her insistence, he bought the house on Lovering Place. In all, they had lived and toured together for over a year at the time of his illness. Sullivan was badly frightened by his brush with death. He told one visiting priest that he and Annie were married, and denied it to another. Then there was his mother, righteously appalled at the spectacle of her son cohabiting out of wedlock. The shaken champion made his decision—"I married her for religious purposes"—and Annie got her man. John L.'s iron constitution got him out of the sickbed, and they were married on May 1, 1883, at Saint Patrick's Church in Roxbury, by the Reverend Joseph H. Gallagher. Sullivan gave his age as twenty-five (one year too many) and his occupation as "plumber." Annie said she was a year older, gave her name as Bailey and her home as Centerville, Rhode Island, and said she had no occupation.[38]

It was not a marriage made in heaven. Annie was imposing, even handsome, and she readily gave as good as she got with her temperamental, obstreperous spouse. Both of them drank; it is possible that their connubial bliss was at least partially marinated in alcohol. And Annie had a local reputation as a loose woman, which is not helped today by the speed with which she let John L. inveigle her into the Hawthorne (or vice versa). In April 1884 she gave birth to a son, John Jr., at the Lovering Place house, but by that time the marriage, such as it was, was shattered.[39]

Within a month of the wedding, reports circulated that a drunken Sullivan was beating his wife. In this, the champion did not depart markedly from others with his ethnic background; the evidence on the nineteenth-century Irish is loaded with depictions of brutality toward wives. A pattern developed; the two would scrap in Boston; Annie would flee to the home of relatives near Providence; John L. would follow, a reconciliation would ensue, and Annie would return to Boston, whereupon the entire cycle would start again. She went with him on many of his trips, including the grand tour of 1883–84, but there was always squabbling. The most sensational story emerged in June 1883 with gossip that the champion had smashed the furniture in the Lovering Place home, beaten his wife, and fled from justice. Annie alleged that her husband had destroyed over five hundred dollars' worth of furniture and had beaten her so badly that she could not get to the police station to report the assault until the next evening. Circumstantial evidence favors her account, if not the extent of damages, because on the night she reported the incident to the police, June 8, Sullivan left Boston for Providence, where he stayed for three days.[40]

No warrant was ever issued for John L., and the particulars of the tale may have been untrue. But the generally violent pattern of marital discord persisted. Later in June reports out of Boston said that the champion had brutally beaten not only his wife but also her sister. The *Police Gazette*, which would have been eager to expose anything negative about Sullivan that it could, sent a reporter hustling north. But Fox was disappointed. Both women denied the story completely, and Annie was quoted as saying of her husband, who was in Providence

10. Annie Bates Bailey Sullivan, in later life

watching a baseball game, that "his great misfortune is that he has a heart too big for his body, and is so lavish in entertaining his friends that he sometimes oversteps the bounds of prudence in his sociability and is then a little morose and surly." Shortly after the birth of their son, however, the champion overstepped the bounds of prudence for the last time. Annie packed up the child and moved back to Centerville. Although they would remain married for over a quarter of a century, after the spring of 1884 John L. and Annie were husband and wife in name only.[41]

The reasons for such a marital shambles can only be speculative. Annie had a temper of her own, knew her way around saloons and hotels, and drank at least occasionally. Part of the blame is hers. But Sullivan bears the brunt of the blame for the marital failure. His "good little woman" was unable to sever his bonds with the familiar all-male world, and indeed he did not wish them to be severed. Each visit to a saloon revivified his status within the cult and boosted his self-esteem. He was both unable and unwilling to make the leap from the roistering masculine life of liquor, gambling, and athletics to the placidity and stability of the home. In this sense he was still a juvenile, slow to mature in patterns approved by the middle class. And, like a juvenile, he often responded with violence and aggression when called to account for his actions. His brush with death in April 1883 did not slow down the progress of his alcoholism one whit. By June he was failing to meet exhibition engagements and, in New Haven, spent much of his time in his hotel room with a raging hangover.[42]

To many of his admirers the rumored wife beatings and drunken sprees were regrettable but did not diminish the image of a fighting, manly champion. Amid the debris of his unfortunate marriage, Sullivan was discovering that his fame had developed to the point at which he could make money in endeavors unrelated to boxing, one of the first instances of transcendence in American popular culture. The same week that he supposedly demolished his home and assaulted his wife, he appeared for the first time on stage, in a skit called "Tom and Jerry" at the Howard Athenaeum in Boston.[43] The theater would, in time, prove a natural and at times profitable outlet for his extroverted personality.

A second source of income lay in appearances at baseball games. John L., remember, had been a passable semiprofessional ballplayer as a teenager. Many Irish Americans were in the big leagues by the 1880s, and ballplayers thus were considered only a cut above prizefighters by proper public opinion. Still, baseball "exhibitions" featuring the champion were a natural drawing card. Sullivan loved the game, and he hobnobbed with Red Sox players whenever he could. As to his skills, and his later boast that he could have played professional baseball, skepticism must prevail.

A case in point: On May 28, 1883, John L. appeared in an exhibition game in New York's old Polo Grounds. He pitched for a local semipro team against another picked group of semipros. Over four thousand people showed up. As a pitcher, the champion proved eminently hittable; the opposition swatted his deliveries all over the field. At bat things were a bit better, although critics charged that Sullivan was served "gopher balls" so he could thrill the fans. The box score survives. During the game he made three hits, scored one run, and committed no less than four of his team's ten errors. He batted sixth, all of his hits were singles, and he uncorked three wild pitches, striking out one batter. The catcher, a hapless individual named Reipschlager, stood twenty feet behind the plate—the catcher's normal position at the time—and still had two passed balls. Sullivan's team prevailed, 20 to 15. The *Herald*'s reporter put it best, describing the champion as "a fair sample of an ordinary amateur player." But this missed the point; the bottom line was at the turnstiles, and here Sullivan pocketed $1,585.90 (half the gate) for his afternoon's recreation.[44] He was proving that people would *pay* to see John L. Sullivan do something other than box. Over a thousand fans remained at the Polo Grounds merely to watch Sullivan, now attired in frock coat and beaver hat, drive away after the game.

Nevertheless, and despite his illness, martial strife, and excursions onto stage and ball field, he was champion of the world, and he was expected to fight. By the spring of 1883 two more opponents were on the horizon, and as Sullivan careened from Boston to Providence to New York and back again, he began (in his way) to prepare for them.

## IV

Charles Watson Mitchell was a native of Birmingham, England. Born of Irish parents in 1861, he fought his first bare-knuckle prizefight at the tender age of sixteen for five pounds a side. By early 1883 his ring record stood at eleven wins and two draws, including victories over Tug Wilson and Alf Greenfield. He was a clever, tricky boxer and usually fought at about 150 pounds. Plucky and courageous, he had beaten in one of his early matches a man who outweighed him by ninety-one pounds. Billy Madden had "discovered" Mitchell in his English promotion to find a man who could beat Sullivan. After winning this competition in late 1882, Mitchell toured England. He sailed in March 1883 for New York, where he promptly defeated Mike Cleary in three rounds.[45]

Richard Kyle Fox lost no time in getting aboard the Mitchell bandwagon. Here was someone with a much better record than the unlamented Tug Wilson. His small size made Mitchell the natural sympathetic underdog, and Fox's hounds were soon in full cry. Charlie was boomed as "the greatest pugilist ever seen in this or any other country," although Madden, his manager, frankly admitted, without rancor, that Sullivan was still the best in America. John L. saw the Englishman fight Cleary in Philadelphia, a bout stopped by the police in the third round, and thus was able to take some measure of his man. He kept to his agreement to fight Mitchell in mid-May, only three weeks after his lungs had hemorrhaged. He prepared gingerly under the ministrations of Patsey Sheppard at Chelsea Beach, Massachusetts, while Mitchell and Madden chose the spa at Saratoga, New York, to get ready.[46]

The bout had been scheduled for Madison Square Garden, but the boxers had to tread carefully because the city fathers did not want another fiasco such as the Wilson affair. Thus Sullivan and Mitchell pretended that they were to give an "exhibition," although every betting man in the country knew what was really intended. Interest in the match was at a high pitch, with some giving Mitchell a chance because of Sullivan's illness and lack of training.

Rain pelted down all day on May 14, but the Garden's gates were thrown open promptly at 7 P.M. as scheduled. In the next two hours between eight and ten thousand sodden spectators filed in, the observant among them noting that Clubber Williams was again on hand, supported by ninety policemen. The audience was a Who's Who of the city's political and social scene. Roscoe Conkling, who sat himself on a plank suspended between two barrels, "occupied a position as close to the stage as it was possible to get" and cut a conspicuous figure in long coat and black silk traveling cap. John Reilly, who as president of the Board of Aldermen had been acting mayor only the day before, was in attendance, along with other aldermen, sheriffs, coroners, justices, and City Hall flunkies. Theatrical personalities were noted in abundance, including the ponderous vaudeville impresario, Tony Pastor. The renowned Charles A. Dana took his place at the reporters' table, while bankers and brokers such as William R. Travers, John Lowry, and Lawrence R. Jerome (great-uncle of an eight-year-old English lad named Winston Churchill) chatted easily as they sat waiting. "Tier after tier of silver-headed walking sticks, opera hats, white shirt fronts, and evening ulsters rose to the eaves, while a cloud of tobacco smoke ascended to the roof, obscuring the small boys who dangled their legs from the rafters." A friendly sparring match of four rounds had been advertised; almost everyone hoped for more.[47]

A roar went up as the two fighters appeared and made their way to the rope-encircled platform in the middle of the Garden. Sullivan was naked from the waist up, dressed in salmon-colored, knee-length tights and colored stockings. Both men donned medium-sized soft gloves, which were then ostentatiously examined by Clubber Williams to the accompaniment of hisses from the audience. The preliminaries over, the referee, Al Smith called time.

Sullivan came after Mitchell like a maddened bull, swinging lefts and rights in jackhammer succession. But Charlie, unlike Tug Wilson, did not run. Instead, he slipped under the wild swings and counter-punched again and again. Nevertheless, the champion, with at least a forty-pound weight advantage, clubbed him down several times, but in the middle of the melee Mitchell sent home a quick left that knocked John L. down. For the first time in his career, Sullivan had been solidly floored, and the crowd went wild. The second three-minute round saw Mitchell beaten into the ropes; he fell through the strands and off the stage, wrenching his back. The Englishman went to the deck several more times in the third round, but he rose each time to gamely fight on. At last Sullivan bulled him into the ropes and fell atop him. Mitchell, dazed, struggled to his feet and apparently was willing to continue, but at this point the alert Clubber, who had been lurking in one of the corners, entered the ring and declared a halt.[48]

Sullivan had clearly won but had looked bad and off-form in doing so. Mitchell had as clearly lost but had showed what experienced ring craft could do against the untutored Strong Boy. The spectators were well pleased with the action-filled display of two conflicting styles, and many even applauded Williams as he stopped the fight. As Clubber stepped in, Sullivan and Mitchell shook hands, the champion raising Charlie's gloved mitt and good-humoredly kissing it. Both men dressed in the same small room, surrounded by friends and admirers. Williams sat nearby, swinging his club and telling reporters the match had been getting to be more than sparring, so he had called it off. Sullivan and his entourage headed for Bennett's Saloon, while Mitchell went to Harry Hill's. Both men had good reason to be satisfied; Sullivan took 60 percent of the estimated $16,000 gate, Mitchell 40 percent. After paying off his supporters and sailing through two consecutive nights on the town, John L. still took $4,000 home to Boston on the seventeenth.[49]

The second opponent, unlike the experienced Mitchell, was a complete unknown, but his principal backer was not. There had been a day when the name of Jem Mace was among the most feared in the prize ring. Mace, born near Norwich, England, in 1831, had fought consistently in the 1850s and 1860s, a tough, aggressive scrapper whose face was crosshatched by the results of over a score of bare-knuckle bouts. He came to America in 1869, his trade almost dead in England, and gave several exhibitions with John Carmel Heenan before that unfortunate passed from the scene. He beat Tom Allen in ten rounds in 1870 at Kennerville, near New Orleans, and the next year was matched against Joe Coburn in a bizarre nonfight in which the two men struck fighting poses and nothing else. Later in 1871, in the fight at Bay Saint Louis witnessed by William Muldoon, the same two pugilists battled to a punishing, three-hour draw. Since then, too old to box but still interested in the fight game, Jem had traveled the world, at least that considerable part under the Union Jack.[50]

At one time Richard Kyle Fox had conceived the far-fetched notion that Mace himself could be matched with Sullivan, but even the Proprietor had to admit that a man of Tom Allen's or Joe Coburn's generation could not stand against the champion in a prizefight. Mace and Fox corresponded; in his travels to Australia Jem had stumbled across a giant named Herbert Slade, whom Fox with gleeful lack of accuracy promptly dubbed "the Maori Half-breed." With Slade in tow, Mace arrived in San Francisco on Christmas Day of 1882 and lodged himself and his charge in the Palace Hotel. The "Maori" (who was not) proved to be 6 feet 2½ inches and 225 pounds, a bulky, squarish man who was broad of shoulder and hip. He was twenty-seven, Mace told inquiring San Franciscans, and he had "perfect good nature." Again Fox's war-drums began to beat: Sullivan was eagerly awaiting Slade; they would fight for $5,000 a side; Mace had broken his contract with the *Gazette*; Slade was traveling eastward; Slade displayed wondrous strength and power—and so on, and on.[51]

Fox pushed the pending battle with the Maori so far that in early February he was arraigned in the Court of Special Sessions, charged with aiding and abetting a prizefight. The charge was based on the Proprietor's offer to put up $5,000 on Slade against Sullivan. Fox had to post a bond of $1,000 to keep the peace for one year, a sentence that did not in the least slow him down. He broadcast himself as a neutral with an "all-for-sport" approach to matchmaking. Still, Slade was the coming man, the "Maori Wonder." The *Gazette* breathlessly followed the progress of Slade and Mace across the continent, to Chicago and on to New York. Readers learned that Slade's hand was "a menace to life—large and sinewy, with a grip like a vise." Mace and the Maori were scheduled to give a sparring exhibition in New York on January 29, but Mayor Franklin Edson had the police intervene. Fox's mouthpiece, Charles S. Spencer, appeared in court on their behalf, and the two men were released to the accompaniment of blaring cheers from the *Gazette*. Unchastened, Slade and Mace eventually sparred in Manhattan, Baltimore, and other eastern cities, waiting for arrangements to be made.[52]

Fox backed the Slade-Mace combination with $2,500, and at every stop Mace loudly challenged the champion. For his part, Sullivan had expressed a willingness to fight even before his illness, marriage, and the Mitchell bout. Fox simply ignored the provisions of his bond and kept on calling for the match: "Sporting men have rights which must be respected." The Proprietor eventually cooled on Slade—"his blows are like kisses compared with the sledgehammer thumps of the Boston Boy"—but by early summer the match was made for August 6. Mace and his protégé, who had taken their act overseas, returned from England on July 15 to prepare. Slade trained at Harry Hill's "country residence" in Flushing, Long Island; Hill had become an ardent backer. Sullivan, accompanied by Joe Goss and Pete McCoy, started "training" in Natick.[53]

Once again the site was Madison Square Garden. Vanderbilt, bowing to progress, had installed a few electric lights, but the Garden was still predominantly gaslit, and the crowd that assembled had to cope not only with the miasmatic cloud of tobacco haze but also with blue gas fumes. Despite the summer heat, over ten thousand crammed themselves into the huge wooden structure, while thousands more waited outside for news of the contest. As at the Mitchell fight the previous spring, members of tony clubs, such as the Union, the Union League, and the Knickerbocker, were prominent, and Wall Streeters and Stock Exchange members were scattered throughout the audience. The choice seats near the ring went to a crew of aldermen, city officials, and politicos, whose special badges got them passed through police lines.[54] Only a little more than two years had passed since Captain Starin's barge had sneaked some of the same men up the Hudson River to watch an unknown Boston youth batter John Flood.

The match was to be four three-minute rounds, Queensberry Rules. The winner would take 65 percent of the gate, the loser the rest. Amid the choking cigar smoke and the growing stench of perspiration, the betting on Sullivan at fight time was $100 to $40. Once again Clubber Williams was on hand, now with one hundred of New York's finest to help him keep the peace. Slade had slimmed down to 195 pounds for the bout, and Sullivan, despite working only sporadically in the summer heat at Natick, had pared himself to 193. The two men stepped into the ring around 9 P.M. with the referee, Barney Aaron. John L.'s little brother, Mike, was in the audience, and so was the temporarily reconciled Annie Bates Bailey Sullivan. Goss worked the champion's corner.

Those who favored Slade gave the Australian a chance because of his size and reach, but the minute the fighters, both naked to the waist, met in the center of the ring, everyone in the vast throng could see that a serious mismatch had been made. Slade was far from a natural boxer; he was slow, clumsy, and unaggressive. The champion charged in his usual self-induced fury, and the Maori quickly went down from a right hand to the jaw. Rising, he tried to spar but was blasted clean off the stage. He had to be assisted back into the ring. By this time Harry Hill, who probably had money on him, was screaming himself hoarse at ringside. At the end of the round Slade was slumped in his corner, "blowing like a blacksmith's bellows."

The execution continued. In the second round a blizzard of punches sent Slade down again. Bewildered, and possibly wondering why he had ever let Mace coax him to leave Australia, he had to be assisted to his feet. At this point, to the amazement of the crowd, he turned his back and *ran* from Sullivan. The champion hurried after him and slugged him through the ropes while the Maori's back was turned. Again Slade was manhandled back onto the stage. Groggy, he tried to close and wrestle, and Sullivan knocked him down for a fifth time. Midway through the third round, Slade was pushed against the ropes and decked by a smoking punch to his left ear. He "fell like an ox knocked down with a butcher's axe." He was dragged to his chair by Mace, unable to fight any longer. Clubber Williams had had enough, and so had the crowd. The captain entered the ring and ordered the gloves taken off.[55]

The crowd screamed, "Knocked out! Knocked out!" in a frenzy and mobbed the ring, shaking Sullivan's hand again and again. John L. and Goss, along with a herd of backers, retired to celebrate at their hotel, the Ashland House. The fight netted $11,000, of which the champion collected about $7,000. Sullivan diplomatically told the press that Slade had been the toughest man he had yet faced, while Mace said of his protégé that he had stood his ground pluckily, but "his head was in the way."[56]

## V

Thus far, 1883 with its ups and downs had been a banner year for Sullivan's pocketbook. The box office bonanzas of the Mitchell and Slade fights, when added to his exhibition profits, gave the champion earnings of over $40,000 by August, a sum that could be matched by no one in America, save a few plutocrats and top-notch professional men.[57] No member of the lower class in American history, and precious few others, had ever made money at such a clip. It was time to celebrate.

The day after the Slade triumph Sullivan was back in Boston to realize a dream. Ever since he had begun to make money in the fight game, the summit of his ambition, in the sense of personal property holdings, had been to open a saloon. The idea was hardly new; indeed,

11. Herbert Slade ("the Maori") (1883) (William Schutte Collection)

it was in the mainstream of the prizefighting tradition. But his own saloon would bind him to the comfortable, familiar masculine world as well as make him a person of substance, as understood by his peers. He would be a businessman as well as an athlete.

During the spring of 1883, shortly after his marriage, Sullivan bought a building on Washington Street for $15,000, including $4,000 for the purchase of the lease. The structure had formerly housed a shoe store run by a man named John P. Dore. During the summer Sullivan poured thousands of dollars into remodeling the building. This was to be, after all, the Champion's Saloon, and he wanted it done right. Sullivan's goal was to rival the posh Hoffman House bar in New York City. The establishment had to stand out, because Washington Street was an almost continuous row of grogshops and bars already. In a seven-block stretch between Franklin and State streets were no less than seventeen saloons. Sullivan's place would be within two blocks of City Hall and almost that close to the Court House and City Prison.[58]

On Tuesday, August 7, the establishment at 714 Washington Street opened for business. Sullivan, who had been greeted with tremendous enthusiasm by a crowd at the railway station earlier in the day, went immediately to the saloon with his brother, Mike, and a friend, Frank Moran. The crowd in the thoroughfare was so great that every cop from Station Four was detailed to keep order. Sixty foot patrolmen and seven mounted policemen had their hands full with a mob that jammed the street for a full block and beyond. Cautious residents of the South End were forced to take roundabout routes to their homes. Word had gotten out that the champion would be offering free drinks, which at least partially accounted for the size of the throng.[59]

Over the door hung a simple sign in bright gilt letters: "John L. Sullivan." The curtains were raised in the windows at 7 P.M., and the new owner was ready for customers. "Only those whose dress was of the regulation flash order were permitted to pass the guard at the door and enter the saloon," sniffed one correspondent. In order to disperse the legion of children trying to sneak in, the guards drove them off by squirting soda from a siphon into their faces. The *New York Daily Tribune*, in a burst of exaggeration, estimated the mob at twenty thousand "howling ruffians," who completely blocked the street from Boylston to Hollis.[60]

Inside, "it was as difficult for a man to get across the room as for a herring to get from one end of its box to another." The evening was exceedingly hot, and tobacco fumes mingled with the odor of fresh paint: Dore's Shoe Store had not been large, only forty-five feet deep, and the thirsty mob was packed shoulder to shoulder. The front of the room had been partitioned by wood and glass into a small office, and here Sullivan presided. Many prominent saloon owners and liquor dealers showed up, as one of them said, "just to shake the hand of John L. Sullivan."[61]

The centerpiece of the saloon was the main bar, a beautifully carved monolith of polished mahogany extending down one side of the room, over which presided Tom Bogue, a former prizefighter. Behind the bar, encased in enormous mahogany frames, were three French plate-glass mirrors, ten feet by seven feet, the largest that could be found. Each pillar separating the mirrors supported golden gaslit globes of a delicate, "peculiar" pattern. A fine mahogany ice chest was built into the wall at the rear of the room. The champion's initials were carved in the frosted glass border of each front window and etched into each bar glass.[62]

Floral displays were everywhere. The walls were studded with pictures, most of them of fighting scenes. One of the windows displayed a crayon drawing of Sullivan in ring attire and attitude, while the other featured a testimonial concerning John L.'s fighting colors. The only painting was a garish depiction of Venus rising from the sea, promoted as being "from the brush of Theophile Constan of Paris." While free-loading was the order of the day on this festive occasion, both beer and liquor had a set price, and drinkers were charged double for the better brands. As befitted a man's bar, no mixed drinks could be had at all.[63]

When the bar was opened, the mob immediately broke down the heavy brass railing lining its length, smashed some glassware, and did other damage. Extra police were summoned. Several people were arrested for disorderly conduct, including the boxer Tim Drohan. At least one hundred law officers worked to quiet the rowdies inside and disperse the curious outside. Around 9 P.M. a line of police established themselves across the entrance, admitting only those known to be Sullivan's cronies; this tactic somewhat reduced the press of people inside. By midnight comparative quiet had been restored.[64]

John L. Sullivan was in his element—treating, toasting, telling tales. A friend later claimed that the champion had had nothing stronger to drink than seltzer water during the evening, but this was not in character. One reporter observed that "Sullivan at ten o'clock was able to talk and keep on his feet, but he was pretty well 'sprung.' " Sometime during the course of the celebration, another reporter cornered the tipsy owner in the cool cellar of the building and asked him about the cost of all this. John L. replied that the saloon had cost $20,000 to outfit, an enormous sum that had been only partially paid. In addition, Sullivan had to bear the significant upkeep of the establishment by himself. The business took in over $3,000 its first three days of operation, which was a good start. It remained to be seen if the cham-

12. The Washington Street saloon, mid-1880s. Sullivan is at the far end of the bar. (William Schutte Collection)

pion's management skills were equivalent to those he displayed in the ring.[65]

For the moment there were no money clouds on the horizon. The Great John L. basked in his triumphs. Since conquering Paddy Ryan a year and a half before, he had beaten ten men in prizefights and given a score of exhibitions. No one had come close to defeating him in the ring; not even the knockdown by the crafty Mitchell had diminished the aura surrounding the Great Knocker-Out. He had drawn all levels of society to his bouts, which had taken place, unlike the fights of his predecessors, in urban settings before generally large audiences. Not yet twenty-five, he was living life to the fullest, and most of it in public. There was, in short, nothing pianissimo about John L. Sullivan. He fought tough, drank hard, and had begun to sign his name "Yours Truly"—always open, always honest, always "on the level." His generosity as well as his profligacy were already legendary. If his flaws were gargantuan, so too were his talents, or so it seemed to his admirers. He could even be joined to a Walt Whitman parody, as with this bauble in the old *Life* magazine:

Oh, J. Sullivan! Oh, J. Sullivan!
Oh, John Lycurgus Sullivan, all hail!!
Thou Bottomless infinitude! Thou god! Thou you!
Thou Zeus with all-compelling hand!
Thou glory of the mighty Occident! Thou Heaven-born!
Thou Athens-bred! Thou light of the Acropolis!
    Thou son of a gambolier!
59 inches art thou around thy ribs; twice twain knuckles
    hast thou; and again twice twain.
Thou scatterest men's teeth like antelopes at play.
Thou straightenest thine arm, and systems rock, and eye-balls
    change their hue.
Oh, thou grim granulator! Thou soul-remover! Thou
    lightsome, coy excoriator!
Thou cooing dove! Thou droll, droll John!
Thou buster!
Oh, you! Oh, me too! Oh, me some more!
Oh, thunder![66]

What worlds were left to conquer? Amid the whirling carousel of fights, drinking sprees, domestic quarrels, and sporadic training, Sullivan realized that his fame and prestige were, at bottom, dependent on what he did with his fists. Even as he acknowledged the tributes of the Boston faithful in his jam-packed saloon, a plan was being shaped for an athletic expedition the likes of which the country had never seen.

# CHAPTER SIX

# The Grand Tour
## (1883—1884)

Sometime during the spring and summer of 1883, while John L. Sullivan was thumping Charlie Mitchell and Herbert Slade, a grandiose idea was conceived. Its progenitor may have been Sullivan himself, but the more likely candidate is Al Smith, the man who had refereed the Flood fight and the Sullivan-Mitchell match in the Garden. Like Mike Donovan and William Muldoon, Smith had gone for the Union in the Civil War, soldiering throughout with an Ohio regiment. After the war Al drifted to Saint Louis, and there and in the other rough and growing commercial cities along the Mississippi he rubbed shoulders with pugilists like Tom Allen and Mike McCoole. Broad-shouldered and six feet two inches tall, Smith turned to rough-and-tumble fighting himself. By the mid-1870s he was an experienced bare-knuckler, with victories over men with regional reputations, such as Pat Conley and Jake Powell. In 1883 he was in his midforties and no longer fought, but he had become a trustworthy staple of the sporting culture and widely accepted as adept at scheduling and refereeing fights.[1]

Smith's great conception was another tour, but this time on a scale never attempted before by any American. He proposed to put Sullivan on the road not just for a few weeks but for *eight months*. Beyond this, John L. would visit practically every part of the country; he would literally make a "swing around the nation." Although politicians like Stephen A. Douglas and Andrew Johnson had toured throughout the areas east of the Mississippi, no one, politician, entertainer, or otherwise, had traveled America to such a degree. As the champion bathed in the liquid aftermath of the Slade victory, Smith was busy at the telegraph office. Much advance work had to be done.

Finally, the plans were set. On September 18, in the Gilsey House in New York City, the tour was announced. The champion, sporting the dazzling gold watch and chain given him in March, faced reporters

13. Al Smith, Sullivan's manager on the Grand tour (William Schutte Collection)

with Smith at his side. Sullivan was content to let Smith take charge of things. He admitted that after the tour left Baltimore, "I have no idea where we go to." He realized that they were somehow to get to San Francisco but probably had little notion how that was to be achieved. Annie would be with him, Sullivan announced. He had given up the "flowing bowl," and his "good little woman" would look after his interests. Sullivan and Smith had a contract for the duration of the tour. After paying a fixed salary to the fighters and others in the "combination" traveling with them, the two men would split the proceeds.[2]

The day-to-day task of running the Washington Street saloon had already begun to pall on John L. In the five weeks since its opening the establishment had taken in about twenty-five thousand dollars, but there were expenses, not the least of which were the cost of liquor and beer, six bartenders, and his brother, Mike, who ran the cigar stand. Sullivan was eager for a change, but in all likelihood he had no idea of what the industrous Smith had arranged for him. The tour encompassed twenty-six of the thirty-eight states, the District of Columbia, five territories, and British Columbia. From September 28 to May 23 the champion had contracted to appear at least once in no less than 136 cities and towns, in 22 for two-day appearances and in five for several days. Smith thus had scheduled a grand total of 195 performances for the combination in 238 days.[3]

The pace would have to be breakneck, at a speed never achieved by any American tour of any kind over such a length of time. Only one development made it possible: the railroad. As far back as 1850 Congress had begun a policy of aiding the new industry with lavish land grants and had permitted railroad construction firms to import cheap Chinese labor under contract. After the Civil War the country's rail network had both broadened (main lines) and deepened (trunk and feeder lines), so that by 1883 Americans could boast of a truly national system of transportation. Between 1870 and 1880 railway mileage had almost doubled, from 54,000 to 93,000. Some of these lines were poorly constructed, their stock was mostly water, and a few were little more than playthings for eastern speculators, but the trains still ran, and for the most part (the pride of the industry) they ran on time. The great transcontinental centerpiece was the Central Pacific–Union Pacific system, completed in 1869. But by the time Sullivan and Smith launched themselves on tour, the Northern Pacific was running from Duluth to Portland. The Southern Pacific (which had absorbed the Central Pacific) had connected Los Angeles with El Paso in 1882, and from there a traveler could move on to Kansas City, Fort Worth, or New Orleans.

The railroad would not only provide the pugilists with access to the Great Plains, the Rockies, and the Pacific Coast. It would also enable them to visit nooks and crannies of America that had never seen a boxing "exhibition," much less a prizefight. Every major American city west and south of New York and Philadelphia was on the itinerary, but Smith had not overlooked the tank towns. Sullivan would go to Altoona, Pennsylvania, Steubenville, Ohio, Danville, Illinois, Keokuk, Iowa, Oshkosh, Wisconsin, and Winona, Minnesota, among his dozens of stops east of the Mississippi. In the vast West, where almost everywhere communities were small and hopes were high, there would be more of the same. For the first time, John L. would come face-to-face with small-town Middle America.

The small towns through which the tour would journey were, in general, on the defensive in 1883. Many of them had ceased to grow, and some of their most promising youngsters were being lured away (the railroad made it easier) to the city. East of the Mississippi the former urban boomlets, each tiny collection of houses a potential metropolis, were fading into the past. It was still the land of the general store, temperance leagues, community-sponsored baseball, and Protestant fundamentalism, but already—before the horseless carriage, the motion picture, and the radio—the city was feared as a place of vice, an immigrant-infested sewer, an all-consuming Moloch.[4] And here would come Sullivan, with his boxing "exhibitions." How would an urban easterner of Irish Catholic heritage, promoting an outlaw sport, play on Main Street? Smith, for one, was confident.

The combination would feature boxers other than Sullivan. Herbert Slade signed on, at $200 a month, and paid Jem Mace $300 to break his contract with the Englishman. The former Jersey City coroner, Steve Taylor, was the other heavyweight. Two scrappy lightweights, Pete McCoy and Mike Gillespie, rounded out the pugilistic crew. Smith would go, of course, most of the time serving as advance man. Sullivan's friend Frank Moran, who had been around the fight game for years, would serve as master of ceremonies. Jack Menzinger, whose name would be mangled in a bewildering variety of ways by reporters along the route, would handle the finances. With Annie, who was now pregnant, the little band numbered nine.[5]

To hype the tour and draw the crowds, Sullivan and Smith announced that at any time during his travels the champion would box *anyone* four rounds under the Queensberry Rules for $250. John L. was literally challenging all of America to fight. This challenge made arrangements complete; with Smith riding point as advance man, the group set forth on September 28—"the Great John L." was coming to town!

# I

After a two-day appearance in Baltimore the troupe rolled south, into the former heart of the Confederacy. On October 1, in Richmond,

Virginia's Mozart Hall, Sullivan performed before three hundred people, including some "aged and moss-backed old sports," to "general satisfaction." The champion, despite stepping on a furnace register and breaking it during his scuffle with Taylor, was pronounced impressive by the locals. The group had set the pattern of their performance: With Moran doing the introductions and Menzinger tallying the house, Taylor would first spar with Gillespie, then Slade with McCoy. Sullivan would next be introduced, to box with Taylor. Penultimately, the two lightweights, McCoy and Gillespie, would go at it, and John L. and Slade would wind up the evening. All the fighters wore tights and appeared naked to the waist. Each exhibition was to be three three-minute rounds with gloves; the total entertainment (as advertised) thus came to forty-five minutes of sparring, which was forty-five minutes more than most in their audiences had ever seen.[6] At times two local amateurs would meet to fill out the bill.

Next, on to Petersburg, Virginia, scene of Grant's relentless siege of Lee in the waning months of the war, then to Norfolk and back to Washington, D.C., for two appearances. The early crowds were good and attentive, and in the capital Sullivan drew many prominent people. Still, there were no challengers. Up to Harrisburg, Pennsylvania, where a certain E. Z. Wallower attempted to stop the exhibition at the Opera House. As if to prove his harmlessness, John L. umpired a local baseball game that afternoon, and in the evening he played to a full house stippled with brawny iron puddlers and steel workers. There was much hemming and hawing among several of these muscular laboring men, but in the end no one had the nerve to get up on stage with the champion.[7]

The group began to settle into the routine: check in, check out, each morning to the depot early, and so to the next town. Onward the train rolled through Pennsylvania: Reading, Lancaster, Pottsville, Wilkes-Barre, Scranton, York, Altoona, McKeesport, Allegheny City. Each night a new stage, a new audience to take the measure of the champion. In Pottsville the first trouble occurred. Two of the fighters (Sullivan denied being one) and two locals raised a rumpus in a whorehouse, and the entire troupe entrained one step ahead of the law. Two nights later, in Scranton, Sullivan refused to spar, charging that he had been shorted $100 of his $250 guarantee by the promoter, S. E. Whipple, proprietor of the Lackawanna Valley House. The cold rain falling on the outdoor ring may have had something to do with his decision. The disappointed crowd rushed the box office, ineptly defended by Menzinger, and lifted many of the cash boxes, which finally came into the possession of a mysterious horseman who spurred away amid a shower of stones and sticks. Everyone wanted his fifty cents back. A surly mob surrounded Sullivan's hotel. When the champion tried to get his hair cut later that day, two policemen tried to disperse the threatening townspeople and were beaten. Sullivan fled the barbershop and hid in the hotel, around which the crowd, made up largely of enraged miners and steelworkers, surged until nearly midnight.[8]

Leaving the troublesome citizenry of Pottsville and Scranton behind, the pugilists appeared in York and Altoona without difficulty, although in the latter community Sullivan almost got in a scrap when, as he and Annie were dining, he overheard people at an adjoining table wondering how a woman that pretty could marry such a fellow. Finally, in McKeesport, the first challenger appeared: James McCoy, a puddler from Sharpsburg. By this time Smith and Sullivan had decided to double the prize to five hundred dollars to attract challengers. McCoy, at 160 pounds to Sullivan's 200 plus, was at least colorful: when he bared his chest, he revealed a torso embossed with tattoo work representing flowers, anchors, snakes, and flared-mouth dragons. Before the audience had time to appreciate this spectacle fully, McCoy weakly pawed at Sullivan's mouth to open the bout. The champion responded with a right and left, and the puddler lay sprawled on the stage. The "fight" had taken twenty seconds.[9]

After a dip across the border to Youngstown, Ohio, the combination played Allegheny City, on the outskirts of Pittsburgh, for two days. As with most of the performances, no ring was set up. Usually there would be a raised stage, with a chair placed at either end for the boxers to rest on between rounds. Frank Moran would come out to warm up the audience and sprinkle some rosin on the boards, and sometimes he would make a show of refereeing, but by this time the fighters know each other's ring habits so well that the sparring was taking on elements of choreography. The crowds were especially good in Allegheny City; over four thousand showed up the first night at the city Coliseum, and Menzinger was kept busy scraping money into handkerchiefs and emptying the pile into the cash boxes every half hour. In the audience lawyers and physicians sat beside Fifth Ward toughs and slum bullies from the Steel City. A reporter noticed a solitary woman (Annie?) seated in the second row. The act went off without a hitch, and clerks at the Monongahela House said the pugilists had been orderly off stage as well, keeping to their rooms and smoking cigars. Sullivan passed the time extolling the science of self-defense to reporters and praising the importance of boxing to men in public life, such as John Morrissey, Roscoe Conkling, and Zack Chandler.[10]

Pennsylvania behind them, the travelers rode the little Panhandle line to Wheeling, West Virginia. Sullivan was moving now into the Old Midwest. Although Wheeling was a grimy industrial town, it treated the champion's advent as Middle America treated a circus visit. Hundreds flocked to the McClure House on the evening of his scheduled arrival, only to be told that Sullivan would be coming in the next day. A critical local editorial did nothing to dampen enthusiasm. The next day, a large troop of admirers and the merely curious followed John L.'s carriage from the station to his hotel. Many flattened their noses against the windows of Hollinger's Shop to see him finally get his hair cut. That night, a crowd of over two thousand filled Charley Shay's Theater.[11]

Almost everywhere it was the same: At the railroad station, official greeters, at times including the community's leading men. At the hotel, punctilious service. In the streets, crowds of men and boys eager to get a look at the Boston marvel. Audiences everywhere were composed of a mix of the better sort and riffraff, and occasionally some women attended. In Ohio, Steubenville and Newark opened their doors. In Columbus, Smith placed a newspaper ad claiming "an ovation at every point. Thousands turned away from each performance from the largest amusement houses in the country." It was not far from the truth. By the evening of the combination's arrival in the Ohio capital, the corridors of the Neil Hotel were crowded with the curious, both gentlemen and toughs. While rain cut attendance to five hundred, members of the City Council were at the show in City Hall. Smith had raised the price for better seats from fifty cents to a dollar.[12]

On to Dayton, and then to Cincinnati, scene of the Christmas Eve clandestine bout against Donaldson almost three years before. A week of good behavior apparently was Sullivan's limit. Smith was now forced to deny reports that the champion had been drinking again. In contrast to the whispered secrecy of the Donaldson bout, John L.'s name was emblazoned across the width of local papers in big black type. At the Coliseum Theater each member of the audience received a "personal license," which said that if the holder became objectionable during the performance, he would be shown the door. Rain kept the well-behaved house to about two-thirds capacity. Although most were satisfied, the few who had seen Sullivan before noted that he looked rumpled and was "getting somewhat baggy in the lower portion of his trunk." Smith's promotions were still packing them in, though. He had lithographs printed bearing John L.'s likeness, with a space labeled "next" across from the champion's picture for the next victim.[13]

Across the Ohio to Louisville, where Sullivan performed in a hall "filled to overflowing" with enthusiastic fans, incuding the city's mayor, Charles D. Jacobs. Then into Indiana, and another big crowd at the Park Theater in Indianapolis. He was deep in the heartland now, and still the crowds came. Terre Haute and Lafayette in Indiana, Danville in Illinois, and finally, in early November, a welcome four-day stayover in the Saint Louis area.[14]

In East Saint Louis, Illinois, Sullivan got his second challenge. Before a motley crowd of three hundred mill workers and other East Siders in Flanigan's Hall, he faced a somewhat experienced local boxer named James ("Gypsy") Miles for $500. Miles had plenty of gumption, but his size (5 feet 7 and 135 pounds) made the contest potentially dangerous. Moran offered to match him with Pete McCoy for $200, but Gypsy wanted the champion. From the opening blow the audience was yelling for John L. to stop. The police, in fact, cut short the slaughter after only twenty seconds. A dazed Miles inquired, "Isn't it two minutes?" Then he lunged for Sullivan, who blasted him off the stage, his head ending up wedged between the rungs of a ladder. Gypsy disentangled himself and appeared ready for more, but everyone saw that he had had enough. Miles stumbled off to wild applause, having burnished his image in the local cult of masculinity.[15]

The next day Sullivan appeared at Sportsman's Park in Saint Louis. His host was Chris Von der Ahe, the eccentric owner of the Browns baseball team, "half-genius and half-buffoon." Von der Ahe was prospering, his beer garden was popular, and the Browns, finishing second in the American Association with a 65-33 mark, had made him over fifty thousand dollars during the 1883 season. Sullivan would keep the crowds coming.

Despite the lateness of the year, over five thousand people showed up. The Browns divided sides and mingled with local semipros to form two teams. Sullivan pitched and played shortstop. To give him more appearances at the plate, the Brown's team captain and soon-to-be manager, the tall and talented Charles Comiskey, batted John L. first. As perhaps the most muscular leadoff batter ever to appear on a diamond, Sullivan went hitless in four at bats. In the field he had two assists and an error, a decided improvement over his Polo Grounds performance the previous spring. He pitched for five innings and was hammered, giving up eight runs and managing to strike out one. Throughout the contest, during which Sullivan's side was demolished 15 to 3, the spectators watched with great good humor. At the finish the champion was surrounded by a large crowd and could barely make it to the dressing room. For his afternoon's work Von der Ahe guaranteed him 60 percent of the gate, which came to over fourteen hundred dollars.[16]

The pugilists had their first real trouble with the law in Saint Louis. On November 7, after two days of routine sparring in front of large crowds at the People's Theater, Sullivan and Taylor were arrested on warrants charging them with violating a state law that prohibited sparring and boxing exhibitions. John L. posted bond for an appearance in the Court of Criminal Corrections and promptly absconded. "Our only alternative was to abandon the California trip, or forfeit the bonds," he later wrote. "Of course we preferred the latter."[17]

The bond-breakers proceeded onward, up the broad valley of the Mississippi: Quincy, Illinois; Keokuk and Burlington in Iowa; then across Illinois to Chicago, though Peoria, Galesburg, Mendota, and Streator. The rumors of the champion's boozing were growing. The *Cleveland Herald*, noting that Sullivan's habits were causing trouble everywhere on the tour, declared that "it is about time that press and public 'sat down' on the lionizing of this disreputable individual." For his part, John L. contended that "I don't drink much, say five or six glasses of ale a day and a bottle for dinner, if I feel like it."[18]

Regardless of his disclaimers and in spite of the almost nightly sparring activity, he was putting on weight rapidly. The combination played Chicago for two profitable days, opening at the Battery D Armory before a vast audience of nine thousand, of whom perhaps four thousand were crammed in as standees. One reporter observed that the newly acquired girth of the champion suggested "the prize bullock, King David, in the fat stock show." Still, the performances were deemed more than adequate. John L. and his companions cleared over eighteen thousand dollars in the two nights in the armory.[19]

North to Wisconsin: Racine, Milwaukee, Fond-du-Lac, Oshkosh, Eau Claire—five communities in five days. Then once again across the Mississippi, to Stillwater, Minnesota, and on to Saint Paul. There, a third challenger materialized. He was Morris Hefey, a railroad engineer, and unlike the diminutive McCoy and Miles he had size: 6 feet 1 and 195 pounds. Unfortunately he had little else. Sullivan charged squarely at Hefey and drilled him to the back of the stage. The railway man managed one blow to John L.'s neck and was promptly knocked down again. Following a third trip to the floor, he refused to fight anymore. Time elapsed: thirty seconds. The next day in Minneapolis, prior to performing before a packed audience in Market Hall (everyone was now paying one dollar apiece, and Menzinger's coffers were swelling), Sullivan unburdened himself to a reporter. Wreathed in cigar smoke, he bragged that his seventeen-year-old brother, Mike, would grow to be a better man than John L. ever was. As to politics, the Democrats would win the White House in 1884, and the man would be Samuel Tilden, the former New York governor, who had lost the disputed 1876 presidential election to Rutherford B. Hayes.[20] The public was finding out more about his habits and personal preferences with each passing day.

Down the Mississippi this time: Winona, Minnesota, and La Crosse, Wisconsin; then McGregor, Dubuque, Clinton, and Davenport in Iowa. In the latter city a blacksmith named Mike Sheehan was brought forth, billed as "the strongest man in Iowa." Sheehan was thirty-five and was seconded by his two teenage sons. Sullivan later claimed that Mrs. Sheehan had come to his hotel before the fight to plead with him not to meet her husband, because she had five children, her man would kill Sullivan, and she did not want a murderer for a spouse. The results were somewhat different. Within seconds the blacksmith was pelted in the cheek, nose, and jaw and sent spinning toward the rear of the stage. With this, the strongest man in Iowa sheepishly pulled off the gloves and retired, content with a gift of one hundred dollars from Sullivan.[21]

Across the rolling farmlands of the Hawkeye State, the towns strung out to the west along the railroad like beads on a string: Muscatine, Marshalltown, Oscaloosa, Ottumwa, Des Moines. In the state capital over two hundred people milled around in the vestibule of the Morgan Hotel, hoping for a glimpse. On to Nebraska, riding the Rock Island Line. After a short trip to Lincoln, the combination performed at Boyd's Opera House in Omaha. The place was jammed with all grades of local male society, and as they had done at many of their stops, the pugilists sparred to the strains of an orchestra. The *Daily Republican* sent an enterprising reporter, who was surprised at Sullivan's regular, unmarked features. The champion was judged "not as bad looking as he will be when he gets his nose flattened a few times, has his lip split in half a dozen places, gets a cornice factory over his peepers, and loses a few nippers from his bread basket." The reporter actually polled the spectators on their opinions of Sullivan's athletic skills and morals. Of the published replies, forty-five gave responses favorable to the champion, nine were undecided, and fourteen submitted decidedly unfavorable observations.[22]

With this rough-and-ready public opinion poll in their wake, John L. and his entourage proceeded down the Missouri River toward Kansas City, through Council Bluffs, Iowa, and Saint Joseph, Missouri, then on to Atchison, Leavenworth, Lawrence, Topeka, and Wyandotte in Kansas. Not thirty years before, these Jayhawker towns had been the core of "Bleeding Kansas," a battleground for abolitionist and proslavery forces that had helped tear the nation apart. Now they had receded quietly into Middle America. In Atchison there were rumors that a policeman would face Sullivan, but no one materialized. There was a growing rift in the combination. Slade was tiring of the endless traveling and one-night stands, and he sparred weakly against Pete McCoy, a much smaller man. John L. and Annie were fatigued as well, avoiding the crowds at the depot in Topeka. Occasionally a reporter would seek her out. A Topeka journalist approvingly noted that "like a true wife, [she] speaks always well of her husband." Annie was learning the art of public relations, of putting on a front. Actually, she was increasingly discouraged by John L.'s periodic relapses with the bottle.

In addition, McCoy and Gillespie had conceived an intense dislike of each other. The two lightweights had become the best part of the act, usually giving audiences three solid rounds of hammer-and-tongs sparring.[23]

The one-day stop in Kansas City, on December 22, concluded the initial part of the tour. There was no doubt that Sullivan was disintegrating steadily, with his weight increase and his recurrent binges. But to many who had seen him, it made no difference. He was the champion, the master of ring science, the apotheosis of fighting manhood. Each of his four challengers thus far—McCoy, Miles, Hefey, and Sheehan—had been rank novices, the work of a few seconds. In Boston his popularity remained undiminished. His friends, through the proxy of brother Mike, presented him a three-hundred-dollar clock, in absentia.[24] Their man was beating the nation.

But now John L. Sullivan was entering *terra incognita*, that vast half of the country that few Americans had ever seen. Even now, in parts of the West, marauding Indians prowled, struggling to avoid cavalry units detailed to herd them onto reservations. Overnight mining camps abounded, filled with the toughest scourings of the continent. Cattle ranchers, sheep men, and farmers all strove to wrest a living from the rugged environment. Outlaws and badmen still pocked the landscape, though their day was drawing to a close. Throughout the mountains, plains, and deserts from the Mississippi to the Pacific Ocean, savagery and civilization were yet at loggerheads. What sort of welcome could a little group of eastern city dwellers expect amid such overwhelming and diverse scenes? Al Smith was already in Denver, announcing the impending arrival of the American Hercules. Two days before Christmas, Sullivan with his aggregation boarded the Kansas Pacific and headed west, toward the towering Rockies.

## II

The high prairies through which they passed were almost devoid of buffalo. The shaggy beasts had been practically obliterated in a prolonged mass slaughter some ten years before. Part of their meat had fed the very crews who built the Kansas Pacific. No more Indian bands followed the seasons and the giant herds. The Sioux and Cheyenne had been confined to reservations. Over seven years had passed since their warriors had cut down Custer on the Greasy Grass. Only a stark, frozen, winter landscape greeted the travelers, punctuated occasionally by a clapboard farmhouse or the outlines of a "soddy." They were entering a new world.

Sullivan arrived in Central City, Colorado, on Christmas Eve. Like all the Rocky Mountain mining camps, the community had had its twists of fate since the first gold strike in the late 1850s. By 1868 the placer miners were back to conducting small-scale operations, and wise men proclaimed that Colorado was past its flush days. One traveler to Central City about that time had noted the deserted mills, idle wheels, and empty shafts. But the town was coming back. The city fathers had lobbied hard for the branch line of the Denver Pacific that carried the pugilists up into the mountains. Mining became more efficient and professional. and, although the old wildcat days were gone, Central City still retained some of the characteristics of a boom town. Its pride and joy was its Opera House, and there Sullivan and the combination performed for a large crowd on the night of their arrival.[25] It was an auspicious beginning. John L.'s name was known and celebrated even here, in an area that had known only the Indian and the mountain man thirty years before.

On Christmas Day the boxers gave two performances in Denver. The capital of the state, the newest in the nation (1876), was booming. Denver was a transportation and financial center, standing at the crease where the High Plains exploded into the Rockies. It had a fancy new Exposition Building, optimistically constructed so far from downtown that trains were run to the site. Sullivan drew over seven thousand to the cavernous barn for the two shows, despite the day and the distance. His first big western crowd included cattle kings, merchants, miners, and professional men. Here Sullivan was recognized readily; "his portrait has long been familiar in Denver." In late afternoon, howling winds swept in, cutting the evening attendance to about two thousand.[26]

While in the dressing room in the Exposition Building, Sullivan saw a twin-triggered double-barreled shotgun lying on a table. An avid hunter, he picked up the piece out of curiosity. Told the weapon was not loaded, John L. playfully pointed it at Mike Gillespie, who was standing nearby, and pulled one of the triggers. Click. He swung the muzzle to aim it at a table and pulled the second trigger, blowing the table to kindling. Gillespie, whose left sleeve was riddled with buckshot holes, was scared stiff. Sullivan himself was badly shaken, and he refused to handle weapons of any kind for some years.[27]

Perhaps this accident triggered the spree that followed. For the next week the champion was seldom sober. In fact, the entire gang went off the wagon. Sullivan brawled with Pete McCoy, who had been called "by far the best-natured and most popular man" in the combination, and Slade was involved in a ruckus in which pistols were flashed. Even so, they managed a performance in Buena Vista, Colorado, the day after Christmas. Then on to Leadville, the town's reception committee clambering aboard at Buena Vista only to find John L. asleep in his railroad car. Leadville was percolating; its boom had begun in 1877, and in six years the population had gone from two hundred to fifteen thousand. The town was the second city in Colorado, with thirty miles of streets, gas lights, thirteen schools, five churches, and three hospitals. Its annual production of silver was second only to that of the fabled Comstock Lode, and it surpassed that of any foreign country except Mexico. As a sideline, the community's lead output rivaled England's. A considerable part of its prosperity came from fines on houses of prostitution, which amounted to little more than a business tax. A local couplet was appropriate:

> It's day all day in the day-time,
> And no night in Leadville.[28]

Here was a community made for Sullivan. The pugilists, despite the contretemps on the railway car, were given a civic parade, right in the midst of a mountain winter. Large banners were strung across the streets and in saloons. "Sullivan, the champion, is Leadville's guest." After the performance at the Zoo Theater, Leadville's guest got roaring drunk. He pushed Pete McCoy around, and the smaller man responded by smashing a chair over the champion's head. John L. reacted violently, seizing a lighted kerosene lamp and hurling it at McCoy. A real tragedy was averted only because the force of the throw blew out the flame. When the city marshal tried to collar him, Sullivan started punching and was stopped only by threat of firearms. Throughout the day of December 28 he kept to his hotel room, but that night he started again, culminating his evening by slipping on an icy sidewalk and injuring his stomach on the wooden edge.[29] In these moods no one could do a thing with him. He was a surly drunk, quick to take offense and quick to anger. The belligerent part of his character was released by alcohol.

The binge went on for three more days, through a trip back to Denver and a stay at Charpiot's Hotel. A scheduled second Denver exhibition was canceled. At last, on January 2, a barely sober champion and his retinue boarded the train for Cheyenne. Wyoming Territory passed quickly under the wheels of the Union Pacific's locomotive—Cheyenne, Laramie, and Rawlins in three days. Along the way the group steamed past the spot at Green River where John Carmel Heenan had died, lonely and forgotten, ten years before. Then through the Wasatch Range and down to Salt Lake City.[30]

Most Mormons could not have cared less about John L. Sullivan. Their organ, the *Desert Evening News*, did not print a single word concerning the combination. But there were others in the kingdom, and many of these, as well as a few Mormons, responded to Al Smith's publicity. Smith had lived in Salt Lake City shortly after the Civil War and was popular there. He told his Utah friends that Slade had become involved in a drunken brawl in Denver but that all the stories about Sullivan's boozing were untrue. Large crowds, as usual, clogged the Walker House, where the champion stayed, and the Opera House, where a good-humored audience paid a dollar apiece to listen to the orchestra and watch the show.[31] John L. was temporarily back on track.

Now the combination made a detour, moving up through Ogden, Utah, to Butte and Helena, in Montana Territory. Sullivan returned to Butte for a second time on January 12. Like Central City and Leadville, Butte had been through its share of hard times. But now it was thriving once again, thanks to aggressive local merchants and bankers and new ore discoveries. The community, it was found, sat above a trove of silver and copper. Butte shared the rip-roaring style of the Colorado mining camps, but the city and its new neighbor, the smelter works of Anaconda, were industrial centers on their way to becoming "company towns." Tense and often violent struggles between labor and capital thus gave Butte an almost eastern flavor. Here Sullivan faced his fifth challenger, a Texan named Fred Robinson, who had come north hoping to strike it rich in the bonanza. Robinson may have had some ring experience; he was described as a "middleweight" and weighed 153 pounds. John L. by this juncture had puffed up to 225 pounds. The weight disparity was reminiscent of the "fight" with Gypsy Miles back in Saint Louis. For the first time, the champion offered one thousand dollars to anyone lasting the four rounds. Alas for Robinson, it was no contest. Before an audience of two thousand, he was knocked down seven times in the first round, once completely through the ropes. He grittily held on, but in round two he was decked eight more times, and Sullivan was declared the winner.[32]

The troupe returned to Salt Lake City, where brother Mike joined up. He would travel along to San Francisco and then accompany Annie, by now six months pregnant, back to Boston. Now numbering ten, the company rolled on into the high desert, past the Great Salt Lake and thence to Nevada: Reno, Carson City, Virginia City. By this time the constant traveling was getting to everyone except young Mike. In Reno the combination gave a lackluster exhibition, leading to accusations of "hippodroming." The audience left somewhat chagrined, but, as one observer said, "They saw Sullivan." Over the rails of the Virginia and Truckee, now, and into California at last. First Nevada City, then into the lush valley below: Sacramento, Stockton, San Jose. On January 25 they arrived in San Francisco.[33]

The Bay City was a multiple phoenix. It burned down as if on schedule and each time rose better than before. Already, with the possible exception of New Orleans, it had the most highly seasoned personality of any American community. San Franciscans were eager to see Sullivan. Fifty policemen were detailed to keep order upon his

14. John L.'s younger brother, Mike (mid-1880s) (William Schutte collection)

arrival; over six thousand flocked to the station to watch him alight. Fully one thousand men and boys walked in the wake of his carriage on the way to the Palace Hotel, which was soon besieged by admirers.

Unfortunately, although Smith's advance work attracted four thousand people to Mechanics' Pavilion that evening, the event was soured by rampant ticket speculation. As it was, the asking price had escalated to $2.50, a fivefold inflation over the early charges in the East. In addition, the weary pugilists had told Moran to hold their rounds to one minute apiece. Only half as many people came to the next fight, in spite of lowered prices. As Sullivan and Taylor sparred in the drastically shortened exhibition, the audience hissed Moran each time he ended a "round." John L. lost his temper, advanced to the ring ropes, and spoke savagely to the crowd. Those who hissed were loafers, he said; if they did not like that name, they could have a sock in the jaw. It was not his finest hour in public relations. He also managed to insult a certain Patsy Hogan, Richard Kyle Fox's man in San Francisco, and the purple prose of the *Police Gazette* was unleashed on him once again. Fox immediately commissioned drawings of women "mashed" on Sullivan; of the champion drinking, "surrounded by dudes"; of a battered victim; of gunplay at a western reception; and, as the *pièce de résistance*, John L. involved in a barroom brawl.[34]

His western popularity at a new low, Sullivan gave a pair of exhibitions across the bay in Oakland and then took ship for an expedition up the fogbound, treacherous lee shore of the Oregon coast. On February 1 he was in Astoria, Oregon. There, before a packed house, he met the "Astoria champion," a hulking French-Canadian fisherman named Sylvester Le Gouriff. For the first time the champion confronted a behemoth; Le Gouriff, who spoke little English, weighed over three hundred pounds. Nevertheless, Sylvester proved a complete innocent in ring craft. John L. knocked him down twice in twenty seconds, and he remained unconscious for over ten minutes. Upon recovering, the fisherman told friends that he could break boards with his bare hands, but Sullivan could break stone walls.[35]

The next night in Portland was a success, as well. Sullivan's ship, the *Fleetwood*, was welcomed at the dock by a large crowd. The New Market Theater was packed, over three hundred people sitting on the stage. The *Morning Oregonian* was moved to publish a multistanza poem, the "Song of the Slugger," in John L.'s honor ("I'm a chick you must not sass, for I come from Boston, Mass.").[36]

On to Tacoma, Washington Territory, and then Seattle, a raw, timber-built city at the farthest reaches of the nation. This time the *Emma Hayward* bore him to the dock, where over two thousand awaited, including the community band. A large percentage of Seattle's "solid men and best citizens" were on hand. Despite the champion's corpulence, a callow reporter was awestruck by his first sight of Sullivan: "No ordinary man has any chance at all before him, and it is idle, foolish, to talk otherwise." Nevertheless a lumberman named James Lang gave it a try that evening, emboldened by the thousand-dollar offer. He was battered to the floor twice in seven seconds and quit. The combination then performed in Vancouver, British Columbia, and in Seattle a second time. Everything was once again going smoothly. From Seattle the tour dipped inland by rail once more, to Dayton and Walla Walla, then down the mighty Columbia to Dallas (the Dalles) and Portland, Oregon. By February 18, buoyed by the renewed applause, Sullivan was back in San Francisco for what turned out to be the longest stop on the trip, twenty-two days.[37]

So far the West had presented John L. with amateurs only: Robinson, Le Gouriff, and Lang. But now a professional prizefighter offered himself. He was another (and unrelated) Robinson, George M., member of the sports-minded Olympic Club. Robinson had boxed and beaten Slade the year before, during the San Francisco stopover of the Maori and Jem Mace. He arranged the bout through Al Smith, the latter agreeing that if Robinson stayed the four rounds he would receive five hundred dollars and a healthy share of the gross receipts. If not, he would get only one-third the gross. Looking toward a real fight at last, Sullivan patched things up with Patsy Hogan, declaring Hogan's saloon his headquarters for this stay and making inroads on Patsy's liquor supply.[38]

Five days after his arrival, and during the Robinson negotiations, Sullivan's combination lost its first fighter. Herbert Slade had tired of, as he put it, being nightly pounded by John L. from hell to breakfast for only fifty dollars a week. An enraged Sullivan sought him out in Harry Maynard's notorious dive. Seizing the Maori, he butted him in the face. They brawled until the police arrived, to find a drunken Slade lying atop an equally inebriated champion. Back East, the *Virginia Chronicle* moaned that almost everywhere in the West, Sullivan "has almost invariably exhibited the brutal side of his character—the people are getting disgusted with him." Certainly Slade was; he left the combination amid rancorous name calling on both sides.[39]

Slade's departure proved inconsequential. The prospect of a real fight drew the previously alienated San Francisco fans like a magnet. On March 6 Mechanics' Pavilion was overwhelmed by a mob. Over twelve thousand eventually got inside after the doors opened at 5 P.M., while five thousand more milled around in the streets. One hundred police officers had difficulty in handling the mass. The best tickets were going for five dollars. In the center of the building stood a twenty-four-foot ring raised four feet from the floor. The structure was provided with something called the Williams Safety Extension, or Automatic Ama-

teur Catcher—perhaps the first use of a ring apron. From ringside, tiers
of seats rose sharply, their occupants packed in like sardines in a box.
Over these loomed the galleries, five rows deep. Above everything
scrambled adventurous boys, who perched on beams, dangled from
the rafters, and scrunched themselves into window sills. Shortly before
the fight the crowd was mesmerized by a man who coolly walked on
a platform near the ceiling, some eighty feet high; he finally sat down
directly over the ring, legs dangling. This individual's task was to ring
the bell, which he did enthusiastically throughout the bout.

Sullivan took this opponent somewhat more seriously than the previous seven. Robinson had been training for the previous two weeks
while Sullivan was migrating from saloon to saloon. But John L. had
cut back his drinking after the clash with Slade and his weight had
fallen to 205. Robinson was still the much lighter man, at 170. The
champion, for the first time on his tour, had cropped his hair short
once again, indicating he was intent on his work.

The throng murmured with approval as both men climbed into the
ring, Robinson clad in red tights under a long overcoat. It was to have
been a fight with three-ounce gloves, but the authorities insisted on
eight ounces. When this change was announced to the house, it brought
forth prolonged hissing. The referee, Thomas Chandler, took his place.
Each side was permitted its own timekeeper, in addition to the bell-
ringer in the rafters, and Sullivan's was none other than his friend
William Muldoon, who happened to be in San Francisco at the time.

As the two boxers met, everyone in attendance could see that Robinson had studied Tug Wilson's book; in fact, it was the Wilson fight
all over again. During the first round the challenger slipped and dodged
all over the ring, falling down eight times in the process. The second
round saw more of the same, with John L. becoming increasing frustrated by his inability to land a solid punch. By the third Sullivan was
at last getting home with some shots, but he had not fought this long
in earnest at any point in the tour and was obviously tiring. Robinson's
backers were jubilant. In the final round John L. lost his composure
and got his tormentor in a headlock, which was allowed under the
London Rules but not by Queensberry. With Robinson thus immo-
bilized, Sullivan drove him to the floor. But it was not a knockout.
Robinson continued to drop until the end, and lasted the fight.[40]

Most of the natives felt the hometown man had disgraced the city.
Sullivan, the obvious victor, was loudly cheered, and Robinson, as
loudly booed. The *Chronicle* lambasted Robinson for "showing the
white feather" and reported that he had dropped to the canvas no less
than sixty-six times in four rounds, meaning that Robinson had gone
down, on average, every ten seconds, which would have made him
more yo-yo than human. Patsy Hogan described the fight as "the most

disgusting fiasco ever witnessed in this city." Whatever it was, both men made money. The gate had topped $20,000; Sullivan took $10,000 and Robinson $5,000. The money was the only thing the challenger received; his local reputation was gone. The day after the fight he and Steve Taylor got into a fracas in the barroom of Baldwin's Hotel, and shortly thereafter George M. Robinson was unanimously expelled from the Olympic Club.[41] Such were the penalties for "showing the white feather" in the all-male world.

Regardless of the seriocomic outcome, the match had been good for Sullivan's pocketbook. With the windfall he paid off the remaining mortgage on the Washington Street Saloon and sent $5,000 back home to his mother.[42] Annie left for home as well, escorted by the loyal Mike. Now down to seven—Smith, Moran, Menzinger, and the four remaining fighters (Sullivan, Taylor, McCoy, and Gillespie)—the combination headed southward on March 11 aboard the Southern Pacific.

For a full week the group relaxed in Southern California, which was still a lazy, lethargic quilt of small farms and ranches. The fighters performed to small crowds in Los Angeles and San Bernardino, both communities being little more than villages (although Los Angeles was then in the midst of the first of several real estate booms). Then across the desert, following the valley of the Gila River most of the way, to Tucson in Arizona Territory. They arrived only days after the tough and vicious Apache leader, Geronimo, had been met at the Mexican border by the U. S. cavalry and, with his eighty followers, escorted to the San Carlos Reservation. For the first time in years all the Apache war bands were sequestered, at least temporarily, and the Southwest was relatively safe. The residents of Tucson, including the community's "representative men," therefore gathered at the Park Theater to see the pugilists. With Slade gone, Sullivan was now sparring first with McCoy and then winding up with Taylor. The fighters were loafing by now, merely going through the motions. The act was badly cribbed, as well; one Tucson observer timed Sullivan's three rounds with Taylor as lasting forty-two, thirty-five, and thirty seconds.[43]

Next to storied Tombstone. This dusty collection of adobe and brick was a national sensation, famed alike for its silver output and its anarchy in the streets. The Earps and Doc Holliday had met the Clanton gang at the OK Corral less than three years before, and the wild days were still in progress. There had been a payroll holdup of a copper mining company down in Bisbee, only a few miles from the border, and four people had been killed. Five of the "Bisbee bandits" were housed in the Tombstone jail, and the curious pugilists asked to see them. The condemned men and the boxers got along famously, laughing and joking with one another. One of the murderers, Tex Howard, avowed that their jailer, a diminutive sheriff named Ward, could beat

Sullivan. "How's that?" John L. responded. "He don't look like a fighter." "Well, he ain't," drawled Tex, "but he'll knock five of us out in one round next Friday morning, all the same." And so it was: Tex and his compatriots were hanged on March 28.[44]

Sullivan did not stay around to see the gallows do its work. The combination was off to Deming, in New Mexico Territory, where only a few years before "Billy the Kid" (William Bonney) had been a byword for ruthlessness. In Deming and El Paso, Texas, the boxers gave small shows, as they had in Tombstone, and then switched from the Southern Pacific to the Texas & Pacific and headed for Dallas via Fort Worth, Denison, and Sherman. Then south again, through Corsicana, Waco, Austin, and San Antonio. Heading east once more, they appeared in Houston before reaching the Gulf Coast at Galveston. The combination had gone through Texas like a whirlwind, appearing in eleven communities in thirteen days.

The western swing was over. In a little more than three months Sullivan's aggregation had appeared in every state and territory of the plains, mountains, and Far West with the exception of the Dakota and Idaho territories and the Indian Territory, which eventually became Oklahoma. Measured merely by a graph of mileage versus time, their achievement was breathtaking. Naturally, the pace was telling on everyone. Slade was gone, Smith was often absent in the next city doing the groundwork for their arrival, and there were the tensions usual among people cooped up in one another's company for extended periods. John L. was drinking, too, not steadily but sporadically, and no one in the combination knew when his craving for alcohol might flare up again. But they were making money; for Sullivan and Smith, the amounts were fabulous by the standards of the day. These two would glean more from their project than the great majority of the miners in the far-flung western camps and towns would earn in a lifetime. Measured by this yardstick, the Grand Tour was already a success. But there were still thousands of miles to go; the Southland lay ahead.

## III

Galveston was more Gulf than Texas. Its oppressive summer humidity was only occasionally lifted by a coastal breeze, and its main businesses were shipping and cotton. The travelers were eager to get back to a familiar city; they had swept through the Longhorn State looking forward to a rest in New Orleans, and Sullivan had yet to be challenged by any of its residents. A large audience witnessed the act's debut at the Tremont Opera House on April 9. The Galvestonians had never seen professional pugilists and rubbernecked at the ring costumes. No ladies were present, but to the surprise of those who anticipated an assemblage of toughs, the respectable citizens were in the majority.

The following evening an unexpected challenger appeared. Al Marx, a six-foot, twenty-three-year-old Pennsylvanian, decided to have a go at the champion. Marx had worked for a time in Kansas before coming to Galveston the year before; he was employed in a local cotton yard. The crowd, on seeing him mount the stage, cheered loudly but expected the worst: Marx was beefy, chubby-faced, and had a "soft look." He was knocked down three times in fifty-five seconds, an ordeal that ended with him curled in a fetal position and Sullivan, looming over him, asking if he wanted more. Afterward, Marx compared the champion's blows to "standing under a pile-driver encased in a football."[45]

At last, New Orleans. Here the pugilists were in familiar surroundings again, Sullivan in particular having made many friends during his stay in early 1882 while training for the Paddy Ryan fight. Al Smith had arranged for a boxer named Johnny Reilly to join them there, but Reilly was ill. A hurried wire to New York produced Mike Donovan, who once again brought the number of performers to five. Sullivan greeted reporters in his suite at the St. Charles, expansive and ebullient, gulping ale by the bottle. He received word that Annie had given birth to a ten-pound boy, John, Jr., on April 12. The newspapermen noted the champion's weight, now back to 230, and his luxurious mustache. In response to questions about the tour, Sullivan exaggerated only slightly, claiming he had knocked out twelve men to date (there had been eight knockouts, plus the victory over George Robinson). The profits were over $100,000, he said, which was close to the truth. He would quit the ring within six months.[46] This last was a constant refrain on the tour, reflecting both pressure from Annie and his growing exhaustion with the hectic schedule.

The two New Orleans exhibitions were successful. Now the performing order featured Donovan and McCoy in the opening bout, then Taylor and Gillespie. Sullivan would be introduced, to spar with Donovan, followed by the continuing crowd favorites, McCoy and Gillespie. Sullivan would close by boxing Taylor. John L.'s hotel, as usual, was packed with gawkers, and as he progressed to the theater for each performance, a crowd of men and boys ran screaming after the carriage, shouting his name. The performances, scaled from fifty cents to one dollar, were sold out, and hundreds were turned away. Al Smith was all smiles.[47]

Over the Louisville and Nashville now, the same line that had borne Sullivan to the Ryan fight two years before, and on to Mobile, Alabama. There the citizenry was disappointed by the sparring; like many other crowds, particularly those in the West, they expected blood. Nevertheless, paunch and all, John L. was still impressive. "He is a powerfully-built man and the muscles of his shoulders work like machinery." Next, Montgomery and then into Georgia, through Columbus and Macon to Savannah. The crowds in the old Confederacy were substantial, mobbing the champion at the railway stations and hotels.[48] Southern hospitality was everywhere in evidence, and John L. responded in fullest measure.

By the time he left Savannah he was dead drunk, having to be poured off the train in Charleston, South Carolina, and hurried to his hotel. Despite a sheeting rain a large crowd kept a vigil outside, while the hall inside was comfortably filled with local sportsmen. When he finally got to the Academy of Music for the performance, Sullivan still was intoxicated; when announced, "he waddled from the wings like a very fat and very drunken duck." The audience began to hiss as he lightly sparred with McCoy (a temporary change in the routine), and John L. stopped, confronted the crowd from the stage, and admitted he had been drinking. Some cheering greeted this confession, but when the champion came out for the last match with Taylor, the disappointed spectators began to file out, leaving a half-empty house.[49]

Back into Georgia, through Augusta to Atlanta. The binge was still in progress. Attendees at DeGive's Opera House were told that Sullivan was "sick" in his hotel room. Eventually he showed up, to stagger through three rounds of charade with Taylor, the crowd hissing all the while. The orchestra's music was the only redeeming feature, as the whole show lasted only forty-nine minutes. The Atlantans had been gypped. After the bouts a reporter found the other boxers trying to help John L. over what the champion called an attack of "vertigo."[50]

Finally, he began to sober up and regain his normal spirits. In Chattanooga, Tennessee, a rumor got started that Sullivan was an impostor. When he appeared on stage, the local police demanded that he establish his identity. John L. blazed back with the challenge that if any man in the house could face him for five minutes, that person would get one thousand dollars. The show went on. By this time, however, the combination had raised expectations in its audiences that could not be satisfied. Al Smith was increasingly preoccupied with baby-sitting for the well-oiled Sullivan, and he had hired a new advance man named Hugh Coyle. Coyle was proceeding throughout the Southland, loudly advertising that the boxers were in tip-top shape and that "there would be no playing" in their act. Crowds thus were inevitably being disappointed by the travel-weary quintet. Everywhere there was a letdown, in Birmingham, Nashville, Memphis.[51] And no challengers were coming forward to give a fillip to the entertainment.

At last another victim was found, in Hot Springs, Arkansas. He was Dan Henry, a solidly built Irishman but a ring novice. Sullivan, billed in Arkansas as "the modern Samson," knocked him out in the first round. The positive side to Coyle's fanfare had now begun to produce a renewed interest in contesting the champion. Frank Moran was ill, and Menzinger was handling the announcing chores as well as taking tickets, but the group kept going. There were no takers in Little Rock, but there Sullivan received word that a bricklayer, William Fleming, was awaiting his return to Memphis.[52]

Fleming was a bit of a local character. His friends claimed he was tough as nails, offering as proof the fact that he had fallen four stories from a scaffold, landed on an iron sidewalk grating, and escaped uninjured. He was serious about meeting Sullivan, training by drinking nothing but soda water and punching sandbags. The evening of the fight, however, his resolution weakened somewhat, and he downed several drinks before going to the Exposition Building to confront the champion.

News that a Memphis native would go for the thousand dollars packed the house. The standing crowd was four rows deep and overflowed onto the stage. Over three thousand people, by far the best audience since New Orleans, formed "a swaying mass of perpendicular humanity." As a preliminary they were treated to a "coon fight" between Nelse Scott and Bill O'Neill, as well as the sparring matches of the combination. Finally Frank Moran, now back on his feet, was on stage and introducing Fleming as an amateur boxer of Memphis and Sullivan as "champion pugilist of the world"—the standard opening. Both men stripped to the waist and put on soft gloves. Fleming appeared to be somewhat slender, especially when seen beside Sullivan, but, after all, he had *trained*. They squared off. Immediately John L. sent a right hand whistling in under Fleming's jaw, and the bricklayer fell like a clod, his back slamming into the chair in the corner and his side striking the hard pine floor with a dull thud. Sullivan stripped off his own gloves and called for aid. A pitcher of water was emptied into Fleming's face, a glass at a time, and finally he recovered. William Fleming had the distinction of being Sullivan's (and perhaps anyone's) quickest knockout: two seconds.[53]

The very next day, in Nashville, Sullivan received another challenge, his third in four days. His advertised opponent, one William E. Stern, declined to appear, so in his place a man named Enos Phillips volunteered to go on. Over fourteen hundred people, chiefly "the best citizens of Nashville," were gathered in the Buckingham Theater for the bout, and there would have been more had news of the match not been generated at the last second. At his first glimpse of Phillips, Frank Moran was appalled. The Tennessean was little more than a beardless stripling of 150 pounds. Moran tried to convince him to fight one of the smaller men in the combination: McCoy, Gillespie, or Donovan.

Sullivan would outweigh him by eighty pounds. But Phillips, like Gypsy Miles in St. Louis, wanted a reputation; bring on Sullivan!

Sullivan himself wanted no part of it, especially when he saw the youth carefully take off his hat, coat, and vest, preparing to fight in his shirt sleeves. For three rounds John L. moved cautiously around the stage and lightly sparred with Phillips, a display of generosity appreciated by the crowd. But enough was enough, especially when a thousand dollars was at stake. In the fourth Enos was suddenly confronted by the champion's bull-like rush, and what had been light taps turned into pile drivers. Sullivan battered the hapless lad into the wings three straight times. Finally he cornered him against the backdrop and had started Phillips's nose bleeding when the chief of police emerged from behind the scenes and led the protesting young man from the stage.[54] Like Miles, Enos Phillips had proved himself.

After Nashville it was north to the Ohio River and down to Saint Louis again, via Louisville, Cincinnati, and Evansville, Indiana. In Louisville the enthusiastic Coyle did his work so well that the locals were convinced the other members of the combination were paid by Sullivan not to spar but to be knocked senseless by the champion on a nightly basis. The ultimate revelation, of a badly out-of-shape pugilist, still did not dampen their warm welcome. There was talk that Sullivan would fight Mervine Thompson of Cleveland. Although the champion was willing, he said that Thompson was a "nigger" and that he, John L., would pass him by on the street. Nothing came of the match. Meanwhile, Pete McCoy, who for months had endured Sullivan's drunken rages and scrapped away with Mike Gillespie, amicably left the combination for a prizefight with Duncan McDonald in Montana.[55]

The second stop in Cincinnati produced a mayoral intervention against sparring, so Sullivan agreed to play baseball in a game between two amateur clubs. Nearly four thousand people were in attendance, paying twenty-five cents each, to see John L. pitch, but a downpour broke up the contest in the second inning. In Saint Louis the combination sparred before a crowded house, including Buffalo Bill, at the People's Theater. To replace McCoy, Al Smith had arranged for Florrie Barnett, a pudgy heavyweight, to spar with Sullivan. For the rest of the tour Barnett and Donovan would open, followed by Taylor and Gillespie. Sullivan would first spar with Barnett; then after Donovan and Gillespie had appeared, John L. would conclude against Taylor. The Saint Louis stop was enlivened by the surprise appearance of Tom Allen in the theater. Allen was promoting a local fighter, Fred Zachritz, and loudly denounced Sullivan's reluctance to fight his man right there. Sullivan could not oblige; although his bond had been lifted from the arrest in November, he knew he would be forced to pay and possibly wind up in jail if he put on the gloves for real with Zachritz. To the disappointment of the spectators, the fight never came off.[56]

The last lap, now, up through Illinois into Michigan. Everyone was exhausted. It was spring, and to a man they wanted to get home. As a result, their final appearances had the look of travesty. The combination drew poorly in Springfield, Illinois—a dozen businessmen surrounded by local hoodlums. Al Smith was almost arrested, but the show went on, while a weary-looking group of sad-eyed fiddlers dosed out music. Only 250 people showed up, including perhaps 50 youngsters who sneaked onto the roof of Amory Hall to peep through the skylights. Only two hundred dollars was in the pot when Menzinger finished counting. Much the same happened in Bloomington, Illinois, and in Michigan along the way to Detroit: Kalamazoo, Grand Rapids, Saginaw, Bay City, and Jackson. The disparity between Coyle's advance publicity about the terrific hitting that was coming to town and the actual shuffling and pawing of five weary fighters was ludicrous. In Detroit the large and socially respectable audience was disgusted with the light sparring, and one reporter grumbled that "the mighty Sullivan . . . is as fat as a prize hog."[57]

It all ended with a whimper, but exactly on schedule, as Sullivan sparred Barnett in Toledo on May 23, 1884. From there John L. headed home, via New York, and was back in Boston four days later. Welcomed by a small band of friends, including City Councilman Thomas Denny, the champion significantly went, not home to his wife and baby, but to his saloon. Finally he reached the Lovering Place house and for the first time saw his son. The *Police Gazette* fancifully pictured him "at home again," dandling John, Jr., on his knee.[58]

## IV

Al Smith lost no time in trumpeting the success of the Grand Tour. The promoter himself had prospered mightily, taking in at least forty thousand dollars in return for what had been, for him, almost a solid year of planning, huckstering, and pampering grown men. But the signs of a split between Sullivan and Smith were evident. Al had had to play nursemaid once too often during John L.'s sprees. Only with difficulty had he kept the tour on track in the numerous instances— Pottsville, Denver, San Francisco, Savannah—when his charge had gone off the wagon in a big way. Smith had frequently seen Sullivan perform drunk. As a member in good standing of the cult of masculinity he admired the champion's resilience; as a businessman he was disgusted.[59] The two men would never work together again.

Indeed, the nation had been treated to Sullivan at his worst. The presence of Annie for half the tour had not diminished the champion's

capacity for boozing in the slightest. In his melancholic spells of al-
cohol-induced rage, John L. was fit company for no one, not even his
fellow boxers and friends. Helpless, they could only watch each binge
run its wildly careening course—if some of them did not join in themselves. Amazingly, only one performance is known to have been canceled because of Sullivan's excesses: the second appearance in Denver.
This meant, however, that audiences throughout the country were often
treated to a shambling drunk walking through a stage act, rather than
a muscular advocate of the manly art crisply showing his stuff. The
performance in Charleston was probably the nadir, but there had been
many other low points.

He did it all so *publicly*. There was no ambiguity whatsoever about
John L. Sullivan. When he was drunk, people saw it, and when he was
at the top of his form, people saw that, too. The other side of the coin
was his open, honest disposition, coupled with his warm, sincere generosity. Several times during the tour local men would come forward
to fight, not to win the $1,000 but to gain themselves a name in the
community. The champion would refer them to McCoy or Gillespie
and give them a gift of twenty-five or fifty dollars. The stubborn ones,
like Gypsy Miles or Enos Phillips, had to be dealt with, but everywhere
his liberality, in the ring and in the saloon, was on display. He shared
his bounty with his parents, as well, making sure that they were secure
in the ownership of their home. In Boston his fame was even more
pronounced. It was rumored that business in the Washington Street
saloon had increased 60 percent since his return from the exhibition
tour.[60]

What had really been accomplished? The most amazing thing, perhaps, was that Smith had miraculously kept his wayward outfit to the
backbreaking schedule. As to the fights, Sullivan would eventually
claim that he had knocked out fifty-nine men. Frank Moran, years
later, placed the number at thirty-nine. The actual number of knockouts was eleven—James McCoy, Miles, Hefey, Sheehan, Fred Robinson, Le Gouriff, Lang, Marx, Henry, Fleming, and Phillips—and there
was one other victory, over George Robinson. But the numbers did
not matter as much as the accomplishment. Sullivan could rightfully
say he had challenged America, and won. Few noted that the victories
had come over the likes of iron puddlers, railway men, fishermen, and
cotton workers.

As to profits, Moran estimated them at $110,000 after expenses to-
taling $44,000 were subtracted. John L. placed the total receipts at
$187,000 and the expenses at $42,000.[61] In actuality he probably had
cleared over $80,000 for himself as a result of the project. In 1884 the
president of the United States, Chester A. Arthur, was paid $25,000 a
year, a sum that had not changed since Washington's day. A good city

lawyer might make twice that much. Physicians, as a rule, lagged far behind. A university professor, if he was lucky, might make $2,500. No professional athlete in modern history had ever enjoyed such commercial success. The only other professionals in the country, pedestrians, cyclists, and ballplayers, barely eked out a living. Mike ("King") Kelly ("Slide, Kelly, slide!") would receive a top-drawer salary of $5,000 to captain the Boston Red Sox in 1887.[62] Sullivan had become a money machine.

Even more importantly, the Grand Tour brought a famous public figure into the byways of America. Main Street was able to *see* the champion. Beyond that, he was celebrated. Everywhere, regardless of the size or location of the community, the nation's males turned out in huge numbers to get a gander at the Great John L. They flocked to the railway stations, laid siege to the hotels, and jammed the theaters. Conservatively estimated, over one hundred thousand men and boys actually laid eyes on the champion during the tour. Only four years before, in Cincinnati, he had fought John Donaldson before thirty people for a handful of change. Now, his name was familiar in every corner of the country. They *knew* what he looked like in Savannah, Tucson, and Walla Walla. In and of himself, John L. Sullivan had become big business, a celebrity, and a public disgrace, all rolled into one. He was at the apex.

# CHAPTER SEVEN

# Life at the Apex:
# Time of Troubles
# (1884—1887)

On the surface, all was well with the champion. He had returned from an epochal and successful tour of the entire country to the arms of his wife, who had just given him his son and namesake. All Boston knew his name and where he lived; the substantial three-story brick house at 4 Lovering Place bore a big silver plate on the door with the name "Sullivan." Inside, Annie had found room for the homely overstuffed furniture of the period amid the clutter of her husband's sporting pictures and costly presents from admirers. John L. Sullivan's working-class parents lived in middle-class comfort in the three-story wooden row house on Parnell Street. The champion was a businessman, with a supposedly prosperous saloon. He was a member of Boston's swank Cribb Club, "the most high-toned athletic organization" in the city. He had friends, it seemed, almost everywhere. Superficially, his life skirted the boundaries of the idyllic. Sergeant Daly, of Boston's Second Precinct (John L.'s district), offered the following observation to an inquiring reporter:

> Sullivan is a very peaceful man at home, and only got into trouble with our officers once when he was tormented by a man, and he struck him, breaking his jaw, which he afterward paid for. [This was the saloon assault on Charles Robbins in April 1882.] He is thought well of here by all, and has many good friends among the upper classes, who will give him anything he asks for.[1]

Despite the seemingly placid domestic existence, the truth was that Sullivan's home life, despite the new baby, was fractured beyond repair. His drinking habits were only becoming worse. And against him the forces of "law and order" were marshaling once again. The years just ahead, while chockablock with the rewards of fame, would provide him with little but trouble, both in his public and personal life—and most of it he would bring on himself.

I

John L. agreed to spar with Charlie Mitchell on June 30, 1884, at Madison Square Garden. The match, under the Queensberry Rules, should have been a crowd-pleaser, as fight fans remembered Mitchell's cunning effectiveness against the champion the previous year. Billy Madden, who now ran a saloon on Thirteenth Street, was confident Mitchell could win. Both men established training camps and set to work, in Sullivan's case with something less than total dedication.[2]

On the scheduled night over five thousand people showed up, testimony to continued popular interest in the champion. Rumors had been flying that Mitchell had malaria and that Sullivan was on an extended debauch. The weather was very warm outside, and the Garden atmosphere was unusually foul. On top of this the crowd, which paid two dollars for general admission and up to twenty-five dollars for box seats, was forced to swelter for almost three hours until John L. appeared. Among the impatient throng were the Garden's owner, William H. Vanderbilt; dapper Roscoe Conkling, wilting rapidly in the muggy heat; and the usual assortment of aldermen, judges, and city politicians.

When Sullivan finally shambled toward the ring, the crowd could see easily that he was drunk. Gossip sped around the hall that he had been drinking wine at the Ashland House. Ascending to the ring and leaning unsteadily on the ropes, the champion sheepishly addressed the house in words recorded by several reporters: "Gentlemen, I am sick and not able to box. The doctor is here, and this is the first time I have disappointed you." Even the most fight-hardened fans were shocked. Attired in a somber suit of black, Sullivan, with mustache gone, displayed bloated and out-of-focus features. With unkempt hair, unshaven face, and half-closed, bloodshot eyes, he was the very picture of a man at the end of a binge. Alderman Thomas J. Denny of Boston rose and screamed: "John! Don't have it! Fight him!"

The master of ceremonies, William O'Brien, tried to quiet the crowd, announcing that Dominick McCaffery was ready to take Sullivan's place. The doctor mentioned by John L. tried to say a few words in exculpation, but his voice went unheard in the rising chorus of disapproval. The champion left the stage amid uncomplimentary remarks from all sides. Angriest of all were the vendors, who now lost their market for sliced watermelon, lemonade, roasted peanuts, candies, ice water, chalk statues, and pictures of Sullivan and Mitchell. Amid the furor Clubber Williams, on hand as always, had his pockets picked and lost his watch.[3]

It was a fiasco. Sullivan fled to Boston, accompanied only by Annie, brother Mike, and the steadfast O'Brien. Annie loyally maintained that her man had not been drunk, but only sick. Numerous witnesses told a different story. The day before, John L. had left Boston with Annie, Pete McCoy, and about thirty assorted sportsmen, drinking their way to New York. Things got so bad that McCoy tried to stop the spree by throwing a brandy bottle out of the railway car window, but to no avail. The boozing continued all night in room 61 of the Ashland House and into Monday, the day of the fight. Some said the champion had been drinking since the previous Wednesday. Others claimed he had been involved in two Boston saloon scraps, on Thursday and Friday nights, in one of which a pistol was flashed. At any rate, the New York fight crowd was enraged, the more so because it was said that John L. had taken two thousand dollars of the gate money back to Boston with him. The metropolitan press lost no time in conveying the details of the humiliation to the rest of the country.[4]

"He has forever disgraced himself in the eyes of the general and the sporting public," thundered Richard Kyle Fox. The manager of the Ashland House intoned that Sullivan and his buddies would not be welcome at his hostelry again. For the first time, no triumphant reception from the Boston faithful awaited him. An official of the Manhattan Temperance Union announced that he intended to go to Boston to win John L. over to cold water. The *Daily Tribune* asserted that good would come of all this, that Sullivan's excesses would check ruffians and lessen lawlessness. Even the ultraloyal Boston fans were put on their guard, and a poet among them issued a warning:

> A swollen head, the papers said,
>   Had caused our John to flunk.
> It wasn't beer or sudden fear—
>   'Twas just a champagne drunk.
>
> Take heed, dear John—your name's not gone
>   To seek oblivion's rest;
> With strength refuse the festive booze,
>   Add honors to your crest.
>
> The braggart bold who caught a cold,
>   One week the fight before,
> Would homeward flee, were he to see
>   You were yourself once more.
>
> For Boston's sake, this advice take,
>   But chiefly for your own;
> And if you do we'll raise you to
>   The pugilistic throne.[5]

Sullivan knew he had stumbled badly. Years later he would remark of the Mitchell fiasco that "I was in no condition to fight." Despite his considerable circumspection in arguing that he had thought his opponent unable to appear, and despite his claim that numerous counterfeit tickets had made refunds to the angry audience impossible, John L. realized that he had come across that muggy June evening as a drunkard and a swindler. "I grew careless in eating and drinking," he said with bravura understatement, and "was incapacitated through sickness, caused by my own fault." Throughout the summer he did nothing to redress the shambles he had made of his already suspect reputation. In fact he showed up at an August benefit for the loyal alderman, Tom Denny, in Boston's Institute Building in much the same condition he had displayed earlier in the Garden. This time, in front of twenty-five hundred people, he managed to tamely spar with McCaffery, Steve Taylor, and Denny himself, but his intoxication was evident to everyone.[6]

In the classic pattern of the alcoholic, John L. was rapidly alienating even his closest friends. Al Smith had had enough. After shepherding Sullivan around the country for the better part of a year, he had witnessed the debacle in the Garden and sadly announced he would have nothing further to do with the champion—a considerable assertion, given the small fortune Smith had reaped from the Grand Tour. So Sullivan was rudderless, both professionally and personally. He passed his time playing baseball, in one game between two "wine clubs" managing to get conked in the head by a thrown ball as he ran to first base.

In the early fall of 1884 he took on yet another "manager," a gambler from Chicago named Patrick F. Sheedy, whom he had come to know through Parson Davies. Sheedy was a loud-talking, brassy promoter when he was not flicking pasteboards across a gaming table or betting on horses. Like John L. he had been intended for the priesthood as a boy, but the cassock obviously had not taken. Sheedy, with what truth nobody knew, claimed he had never used tobacco in any form. He was as tall as Sullivan and almost as heavy, his broad, smooth face continually creased in a smile. Sheedy was every inch a hustler and a dandy, his high forehead capped by long, wavy, black hair and his dress of the appropriate flash.[7] This was the man who would be with Sullivan for the next three years. He was a considerable distance from the admiring, friendly Madden and the hardworking Al Smith. Indeed, he might have been Central Casting's idea of the glad-handing fight manager with heart of stone.

A hustler Sheedy might be, but he was no fool, and he soon realized that the Sullivan image needed a quick refurbishing. There had been autumn floods in Ohio, and Pat cleverly arranged for John L. to spar with John Laflin in the Garden on November 10 for the benefit of the victims. The fight was scheduled for four rounds under the Queensberry Rules. The promoters, with painful memories of the abortive Mitchell affair, arranged for every ticket to have a coupon attached in case refunds were required. Sheedy got Patsey Sheppard to once again force John L. into training, and Patsey, by now experienced with the wiles of his charge, allowed Sullivan only a few bottles of ale a day, crammed him full of beefsteak, mutton chops, and toast, and exercised him so much that he slimmed from 231 pounds to 196.

Sullivan wore a two-day growth of beard into the ring, but he was in better condition than he had been in a year. That was fortunate for him, since the Society Adonis was a bigger man, standing six feet two and weighing over two hundred pounds. Laflin, of course, remembered Sullivan from their three-round exhibition back in March 1883, and the New Yorker intended a surprise. The problem was his age: he claimed to be thirty-six but was probably forty-two, much too antiquated to face Sullivan when the champion was anywhere near fighting trim. Once again, however, John L. packed the Garden; over five thousand people came, many curious to see whether Sullivan's summer disgrace was only a passing storm. Sheedy and the other promoters had kept the ticket prices at the same high levels, but this deterred no one. Clubber Williams, with his one hundred picked constables, again oversaw an audience sprinkled with politicians, bankers, brokers, pugilists, at least one general (Anson McCook), and a man who rivaled Sullivan as a national celebrity—Thomas Edison, then at the peak of his inventive powers.[8] Aristocratic types from Murray Hill and the Union Club occupied the twenty-five-dollar boxes, although they were separated from the hoi polloi only by a small railing. A bluish fog of cigar smoke was only dimly cut by the yellow rays of the building's many gas jets. White-aproned waiters scurried about, yelling, "Orders, gents, gimme y'r orders."

The crowd rapidly created pandemonium as the referee, Mike McDonald, brought the two men together. The Society Adonis sported a slight, curling mustache and smiled in a "sickly way" as he advanced to the center of the ring. Laflin tried a bear hug, but Sullivan instantly pounded him down in a corner. One of Laflin's seconds, Billy Edwards, helped him to his feet (a violation of Queensberry Rule Six, but no matter) and Laflin managed to last the round. In round two the older man was knocked down three times, and Sullivan slugged him once while Laflin was on his knees (another violation). Laflin was staggering, and by now the mismatch was apparent. John L., to spectators at ringside, was "blowing a trifle," but he appeared composed. Laflin tried more hugging tactics in round three but was knocked down again by an obviously tiring champion. In the final round John L. wrestled Laflin down (yet another violation) and then drove him into the corner with such force that the head of the Society Adonis shivered the ring post. That was enough. The champion, badly winded, had nevertheless proved that his fists could still bring a man down, and that was all the evidence many of his followers seemed to need. After enjoying a post-fight massage with whiskey, Sullivan pocketed almost eight thousand dollars after expenses.[9]

Sheedy's first exercise in rubbing some of the tarnish off the champion's crown had been a success. The flood victims had their money, Sullivan and Sheedy had theirs, and John L. had been welcomed back to New York. With the indignant Ashland House closed to them, the boxing entourage had pitched camp at the Monico Villa, way up on 146th Street, and there Sullivan greeted a continuous stream of admirers arriving in anything a horse could draw: buggies, coupes, barouches, sulkies, even dog carts. One correspondent counted over one hundred calling cards left by female admirers. "John L. Sullivan is the biggest man in town," asserted a special dispatch on November 15.[10]

## II

The law-and-order crowd remained unimpressed—doubly so, because the irrepressible Fox had arranged for a real prizefight under their very noses, and only a week after the benefit for the wretched Ohioans. This time Fox's protégé was another Englishman, Alf Greenfield. Born in Northhampton in 1853, Greenfield was a stocky 5 feet 8 and 162 pounds, with little prize-ring experience. He made his home in Birmingham, where he had originally worked in a rolling mill, and there he received thirty pounds from Fox, who obligingly booked his passage on the steamer *Oregon*. It was Fox's intention that the two boxers fight for something called the *Police Gazette* Diamond Belt, a gaudy affair fifty inches long, eight inches wide, and riddled with two hundred ounces of silver and gold. A ring in the center of the belt was encircled by diamonds, the top featuring a fox's head. The whole was valued at twenty-five hundred dollars, and no one could accuse the Proprietor of lacking promotional zeal. As he had done with Tug Wilson, Fox cordially greeted Greenfield when the *Oregon* docked on November 2.[11]

Sullivan, for his part, stayed on in New York, accepting the admiration of the crowd. Seemingly, he was back in the good graces of his fans. "The lamentable feature of these gatherings of worshippers at the shrine of the slug-god," wrote one disgusted reporter, "is the presence of boys in throngs. Imagine the burning desire of the little rascals to grow up into prize fighters!" Another scribe saw one small urchin tentatively approach the champion and ask his hero what he ate and drank. Blood, nothing but blood, responded John L. "I drain a boy about your size three times a day." The diminutive questioner promptly scrambled away.[12]

As Sullivan basked in this warmer sunlight, plans were afoot to ensure that a "Mitchell fiasco" or even a "Laflin exhibition" would never again take place in New York City. Indeed, Clubber Williams had almost stopped the Laflin fight in the third round; now the authorities planned a crackdown. On November 14 Mayor Franklin Edson wrote the Police Board asking it to prevent all further boxing exhibitions. "I believe that such exhibitions are disgraceful to the city in the higher degree, demoralizing to young men, and in their tendency leading to disrespect of law and order." The next day the obedient Inspector Thorne, who had dispatched the Harbor Police to fruitlessly pursue the fight crowd the night of the brawl on the barge with John Flood, appeared at the Jefferson Market Police Court to assert that he had reason to believe Sullivan and Greenfield were about to violate Section 458 of the Penal Code. This tiresome bit of legalese read as follows:

A person who, within this state, engages in, instigates, aids, encourages, or does any act to further a contention or a fight without weapons between two or more persons, or a fight commonly called a ring or prize fight, either within or without this State, or who sends or publishes a challenge or acceptance of the challenge for such a contention or fight, or carries or delivers such a challenge or acceptance, or trains or assists any person in training or preparing for such a contest or fight, is guilty of a misdemeanor.[13]

The omnibus quality of Section 458 was obviously intended to end prizefighting in the state of New York, but almost everyone had winked at the statute for years. Fox alone would have accumulated enough warrants to paper the walls of his sumptuous offices. Now, however, New York City was in the midst of one of its occasional spates of reform, and Mayor Edson was listening to those ardent advocates of "good government" who believed that the city could be morally purified by eliminating undesirable elements, chief of which was the prizefight crowd.

Accordingly, on Thorne's complaint, Sullivan, Sheedy, Greenfield, and Fox were duly arrested and brought to Judge Patterson's chambers that very afternoon. Both pugilists sturdily contended that they would not fight for a knockout but only for "points." The case was carried over to the State Supreme Court on Monday, November 17. There, Judge Barrett admitted that the "legality" of these exhibitions was difficult to determine in advance. He decided to let the match take place, but ordered that "the blows are to have no relation to the injury or exhaustion of either party." If the fighters went too far, the police were to stop the fight. The charade thus played out, John L. and his entourage left the court building to stamping and shouting from a crowd that flowed out into City Hall Park, increased by an excited mass of youngsters. The fight was on, for the next night.

With the press reporting every detail of the legal wrangling, over seven thousand were drawn to the Garden on Tuesday evening. Edson's efforts had not deterred the swells. Several members of the Union Club showed up wearing the same gloves and apparel in which they had appeared at the wedding of one of the Astor daughters that afternoon. Lord Roscoe Conkling was there as usual, but so were the philanthropist Henry W. Sage, the merchant prince Isidor Straus, the oil and railroad baron Henry M. Flagler, the magnate Cyrus W. Field, and prominent lawyers like Elihu Root and William M. Evarts. Still the hall was only partially filled, as many fans had heard that the bout would be called off. All present could see that Greenfield was but a carbon copy of Tug Wilson, a pudgy torso surmounting a spindly pair of legs.

Initially both fighters appeared tentative, jabbing away at each other and perhaps remembering their fervent promises before Judge Patterson. Greenfield got in a few rights, but as the first round ended, John L. was picking up the tempo. At the start of the second round the champion, now fully into the contest, hurled himself out of his corner and began to pummel away at Greenfield, the Englishman clinching as much as he could. A cut appeared over Alf's left eye, and action in the clinches produced bleeding from behind Sullivan's left ear. Suddenly Greenfield was pinned against the ropes, fighting courageously but clearly outgunned.

At this point, well before the end of the round, Clubber Williams stepped into the ring and separated the two men. He then spoke to the master of ceremonies, Billy Williams of Boston, and Williams was forced to announce that the fight was over, Sullivan had won, and both pugilists were under arrest. The crowd responded in a fury at being denied its treat. A squad of Clubber's men escorted the two fighters to their dressing rooms at the Madison Avenue end of the Garden, listening to a stream of epithets from the handlers and angry fans all the way. After Sullivan and Greenfield had dressed, Clubber and his cops led them out into an unseasonal, hail-like snowstorm. With Williams in the van the column stoically marched across Twenty-seventh Street to Broadway, then north three blocks to the Thirtieth Street Station House. Over a thousand fans accompanied the procession, screaming and jeering at the police. Along the way horsecars and yellow cabs were ordered to halt to make way for the unruly parade.

At the station house both fighters were booked for violations of Section 458, and by now they were in a surly mood. Detective Price, as evidence, displayed four bloody boxing gloves. Sullivan, chewing sullenly on a toothpick, gave his occupation as liquor dealer. Harry Hill made Sullivan's bail, and Fox did the same for Greenfield, but the lesson was crystal clear to the fight crowd. Hill and Police Super-

15. Clubber Williams stops the Sullivan-Greenfield Fight, *National Police Gazette*, December 6, 1884 (William Schutte Collection)

intendent George Washington Walling, on opposite sides of the Section 458 issue, solemnly agreed that this was the end of manly sport in New York City. Fox's sports editor, William Harding, moaned that all that was left was "a quiet time, with a few friends and bare fists." It was nearly midnight before the station house was cleared of the pugilists and their hangers-on. John L. was smuggled into the street through a side door but was pursued by a crowd of curiosity-seekers for blocks.

The next afternoon Sullivan and Greenfield pleaded not guilty and were held on one-thousand-dollar bail to await trial. Greenfield admitted that he was illiterate and helpless to post bail unless a backer came forward. Finally, after Fox, Hill, and a Sixth Avenue liquor dealer named Billy Bennett were rejected as bondsmen, a Canal Street shoemaker, William Beneke, proved agreeable to all sides. By this time Sullivan had recognized that the authorities were at last serious about Section 458, and he and his friends registered deep disgust with the entire proceedings. District Attorney Peter B. Olney, the quintessence of a "good government" official, refused even to admit Fox, Hill, and Bennett to his office to discuss the case, on the ground that they were sporting men.[14]

What had happened? Section 458 had been on the books since 1859, but only recently, in the wake of the Mitchell affair, had it been exhumed by local ministers and, of all organizations, the Society for the Prevention of Cruelty to Animals. The charm of Section 458, for the authorities, was that it nowhere mentioned fists, and thus it rendered moot the prizefighters' defense that they were offering only a gloved exhibition. Seemingly the authorities had Sullivan at their mercy, but they had not reckoned on the intrinsic strength of the cult of masculinity.

That strength was shown within days, at the jury trial on December 17. John L., a diamond stickpin blazing in his cravat, appeared clad in a blue pea jacket and light blue pants; bystanders in the packed courtroom whispered that the champion's sartorial weakness was trousers and that he possessed many pairs, mostly in shades of blue and yellow. The all-male jury was solidly middle class. There were two bookkeepers; five merchants—one in drugs, two in lace, and two in silks and millinery; two brokers; a builder; a machinist; and one man whose occupation was unknown.

These jurors were exactly those elements of the "respectable" population who most tended to tolerate prizefighting. Greenfield's attorney, William F. Howe, was as shrewd as they came, a "Tombs shyster." (He once convinced a jury that his client in a murder trial had pulled the trigger accidentally not once but half a dozen times.) Howe quickly recognized the nature of the case and rejected several potential upper-middle-class jurors for cause.

The twelve heard Superintendent Walling testify that he had ordered the arrests. Then Clubber Williams and Inspector Thorne told their stories, but both men, surprisingly, characterized the fighting as mild. The jury was given the gory gloves to handle. The next day Sullivan's lawyer, Peter Mitchell, produced a stream of witnesses, led by Harry Hill, who insisted that the sparring had been tame, even gentle. Greenfield and Sullivan testified to their undying friendship. Asked by District Attorney Olney if he had been angry during the exhibition, John L. told a whopper: "No, sir. I have never been angry in any of the engagements I have been in." After closing remarks the jury members filed out, obediently taking the blood-soaked gloves with them.

They returned eight minutes later with a unanimous verdict of not guilty. They found that the exhibition had *not* been a "contest for physical supremacy." Olney, who had found other things to do on this second day of the trial, was outmaneuvered, and the cult of masculinity stood fast. There was never any danger of the maximum punishment—one year in jail, a fine of $250, or both—but a conviction would have served the purpose of the good-government men, a clear warning for prizefighters to stay out of New York City. Now, however, Sullivan had for the moment emerged triumphant. Clad this day in trousers of a delicate shade of purple with maidenhair fern design, he regally accepted the courtroom congratulations of his admirers. A young man seeing him at this time registered an impression he carried for half a century: "The high-bridged nose, the broad, jutting chin and the big-boned jaws were strong as carved bronze. Long exposure to sun and wind had stained his cheeks a vivid red. [The observer did not know about the boozing.] He radiated vitality and mastery."[15]

Indeed, as the outraged antiboxing press put it, the trial had been a "roaring farce." Beyond doubt, Sullivan, Greenfield, and their backers had violated Section 458. A popular middle-class organ, *Frank Leslie's*, put the indictment squarely in an unsigned editorial written after the charge but before the acquittal:

> The "science" of pugilism has been making great progress within the last few years, especially in its audacity. These knockdowns and beatings, in public halls and under the protection of the police, have become quite too common. They would not have been permitted twenty years ago, except when skulking in some secret den, and the fact that they have recently been tolerated and widely patronized marks a decline in the sensitiveness of the community. It is well that the police have at last awakened to their duty and put a stop to these fights, arresting the principals and holding them for a breach of the peace. A "boxing bout" in Madison Square Garden, with $10,000 gate money, is nothing less than a prizefight under the protection

of the authorities, and the wearing of gloves does not prevent the violation of law and the disgraceful outbreak of brutal passions. It is time we got back to the old methods. Let prizefighters be once more regarded as outlaws, and not as public "entertainers."[16]

Despite the acquittal, then, Section 458 remained on the books and retained its full capacity to harass, if not convict, pugilists seeking to ply their trade in New York City. The handwriting was on the wall for John L. Sullivan, and during December he turned his attention elsewhere, appearing at a play called *The Lottery of Life* at Brooklyn's Academy of Music and sparring with Mike Donovan between acts. Attendance was very slim, particularly around New Year's Day, and the management decided to close. Sullivan cleared a little over four hundred dollars, profits which would not come close to supporting his spendthrift life-style.[17]

The drinking continued even as John L. and Sheedy arranged a rematch with Greenfield in Boston. The purpose for both men was a quick payday; the champion prepared with "a shave and a shampoo" and continued to drink up to the night of the contest. The two men met on January 12 in Institute Hall under the same terms, except that this time Alf had been smart enough to insist on a 65-35 split of the gate. The attendance was modest, the police were conspicuous, and all the crowd saw was the Englishman dancing away and hugging for four rounds. Even ardent Sullivan fans were displeased; their man was only going through the motions. Beacon Hill and Commonwealth Avenue types stayed home. The *Boston Herald* printed an ominous front-page lead: "John Lawrence Sullivan is losing his popularity as a pugilist."[18]

In growing desperation Sheedy had set up a snap rematch with Paddy Ryan, figuring that a replay of the championship fight would be a certain crowd-pleaser. Paddy had fallen on hard times, unable to hold a steady job; his Chicago saloon had burned down, and he badly needed a payday. He had been pestering John L. for a rematch since the fall of 1883. Ryan, the youngest of eleven children, was trying to support his eighty-year-old mother as well as his own family. The problem: Paddy was overweight and out of shape. Any match without considerable training time for both fighters would be a charade. Sheedy nevertheless took the chance, booking the Garden again on the hunch that William R. Grace, who had returned to the mayor's office in New York City, would be more lenient than Edson.[19]

The publicity drew over five thousand people on January 19. Once again there was generous evidence of silver-headed walking sticks, opera hats, starched white shirtfronts, and evening ulsters. The dependable Conkling was there along with a delegation from the Union Club. Tucked away in a clutch of pugilists was the forgotten John

Flood, no longer "the Bull's Head Terror." Ominously, the police circulated everywhere; Clubber Williams, sporting new gold stripes on his cuffs, and Inspector Thorne were primed to do their duty. Mayor Grace had given the police orders every bit as intractible as those previously issued by Edson before the first Greenfield fight: stop it if they start slugging.

The two fighters barely got a chance to use their four-ounce gloves on each other. Ryan sparred briefly, clamped an illegal neckhold on Sullivan, and then got tattooed for a few seconds before Thorne, who had been standing at ringside, climbed in and stopped the match. Time elapsed: thirty seconds. John L. had appeared badly overweight and winded, even in this brief period. The abortive bout had given both men a windfall profit—Sullivan had generously guaranteed Ryan half the gate—but that was all.[20]

That same day, up in Boston, the Board of Aldermen voted that no licenses for sparring matches would be issued except by unanimous consent. In effect, this closed the Hub to Sullivan at the same time that the New York authorities had made their opposition to prize-fighting crystal clear.[21] The champion had lost the official backing of his hometown just as the press capital of the nation, New York, was closed to him by Section 458. Except for mild exhibitions, he would never box professionally in either city again. It was a shattering double blow, and there was nothing John L. could do about it. He had been denied the right to fight for money in the two most important communities in the country.

## III

Overweight, restless, and drinking constantly, John L. Sullivan lurched from disaster to disaster. Two days after the Ryan match he was back in Boston, driving his carriage down Beacon Street, when the team bolted. John L. lost control and was thrown from the vehicle, which was smashed to flinders before the horses were halted. His head was badly gashed, and he had to be taken home. The following day, the worse for wear, he got into a row in the Delmonico Exchange, butting a youngster in the head. Completely liquored up, he then turned on a bystander who had reproached him, and knocked him cold. This led to a general melee. Eight officers were summoned, and the bartender actually drew a revolver before John L. was subdued. No charges were filed, apparently, but at the end of January there was Sullivan, in Police Court, charged with having abused a horse (not the runaways) on December 28. A witness swore he had seen Sullivan kick one of his carriage team three times in the underribs as it stood in harness and also strike the horse several times with his fist. Another bystander and a patrolman testified to the same effect. John L.'s counsel lamely responded that there had been no abuse, that the horse had been a runaway and a bucker. The fine was one hundred dollars and costs.[22]

John L. rootlessly careened from Boston to New York to Philadelphia during the next two months, spending a lot of time with Arthur Chambers and his other cronies in the Quaker City. He signed for another fight with Ryan in June, "somewhere in Wyoming territory," but this never came off. On March 24 Joe Goss, one of his closest friends in the fight game, died of Bright's disease of the kidneys and liver in his room above his Boston saloon, the Saracen's Head. Although Sullivan's career on the road had separated the two men for a good part of the preceding two years, the loss of the gruff ring veteran (Goss was only forty-six) cut deeply. Sullivan provided a mammoth floral tribute for Joe's burial at Mount Auburn cemetery.[23] Goss's early death, from an alcohol-related disease, should have been a clear warning to John L., but he took no heed.

In the meantime Sheedy had lined up a match with Dominick McCaffery in Philadelphia. He had worked through Frederick A. Bancker, a Pinkerton employee who doubled as a sports correspondent, and Bancker promised to bring the authorities around. But Mayor William B. Smith, taking his cue from New York City, Boston, and some very vociferous local opponents of prizefighting, refused to condone the match, which had become a political hot potato. Both fighters were arrested and placed under five-thousand-dollar bond apiece. Ticket receipts had to be refunded. The sporting fraternity was outraged, but there it was: a third major city had been closed to Sullivan in the space of three months.[24]

On top of this, the champion at last had to face the impending dissolution of his marriage. On February 24 Annie Bates Bailey Sullivan filed a petition in the Supreme Judicial Court of Massachusetts asking for a divorce from her husband on the grounds of cruel and abusive treatment and "gross and confirmed habits of intoxication." Through her attorneys, Ben Butler and Frank L. Washburn, she also asked that John L.'s property be attached for twenty thousand dollars to ensure the support of John, Jr., and herself. The judge granted her a restraining order prohibiting her husband from inflicting bodily injury on her pending the appearance of the case in court.

In asking for a divorce, Annie unwittingly involved herself in the most public celebrity divorce case in American life since the celebrated Beecher-Tilton scandal over ten years before. Although recourse to the divorce courts was increasingly common for middle-class women, who were slowly becoming the legal beneficiaries of the increasing sanctity of family life and the cult of domesticity, such a step was extremely rare for those lower on the social scale, particularly the working-class

Irish.[25] But the boozing, the beatings, and the separations had taken their toll; Annie had had enough.

Inevitably, the press had a field day. On May 27, after a two-day continuance, a horde of the curious joined a legion of reporters in the Supreme Judicial Court Building to hear the Sullivans air their dirty linen in judicial hearing. No one was disappointed. Augustus Russ had replaced Butler as one of Annie's attorneys, while John L. was represented by Charles D. Whitcomb and Thomas E. Barry. Sullivan, probably for religious purposes and out of pride, was determined to contest the divorce. John L. countercharged cruelty and intoxication on the part of his wife.

As the complainant, Annie told a piteous tale, describing several occasions when her husband had beaten her, in one instance marking her face so badly that she had to use house paint to hide the bruises from her friends and the public. After she had left Sullivan several times, Annie testified, they permanently separated on December 8, 1884, she taking their son with her. On cross-examination, Barry elicited the story of her first marriage, although Annie could not remember when she had married Bailey. Barry then set the general tone for the case when he suggested that Annie's friends were "women of ill repute" and asked if she had had any "obstetrical trouble" before her marriage to Bailey.[26]

Annie stood her ground. She was dressed to the nines for the occasion, her imposing figure laced into a close-fitting dress. A black and yellow bonnet was perched saucily atop her head, supporting a decorous half-veil of black. Belying her background, a pair of small diamond drops glistened in her ears. Either Russ and Washburn understood little of courtroom psychology, or Annie had refused to appear as the abused and downtrodden female. She spun a series of vignettes, each one depicting John L. as a cross between a rampaging brute and a confirmed tosspot. She claimed he had hit her during the Grand Tour, even though she was pregnant, in Leadville driving her out of their hotel with a pitcher and in Montana kicking her and throwing objects at her. The worst incident occurred in Natick, Rhode Island, on August 31 of the previous year, said Annie; John L. assaulted her in a drunken rage in front of his brother, Mike, and an outsider, Matilda Adams. Mrs. Adams was produced and corroborated Annie's story. Then Annie's two brothers, Henry and William, appeared to support their sister. Henry, in particular, showed himself a bit of a freeloader and an ingrate (as an unemployed machinist he had stayed with the Sullivans for four months, and had accepted gifts of clothing from John L.), but both men nevertheless offered vivid descriptions of a berserk, liquor-soaked champion.[27]

After the Bates family finished, it seemed to some spectators that Sullivan was a clear and present danger to all of society, never mind the wife. But Annie had slipped, or her attorneys had carelessly let her do so. For one thing, she appeared entirely too composed and well-dressed to satisfy the on-lookers, some of whom put her down as a mere money-grubber. For another, she had freely admitted her husband's generosity: "Mr. Sullivan used to give me most of his money; it was his custom to do so." She admitted she had "a few thousand dollars" from Sullivan on deposit in several savings banks.

The next day was John L.'s turn. He told the story of their meeting and the quick trip to the Hawthorne Hotel, of their living together, of his illness and eventual proposal of marriage, speaking in soft, measured tones as his attorneys carefully led him over the jumps. From the champion's perspective, the major problem with their marriage was Annie's sponging relatives. He said he did not mind supporting two or three, but not "the whole of Rhode Island." Claiming he never drank to excess ("I've been full, but never drunk"), John L. was forced to admit the horse-abuse case, which was still fresh in everyone's mind. "The horse overturned the sleigh, and I hit him a slug on the side of the jaw." In response to a question from one of Annie's attorneys, he then vehemently denied he had ever been in Lida Pierce's, an infamous Boston rookery.

Then came a cavalcade of character witnesses. Mike said he had never seen his brother strike Annie; indeed, he had seen Annie hurl bottles at John L. Annie was fond of brandy punches and wine, avowed Mike. Frank Moran affirmed that the Sullivans were a loving couple during the Grand Tour. Sullivan's sister, Ann, supported her brother down the line. Albert Stickney, the hack driver who had figured in the introduction of the two principals, darkly intimated that he had taken Annie riding several times after her marriage with a certain "Zack Hollingsworth," and he suggested that Zack and Annie were more than casual friends. It was left to Annie Durgin, who had known Annie Sullivan for over ten years and who kept house for the couple at 4 Lovering Place, to provide a suitable finale. Annie Sullivan, said Mrs. Durgin, was in the habit of having liquor brought in by the case, a considerable amount of which the mistress drained herself. As for John L., Mrs. Durgin testified that on the Sunday in December after Annie left her husband for the last time, he was visited by a woman named Lottie Boswell. The pair went into "Mrs. Sullivan's room," claimed the witness, and she knew not what ensued there, but when Mrs. Boswell left she took with her a large roll of bills.

By this time the crowded court was completely agog, more so than if it were a sensational murder trial under Judge Charles Allen's gavel. Many curious members of the Boston bar in attendance were so noisy in their whispers over the ripe testimony that the judge grew testy and ordered no more people admitted to the courtroom. No one could top Mrs. Durgin, and Allen recessed to consider his decision. On May 29 he rendered his verdict: By her actions Annie Bates Bailey Sullivan had "condoned" the offenses of which she accused her husband, such as striking him and joining him in drinking. She had admitted sleeping with him for three weeks after the Natick scrap. Much of Annie's testimony was uncorroborated, and John L. denied it. "No doubt Sullivan drank to excess," reasoned the judge, but his habits could not be called "gross and confirmed." The champion had been generous with money for his wife, as Annie had admitted on the stand and as her dress silently but eloquently testified. The case therefore was dismissed; Annie's divorce suit had failed.[28]

In one sense, Annie had been fighting a hopeless battle. The burden of proof rested on her, and she could not muster enough believable witnesses to offset the pungent tales about her own behavior. The future of John, Jr., never entered into the deliberations. It was male-centered law and a male-centered verdict, fully consonant with many legal decisions of the age. Nevertheless, for the Sullivans it was the end. Annie retreated with her son back to Rhode Island, while John L., bereft of family, went on his way. He might have sent money from time to time, but the ill-suited couple never lived together again. Their marriage would last on paper for twenty-three more years, and Sullivan, to his credit, may have been properly ashamed. He mentioned not a word of either wife or son in his autobiography.

## IV

John L. lost little time getting back to the ring. It had been half a year since he last put up his fists, his longest hiatus yet, and he badly needed a place to fight. One was found by the industrious Sheedy in Chicago, a rough-edged city that had little truck with the blue-nosed attitude of Boston, New York, and Philadelphia toward prizefighting. The champion arrived with his entourage on June 12, immediately indulging in a Turkish bath and then taking in a ball game and the theater. He was still overweight and had two painful carbuncles on the back of his neck, which forced him to hold his head in a strained and unnatural position.

The following day it became apparent that Chicago still loved Sullivan, regardless of what the eastern municipal authorities had done. Sheedy had arranged an open-air match in front of the grandstand of the Chicago Driving Park against a popular young fighter, Jack Burke, "the Irish Lad." Washington Boulevard was thronged with rigs on their way to the fight, everything from sulkies to four-in-hand wagons. At the park a twenty-piece brass band tooted away between events, of which the boxing match was the conclusion. The shirtsleeve audience swelled to over twelve thousand. The festive early-summer atmosphere was heightened even more as John L. made his entrance through the arched gateway of the clubhouse and walked two hundred yards to the ring, pursued every step by the strains of "See the Conquering Hero Comes." His colors were somewhat subdued, a flesh-colored silk shirt over white tights. The carbuncles had been removed that morning, two pieces of black court-plaster marking the sore areas.

After the two sides settled on their referee, a local sportsman named Sherm Thurston, the gloves were ostentatiously examined by two police officers. Then Sullivan turned to face the Irish Lad, who weighed only 170 to the champion's 230. Obviously, Burke's only hope was to outlast his grossly out-of-shape opponent. In the first round Sullivan rushed out as usual, clinched, and threw his man. The inexperienced referee was not about to call a foul on the Great John L., and Burke wisely counterpunched his way through the round. In the second, Sullivan rabbit-punched the Lad in the back of the neck. He seemed to be holding back, aware that a police officer, Lieutenant Ward, was stationed at ringside. During round three Burke socked his cautious opponent solidly on the chin; Sullivan, scowling, started to advance but backed off when Ward leaned over the ropes and cautioned, "John!" Still, by round four the late-afternoon sun, his sore neck, and the aggressive young Burke had tormented John L. enough. He floored the Lad with a solid body blow and then drove him down again with a rain of right hands; Burke, now feeling the enormous disparity in weight and power, dropped twice more in his corner to avoid punishment. The fifth round was more of the same, at the end of which Sullivan was declared the winner, to the sound of good-natured cheers and countercheers from the grandstand. John L., who received 65 percent of the gate, bragged that "I never trained a day for this event," but even so, "Burke was but a mere boy in my hands."[29]

Such a warm welcome from his Chicago fans led Sullivan and his pals on another tear, and a better part of the Burke gate money had slipped through their fingers by the time they staggered home to Boston on June 22. Thus the need for another match that summer, and Sullivan finally contracted for a bout with Dominick McCaffery, who had been clamoring for a fight since the cancellation in Philadelphia. With some unease, since the city fathers there remembered the clandestine Sullivan-Donaldson match back at Christmastime 1880, the promoter George Campbell chose his home, Cincinnati, as the locale.

McCaffery, born in Pittsburgh in 1863, had rebelled against seminary life and had taught boxing for a short time at, of all places, a Quaker school in Media, Pennsylvania. He owned victories over Mike Cleary and Sullivan's *bête noire*, Charlie Mitchell. Dominick was a serious young professional and knew the champion's style well, having seen John L. fight several times and having sparred with him a year before at the Denny benefit. The fight would be with three-ounce gloves and McCaffery wanted to make the most of his opportunity. A small fighter at 5 feet 8½ and 165 pounds, he trained hard at the Bowery Saloon in Cincinnati, the spot where Tom Allen had prepared for his fight with Joe Goss in 1876. Daily the challenger ran, walked, took rubdowns, punched the light bag, and washed down porterhouse steaks and soft-boiled eggs with quantities of ale. He exuded confidence. "I'm ten times the boxer Sullivan is."[30]

For his part, Sullivan roistered on throughout the summer. He sold the Lovering Place house, Annie having taken most of the furniture and bric-a-brac with her, and bought a new residence at 7 Carver Street. Only two weeks before the fight, he was laid up there with a "severe sore throat." Meanwhile, the Cincinnati watchdogs were preparing their welcome. When John L. finally arrived on the Beeline Express and was hailed by a large crowd at the station, he was promptly arrested at the instigation of the Law and Order League and taken before a Court of Common Pleas judge under a local statute authorizing any citizen to call on a constable or police officer to arrest one or both of the principals when a prizefight was contemplated. McCaffery, for some reason, was not taken into custody. Before Judge Huston, Sullivan stoutly claimed that only a sparring exhibition was intended. He therefore was released, although the court allowed that the fight would probably come off anyway, obviously expecting the champion to forfeit his one-thousand-dollar bond.[31]

Actually, Sullivan had done some training, in response to rumors about McCaffery's serious preparation. Frank Woodman, a Boston merchant who owned a farm near Searsport, Maine, a little hamlet well up the New England coast, had invited him north to get in shape, and there John L. had pared himself from 237 to 208 under the August sun. The notion that two well-prepared gladiators would meet in their town drove Cincinnati sports fans into a blaze of excitement. Locals estimated that over six thousand outsiders had arrived for the fight. Excursion trains poured in from New York, Chicago, Pittsburgh, Atlanta, and New Orleans. Gambling men were everywhere, offering Sullivan at 5 to 3. A mob assembled outside a local bar merely to stare at the champion as he took his fill. Seats were going for fifteen to twenty dollars a crack. In the midst of the frenzy, Sheriff Beresford responded to a query from the Law and Order Leaguers by saying that he understood the contest was to be a sparring match and "volume 81, page 203 of the Ohio laws permits this."[32]

The sympathetic sheriff even helped arrange the site, just outside the city limits at Chester Park, a half-mile race course surrounded by high fences and famed as the training grounds of the trotter Maud S. On August 29 a goodly share of Cincinnati made its way to the park, over three thousand gate-crashers eventually swelling the crowd to over fifteen thousand, one of Sullivan's biggest. Trains ran from the city at one-minute intervals. The waiting throng swilled beer and gulped ham sandwiches. It was composed of almost every element of society— lawyers, physicians, businessmen, brokers, bankers. Members of both the City Council and the Board of Aldermen showed up. Neighboring housetops and shed roofs were littered with people. Some twenty hack-loads of "ladies" arrived, to be provided with beer and ginger ale by their lovers and admirers as the doxies perched on their carriages to get a better view. Three shell-game operations at the gates did a windfall business. It was rumored that the best seats were going for an astronomical two hundred dollars. A strong group of Pittsburgh ironworkers, many sporting pistols, gathered near the ring to support McCaffery.

The crowd was entertained by local boxers until at last, at 5 P.M. amid shouts of "Sullivan is coming!" the champion arrived, a roll of fat around his middle giving evidence that the self-induced Searsport regimen had been only partially effective. Quickly, Billy Tate of Toledo was accepted as the referee. Loud-mouthed Charlie Mitchell, in McCaffery's corner, tried to upset Sullivan by taunting the champion and challenging him to fight, but Sullivan ignored his tormentor and geared himself for the job at hand.

For the first three rounds Sullivan pressed forward in his usual style, pushing and slugging the smaller man all over the ring. John L. kept banging his opponent into the ropes. McCaffery went down several times and was groggy at the end of round three. Both men, despite their training, were wilting in the August heat. By round five McCaffery had gained a second wind and managed to spar, although he was floored once and was back on the ropes most of the time. The challenger was bleeding from under the right eye and the corner of his lip. At the start of round six Sullivan wrestled him to the deck and pinned him. At this artless and illegal move, Tate stopped the fight and gave the decision to John L. When William Muldoon, the master of ceremonies, announced the decision, the highly pleased crowd rapidly disintegrated into fevered arguments over the relative merits of the two pugilists. Dominick's brother John tried to pistol whip Arthur Chambers at ringside, and the exhausted boxers had to combine to break it up.[33]

Both fighters bragged after the fight, but for McCaffery it was no payday at all, and his supporters groused about Billy Tate's decision for months. Sullivan took home almost six thousand dollars, about

60 percent of the gross. For two days everyone celebrated in Cincinnati, John L. and his opponent attending a National League game between the Red Stockings and Pittsburgh. Campbell eventually gave McCaffery a gift of one thousand dollars, and the Pittsburgher boasted that he had stayed in the ring with Sullivan longer than any man before him—which was true, although Flood had lasted eight rounds, Ryan nine, and Donaldson ten under the London Rules.[34] Sullivan, momentarily content with the fat payday, would not fight again for over a year.

Both the Burke and McCaffery bouts had been summertime extravaganzas, but now the season was closing in on the champion, and the biggest indoor arenas of the East were barred to him. Also, despite the failure of the Law and Order League in Cincinnati, similarly minded citizens remained alert. In September John L. stopped off in Cleveland and pitched in a Sunday ball game at Brooklyn Park before three thousand spectators. He gave up eight hits and lost 2 to 0, but the real story was the response of the local Law and Order League, which had generated a citizen's ordinance similar to that of Cincinnati. As Sullivan was about to step into a hack at the end of the game, he was arrested for violating a "blue law" against Sunday baseball. It was an obvious harassment; no other player was collared. Yet John L. was forced to make bond, plead guilty, and pay a fine of ten dollars. In addition to the lack of places to fight and the obvious rage of antiboxing people, Sullivan had to contend with himself. Back in Boston he was pitched from a buggy and slightly injured.[35]

In July the champion had signed a contract with the Lester and Allen Minstrel Show for the 1885–86 season, clearly recognizing that the McCaffery fight would be his last for some months. The terms were exceptional for that time, $500 a week for twenty weeks. Lester and Allen, to protect themselves against John L.'s drinking escapades, forced him to agree that if he failed to appear for a scheduled performance, he would forfeit $700. Both parties gave a $10,000 bond not to break the engagement. It was a lucrative contract.[36]

Sullivan's task with the minstrel show was a role he had tried earlier, that of "model statuary." Actually, John L. loved to pose. He had stood for photographic portraits in June at John Wood's Broadway gallery in New York City, a four-hour session that exhausted him. Among Wood's shots was a full-length view of the champion, bare to the waist in an aggressive fighting stance, his short-cropped hair and ferocious scowl the very image of pugilistic aggressiveness. It was an immediate best-seller, appearing on cards and above bars for years. Sullivan also toyed with the idea of having a marble bust made of himself.

16. John Wood's photograph of Sullivan, probably the most popular picture ever taken of the champion (1885) (William Schutte Collection)

Now, however, he was to pose for audiences. The rage for *"poses plastiques,"* imported from France, had hit the American popular stage. In its purest form, model statuary presented live single figures or tableaux arranged with supposed artistry to convey some aesthetic ideal. In actuality the device had become an excuse for displaying the human form undraped as far as convention would allow. The more outrageous acts, to the righteously offended, bordered on burlesque. Sullivan had been a success at the racket early in June in Boston's Howard Atheneaeum, posing as a living statue, the Fighting Gladiator. One critic praised the hero, although noting that John L. was "carrying about rather too much beef." Richard Kyle Fox depicted the champion spread across the *Police Gazette's* pink pages as Perseus slaying Medusa, as a classical orator, as a discus thrower, and as a Roman soldier with a short sword and shield—each pose offering a plenitude of Sullivan arm and thigh.[37]

On September 20 the minstrel show hit the road, Sullivan the headliner. Audiences were consistently good, so much so that in Chicago John L. signed a three-year contract with John G. Cannon, the former manager of the popular vaudeville team Harrigan and Hart, to tour the world doing the same thing, commencing in the spring of 1886. Nothing came of this agreement, as the rage for poses died as rapidly as it had been born, but in the meantime Sullivan was making big money. As he attracted the crowds, his weight ballooned to 245, his heaviest yet. William Muldoon joined up and displayed his muscular torso in several scenes with his friend. The apostle went so far as to adopt a bit of the champion's life-style as his own; in December the two men were arrested in Cohoes, New York, for assault. They made their bail and John L. was acquitted, although Muldoon was fined fifty dollars. A month later Tommy Lee, a New York thirteen-year-old, made headlines by alleging that Sullivan had hit him in the mouth with an umbrella.[38]

The supposed assault on the youngster took place while the heavyweight champion of the world was appearing at the Third Avenue Theater in New York as "the best formed man in the world." It was the season for beefcake in the metropolis: Charlie Mitchell was appearing at the Grand Opera House billed as "the handsomest and most symmetrically formed man living," and Dominick McCaffery ("an athletic figure") was down at William's Dime Museum in the Bowery. But it was John L. who packed them in. Audiences saw the master of ceremonies, William Kellogg, introduce each pose. Kellogg would intone, "the Gladiator in Combat," and the curtains would part, revealing a scantily attired Sullivan, ill at ease in white tights and wig, with hands up, chest forward, head back. Whisk—the scene ended. "The Dying Gladiator," and once again the curtains opened, to reveal

17. William Muldoon, about the time he and Sullivan were appearing as "living statuary" (about 1885) (William Schutte Collection)

Sullivan recumbent, with head drooping and arms supporting his last breath. And so it went, through "Hercules at Rest" and "Cain Killing Abel," the critics not revealing which of the last two roles John L. assayed. By turns he portrayed "the biggest undressed heroes of antiquity," although his audiences were uneasy with his immobility; they wanted *action*, and they got static poses. Nevertheless most went away pleased and impressed with the way the figures had been staged; such was the nature of "plastic art" in that precinematic age.[39]

At the end of his New York modeling engagement, Sullivan at last reconciled with Billy Madden after their three-year spat. Over several bottles of Bass Ale at the Hoffman House, John L. candidly admitted that his split with Billy had cost him not only a firm friendship but also a great deal of money. Then the show was on the road again, crowds everywhere eager to shake Sullivan's hand after each performance. During the next three months they were up and down the eastern seaboard and into Canada, with the champion posing almost nightly and drinking up his profits almost as fast, even though he claimed to have become "part owner" of the show by the end of the tour in Chicago in May 1886.[40]

Thoughts of fighting again were still in the back of his mind. He kept insisting, even as his girth swelled, that he would fight anyone but that it should be in private to avoid the law. There was talk of a match against the aged Jem Smith, which Fox in his ceaseless search for anyone who could beat Sullivan naturally plugged. Fox and Sullivan actually talked over such a bout in February, but nothing ensued. More speculation surrounded rematches with Paddy Ryan and Charlie Mitchell, but John L. could do nothing while under his heavy bond to Lester and Allen. Finally, at the end of the tour in Chicago, Pat Sheedy popped up again and agreed to arrange a fight for the champion, preferably with the insufferable Mitchell.[41]

## V

Sullivan's saloon on Washington Street, which at first had made money, was now at best a break-even proposition. After the initial satisfaction of ownership wore off, Sullivan paid little attention to his property. He may have sold part of it to his brother, Mike, in December 1884. At any rate, the inexperienced young man was managing it on a daily basis by the spring of 1886, and without John L. to attract customers, business was falling off. In May the champion sold his bar, claiming a 100 percent profit.[42]

Sheedy had lined up a fight with Mitchell. At first arranged for Chicago, it was rescheduled to take place in dangerous territory, at New York's Polo Grounds, on July 5. Meanwhile, Sullivan claimed to have his weight down to 215 and to be drinking nothing but seltzer water. If so, the abstinence was temporary. In late June he got into another saloon row with a gambler named Michael Meehan at a dive called the Perkins on Boston's Fremont Street, choking the man until other patrons pulled him off. The affronted Meehan quickly swore out a warrant for assault and battery in Municipal Court, and Sullivan prudently decamped for New York City.[43]

Mayor Grace was still in office, and he still refused to have any truck with Sullivan or his crowd. The mayor ordered the fight canceled. Sheedy, unfamiliar with the byzantine world of New York politics, pleaded his case to such Tammany sachems as Richard Croker, John Scannell, and Edward Cahill, which only enraged the mayor further, as he was now convinced that Sullivan was hand-in-glove with the dissolute remnants of the old Tweed gang. Sheedy retreated to his home in Chicago to lick his wounds and indulge in his primary occupation, making book at the local racetracks. In opposing the fight, the *New York Times* moralized as follows for its predominantly middle-class readers: "While there would no doubt be some respectable persons present, drawn by no more respectable motive than a desire to look at the athletes in training, every blackguard and thief in New York who could scrape the entrance money together would undoubtedly be there, and a judicious earthquake that should swallow up the whole assemblage, while it might do some harm, would do an incalculable deal of good."[44]

By now the champion had not laced the gloves on in earnest for almost a year. He had bought into Billy Bennett's saloon business in New York but was at best a silent partner. Restless and unoccupied, he had Sheedy line up another national tour for the 1886–87 season. This would be nothing near the whistle-stop frenzy of the Grand Tour; well fewer than one hundred appearances were planned. Steve Taylor signed on, as did several new faces: George La Blanche (a tough customer billed as "the Marine"), Joe Lannon, Jimmy Carroll, and Patsy Kerrigan. John L. intended a far more relaxed pace, with a few select fights along the way. Theoretically he was to work himself back into condition gradually as he went.[45]

One fight, however, would not wait. The police canceled a scheduled bout with a Pennsylvania boxer named Frank Herald ("the Nicetown Pet") that had been scheduled for Union Park, New Jersey, in late August. The promoters frantically tried to reschedule the contest in Brooklyn, but they ran into a stone wall. Herald's backers then proceeded to outrage the champion by declaring that John L. was afraid to meet their man. Sullivan had been hearing this sort of talk from Charlie Mitchell for years, and he immediately entrained for Pittsburgh, following the departing Herald crowd by an hour. There, a match was quickly arranged for Allegheny City, across the river from the steel town, on September 18.

John L. outweighed his opponent by forty pounds and intended to make short work of him, almost as if Herald were a surrogate for the voluble Mitchell. Before three thousand people at the Coliseum, the two men pounded away at each other during the first round, Sullivan's bulk forcing Herald over the ropes. Herald came out strongly in the next round, but Sullivan got him in a neckhold and slammed right hands at his prisoner's head until the smaller man slipped away and got in one good shot to the champion's eye. This served only to madden John L. further, and he rapidly decked Herald with an uppercut. The Pet was quickly on his feet and clinched; all semblance of boxing skills on either side vanished At this point the police, under pressure from a local committee of clergymen, separated the two and Sullivan was declared the winner. The receipts were pegged at five thousand dollars, John L. taking 20 percent.[46] The fight scarcely was pretty, but for a man who had not fought in over a year, it was a notable effort.

The talkative Sheedy had managed to arrange one sure match for Sullivan on the tour, a third fight with Paddy Ryan. Paddy, as impoverished as ever, signed a contract with Sheedy in Chicago early in the fall for 25 percent of the pot. The two pugilists were to meet in San Francisco before the end of the year. Meanwhile the combination set out, commencing in Racine, Wisconsin, and moving on to Minneapolis. Sullivan did very little sparring, but the crowds were fairly good, drawn by news of the Herald fight and word that John L. had repeated his earlier universal challenge, depositing one thousand dollars earnest money with the *New York Clipper*. The fighters were pursued by the barking editorials of the *New York Times*: the Ryan match was a farce, and the public was being swindled by the antics of the combination.[47]

In the midst of the westward swing, Sullivan received crushing news. On October 28 John, Jr., died of diphtheria in Centerville, Rhode Island, a town outside Providence where Annie had made her home. The boy was only 2½; the dreaded disease, for which no vaccine had been developed, had raced through his heretofore sturdy body in just four days. Annie was devastated, and she bitterly told reporters that though she and John L. were still legally married, the "wife" who had registered with her husband at a Milwaukee hotel was certainly not her. As for Sullivan, he said not a word for public consumption and kept his grief so close that few remembered or ever knew that he once had a son and namesake. Years later, Sullivan's brother-in-law showed Hype Igoe of the *New York World* a chest full of the fighter's most cherished possessions. There, amid the paraphernalia of belts, canes, ring tights, boxing shoes, and assorted gewgaws, was a picture of John,

Jr., set in a deep-set, glass-covered frame with white wax flowers pressed under the glass.[48]

There was nothing he felt he could do, no words to send to the estranged Annie, so the tour pressed on, eventually pulling up in San Francisco in early November. Here Ryan was waiting. Sullivan and Sheedy had scheduled the Mechanics' Pavilion for November 13. John L. and the San Franciscans had had their ups and downs, but the champion had not fought in the Bay Area since the George Robinson bout back in 1884, and the fans were eager to see him once more, even pitted against his perennial punching bag.

By 6 P.M. on the following day the crowd had begun to gather, five hours in advance of the scheduled start. Over nine thousand people eventually crammed into the Pavilion, men on all sides clamoring wildly for tickets, which were scaled between one and two dollars. The audience endured an interminable siege of nine preliminary bouts, and it was nearly midnight as John L. and Paddy made their way to the ring.

The fight was scheduled for four rounds, Queensberry Rules. Sullivan, if not Ryan, had been encouraged by the fact that though the police would be present, no rumbles of civic discontent had surfaced. The champion intended a convincing victory, as Paddy, like himself, was in only mediocre condition. Both men came out slugging, Ryan swiping John L. across the cheek and priming the champion into even more than his usual first-round cannonade. They banged away at each other for a full minute, the most severe sustained fighting Sullivan had done since the McCaffery battle, before Ryan backed off, badly out of breath. Paddy gamely came back in the second round to force the fighting, but those closest to the ring could see that his punches already lacked snap and timing. John L. skillfully counterpunched (not his usual tactic) and downed Ryan amid loud applause. Rising, Ryan tried to clinch but went down twice more. At the beginning of round three Paddy was still getting in some shots, but Sullivan's stamina was telling. Suddenly the champion sent home a whistling right hand to Ryan's jaw, sending him spinning into the ropes and down. He staggered to his feet and dazedly poked at Sullivan's face with an unsteady left. The response was another clout on the jaw, and Paddy crumpled to the canvas.

The police rushed in, but John L. waved them back, majestically lifted his fallen foe, and carried Paddy to his corner. Propping him on a stool, Sullivan gave Ryan a drink from a bottle and wiped the blood from his face, all the while fanning him with a towel. Such solicitude produced a supreme moment; the crowd went absolutely berserk as cheers for John L. shook the rafters. Fox gave over the entire front page of the *Gazette* to a lithograph of Sullivan, face full of concern, offering succor to the unconscious Ryan. Sullivan's net for his late night work was about nine thousand dollars. Paddy got his pummeling, as expected, but he got his payday, too—twenty-six hundred dollars.

Sullivan, despite the drinking, the assaults, and the family problems, seemed with this smashing triumph to rise again in the esteem of his worshippers. When the news of John L.'s victory flashed across the nation to New York and hit the morning papers, a grizzled old boot-black in front of Sullivan and Bennett's saloon at the corner of Sixth Avenue and Thirty-second Street was heard to shout: "Crown him King! Crown him Lord of everything!"[49]

## VI

After umpiring a baseball game in Alameda to pick up a little extra cash and being refused a permit to appear in Victoria, British Columbia, Sullivan hit the road for the long trip back home. Ryan declined an offer of five hundred dollars a week to join him, and became a saloon keeper on Market Street. Along the way the combination made several of the old Rocky Mountain stops. Butte, Montana, and Leadville, Colorado, each gave Sullivan a good house, and John L. appeared in Colorado Springs alongside a local Presbyterian pastor, who lectured on physical fitness while the champion assumed various poses to demonstrate the same. In Denver during Christmas week Sullivan met a Montana fighter, Duncan McDonald, billed as the "champion, Northwest Territory." Sullivan sparred his way through a relaxed four rounds with the much smaller man (who had earlier in his career fought a thirty-four-round battle with little Pete McCoy), the fight being declared a draw.[50]

After a stopover in Kansas City, the combination moved up again to Minneapolis, where Sheedy had arranged a six-round match with Patsy Cardiff, an experienced fighter who was Sullivan's height but weighed about thirty pounds less. Cardiff, like Tom Allen and Al Smith before him, was a veteran of scraps up and down the tough river towns. Only twenty-four, he fought a bare-knuckle bout with Jim Good on a flatboat in the Mississippi River near Saint Louis in 1885 and knocked him out in three rounds. The previous summer he had dueled to a punishing draw with the ubiquitous Mitchell in Minneapolis. He was, despite his origins in Peoria, Illinois, a local favorite, and he was determined to put up a better fight than the novice Morris Hefey had done in Saint Paul during the Grand Tour.

A crowd of over seven thousand showed up, braving the January cold and filling the Washington Rink from end to end. Minnesota's lieutenant governor, C. A. Gilman, attended, as did the mayor, A. A. Ames. A delegation all the way from Devil's Lake, out in Dakota

Territory, was hopping mad at being scalped for one hundred dollars a ticket. No preliminary bouts were offered, as the locals wanted 50 percent of the gate to spar with members of the combination, a demand Sheedy refused. After the band played the requisite patriotic air, the fighters squared away. The quicker Cardiff proved adept at avoiding Sullivan's rushes and blows, at one point in the first round dodging a wicked left to the head that glanced off the point of his shoulder. For the next three rounds Sullivan sparred cautiously, using his right hand only. In the fourth round the pugilists circled each other warily, not a blow being struck. The crowd began to hiss their disapproval. John L. continued to lead weakly with his right the next two rounds, and finally Cardiff rushed at him, raining lefts and rights and forcing him across the stage into the ropes. Time quickly was called, and the affair was declared a draw.[51]

Something was obviously wrong. After the fight Sullivan, accompanied by his "wife" (whether she was the same woman who registered with him in Milwaukee is uncertain), returned to the Nicollet House and had his left arm examined by Dr. T. F. Quimby. John L. was in excruciating pain; the arm had swelled to twice its size. A fracture of the radius was diagnosed, and Quimby set the bone. The entourage quickly left the Twin Cities, as Cardiff held court in his saloon, surrounded by a crowd of jubilant friends. He had just taken a quarter of the healthiest gate of his life, about ten thousand dollars, from his match with the champion. Sullivan, his arm in a sling, acted as master of ceremonies for the rest of the boxers as they performed along the Red River Valley, in Fargo and Grand Forks, North Dakota, and Winnipeg, Manitoba. He attributed the fracture to the subzero weather on the Northern Plains, which had made his bones brittle.[52]

Within a week he was back in New York, the arm still painfully swollen. He went to Dr. Louis F. Sayre, a Fifth Avenue physician, who immediately saw that the bone had not been set properly. Sayre said the arm would have to be broken again and offered ether, but John L. refused. The doctor summoned his sons, Louis, Jr., and Ridgeway, who were also physicians. The younger men held Sullivan's arm immobile just above the elbow while their father grasped the fighter's left hand as if he were about to shake it. Giving the wrist a sudden wrench forward, he snapped the radius again. Sullivan's face twitched slightly, but he uttered no sound. Sayre put the arm in a plaster of paris cast and arranged a black silk handkerchief as a sling while John L. chatted calmly with his brother and two friends. By late March the physician pronounced the arm almost healed.[53]

The combination resumed the tour in Hoboken, New Jersey, although Sullivan's arm was noticeably still tender, and he did only light sparring. Within a week the group was in the national capital, where a large crowd applauded his every move even though he kept favoring the left. Once again his weight had risen; at 235 pounds he was short-winded and more than pudgy, but no matter. Attired nattily in black four-button cutaway coat and light trousers, he made the rounds of his favorite Washington haunts from his base at the Harris House. The city was wide open and very much to his satisfaction. In the previous five years, while the population had increased 15 percent, there had been a 40 percent rise in the number of licensed saloons and liquor wholesalers and a 90 percent increase in licensed billiard and pool halls. Countless cribs operated illegally.[54]

The current occupant of the White House was Grover Cleveland, by virtue of his victory over James G. Blaine ("the continental liar from the state of Maine") in what had been the dirtiest presidential contest within memory. Married to the beautiful young Frances Folsom the previous year, Cleveland had evolved a custom of receiving the public on Mondays. Wednesdays, and Fridays at a White House reception, and to this event on April 4 Sullivan, Sheedy, and the rest of the combination decided they would go. Cleveland was a hard-working president but a private man. The handshaking was an ordeal for him; he did it only as a duty. In that simpler age practically any American could hobnob for an instant with the country's leader.

The pugilists arrived fifteen minutes early and stood uneasily amid the rest of the crowd gathered in the East Room. Sullivan, clad in a fine black suit and standing under the great gas chandelier in the center of the room, quickly became the center of attention after an alert reporter spotted the unusual guests. By the time Cleveland entered, expecting the usual respectful silence his considerable bulk and high office commanded, the room was a hubbub of prizefight chatter. Sheedy, never at a loss for words, immediately introduced himself and then introduced John L. to Cleveland. Pat did most of the talking, observing tactlessly that the president had been gaining weight and offering him a four-round go with Sullivan. Cleveland listened in good humor, and then the unlikely group of boxers moved on down the line.[55]

Only a minute or so had passed, and Sullivan regarded the whole thing so lightly that he did not mention it in his autobiography. Cleveland, of course, took it in stride as part of his job; he shook hands and exchanged pleasantries with hundreds of people each week. But the sporting press noticed, and so did Sullivan's fans. The Irish-American son of a Boston laborer, the drunk, the wife-beater, the bully, had shaken hands with the president of the United States in the White House. Not even John Morrissey, with all his political connections, had pulled that one off! It seemed yet another triumph for "our John."

From Washington the tour circled north, continuing into late spring. Now, however, clouds of disapproval began to form again, and Sullivan found the East as forbidding as when he had left. Remembering the Herald fight, the mayors of Pittsburgh, Allegheny City, and Erie denied him licenses to perform. So did the authorities in Springfield, Ohio. Likewise in Syracuse, Rochester, and New Haven. The *New York Times*, which editorially dogged the combination all spring, noted with approval that "this repeated action of the Chief Magistrates of different cities in the interest of decency is encouraging, and calculated to inspire the hope that in time even New York may refuse to tolerate the disgusting and demoralizing exhibitions which the Sullivan combination has been given [*sic*] throughout the country." Everywhere the "better class" of citizens were reported to be enraged at the appearance of pugilists in their midst. Said one of these, in Rochester: "I think it is an outrage that a strolling band of prize fighters should be allowed to come here and essay to run the city, dictate to the mayor and block the streets nightly with gangs of roughs. It is an outrage and the people should rise up against such disregard of law, order, and decency."[56]

The people rose up enough so that Sullivan and Sheedy were forced to curtail the New England portion of their tour, which finally floundered to an end in Brockton, Massachusetts, on June 9. The finish was, however, unlike the liquor-soaked dissolution of the Grand Tour; in addition, Sheedy showed a greater tolerance for John L.'s peccadillos than had Al Smith, and the two men agreed to remain business partners and cast about for new opportunities.[57]

So it was home to Boston, after another long absence. There, the ring was still closed to him, but the local faithful spent the summer planning a suitable tribute for their hero. At last, on August 8, Sullivan's moment came—his proudest in all his years among his hometown friends.

The local guardians of masculinity had hit on the notion of a championship belt, not in itself a new idea, but this one would outshine Richard Kyle Fox's bauble as the sun did the moon. Dozens of loyal followers contributed to its manufacture, some offering hundreds of dollars. Eventually valued at eight thousand dollars—at least four times the annual wage of a skilled workingman—the belt was a marvel of metal and inlay work. Its centerplate was a large shield surmounted by six flags, two each for America, Ireland, and England (how the Union Jack got included was a mystery). On the front of the shield, in large, raised block letters, was embossed the inscription: "Presented to the Champion of Champions, John L. Sullivan, by the Citizens of the United States." It was suitably dated July 4, 1887. Sullivan's name was encrusted with no fewer than 256 diamonds. Above the name a three-carat diamond was set. Other, smaller stones surrounded the shield.

The belt itself consisted of eight connected panels, four on either side of the shield. Portraits of Sullivan and Sheedy were on the flanking panels, and the others held scenes of Sullivan, Irish symbols such as the harp, shamrock, and flag, and the American shield and flag. All the panels were checkered with diamonds. The belt itself was of solid fourteen-carat gold and weighed almost thirty pounds. The total length was almost four feet, enough to encircle even Sullivan's girth. It was, in short, a masterpiece and a fitting icon for the man to whom it was presented.[58]

The big evening came off as scheduled in the Boston Theater. Sheedy promised total decorum and only the lightest sort of sparring, and he had wangled the necessary unanimous consent of the Board of Aldermen for the exhibition. Over three thousand attended, many from throughout New England, and three hundred more were stacked on the stage behind the dais, among them Sullivan's proud father, who sat near Mayor Hugh O'Brien. Sheedy, attired in clawhammer coat, was the acme of hospitality. Despite his rude manners he could put on a good show, and this was his tour de force. When the curtains parted the massive belt lay on a table in the center of the stage, whereupon the promoter stepped forward and spoke. His tone was perfect— polite, sincere, thankful, and registering pride in Sullivan's accomplishments. A poem entitled "Our John" was read. Then Sullivan entered to a long ovation and sparred gently with Mike Donovan and Steve Taylor.

After a short break to allow the champion to change into formal wear, complete with wide-lapelled vest, stiff bat-wing collar, and diamond-studded cravat, the presentation took place. Sullivan was at his best, with fresh haircut and trimmed handlebar mustache, completely sober. He stepped forward with Sheedy and Councilman William Benjamin Franklin Whall, "the Cicero of the North End," as the band played the newly popular "Hail to the Chief." Whall, with a politician's prerogative, offered a few remarks. He was proud of John L., proud of Boston, and did not give a damn for prudish Back Bay bluebloods. ("Puny dyspeptics with colossal heads never deserved a nation.")

Sheedy then took the belt from the mayor's box, where it was being admired, and the promoter and the politician, both unabashed Irishmen, clasped it around Sullivan's broad waist. The champion took it as his due, and gave a few words of thanks in a clear, firm voice. He reaffirmed his love for Boston and affection for his pals. Concluding, in the pattern he had made famous, he said, "I remain, as ever, your devoted friend, John L. Sullivan."[59]

## VII

It was a love feast, and Sullivan's position among his own was once again secure. The mid-1880s had been rocky years for him. His wife was permanently estranged, and his only child dead. The major cities of the East were closed to his profession, and at least part of the metropolitan press was in full cry against him, once again led by Fox's *Police Gazette.* He showed no sign whatsoever of changing his drinking habits, and his sudden, destructive outbursts of temper could occur whenever he touched a bottle. His last two fights, with McDonald and Cardiff, had been draws. After a summer with no bout scheduled, his weight was constant at a decidedly unathletic 240 pounds. All in all, he was the picture of a successful prizefighter at the end of the road, rich in victories and memories, with the approbation of his hometown as his signature.

The problem was that there was nothing to retire *with.* Not yet twenty-nine, Sullivan continued the hard-living habits that had given him the body of a man at least ten years older. More to the point, the tour with Sheedy had proved that he was still a drawing card. In fact, since 1884 John L. had grossed over $200,000, including profits from the Boston saloon and the partnership with Billy Bennett, the various fights, and the very rewarding contract with Lester and Allen. This averaged out to over $60,000 a year, a sum matched only by a handful of professionals, such as corporation lawyers, and exceeded only by the smallest number of industrial tycoons, men of the stripe of Carnegie and Rockefeller.[60]

But very little of the money remained. It had filtered through his wallet like water, spent in saloons from coast to coast, given or loaned to friends (never to be repaid), and, in all probability, occasionally lavished on prostitutes and "traveling companions." Indeed Sullivan oversaw an informal galaxy of impecunious and always needy satellites, a group starting with his parents and brother and extending outward to friends, associates, and hangers-on, all of them orbiting about the sun of his pocketbook. It was a pattern to become all too familiar in the boxing world, perhaps culminating in the greedy menagerie of Muhammad Ali, but John L. was the first, and he lavished money with an open and ready hand.

He was far from bankrupt, but somehow he had to keep the money coming in. His not inconsiderable ego was by now totally congruent with what he achieved in the ring. All else stemmed from this—the theater crowds, the civic awards, the adoring hordes of small boys, the gaping adults at every train station and hotel, the ready army of reporters who tracked his every move. He could not give up boxing, not now, not "undefeated." The fame, the celebrity, and even the notoriety were too much. They bore him onward like some great ocean wave, he more their captive than their master. As much a creature of the moment as any man ever was, John L. Sullivan gloried in the attention of the Gilded Age.

## CHAPTER EIGHT

# The Unfinished Hero:
# John L. and the Gilded Age

The business of being an American hero is a difficult one at best. Democracies, more than other societies and cultures, create their heroes for use and discard them readily and even cruelly when they no longer seem to serve their purpose. The heroic may translate into fame, power, or wealth, but democracies also are fickle. They may award the heroic diadem easily, far too easily in modern times, but they often compensate by withdrawing it overnight. Cultural heroes tend to be transient figures, leaving the public stage as the needs and demands of their culture change.

The Gilded Age was the first period in American life in which a truly popular culture emerged, knit together by a national press, the telegraph, and the railroad. The era was one of considerable social tension, riven by economic uncertainties and beset by concerns of wealth and status. Many of the traditional patterns of the American hero were in short supply. Already a generation had grown up that knew the great American epic of Civil War only as history. Political leadership at all levels tended to the mediocre, and the military had, for the present, no new worlds to conquer. At the same time the nation's demography was changing dramatically. America was becoming more urban and more industrialized with each passing year. Immigration policy, unrestricted except for Orientals, was also giving a far more varied cast to the population. The older verities concerning heroism were not, of course, being discarded. Washington and Lincoln remained highly useful models. But to the common man they seemed increasingly remote, even austere.

This newer America shaped its own images of the heroic, and in so doing it reflected many of its own ideals and problems. It was no accident that the first and most prominent of the cultural heroes to be created by the Gilded Age was an ethnic and a man of the city. It also was no accident that his accomplishments were couched in the metaphors of industrialism, nor that his excesses were damned in the language of traditional morality. John L. Sullivan, perhaps more than any other American of his era, sustained an intimate, if troubled, relationship with the public that helps to chart the swirling and treacherous social currents of the Gilded Age.

# I

His name, his face, and his deeds were now known throughout the land. He was the most prominent sporting hero America had produced, and neither he nor anyone else knew quite how to handle the novelty of his fame. The role of celebrity was doubly difficult to handle. Not only had no previous sporting figure undergone the intense scrutiny and reporting that became Sullivan's lot; no member of an ethnic and religious minority had ever shone so brightly in the public eye. Beyond this, John L.'s practice of his occupation, so far outside the mainstream of dominant middle-class mores, manners, and ideals, managed to fascinate and offend at the same time.

In truth, he accepted the attention with relish, accepted it greedily. By the mid-1880s he had little private life and did not seem to mind a bit, except when he felt that his drinking was being overplayed by the press or that his beloved sport was being misrepresented. As a public figure, however, he was learning that fame exacted a price, one that Milton had sketched over two centuries before:

> Fame, if not double-faced, is double-mouthed,
> And with contrary blast proclaims most deeds;
> On both his wings, one black, the other white,
> Bears greatest names in his wild aery flight.[1]

The Gilded Age was the first period in American history when sports and games moved away from casual amateurism in the direction of organization and professionalism. Athletes, along with another despised out-group, actors, edged slowly but noticeably in the direction of social tolerance. So long as they conducted themselves "as gentlemen and true sportsmen," the chance of acceptance by the middle class was theirs. Whereas the English demonstrated social stratification in attendance at their prizefights as late as the 1890s, Sullivan's popularity transcended class barriers and raised him to a level reached by no previous sporting figure. For proof, his adherents needed to point no further than the East Room of the White House on that April day in 1887, with its unforgettable scene of the pugilist shaking hands and exchanging jollities with the president of the United States.[2]

Increased acceptance of athletes was smoothed by a process of which most Americans were scarcely aware, a redefinition of the proper public and private spheres of life. The prime instruments of this redefinition were the lithograph and the photograph, which produced images that heretofore had been private, or at least the property of a limited circle, and made them artifacts for mass consumption. In addition, the human body was now treated more forthrightly than ever before, although hardly with the prurient sensationalism of a later age. Eadweard Muybridge, one of the grandfathers of the motion picture, in studying human movement at the University of Pennsylvania in 1884–85 produced over 100,000 negatives. These photographs included sporting activities among other forms of action. Interested in the kinetics of muscular and skeletal structure, Muybridge included numerous examples of the "disciplined use of nudity," a frank examination of the human form within the framework of scientific inquiry. Such ethically neutral studies aided in redefining modesty as well as supporting the acceptance of honest and open athletic endeavor.[3] At least part of this process could be translated into the popular culture, as Sullivan and William Muldoon demonstrated when they posed with the Lester and Allen minstrel show.

Photography and lithography quickly spread Sullivan's likeness far and wide. His first solo portrait, an engraving, appeared in the *National Police Gazette* in 1881, shortly after his triumph over John Flood. For the first time Fox's readers saw the fighting pose, the jug ears and beetling black brows, and, a bit incongruously, a dandyish pencil-thin mustache. From then on he was a steady subject for the camera or the portrait artist, whether sitting in John Wood's New York studio or providing the action for countless drawings, lithographs, and engravings. The flood of likenesses rapidly saturated the masculine world, no saloon being complete without at least a head of the champion on display. For years Ritzman's famous photography shop window on Broadway near Madison Square was filled with pictures of notables of the day, and here John L. consorted with the likes of the Prince of Wales, Lillian Russell, Frances Folsom Cleveland, P. T. Barnum, and the actor Joseph Jefferson—a true democracy of the camera. His visage appeared in ads for books and boxing exhibitions, on ticket stubs, and on walls and doors of every city in which he fought. He was even a fireworks display; after his fight with Tug Wilson the crowd enthusiastically applauded blazing images of the two pugilists that crackled for a bit and then exploded.[4]

Sullivan's strong ego, linked to his strength and his string of victories, was naturally bolstered by the constant recognition and approbation. He had shown a considerable streak of vanity even as a youth, and by now it had swelled into a major component of his character. He exulted in the dozens of nicknames bestowed on him by his fans. In his autobiography he coyly listed no less than thirty-four of these ("not with the idea that I endorse them myself"), among them the Boston Hercules, Knight of the Fives, Trip-hammer Jack, and His Fistic Highness.[5] His saving grace was that his vanity was open and honest. He admired himself inordinately, and it seemed completely natural to him that others should share that sentiment.

Beyond the pictures and the laudatory nicknames were the numerous written effusions to his powers, some of them half-mocking, most of them adulatory, and all of them an aesthetic nightmare. Poems appeared with metronomic steadiness, celebrating the supposed quintessence of the champion. Let only one of these, "The Famous Knocker-out" (also and unfortunately set to music), stand for all the rest:

> You valiant Sons of Erin's Isle,
>     And sweet Columbia too,
> Come, gather 'round, and listen while
>     I chant a stave for you.
> Oh! Fill your glass up, every man,
>     With Irish whiskey, stout;
> And drink to John L. Sullivan,
>     The famous "Knocker-out."
>
>               *chorus*
> Oh! The chorus swell for bold John L.,
>     We'll fling it to the breeze,
> Yes, shout it loud, so England's crowd
>     Shall hear it o'er the seas;
> The great and small, he's downed them all
>     In many a clever bout;
> Hurrah for John L. Sullivan,
>     The famous "Knocker-out."
>
> They sent men here from England's shore,
>     The best they could produce,
> The great John L. to try and floor,
>     but 'twasn't any use.
> Try how they would, they never could
>     Give Sullivan the rout,
> For like a giant there he stood,
>     This famous "Knocker-out. . . ."[6]

The execrable poetry, along the lines of "The Famous Knocker-out," "Our Champion," and many others, was bad enough, but Sullivan was also the subject of songs, in an age when the burgeoning sheet music industry was turning into Tin Pan Alley. From one of the most popular hits of the day, Maggie Cline's "Throw Him Down McClusky," to the most wretched jingle, tunes with John L. as the centerpiece rang through the popular culture. Not all of these were positive in tone. He appeared in a black spiritual and was found wanting: "Tell John L. Sullivan he'll have to be a better man if he wants to climb de golden stairs."[7]

In short, every avenue of communication tying together the popular culture brought his name before the public. He had won no elections, no military victories; he was not in the forefront of any crusade. Yet there he was, arguably the most popular man in the United States. Indeed, Sullivan's popularity—its scale, intensity, and persistence—had never been seen in the United States, at least for one of his social background. Without doubt, in his heyday he "was as popular a sporting character as the world possessed." Crowds would wait hours just to glimpse him or, even better, shake his hand. One of these people, a hulking Illinois miner, was perhaps the man who coined the phrase "This hand shook Sullivan's!" (Which, in turn, rapidly became the famous line "Let me shake the hand of the man who shook the hand of John L. Sullivan!")[8]

The fervid nature of Sullivan's support was surprising to many, and a bit unsettling as well. A young reporter, visiting a Tacoma theater to see John L. in a play, light-heartedly asked his neighbor if he thought Sullivan was the best-known living American, and was surprised by the suddenness and vehemence of the answer: yes, beyond a doubt. The champion's fellow pugilists agreed. They all clamored to fight Sullivan for the money and the fame that came with stepping into the ring with John L. For most of them, men like Jack Burke and Patsy Cardiff, it would be the greatest single payday of their lives. For the innocents who were quickly battered to the canvas, like Gypsy Miles and Enos Phillips on the Grand Tour, it was enough to have touched gloves and stood against him, man to man.[9]

Sullivan's popularity had a sexual, not a class, basis. It spread through every stratum of the cult of masculinity, and where it crossed sexual lines it included only the feminine adjuncts of the cult, such as prostitutes or a few working-class women. It is true that his most rabid following was among his fellow Irish Americans, and since in terms of contemporary American patriotism and nationalism the Irish may have looked superior to newer immigrant groups, such as Italians and Chinese, Sullivan may have profited accordingly as his ethnic group painfully gained some respectability. But to identify John L.'s following with immigrants and working-class men *only* is to ignore his standing among many American males regardless of background. Sullivan alone had done much to erode the traditional localism in which sporting identities sprouted and flourished. As he was the first to take individual sporting celebrity from the neighborhood to the nation, so he was the first to take boxing from the back alley and gutter into the urban arena.[10] Despite his behavior and despite the onus of law, he had

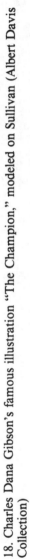

18. Charles Dana Gibson's famous illustration "The Champion," modeled on Sullivan (Albert Davis Collection)

become at least partially "respectable." In so doing, he made boxing partially respectable as well, and with his numerous tours and exhibitions he helped to bring a more businesslike basis to the sport.

In England a temporary allegiance between the working classes and the aristocracy had produced the golden age of Regency boxing. No such social structure existed in America; the common denominator of Sullivan's appeal was masculinity. His virtually all-male audiences and admirers included individuals from every social background and calling that American life had to offer, just as his many detractors, both male and female, spanned the social spectrum. Sullivan himself was proudest of his association with men like Conkling (he called the rascally Lord Roscoe "a warm and constant adherent of mine"), but he drew from a far wider company than slightly off-color politicians. As a cub reporter, Arthur Brisbane was assigned to Sullivan's fights by his bosses on the *New York Sun* simply to get the names of prominent people in attendance, and he found plenty to report.

The champion was recognized as readily among the middle class as among the working class. With his arm in a sling after the Cardiff fight, he visited his friend John C. Kiernan, a high-ranking Tammany sachem, to get the politico to identify him for purposes of cashing a check. Kiernan ushered his guest into the north gallery of the New York Stock Exchange, whereupon the floor brokers immediately gathered with upturned faces to shout their greetings. Although Sullivan declined the opportunity for a speech, the men of Wall Street mobbed him as he made for his cab, the well-wishers elbowing the merely curious.[11]

This sort of public show was common enough, but the sporting press and even the respectable metropolitan dailies carried his exploits into practically every literate home in America. In these John L. found a following as well, sometimes in the most unlikely places. William Lyon Phelps, who later taught literature at Yale for years, was in the habit of reading the news to his father, an orthodox Baptist minister. "I had never heard him mention a prize fight," remembered the younger Phelps, "and did not suppose he knew anything on that subject, or cared anything about it." One day the son noted briefly the results of one of Sullivan's famous bouts and turned the page. The minister leaned over and said earnestly, "Read it by rounds!" Sullivan's penetration of the middle class was smoothed by the propensity of the American male for fraternizing in social and civic clubs. John L. himself was a member of several predominantly middle-class groups, such as the Elks, although he enjoyed most his associations with more rakish organizations, like New York's Chuck Connors Club, which was riddled with Tammanyites, gamblers, newspapermen, and sporting figures. The champion counted several close friends among the middle class, particularly among the few emergent Irish Americans; for example, he sparred on occasion with the widely respected John Boyle O'Reilly.[12]

The natural capstone to his popularity might have been expected to be a life in politics following the end of his ring career. John Morrissey had provided the precedent, and Sullivan himself developed political notions from time to time, although he modestly refused to admit "any aspirations of that sort." After the Grand Tour had roared through Altoona, Pennsylvania, the local paper resignedly noted that "none of Sullivan's admirers will die happy until he is elected to Congress." At one time he was rumored as anxious to be mayor of Boston, and his cronies regarded him as a shoo-in for alderman. He had the instinct for ward politics, without doubt, once buying two hundred tons of flour to distribute among Boston's poor. Whatever political aspirations he had reached their peak in 1889, when he announced himself as a candidate for Congress, his speech written by Arthur Brisbane.

Superficially, Sullivan was an ideal candidate. He was a lifelong Democrat, despised the reforming variety of Republicans called Mugwumps, and had undoubted popularity and voter appeal. But unlike Morrissey, he had no well-oiled political machine behind him, and, also unlike Morrissey, he cared not a whit for the hard, daily grind of local political life. Too impatient and blunt to savor the thrills of political intrigue, he also had the decided handicaps of his boozing, brawling, and marital breakup, all of which were public knowledge. The upshot was that he was denied the nomination by the local power brokers in Boston, which did not concern him overmuch. He continued to keep a strong interest in politics, like most American males, and would pronounce loudly and at length on the leading issues of the day. He also continued to cultivate friends and acquaintances among leading lights of both parties, culminating in his relationship with Theodore Roosevelt.[13]

Regardless of his failure to become a political figure (an occupation for which, given the character of politics in the late nineteenth century, he was not particularly ill suited), Sullivan remained a highly popular icon. The man who eventually ended John L.'s ring career, no mean egoist himself, admitted that Sullivan's popularity was exceptional. Many Irish Americans hated James J. Corbett, one of their own, "just because I had the insolence to fight him." No once could challenge Sullivan for good nature, generosity, and honesty, or so it seemed. Corbett sadly recalled his inability to capture the crowd in the way John L. did: "I was always more controlled and a little too businesslike, perhaps, to vie with him in popularity." This nagging thought clung to Gentleman Jim to the very end of his life: "You can't destroy a public hero without it being resented."[14]

To be sure, Sullivan's popularity and standing with the American public were far from universal, and they fluctuated with the news of each barroom brawl, display of public intoxication, or abuse of a helpless animal. There were always those eager to say, with Corbett's manager, William A. Brady, that "he never really earned the place he occupied in public esteem."[15] Yet there he was, warts and all, at the center of public attention in the Gilded Age, a peculiar sort of hero in an era unusually bereft of traditional heroic figures—but a hero nonetheless.

## II

American heroes traditionally appeared in several guises. Military figures had always been noteworthy, from Washington through Jackson to Lee and Grant. Politicians also ranked highly, but they tended to have a more regional than national flavor, like Calhoun, Webster, or Clay. Only Lincoln, at the price of martyrdom, truly transcended these limitations. There were frontiersmen, like Daniel Boone and Davy Crockett; inventors, like Robert Fulton, Samuel F. B. Morse, and Cyrus McCormick; even, for a growing audience, heroines of the caliber of Lucretia Mott, Elizabeth Cady Stanton, and Harriet Tubman. "The democratic appetite for heroes was apparently insatiable." As American society produced new social roles or ways of making a living, some individual would inevitably be selected as the archetype against whom all others would be matched. The archetype, to be heroic, had to foster admiration and, as far as behavioral patterns went, emulation as well.[16]

The industrial age produced a new constellation of heroes, none of them more respected than Thomas Edison, the pragmatist-as-inventor. But the newer pattern of the heroic lay with the accumulation of money, pure and simple. Industrialism spawned the millionaire, distinguished not only by his wealth but also by the Darwinian struggle he had supposedly undergone to win it. One newspaper, by 1892, was able to tot up no less than 4,047 members of the species, the majority in trade or transportation—although financiers and industrialists were rapidly increasing. These great sums were being accumulated in fewer and fewer hands, as well; by the turn of the century 0.35 percent of the population controlled 75 percent of the wealth of the country. Such concentration meant that the millionaire had his enemies, and as a symbol he was so loathed that many observers predicted class war, capital against labor, the first skirmishes of which had already been seen on the railroads and in the steel mills. Yet the accumulation of money was widely respected as both an art and a skill, to the extent that William Dean Howells had a character in *A Traveler from Alturia*

(1894) remark, "I don't think there is any doubt but the millionaire is now the American ideal."[17]

The older models of success, involving the achievement of competence in one's chosen walk of life, were still present in America, particularly in the countryside, but in the cities they were rapidly being superseded by more acquisitive and status-oriented concerns. The nature of the *deed*, that act by which one registered success or even ascended to the heroic, was changing as well, becoming more public and inclusive in consonance with the increasing social and cultural complexities of the era. Generals and presidents still counted for much, of course. But the pantheon was being enlarged, not only by the broadening communications and transportation networks but also by the public's increasing acceptance of alternative versions of the hero and the successful man.[18]

Despite the change, one constant remained: the hero reached the summit through *individual* struggle. The Greeks had initiated this notion in Western civilization, their festivals ignoring team sports and demanding supreme individual effort. The effort was focused on character, the ennobling virtue of the athletic contest. This idea waxed and waned over the centuries, but in the industrial age it burst into full bloom once again. At first, it did not have the aid of the promotional techniques and marketing strategies that became inseparable from the cultivation of celebrity appeal in the twentieth century. Nevertheless, the idea in connection with modern sport moved the heroic accent from character to deeds, and in consequence the nature of the appropriate heroic deed changed as well. The traditional emphasis on the individual, coupled with the revamped and more culturally tolerant estimation of the deed, produced the athletic celebrity, the sports "star." The change was spurred along by clever promoters like the baseball pioneer Albert G. Spaulding, who organized "all-star" touring teams built around the fame of one man and serving to confirm individualism in both its mythic and realistic patterns.[19]

Of all forms of sport, boxing was most fundamental, even primal, in terms of its individualistic appeal. No other sport presented participants in such basic opposition, and no other sport was so simple in its purpose. As the most highly individualized of all sports, boxing had considerable psychological fascination in an age when the individual seemed to count for less amid the unchecked processes of urbanization and industrialization. The "contemporary passion for the deed" meant that boxing's popularity could interest even its critics, calling forth vituperation and admiration in the same breath. At the grass-roots level, individual initiative remained of prime importance, and throughout the cult of masculinity that individual who asserted himself against the odds was held in high esteem.[20]

John L. Sullivan both profited from and helped to shape this redefinition of the heroic. Several strains in American life led to this development. The age admired force and strength; its citizens were, after all, conquering a continent and reshaping its very mold through the twin genies of industrialization and technology. Sullivan personified nothing if not brute force and muscular power; he was "perfection itself . . . perfectly cultured in his profession. . . . he . . . can knock a man down with as much ease and grace as an accomplished lady can gently and languidly handle an opera fan. . . . all comes as natural and easy as the balmy breezes of May." Even outside the ring, John L.'s feats of strength were routinely reported. Once, it was said, he visited a blacksmith and noticed the iron bar from which the smithy hammered nails. Taking up the bar, he bent it into a semicircle over a brawny forearm and then supposedly bit a piece off it. Another time, tricked into a handshaking contest with a huge Illinois miner, Sullivan was said to have "leaned over and single-handed raised [him] three feet from the ground and swung him lightly twenty feet away." If his teeth were steel and his hands were a vice, his lungs were bellows; he could blow a silver dollar several yards across a room.[21] Such tales were legion, only increased with the telling, and swelled the chorus praising the champion as the virtual embodiment of irresistible force.

Some people also heralded Sullivan for his physique alone. Almost everyone admired perfection, but it was an age that liked *substance* in its public men. The dining habits of most Americans were colossal; no one had heard of calories, carbohydrates, or cholesterol, and as a result, most of the prominent males of the period projected a certain ponderous beefiness. From James Garfield to William Howard Taft, no American president resisted overmuch the blandishments of the dinner table. John L. was cut from the same cloth, eating and drinking with reckless abandon, and his excesses produced a frame that might seem laughable today but was perfectly acceptable in the 1880s as the apotheosis of a manly physique. Thus, "he is not a model member of society, but he is a model of physical culture." Here is John Boyle O'Reilly's description:

> Look at the Statue [*The Boxer*, recently completed in Boston]; that is Sullivan, life, body, and spirit. See the tremendous chest, filled with capacious lungs and a mighty heart, capable of pumping blood everywhere at once. See the ponderous fist and the massive wrist; and the legs and feet—ah! there you see the limbs of a perfect boxer—light as a dancer, firm as a tower. And then, look up to the buttressed, Samson neck, springing beautifully from the great shoulders; look at the head—large round as a Greek's, broad-browed, wide-chinned, with a deep dimple, showing the good nature, and a mouth and lips that ought to be cut in granite, so full are they of doomful power and purpose.[22]

Strength and physique, yes, but it was what Sullivan did with these attributes that held his admirers spellbound. Over and over, the dominant metaphors of the industrial age were used to describe him. He seemed a "magnificent machine of flesh and blood." To a young reporter seeing him for the first time at the Greenfield trial he was "the most wonderful engine of destruction I had ever seen in human form." Statics gave way to kinetics as observers hymned the raw energy of Sullivan in motion. O'Reilly believed that John L.'s superiority lay in his "extraordinary nervous force"; the champion was "as distinct from other boxers as a bull dog is from a spaniel" and in battle was "as fierce, relentless, tireless as a cataract."[23]

Sullivan himself was supremely confident in his power. When younger, he said, he used to hit men under the ear but soon learned the efficiency of a blow to the jaw. Here was "a sure spot to hit a man, and it is less likely to get you sent up for manslaughter." All very precise, scientific, and ultimately unstoppable. Always a staunch advocate of boxing as a science, John L. cultivated the image of himself as a precision fighter: "My objective point in hitting is the corner of a man's shoulder, and if he ducks his head he is bound to get it in the neck. A man will break his dukes if he goes hitting at his antagonist's skull." Indeed, his fear for his hands conditioned much of his "science." Billy Madden recalled that during their association the raw young slugger had injured his knuckles repeatedly and had "soft" hands. Thus Sullivan favored the use of gloves, keeping the machine under control, and was duly applauded by O'Reilly and many others for his supposed forbearance.[24]

The Gilded Age also celebrated the ethic of self-improvement, and here John L., swimming upstream against a torrent of his own evidence to the contrary, sought to present himself as a Spartan during training and a man of moderation at all other times. His guide to improving the human machine began with sound sleep in an airy, well-ventilated room. "I do not believe in having a trainer sleep in the same bed with the person training. . . . a man can sleep better alone and will not be obliged to inhale the breath of the other man." He would prepare himself a "dose of physic," compounded of about fifty cents worth of zinnia, salts, manna, and black stick licorice. Repeated use of this purgative was followed by an application of liver pills (John L. believed in nostrums to the end of his life), and then he got down to work.

Sullivan's ideal regimen, which he seldom if ever followed, involved regular habits, careful attention to personal cleanliness, and a heavy meat diet punctuated by large quantities of celery ("a man can eat plenty of celery"), which he believed was good for the wind and nerves. For exercise he recommended long walks, dumbbells, punching a bag, and jumping rope. He usually had no "sparring partners" in training

19. Confident, poised, and on his best behavior. John L. at the peak of his powers (about 1888) (William Schutte Collection)

and relied mostly on instinct for his ringcraft. Vain about his speed, he once bragged that he had run 100 yards in 10.5 seconds. He dreaded overtraining, which he claimed reduced fighters to desiccated "human greyhounds," but in truth he was never in danger of this particular peril. "There is such a thing as a man overworking himself and growing stale," and against this threat he advocated cards, pool playing, cigar smoking, or "any other little amusement." When out of training he frankly admitted his fancies: "I take things as easy as possible," including sleeping late, eating whatever food he chose (by which he meant food *and* drink), attending theatrical performances, and smoking "as many cigars as I feel like smoking."

John L. considered that from six to ten weeks was enough to train any man for a prizefight. "My one golden rule in conditioning is to disregard my weight altogether"; that is, if he felt good, he was ready. Of course, he said, "a man who drinks should not expect to be a fighter, that is, if he drinks to excess. Drinking makes a man fat." This deadpan lie should not belie the key to his own life-style embodied in his training regimen: "My whole existence and manner of living is guided by nature and nature only"—thus Sullivan's particular version of "the machine in the garden."[25]

Above all in the Gilded Age, the machine was the embodiment of stark power, the abrupt multiplication of human energy that fascinated everyone and repelled a few, such as Henry Adams. For his public, John L. was the vital essence of power, a lethal engine of destruction against which no man could stand. As a machine was fearless, so was Sullivan. On this score even his enemies gave him his due. "There is hardly a more disreputable ruffian now breathing than . . . Sullivan," remarked the *New York Tribune*, "but with all his brutality, his coarseness, and his vices, he certainly is not afraid of meeting any living man with his fists." The result was the ultimate decisive act, the knockout blow. This is what thousands came to see, and when Sullivan delivered, they were fulfilled.[26]

At its base the relationship between fighter-hero and fan was pure atavism, an instinctive worship of force and dominance. Some even saw Sullivan as unrefined aggressive energy, "reminiscent of prehistoric man, the cave-dweller, stone axe in hand, battling indiscriminately, fighting his way to his goal, fulfilling his desires, good or bad, and conquering by sheer audacity, an irresistible arm and a heart that never knew fear." By this view instinct called out to instinct at an almost subconscious level, earning John L. the grudging admiration even of those who loathed his lifestyle. The Gilded Age was awash in the ideas of social Darwinism, that peculiar perversion of Darwin that advanced biological arguments to justify status differences and social injustice. Whether one was a coal heaver, preacher, or millionaire, if one believed that life itself was a struggle, then Sullivan was at once the most fundamental warrior around and the example par excellence of the rewards of victory.[27]

This particular machine had a mind, and it appeared to all that Sullivan possessed incredible confidence and will power, an urge to triumph that transcended the limitations of the human frame. "When I started out boxing," he recalled, "I felt within myself, as I do now, that I could knock out any man living." In any fight, his fundamental purpose was to bend the other man to his inexorable will; his opponent was "second to me at every stage." As for victory, none of the "joys of competitive sport" for John L.: "I go in to win from the very first second, and I never stop until I have won. Win I must, and win I will, at every stage of the game." He cultivated also the aura of invincibility: "I have never felt a man's blow in my life." Victory, decisiveness, culmination, conquest! Draws were intolerable; there should be a winner of every fight, and if officials were uncertain after the scheduled number of rounds, then the fight should continue until they were convinced of one man's mastery over another. These attitudes not only concerned boxing, they extended to other areas as well. They were not new in American life but were now simply raised to their highest pitch yet. After all, even Benjamin Franklin remembered that "when I was a boxing boy, it was allowed, even after an adversary said he had had enough, to give him a rising blow."[28]

Metaphorically, of course, the strength and will espoused by John L. at his saltiest could have been tolerated by no society outside the prize ring. Nietzsche aside, the result would have been anarchic chaos, and everyone, including Sullivan, recognized this. No one wanted a locomotive, serviceable enough in its proper sphere, running amuck through his living room. Therefore the champion established a fallback position that lacked the atavistic appeal of the primitive but spoke directly to the conscious bonds of the cult of masculinity. Throughout his life he posed as an advocate of self-defense in a social context rather than as the awesome, unstoppable ring machine that both he and his admirers believed him to be:

> It is very much better for the young, as well as the old, to possess the knowledge of the manly art of self defense than it is to have them resort to knives and guns. It shows conclusively that if we all know how to protect ourselves with Nature's weapons, the fists, which God gave us—one and all—to protect ourselves with, there would be less use for fire-arms and knives and less people in the penitentiary today.
>
> Boxing is something that quickens the eye and makes the brain active and improves every muscle in the body and, above all, gives a man or woman confidence. You very seldom hear of a man who understands how to handle himself with his fists carrying a gun, and, if he is in any kind of

a heated argument, is always very cool and collected and never loses his temper, knowing at all times that he can defend himself.[29]

Thus the hero professed his ideals, as well as his self-control. Self-defense was fundamental to a smoothly functioning society. The manly art diminished violence and created confidence. Far from a threat, boxing was integral to concepts of self-esteem and self-worth. Sullivan kept this mantle of teacher and prophet wrapped close about him to the very end, even as his actions spoke thunderously louder than his words. But it was a useful pose, not only to the champion but also to society at large, since through it everyone could be reassured that the machine had its limits and pugilism was, anyway, only an exercise in the necessity of self-protection.

Sullivan's deeds within the ring meshed with his era's demands for the heroic. Yet if the classic hero was "a personage of idealized virtues," then here Sullivan parted company. He was *sui generis*, the first of his kind. Probably no one took the trouble to analyze the roots of their affection for or allegiance to him; he simply *was*, and in so being he became, for a moment, a national celebrity. He was known not only for his deeds but for his personality and his fame as well—"known for being known." He was the subject of constant gossip and speculation, the focus of praise, damnation, and oracular interpretation. Instant legends spun about him, passing from barroom to pool hall like tales told around ancient campfires. Far from a monument, he was all too common, all too *alive*, a public symbol like none seen before, especially in urban America. True, his special identity was with the Irish, but this was a convenient dustbin into which his critics could sweep him when all else failed. Actually, his appeal was well-nigh universal within the male world, because he spoke so deeply to newer masculine ideals for action before thought, victory before compromise, the deed above character itself.[30]

His closest compeer was a legend himself, Mose the Bowery B'hoy, "America's first urban folk hero." Mose was a stage character, a rough-hewn Irish rake and dandy. He was part and parcel of the city, a fireman who squelched flame with machines and a pugnacious rough-and-ready brawler who conquered men with his fists. A knight-errant, Mose left no baby unsaved from a flaming second-story window and allowed no man to sully the reputation of a fair Irish lass. He was a bundle of appealing contradictions—lovable and violent, rakish and oafish, gentlemanly and obscene. Mose was thus an ambiguous figure, and his problematic character was defined by his public in several contradictory ways at once. He could simultaneously seem to be the manly hero, the political fixer, the courtly gallant, or the tipsy plug-ugly.[31]

Sullivan's public persona shared the same ambiguity. A few of his more unabashed admirers might have tried to emulate him in some way, but most of them lived vicariously through him, as a partial role model or hero. Positive virtues he had in abundance—courage, honesty, and candor, for example. Also, he was the best at what he did, certifiably a "champion" and a winner. And he "won" not once but over and over, in different contexts and for more than a decade. Heroes, observed the historian Carlyle, have their season, and the Gilded Age belonged to Sullivan.

However, there were all those negatives, aspects of his character that even his most steadfast fans might downplay or dismiss but could not ignore. Alexandre Dumas had asserted that there were *"deux classes d'imbéciles qui ont beaucoup de choses en common."* One of these was the hero, the superman, the invincible champion, defined as such not by himself but by the group for which he performed. He was supernormal, in contrast to the subnormality or the countermorality of the villain and the general lack of intelligence, competence, or sobriety of the fool. John L. Sullivan may never have seen his alter ego Mose perform (the Mose character was a standard of the mid-nineteenth-century popular theater), but if he did, the Bowery B'hoy's stage antics would have given him as much laughter as a sense of admiration. For Mose, regardless of his steadfast courage and his noble deeds, was also a fool.[32]

## III

In metaphors and fairy tales, size and power are almost always accompanied by lack of intelligence. Brains are the little man's defense, while "slow wit is the tragic flaw of the giant." Societies tend to find strength and intelligence, when coupled in the same frame, to be a bit overwhelming or even intolerable. John L. Sullivan was extraordinarily sensitive to the charge of stupidity, which was made against him probably above all other men of his generation:

> They do not consider the pugilist as anything more than a brute, and thought a man of muscle and science could not be gifted with brains as well; and on this account I wish to show ... that ... [I] am gifted with ordinary ability, and [am] conscious of being something more than a pugilist. I want them also to understand that, while not of an egotistical nature, I have fair amount of common sense, and, with a Boston public school education, can give an intelligent opinion on almost any subject, and conduct myself as a gentleman in any company.

Many of his public scraps were started by slurs against his intelligence, and he often declaimed, as he once did before a crowd of Chicago grain men and Harvard students in the billiard room of Young's Hotel in Boston, that he was no brute and wanted to be known as a gentleman.[33]

Some admirers expanded this moderate, defensive assertion and made John L. look like a cross between Demosthenes and an Ivy league professor. "He was a very well read man," wrote one, "and preferred any time to discuss Shakespeare, Gladstone or Parnell to talking fight." The champion had his philosophical moods, said another, and when so engaged "preferred long words, hunted for them carefully, and would not accept suggestions or substitutes." Supposedly he read Marcus Aurelius, pondered Socrates, and was fond of relating classical thought to his ring experiences. Classical allusions to his physique were routine ("His head sits on its columned neck, as proud as that of Ajax when he braved Jove's cloud and laughed at lightnings!"), but most of the intellectual references contained more than a dose of sarcasm.[34]

Obviously, Sullivan was far from a learned man, but he and his fans compensated by promoting native instinct over book learning. For his detractors, juxtaposing the mindless brute with his pretensions to thought provided a useful defense against John L.'s physical dominance. The truth concerning his mental abilities obviously lay between these two poles, but what stands out poignantly is the desire of the outsider to be accepted in the world of intellect, which would always reject him out of hand. Not until a later generation inflated Gene Tunney as a student of English literature would the fight world meet academe, and even then it was a temporary marriage of the bizarre, with banns posted by the sensationalist press.

Coupled with Sullivan's lack of intelligence was his supposedly childlike character. By reducing him symbolically to the level of a child, the Gilded Age lessened John L.'s ability to terrorize or threaten and rendered him harmless in the real and meaningful world of adults. The champion directly encouraged the tendency with his frank and open behavior. He was completely unashamed of his body and would often appear naked in his dressing room in front of reporters and other males. He allowed several full-length nude photographs of himself (rear view) to appear in his autobiography. Fond of playing the role of the "natural man," unadorned and unencumbered by the common hypocrisies of society, he was candid, blunt, and without affectation, deception, or guile—deliberately cultivating the innocence of a child. "If Sullivan cannot express himself after the sentimental manner of Sterne, or attempt to gammon any of the tender part of society with the platonic taste of Rousseau, and wind up with the speciousness of a Joseph Surface, he can be backed against them all at high odds for his possession of genuine feeling." In this he was nature's nobleman, displaying "much of the majesty Carlyle ascribes to the primal king."[35] Here was either honesty unadorned or simplemindedness, depending on the point of view.

Like a child, he would often burst out singing at unexpected moments, tunes such as "Oh, White, White Moon" being delivered in a gravelly roar. He took a childish delight in the cascade of gifts, from the most trivial to the grandest jewels, and would often proudly display his latest acquisition to friends and reporters. By the late 1880s he had been the recipient of countless watches, pins, medals, and likenesses and was accustomed to seeing himself as a centerpiece of that orgy of praise, the prizefighter's "benefit." The really valuable awards, such as the great Championship Belt, he cherished inordinately. At every ceremonial occasion he was deeply moved, even when a character named "Smiling Albert" gave him a sponge-shaped piece of copper matte from the Parrot Smelter in Butte, Montana. He was said to be fascinated by valuables, spending hours playing with them in Diamond Jim Brady's Fifty-seventh Street apartment. Diamond Jim reputedly gave John L. gifts of stickpins and rings, much of which went to buy liquor, and often had to coax him from bars with promises of diamonds. "The sight of Jim luring the fighter into a hansom cab was reminiscent of a farmer enticing a recalcitrant chicken into its coop with kernels of corn."[36]

Sullivan deeply loved animals, and he went out of his way to see vaudeville acts featuring goats, dogs, birds, and monkeys, although horses apparently did not rank highly in his zoological pantheon. He kept dogs around him constantly, particularly in his later years, favoring collies. Insatiably curious, he had a proclivity for visiting odd places—the visit to the Tombstone jail being one such instance. Indeed, condemned men held a special fascination. On his way to the championship bout with Ryan, he stopped off in the nation's capital and was taken to see Charles Guiteau, then being held for the assassination of President Garfield. Five years later he visited Chicago Police Headquarters to view four of the accused Haymarket anarchists. In 1891 he was given a special chair near the jury box to witness the trial of several Italians in New Orleans for the murder of an Irish police chief. He seemed fascinated by celebrity, particularly of the criminal kind.[37]

Sullivan's love of excitement and games also reflected his childlike quality. He was fond of taking dares, once letting a trick shooter named Dan Murphy blast away at a quarter held between his thumb and forefinger. Murphy had a checkered track record. He had previously exercised his skill on a fighter named Ike Weir ("the Belfast Spider"), leaving Weir with a bloody pair of digits. Undeterred, Sullivan let Murphy fire away, in the process receiving a painful injury to his hand. When he began to use weapons himself again, years after his near-fatal incident with the shotgun in Denver, he developed into a fine wing shot. John L. loved to chase fire engines, too. While never settled enough in any community to be a volunteer fireman, he could not resist a good blaze. Once, railroading through Indiana, the Sullivan combination was forced to stop by a fire hose athwart the tracks. Tracing it to the scene of the fire, John L. was soon helping to carry out household goods before a goggle-eyed crowd.[38]

He seldom if ever gambled, preferring any contest of physical skill. Of course, baseball was a lifelong love. He never really shed the dust of the Boston sandlots and even late in life was a frequent visitor in the Red Sox dugout. In city after city he would appear with local teams, drawing thousands to see his decidedly mediocre play. He often acquired minor injuries on the ball field, but nothing diminished his zeal for the game. In 1885 he even organized a short-lived traveling team of his own. And if he did not play, he umpired, thoroughly enjoying the role of arbitrator.[39]

All of this had its positive side, to be sure, a refreshing, exuberant element that fed directly into his popularity. But it also gave him the reputation of a man who had never really grown up, a permanent case of arrested development who could never be taken seriously in any aspect of adult affairs. In this way he could be rendered almost harmless, unworthy of the consideration of reasonable, practical men.

There was more, however, much more; the darker side of power and brutality could not be whitewashed so easily. If Sullivan was a stupid oaf, still he might take apart an opponent or a barroom. If he was only an inquisitive, greedy child, still he could profane by his mere presence. His contemporaries in the upper and middle classes tended to cultivate an internalized ethic of self-control; John L. too often lived out of control. In short, he seemed to many to be a profligate of the grandest sort, perhaps the greatest sinner of his age. There was a certain amount of social hypocrisy involved. As a famous sociologist once noted, "Some Americans do most of the sinning, but most do some of it." The catalog of John L.'s sins was long and astonishingly varied, but even so he became as much a symbol of sin as an active participant.[40] And, wickedness (as always) held a certain allure.

Most cultures closely correlate evil and ugliness. Not everyone saw in Sullivan's muscular bulk the perfection of Hercules or the symmetrical beauty of classical sculpture. Reporters would dwell on the heavy black eyebrows or the slightly prognathous jaw, or attempt to sketch his features with adjectives such as dull, heavy, gross, or coarse. To one observer of his early career "he looked like an overgrown youngster, with no hirsute concealment of the ugliest mouth I ever saw gashed in a human countenance."[41] A brute *had* to be ugly.

Making the brute more comical were his endless boasting, his vulgar efforts to dress in style, and his clumsy attempts to act respectably. John L.'s firm confidence in his abilities, the public model for practically every boxing champion since, often drifted into outright bragging. Much of this, to be sure, went down smoothly with his fans. Socially, boosters and braggarts have time-honored functions; they serve not only as clowns but also as heralds of pride and accomplishment. Sullivan was a four-square American patriot, and this side of his boasting had a certain attraction. Personally, however, his favorite subject (himself) was too often the hero, too much the gentleman. He would never admit that he had been pressed by any of his ring adversaries. "None of them ever gave me any trouble," he responded to one inquiry, proceeding to make the incredible claim that Paddy Ryan was the toughest man he had faced.[42]

He was a flashy dresser, displaying a consistent sartorial bad taste that in itself was remarkable. A typical meet-the-press outfit might feature tight-fitting salmon-pink trousers with two-inch checks of white and black, a blue waistcoat speckled with red and black spots and lined with white stripes, and a Prince Albert cutaway. He was a walking rainbow in an era when most men attired themselves in somber blacks and browns, and he could preen like a peacock over a thousand dollars' worth of suits in New York: "I've got the prettiest clothes you ever saw."[43]

Much of the time he tried hard to be polite, and much of the time he succeeded. When sober and on his best behavior he exuded a joviality and consideration for others that were unfeigned and usually reciprocated. In this condition he was chivalrous and mannered to a fault, and he could enjoy repartee with the likes of Grover Cleveland, Theodore Roosevelt, and the Prince of Wales. He was "a regular Lord Chesterfield," according to one English journalist.[44] But the comments on his manners often masked the unspoken phrase "for a fighter." It was these obvious attempts to ape ways of life into which he had not been born that led to the mockery and deflating barbs at his ego. And like most *arrivistes* he only kept on trying, seemingly oblivious to the scorn but deeply hurt by his failure to fit in with the "right crowd." The result often came in vehement outbursts against the "swells" and "snobs" who were not man enough to confront him face to face.

His temper was hair-trigger and volcanic; he was quick to resort to violent behavior. His most immediate method, surprisingly, did not involve his sledgehammer fists. He would grab his tormentor by the lapels and butt him in the head, as he had done to Herbert Slade in San Francisco. He was always ready to back up any altercation with punches, a habit strengthened by the victim's obvious tendency to cower before the heavyweight champion of the world. Many of his flare-ups came in the most trivial circumstances, as when he squabbled with a Sante Fe Railroad conductor over ticket fare and was allowed to ride free from Newton, Kansas, to Topeka. His well-earned reputation as a bully was enhanced by his readiness to use any weapon that was ready at hand, short of a gun. After the shotgun incident in Denver he was nervous around firearms and never carried them himself, believing adamantly that any man worth his salt did his fighting with his fists. Nevertheless, he was not above the use of weapons, once supposedly permanently injuring a San Francisco character named Oofty Goofty by slugging him in the back with a billiard cue. The stories of his hitting the youngster in New York City and mistreating his horses followed him for years.[45]

Most of this violence was a direct result of his alcoholism, and in the classic pattern of the alchoholic his behavior patterns would become much worse before they got better. His drinking was, in part, learned behavior, a masculine license to function in the male world, but beyond that, lacking solid psychiatric evidence, there can be only speculation. As in his attitudes toward the slurs on his intelligence, Sullivan was extremely sensitive on the subject of his drinking. "I never drank because I like liquor," he said, "and never took a glass of whiskey that it didn't burn my throat, and I never drank a glass of wine without thinking of the consequences. Why did I drink, then? Why, sociability." Ever since the abortive Charlie Mitchell fight in the summer of 1884, the fact that the most famous sporting figure in America was a drunkard had been public knowledge, but John L. did absolutely nothing to remove this particular incubus from his back. For one thing the image of a stand-up, two-fisted drinker served him well among certain segments of the cult of masculinity. For another, the temperance advocates who constantly sought to bring him within the fold seemed to him a weak-kneed lot of milksops. And for a third, he could not stop.[46]

Thus his public career was a veritable parade of drunken escapades, most of them reported fully, if sometimes distortedly, by the nation's press. Loud, boisterous behavior was the least of it. In practically every city in the Union he drank, quarreled, came to blows, and often ended up standing sheepishly before a magistrate and paying his fine. His rambunctiousness was not confined to bars, either. Whether as a reckless carriage driver or an obnoxious drunk careening down some sidewalk, he seemed to be a constant public menace, an endless burr under the blanket of civil order and decorum. Such an example was a carriage accident in Boston, in which Sullivan's vehicle crashed into one driven by a man named Marsh, resulting in a slight injury to Marsh, a consequent pressing of charges, and a night in jail on drunk-and-disorderly charges plus a five-dollar fine for Sullivan. Many of these escapades were wildly inflated in the telling (supposedly he once strangled a wildcat after downing a pint of whiskey), but enough of them are documented to make the point that John L., when boozed up, was a threat to anyone around him, including himself.[47]

The core of Sullivan's violent personality was not, such tales to the contrary, schizoid. He was not mentally aberrant and bore no grudge against society. Despite appearances, he did not veer wildly from "good John L." to "bad John L." But his ring achievements and the constant adulation had caused him to erect a formidable fortress of self-identity, a monumentally egocentric vision of himself that he probably fortified in alcohol. Any breach of this image by *anyone*, whether outsider or confidant, deserved retribution. He ruined many friendships, such as those with Billy Madden and Al Smith, through his obstinate refusal to accept criticism and his outright rejection of anyone trying to save him from himself. While the good times lasted and the money kept rolling in, he could get away with it, but he could never hide from people who called him a stupid brute, regarded him as a child, feared him as a bully, or, worst of all, dismissed him as an alcoholic. It was one of these who described the champion as "a son-of-a-bitch of the first water—if he ever drank any."[48]

## IV

And yet there was something powerfully appealing about him to his generation. All his faults—including the one most difficult to document, the womanizing—were widely known throughout the popular culture, and lest his public be disposed to forget, John L. was disposed to provide a flagrant new lapse every few months or so. His was the naughty charm of Peck's Bad Boy, and although his destructive rages rarely played well among the middle class, his vices held the thrill of the profane.

Sullivan was hemmed in by none of the Calvinist principles, particularly the ethic of hard work, saving, and deferred gratification. With the death of John, Jr., he had no posterity to provide for, although it is fair to say he saved as little at the beginning of his career as he did toward the end. Stocks, bonds, insurance, savings accounts—each of these hedges against a rainy day were alien to his nature. He seldom saw more than a few days into the future, content to take what came. His attitude toward money was that it was to be spent, not saved, and he chose to spend within the parameters of the cult of masculinity. Except for his clothes and jewelry, he spent little on the status symbols his kind of wealth could afford—a fine home, for example. Instead, his paydays, as large as some of them were, evaporated into the air like water under a desert sun.

Sullivan, by all accounts, was an exceptionally open-hearted and generous man. This, along with his drinking, meant that the size of his pocketbook swelled and deflated with systolic regularity. Some of his fights, such as the match with Frank Herald, were frankly scheduled

20. John L.'s generosity was celebrated throughout the popular culture, as in this *National Police Gazette* illustration, 24 April 1886   (William Schutte Collection)

because he, rather than his opponent, needed a payday. He became an inveterate borrower as well as a loaner of money, one's willingness to share being an important denominator in his world of men. At different times he owed money to every boxing promoter he ever worked with, including Billy Madden, Al Smith, and Pat Sheedy. By 1892 John L. conservatively estimated he had made half a million dollars in the previous decade—and he was close to dead broke.[49]

The public saw only his ability to make money, the seeming ease with which he amassed his thousands. He was *expected* to spend; it was part of his social role, and anything less than lavish would be miserly. After all, he made in a few minutes what other men labored for years to attain. One contemporary tale has a small boy approach his father, an author:

> "Papa, how long did it take you to write this book?"
> "Nearly a year, my boy."
> "Did you work very hard at it?"
> "Every page has my heart's blood on it."
> "Ain't that queer? I don't see any."
> "No, you don't see it. Nobody else seemed to either."
> "Did you make any money out of it, papa?"
> "Oh, yes (drearily), I made about $250."
> "Is that all. Why, this paper says 'John L. Sullivan made ten times that much in one night by knocking a man down a few times.' Why don't you learn to be a fighter? Or why don't you keep a saloon? The saloon-keeper's boy dresses betterin' I do."[50]

John L.'s image as a spendthrift was, alas, all too true. Corbett's manager would write later that "during all his career, Sullivan never made any great amount of money," that the first big American fight purse was the Corbett bout. For sheer amount this is true enough, but this statement ignores the several times that Sullivan took home more than ten thousand dollars from a single day's work, as well as the ancillary profits he made from well-paying ventures such as that with Lester and Allen. Once again, Sullivan's income, sporadic as it was, should not be judged against the earnings of the plutocrats of the industrial age but against paydays typical of members of his social class and background. By this comparison he made heaping amounts of money. Although he associated with many gamblers, most of his profits went not to them (some of the sharpers, such as the famed Richard A. Canfield, cared nothing for sports) but to marginal business enterprises and, above all, to family, friends, and even strangers.[51] He was as prodigal with his funds as he was careless about his health.

By the mid-1880s he was virtually the sole support of his family, with the exception of his sister, Ann, who had married a workingman named James Lennon in 1880 and was busy rearing a brood of her own. He gave his parents thousands of dollars and provided them with a comfortable home. His brother, Mike, who was proving incapable of earning a living on his own, had to be provided for, with jobs such as helping to run the Washington Street saloon. Even Annie Sullivan, before their split in 1885, had been treated most kindly, by her own admission, with gifts of money and jewels.

With his friends he was an open spigot, pouring forth money in every direction at the slightest opportunity. He stayed at the best hotels, tipped lavishly, and bullheadedly refused to let any barroom crowd spend a cent while he was buying. Eventually he became a willing captive of his generosity; it was part of his social role, even if it bankrupted him. Only rarely did the purse snap shut, and then only when he felt the integrity of a friendship had been violated, always by the other person. When the ex-felon Joe Coburn died, alone and penniless, Sullivan wired Pat Sheedy five hundred dollars thinking it was for his former manager. But he withdrew it on finding out it was not for Sheedy but for funeral expenses for old Joe, against whom John L. had nursed a grudge ever since Coburn's ill-chosen remarks to a reporter about the champion's character. With all his borrowing, Sullivan tried his best to repay his loans, often stuffing a fresh pay envelope directly into the pocket of a benefactor, as he did with seventeen hundred dollars he owed Sheedy—a debt that was promptly paid even though the two men had split the previous year.[52]

Beyond the network of family and friends, he distributed money far and near to charities, worthy causes, and complete strangers. Hibernian activities, Democratic political campaigners, and male social clubs found him a willing giver. He was at his best (or worst) in a bar, where his reputation as a soft touch had to be sustained in public. Once in James Cusick's New York saloon, he was approached by a Sister of Charity for a donation and, thinking of giving her a fiver, handed over a fifty-dollar bill. When a friend pointed out the mistake, John L. airily told her to keep it. He routinely gave wood, coal, and flour to poor families in the Boston area, not all of this connected with his fledgling political aspirations. Stories abounded, many of them true if embellished, of his kindness to the unfortunate. Panhandling bums, aged women who could not afford even the simplest funeral arrangements, crippled bootblacks, and pugilists down on their luck—Sullivan helped them all.

Many of these tales had more than a passing resemblance to the melodramatic theater of the era. John L. loved the theater, and he probably modeled some of his behavior patterns on the florid emotionalism so common on stage. Hearing that a poor widow had been evicted from her home because she could not pay the rent, the champion paid the rent plus six months in advance, filled her locker with food and her cellar with coal, and gave her twenty dollars to boot. Mike Donovan recalled that panhandlers would buy tickets for trains on which Sullivan traveled, just to get the chance to touch him for a handout. If he was in the mood, John L. would press cash even on those who did not want the money, as he did with a seedy, threadbare Methodist minister who left Sullivan's train with one hundred dollars for his small Alabama church.[53]

John L.'s views on chivalry and fair play were fully consonant with his openhearted character. Even though he routinely consorted with prostitutes and went through an impressive list of "traveling companions" during his career, his attitudes on women reflected the virgin-whore duality of the Gilded Age. His self-image led him to champion victimized females and damsels in distress. He was unfailingly courteous to the "better sort" of woman and missed no opportunity to defend her honor or, literally, save her. Once on a steamer going from Belfast, Maine, to Boston he saw a young woman, "evidently somewhat crazy," hurl herself overboard. Sullivan had to be restrained from diving in after her and then was ordered out of the lifeboat being lowered for the rescue. Following her safe recovery, he reflected that "being a woman and somewhat crazy, she might have made trouble for me in the water; but I am a good swimmer, and I think I could have saved her."

Again, the melodramatic quality was uppermost, as in the tale of Sullivan in England, strolling hotelward from London's Haymarket Theater and seeing a poor working girl being accosted by a hulking brute. Quickly, John L. bounded across the street, seized the burly wretch by the throat, and hurled him into the gutter a dozen feet away. As he escorted the half-fainting girl to a cab, there ensued this choice bit of Late Victorian dialogue:

He: "Hurry home, little girl, hurry home now! This is no time for you to be out!"

She: "Oh, sir (sobbing), how can I ever thank you! And I'm so afraid that ruffian will harm you! You know, sir, he's Big Jem, 'the Holgate Hurricane,' they calls him, sir!"

He: "Never you fear for me, my girl. I'm Sullivan, the American, and we don't allow unprotected women to be insulted over there!"

She: "What, sir, the great Yankee Sullivan they talk so much about——"

He: "Yes (grinning), and Yankees don't insult poor girls. Now be off home with you!"

Another time he was said to have rescued a woman, an American abroad, who had slipped in front of a powerful dray horse at Charing Cross. The lady's son, who saw the whole thing, was duly grateful: "no man in my hearing shall ever abuse prize-fighters!" As for his mother, while practically unconscious she nevertherless was able to deliver this soliloquy:

> What! Is this Sullivan the prize-fighter? Oh, sir; to think how I have abused you and how I have warned my son to have nothing to do with this modern "slugging" but to stand by the duelling creed of his forefathers! Mr. Sullivan, I do not believe many duelists would or could have done what you did today. I thank you from my heart, and from this time on, Southern woman as I am, the man who fights with his fists shall have honor at my hands![54]

The point is not that anyone really talked in these orotund tones from the melodramatic stage, or even that the incidents ever happened. Sullivan's image of himself was heavily laden with chivalrous, protective attitudes toward women and gave to his sexual life the quality of hypocrisy and the masculine double standard. Thus, admiring males could wink at his sexual peccadilloes while agreeing with his noble vision of the helpless woman. The poor creatures needed male protectors, and who better in this role than the heavyweight champion of the world?

He was also a wholehearted advocate of fair play, which to him meant honest, open competitition, each man to his individual resources. In his own bouts he loafed occasionally, particularly under the strain of the Grand Tour, but he usually gave all he had, in violent bursts of energy summoned from somewhere deep within. He loathed the notion of "fixed" fights or prearranged outcomes, practices that were unfortunately all too common in the bare-knuckle era. Jem Mace once wanted a guarantee that John L. would let him stay the four rounds, but Sullivan would have none of it. "If Mace can whip me, let him do it. If I can whip him, so much the better. I will try to knock his block off from the moment I enter the ring until I leave it." Such strictures went for others, too. While seconding Pete McCoy in a fight against Dominick McCaffery, John L. tangled with McCaffery's seconds when he thought they were cheating. A bit of a bully himself when intoxicated, Sullivan could not stand overbearing, browbeating behavior in others and was given to "chastising" such disturbers of the peace, as he once did with a local blowhard in Mount Clemens, Michigan.[55]

Common American strains in Sullivan's time and thereafter were to use humor to deflate pretension and to laugh at the expense of social underdogs. John L. was the butt of countless jokes and satires, not only as a brute or buffoon but also as an Irishman. He was exceptionally sensitive on this score and accordingly disdained many of the social airs of the middle class. At times he declared his way of robbing people about as clever as that of more elevated professions, say, Baptist preachers.[56]

His own sense of humor was puckish, racist, and cynical. He was fond of jokes of the traveling-salesman variety, and "nigger humor" was a staple in his repertoire. The misfortunes of others were fair game, too. After Ryan blamed his hernia for the loss of the championship, Sullivan penned a squib to the *New York Clipper*, "truss-ting that Mr. Ryan's 'excuse' for losing the fight may not prevent him from meeting me [again]." He loved practical jokes, the more heavy-handed, callous, and crude, the better. Once aboard ship with his sparring partner, Jack Ashton, he noticed Ashton leaning over the rail. Borrowing a gold-headed walking stick from a bystander, he struck his friend's rear end with such force that the stick shattered into splinters. The bystander was given five dollars for his trouble, and Ashton was left to reflect on the perils of travel with Sullivan, much as the members of the Grand Tour had done. John L. would practice his sense of fun on strangers, too, as when he playfully barred a depot door in Iowa until he could reach the train himself, leaving other passengers without passage. He would abuse black waiters, mockingly threaten friends with firearms, or pinch a man's arm until it was black and blue, all in the name of good fun.[57]

Sullivan was also a noteworthy raconteur and was highly regarded as a tale-spinner, especially when the subject was Sullivan. He eventually refined his humor and his storytelling into a passable vaudeville act, and he grew adept in later years at telling stories on himself. When in a self-deflating mood he could be positively endearing, but particularly in his early years such moments barely concealed his anger at those presumably above him on the social scale, nor did they hide for long his penchant for crude physical humor. Regardless, he was (when sober) a hale fellow well met, and this, along with his generosity, sense of chivalry, and love of fair play caused him to be adored as much as feared. He was the stuff of legend.

# V

Sullivan's behavior was made for exaggeration, and apocrypha convoyed his passage through the Gilded Age from the moment he became champion. He assiduously helped in manufacturing the more positive aspects of his own legend, creating an urban counterpart to the frontier boast and brag common to earlier generations. But most of the bunkum was produced by others. If it was fighting, John L. was the best; in boozing, he could drink more and hold it better; and if you discussed the fair sex, he had shagged more than any man around. Congruent with the values of his age, the accent was on quantity: more knockouts, more bottles polished off, more women skewered.

In the world of the prize ring he was beyond compare. His punches had the power of steam engines, and his opponents were inevitably flattened. The number of his knockouts was inflated dramatically, many Americans believing he had kayoed two hundred men during the Grand Tour. Like authentic frontier heroes he not only made the big brag but made it stick, as when, still a small boy in school, he supposedly passed the following note among his classmates:

> My name is John L. Sullivan. I whipped every boy at the Concord Primary, and I can whip every kid in this room. I'm going to do it too. Read this and pass it on.[58]

Apart from his physical dominance, the stories that clung closest to him had to do with his drinking. He was denoted "one of the greatest souses who ever lived"—a title not without esteem within the cult of masculinity. In truth he drank publicly and often, and his tastes were eclectic, running all the way from beer through gin to finer wines and brandies. He drank alone or with companions, and he was known to go on alcoholic binges lasting for days. His consumption was considered prodigious—if not enough to float a battleship, at least a medium cruiser. He was said by one account to have drained sixty-seven gin fizzes at a single sitting. Another had him polishing off fifty-six of the same within an hour. A third claimed he had gulped one hundred drinks at a bar and left under his own steam. To prove his capacity, he supposedly engaged in drinking contests at the drop of a bartender's apron, once losing a champagne duel to a San Francisco trollop named Tessie Wall in the bar of the Cremorn dance hall.[59]

His sexual skills, measured in the indefinite dimension of numbers of mistresses and lovers, were held remarkable in their variety. Like many men of his generation he occasionally paid for sex and may have been introduced to the pleasures of the bed by Boston prostitutes. The available evidence, while extremely slim, indicates he believed that women in a sexual relationship were for use and display but little else. His was a decidedly masculine world, and while women were fine objects to worship or defend, they had no function whatsoever in male decision making or rites of passage. His female associations, so far as is known, were all from the twilight world of prostitution, from the slightly illicit stage, or from his own social background. Only late in life did he settle down with a "good woman."

Brawling, boozing, and wenching hardly provided exemplary role models for young American boys, and the incredible feats of Sullivan in these areas were pilloried by press and pulpit for years. It was easy enough for the gentility to puncture the numerous lies and exaggerations surrounding him, but if they did so, they only made him less the devil and more like themselves. Thus, most of his critics preferred to believe the worst, and the negative elements of Sullivan's legend, like the positive, reverberated throughout the popular culture. Indeed, people could take a single fact, such as his undeniably prodigious drinking, and praise or damn it as they willed. John L. was a useful symbol not only for Irish underdogs and apostles of rugged manhood; he also served those who hated or feared what he seemed to be.

Sullivan was a transitional figure in American sport, the last of the bare-knuckle breed and a harbinger of the newer boxing science. In an age that sought to discipline itself in the school, the factory, and the office, he seemed a wild throwback to a more ungoverned time. Above all, he made the figure of the lower-class mauler a cultural hero—never entirely respectable, but never completely outside the law, either. He cut across the grain of athletic idealism like a rampaging buzzsaw. The young athlete was supposed to be both sexually and morally pure. He neither gambled, smoked, nor drank, nor did he chase women, of whom only two mattered, Mom and The Girl. He was modest and self-effacing and readily sacrificed himself for the greater whole, such as the team. The unwritten "sportsmen's code" that embodied this idealism was part of Sullivan's code, too. But no one would argue that he came near to living up to its standards.[60]

There were many reasons for John L.'s popularity, but probably the most important was his openness, both about himself and about the world around him. His speaking voice was deep and mellow, "as resonant as a cathedral bell," and as the years passed and the booze sandpapered his throat, his tone became deeper and more reverberating still. He spoke with just the hint of a brogue, gleaned from his parents, that underlaid a broad Bostonian accent. The combination added a certain charm for those who were inclined to listen. Sullivan used this instrument throughout his life with considerable effect. Although not a natural public speaker, he appealed directly to his audiences with his undoubted candor. His honesty stopped short of flatly admitting his alcoholism; this he could not bring himself to do for many years. But apart from this painful exercise in self-awareness, he was as direct and forthright as any public American had ever been, and in a society of greater complexity and growing individual anonymity, this was both significant and refreshing.

After his fight with Frank Herald, Sullivan advanced to the ropes and said a few words in praise of his vanquished opponent, as was his custom. He ended by saying "with these few remarks I am yours, truly, John L. Sullivan." The phrase went down so well that he used it as an envoi ever after. For he *was* theirs, big-hearted, courageous, and honest. Like his flaws, his virtues had the dimension of legend; there seemed nothing small about him.

He had to be swallowed whole, or not swallowed at all. And always (as he loudly proclaimed to the end of his life), always he was "on the level!" Many guardians of American culture in his day, increasingly uncertain about a sense of self, displayed a "dread fascination" with deceit and imposture.[61] Yet here was Sullivan, roaring through life at full throttle, relentlessly blaring his candor and sincerity. A barbarian and a renegade he might be, but he never prevaricated, never quibbled, never stalled. His very longevity in the brutal fight game offered reassurance that come what may, there would always be John L. Sullivan, as constant as the morning light, and he would always be the champion, mirroring many of the tensions, conflicts, and aspirations of the Gilded Age—America's own unfinished hero.

CHAPTER NINE

# The Champion Abroad
## (1887—1888)

I

In the weeks following the presentation of the Championship Belt, Sullivan grew restless and irritable. Although the 1886–87 tour had been financially successful, his injury in the Cardiff fight had made him less than eager to step in the prize ring again, and he felt he had, for the moment, exhausted the touring possibilities in the United States. In addition, he was at odds with his manager, Pat Sheedy, who had guided the last tour and borne the brunt of Sullivan's wrath over the string of cancellations in the East.

The two men split in the late summer of 1887. Sullivan disliked Sheedy's flamboyance and play for credit in the press, and John L.'s refusal to train and his nearly constant drinking annoyed Pat. In addition, Sullivan felt shortchanged in their financial dealings. Sheedy, for his part, later claimed that the champion had run up gigantic "training bills" that his manager was expected to pay. Sheedy left September 10 for London on the *Servia*, possibly to drum up new fighters to manage. His departure may have given Sullivan the idea to go abroad himself and open up new "markets" for his prestige, as it were. Reports circulated that his friend Jim McKeon of Boston was now his "business associate," but if so, the two men only went through the motions of looking for fights in America. In September John L. made the decision to stage a European tour and arranged for a Montreal sporting man named Harry S. Phillips to manage his affairs. Said the champion, "I am going to Europe to make money."[1]

At least part of the press was glad to see him go. The previous tour had proved to be far from a pinnacle in Sullivan's public relations, and perhaps it was time to get out of town. The *Omaha Chronicle* put it best:

John L. Sullivan, the mightiest slugger and the most discourteous brute of them all, would have fared better in a financial sense if he had cultivated good manners as well as muscle. His arrogant treatment of the reporters erected against him an enmity more formidable than anything he ever faced in the rope ring. In the heyday of his success the press reported every misdemeanor he committed, and he now acknowledges the mistake he made when he began to fight the ubiquitous pencil pusher. He was shoved into notoriety by the press, and by the press he has been forced to relinquish his championship honors and sink into comparative obscurity. And from the tone of the press it is reasonable to infer that it will keep him there. If the young prize fighter is ambitious to attain prominence in his profession he should devote as much of his time to studying the rules of social etiquette as to swinging the club or punching the bag.[2]

John L.'s troubles were soothed somewhat by the fact that, sometime in 1886, he had taken a mistress. Ann Livingston was a well-proportioned, heavyset, blonde woman a few years older than Sullivan. The press would eventually have a field day with their relationship, the *New York Sun's* Boston correspondent heatedly reporting that "her well-developed, voluptuous figure, and bright, sensuous, half saucy beauty made her a splendid match for the ideal physical man." Livingston had been with John L. for at least part of the previous tour (she may have been the woman who registered with him in the Milwaukee hotel at the time of his son's death), and tales had emerged of her having steadied the champion during his drinking bouts.

Like the other Ann, Sullivan's estranged wife, Livingston had a suspect past. Her real name was Anna B. Nailor. About 1876 she met and married a Boston confectioner and part-time actor named Frank (or Fred) Anderson. At the time, she was appearing in the chorus of *The Corsair* at Boston's Globe Theater. She adopted the married name of Anna B. Anderson and kept the stage name of Ann Livingston. The Andersons had a daughter, who was about ten years of age when Ann met John L. The couple began divorce proceedings in 1883, both charging unfaithfulness, and the husband was ungallant enough to allege that his spouse had a "romantic history." Once free of her confectioner, Ann squirreled their child away with his parents in Providence and moved from chorus line to chorus line, in one of which she was working when Sullivan met her.[3]

By the fall of 1887 John L. and Ann were living together, and it was natural that she would accompany him overseas, although he said not a word about her in his autobiography. Sullivan, Phillips and his wife, and Ann were joined by Jack Barnett, who would act "somewhat in the capacity of companion and secretary," and Jack Ashton of Providence, who would serve as the champion's sparring partner. The party sailed from Boston aboard the steamer *Cephalonia* on October 27, seen off by a large crowd of sportsmen that included John L.'s father

21. Ann Livingston, in costume for a *National Polize Gazette* illustration (Nat Fleischer, *John L. Sullivan, Champion of Champions*, opposite p. 110)

and brother. Sullivan's cabin was a riot of floral tributes, and old Mike bade him good-bye from the pier while wearing the colors his son had borne in the first match with Paddy Ryan. Some of John L.'s more fervent boosters chartered two tugs, which chuffed along for some distance in the wake of the ship, firing a final salute from two brass cannons as the *Cephalonia* cleared for the open sea. One sour editor noted that John L.'s departure "was attended with an amount of cheap pomp and circumstance."

The *Cephalonia* enjoyed a smooth passage. She made land at Queenstown, Ireland, where John L. told a reporter he would return to America as champion of the world or die.[4]

## II

On Sunday, November 6, the ship headed in for Liverpool. Phillips had made previous arrangements by cable, and a few prominent members of the English sporting crowd, including Arthur Magnus, Johnny Curran, and Alf Greenfield, boarded a tug to meet the champion outside the harbor. This group, in turn, had spread the news of the hero's impending arrival, and when the *Cephalonia* docked, thousands of enthusiastic fight fans were waiting for a glimpse of Sullivan. The crush was so great that John L. and his friends required a bodyguard to get to the four-in-hand that would take them to the Grand Hotel. There was a contretemps with customs officials over the Championship Belt, which Sullivan had intended to display in exhibitions throughout the British Isles. The bureaucrats wanted £120 ($600) as the price of admission, which John L. refused to pay, and the gaudy artifact remained sequestered in the queen's bonded warehouse until his departure the following spring.[5]

Not everyone was pleased with his arrival, by any means. Most of the better sort simply ignored it, and an English newspaper printed a full-page cartoon showing a fat, cigar-smoking John L. in fighting togs being challenged to fight by Honest John Bull, who was saying that "this glove business won't work over here, so come off." No matter; Sullivan was mobbed on his departure for London, and his train drew throngs as it passed through Crewe, Rugby, and Willesden before arriving at London's Euston Station. There the press of people made it impossible for him to reach his assigned carriage; many scrambled to the roof of his railway car for a better look. In desperation, and with a presentational bouquet in hand, he bolted for a nearby funeral coach, the bottom of which immediately collapsed from the weight. Finally he fought his way to the offices of the *Sportsman*, which served much the same function for the British as the Big Three of sporting journalism did for Americans, and from the building's upper window made a brief thank-you speech to a crowd estimated at five thousand. It was, sniffed the stylish *Pall Mall Gazette*, the "apotheosis of the bruiser." The paper noted that although William Ewart Gladstone, who was currently between terms as prime minister (having given way the year before to Lord Salisbury on the issue of Irish home rule), could draw immense crowds at provincial railway stations, only Sullivan could draw them in blasé London.

John L. and his tiny entourage took lodgings at one of the fashionable hotels in the West End. He was the "lion of the hour," and to his rooms came several members of the aristocracy, residents of the fashionable Belgravia district, and delegations of working-class admirers from Whitechapel. He dined with the upper crust, causing one astonished observer to moan that "this worship of brutality and muscle is merely an unhealthy sign of the age."[6]

Sullivan had landed in the midst of a country sunning itself in the high noon of Empire. From pole to pole the Union Jack flew over fully one-quarter of the earth's surface, guarded by a far-flung fleet and Tommy Atkins. There might be labor unrest at home and troubles with the Irish (there were *always* troubles with the Irish), but the British had just given themselves over to a summer orgy of self-congratulation, Queen Victoria's Golden Jubilee. The sovereign had been through an exhausting schedule of prayer services, ceremonial appearances, and military reviews, culminating in the great display at Spithead, where the assembled naval might of imperialism, from armored battleships to training brigs, filed before its queen. For Victoria, and for her subjects, it was a "never-to-be-forgotten year."[7]

The English had just had their fill of another kind of American celebrity—William F. Cody. "Buffalo Bill" had been a smashing success with his Wild West Show during the jubilee summer. He could have taught Sullivan a thing or two about public relations. Victoria herself had been most pleased with her command performance, even rising from her seat and bowing respectfully as the American flag was paraded. A few weeks later Cody drove the Deadwood stage during a simulated attack by Indians, his excited passengers being the crowned heads of Denmark, Greece, Belgium, and Saxony. In all, hundreds of thousands of people flocked to see the show: a lively panoply of Indian attacks, pony express riders, wagon trains, wonder horses, and trick shooting. Buffalo Bill was the toast of London. His caravan headed out to play the provinces just as Sullivan arrived. Back home, *Life* noted that America was doing a great deal for her British cousins, sending them first the flamboyant westerner and then the city-bred pugilist.[8] There is no evidence that the two celebrities ever met, but in 1887 they gave the British at least a taste of two Americas: the romanticized West and the immigrant-leavened city.

Sullivan's first public appearance took place in a large room in Saint James's Hall on November 9. Prices were doubled, but the place was still crowded with enthusiastic spectators eager to see the marvel who had bested three of their countrymen: Tug Wilson, Charlie Mitchell, and Alf Greenfield. Old Jem Smith introduced John L., who then sparred lightly with Ashton and three other boxers. Although the champion was overweight and clearly out of condition, he was repeatedly applauded.

For the next two weeks he, like Cody, toured the provinces, and his sparring routine received excellent receptions in Birmingham, Manchester, and Wolverhampton before predominantly working-class audiences of English and Irish males. He appeared in a variety of other Midlands towns and then moved up to Scotland and Glasgow, Dundee, Aberdeen, and Edinburgh. The pace was reminiscent of the Grand Tour, but Sullivan was not making the ultimate challenge to all comers. Only once, at his lone stop in Wales, Cardiff, did he take on a local man eager for fame. This bout was more an exhibition than anything else, and John L.'s opponent, one Samuels, called it quits after two rounds.

His greeting everywhere was astounding. Over nineteen thousand people came to see him during his two nights in Birmingham. The local *Gazette* observed that "his admirers—and they are many—[gave] him a welcome scarcely accorded to a royal prince." In Cardiff he was proud to be told that not even Gladstone had drawn a larger (or more decently behaved) crowd when he visited the year before. Englishman, Irishman, Scotsman—it made no difference. For the moment, the British Isles belonged to Sullivan. After two and one-half whirlwind weeks he returned to London for a twelve-night stand on the great central stage of the Royal Aquarium.[9]

His press coverage from the middle-class sheets was almost nil, but the audiences came nonetheless. The *Pall Mall Gazette*, other than a few sneers, had nothing to say, and the popular *Illustrated London News* ignored him completely, concerned as it was with following the activities of the social set, in particular Edward, Prince of Wales. The *London Times* and the *London Daily Telegraph* had begun covering sports, just as had the great metropolitan dailies in the United States, but they limited themselves to activities such as horse racing, chess, billiards, cycling, and rugby. What little attention Sullivan received came from the penny sheets, designed for the increasingly literate working class. These generally admired him but were not exactly incisive in their reporting. To local reporters throughout England, for example, Ann Livingston was constantly presented as John L.'s wife, and the masquerade continued even after Richard Kyle Fox blew the lid off with screeching *National Police Gazette* headlines in December.

Nevertheless, Sullivan found that his appeal within the male world translated nicely to the British Isles. He found the same gaping crowds, the same eager reporters, the same mix of approbatory men and boys from all walks of society. He was feted by masculine social organizations wherever he traveled and became a member of the exclusive Pelican Club in the presence of nineteen English peers. In most places there were gifts as well, ranging from worthless trinkets to valuable jewelry. The Pelicans chipped in with a stickpin and matching waistcoat buttons. Such friendliness had its social limits, of course. The story went around that one of Lord Beresford's daughters wanted to see the champion, not as a guest but just as a curiosity, and that she was willing to pay handsomely for his pains. John L. refused, and the young lady never gazed upon his muscles.[10]

As Sullivan was preparing to leave the Pelican Club after his chummy evening with the members, he was approached by a nattily attired messenger bearing the following missive:

> St. James Barracks
>
> My Dear Mr. Sullivan—I have great pleasure on behalf of the officers of the Scots Guards in inviting you to breakfast in our mess-room tomorrow at twelve o'clock, and subsequently to meet H.R.H. the Prince of Wales, who has repeatedly expressed the desire to make your personal acquaintance.
> > Very truly yours,
> > Clifford Drummond
> > Captain Scots Guards

This from a regiment whose lineage went back to 1642, as a band loyal to King Charles. Its history was long and noble, ironically riven with occasional campaigns against the Irish. Largely officered by privileged young aristocrats, the Scots Guards were among the military elite in Britain. Sullivan accepted at once.

On December 9, a glowering, foggy day, Sullivan arrived punctually, dressed in somber black, and quickly found that the Guards knew how to set a table. Cold salmon, hot cuts of beef, and cold joints were served, washed down with bitter ale, porter, and light French wines. Toasts were made all around, and all drank silently to the health of Tom Sayers and John Carmel Heenan, whose epic battle in 1860 was well remembered by the sporting gentry. As guests, the young aristocrats had invited friends from their brother regiments, the Grenadier and Coldstream Guards. Lord Randolph Churchill, then at the start of his tragic downhill slide from power, was present as well.

Shortly after three o'clock word came that Edward had arrived at the nearby Fencing Club. Extremely popular, the Prince of Wales gave no end of concern to his mother and no end of delight to the public, which knew he was fond of amusing himself with the gaming tables, good food and drink, and women not his wife. His primary business, like that of all heirs to the throne, was waiting for the sovereign to die; since in Victoria's case this was turning out to be a very long process indeed, he was determined to enjoy himself to the utmost while waiting his turn. Yet he was far from a wastrel or a profligate. Most people marked him as a friendly, unassuming man whose inquisitive charm entranced almost everyone.

John L. found the prince dressed in black cutaway, gray trousers, gaiters, and thick-soled walking boots, toasting himself in front of an open wood fire. The introductions were made by Edward's private secretary, Sir Francis Knollys, and the heir to the British throne shook the hand of the Boston Irishman heartily. Edward was quite familiar with many of Sullivan's fights and particularly wanted to know about the first battle with Paddy Ryan. Sullivan by all accounts (including his own) was perfectly charming, asking the prince at one point when he had last put up his dukes. Following the banter, which lasted for almost twenty minutes, Edward, his retinue, and the glittering young officers watched two bantamweights spar, followed by Jem Smith and Alf Greenfield. Sullivan and Ashton offered the final exhibition of the day. Socially, it was the most exalted group before which he would ever perform, and polite, too—whenever Edward clapped his hands, all present dutifully joined him in applause. When it was over, John L. and the prince shook hands again and wished each other well.[11]

The memory remained a rosy glow with Sullivan always. His father's generation of Irish had been light-years removed from royalty. Now he had swapped quips with the man who would one day symbolically head the greatest empire of them all and, in addition, had received from him a pair of garnets and a matching set of emeralds. The meeting produced the usual amount of Sullivan apocrypha, most of it centering on the juxtaposition of John L.'s open, candid manner with the snobbish ways of English court society. One account had him almost causing a war by his lack of deference; another had him bidding farewell to the prince with the offer "If you ever come to Boston be sure and look me up."[12]

The next day he was off to Ireland, the trip as much sentimental as financial. The Catholic Irish had been through some very rough times recently; the more extreme among them had taken to killing Englishmen. The failure of Gladstone's home rule bill had spread further bitterness through a country that was economically one of the most backward in Europe. Thus Sullivan, an Irishman who had been celebrated in England and had defeated every Englishman he had met in the ring, was a welcome and useful totem. Almost fifteen thousand people gathered at the steamboat landing in Dublin to welcome him. Two full brass bands blared away, vying with each other in energy, enthusiasm, and noise. Sullivan proceeded to Grosvenor's Hotel in triumph to the strains of "See, the Conquering Hero Comes!" and "The Wearing of the Green." The horses had to move at a snail's pace, so thick was the crowd.

At the hotel, the faithful would not quiet down until the hero stepped onto the veranda and delivered a short speech. "I thank you for your kindness to me this evening," he said. "As a descendant of Erin's Isle, I will endeavor always to prove myself worthy of your attention and to uphold the honor of my father's native land." At least that is what he remembered, or wished, he had said, but whatever words he used they were sufficient; tumultuous cheering followed, and then the bands struck up again and marched off, followed by most of the crowd. They had heard the voice of an Irish *man*. As for Sullivan, "I was much moved by this reception in the land of my forefathers."

More of the same followed, in Waterford, Limerick, Cork, and even Belfast, with its large Protestant population. The impoverished Irish supported him generously at his exhibitions, and Sullivan, in turn, fell in love with the quaint ways of his ancestral homeland. Of course, he kissed the Blarney Stone. In particular John L. remembered visiting a place called "Donnelly's Hollow," a natural amphitheater in Kildare, which could seat thousands on its gentle grassy slopes. There the famed Irish champion, Dan Donnelly, had defeated an Englishman named Cooper, and, the Irish being Irish, the spot retained a touch of magic. Each visitor to the Hollow was asked to put his feet in the footsteps made by the two men as they had toed the mark, and thus the imprints in the soft green sod became permanent, a particularly Irish form of memorial. Sullivan added his prints to those of the thousands who had been there before him.[13]

He rejoiced in such a welcome in the land of his forebears, but there is no record of his having visited Tralee, his father's home, or Athlone, his mother's country. Still, it was an emotional homecoming of sorts, and both Sullivan and his hosts were deeply moved. Although a complete American, the champion was readily accepted as an exemplar of Irish manhood. Desperate for heroes, despising the English, and tolerant of a man who was fond of a dram, the Irish took John L. to their hearts. It was the high point of his stay in Europe.

## III

The exhibition tour in Great Britain closed with an appearance in Portsmouth in January 1888. By then Phillips had arranged for a prize-fight matching the champion against his old tormentor, Charlie Mitchell. Sullivan would have preferred to go through the entire tour without defending his title, simply making appearances and counting the gates, but Europeans, like Americans, wanted to see him fight. In addition, two pressures were driving him back into the ring. The first was the constant one, money. His tour was profitable, but he was running through the proceeds as fast as they came in, and Ann Livingston was not an inexpensive mistress. Second, his opponent would be the loathsome Mitchell, or as John L. called him, the "bombastic sprinter." The champion felt he had three bones to pick with Charlie—the first over Mitchell's tactics in their initial match; the next over the abortive second bout, Sullivan having come to believe he had shown up drunk only because he thought Mitchell would not fight; and the third over Mitchell's undoubted talent for goading the bigger man in the sporting press. Charlie knew John L.'s sore spot—his vanity—and he never lost an opportunity.[14]

In November 1887 Mitchell posted $1,000 with *Sporting Life*, a London sports sheet, as earnest money. He was eager to meet John L. again, and felt that under the right circumstances his run-and-delay tactics, coupled with greater stamina, could bring him victory. The two antagonists and their backers got together at a sporting house in London shortly before Sullivan met the Prince of Wales. After nearly three hours of wrangling they agreed to a match for $2,500 (£500) a side, and each deposited $500 with a bookie and hotelier named Harry Bull, whose real name was "Chippy" Norton. Mitchell chattered incessantly during the entire process, thoroughly enraging Sullivan.[15] Charlie figured he would be facing an overweight, aging, and uninterested fighter. In addition, the agreement was made under the London Rules, and Mitchell knew John L. preferred the gloves.

Sullivan indeed was saddled with his usual out-of-condition flab; when he began his training regimen at Bull's Royal Adelaide Hotel in Windsor on January 26, he weighed 230. His pocketbook nearly depleted as a result of his parties of the previous two months and his usual generosity (he had recently presented a diamond locket to the Liverpool bookmaker Arthur Magnus in gratitude for his role in arranging Sullivan's reception there), John L. needed a victory over Mitchell to show a significant profit from the tour. Mitchell trained at the St. Mildred Hotel in a hamlet called Westgate-on-Sea, about sixty miles from London, and continued chirping away at Sullivan. "When Sullivan licks me," boasted the challenger, "you'll see white blackbirds in O'Connell Street."[16]

Bull and Magnus were Sullivan's chief supporters. Driven both by his need for money and his hatred of Mitchell, he relied on the two bookies to keep his meals coming while he sloughed off the fat. He was up every day at 6:30, plunging himself into a saltwater bath. Then he began a six-mile walk in the predawn winter darkness, clad in heavy flannels. Sometimes he walked the thirteen-mile round trip to Maidenhead and back, afterward exercising with dumbbells. He had an early

22. Charlie Mitchell (about 1885) (William Schutte Collection)

afternoon dinner, sticking mostly to light foods, and then did more "road work" or punched the speed bag during the afternoon. After supper he walked some more. The routine was light, and he had no one to supervise his activities except himself. Still, the weight came off, and by the beginning of March he had lost thirty pounds.[17]

Privately, Mitchell knew he was overmatched if Sullivan entered the ring in anywhere near prime condition, but he remained confident. "I think I shall win," he wrote to a friend in New York City. "Of course, there is nothing certain—only rent day and death. Should the fight result in my favor, I suppose they will say Sullivan was drugged." Charlie worked hard in training, one of his advisers being Jake Kilrain. He had the backing of a squadron of English sportsmen and was highly popular throughout the British Isles, whereas John L., although he had many backers, "chiefly among the plebian class," had not been able to attract any sort of aristocratic following despite his appearance before the Prince of Wales.[18] The challenger played his role of plucky underdog to the hilt.

The location of the fight was a problem. The original contract had been left deliberately vague on this point, mentioning neither the time nor the place of the match. Sullivan and Mitchell obviously hoped to pull a fast one in the best tradition of English prizefighting, waiting until the last minute to announce a locale, probably well out in the countryside. The seconds thus had been given the liberty of choosing the time and place, with Sullivan insisting only that the bout occur within one thousand miles of London and not interfere with any of his previous engagements. Indeed, he had been very lenient with Mitchell's terms, needing the payday as he did. Specifically, John L. had wanted a sixteen-foot-square ring, which would leave less space in which the "bombastic sprinter" could maneuver. Charlie, knowing on which side his bread was buttered, insisted on twenty-four, and after acrimonious discussion it was so agreed. But the English authorities no longer had a blind eye turned toward prizefighting, and the pressure to stop the match was strong. Mitchell at last arranged to be arrested on March 2 and allowed himself to be hauled before the local magistrate at Chertsey. There he was bound over for two hundred pounds, and righteously swore that he did not intend to break the peace in England.[19]

The two principals, despite Mitchell's disclaimer, could still have pulled off a match on English soil, but it would have been extremely risky. Thoughts began to center on France, for no apparent reason other than it was conveniently located right across the English Channel. Mitchell's father-in-law and chief backer, a somewhat disreputable publican named Pony Moore, grew to favor this change in venue, so early in March an odd assemblage of bookies, newsmen, and fight fans began to scout northern France for a suitable location. It was tentatively agreed that the ring should be staked on an island in the Seine near Vernon, but this idea was abandoned when the French police, admittedly a bit slower on the uptake than their English counterparts, got wind of it. Still, Mitchell and Sullivan both crossed the channel, Charlie getting seasick on the way, and both were said to be ready at a moment's notice. Ann Livingston had been left behind, as this was man's work. It was raining constantly; the vagrant herd of sporting men swarmed like devouring locusts through the quaint villages of Picardy, yelling at their hosts in English and receiving blank stares in return. The authorities did not know where the fight was to take place, for the very good reason that the backers did not know themselves.[20]

Among the disorganized little band were two young correspondents destined to be leading lights in American journalism, Stephen Bonsal of the *New York Herald* and Arthur Brisbane of the *New York Sun*. The two made a gentleman's agreement that they would share information about the fighters during the hectic days leading up to the match, but once the two boxers stepped in the ring, all bets were off. As allies of the pen, the two reporters accompanied Sullivan on the morning of March 10 when he visited the great cathedral at Amiens, Bonsal noting that Sullivan took the numerous sculptured images of saints, apostles, and crusaders to be famous fighters of the past. When they rejoined their group after the cathedral tour, it was evident something was afoot, and for that very afternoon. A place had been found! Everyone scurried for carriages and sped into the countryside, only the leaders knowing for sure where they were going.[21] Sullivan was headed for the weirdest fight of his career.

## IV

A London sports reporter named John Gideon had ferreted out the site. It was a moist plot of ground facing the stables on the estate of one of the most famous names in France, Baron Alphonse Rothschild. This particular Rothschild was the undisputed head of the French branch of the great banking family, a collector of valuable art, the man who had provided a food supply to starving Paris in 1871, and the guarantor of a five-billion-franc indemnity to Prussia in the wake of the French defeat in the Franco-Prussian War. Small, stout, and highly capable, Baron Alphonse was said to own the best pair of mustaches in Europe. But he was not known as a boxing fan, or even a sportsman, and the grounds of his estate may have been used without his knowledge.[22]

The strange, excited little procession arrived at the great estate, located north of Paris near Chantilly, after wending its way over hill and down dale for half an hour. No police were in evidence, the fighters and their backers having ostentatiously bought tickets for Paris that morning at the Amiens station, boarded the train, and then sneaked off at Creil, a little town twenty miles from Paris. Sullivan's supporters had thrown scarves about their necks, displaying an American flag decorated with an eagle, shamrock, and Irish harps. In the distance they could see the curious old church clocktower in Creil, but just barely, for it was pouring rain.

Quickly the ring, composed of ropes and stakes carried in bundles to the spot, was pitched on a grassy slope near the edge of the woods abutting the stables. Around forty people, including the two fighters and their backers, had made the abrupt trip. Sullivan showed up with a jaunty traveling cap and a big rug wrapped around his shoulders. Ashton, his second, carried a large tin can of water, and George McDonald, who had helped him train, lugged sponges, a pail, and a bottle of brandy. A handful of curious Frenchmen gathered to look from a distance, "as we would select to look upon a hyena fight," wrote Brisbane. Without much ado a man named George B. Angle, said to have worked at the London Stock Exchange, was selected as referee.[23] It would be a fight in the old style.

Both men shivered in the chill, biting air as they stripped to their fighting togs. Mitchell won the toss for choice of corners and shrewdly kept his own back to the driving wind and rain. The hardy group of spectators bunched around the single strand of ring rope, making knowing remarks about the effect of the weather. Odds on Sullivan, such as they were, ran at 3 to 1. One of Mitchell's seconds, an English boxer named Jack Baldock, rubbed ground resin into his man's fists, while the other, Kilrain, perhaps pondered his future chances against the Bostonian. As an oddity, a stake bearing the colors of both men was driven into the ground at the scratch line. At 12:30 the fighters toed the line, Sullivan wearing a silk handkerchief embroidered with stars and stripes about his waist. The rain by now was coming down in torrents.[24]

They began by sparring cautiously. Sullivan counterpunched successfully and hit Mitchell several times in the head; Charlie quickly dropped to his knees to avoid further punishment. Mitchell came out thirty seconds later pecking at Sullivan's eyes, but John L. ended the round by knocking his opponent down with a whistling right to the head. They grappled at the beginning of round three and separated by mutual consent, both laughing. Beneath them the ground was being churned to suet by their feet. Sullivan yelled at Mitchell to stop running and knocked the smaller man, lighter by at least thirty pounds, in the temple, driving him down again. So far, John L. was doing pretty much as he pleased, and his corner made a plea for a decision. Angle refused, and almost everyone thought the fight would be quickly finished, in one or two more rounds at most.

Charlie had a rapidly swelling lump on his temple as he came out for round four. Sullivan slammed him over the left eye and sent him down; he pounded the challenger on the head again to end rounds five and six, and both men grappled and fell to end the seventh. Sullivan walked to his corner after every round, where a tough little English fighter named Sam Blakelock was literally serving as his "chair," crouching on his hands and knees so the champion could rest himself. But Sam was growing discouraged, not so much from the inclement weather but because he had bet his savings that John L. would win in thirty minutes. As for Mitchell, he never shut up. Every time he was carried off in the arms of his seconds he would turn his bruised, swollen face to Sullivan and shout, "Not yet! You haven't whipped me yet!" In his corner Baldock exhorted him to remember the little children at home, all the while mumbling poetry and little snatches of song interpersed with vile profanity. Brisbane, standing soaked at ringside, thought Jack was "probably the most perfect specimen of a depraved gray-haired man that was ever seen."

John L. was growing impatient, the more so because he had badly bruised his right arm during one of his wild swings at Mitchell's head in the fifth round. In addition Mitchell was wearing half-inch spikes for better footing, and in the process of give and take during the fight these raked Sullivan's lower legs until they were sheeting blood. What was more, Mitchell kept coming back. Charlie, a notorious low puncher, delivered several blows below the waist in round eight and then drew first blood with a blow to the champion's head, quickly falling down to avoid a return.

And so it went, as the rain poured down and the small group of spectators, now drenched to the skin, shifted restlessly. In rounds nine through nineteen, Mitchell punched a few times and then went down, either intentionally or from one of Sullivan's powerhouse rushes. John L. was turning more savage the more his foe escaped; his punches became wilder and wilder, few of them finding their mark. Even worse, Mitchell kept laughing, taunting him, while Pony Moore screamed invective from his son-in-law's corner. From rounds nine to fifteen, one of them lasting twenty-five minutes, the rainstorm became so severe that everyone except the fighters and their seconds took shelter in a nearby shed. But the battle kept on, by now a watery nightmare for Sullivan. He was tiring badly and shivering, and his teeth were chattering. He steadfastly refused doses of brandy offered by Ashton between rounds.

At last the sun emerged, and Sullivan recovered somewhat. By now it was round twenty. Suddenly three men in uniform with guns appeared, and the cry of "gendarmes!" was raised, but they turned out to be three of the baron's gamekeepers and quickly joined the remote cluster of their countrymen to watch the strange duel. Charlie kept on coming, kept on punching, kept on sliding to the ground, which by now was a quagmire. The rounds passed—twenty-five, thirty. Every once in a while Mitchell would score; neither man tried to wrestle, Sullivan being too tired and Mitchell too clever to place himself in such close quarters with the stronger man. Thirty-five, thirty-six, thirty-seven, thirty-eight—Sullivan alternated between rage and good humor, occasionally congratulating Mitchell for a good blow ("That's a good one, Charlie") and then yelling at him to stand and fight.

By now it was midafternoon. Mitchell was uncut, but his face was a mass of reddish-purple lumps and bruises. John L.'s nose and mouth were bleeding slightly, but he refused to have his mustache removed. The ground was now impossible; only about eight feet square remained on the upper slope where the two men could find any kind of purchase at all for their feet. The spectators were getting impatient; sometimes Charlie would simply walk about the ring, Sullivan standing still. Four times they mutually agreed to retire to their corners to get the mud off their shoes and take a drink. Mitchell still seemed fresh and still twittered away, while Sullivan, in increasing pain from his damaged arm, was rapidly losing interest in the contest. It was a soggy standoff.

After an exceptionally tedious thirty-ninth round, Baldock suggested to Mitchell that he ask for a draw. Charlie thought a moment and then said, "Well, let us shake hands or fight on, as John likes." Sullivan later claimed he had wanted to fight on, but all the other witnesses agreed he was bone-tired and readily acceded to the draw. Over three hours had elapsed since they had squared off. The two men shook hands, the crowd joining in. Everyone was glum, as no money had been made, and Sullivan's backers sadly admitted how "done up" the champion seemed. Mitchell, on the other hand, was merry as a cricket. His tactics, aided by the abominable weather and the large ring, had worked again. Brisbane and Bonsal, by now frozen stiff, both raced for the nearest cable office.[25]

## V

The French police had not been completely hoodwinked. The events of the previous week, what with small herds of braying Anglais moving hither and yon looking for a suitable site, had not exactly kept the impending match a secret. As the pugilists and their dispirited followers left the Rothschild estate, several gendarmes surrounded their carriages with drawn swords and carbines and arrested practically the entire bunch; only Jake Kilrain managed to escape. They were taken immediately to Senlis, a substantial town about six miles from the fight scene. There everyone was hauled before the magistrate, who was so favorably impressed by their stories that he let them all go—all, that is, except Sullivan and Mitchell. As the majority of their pals made straight for London without any loss of time, John L. and Charlie were packed off to cells, and their seconds, McDonald and Baldock, were released on their promise to reappear the following morning, a Sunday.

Around midnight Brisbane arrived, having filed his story. He had a French doctor in tow, and the medical man quickly went to work. The two fighters were in separate cells, cold, damp, and hungry, without any covering to their beds. John L.'s knuckles were badly swollen, the skin rubbed raw. Mitchell's body was a mass of contusions; his knees were still bleeding from his forty or so falls during the match. The doctor did the best he could, which was not much. Brisbane, whose French was far from elegant, thought the Frenchman believed the two men had tried to murder each other. Actually, the fighters were lucky. The French code provided only a simple fine for prizefighting, a factor that had made the move across the channel attractive in the first place. Also, magistrates were not empowered to imprison, although they could temporarily incarcerate disturbers of the peace, as the Senlis magistrate had done.

Thus on Sunday morning, March 11, the two aching pugilists posted bond of one thousand francs and then made their way to the Hôtel du Grand Cerf, where they, their seconds, and the few remaining backers (including Kilrain) sat down to a champagne breakfast. Sullivan did not want to stand trial; he feared French justice and saw no reason to spend any more time in French jails. Accordingly, he took the first train to Paris, thence to Calais and back to England. He was sentenced in absentia to three days in prison and a fine of two thousand francs. Mitchell remained to stand trial and served the sentence. John L. recovered from his injuries at Arthur Magnus's home in Liverpool.[26]

Brisbane and Bonsal had been the only two reporters at the peculiar contest. None of the big English papers, such as the *London Times* or the *Manchester Guardian*, had been concerned. The invasion of France had taken place so rapidly that the French press, not overly interested in prizefighting anyway, provided no coverage. In fact, the fight took place in the shadow of the death of the aged German emperor, William I, on Friday morning, March 9. *Le Temps*, *La Dèpêche de Toulouse*, and practically every other French paper were given over to coverage of this event, and the English press, led by the *Illustrated London News*, followed suit. In short, the most intense interest in the draw was found in the United States, and there it rested on the accounts in the *Sun* and the *Herald* provided by the two young reporters.

Most of the American press rubbed it in, criticizing John L. for being unable to take out "Little Charlie." Many fight fans believed he was finished. A *draw*, after all, not only ran counter to American notions concerning victory but also contradicted Sullivan's widely known attitudes toward pugilism as the fundamentally decisive contest. There were thoughtful comments on Sullivan's conditioning and his supposed lack of stamina. Some believed he had bribed the referee to end the fight. Richard Kyle Fox, who had been trumpeting the virtues of Kilrain for months, announced that the draw had only proved that Jake was the true champion.[27]

There were excuses. Sullivan griped about the twenty-four-foot ring. The faithful John Boyle O'Reilly hoped the fight would be "the last of its brutal kind" and offered the basic apology:

A cold rain was falling, and Sullivan became chilled, and in the thirty-fifth round he had a fit of ague. He was overtrained [!]; he had hurt his right hand; he was too heavy to plough through the mud after his running adversary, whom he could not catch; so he agreed to end the contest by a draw.

The indecisive fight always rankled with Sullivan, but Mitchell's twinkling good humor about it all (he had fought in France before and was used to the wrist slaps of the French authorities) eventually won him over. The two men at last became good friends, even though Charlie would second Kilrain a year later in an even more epic match against the champion.[28]

Sullivan had had enough of Europe. On April 12 he boarded the steamship *Catalonia* in Liverpool with his retinue, including Ann Livingston. During the crossing he was drinking again. He and Ann had a stateroom next to a missionary named W. R. Manley, who was returning from India. Manley heard the couple quarreling every night, but he denied a story that John L. had become so irritated with the missionary's four children that he had threatened to throw them overboard. Sullivan did show his displeasure at something, however, by pinching a steward's arm black and blue.[29]

At last the *Catalonia* made Boston, on April 24. The greeting for the hometown hero was as effusive as had been the celebration accompanying his departure. Tugs and private yachts filled with admirers escorted the ship to her berth. John N. Taylor, the sports editor of the *Globe*, scored a scoop by telegraphing the first sighting of the ship, clambering aboard the *Catalonia* from a tug to shake Sullivan's hand, and interviewing the champion before his journalistic rivals had left the wharf for the quarantine anchorage. Within hours eager Bostonians were reading Sullivan's version of the European tour. When the ship finally cleared quarantine and docked, a large crowd cheered as John

L. descended the gangway and blocked his coach's path up Washington Street in order to get a look. They saw a haggard man, exhausted from a rocky ocean voyage and continuous squabbles with his mistress. "He looked to weigh about 280 pounds, and was as fat as a North End Boston alderman." It mattered little to him; he was home.[30]

## VI

The tour had been a mixed success. Sullivan had given fifty-one exhibitions in all, including the highlight before the Prince of Wales. He had made over five thousand pounds, about twenty-five thousand dollars, which he admitted was "an extraordinary sum considering the condition of the kingdom and the small wages paid workingmen." Everywhere he had received a hearty welcome from local sporting fraternities and laborers. Many of his shows had turned away ticket seekers. Ireland had been particularly lucrative; "I can say that I made more money in one week there than in six weeks in England." In addition the Irish had given him a tweed suit, forty-five letters asking him to give benefits for charitable institutions, seventeen blackthorn walking sticks, and, because they were Irish and he was Sullivan, four jugs of whiskey. True, he had been almost ignored by the aristocracy, except for the prince and the elegant young men of the Scots Guards, but he claimed he had frequently seen one of the royal princesses and her daughter in their carriage, and that they had looked at him after their coachman had pointed him out. John L. had even (he said) seen the queen near Windsor. Victoria "looked out to see me as I passed along, and made comments which I did not hear."[31]

Against all this—the money, the ready celebrity, the gifts—there had been the disappointing draw with Mitchell, continued drinking, and the fresh disintegration of personal relationships. Sullivan and Ann Livingston were on again, off again, the champion displaying the same propensity for argument with her that he had with his wife. He owed Harry Phillips money, for despite the enormous sums made on the tour he had gone through it all, and then some. Over three thousand people attended a testimonial for Sullivan at the Music Hall on May 15, during which John L. sparred with Ashton, but Phillips attached the bulk of the proceeds to cover Sullivan's indebtedness to him. Like Billy Madden, Al Smith, and Pat Sheedy before him, he cut off business relations with the champion, and in terms of management, John L. was once again adrift.[32]

The cyclic ups and downs of his drawing power were at a new low as well. He was given another benefit at New York's Academy of Music on June 4, at which only three hundred people appeared. Some said not enough money was taken in to pay for the theater's gas, let alone the printing and advertising bills. The New York press agreed he was finished as a drawing card; they saw a fat, flabby champion spar lackadaisically with Mike Donovan and Ashton, then make a short, embarrassed thank-you speech. (Later that summer still another benefit with Joe Lannon at Nantasket Beach would attract only three hundred.)[33]

For the first time, largely in response to the Mitchell fight and the continuous anti-Sullivan tub thumping of the *Police Gazette*, more than the members of New York's press were beginning to think that Sullivan was through. True, he had not "lost" the championship, but to some he seemed, with his drinking and his lack of conditioning, to be palpably unable to defend it. And, as so often before, Richard Kyle Fox offered an alternative to the dissolute, dissipated John L.: none other than that escapee from the clutches of the French gendarmes, Jake Kilrain.

## CHAPTER TEN

# Farewell to Bare Knuckles: Jake Kilrain on the Mississippi Plain (1888—1889)

## I

If shifting popularity within a nation's culture can be viewed as tidal movements, John L. Sullivan's acclaim was now at another low ebb. Without a manager, he had no one to talk business for him. He had lost his zest for fighting after the embarrassing draw with Charlie Mitchell, and he now refused matches even when they were offered on a platter. At one of the benefits given him after the European tour, a black fighter named George Godfrey was summoned to the stage as a potential sparring partner, whereupon Sullivan, sensitive to charges that he had refused to meet black men in the ring, said he would fight Godfrey anytime (he never did). Other would-be challengers were ignored. He was broke again, the Boston benefits going to pay off the money he had been advanced by Harry Phillips on the tour. In New York he appeared as part of a variety bill consisting of dancers, tumblers, and gymnasts, and he drew poorly. Ann Livingston, unable to endure the drunken rages, had left him.[1]

He had set aside nothing for a rainy day. Unlike millions of other Americans who found it impossible to save because their income was eroded by basic needs for food, clothing, and housing, John L.'s wastrel habits had condemned him to a continual carousel of quick paydays and sudden sprees. In this, he was exceptional among his counterparts only in the amounts of money that passed through his hands. Being broke was all too common among the sporting elements of the cult of masculinity. Few defects of character were attached to this condition; a person was simply "down on his luck" and needed some help from his fellows to restore himself. No less a personage than Harry Hill, once the dominant force among New York's sportsmen, had fallen on hard times, largely due to police interference with the Houston Street saloon. The famous establishment had closed its doors, and Hill himself was in debt for almost eight thousand dollars.[2] But Sullivan's case was different. He was too well-known, and much was expected of him by way of income and display. Whether he wanted to fight or not, he was expected to *earn.*

Bereft of solid offers, John L. turned in an unexpected direction. In June 1888 he was given a partial interest in a traveling show called the John B. Doris and Gray Circus. Sullivan had the notion that it would be known as "John L. Sullivan's Circus": "I have an idea of appearing in the ring with two trick ponies." The press comment ranged from ridicule to outright hostility. Undaunted, the champion took to the road, and he arrived in Boston with his new entourage in the middle of July. "His" circus was pitched at the intersection of Harrison Avenue and Dover Street, not far from John L.'s boyhood home, flanked by a piano factory and an iron foundry. It was a gritty, soiled neighborhood; the tenements and gin mills of South Boston hovered close by. Audiences, mostly children, saw Sullivan enter riding a white stallion, serve as ringmaster, and spar a bit with Jack Ashton. It was not enough. As one of his old admirers put it, "If John L. wants to be popular in Boston again he must fight for it."[3]

Sullivan and John Doris dissolved their partnership by mutual consent on July 19. The champion's try at the sawdust ring had ended in dismal failure, and he never listed it among his profit-making ventures. He was drinking steadily, and for the next month he was totally out of control. On August 11 he was driving his carriage on the Milldam Road in Brighton and careened into another team. He pleaded guilty to a charge of public drunkenness and was fined $6.20, which, given the state of his pocketbook, he may have found difficult to pay. The accident had pitched him on his face, and his blackened eye highlighted more damage than he had received in scores of ring bouts.[4]

Worse was to come. He drank steadily into the early autumn, and finally his maltreated body rebelled. His liver and stomach lining were so inflamed that he became seriously ill with what was diagnosed as "gastric fever." For days he lay near death in a cottage at Crescent Beach, running a high temperature and unable to keep down any solid food. His doctor, a man named Bush, offered little but a sweating regimen under heavy blankets. Ann Livingston turned up to help nurse him, and his mother was constantly at his bedside. (His mistress's behavior was not altogether altruistic; Ann had signed a contract with Harry Phillips to tour in a variety show at seventy-five dollars a week, billed as "Mrs. John L. Sullivan," and now her meal ticket lay deathly ill.)

The press got a bit feverish itself, issuing hysterical reports of a deathbed watch. The truth was bad enough; when reporters were at last admitted to see the victim, they found a sleeping Sullivan with shrunken features and pallid skin. His hands twitched restlessly outside the pile of covers. Ann told the newsmen that he had stopped drinking and staunchly offered the opinion that swimming in the ocean off Nantasket might have brought on the attack.

At one time, a priest was summoned. As with his illness back in 1883, John L. confessed his relationship with the second Ann but refused the priest's request to send her away. He was shedding enormous quantities of fat, partially because his mother's chicken broth brought little but diarrhea. He was given milk and soda every hour and extract of beef every few hours, coupled with an occasional "spoonful of black mixture." These nostrums may have helped, but the key was the purging of the alcohol from his system and the opportunity for his liver and stomach cells to rebuild themselves. Slowly his temperature declined, finally falling four degrees in one day to ninety-nine. Loyalists who did not accept Ann's swimming defense nevertheless surmised that the champion had typhoid fever and refused to give any credence to stories of his drinking habits.

Sullivan celebrated his thirtieth birthday debilitated and on crutches—but dry. He proclaimed that he was firmly resolved never to touch a glass of beer or any form of intoxicating liquor again. He had lost almost 80 pounds (he claimed over 100) in the span of one month; at one time his weight had fallen to 160. Ann was still at his side, celebrated as the loyal nurse-companion. ("Her little daughter . . . received no more of her love and care, if as much, as did the man she loved and with whose fortunes she had cast in her own.") Many took a more jaundiced view. Sullivan's arch-enemy, the *New York Times*, printed a short squib denying that he was all that ill and blaming hard drinking for his stomach disorder.

John L. certainly felt that he had passed through the valley of the shadow of death, proudly announcing that he had defeated typhoid fever, gastric fever, inflammation of the bowels, heart trouble, and "liver complaint." He said he had been given up for lost on two occasions by his doctors (he had run through five physicians, culminating in the harmless Bush) and had suffered "incipient paralysis" for six weeks. At no time did he admit that his drinking had had the slightest bit to do with his condition—the usual denial pattern of the alcoholic. John L. credited his recovery to the ministrations of Bush, twice-a-day rubdowns with oil, and "electric treatment." He saw the trial as a great catharsis: "I came out of my sickness a new man."[5]

A new man was what he would need to be, if he was ever to return to the prize ring. Some of his more sanguine admirers felt he could be honed into shape within three months; others feared that now, with his thirtieth birthday and a severe illness behind him, he was finished. Worse, Richard Kyle Fox was parading a new "champion of the world," convinced that Sullivan had passed his peak. The Proprietor had even commissioned a song entitled "Our Champion," which was sung by the popular Maggie Cline:

> A song for him whose gallant fame still rings around the earth,
> Among our heroes grand, we name this soul of stirring worth.
> A conq'ror brave and tried and true, whose record bears no stain,
> Our hearts and hands we give to you, our champion, Jake Kilrain.[6]

## II

His real name was John Joseph Killion. Four months younger than Sullivan, he was born on February 9, 1859, in the Long Island village of Green Point. His mother came from Athlone, Catherine Sullivan's home, and his father, John J., had been born in Roxbury, Sullivan's birthplace. His youthful pals for some reason tagged him with the moniker of Jake Kilrain, and the name stuck. As a teenager he gravitated to the rolling mills of Somerville, a suburb of Boston, by his own description a "gawky country boy." He soon had to learn to scuffle as best he could with the rough mill workers, most of them Irish Americans like himself. He grew to five feet ten inches and filled out accordingly under the press of the ten-and twelve-hour workdays. By the time he was twenty he was fighting and winning pickup bouts with his fellow laborers. Proudly he remembered the day when "I was champion of the mill."[7]

Kilrain may have met Sullivan during his stay in the Boston area. At any rate, he fought several men who had been early victims of John L., among them Dan Dwyer. Also like Sullivan, Jake developed sporting interests outside of boxing. He became an ardent rower and under his real name won the National Amateur Junior Sculling Championship in Newark, New Jersey, in 1883. When officials found out that "Killion" had fought for money, his title was taken away. He continued to row for a while longer, developing powerful leg, shoulder, and back muscles, but in the winter of 1883 he decided to become a professional pugilist. To this end he left the mills for good and worked at Boston's Cribb Club, where he certainly knew Sullivan, and began to make his way in the fight game. Kilrain possessed significant assets; he had stamina and was whipcord-tough after the years spent rowing and toiling in the mills. He probably never filled out to the 210 pounds he claimed for himself, but he was big enough—sinewy, agile, and possessed of a burning desire to win.

His ring conquests mounted, George Godfrey among them. Kilrain fought draws with Mitchell and Mike Cleary and defeated Frank Herald in one round. Triumphs followed over Ashton and Joe Lannon, both of whom had fought exhibitions against Sullivan. By 1886 he was a nationally known boxer, Fox's latest "coming man." That winter

23. Jake Kilrain (about 1889) (William Schutte Collection)

Fox awarded him the *National Police Gazette* diamond belt and matched him to fight Jem Smith for Fox's version of the world championship. The two men met on a swampy island in the Seine on December 19, 1887, under the London Rules. Ten thousand dollars and the "championship of England" were at stake. For almost three hours Kilrain and Smith battered away at each other, their faces swollen and bleeding and their knuckles in shreds. At last winter darkness brought a halt. The utterly exhausted pugilists had fought an astonishing 106 rounds to a draw.[8]

The Smith fight made Kilrain's pugilistic reputation, but Sullivan was unapproachable, having already signed a contract to meet Mitchell. Kilrain contented himself with witnessing the Chantilly draw, but he burned for a crack at the champion. The differences between the two men were wildly exaggerated by the sporting press, but they existed. Kilrain was a family man. By 1887 he was living quietly in Baltimore with his wife, Elizabeth, and two children. He was prudent; he kept a bank account for each child and had life insurance covering his bouts, with his wife as beneficiary. He also supported a younger sister and his aging parents. His father, a former machinist, was over eighty in 1887, and his mother was almost as old and very feeble (she died in June 1889).[9]

The stable Kilrain thus could be contrasted with the erratic drunkard Sullivan. No one doubted Jake's courage, though, and even before the Smith fight he had found backers eager to match him against John L. Chief among these were a saloon keeper, Charley Johnston of Brooklyn; two other New Yorkers, Jimmy Wakely and Phil Lynch; and, of course, Fox himself. For fight fans it seemed an ideal match, and the careful minuet among the various wheeler-dealers had been going on well before Sullivan left on his European tour. Kilrain had posted one thousand dollars as early as May 1887. Fox had cooperated by unilaterally declaring Jake the champion and dubbing John L. a "quitter." The Proprietor even sponsored a little ceremony in Kiernan's Monumental Theater in Baltimore, awarding Jake the *Police Gazette* belt and asserting that Sullivan was getting bad advice from his manager at the time, Pat Sheedy (described by Fox as "an astute adventurer without capital and without credit").[10]

Sullivan's response to this ploy was not long in coming. He called Kilrain's belt a "dog-collar." Fox and Kilrain's other backers, despite their confident tub thumping, knew that unless they could entice Sullivan into the ring with their man, John L. with all his flaws was still the people's choice. Their strategy became one of delivering a cascade of insults. First Sheedy, then Phillips, were presented as Svengalis to Sullivan's Trilby. The life-styles of the two pugilists were hyperbolically compared, to the constant detriment of John L.[11] The champion's illness intervened. Still, throughout his recovery Sullivan began to think about a match with Kilrain. He was farsighted enough to see the possibilities of a big payday, and this he had not had in more than a year.

Johnston, Wakely, and Lynch were so eager to see the fight that they helped back Sullivan, and accordingly the convalescing John L. posted five thousand dollars on December 7, 1888, to fight Kilrain. Jake followed suit two weeks later, depositing his money with the *New York Clipper*. In the offices of the *New York Illustrated News*, run by his supporter Frederick Willetts, John L. scrawled a challenge in his bold, slanting hand:

> I hereby challenge Jake Kilrain to fight me according to the latest rules of the London prize ring for the sum of $10,000 a side or as much more as he would like me to make it. The fight to take place six months after signing articles, the place of the fight to be mutually agreed upon. I have this day placed in the hands of the Sporting Editor of the New York Clipper the sum of $5,000 as a guarantee of good faith.
>
> John L. Sullivan, Champion of the World.[12]

Everyone concerned decided to make the match outside New York, to avoid the inevitable response of the authorities. They chose Toronto, and there in the Rossin House on January 7, 1889, Sullivan and his new "business manager," Jack Barnett (who had been the champion's "secretary" on the trip abroad), got together with Kilrain's backers. Jake was not present, his interests being served by his biographer, Fox's indefatigable sports editor, William E. Harding. Sullivan's eagerness for the bout was evidenced by his ready agreement to fight under the London Rules. The articles were quickly agreed upon and were stylistically typical of the prizefights of Sullivan's era:

> Articles of agreement entered into this 7th day of January, 1889, between Jake Kilrain, of Baltimore, Md., and John L. Sullivan, of Boston, Mass. Said Jake Kilrain and said John L. Sullivan hereby agree to fight a fair stand up fight according to the new rules of the London prize ring, by which said Jake Kilrain and said John L. Sullivan hereby do agree to be bound. Said fight shall be for the sum of $10,000 a side and belt [the *Police Gazette* belt], representing the championship of the world [Sullivan had lined out a phrase so designating Kilrain, but had agreed to fight for the belt, which he said he would give to some newsboy in Boston], and shall take place on the 8th day of July, 1889, within 200 miles of New Orleans, in the state of Louisiana, the man winning the toss to give the opposite party ten days' notice of the place. Said Jake Kilrain and said John L. Sullivan to fight at catch weights [no weight limit]. The men shall be in the ring between the hours of 8 A.M. and 12 M., or the man absent shall forfeit the battle money. The expenses of the ropes and stakes shall be borne by each party, share and share alike . . . .[13]

Jake's backers felt they had made an excellent deal. They knew their man would be in condition, and Sullivan's lax training habits were notorious. Besides, John L. had not won a decisive prizefight in over two years, since his pasting of Paddy Ryan in San Francisco. Kilrain had the desire, the backing, and the edge, they believed. He would be fighting a man who had been badly weakened by illness for the biggest single purse in the history of the prize ring: twenty thousand dollars, winner-take-all.

## III

The challenger went to work immediately. He was rusty, not having fought since the Smith bout. This was Kilrain's big opportunity, and fierce competitor that he was, he was determined not to muff it. His backers did their part as well, promptly depositing the remaining five thousand dollars at the *Clipper* office on April 15. Sullivan, with a large delegation in tow, personally delivered his stake three days later. After much discussion, everyone agreed that a bookie named Al Cridge, a former carpenter from Paddy Ryan's hometown of Troy, would hold the stakes. Kilrain continued to let his backers do his talking for him. He even spent some time overseas, coming home in early June only because of the death of his mother. On his return he left the *Police Gazette* belt with Cridge, who placed the icon, wrapped in blue velvet and tucked into a valise, in a safe-deposit vault. At the same time Jake's backers won the coin toss for deciding the location of the fight; for the moment they kept their choice to themselves.[14]

As Kilrain assiduously sweated himself into condition and mourned his mother, the news from the Sullivan camp was in sharp contrast. A man named Jack Hayes had been engaged to train the champion. Sullivan reported that Hayes had him walking twelve to fifteen miles a day, getting rubdowns, and taking three-hour naps. In the early afternoon he would head with Barnett and Hayes for Tom Hagerty's or M. T. Clarke's, two popular Boston groggeries. In these places he would either demolish a few bottles of Bass Ale or drink the harder stuff. His old habits were back, and his weight was up to 215 and climbing. He talked of another exhibition tour, to end in New Orleans just before the fight. Soon even this slack "training" tapered off, and he was boozing as fiercely as before. His brother, Mike, tried to get Hayes to force John L. back into training and finally enlisted Barnett in the cause. One evening Hayes and Barnett, trainer and manager, actually came to blows over the issue, and the police had to be called to break it up twice while, in a nearby saloon, an oblivious Sullivan drank steadily on.[15]

Clearly, Hayes had to go. John L. was once again into a heedless round of saloons, testimonials, and very occasional workouts. In desperation, the champion's backers turned to the firmest apostle of physical fitness they knew: William Muldoon. The challenge appealed to Muldoon, as he had known Sullivan for years, toured with him, and developed a theory that John L. had never been properly prepared for a fight. After much wheedling the "Big Fellow" was packed off to Muldoon's farm near Belfast, New York, in the company of Barnett and Mike Cleary. There Muldoon waited with a clearly defined program, but by this time less than two months remained before the match.[16]

As Muldoon obliquely phrased it, Sullivan was "a man who makes flesh rapidly." When he arrived at Belfast, the champion weighed a flabby 240 pounds. He required a regimen to turn fat into muscle, not one to merely lose weight. Muldoon's program was a combination of carefully supervised routine and common sense. A grumbling John L. was first put to work alongside the apostle's farm hands. For days he sweated with them in the field, hewing to their hours, eating alongside them, and ultimately collapsing into bed, weary with fatigue. He chopped down trees, helped with the plowing, even milked the cows. Slowly his muscles began to harden and his wind to improve. He did not lose much weight, but his fluid retention was much less under the enforced discipline. At the beginning a few dozen rope skips were enough to tire him; at the end he was doing 800 to 900 repetitions at a time. Gradually Muldoon moved him from field work into serious training with the punching bag and a twelve-pound medicine ball. He walked and ran daily.[17]

Muldoon was no fool, nor was he a quack on the subject of physical fitness. He knew John L. was an alcoholic; thus he kept his charge away from whiskey and so busy from dawn to dusk that John L. had little time or inclination to fall into the standard pattern of complaint and self-pity. An exhausted Sullivan was happy to accept rest and refreshment in whatever form they came. Nevertheless, John L. rebelled from time to time. At least once he fled into Belfast for a night on the town, leading to a row with his mentor and resulting in an even stricter schedule. Sports fans everywhere were riveted on the news from Muldoon's farm. Was the apostle performing a miracle or merely wasting his time, given Sullivan's colossal capacity for dissipation? In mid-June the odds shifted from 6 to 4 for John L. to 5 to 4 against him.[18]

Later it would be said that Muldoon's masterful mind had "compelled the big giant from Boston to obey him like a child." This claim was exaggerated and overwrought, but it was true that, for the first and only time in his life, Sullivan was training thoroughly under the inspired guidance of a man who understood the rudiments of physical culture as well as anyone of his era. Muldoon concentrated on Sullivan's legs and wind. The two men wrestled constantly to get John L. used to the grapple and grab of the London Rules. The apostle was a bit of a psychologist as well, talking constantly about how hard Kilrain was working and what would happen should Sullivan lose the crown. He kept Sullivan off tobacco and dosed him regularly with a "first rate purgative," a vile concoction composed of equal parts powdered rhubarb, calcined magnesia, and powdered ginger. The diet was heavy on protein and light on carbohydrates.[19] By early July the champion was down to 209, as quick and strong as he had ever been.

At last the two men headed for New York, where they had previously given wrestling exhibitions. Kilrain was in town as well, sparring with his second, Mitchell, for the relief of the victims of the disastrous Johnstown Flood in Pennsylvania. Muldoon's deal with Sullivan's backers was risky, and he intended to accompany his charge all the way to New Orleans. The apostle had paid all the training expenses, and if Sullivan lost, he would get nothing and be out of pocket hundreds of dollars. If John L. won, Muldoon was to get a substantial share of the forfeit money, a hefty cut out of ten thousand dollars. Despite John L.'s flagrant abuses of his body, Muldoon liked him enormously, was saddened by his chronic dissipation, and viewed him as an ideal test case for his theories of physical fitness. As for Sullivan, he would frankly acknowledge that he had never been trained so well.[20]

# IV

As the two contestants rounded into shape, the sporting world had not been idle. In New Orleans two local gamblers and promoters, Bud Renaud and Pat Duffy, had been furtively looking for a suitable fight location. They were bucking a tirade of antiboxing sentiment in the Crescent City; the influential *Picayune* was firing a barrage of editorials deploring the match as a deification of brute strength. Still, New Orleans was becoming increasingly tolerant toward prizefighting and indeed was well on its way to earning its late-nineteenth-century title of "city of sin." The notorious Storyville district was in the process of formation, and high-priced bawds were a staple of the local scenery. Sports of all types, including cockfighting, were permitted. The state of Louisiana helped attract the sporting crowd by running a lottery, to which thousands subscribed. In short, Louisiana was wide open, to the deep chagrin of its "better citizens."

Governor Francis T. Nicholls was convinced, however, that Sullivan and Kilrain were too much, and he was determined to stop the match. His fellow governors also were up in arms; opposing prizefighting was good politics. Robert Lowry of Mississippi offered troops to Nicholls, just in case Louisiana needed help, and he finally posted a reward of one thousand dollars for the two pugilists. Lawrence T. Ross of Texas stoutly declared that the fight would not take place there. Arkansas's James P. Eagle announced that he would use "all lawful means" to stop it. When Thomas Seay of Alabama heard a rumor that Renaud and Duffy had been sniffing around Mobile County, he wired the sheriff there not to permit the fight. "It is a felony. Take precautions as you deem necessary to prevent or punish." From as far away as Nebraska, Governor Joseph Evans gave evidence that his state would be closed to the match. As for Nicholls, he called for the Louisiana Field Artillery and the Louisiana Rifles to stand ready.[21]

Interest in the bout was building rapidly, and the vehement denouncements of the governors only served to catapult Sullivan and Kilrain from the sports pages to page one. In Chicago, the Reverend Mr. Brobst of the Westminster Presbyterian Church took a different view in a sermon on "Prize Fights." The world had advanced, he said, using John L. and Jake as proof:

> Look at the preparation these two men have gone through. A short time ago they were drinkers, sensual, beastly. But for weeks and months they have been temperate—they have denied themselves. They have passed through the severest training. Talk about taking up your cross, Christians! You ought to be ashamed of yourselves. Take a lesson in hardship and denial from these pugilists! Think how they have worked to be ready for a fight which may last only a half hour. . . . We are called on to suffer. Learn how to do it from these pugilists.

As the fight drew nearer, lengthy press comment appeared daily. Betting was heavy and transcended national boundaries. Jacob L. Doty, the American consul in Tahiti, reported that large sums were being wagered by the Polynesians, with Sullivan a great favorite.[22]

In early July the champion set forth for New Orleans, the site for the fight still undecided. Curious townspeople and farmers gathered to greet his train as it whistle-stopped through New York; the Rochester depot was crammed with supporters. There was an equally grand reception in Cincinnati. By the time the caravan pulled into Gentilly Station, a mile outside New Orleans, the fight had become a national sensation. Muldoon installed his man in a boarding house on Rampart Street, guarded him zealously from eager well-wishers, and put him on a mild schedule of exercise to keep him in tone.[23]

A raucous cascade of fight fans descended on New Orleans, many of them coming in chartered railroad cars. Fox arranged for an entire train to run over the Baltimore and Ohio and Queen and Crescent systems. Johnston and Wakely were there, of course; so were the loyal Frank Moran, Joe Coburn, and dozens of Sullivan's friends from New York and Boston. Kilrain arrived with a retinue that included Mitchell,

Dominick McCaffery, and Johnny Roche. Rumors flew that the fight would be in Mississippi. Governor Lowry asked permission of Governors Nicholls and Seay to let armed militiamen through their states to intercept the pugilists. Governor Ross wired the sheriff of Orange County, located on the Sabine River where the Southern Pacific from New Orleans entered Texas, to be on the lookout.[24]

Nicholls had his problems, even had he wanted to comply with Lowry's request. Only two companies, totaling sixty-five men, were on the militia rolls in New Orleans, and the captain of one of them, Battery B of the Louisiana Field Artillery, had been mentioned as a possible referee for the fight. Now that the rumors were centering on Mississippi, Nicholls was more relaxed but still vigilant. Lowry, for his part, pushed himself into a frenzy of activity. He ordered three companies of militia to defend the state line against invasion. The Jeff Davis Volunteers of Fayette were reported mobilizing on the Northeastern Road, while two companies guarded Pass Christian and Bay Saint Louis on the Seacoast Route. Nicholls had to rely on his minuscule militia, and the Louisiana Rifles appeared less than trustworthy. The unit was composed of members of the Young Men's Gymnastic Club in New Orleans; they had feted John L. on his arrival. In addition, the militia commander, Major General John Glynn, was general manager of the Northeastern Road, which had just signed a contract to supply excursion trains to the fight. Two excursion cars were already booked. The exasperated Nicholls could not even find rail transport to move his troops.[25]

All in all it was broad farce, a scene worthy of Plautus at his best. As the first week of July ended, the only questions were those of surprise and timing. Having invested so much in proclamations upholding public order and morality, Lowry and Nicholls had placed themselves in the national eye, right alongside Sullivan and Kilrain. Americans centered their attention on New Orleans. Would the great contest occur?

## V

Occur it did, and with the rapidity of summer lightning. Unfortunately for the reputation of Governor Lowry, the rumors concerning Mississippi were all too true. Renaud and Duffy had been piling up a small fortune for a month, charging ten dollars for general admission and fifteen for ringside seats to fight fans who had not the slightest idea where the match was to take place. Only the promoters knew, and they kept the location a secret until July 7, the day before the fight. Their angel was Charles W. Rich, a wealthy young Mississippi landowner who controlled thirty thousand acres of prime pine land and owned a large sawmill. Rich was eager for the publicity and actually offered his property to Renaud and Duffy.[26]

On the night of July 7 Rich put twenty black laborers to work by the light of sputtering pine torches. The site he chose was about half a mile from the railroad, on the highest of the hills behind his estate, which was located in the hamlet of Richburg in Marion County. The area was grassy, level, dry, and firm, and a slight rain had packed the sandy soil. The men toiled steadily, driving eight-foot ash stakes into the ground only with difficulty. They then linked them together with high-grade, $1\frac{1}{16}$-inch manila rope. Outside the twenty-four-foot ring they speedily erected similar enclosures for backers and seconds. Fully conscious of the press, Rich even had a small area roped off for reporters to the east of the ring. Finally the men nailed together a scaffolding for fresh-cut plank bleachers (only the best pine from the sawmill of Charles W. Rich), which eventually rose twelve tiers high and could accommodate a crowd of well over one thousand. As dawn tinted the summer sky the work was finished, and the heretofore virgin woodland had become a miniature three-sided arena.

In New Orleans on the evening of the seventh, the fight crowd scurried to the depot. Renaud and Duffy had chartered three trains, one for the fighters and their entourages and two for the fans. The promoters kept the destination secret until the journey began, and a merry, conspiratorial air blanketed the entire proceedings. The Louisiana attorney general and the New Orleans chief of police rode one of the trains to the state line to ensure, as they said, that no fight would take place in Louisiana. One reporter dryly noted that "as they failed to return it is presumed that they continued on the way with the others." The pugilists' train was away from the station first; its occupants spent a rather uncomfortable night in Richburg, where Rich himself played host to Kilrain, and Sullivan stayed in the home of Rich's chief clerk.[27]

The other two trains, rolling slowly through the black delta country-side with their eager cargo, did not arrive until well after sunrise on July 8. A band of armed men had challenged them at the Mississippi line, but they had chugged right on through at a sedate twenty-five miles per hour, and no shots were fired. The fight had originally been scheduled for shortly after daybreak, but the excursionists' delay moved the time back to ten o'clock, allowing both fighters a chance to eat and limber up. Little time was needed to get loose, because it became readily apparent that the day would be steaming hot. By ten the thermometer was approaching one hundred degrees. The slender pines provided little shade, and what little there was fell well outside the ring. Undaunted, the fans debarked, marched the half-mile to the open-air amphitheater, and placed themselves on boards already oozing sticky pitch. By fight time almost two thousand people were seated, and around seven hundred stood on the open side of the ring. Some blacks climbed to the roof of their nearby meetinghouse to get a better view.

Kilrain arrived first, accompanied by his seconds, Mitchell and Mike Donovan, and threw his hat into the ring. Sullivan was on hand within moments, seconded by Muldoon and Cleary. John L. was wrapped in a Turkish bath rug, and Cleary waved an American flag over his head. Both fighters had "bottle holders," a key office for such a scorching day. Sullivan had chosen Tom Costello of Cleveland as his umpire and time keeper, and Kilrain's choice for this function occasioned comment. Jake had selected none other than the notorious William Barclay ("Bat") Masterson, currently operating out of Denver. Bat was an ardent boxing fan; he would at one time control a significant amount of the boxing in Denver, and he eventually became a New York sports-writer. He had watched John L. whip Ryan back in 1882. Masterson's gunslinging days in Dodge City were still fresh in everyone's memory, and he had been hired as Kilrain's bodyguard during the stay in New Orleans. Bat had bet heavily on Kilrain.

After a short discussion, John Fitzpatrick of New Orleans, a popular politician and future mayor, was appointed referee. (It was later dis-covered that he had bet seven hundred dollars on Sullivan.) After the toss for corners, inconsequential given the lay of the land and the high summer sun, there was a brief delay as the local sheriff strode to the center of the ring and commanded peace in the name of the state of Mississippi. This perfunctory notice served, he retired to the side-lines to watch the fight.[28]

Mike Donovan, in Kilrain's corner, later swore that his fighter had been beaten before the fight started, acting "more like a man going to his own execution than a man who was going to fight for the cham-pionship. He was covered with a nervous sweat, and his eyes were glazed." Maybe so, but Jake had a strategy, and he intended to use it. He had seen the way Mitchell avoided Sullivan at Chantilly and forced a draw. At the least, Kilrain, about twenty pounds lighter than Sullivan, hoped for this. But the challenger was bigger and stronger than Mitch-ell, and he planned to slip in his damaging blows as the fight wore on.[29]

Both men were bare-chested, clad in fighting tights and leather shoes. Sullivan's breeches were green and covered to calf height by white stockings. In unconscious irony considering what was in store for him, Kilrain wore black tights and blue stockings. Each was buttressed by a strengthening plaster extending from the groin to about four inches above the top of the tights. The plaster was composed of equal parts of pitch and beeswax spread thinly on sheepskin, and gave the two men the odd look of two partially armored knights. John L. kept to his usual practice, when fighting seriously, of shaving his mustache and cropping his dark hair almost to a stubble. Observant spectators noticed flecks of gray in what remained. At 10:13 Fitzpatrick, with the politician's sense of drama, drew a line with his cane on the turf and summoned the fighters to scratch. Sullivan and Kilrain bowed to each other, retired to their corners, and advanced as Masterson yelled out "time!"[30] It was to prove, although no one could then know, the last bare-knuckle championship prizefight in the United States.

# VI

Both boxers briefly assumed a pugilistic pose as the crowd grew breathlessly silent under the blazing sun. Then Sullivan feinted and let fly a left, which Kilrain easily slipped under. Jake immediately grabbed the champion around the neck and hurled him to the ground with a hip toss, falling heavily on John L.'s chest. Fifteen seconds! Kilrain smiled as he took his chair, the prefight tension ebbing a little, but Sullivan stood disdainfully in his corner, waiting for the call.

They banged away at each other for the next two rounds, Kilrain slipping in low blows that some spectators saw as deliberate. Sullivan slammed him down with a hip toss to end the second, and he was himself twisted down after a series of clinches in the third. The fourth round was the longest of the fight, over fifteen minutes, and during it John L. hammered away at Jake's head while taking an occasional shot to the body. Both of them were sweating freely now, and Sullivan was becoming exasperated as Mitchell's influence on Kilrain became more and more evident. Sullivan taunted Kilrain to "fight like a man" as Jake attacked and evaded, and at one point he screamed at Mitchell, "I wish it was you I had in here, you sucker!" Despite Jake's tactics, the heavy blows to his head and chest were taking effect; he was again thrown to end the round. Each time he sat in his corner, he could look across at Sullivan leaning on the opposite ring post, arms folded and bright black eyes ominously boring in on his target.

Mitchell had warned Kilrain against John L.'s lethal right hand, and Jake tended to circle away from it. This action made his own right more effective if the champion ever dropped his guard, and this he did in round five. Kilrain smashed Sullivan's nose and drew first blood, along with approving murmurs from those closest to the ring. Kilrain's reward was a stinging blow to the head that knocked him down; he was dazed as he was carried to his corner.

From the sixth round onward the contest was not between Sullivan and Kilrain. It became, in fact, two contests, each man testing his willpower to the utmost. For Jake, the ordeal became one of simply showing up for the next round, hoping that Sullivan would make a

24. Sullivan, on left, grapples with Kilrain in this rare photograph. It is early in the fight, as both men are still wearing their "strengthening plasters." (William Schutte Collection)

mistake or give up. For John L., it became a battle against his own impatience and the searing Mississippi sun. Kilrain was a beaten fighter after the first twenty minutes, Mike Donovan's observations aside, but he was about to stage an epic practically unrivaled in American sport, and in his struggle he took Sullivan along with him. By now the pine pitch was literally bubbling out of the bleacher seats. The presence of so many people had added even more heat (some later claimed that the temperature had reached 115 degrees), and the usual Gulf humidity saturated Rich's makeshift arena. For the fighters the ring was turning into hell at midday.

Kilrain began to fall deliberately to end the rounds. From time to time he would feel a fresh rush of strength and fight effectively. He tripped John L. to end the seventh. But Sullivan kept tapping fresh reserves, too, reaching into the well of energy Muldoon had built for him during the weeks on the Belfast farm. He launched frequent haymakers, and sometimes one would land. By the eighth, Kilrain's face was becoming swollen and disfigured, and red splotches appeared on his chest where John L. had thumped him. By the tenth the crowd was grumbling over the challenger's unwillingness to come to close quarters. By the twelfth it was hissing him. Still Jake kept falling, more quickly now. John L.'s strengthening plaster had melted almost entirely off and hung down obscenely over his tights. Nevertheless, he stayed fresh while Kilrain was visibly weakening.

On it went, as the sun ascended to its zenith. Fifteen, twenty, twenty-five rounds. Every once in a while Sullivan himself accidentally slipped to end a round. But mostly it was Kilrain who stopped, eager for a rest from the pummeling. Sullivan was screaming at him: "You're a champion, eh? A champion of what?" Still, Jake kept coming back and occasionally landed a stinging blow. Despite his fatigue he was still dangerous, and Sullivan knew it, stalking him very carefully and uncharacteristically husbanding his energy, another strategic gift from the time spent with Muldoon. Once, after about forty minutes, Muldoon asked John L. how much longer he could stand the heat, and was met with the fierce response, "I can stay here until daybreak tomorrow."

By the twenty-eighth round the champion had worked himself into a rage. A lump was growing under one eye, and Kilrain had managed to throw him again two rounds before. Jake suddenly staggered him with a sharp punch to the swelling eye, which produced the familiar bull-like rush and a smash to Kilrain's jaw. This was Jake's plan, to madden the champion and lead him to exhaustion, but how much more could he himself take? Between rounds, Kilrain and Mitchell decided that their only hope was for Jake to go for Sullivan's eyes and close them both with repeated jabs. Masterson was doing his part by arguing with Costello after each round and thus giving Kilrain precious extra seconds to rest.

Past the thirtieth round they went. Kilrain sometimes slumped to the turf without being hit, craving a few more seconds in his corner. In the thirty-sixth John L. appealed to Fitzpatrick to end the fight, with no result. By now Kilrain had to be lifted bodily out of his chair by his seconds and propelled toward the scratch line. He was utterly exhausted. The spectators were howling their displeasure. At the end of the forty-first round William E. Harding, Fox's representative, ostentatiously left ringside, convinced that his boss's man could not win.

Yet, incredibly, Kilrain kept going. He got up, he punched at times, he still managed to dodge some of John L.'s blows. He even gained some support when Sullivan ended one round by trying to sit on his opponent's head. In addition, Jake's spikes had torn into Sullivan's shoes repeatedly, until the leather uppers were hanging in long strips about the soles and the champion was standing in his own blood. At last came a seeming miracle for Kilrain and his fans: five seconds into round forty-four, John L. suddenly and unaccountably began to vomit, and to those familiar with his drinking habits and his illness, it seemed to be proof that his stomach was gone—and with it, the championship. Heartened, Jake quickly asked, "Will you draw the fight?" Stomach still heaving, John L. roared, "No, you loafer!" and went at him again with both hands. For the next three rounds the old Sullivan rage was back, and Kilrain dropped each time.

Fifty, fifty-five, sixty—John L. had fully recovered from his upset stomach, and Kilrain was plumbing new depths of exhaustion. Jake was drinking whiskey steadily between rounds, eventually consuming over a quart. The midday sun beat down mercilessly, and both men had huge blisters on their shoulders and arms, crisscrossed by red welts raised by the bare-knuckle blows. Sullivan was laughing derisively now, and Mike Donovan had to continuously prod Jake to come out and fight. The champion refused to sit in his corner between rounds and kept insisting that his bottle holder keep his back "good and wet." John L.'s eye was swollen almost shut, but Kilrain had no strength left to work on it. He could manage only one or two weak blows in each round and went down at every opportunity.

Sixty-five, seventy—at ringside Charley Johnston offered to bet five hundred dollars to fifty that Sullivan would win, but he found no takers. Kilrain's midsection was a mass of bruises, and John L. was firing in shots to the face at will, crunching blows to the cheek and jaw. Jake was flailing all over the ring, trying somehow to trip his heavier opponent and bring him down. Failing this he was running constantly, clearly beaten but propelled onward by some fierce inner instinct that would not let him quit.

Despite the temperature, his own injuries, and his stomach trouble, John L. seemed fresh. His blows were solid, well-aimed, destructive. It was obvious to everyone that Kilrain's Mitchell-inspired tactics had failed and that the champion, thanks to Muldoon, was in the best condition of his career. The last five rounds were a prolonged death knell for Kilrain's hopes. In the seventy-fifth Sullivan belted his opponent about the ring as he pleased, once again the irresistible fighting machine of his boxing youth. It was enough. Kilrain was dazed, scarcely conscious. Although Mitchell wanted him to continue, he refused to come to scratch for round seventy-six, and Mike Donovan, at long last, resignedly took the sponge from the water pail in Jake's corner and threw it into the middle of the ring.

John L. immediately hurtled across the turf toward Mitchell, daring him to fight. Charlie, who had been screaming "foul!" throughout the bout, started forward, but cooler heads separated them. There were plenty of guns in the crowd, and John L. came close to triggering a melee that might have ended in a bloodbath. As it was, Cleary and some others coaxed him back to his corner. It was past high noon on the Mississippi plain. Two hours, sixteen minutes, and twenty-three seconds had elapsed, and John L. Sullivan was still heavyweight champion of the world.[31]

## VII

The bystanders immediately sensed that they had witnessed something special. They stormed the ring and took everything not nailed down. Sullivan's soft felt hat, which he had shied into the arena at the beginning of the fight to join Kilrain's, went for $50. The buckets that had held the ice water sold for $25 each. The crowd demolished the ring post that had held John L.'s colors; the splinters brought $5 apiece. The ring rope was quickly hacked to bits and its remnants sold. Towels and sponges disappeared. Even the turf was dug up and later peddled in little parcels as mementoes. Sullivan's drinking can, from which he had taken only water during the ordeal, was grabbed by Louisville's fire chief, who supposedly refused $1,000 for it.[32]

The news was flashed to the nation as soon as reporters could get to a telegraph key. "THE BIGGER BRUTE WON," screamed the *New York Times*—but it gave Sullivan page one. The *Boston Pilot* at last grudgingly admitted John L. to its pages, and even the proper *Boston Evening Transcript* squeezed out thirteen lines, although five of these dealt with the failure of the authorities to interfere. In Kilrain's hometown, Baltimore, the newspapers had issued hourly extras, and crowds had packed the streets around the press offices, only to be told in midafternoon that their man had been beaten. New Yorkers had crowded into Park

Row and waited patiently for hours under the summer sun to look at the bulletins. Thousands of bogus newspapers claiming to bear fight news were sold that evening.[33]

At the White House the small band of assigned reporters was surprised by an official inquiry concerning the news of the fight. Whether the request had come from the current resident, the stodgy and stand-offish Benjamin Harrison, was not known. Once Sullivan's victory had registered, the celebrations began. In Baltimore a troop of small boys paraded on Baltimore Street, cheering for John L., while knots of sullen Kilrain backers watched from the sidewalks. Long after midnight, New York saloons were jammed with men drinking and cheering for Sullivan. Boston rose to the occasion as well. "I am glad that Sullivan has redeemed himself," commented John Boyle O'Reilly. "His equal as a boxer never entered the ring in ancient or modern times." Journalists like Charles Dana of the *New York Sun* were at last convinced, even against their will:

> A wonderful specimen is this Sullivan. He is a man of naturally extravagant and exaggerated powers in almost every way. He might be called a sort of extremist. He dines like Gargantua. He drinks like Gambrinus. He has the strength of Samson, and the fighting talent of Achilles. When he moves it is with a child's ease, and he hits with a giant's force. And all these qualities are contained in a figure so compact and balanced that it impresses the eye more with its symmetry than its power. If any one thinks that the physique of the human race is degenerating, let him consider the great John L. He should be reassured.[34]

In Mississippi the wonderful specimen and his vanquished opponent had more immediate concerns. Kilrain was horribly sunburned and so badly beaten that he had trouble climbing into a buggy to be conveyed to the press train. Once aboard, Donovan sat himself next to Jake, hoping to cheer him up. Kilrain groaned in agony and despondency throughout most of the journey back to New Orleans, blaming himself for letting down his friends and supporters. He slumped in his fighting togs near an open window, shoulders bare and blistered, blood flowing down his face and mingling with his tears. The next morning, with Mitchell, Pony Moore, and Johnny Murphy, he fled New Orleans, fearing arrest. Eventually the quartet reached New York, where Mitchell and his father-in-law departed for England, leaving behind an angry Kilrain, who felt that Mitchell had come close to urging him on to pugilistic suicide. Broke and bruised, Jake went to ground temporarily in Virginia, hiding from the law.[35]

The authorities were indeed in full pursuit, and their big fish was Sullivan. The champion was in naturally high spirits following his triumph. The proof of his conditioning lay in the fact that he had sloughed off only six pounds during the unequal but prolonged contest.

His train left Richburg an hour after Kilrain's, and in the interim an alarm spread that the militia was coming. Sullivan was already aboard, a coat slung over his shoulders and his hands badly swollen. Hearing the hue and cry, he immediately piled out through the train window and hid behind a thicket. When his friends finally found him, they brought along pants and a jacket, and thus attired, the banged up but happy champion arrived at last back in New Orleans. That night he enjoyed a hot mustard bath and took stock of his injuries, which included the cut under his swollen right eye and a damaged lip. Then he celebrated, boozing most of the following night at the Young Men's Gymnastic Club and throwing money out of a window to a mob of boys.[36]

Two days later John L. learned that a Mississippi sheriff had arrived in New Orleans with a warrant for his arrest. With Johnston, Muldoon, Cleary, Duffy, and a few others he fled for the depot, booking a car for Nashville. The sheriff was on the ball and wired ahead; in Nashville a squad of policemen boarded the train. They took one look at John L.'s swollen face and hands (the champion claimed his name was "Thompson"), clapped him in handcuffs, and after a short struggle deposited him in the local jail. This establishment "was more like a rat pen than anything else," remembered Sullivan, and he was discomfited by the fact that blacks shared cells with whites. He was released the next morning, as he had been arrested without warrant and misdemeanors in Tennessee were not extraditable. Nevertheless, this was just the start of a long legal struggle that eventually cost him forty-five hundred dollars. After a grand celebration in Chicago, he came to rest in New York, where he believed he was beyond the clutches of Mississippi law.[37]

He was wrong. On the evening of July 31 he was arrested in New York City, charged with violating a Mississippi statute against prize-fighting. The possible penalty was a fine of one thousand dollars and imprisonment for one year. Sullivan was escorted under guard to Purvis, Mississippi, where he was turned over to Sheriff W. J. Cowart. A few days later Kilrain was arrested in Baltimore. On August 16, in a ramshackle courtroom in Purvis, Sullivan was found guilty of one count of prizefighting and sentenced to one year in jail. The champion was found innocent of a second charge, assault and battery, and his defense, that he was ignorant of the law, was found unconvincing. He made bond and returned to New York, while Kilrain's bond was made in his absence by Charles Rich and a man named Carborough. Jake agreed to come south for his trial in December.[38]

The legal fallout was heavy. In proceedings held in the Purvis mayor's office (which also doubled as a barbershop), Fitzpatrick, Renaud, Rich, and several of Rich's employees were arraigned for aiding and abetting a prize fight. Renaud was eventually fined $500. Governor Lowry, having been unable for all his public alarms to stop the fight, was intent on punishment, especially since it was so flagrantly obvious that money had changed hands on the results. Al Cridge had turned over the $20,000 in stakes, forty $500 bills, and John L. had also received his "dog collar." But his expenses were heavy. Thousands went to his backers: $3,000 to the *Illustrated News* and $2,500 each to Johnston and Wakely. Muldoon, who split with Sullivan after the fight (the two were reconciled in 1897), had to be content with $2,000. This left the champion with $10,000, but almost half of this went for legal expenses and hundreds more on celebrations all the way from New Orleans to New York City. As a result, Sullivan probably netted only $4,000 or so from a fight worth twenty grand. The Mississippi authorities, however, saw only the larger sum and, outraged by the open flouting of the law, were determined to make him pay. When Lowry heard that John L. had been billeted in a private home in Jackson while awaiting trial, he ordered the champion jailed, and this was done.[39]

The governor, however, was face to face with the imperatives of the cult of masculinity. Try as he might to make the case against Sullivan, he ran into roadblocks at every turn. For example, six of the jurymen at Purvis also were named as witnesses—they had been at the fight— and they saw to it that the second count, that of assault and battery, was thrown out. Lowry, a widower with twelve children, did not lack courage or obstinacy—he had been a Confederate cavalry colonel under Nathan Bedford Forrest—and was increasingly sensitive to the sneers of the national press as he tried to punish the two pugilists. Nevertheless, the case dragged on into the winter months without result. Warrants were sworn out for everyone imaginable—Harding, Cleary, Muldoon, Donovan, Johnston, Wakely, even "Handsome Dan" Murphy, Sullivan's bottle holder.[40] But all remained exasperatingly beyond the reaches of the law; all, that is, except for Kilrain and Sullivan.

In December, Kilrain, as promised, returned to Purvis and was tried on the same two counts as Sullivan. This time a local jury reversed the findings. Jake was found not guilty of prizefighting but guilty of assault and battery, giving the sporting press more chances to laugh at the inconsistencies of Mississippi justice, especially since most of the assault and battery in the fight had been committed by Sullivan. Kilrain was sentenced to two months' imprisonment and a fine of two hundred dollars; he appealed. In March 1890, the appeal having failed, Jake was released to none other than Charles Rich to serve his sentence under the state's prison contract system. This type of imprisonment was not onerous; Kilrain wired the *New York Sun* that "my friend Charlie Rich, with his usual knack of fixing things, brought me here with him without my having to serve a minute. I will spend the next two months with him." To the wire was appended the following: "Nothing is too good for Jake at Richburg. Charlie."[41]

As for Sullivan, his case went on appeal to the Mississippi Supreme Court. This body, in March 1890, reversed the judgment of the lower court, quashed the indictment, and held Sullivan to answer under his current bond of one thousand dollars at the next term of Marion County's Circuit Court for such indictments as might be returned against him. The justices' reasoning was a masterpiece of tortured legal logic. They cited the indictment as faulty. That document did not show that the fight had been public or that Kilrain had fought Sullivan (only that Sullivan had fought Kilrain!). Both of these facts, they asserted, were required under the state's 1882 statute against prizefighting, which admittedly was weak and vaguely written.[42]

Governor Lowry must have been apoplectic. Sullivan never served a day in jail on his sentence, Kilrain enjoyed a vacation on a Mississippi estate, and the rulings of two Mississippi juries were in exact contradiction. John L. did not get away scot-free; "such indictments as might be returned" were indeed rewritten and resubmitted, and on June 25, 1890, Sullivan pleaded guilty in Purvis and was fined five hundred dollars. As for Lowry, he became the unwilling star of a mock-Shakespearean drama that circulated throughout the gleeful northern sporting press ("All this is passing strange. Must I set free the fighter who's defied our laws?") and the equally unwilling symbol of the weakness of statute law in the face of popularity and celebrity appeal.[43]

## VIII

"I'm getting too old," Sullivan told a New York reporter after the Kilrain fight, "and fighting under the London Prize Ring Rules is too risky. I was anxious to fight this time but I never want to fight again." He spoke truly. The training had been boring if necessary drudgery; the fight itself had been an ordeal worse than any he had undergone; and his debts and legal expenses had almost erased his winnings. He was proud of his newfound physical fitness, though, claiming that an unexpected jolt of whiskey from his handlers (after he had been drinking only water) had caused him to throw up in the forty-fourth round, but he ignored the challenges that once again came in, such as the one from Jem Smith. Boasting of his victory, he called Kilrain a dirty fighter for his low blows and spiking, registering himself as the John L. of old: "If Kilrain had stood up and fought like a man I think I could have whipped him in about eight rounds."[44]

Indeed, Sullivan had scaled new peaks of popularity. He had convincingly proven his durability and invincibility. Fresh doggerel was cranked out by the ream to celebrate his glory ("Proclaim it over land and seas—SULLIVAN, CHAMPION OF THE WORLD!"), and he was once again the toast of every saloon in America.[45]

"Our John" was again proved unbeatable, the force that could not be stopped. The Sullivan-Kilrain match would pass quickly into legend. It would become famed as the last bare-knuckle prizefight, which it was not—bare-knuckle bouts would be held (illegally) at least into the 1930s—and as the longest fight ever, which it also was not, either in time or in rounds. But the epic scale of the battle on the Mississippi plain would only grow with the telling, becoming a Homeric sporting legend of struggle and endurance. Jake and John L., in the furnace of Charlie Rich's jerry-built arena, had unwittingly fashioned both the farewell to a sporting way of life and the creation story of modern American prizefighting.

# CHAPTER ELEVEN

# The Thespian
## (1889—1892)

In the three years after the Kilrain match Sullivan did not once defend his title. Instead, his interests turned elsewhere, in the direction of a stage career. Clearly, he was trading on his fame in the prize ring to make money in a new pursuit. Just as clearly, he was tired of fighting. He hated to train, and indeed many of his fights had been conducted when he was badly out of condition. He wanted no more of the regimen of paring off weight or the demanding routine of self-denial.

John L.'s dilemma, however, was the classic one that many later athletes, and especially boxers, were to find so difficult. When does a sports figure give up the one thing that has made his fortune and his reputation, that has, particularly in Sullivan's case, become the leit-motif of his life? As the months passed, John L. avoided the question. He began to see himself as *of* the fight game but not *in* it, and his natural openness and fondness for posturing found a new home in the theater. His renown remained intact, yet the pressure was always on him to defend the crown.

John L.'s racial attitudes restricted the range of his opponents to white fighters, but even there he could have made matches with several good boxers, had he wanted to. He did not. The theater developed into a lucrative source of income, at least at first, and this success reinforced his cool attitude toward the prize ring. Another indication of change came with a stillborn attempt to enter politics, and yet another was his willingness to leave the country on a theatrical tour. In short, John L.'s mind was on a new walk of life. Doubtless helping to speed along the process of disassociation from boxing were twin emotional shocks he received in quick succession: within a little over a year Sullivan lost both his parents.

# I

Catherine Kelly Sullivan had been seriously ill for years. In the late afternoon of August 30, 1889, she began to fail quickly. Her husband, at the bedside, immediately sent for a priest. Even as the last rites were being administered, the family frantically tried to find its most famous member. John L. and his brother, Mike, were at Crescent Beach. On receiving the urgent telegram, they immediately took a train and arrived at the Parnell Street house minutes too late. With her husband, her daughter, Ann, and Ann's husband, James Lennon, at her bedside, Catherine died peacefully at 8:30 P.M.[1]

For the champion it was a shattering blow. He broke down and cried. Then, stolidly, he gathered himself and took care of the funeral arrangements. With the rest of the family he mourned during his mother's funeral and accompanied the cortege to the family plot at Mount Calvary cemetery. Despite her invalidism, Catherine had been very popular in her neighborhood, and the Highlands turned out in force to observe her passing. Fully one hundred carriages, filled with friends, followed her remains to the burial grounds. John L., from all accounts, was her favorite child, and the bond between them had been very close. Although his mother had not attended any of his fights, she had proudly followed his ring career, worried over his carousing, and always provided ready support during his numerous scraps, marital and otherwise. Now this fundamental bond was broken, and Sullivan truly grieved for the first time in his life. He was told, whether truthfully or not, that his mother's last prayer had been that he give up his dissipated habits, and the story went around that he had refused several offers of liquor during her wake.[2]

The impact of his mother's death stayed with Sullivan for months. He was reluctant to attend a benefit for himself at New York's Academy of Music on September 9, as he was trying seriously to observe the lengthy Irish period of mourning, but he came anyway. Despite poor advertising the benefit drew a large crowd of gentlemen and ladies, and John L. concluded the evening by sparring three rounds with Mike Cleary. Very subdued and given the complete sympathy of the audience, he was well-received and concluded with a short, graceful speech.[3]

The exhibition in no sense marked a return to the ring. John L. was weary of prizefighting, but he could not see any distinct way to retire finally from boxing and still maintain both his status and his ability to earn money. As the autumn of 1889 turned to winter, he began to drink heavily again and started to renege on scheduled events. He failed to appear at another benefit for himself at the Clermont Avenue Rink in Brooklyn. After the New Year he did manage to attract a large crowd to an exhibition at Henry Miner's theater in New York City, but his heart was not in it. Every once in a while he would make noises that he was eager to fight again; Pat Duffy was authorized to make a match for him. There was talk of a bout with either Joe McAuliffe or Frank Slavin of Australia. But John L. remained idle. The legal wrangles in Mississippi were dragging on, and he covered up his lack of interest in fighting with a declaration that he stood ready to meet any man in the world, "white or black," if the price was right. He was thinking in terms of another payday on the Kilrain scale—twenty thousand dollars—and this did not materialize.[4]

Compounding his problems, he continued his pattern of splitting with former associates after specific ventures. This time he parted with William Muldoon, the man most responsible in preparing him for Kilrain, because Muldoon had demanded a fixed percentage of future fight gates for his services and John L., with legal expenses piling up, declared himself fed up with the "percentage business." He was once again without any management whatsoever, and fell readily into his old manner of blaming whatever promoter was involved for poor turnouts at exhibitions. His alcoholic habits were back within days of his mother's funeral; one reporter interviewed him in a New York saloon as he was drinking with his father one week after her death.[5] Drowning one's sorrows in alcohol was an old Irish custom, but John L., in truth, needed no such excuse.

With the booze, the drunken sprees returned. Late in 1889 the champion found himself in company with Tommy Kelly, a fighter; John Ryan, a Boston gambler; and one Tom Keefe, alias Shea, who had just been released from prison after serving three years for highway robbery. John L. quarreled with Shea in a barbershop, upon which Kelly attacked Shea with a razor. A drunken Sullivan managed to stumble away before the police arrived. Shea was found badly slashed, and Kelly was arrested. Such tales did much to weaken the public support he had earned with the triumph over Kilrain. The Columbia Athletic Club in the national capital wanted John L. to put on an exhibition, but the older, more conservative members took note of his continued predilection for public disturbances and had their way in denying his appearance.[6]

During his slide back into dissipation—or what might more honestly be termed his continued drinking, only momentarily interrupted by the death of his mother—Sullivan flirted seriously with the political arena for the only time in his life. In September 1889 he publicly announced his interest in a congressional seat. His statement, probably drafted by the reporter Arthur Brisbane, was nevertheless unvarnished Sullivan, and it was further proof that John L., although proud of his ring career, was now interested in putting distance between himself and the manly art. As the most revealing of all his public statements, it also compactly describes the champion's self-image:

A good deal has been said about my becoming a candidate for Congress. I write to say that after thinking the matter over I have decided that when the time comes to elect new Congressmen in Boston I will be a candidate on the democratic ticket if nomination is offered to me. There are several reasons which have induced me to adopt this course.

In the first place I have always supported the party and always voted for it. I am sound as far as my political record is concerned, and I feel that I deserve the support of the party on that score.

Then I have personal friends and general admirers enough in Boston to elect me anyhow.

Any man who doubts my popularity with the American people has only to travel about with me to get rid of that notion.

Some may criticize my occupation in life. They don't know what they are talking about. My business is, and always has been ever since I came before the public, to encourage physical culture.

Young fellows don't care for what they read about a lot of small fighters and second rate champions, but the sight of one man with a national reputation and everybody looking up to him fires them with ambition and encourages them in the task of getting up their muscle. Many a young man is bigger and stronger because my example has set him to work.

Then besides, with my matches and exhibitions I have entertained hundreds of thousands all over the country. Also I have furnished, through the newspapers, interesting reading to millions [perhaps the first time a political candidate had advanced his participation in barroom scuffles as a reason to vote for him]. People have got to feel grateful to those who entertain them.

As for my methods in carrying on business and my dealings with other men, who can criticize them? If I make a promise I keep it.

I have always looked after my friends, and no one can accuse me of not acting fairly by him [*sic*]. A Sunday school teacher can't say more than that.

But what I feel to be more important than all else is the work which I have been doing to keep up the reputation of America among other nations.

The best men from everywhere have tried to beat me, but failed, and since I first began I have kept the pugilistic championship of the world in this country.

There isn't a self-respecting American, no matter what tomfool idea he may have about boxing in general, who does not feel patriotic pride at the thought that a *native born American*, a countryman of his, can lick any man on the face of the earth.

It is human nature, and this feeling of patriotism applies especially to Boston, where I was born and where I shall appear as a candidate.

As to my fitness for the place, I can prove that in a few words. A man is elected to Congress to look out for the interests of those who send him there. That will be my motto, and living up to it will be my business.

I know what is wanted by my friends and the citizens of Boston generally and I'll try to get it.

In my travels about this country and Europe I have had as much experience in public speaking as most people. I'll have no trouble about getting hearing in Congress or in making people pay attention to what I say.

A man who can quiet a crowd in Madison Square garden as I have done can make his presence felt in Congress or anywhere else on earth.

I therefore announce now my willingness to enter political life.

This communication, drawn up in consultation with friends and with their advice, is the longest that I have ever addressed to any paper.

I shall be obliged to you if you will print it.

Yours truly,

JOHN L. SULLIVAN
Champion of the World

Boston, September 5, 1889.[7]

This announcement, probably unique among American declarations of political candidacy, appeared foolish only to the degree that Sullivan refused to obfuscate or distort in the classic pattern of the country's political life. Indeed, he *did* have some support. Late in September the leaders of Boston's Fourth Congressional District held a conclave at the Sherman House, along with some ward bosses and a few pugilists. There was, after all, precedent for a prizefighter in the halls of Congress in the person of John Morrissey, and many were less than pleased with the performance of the district's incumbent, Joseph O'Neil. The meeting generated considerable enthusiasm for John L., but the bosses prevailed.

The champion's popularity was undoubted, and a carefully managed campaign might have been able to bring him victory, but his all-too-public displays of drinking and violent behavior were on everyone's mind. In addition, he had not done his spadework in the wards. As a result, his announcement came with the suddenness of a desert rain shower and with about the same nurturing effect. There were doubts, not so much about his ability to win a political race but about his own serious intentions as a candidate. Outside of Boston, his political ambitions were treated with general ridicule. From far-off Montana Territory a man with political ambitions of his own, Theodore Roosevelt, penned a gossipy letter to his friend the Boston blue blood, Henry Cabot Lodge. "Dear Cabot," asked TR, "is Sullivan really going to run for Congress? I think it is the most exquisite bit of humor if he does."[8]

John L. was not to run. The grand soufflé of his political announcement and his dreams of public office collapsed under the harsh realities of ward politics and his own excesses. The announcement itself survives as an intriguing insight into Sullivan's ego and sense of self-worth.

One parent gone, tired of the ring, and rejected in politics, the champion sustained a further loss just over a year after his mother's death.

In the early morning hours of September 7, 1890, his father died of typhoid pneumonia. Mike's death was a tragic reprise of Catherine's. Only a week before he had left the old home on Parnell Street for a smaller house at 26 Sawyer Street and immediately fallen ill. His daughter, Ann, nursed him, as she had her mother. Once again John L. was out of town, appearing on stage at Niblo's Gardens in New York. He came as quickly as he could, on the Shore Line, but again he was too late. "JOHN L. NOW AN ORPHAN," blared one headline, and a creative reporter quoted the champion as follows: " 'My God!,' said he, ' 'tis too bad. A year ago today poor mother died.' "

Old Mike had been popular too, his feisty manner and combative attitude his most obvious inheritance to his son. Based on oft-told tales of childhood punishments, he gloried in the title of "the only man who ever whipped Sullivan." Over three thousand people attended his funeral services in Roxbury's Saint Patrick's Church, and he was laid to rest beside his wife at Mount Calvary. In no way had Mike been a success in life, but he had been his son's staunchest fan, habitually visiting Boston's newspaper row in search of bulletins whenever John L. fought. Less positively, his temper and his drinking habits had been passed undiluted to his famous offspring. Sullivan had been closer to his mother, but Mike's death was also wrenching.[9]

For the champion it had been a dismal twelve months, bracketed by the deaths of both parents and pocked by legal difficulties and drinking sprees. He now had no real confidant, no one on whom he could rely. Billy Madden was long gone, Muldoon was estranged, and Al Smith and Pat Sheedy were adamant in their refusal ever to work with him again. As if to punctuate his alienation from his surroundings, one of his oldest acquaintances in the fight game, Joe Coburn, died at the end of 1890.[10] By then John L. had been embarked for some months on what he hoped would be a new career, one that would keep his name and reputation before the American public. For the first time he made a serious venture onto the stage.

## II

The melodrama was a much-beloved staple of the late-nineteenth-century theater. It had long since been freed from pretentious literary conventions by the egalitarian preferences of its American audiences, but in turn Americans created an extremely rigid set of dramatic principles that they preferred to see on stage. By 1890 the melodrama was unfettered in time and space; its subject matter was equally diffuse, although often centering on the family. In this sense it offered a theater of variety, its tone comic or serious, its conclusion happy or tragic. But above all the melodrama was a device for contrasting Vice and

Virtue, in whatever form, although which of these two symbolic roles John L. would aspire to may have been a matter of debate.

Heroines were never so fair, heroes never so bold, villains never so dastardly. The purpose of Vice was to tempt Virtue, only to be foiled in the final act. The melodrama created characters "better than saints, or worse than devils," but it was also replete with convoluted plots, Shakespearean asides, and stock situations that audiences loved for their very familiarity. Melodramatic subjects constantly tortured social reality, but in turn they voiced moral and intellectual ideals to which most Americans firmly subscribed.[11] This was the theater, and the form, in which Sullivan hoped to make his way.

His previous experiences on the stage had been set-piece perform-ances, usually involving sparring or, on occasion, posing—as in the *poses plastiques* of 1885. Now he meant to try his hand at *acting*. John L. was not the first boxer to appear on stage in an acting role. Many pugilists had gone before him, among them Jem Mace, who in 1870 played Charles the Wrestler to E. L. Davenport's Orlando in *As You Like It* at Niblo's Gardens. But Sullivan was the first boxer, and prob-ably the first athlete of any kind, to appear in a starring role on the American stage, the lineal ancestor of hordes of later athletes who made the transition from arena to stage or screen, with mixed results.[12]

Even as his Mississippi court case was dragging on, John L. had taken his first tentative steps in this new direction. Needing money, and with no desire whatsoever to fight again, he met an actor-manager named Duncan B. Harrison, who was eager to capitalize on Sullivan's reborn image after his victory over Kilrain. Harrison offered the cham-pion a six-week tour in a vehicle called *The Paymaster*, for one thou-sand dollars a week. Neither Harrison nor Sullivan felt that John L. needed to be burdened with acting lessons. Sullivan took along his sidekick, Joe Lannon, who received the excellent sum of three hundred a week himself, and the two men put on a sparring match to end each performance. The tour did good business; it was a stopgap to tide John L. over until something better came along, but his appetite for the stage was whetted, and he became convinced he could make good money in a theatrical career.[13]

Harrison, a burly, strapping man who, when Sullivan met him, went everywhere accompanied by a small white puppy, evidently agreed. In the late summer of 1890 he and Sullivan formed a partnership in a play called *Honest Hearts and Willing Hands*, which Harrison had written with Sullivan specifically in mind. The plot is pure melodrama, heavy on action and monologue. It is set in Ireland and centers on the two Daly brothers, John (Harrison) and James (John L.). John is in love with Emily Paignford, the niece, ward, and heir of General Dare (wards had incredible difficulties in melodramatic plots); James, a blacksmith, loves Martha, "a girl under a cloud." The villain is Arthur Dare, son of the general. True to the complete lack of scruples common to his calling, he has designs on Emily, kills his father for the inheritance, produces a pistol with the name "Daly" on it, and tries to fasten his odious patricide on the two brothers.

But: all is not lost! When police come to arrest the brothers, James (Sullivan) stands in the door and disgorges himself as follows:

> Stand back! A man's home is his castle and I will protect mine. I promise to brain the first man who attempts to enter here or search my house! I never break my word! My brother is not here! He is no murderer! If you want the man who murdered General Dare (pointing to the nasty Arthur), take him! There he stands!

Unfortunately, it is only the second act (there were five in all), and Arthur still has foul deeds to perpetrate. He matches a professional pugilist, Pug O'Brien (Joe Lannon again), against James, hoping to drive the hero out of town; Pug is offered two hundred pounds to beat the blacksmith. He fights with loaded gloves, but James knocks him out in three rounds—exactly the length of the exhibitions Sullivan and Lannon were accustomed to giving together. The finale is neatly packaged, in the best melodramatic tradition. John Daly gathers evidence to convict Arthur and wins Emily, while Martha, despite her cloud, is united with James. One reviewer, tongue only slightly in cheek, commented that "the plot is ingenious; the mystery deep; the gloom black as ink."[14]

*Honest Hearts and Willing Hands* opened in Bridgeport, Connecticut, on August 28, 1890. Proctor's Theater was crammed for the occasion, and the eager audience included sporting men from all over New England. They came to see Sullivan, and see him they did; John L. appeared in every act but one, although some of his pals noted that his stage outfit of white sweater, velvet knickerbockers, and white stockings did not seem in keeping with the blacksmith's trade. The champion was nervous at first and muffed a few lines, but he improved as the play went on; by the conclusion he was in full sail, and proudly stepped before the final curtain to accept a handsome floral piece. He made a short speech in which he modestly disclaimed any resemblance to the famous Edwin Booth and announced that he had given up the ring and was going to be an actor.[15]

With this brief seasoning, Harrison's troupe assayed the big time, opening at New York's Niblo's Gardens on September 1. Sullivan was greeted with deafening cheers, moving one critic to observe that "the appearance of a really fine-looking young actor like Mr. Sullivan, with good broad shoulders and well-developed limbs, is a grateful surprise to habitual theater goers." The quality and timbre of his voice also were given favorable recognition. Beyond that, however, the New York debut did not impress the reviewers.

One obliquely wrote that "Mr. Sullivan understands the value of repose, one of the secrets of good acting." In fact, John L. performed like a wooden Indian; he tended to entangle himself in lines like "What! Not gone yet? Get out or by heavens I will choke you!" He was so intent on his speeches that, when the audience interrupted a sentence with applause, he doggedly retreated to the beginning and started again. No matter; the opening-night house was full of Sullivan admirers—it had about it, said one observer, "the decided flavor of the ring and the race course"—and they patiently watched their hero work his plodding way through Harrison's tortured plot, which contained three rescues, two robberies, two forgeries, one murder, one disputed will, one accident, three sets of lovers, two villains, and, at last, one probable hanging (Arthur, of course). The audience called continuously for "John L.!" after each of his scenes, cheering him to the rafters despite the fact, apparent to everyone, that he was as grossly overweight as he had ever been (one reporter exaggerated only slightly when he described the champion as weighing three hundred pounds).

Sullivan was obviously far from an accomplished actor; indeed, he was no actor at all, but simply struck one self-conscious pose after another while attempting to declaim his lines. Critics had fun with his reference to Booth in Bridgeport, making mock comparisons of John L. with the great tragedian. Indeed, Harrison's pompous prose was almost an unintended satire on the melodrama itself, and one reviewer noted that "Mr. Sullivan was quite as good as the play." Nevertheless, his fans readily responded when he at last laced on the gloves against Lannon, and his brief curtain speech, which he was to make throughout the tour, brought down the house: "Ladies and gentlemen: I thank you kindly for the very great applause with which you have greeted my first attempt in this line of business. Thanking you again for your kind applause, I remain your obedient servant, John L. Sullivan."[16]

*Honest Hearts and Willing Hands* toured the country during the 1890–91 theatrical season. John L. trod the boards in most of the major cities in the land, all the way to San Francisco and back. In Cincinnati the famed actress Helena Modjeska witnessed his performance. She commented that "he speaks his lines naturally, and one likes that bluff, hearty manner—of course, he hasn't the gracefulness of gesture and business, but he is very good." During the tour he met the captivating Lillian Russell and, like practically every other male who crossed her path, was absolutely smitten. He amused himself on the side by pitching in an occasional baseball game or acting as umpire. In addition he and Lannon, on their own, offered occasional three-round exhibitions, as they had done during the earlier run of *The Paymaster*. On the negative side, he was drinking steadily, although seldom enough to impede his performances; indeed, the booze may have helped to loosen him a bit as he learned the rudiments of stagecraft. When the troupe appeared in Taunton, Massachusetts, John L. was reported to have been so drunk that he fell through a window at the City Hotel. On another occasion it was rumored that he had kicked Harrison in the back, injuring his partner's spine and temporarily forcing him out of the play.[17]

John L. found that he loved the footlights and the applause. It was a far easier way to make a buck; the theater did not seem to require the self-denial of training and the fierce expenditure of energy that the prize ring demanded. At the end of the touring season he and Harrison split profits of thirty thousand dollars. He was not making money on the scale of Booth, but he was much better rewarded than most headliners. As a result, Sullivan became dead set on a stage career.[18] Yet, as always, his admirers wanted to see him *in the ring*. Once again, a new contender had been found, an excellent heavyweight named Peter Jackson. One problem with the match was the champion's newfound interest in the theater; another was Jackson himself. Peter Jackson was a black man.

# III

American blacks in 1890 were far from the promised land offered by the constitutional amendments of the post–Civil War period. Not only were the long-denied rights and freedoms of the ex-slaves slow to ensue; in most cases they were receding, due to Jim Crow laws and public intolerance. Racism was not an attitude of the white South alone; the vicious virus of racial discrimination underlay the social practices of many in the North and West as well. In the face of both statutory repression and unstated (but very clear) social bias, blacks were forced into ethnic subcommunities, both urban and rural, and bound together by a shared culture of social experience, economic hardship, and religion. In the process, they formed black athletic organizations.

Baseball was the most popular team sport of urban blacks, and it was not unusual for teams of black and white amateurs or semipros to play each other, although such games usually took place before segregated bleachers. In the major leagues, two black brothers, Fleet and Weldy Walker, played briefly in the American Association until rising racial bigotry, probably led by the famous Cap Anson, forced them out. Players suspected, for whatever reason, of being Negroes were hounded from white baseball. Even before the turn of the century the majors were lily-white, and except for a few Indians and "Latins" they remained so for fifty years. The result was the formation of all-black leagues in which many excellent athletes, forever denied a shot at the top echelon, performed.

The same was true in almost all other sports. Evidence is sparse concerning black athletics before 1900, but it is clear that black sub-communities fostered athletic organizations, supported them as best they could, and cheered their heroes with all the fervor whites reserved for their own stars. Prizefighting within black communities was common, and black boxers found that they could, on occasion, make matches with white men.[19]

For years the major black challenger to Sullivan had been George Godfrey. The champion was in the habit of announcing that he would meet Godfrey in the ring anytime, if the purse was right, but he never came close to doing so. When *Honest Hearts and Willing Hands* reached San Francisco, Godfrey was waiting. He declared that the champion had drawn the color line against him and challenged John L. to fight for ten thousand dollars a side and the gate. The California Athletic Club agreed to stage the fight and underwrite the purse, but Sullivan was not interested, and Godfrey had trouble finding backers for a sum that many American black families could not accumulate in a lifetime. Sullivan continued to insist that, if the money was right, he would fight any man, white or black.[20]

The reality was otherwise. John L. had been reared in an ethnic neighborhood almost devoid of blacks, and his racial attitudes were fully consonant with his social background and time. His own self-image demanded that he declare, often and loudly, that he was ready to meet all comers, but unlike some of his fellow white pugilists, he could never bring himself to face a black in the prize ring. His reluctance had nothing to do with fear of any specific black fighters. He regarded himself as not only a champion but a *white* champion, and this attitude only hardened with time as he crisscrossed the country on his many tours and saw blacks only in their menial roles as janitors, hotel porters, and washerwomen.

It was Peter Jackson's misfortune that he was forced to confront the twin evils of institutional and personal racism. By most accounts the greatest black fighter of his era, he is almost forgotten today in the fanfaronade surrounding the swaggering Jack Johnson, but he was a worthy precursor of the first black heavyweight champion. Jackson was born on the island of Saint Croix in 1861. His parents emigrated to Australia when he was six. When they returned to the Caribbean, he stayed behind, becoming first a boatman and then a sailor. Like Kilrain, he competed in sculling matches. A natural athlete, he developed a marvelous physique by competing in a sport much celebrated in Australia, swimming. He began his career as a prizefighter in 1882 and usually fought at 190 pounds, although he could go ten pounds either way. For the next decade he fought frequently, usually pummeling his opponents into submission, and in the process he met some of the very best. In 1891 he would duel to a four-hour, sixty-one-round draw with James J. Corbett.[21]

But Jackson's grandest ambition was to get John L. Sullivan into a prize ring. He was rebuffed time and again, a particularly maddening process since other good white fighters, like Corbett, Joe McAuliffe, Patsy Cardiff, Jem Smith, and Frank Slavin, had agreed to meet him. Jackson defeated them all, with the exception of Corbett. In addition, he was clearly the best of his race, having demolished George Godfrey in nineteen rounds in 1888. Jackson was not without a certain wry wit in the face of John L.'s adamancy; he once said that he would not object to the champion's color if a match could be arranged.[22]

It was not to be, and the man whom the Australian boxing authority W. J. Doherty called "the greatest I ever saw fight" passed his pugilistic prime without even getting a crack at the championship. Jackson's last years were sad ones. Denied the opportunity to reach the pinnacle of his profession, he appeared in vaudeville and did minor exhibition bouts. In 1893 he played Uncle Tom in his own touring company for three unsuccessful months. Four years later found him in London, where he opened a boxing school; it failed almost immediately. Desperate, he tried for a comeback in the ring, only to be blown away in three rounds by a rising newcomer, James Jackson Jeffries. The once-proud athlete sought relief in the bottle. Within months he was a physical wreck, eating only when friends came to his rescue and cadging sleeping space in the back rooms of saloons. In his final days he returned to Queensland, Australia, where his alcohol-weakened body succumbed to tuberculosis on July 13, 1901.[23]

As for Sullivan, he treated Jackson and his aspirations with disdain. Once, speaking of a possible rematch between Corbett and Jackson, John L. remarked that "the nigger is a great sport, a high roller, and is probably not in the best of condition." Sullivan's cult of masculinity had little use for black ambition, and John L.'s fans were as staunchly protective of boxing "purity" as their hero. When Jack Johnson began his boxing career in the 1890s, he was severely beaten by a gang of Boston Irish toughs who resented his negative opinions about Sullivan and his boxing abilities.[24] In this sense Sullivan only reflected the strong, and rising, racial barriers of his era.

In a second sense, however, John L. flawed his own image by refusing to take on "all comers," despite his oft-stated willingness to do so. By denying men like Peter Jackson a fair shot, he denied them the chance to achieve that which was ostensibly open to everyone in the rough-and-ready democracy of the prize ring: the opportunity to be the best. In this sense he made men like Jackson nonpersons in the boxing world, because they might aspire but never accede to the crown. Sullivan, despite his proud boasts of egalitarianism, never saw any hypocrisy in the stance he took. To him, the championship was his most precious possession; when it passed from him (and who knew when that day would come?), it would go to another white man. Firm in his conviction, he would eventually make a public challenge in which he included "all fighters—first come first served—who are white. I will not fight a negro. I never have and never shall."[25]

## IV

In the midst of his travels with *Honest Hearts and Willing Hands*, Sullivan signed an agreement with the Australian firm of MacMahon Brothers to go to Australia for a theatrical tour, beginning in June 1891. Duncan Harrison, who arranged the agreement through a theatrical agent named John R. Rogers, would come along. The Mac-Mahons, a pair of Australian theatrical entrepreneurs, Sullivan, and Harrison had visions of a profitable presentation of their play in Sydney, followed by a money-making tour of Melbourne and the sticks.[26]

Before he left, John L. dropped by Paddy Ryan's San Francisco saloon to see his old foe. Paddy, as usual, was on his uppers; he was no businessman, the bar was failing, and he begged Sullivan for a fourth fight. The champion put him off—maybe, he said, after he returned. "I haven't much to keep me here," Paddy pathetically replied, "and if you will agree to it I will remain."[27]

Ryan was among the three hundred or so who gathered at dockside the next day, June 26, to see Sullivan on his way aboard the *Mariposa*. John L. was in his element, hosting a bash for his friends that began on the dock, moved onto the ship's deck, and lasted for two hours. He rambled on about whom he would fight when he returned, directed Jimmy Wakely and Charley Johnston to match him against Frank Slavin, and roared that he would quit drinking the moment the ship left the pier. Spying Peter Jackson in the throng, he began bragging about how he could lick the "nigger."[28]

At last the roistering guests were bundled down the gangway, and Captain Haywood headed the *Mariposa* out of the bay. Jack Ashton was along as a possible sparring partner for John L.; he was to fill Lannon's stage role. Frank Moran, the MC of the Grand Tour, completed the quartet, but he was taken ill aboard and remained shaky during the entire voyage. Six days out they made Honolulu, where Sullivan was visited in his hotel by King Kalakaua's sister. In Samoa the champion viewed the wreckage of the German and American ships that had been strewn about Apia Harbor two years before by a savage hurricane. Curious natives gave him a nickname that John L. was told meant something like "Great Chief."[29]

The *Mariposa* made anchor in Sydney Harbor on July 20. She was late, and the scheduled reception arranged by the MacMahons had to be canceled. Still, a large crowd gathered on Cowper's Wharf to see the American Hercules, even as John L. stayed aboard to attend to the ailing Moran. The next evening Sullivan was welcomed at a banquet in Sydney, and the day after that he attended a featherweight prizefight at the Amateur Gymnastic Club Rooms, where he got a "splendid reception." Sports-minded Australians were anticipating a match between John L. and one of their own, but he cooled their ardor somewhat by announcing that he would not fight in Australia. This initial statement even angered some of the natives, because a suitable challenger existed in the person of Joe Goddard, "the Barrier Cyclone." Goddard immediately challenged Sullivan, but John L. replied that he was visiting Australia solely in a "theatrical capacity" and lamely added that he was under contract not to fight.[30]

The next week was spent gathering up supporting players and rehearsing for the theatrical debut. John L. made good use of the bar at the Australian Hotel during this period. He cut such a swath here and in surrounding watering holes that one reporter was moved to wonder at the seeming paradox of a man who could one moment be tenderly nursing Frank Moran and the next carousing through a succession of saloons. "It served to show that, in describing his career, the American papers had not been so utterly regardless of the truth as they are generally asserted to be."[31]

*Honest Hearts and Willing Hands* opened at Her Majesty's Opera House on Thursday, July 30, and within eight days the thespians were out of town. The dismal flop was not caused by any dislike by Australians of melodrama; they had their own flourishing melodramatic tradition, drawn from the English stage. Although Harrison's posturing prose may have been a mite too much for their taste, the real reason for the debacle was that the locals were interested in seeing John L. fight for real, not brush gloves with Ashton in some trumped-up plot.[32]

Sullivan and Harrison were not helped by the fact that the most famous actress in the Western world, Sarah Bernhardt, concluded her triumphal Australian tour in Sydney on the very night their own play closed. Press comparisons were irresistible; in fact, the critics took the whole thing as a joke. "The Sydney people have refused to take Sullivan seriously as an actor," commented a Melbourne paper, "and they are not inclined to pay theatre prices to look at a man whom they can see daily on the streets for nothing." Harrison did not improve matters when he made a vicious speech from the stage to one lackadaisical Sydney audience, in which he accused the local press of "all sorts of malignity." He ended by asking the sparse crowd if they considered it fair treatment to stab people in the back. After all, he and Sullivan had come all the way from America without professing to be great actors, or even to have a great play. They were simply trying to do their best.[33]

On this sour note the little caravan was off on a jolting nineteen-hour train ride across southeastern Australia to Melbourne, where it was scheduled to play a three-week engagement at the Grand Opera House, opening on August 15. With the wretched news from Sydney preceding it, the troupe never had a chance. *Honest Hearts and Willing Hands* was robustly panned; the theatergoers were bored with the sparring and found the melodrama itself of poor quality. "A considerable proportion of the spectators amused themselves by chaffing the actors and the play." Sullivan's climactic fight scene, said one spectator, "had not been seen in Melbourne since Jack the Fighting Kangaroo left the Waxworks." John L. responded in kind, often stopping the action and threatening the audience if it did not show more respect. It did no good, and the critics had a field day. Sullivan's stage walk was a "gentle prance"; he was inarticulate; he forgot line after line; he was stolidly indifferent to what was going on around him on the stage. The Australian supporting players received what praise there was: "they did their best, and were deserving of sympathy under the adverse conditions of the performance." As for John L., "Mr. Sullivan does not possess a single qualification for the *rôle* of an actor."[34]

The original run was cut short a week, as attendance dwindled to nothing. By now Sullivan was boiling mad. Even though he had had the chance to meet many of the Australian sporting gentry and even to rub elbows with a couple of provincial governors, he was angry at the theater crowd, angry at the press, and angry at being jounced about by the primitive railway system. The MacMahon brothers, for their part, hoped the failures in the big cities could be recouped elsewhere. So, for the next three weeks, the players toured the boondocks for brief stands—Ballarat, Bendigo, Cathlenain, Maryboro, Geelong, and Stahl, surfacing for three nights in Adelaide. The constant travel and continuing poor receptions did nothing to improve John L.'s temper.[35]

By late September they were back in Melbourne. There, the champion refereed a featherweight boxing match and agreed to second Ashton in a prizefight against Joe Goddard. The two men met in a scheduled eight-rounder, under the Queensberry Rules, on October 2 in Richmond's Crystal Palace before a large crowd. At last, the Australian sports would see an American fight. Ashton, however, found that the Barrier Cyclone was no cinch; both men were badly out of condition, but Goddard pressed the fight, Ashton fought defensively, and the crowd cheered when, after the full eight rounds, the local champion was declared the winner by the referee.[36]

It was Sullivan's swan song in Australia. The next day he, Ashton, Harrison, and the now-recovered Moran boarded the *Alameda*, eventually returning to San Francisco on October 26. The Australian tour netted John L. very little, if anything at all, and he never mentioned the voyage in his list of financial ventures. As the Australian sporting paper *The Referee* put it, Sullivan had been to a certain extent marching through hostile country. "John has not made the barrels of money it was expected he would coin here in Australia." For his part, Sullivan was disappointed and a bit mystified. His English and Irish tours had been financial successes, even if he had squandered those profits as fast as he received them. But here was an entire continent rejecting him! "They don't give up [money] to Americans," he said. "I been in Australia and know what I'm talking about." He took refuge in nationalism, arguing that there had been very few "thorough sports" among his hosts. "Anybody that says Australians love Americans is mistaken."[37]

John L. whiled away time in San Francisco, appearing in something called *Broderick Agra* at the Bush Street Theater. Whatever this was, it included a sparring sequence with Ashton, but for Sullivan's final performance a tough local fighter, Joe Choynski, was announced for the "part" of his opponent. Joe was one of the best of his day (he had already lost twice to Corbett—one of these a savage twenty-seven-round struggle—and would later fight both Bob Fitzsimmons and Jim Jeffries), and a large crowd gathered for the three-round "exhibition." Both men appeared in regulation ring costume, Sullivan's physique by now so bloated that the muscular Choynski looked like a mere stripling beside him. By the second round the light sparring was turning to serious punching, and John L. was breathing heavily. All ended well, however; the final round was little but grappling and half-speed punches, and the crowd was well-pleased.[38] This, however, was all the fighting the champion cared to do; there would be no fourth match with Paddy Ryan.

During the interim, Sullivan arranged another tour of *Honest Hearts and Willing Hands*. The troupe opened in Sacramento and whistle-stopped the West, appearing in British Columbia, Manitoba, and numerous other areas. John L. made another contract with Harrison as the group moved eastward. He appeared for a week apiece in Philadelphia and Brooklyn, finally closing in Boston at the Howard Athenaeum on June 4, 1892.[39] Once again he was making money, and once again he was spending it. He was well over 250 pounds now, the heaviest sustained weight he had ever carried. His drinking was in full flower. He was seriously committed to a stage career, and he had not entered the prize ring in almost three years.

## V

Sullivan was always good for an interview, and he spent much of his time with a series of local reporters as he leisurely made his way back home to Boston. Occasionally he spoke as if he were through with the fight game, benignly assessing the skills of the rest of the heavyweight field with Olympian detachment. Often, however, he would deride his competition and, particularly when he was in his cups, still bray that he was more than a match for any man alive. The "gamest" men he ever fought, he said, were Flood, Ryan, Slade, and Kilrain. He admired them all for their pluck and fair play. John L. had only the kindest words for the deceased Joe Goss, whom he called "as true a friend as I ever had." But for Charlie Mitchell the champion had only scorn.[40] The "bombastic sprinter" had given him his most embarrassing moments in the ring and had impishly taunted him, in the press and in person, for years. The mere mention of his name was enough to make Sullivan seethe.

Yet talking fight was all the champion was doing, and his admirers had long since grown restless with their hero's prolonged layoff. John L., wrapped up in his theater engagements, gave every indication that he would not fight again. In the late spring of 1892 he made arrangements with a Boston publishing firm for his autobiography, which was to be ghostwritten for him (probably by Arthur Brisbane, although evidence on this point is far from clear).

Personally, except for some newfound theatrical friends, he was alone. He sought companionship in male social organizations, joining the Newark lodge of the Benevolent and Protective Order of Elks as an "actor." But his constant dissipation was too much for this predominantly middle-class group, and even before he left for Australia, the members had decided to investigate certain unspecified "charges" against him. Many of these worthies were indignant that the pugilist had been allowed to join in the first place. The upshot was that the national head of the order, a Chicagoan named Quinlan, drummed John L. out of the Elks as a person "who is unworthy to associate with gentlemen, and whose conduct has brought shame and discredit upon the order." Quinlan, in his order of suspension, forbade any lodge to admit the miscreant. "THE HORNS TORN FROM SULLIVAN!" shrieked a headline.[41]

His drinking was worse than ever and more public. The national press routinely debated whether John L. could be "saved" from alcohol. At one point it was announced that the champion would try the "Keeley Cure," the invention of a quack who prescribed massive ingestions of bichloride of gold. "If the specific action of the drug needs to be reinforced by any sentimental or moral influences," one editor sarcastically remarked, "the Keeley institute might as well refuse to receive him."[42]

Even Sullivan knew, at times, that his drinking was out of hand. For temperance advocates he had long since become the number one target. In Tacoma, while he was appearing in *Honest Hearts and Willing Hands*, he was cornered backstage by a leading temperance light named Francis Murphy. As Harrison and Moran looked on, Murphy three times urged the champion to sign the pledge; three times John L. refused. Murphy, a sincere, folksy ex-alcoholic with a shock of white hair, kept insisting. Like most alcoholics, Sullivan said he could quit drinking when he wanted to—but not tonight. Despite John L.'s resistance, Harrison, Moran, and W. L. Pond, another member of the company, were convinced. Perhaps to get the insistent temperance man off their backs, these three signed the pledge. Murphy promptly pinned blue ribbons to their coats, and Harrison mailed his pledge to his mother. For his part, Sullivan repaired to a local dive and got roaring drunk. The next night a repentant, hung-over champion appeared at the Theater Comique before a crowd of local sportsmen and sheepishly took the pledge. He then made a short speech, advising others to follow his example.[43]

Francis Murphy thought he had made one of his greatest conquests, but it was not to be. True, and as he often had done before, John L. would go on the wagon for brief periods, announcing his intention to stay dry forever. At times he would even preach temperance to saloon buddies, all the while downing liquor himself.[44] In his more self-conscious moments he fully recognized the grip demon rum had on him; these moments were most conspicuous following one of his prolonged binges. But he always returned to the friendly saloon and the welcoming bottle. Here lay the warmth of companionship, the hearty choruses of adulation, the conviction that he was a man among men.

He was almost thirty-four now. The flecks of gray that had been noticed at the Kilrain fight three years before had become streaks. His stomach was more than a paunch—it was a veritable mountain of flab, the weight of which left him winded after the slightest exertion. He was in no condition for any kind of athletic endeavor, never mind the strenuous demands of the prize ring. And yet he could not give it up, could not walk away from that one thing that gave him purpose, sustained his ego, nourished his very existence. John L. wanted to quit the fight game; all his actions since the battle with Kilrain had pointed away from the arena. But he would not, could not, surrender the crown.

The only alternative, then, was to fight again. An opponent had to be found, a man who could provide a big payday. Once more the champion would have to enter the ring and prove his manhood with his fists, to himself and to the world. He was yoked to the championship; it was *his* and would not be surrendered.

Besides, the man had not yet been made who could whip John L. Sullivan.

## CHAPTER TWELVE

# John L. and the Dude
## (1892)

At his age, John L. would normally have been considered as passing into the prime of life. In his chosen calling, however, he was long since an old man, and indeed no American had ever achieved a championship sporting record close to the duration of his own. More than a decade had passed since the raw young Bostonian had drubbed John Flood on the barge in the Hudson River, a period that seemed forever in the minds of many of his fans. For numerous adoring youngsters, *he had always been* a benchmark of strength and physical dominance.

Sullivan was growing increasingly fond of looking back and assessing his record. Mentally, he had rounded some corner of the past between the Kilrain fight and 1892, and he often spoke as if his ring career was complete. One indication of this new attitude was his autobiography, the contract for which was signed early in the year. When he first announced he was "writing a book," the press generally responded with yawns or smirks, the critics on the *Brooklyn Daily Eagle* adding an acidulous attack on his speech-making abilities and his political hopes.[1] Whoever the ghostwriter was, John L. must have proofread every page of the book, because his personality is dominant throughout. The tone of *The Life and Reminiscences of a 19th Century Gladiator* is proud, vainglorious, and thoughtful by turns, and within it Sullivan tries to take stock of his life in pugilism.

Previous to "my ascending this ladder of fame," wrote John L., boxing was outlawed, vilified, and misunderstood. He claimed, with some justice, to have done much to elevate the sport in the public mind. Sullivan went further, arguing that boxing was conceded "by all good judges of athletics" to be the finest exercise, bar none, for body and mind alike. "All professionals, like myself," he solemnly intoned, "are strong and healthy." On second thought, this sweeping assertion was too much even for Sullivan. He hastily added that "of course, there are persons, I am willing to admit, in this profession, that have made wrecks of themselves through over-indulgence in the flowing bowl, which is more or less suggested by friends partaking of their hospitality."

He went on to display a nice sense of what it meant to live in the public eye: "I have to stand general criticism." He said that he was well aware of the debates over him in the nation's press and that, although the numerous slurs against his character rankled him no end, he fully realized that one of the prices of fame was false or even malicious reporting. Comparing himself to "all public men of the nineteenth century," he maintained that he had stood for the criticism all his life "without the slightest apprehension."[2]

Slightest apprehension or not, the criticism currently coming his way dealt specifically with his reluctance to defend his championship. The outcry at last goaded John L. into action. In March, during his theatrical tour, he issued a choleric challenge:

> This country has been overrun with a lot of foreign fighters and also American aspirants for fistic fame and championship honors, who have endeavored to seek notoriety and American dollars by challenging me to a fight, knowing full well that my hands were tied by contract and honor. I have been compelled to listen to their bluffs without making reply on account of my obligations.
>
> But now my time has come. I hereby challenge any and all of the bluffers who have been trying to make capital at my expense to fight me either the last week in August this year or the first week in September this year at the Olympic Club, New Orleans, Louisiana, for a purse of $25,000 and an outside bet of $10,000, the winner of the fight to take the entire purse . . . . I insist upon the bet of $10,000, to show that they mean business. . . . .
>
> I give precedence in this challenge to Frank P. Slavin, of Australia, he and his backers having done the greatest amount of bluffing. My second preference is the bombastic sprinter, Charles Mitchell, of England, whom I would rather whip than any man in the world. My third preference is James Corbett, of California, who has achieved his share of bombast. But in this challenge I include all fighters—first come, first served—who are white. I will not fight a negro. I never have and never shall.
>
> I prefer this challenge should be accepted by some of the foreigners who have been sprinting so hard after American dollars of late, as I would rather whip them than any of my own countrymen. The Marquis of Queensberry Rules must govern this contest, as I want fighting, not foot racing, and I intend to keep the championship of the world where it belongs, in the land of the free and the home of the brave.[3]

Clearly the memory of his Australian trip still nettled Sullivan; thus Slavin received the place of honor on his list. There was always room, of course, for the infuriating Mitchell. Either of these men would have satisfied John L. as a target. Ponderously and reluctantly he was swinging into gear for yet another title defense. Driven by pride and the continously growing vacuum in his pocketbook, he was heedless of one of the oldest maxims in prizefighting, coined by an English sporting writer almost a century before: "It seems scarcely possible that any man can die in possession of the championship, unless he die young."[4]

# I

When James John Corbett read Sullivan's public challenge, he saw his opportunity. The slender Californian was appearing in a vaudeville sparring routine in Philadelphia, and he immediately begged his manager, William A. Brady, for the seed money to cement a match with the champion. The two men agreed that Sullivan's condition of ten thousand dollars in front money was actually designed to keep challengers away. Together, Corbett and Brady scratched up one thousand dollars. Within a week, Corbett made a trip to Koster and Bial's famous Music Hall in New York, and there he cobbled together the remaining sum from a variety of sporting men. Suddenly, he had the money. Neither Slavin nor Mitchell had given any response at all, and all at once Sullivan was face to face with the whippersnapper, eight years younger than himself.[5]

The moniker the sporting press later fastened on Corbett, "Gentleman Jim," plus the elegant, sassy performance of Errol Flynn in the 1942 motion picture of that name, has obscured the aggressive, aspiring personality of the man behind the nickname. Like Sullivan, Corbett came from American Irish stock; his father was from County Mayo, and his mother from Dublin. He was born September 1, 1866, the son of a livery-stable owner, and grew up in a poor San Francisco neighborhood. The Corbetts were a big clan; ten children lived into adulthood. As in John L.'s case, Corbett's family was never truly destitute, and like John L. young James J. made his way among his peers through street fighting. "We were a very united family," he would remember, and he savored the support of his parents. "A fellow never had better or more affectionate parents than I." But something was askew in this self-assessment. Corbett admitted that the family had had its troubles. His father, Patrick, was given to fits of depression over such things as feed bills, and although Corbett chose to remember the happy times, with the family gathered in song around the piano or his parents footing their way through an Irish jig, there were probably abrupt, violent clashes as well. Patrick Corbett appears to have been a temperamental, sullen man, one of the "Black Irish." At any rate, on the night of August 15, 1898, he would shoot his wife, Catherine, twice in the head as she lay sleeping and then kill himself with a bullet in the mouth.[6]

Corbett's family legacy, so sugar-coated by later writers and by Warner Brothers, was thus at best bittersweet. By his teenage years he was fantasizing about making big sums of money so that he could lift his parents out of their hardscrabble lives and, perhaps, end the bickering at home. His mother dreamed of the priesthood for him, in the best Irish tradition, but there was no money to be made as a man of the cloth. Instead, he unleashed his considerable energy on athletics and won local renown as a sprinter and a gymnast. He very nearly chose to try for a career in professional baseball and might even have made it from the sandlots to the major leagues had not his skills as a ball player attracted the attention of some of the members of the San Francisco Olympic Club.

The Olympic Club was an unusual organization, a classless stew of males from all levels of northern California society who were bound together by their common interest in sports. Within the club's confines gold millionaires rubbed elbows with draymen, and while social distinctions were never absent, the organization offered Corbett an entrée into the sporting world that the Back Bay nabobs of Boston would never have given to Sullivan. The Olympic Club became his support and his school; there he took boxing lessons from the respected Walter Watson, and there he added considerable power to his natural speed and grace. By his twentieth year he had grown to six feet one and 180 pounds, achieving the lean, sinewy proportions that he kept throughout his years in the ring.[7]

In the meantime he had been working to get ahead. One of Patrick Corbett's customers at the livery stable was J. S. Angus, the cashier of the Nevada Bank of San Francisco, and through the cashier Corbett was taken on as a messenger boy, rising after six years to the post of assistant receiving teller. In the bank and at the Olympic Club, young Jim saw how men of fashion dressed and behaved. He made himself a snappy clotheshorse and began to cultivate a luxuriant pompadour hairstyle. Although he was not exactly an Irish version of Sammy Glick, he clearly perceived himself as a young man on the rise.

All in all, he was a bit outside the stereotypical mold of the Irish-American prizefighter. His decision to box professionally, which was made in 1889, was probably prompted by a desire to make more money than he ever could by inching his way higher in the Nevada Bank's bureaucracy. His ambitions grew, fueled not by his limited education (he had left school in his seventeenth year) but by his athletic skills.[8]

Watson showcased his protégé in several "boxing nights" at the Olympic Club, and Corbett developed rapidly. He would never be a power puncher, not with his frame, but he was strong and, above all, he cultivated quickness and stamina. His reflexes proved to be exceptionally fast, and Watson trained him as a counterpuncher. In addition,

Jim attended every prizefight he could. He watched the ring craft of
a wide variety of boxers and reflected for hours on the nature of boxing
as a "science." As an amateur he lost only once, a four-round decision
to a tough middleweight, Billy Welch. As a professional he began with
a series of three fights, all in 1889, against the rugged Joe Choynski.
The police ended the first, Corbett kayoed his man in the twenty-
seventh round in the second, and he won a decision over Choynski
in four rounds in the third.

Other fighters began to take note. Corbett's next major opponent
was Jake Kilrain, who emerged from his enforced idleness on Charles
Rich's Mississippi estate to meet the Pride of the Olympic Club in
early 1890. Jake, not in the best of condition, lost a six-round decision.
The following year Corbett and Peter Jackson drew in a marathon
sixty-one-round bout, but by this time the young San Franciscan was
a fighter of national caliber. He also had attached himself to the mer-
curial person of William A. Brady, who had enough brass for an entire
marching band and was the veritable apotheosis of the word *promoter.*
Brady (who would later blast his way through the early motion picture
industry as head of World Pictures), proved a hard-working manager.
He got Corbett booked into vaudeville houses giving "exhibitions" à
la Sullivan, and he never lost a chance to sound off about the reluctance
of the champion to defend his crown. Much of the "share of bombast"
that John L. allocated to Corbett in his challenge in fact had originated
with Brady, who in addition to his other talents must be adjudged one
of the early masters of the infant art of press agentry. "I never met a
smarter [manager] than William A. Brady," Corbett was to write.[9]

James J. had first seen John L. in 1884, when the champion was in
the Bay Area during the Grand Tour and fought George Robinson.
The seventeen-year-old Corbett (he remembered his age as fifteen)
begged a doorkeeper to let him into the Mechanics' Pavilion for free,
and he sat impatiently for over six hours in the balcony waiting to see
John L. destroy Robinson. The memory of the Olympic Club's ouster
of the defeated man probably stayed with him as well. "There for the
first time I saw the great John L. and conceived a boyish admiration
for his fine physique and courage." Two years later John L. was back
in town, for his third match with Paddy Ryan. Corbett's father visited
the champion's training quarters and "shook the hand." As for Jim,
he watched Sullivan's lopsided victory and began to move beyond
hero worship, to dream of actually meeting the champion in the ring.

In early 1891 Corbett met Sullivan in Chicago, where John L. was
appearing in *Honest Hearts and Willing Hands.* Sullivan, according
to Corbett, was friendly enough but wary, like an old bull guarding his
herd against the threats of younger males. Nevertheless, the two got
along well enough. Sullivan was well-oiled even during his perform-

25. Jim Corbett (about 1889) (William Schutte Collection)

ance, and afterward he and Corbett made the rounds of about ten saloons. Corbett was astonished. His carousing companion seemed to know everyone, and certainly everyone knew him. The crowds trekked after them, watering hole to watering hole. "There was no doubt about his possessing a wonderful personality," the younger man reflected, "and I think he was the most popular pugilist that ever lived." Nonetheless, Corbett ended the evening with the notion that a man with skill and speed, namely himself, could bring down the Titan. From this evening in Chicago on, he set his sights on the championship and worked even harder. He denied himself cigarettes and, unlike the oft-indulgent John L., tried to limit himself to no more than two cigars a day. He cut down his drinking (like Sullivan, he was a complete product of the cult of masculinity), exercised with new intensity, watched what he ate, and got to bed early for proper rest.[10] He now had a goal to match his inner drive.

The two men met again in June 1891 when John L. stopped over in San Francisco on his way to Australia. Corbett had received only $2,500 of his half of the $10,000 purse for the Jackson draw, and his friends had arranged a benefit for him. Corbett went backstage between acts of Sullivan's play to ask if the champion would be kind enough to spar. Sullivan agreed, largely because Jim arranged to split the receipts, but for some reason John L. insisted that the two box wearing formal evening attire. Psychologically, this queer notion was perhaps a register of Sullivan's concern over the potential of the younger man, and the attempt to make a joke of the sparring bout was his way of rendering Corbett harmless. At any rate, both fighters appeared on the stage of the Grand Opera House in soup-and-fish rigs and went through a bloodless four rounds. Jim decided that John L. "was jealous of my growing reputation."[11]

While Sullivan toured Australia, Corbett began to write letters to his own supporters, pleading for them to arrange a match. He wanted any negotiations to be kept private, as "Sullivan is so popular I would rather have the offer come from the Club; I don't want to come out publicly and challenge him. It would look like a grandstand play on my part." He continued his tour with Brady, but his sights were set on John L., a man Corbett himself described as possessing "a magnificent physique, considerable speed for a slugger, ferocious fighting spirit, and a punch as terrific as any man ever uncorked."[12] Nevertheless, after the dress-suit farce on the stage of the Grand Opera House, Jim felt he had the measure of his man. He was stalking the champion, just as Sullivan had stalked Paddy Ryan ten years before, and with the confidence of youth James J. Corbett knew John L. could be beaten.

## II

Another Olympic Club, this one in New Orleans, was eager to see a fight, as much by way of a sporting proposition as anything else. To this end the club's president, Charles Noel, at first attempted to get Sullivan and Mitchell together, but this effort was quickly dropped once Corbett's friends got to work. Sullivan's challenge, coupled with Corbett's surprising ability to raise ten thousand dollars so rapidly, had quick results. On March 15, 1892, the representatives of the two men met in the *New York World* offices and signed fight articles on Sullivan's terms. The fight would be with five-ounce gloves under the Marquis of Queensberry Rules. (Corbett had never fought a bareknuckle bout, and he felt that the use of gloves could only dilute Sullivan's punching power.) The size of the purse immediately caught the attention of sporting America. Sullivan's huge demands had been met, and if the champion was bluffing, he had been called. The two men would fight for a purse of $25,000 and a side bet of $10,000 apiece, a total of $45,000—winner-take-all! John L. insisted on the last part. Members of the Olympic Club agreed to pony up the $25,000 purse; with Corbett's $10,000, this left only the champion's $10,000. Old-time fans rejoiced that their hero would enter the ring again, and Charley Johnston, who had represented Sullivan in the negotiations, had little trouble raising the stakes. Everyone agreed on the well-known turf man, Phil Dwyer, as the stakesholder.[13]

The New Orleans Olympic Club was most satisfied. Founded in 1883 as an athletic association for the young men of the city's Third District, the organization had rapidly made an impact on the Crescent City's sporting life. It began to stage financially successful boxing matches in 1890, holding them in a leased cotton press yard on Royal Street under the novel electric lights. The club reached the pinnacle the following year, when it successfully staged a middleweight title fight between the champion, Jack ("The Nonpareil") Dempsey, and Bob Fitzsimmons; the Australian challenger won in thirteen gruesome rounds. More importantly, the club's members successfully tested the Louisiana law that allowed gloved contests but prohibited prizefights. After winning this case, in September 1891, the members were free to develop the business of prizefighting.

With Corbett and Sullivan signed, the Olympic Club went further. It scheduled what was billed as a "Triple Event," a three-day boxing festival that would culminate on September 7 with the battle for the heavyweight championship. On September 5 the lightweight title would be contested between Jack McAuliffe and Billy Myer, and the following day would see a featherweight championship bout featuring Jack Skelly and George ("Little Chocolate") Dixon, the only black among the six pugilists. That John L. was returning to the ring was news enough, but the extravaganza of the Triple Event immediately created a wildfire of excitement in the sporting world, which the Olympic Club was happy to stoke throughout the summer of 1892.[14]

At the end of his theatrical tour in May, John L. got a medical checkup before commencing training. It was the first thorough physical examination of his life. The doctor, George F. Schrady of New York City, found him in perfect health "except for superfluous flesh around the middle." In his entire practice, said Schrady, he had never seen "such a magnificent specimen of muscular development." The physician gave Sullivan a perfect bill of health, telling the champion that Corbett or any other man who fought him was to be pitied.[15] John L. left the doctor's office convinced that he would be, with training, as good as he had ever been.

The most immediate problem for the magnificent specimen was to rid himself of the "superfluous flesh." He hated this necessity; earlier in the year he told a reporter that "it's training down to fighting weight that makes me dread the fight: it's murder!" Just before his call on Dr. Schrady, John L. visited a Brooklyn handball court owned by his friend Phil Casey. Attired in silk topper, neatly fitted gray suit, a delicately figured colored shirt, and a "standing collar of rather unusual height," he watched a doubles match but did not play. Before leaving, he stepped on a scale—the needle registered 246 pounds.[16]

This weight would have to come off, and fast, but now there was no Muldoon to oversee his training routine. Indeed, Sullivan had no manager at all, only a loose consortium of backers and curious well-wishers, plus his own ideas about what constituted proper training techniques. He delayed the inevitable as long as he could. Throughout June he lounged about the Vanderbilt Hotel in New York, briefly going up to Boston to place a monument on his parents' grave in Mount Calvary. He managed to play some handball games at Casey's courts, and Phil agreed to give him a hand in training. By mid-July they, along with Jack Ashton, had moved to the Canoe Place Inn on Long Island. There John L. trained when he felt like it, but he also studied for a role in a new play and worked with his ghostwriter on the autobiography. Casey, a gentle giant of a man, tried hard to keep the champion to his task, but Sullivan's thoughts were as much on the theater and the literary market as they were on the prize ring. In addition, he had conceived a dislike of the "young dude," as he now called Corbett. People visiting the Canoe Place Inn were treated more than once to Sullivan's old boast that a shave and shampoo were all the training he needed to beat any man living.[17]

For his part, Corbett was working feverishly for the chance of a lifetime. The industrious Brady booked him for a tour throughout the country, and Jim made headlines with his offer to give one hundred dollars to anyone who could last four rounds with him. For weeks Jim plowed his way through the theaters and halls of the nation's cities, sparring himself into peak condition. He was being trained by Billy Delaney, a friend from Oakland, who had sold his business for the opportunity to work with the challenger. On the tour Corbett impressed many with his stamina and rapidly developing ring craft, but he was reminded often that he would be stepping into the ring with a national idol. At the end of the tour, as Jim was boxing at Miner's Eighth Avenue Theater in New York, someone in the gallery called out, "So you're the guy who thinks he can lick John L. Sullivan!" The jeer was punctuated by a bottle hurled across the orchestra, which grazed Corbett's skull and shattered on the floor of the stage.[18]

Such incidents only redoubled the challenger's desire to win. He set up training camp at Asbury Park, New Jersey, and surrounded himself with some of the toughest pugs in the fight game in order to learn the rougher tricks of the trade. He was adopted by a mongrel named Ned, a dog of surpassing ugliness, and the two became inseparable during Jim's many jogs around the area. To reporters he seemed surprisingly relaxed and in control of himself. He often took an afternoon off to bet on the horses at nearby Monmouth Park, and most evenings he could be seen gobbling plates of ice cream at the local parlor. But he always returned to the punching bag, the rope, and his sparring partners. By early September he had pared himself to 178 pounds and had to add weights to his pockets to deceive his backers into believing that he would enter the ring at close to 200.[19]

Young Stephen Crane, then reworking *Maggie: A Girl of the Streets*, was in Asbury Park that summer. He was struck by the ease with which Corbett hobnobbed with socialites like the Willis Fletcher Johnsons and Lily Brandon Munroe, as well as with literary figures such as Hamlin Garland. Crane marked especially Jim's "gentlemanly bearing and quiet manners." It was obvious the challenger was serious about his mission. In Sullivan's camp, close observers were not so sure about the champion. Visitors noted his graying hair and the deep furrows that now seamed his face. During his light workouts with Ashton, they could also see that he was breathing heavily and that the fold of fat around his midsection did not seem to be vanishing. Casey was doing the best he could; John L. was allowed to eat only food carefully prepared by Phil's sister. But the champion's heart was not really in it. Late in August he even began rehearsing his new play, *The Man from Boston*, at a Brooklyn theater.[20]

Also in August, he put the finishing touches on his autobiography. "Having given so much to Corbett in connection with our projected contest," he wrote, "I may say for myself that I never let myself think of a contest till I get into the ring." He presented an image of calm nervelessness: "I can sleep till within a minute of the time to enter. I never lost a pound worrying over anything; I guess all my nerves are in my muscles." He sensed the kind of fight that was ahead of him, saying that a boxer must be ready to change his plan of campaign at the last minute. "A man fights as much with his head as with his hands, especially with such a 'shifty' boxer as Mr. Corbett is reputed to be." His tone was softened, subdued—but the old fire was still burning: "I will only say that, while I have complete confidence as to the outcome, I am conscious that the victory over him, especially as it is for the largest sum ever involved in a ring battle, will not be unworthy to round out a career that has covered three continents and a hundred competitors."[21]

On August 16 John L. went up to Cambridge to get one last thorough physical, from Dr. Dudley A. Sargent, director of the Harvard College Gymnasium. Sargent's report was the most detailed ever done on the champion, and Sullivan thought so much of it that he had it reproduced as an appendix to the autobiography, complete with photographs. Sargent noted that John L. had lost 20 pounds (actually 30) and was at 216. For a man of 5 feet 10½ inches "this weight is considerably in excess of what it should be for a man in good condition, of this stature, and is surpassed by less than one per cent of the persons on my tables." All the girth measurements were "unusually large," from head to calf. Sargent felt (correctly) that John L.'s power came from his exceptionally thick trunk, hips, and thighs. The doctor was surprised at his subject's lung capacity, bettered by only 5 percent of his other patients. What made Sullivan a phenomenon, he said, was that John L. could operate his arms and legs with the "vital machinery" of rapidity usually found in much smaller men. Still, Sargent could easily see the warning signs: "I cannot help thinking that Sullivan's respiratory apparatus is his weak point vitally. . . . The question of how to relieve breathlessness after vigorous exertion is a matter that may concern him as he advances in years." Even so, he remained impressed. Sullivan, he concluded, was an excellent example of "the brawn and sinew that conquers both opponents and environments and sustains the race."[22]

With the medical report, Sullivan put *finis* to his life's story for the publishers. His concluding tone was mildly elegiac and couched in the florid mock-classical prose of which he was so fond:

> And now as I sit calmly at my training quarters at a spot where Long Island seems to reach out in friendship to the Old World. . . . I resolve that after this, my last battle, I shall no longer remain in a position where, in the

words of Byron, "A man must prove his fame four times a year." Just before me stands the colossal form of Hercules that so long adorned the old fighting ship, "Ohio," and as I look on him, I am reminded that I, too, have accomplished my "tasks," and that like him I should take the skin of the lion I captured,—my reputation as a boxer,—and put it over my shoulders hereafter only as a mantle of protection and peace.[23]

The manuscript was packed off to Boston, and John L., finally, turned his attention to New Orleans. He had said, several times before, that his next fight would be his last; this time he meant it. He was tired, not of the crowds and the praise, but of the physical price that had to be paid. His training, he knew, had been at best only half-successful; he was still a good fifteen pounds over his best fighting weight and short-winded to boot. Yet, as the Triple Event grew nearer, the old roaring confidence returned. The Dude was inexperienced, callow, lighter by a good twenty pounds. Once more, then—one more time, winner-take-all!

# III

New Orleans was in a complete dither over the Triple Event. The city now found itself the national center of boxing, to the great pride of the Olympic Club and its sundry supporters, to the considerable distress of the better sort. The local papers denounced the coming festivities, arguing that these would do little to reduce the community's reputation as a "city of sin." Brothel-keepers, whores, gamblers, and hoteliers were eagerly anticipating the influx of well-heeled fight fans. Merchants redoubled their advertising space in the press, and one railroad reported selling three thousand tickets to excursionists. City fathers estimated that over twelve thousand people would be coming from out of town, a commercial bonanza. Street-corner hawkers offered photographs of all the fighters. Thoroughfares were suddenly filled with the sartorial dazzle of the fight crowd. Bystanders saw parades of pink-and-blue shirts, festooned with both polka dots and stripes, along with neckties and scarfs "so gaudy that the very horses in the street shy at them." The Olympic Club had done its part; for forty thousand dollars a spanking new arena, lit by electricity and holding ten thousand people, had been erected to stage the extravaganza.[24]

The "Sullivan Special" left New York on September 1 on the West Shore Railroad. In John L.'s retinue were familiar faces: Charley Johnston, Jimmy Wakely, Phil Casey, and Jack Ashton. Billy Madden was not going. He sadly told a reporter that he still loyally supported his old friend but thought Corbett stood a good chance because of the obvious contrast in ages and life-styles. The trip south was a celebration. All along the route hundreds came to the depot to catch a glimpse of their hero. They were there in Utica, Syracuse, Rochester, Buffalo, and Erie. They continued to come as the Special rolled through Cleveland, Ashtabula, and Dayton. In Springfield, Ohio, a town that had refused John L. a permit to perform during the Grand Tour, over three hundred people crowded the platform, cheering and yelling. Sullivan walked to the back of the train and acknowledged his fans by raising a yachting cap. The cheers redoubled. The crowd could see that his head was close-cropped once again, that he "meant business." Cries of "He's the stuff" continued after the cars lumbered into motion and Sullivan returned to his seat.

When the train rolled through Tennessee, the group divided momentarily. There was still a warrant outstanding for Charley Johnston, stemming from his role in the Kilrain fight, and as a result Sullivan's car with Johnston aboard was detached from the rest of the train in Chattanooga and shunted through the freight yards, while the main section proceeded through the heart of the city. By September 4 they had reached New Orleans. John L. immediately weighed himself; even at this late date he was at 217 pounds. He plunged immediately into a daily routine of exercise, skipping rope and punching a bag. One trainer who had watched him prepare for Kilrain three years before thought Sullivan was 50 percent better than he had been in 1889.[25]

Corbett came by a different route, through the Carolinas, Alabama, and Mississippi. His trip also was attended by enthusiastic crowds, but it was marred in Spartanburg, South Carolina, where the challenger barely escaped arrest because he had chosen to exercise during a brief Sunday stop. In New Orleans, Corbett set up camp at the Southern Athletic Club and began to do some light sparring, amused at the news that some of his old supporters, such as the Californian Tom Williams, were betting heavily on Sullivan.[26]

In fact, betting on the fights, and particularly on the heavyweights, was the main topic in town that week. The excursion trains were coming in by the hour, delivering their cargoes from Chicago, Kansas City, Denver, and Portland. In groups of 50 to 350, the charters unloaded fans eager for the fleshpots of the Crescent City. San Franciscans, avidly looking for action on Pompadour Jim, were there. So, too, were residents of San Antonio, Cincinnati, Columbus, New York, Albany, Wheeling, and Norfolk. A mob of loud Bostonians talked up the merits of their Strong Boy. All in all, it was the greatest conclave of boxing aficionados ever seen.

The betting was running as high as four to one on Sullivan. A local pool room offered $2,000 to $1,200 that John L. would beat Corbett, but got no takers. A few high rollers, looking to an upset, formed betting combinations and backed the San Franciscan. Peter Jackson was in town, billed as the "black heavyweight champion." His sentiments, unsurprisingly, were with Corbett, for if Jim won, then Jackson might get a shot at the crown. Bat Masterson was there, too, still smarting from his financial losses in the Kilrain fight. Now he claimed that Sullivan had met only inferior fighters and that Corbett would win—Bat wagered every dime he had on Gentleman Jim.[27]

The Triple Event kicked off on September 5, with the *Daily Picayune* solemnly asserting that the bouts would be held "as quietly as a theatrical performance"; the police would be on hand to keep order. Many leading newspapers had sent reporters. A writer for the *National Police Gazette* claimed that the "whole civilized world" was anxiously awaiting the results of the great pugilistic carnival. Benjamin Harrison and Grover Cleveland, currently waging a lackluster campaign for the presidency enlivened only by the hell-for-leather oratory of the new Populist party, had for the moment been exiled to the back pages. Telegraphic bulletins by the hour kept the nation informed of the happenings in New Orleans. Even as McAuliffe and Myer stepped into the ring to begin the extravaganza, the *New York Herald* had been forced to observe that "the odium which rested upon the prize ring and the majority of its exponents a decade or two ago, because of the disgraceful occurrences connected with it, have [sic] in a measure been removed, until now the events on hand are of national and international importance."[28] It was true, and it was John L. Sullivan who had made the difference.

Jack McAuliffe had claimed the lightweight title since 1884, when The Nonpareil had moved up into the middleweight class. He and Billy Myer had met before, in 1889, when McAuliffe, fighting with a broken right arm for the last fifty-six rounds, had battled "the Streator Cyclone" to a sixty-four-round draw. Now, before a crowd of sixty-four hundred in the Olympic Club's new arena, McAuliffe showed his skills with a pair of pea-green gloves, laced with red tape. For fourteen rounds he sliced Myer's face with short, sharp blows before finally knocking him out in the fifteenth. The lightweights were great crowd pleasers, and the news was quickly telegraphed to the nation that "the greatest fighter in his class that the world ever saw" was still champion.[29]

The following evening belonged to a new division, the featherweights. Boston's George Dixon had already proved that he was one of the finest small fighters who ever lived. He had won the title the year before (the lighter divisions were never as race-conscious as Sullivan had made the heavyweights) and was so good that his following numbered many whites as well as blacks. To their credit, the members of the Olympic Club were determined to pull off a title match free of race baiting, and this they did, aided by New Orleans's relatively tolerant history of racial intermixture. For the first time, the club admitted black fans to see their Little Chocolate, although it seated them in a special section.

Jack Skelly, on the other hand, was a journeyman, probably the least talented of the six fighters mustered for the Triple Event. For eight rounds Little Chocolate carved him up, battering the Irishman's face until it was no longer recognizable. It got so bad that Dixon's blood-soaked gloves would make a squishing sound as they struck the features of his hapless opponent. A few whites visibly winced. "A darky is all right in his place here," wrote one ringsider, "but the idea of sitting quietly by and seeing a colored boy pummel a white lad grates on Southerners." As a result of the bout, there was much editorial comment, mostly negative, on the propriety of mixing the races in the prize ring. Yet when Skelly was finally able to struggle to his feet after being knocked out in the eighth, the crowd gave Dixon a great ovation. Little Chocolate retired to his dressing room, where he puffed on a cigar and downed two glasses of beer. He would hold his crown for seven more years before finally losing it to Terry McGovern.[30]

The betting pools had parlayed McAuliffe, Dixon, and Sullivan. Two of the champions had won decisively. Now it was the turn of the third, the greatest of them all. All day on the seventh, intense excitement coursed through the streets of the Crescent City. Every public place, from saloon to pool hall to barbershop, was jammed. Visitors of all classes—lawyers, politicians, merchants, gamblers—rubbed elbows and endlessly propounded their particular brand of fight wisdom. Admission prices were scaled from five to fifteen dollars, and every ticket was taken, around ten thousand in all. Sullivan and Corbett would be watched by the largest crowd that had ever gathered to see a prizefight.[31]

He had begun, more than a decade ago, as a pier-six brawler, meeting the likes of John Donaldson, in the curtained-off backroom of a Cincinnati saloon, and John Flood, aboard a dimly lit barge on the Hudson River. Now John L. Sullivan would enter a modern, electrically illuminated arena built specifically for him and men like him. For the Kilrain fight, three years before, reporters from almost every major newspaper in the Union had been present; even more would be at ringside this night. For Kilrain, Western Union had employed fifty operators to handle 208,000 words of special dispatches following the fight. The hands were poised above the keys again; some lines led directly to ringside. Poolrooms and saloons across the country were equipped with receiving sets, and off-duty railroad telegraphers were employed to make sure customers got a round-by-round, minute-by-minute account of what happened. Newspapers readied their bulletin boards for quick broadsides.[32] It was mostly John L.'s doing, this public focus on the prize ring, and now, once more, he was at its center. Across America, on the evening of September 7, 1892, the cult of masculinity was knit together more firmly and efficiently than it had ever been, waiting for the news from New Orleans.

## IV

Corbett was the coolest man in his entourage. He had surrounded himself with experienced fight men: Billy Delaney, Jim Daly, and John Donaldson would be in his corner, and Mike Donovan would be his "bottle holder." Once again, as he had for Kilrain, Bat Masterson would keep time. Most of his backers were nervous, but the Dude exuded confidence and decided to go to the arena in style. Dressed in a light summer suit and cocky straw boater, with bamboo cane to match, he took a carriage. The streets were crammed with people, and from every side all the challenger could hear were murmurs of "Sullivan," "Sullivan," "Sullivan!" Brady, his manager, was infected with the Dude's saucy confidence. Two hours before the fight he bet all the two men had accumulated on their tour—three thousand dollars—on Corbett, with odds of 4 to 1 against him.[33]

The Dude's calm had its source in his own ring experience and in the fact that he had worked for weeks with Mike Donovan at the New York Athletic Club. Donovan, since his years in the ring, had developed into a highly respected teacher of boxing. Patiently he taught Corbett defenses against John L.'s three basic blows: a chopping left to beat down his opponent's guard; a right jab, delivered with tremendous power; and a right cross that usually whistled in on the neck or just behind the ear. His pupil was a fast learner. By the end of their sparring sessions the smaller, quicker Donovan was unable to land a blow on Corbett's constantly bobbing and weaving head. Mike was confident enough in the Dude's skills to have backed him with one thousand dollars of his own money.[34]

Donovan also told Corbett what else to expect when the two fighters met in the ring—John L.'s ferocious, intimidating scowl. On reaching the arena, the Dude tried some gamesmanship. Word came from Sullivan's backers that the champion wanted to toss for corners. Corbett responded flippantly that John L. could take any corner he liked because he, Corbett, was entering the ring last—a violation of the champion's prerogative. This contretemps was solved when Brady won a coin flip. After balking somewhat, Sullivan entered the ring first, to the expected tremendous ovation. Corbett followed shortly, and at last the two men were face to face for the first time since the dress-suit affair in San Francisco. Around them the Olympic Club seats rose up, tier after tier, into the wooden rafters, where they merged with a rat's nest of electrical wiring. Corbett noticed an oddity: the ring was not raised, and its floor was turf rather than boards. He skipped around to check his footing and found it solid.

Sullivan's seconds were busy preparing him in his corner. These were all familiar faces: Charley Johnston, Phil Casey, Joe Lannon, and Jack McAuliffe, the victor of two nights before. The faithful Frank Moran would serve as John L.'s timekeeper. As he waited, the champion sat glaring at Corbett; his head was thrust forward, fists clenched on his knees, eyes blazing. The Dude, forewarned, was bowing right and left, waving, smiling, laughing constantly. "I was trying to convince him that he was the last person or thing in the world I was thinking about."

The referee, John Duffy, called the pair to the center of the ring for their final instructions. John L. stood with arms folded, staring straight at Corbett, bouncing up and down on his toes. Corbett looked at the referee during the instructions. The crowd suddenly became quiet, and those nearest the ring could hear the admonitions against hitting in the clinches and on the breaks. Suddenly, after a few questions to Duffy, the Dude jerked his towel from his shoulders, turned his back on the astonished John L., and yelled, "Let her go!" The audience responded with a larger cheer than when he had entered the ring. By now they were so keyed up with expectation that many could not sit still, and the shifting movements of ten thousand people on wooden seats provided an undercurrent of sound that ran through the arena. The peddlers were well on their way to selling out their cases of ginger ale, sarsaparilla, and soda water. Thousands of cigars were in evidence, and in some parts of the theater fans fluttered in such numbers that they "seemed like a grove of palms ruffled by a gale."[35]

By now John L. was beyond his usual self-induced rage at the apparent indifference of his opponent. More than ever, he was convinced he was facing a glib young coxcomb who needed to be taken down a peg. When Duffy called "time!" he hurtled across the ring at the Dude, eagerly slapping his left hand against his thigh. As Donovan had predicted, he chopped with his left and followed with a right cross. Corbett easily slipped away. He was wary of being backed into a corner. Again the rush, with the same results. Sullivan was having trouble even landing a punch, and so it continued for the first two rounds, as the crowd roared in continuous frenzy, Donovan screamed instructions from Corbett's corner, and the telegraphers at ringside steadily rapped out their codes to the waiting multitude around the country.

In the third, the Dude delivered his first solid shot, a left to John L.'s nose as the champion rushed by him. Blood spurted immediately, the crowd noise redoubled in volume, and Corbett continued to work over Sullivan's nose and jaw for the rest of the round. When John L. at last retired to his corner, his face, arms, and chest were smeared with blood, more than he had lost in all his previous fights together. His nose was broken.

He continued to bleed profusely for the next few rounds, but he also began to recover somewhat. Corbett ignored Donovan's instructions to work on his opponent's fleshy body, instead "jumping around like a grasshopper," to Mike's disgust. "Jim," Donovan pleaded in the corner, "don't you see he's recovering? Go in close to him. He can't hit you." At the start of the seventh Corbett simply beat Sullivan to the punch, sinking rights and lefts into John L.'s stomach, doubling the champion up into a jackknife of agony. But again the Dude did not press in for the kill, backing off, feinting warily, and looking for openings. More and more of his quick hooks were striking home.

By now the crowd could sense an upset in the works. John L.'s lack of conditioning was beginning to tell. He came out for the eighth round puffing hard. He had lost so much blood that people close to the ring thought they saw an ashen pallor spreading over his face. The combination of loss of blood, his inability to hit Corbett, and the Dude's swift counterpunches were all taking their toll. He could barely lift his arms to defend himself, but like Kilrain three years before he was not about to quit. The lighter man danced around him, landing punch after punch over John L.'s lowered guard. This was not Charlie Mitchell, a man who taunted and fled. The Dude had considerable punching power, and his timing was excellent. By the fourteenth Corbett was landing straight shots to Sullivan's battered nose without a return.

John L. was disintegrating as a fighter, before the entire nation. Still he kept on coming, every once in a while saying "That's a good one, Jim," when Corbett fired in a punch. John L.'s face and jaws were repeated targets now, and the amazed fans began to anticipate the kill. In the sixteenth the champion made a desperate rush for Corbett, but the Dude skipped away like a dancing master, making Sullivan's futile efforts look like a game of tag. Maddened even further, John L. ran at Corbett, trying to strike him with his body, his arms so tired he could no longer lift them. Over and over he banged into the ring ropes as Corbett nimbly dodged aside.

Donovan, like so many of the fans present, wanted Corbett to finish it, and fast—anything to prevent John L. from floundering about the ring helpless, no longer able to defend himself, a caricature of the pugilist he had once been. Mike begged Corbett to end the bout, saying John L. "can't hit hard enough to dent a pound of butter." It got so bad that Sullivan would rush directly at his opponent, arms down and chin thrust forward, inviting a knockout. But this was the Dude's hour. He was completely in control, fresh, well aware of what he was accomplishing. He continued to dance and dodge from the seventeenth through the twentieth rounds.

At long last, the iron constitution and raw energy that had served John L. Sullivan so long and so well could do no more. The tree-trunk legs were barely holding him up; his arms ached, even hanging straight down at his sides; he could barely see through his puffed-up eyelids. Dazed, he hardly knew what was happening around him.

But he would not fall. Wavering, he stood helplessly in his corner as Corbett advanced, at last determined to go for the kill. The Dude came on with a rush. John L. was caught flat-footed, too weak to raise his guard. Corbett feinted, then slammed home a right to the jaw. Jim saw his opponent's eyes roll. Sullivan dropped to his knees like a pole-axed steer, but then, incredibly, slowly raised himself to his feet. There he stood, completely defenseless, waiting for the inevitable. Crash! Crash! A left and right to the jaw! John L. pitched forward, landing on his face and chest. Feebly he struggled to rise, but it was no use. Slowly he rolled over on his right side, unable to hear Duffy's count. Eight . . . nine . . . ten. It was over. The unbelievable had happened. John L. Sullivan had been beaten.

The entire house was "still as death." Johnston and McAuliffe picked up Sullivan and carried him to his corner, where they propped him up on the small yellow kitchen chair he had used between rounds. He was not unconscious—no man would ever completely knock him out—but he was so exhausted he could neither move nor think clearly. There was cheering now, wild acclaim for the Dude. John L.'s seconds put ammonia under his nostrils and applied ice to the back of his head and neck. He began to come around a little and tried to struggle to his feet. Johnston and McAuliffe, thinking he wanted to attack Corbett, tried to hold him back. But Sullivan had something else in mind.

Half conscious, eyes glazed and almost closed, he swept the handlers away and stood for a moment, swaying from side to side. He paid no attention to the exuberant Corbett, who was being toweled off on the other side of the ring. Slowly, he stumbled to the ropes, groping with his left hand until he found a grip on a ring post. He held up his right hand; the cheering and applauding stopped instantly. In a low, halting voice, thickened by dehydration and weakened from the pounding he had taken, he spoke:

> Gentlemen—gentlemen, I have nothing at all to say. All I have to say is that I came into the ring once too often—and if I had to get licked I'm glad I was licked by an American. I remain your warm and personal friend, John L. Sullivan.

It was his finest moment in the prize ring. Nothing became him more during his years of dominance in his chosen profession than his manner of leaving it. The simple speech anchored him in the hearts of his admirers once and for all. Many in the crowd were weeping openly. Donovan was convinced he was seeing a man "head and shoulders above all the rest." In defeat as in triumph, John L. Sullivan was "always on the level."[36]

## V

The news sped forth from New Orleans. As quick as the telegraph operators' fingers could move, it flashed across America. To New York, where dispatches had been read from theater stages all over the city, and where a red light had been displayed from the dome of the Pulitzer Building when things looked good for Sullivan, a white light for Corbett. To Washington, where larger crowds had congregated around the bulletin boards than at any time during the race for president. To cities where interest had also been intense: Chicago, Saint Louis, Cincinnati, and Pittsburgh. In San Francisco, crowds danced in the streets. In Boston, fans "vented their sorrow in great howls of disappointment when news of the fight was put on the blackboards." Overseas the story went, on the transatlantic cable. It had a great impact in England, where a young Sandhurst cadet named Winston Spencer Churchill was gratified by Sullivan's defeat.[37] Everywhere men paused, as if attuned to some great cosmic shaking of the earth.

To city after city, the telegraph wires had brought bulletins punch-by-punch, and stentorian announcers had bellowed the news to eager crowds. New York's Broadway was completely jammed between Twenty-fourth and Thirty-fourth streets, and leading lights like Mayor Hugh J. Grant, Richard Croker, and Lieutenant Governor "Blue-eyed Billy" Sheehan had stopped in at the Hoffman House for the latest news. Everyone agreed that the fight had aroused more enthusiasm than a presidential election. Corbett had plenty of backers, and city after city sang and drank his praise until late into the night. Sullivan supporters could be identified by their glum silence. Newspapers rushed special bulletins into the streets. In New Orleans, the *Picayune* ran off more than ten thousand extras and sent out special trains ahead of the regular morning schedules so that readers along the Gulf Coast could get the astounding results with their morning coffee. Doggerel was rapidly struck off, an example being this chorus sung to the tune of the popular "Throw Him Down, McCluskey!":

> John L. has been knocked out! The people all did cry
> Corbett is the champion! how the news did fly.
> And future generations, with wonder and delight
> Will read in history's pages of the Sullivan-Corbett fight.[38]

According to the *New York Times* correspondent, John L. broke down in his dressing room after the fight, sobbing convulsively as his handlers tried to repair his battered face. Be that as it may, he naturally sought to deaden the shock with the bottle. He and his backers returned to his rooms in the St. Charles Hotel and morosely sat up all night drinking champagne and whiskey. At last, around five in the morning, he fell into a restless sleep. When he was awakened at noon, he found his mouth so swollen he could not eat. He did manage to mumble a few words to reporters who dropped by for a postmortem, saying that "Corbett is the cleverest man I ever fought. I am glad, if I had to be whipped, that it was done by an American citizen."[39]

Corbett, of course, was euphoric, but his finest moment was tinged with sadness. Even as delirious fans were showering the ring with hats, coats, canes, belts, and boutonnieres, he found himself staring at the results of his handiwork, lying beaten on the turf of the ring. "I was actually disgusted with the crowd, and it left a lasting impression on me," he remembered. "It struck me as sad to see all those thousands who had given him such a wonderful ovation when he entered the ring turning it to me now that he was down and out." He wanted only to be with his handlers. Quickly he shouldered his way out of the ring and ended up at the Southern Athletic Club, where he ostentatiously drank milk as his supporters whooped it up. This moody, ambitious man was disgusted. "I realized that some day, too, they would turn from me when I should be in Sullivan's shoes lying there on the floor."[40] (He was right. That day came for him on March 17, 1897, in Carson City, Nevada, where he was knocked senseless by the ungainly Bob Fitzsimmons in the fourteenth round.)

For the moment, though, money fell in golden heaps on Corbett, Brady, and the city of New Orleans. The new champion immediately wired $10,000 to his father to pay off the mortgage on the house and livery stable. Later, he and Brady went off on tour in a play, *Gentleman Jack,* written expressly for him. The project netted the partners $150,000 during the 1892–93 theatrical season. The Olympic Club, for its part, made more than $50,000. Over half a million dollars changed hands as a result of the Triple Event; it was a gamblers' paradise.[41] In the upshot, however, it was Corbett's particular tragedy to have dethroned an idol. Despite his youth, good looks, and undoubted boxing skills, he was never a popular champion, certainly not close to Sullivan's stature. Thus his time in the spotlight was clouded by bitterness and some confusion over what his role should be.

As for Sullivan, there was no end of the list of reasons why he had lost. William Muldoon thought he should have gone into training earlier. In spite of the defeat, he declared that John L. was still good for about two more years of fighting. Phil Casey believed that his man had been trained from the hips up, but his legs were gone. Some of the press was less kind. According to the *Hartford Times,* liquor was at fault. True, Sullivan was not a real drunkard, and people should not be too hard on him, but "for him—and for such as he—what other equipment of resource is left?" The *Manchester Union* agreed, and used the weird metaphor of Samson and Delilah to describe Corbett's victory. For the *Lawrence* (Kansas) *Eagle*, it was a simple, instructive morality tale: vice and drink had done in John L., nothing more or less. Dr. Sargent was resurrected to tell his tale of John L.'s physical exam, and he revealed that he had postponed looking at Sullivan in June because the champion was "so abnormally fat and gross." The doctor noted again the "noticeable weakness in his respiratory organs."[42]

Still, the hero's loss had been sadly inevitable, and many took heart with the *Boston Pilot*'s comment that "there is a good deal of real if rude chivalry in the conduct of both gladiators." With marvelous bad timing, John L.'s autobiography was issued the week of his defeat, yet it still sold moderately and introduced him to a new generation of fight fans.[43] But probably the best testimonial to the high esteem in which he was held came ten days after he was beaten.

Sullivan's insistence on winner-take-all had been completely in character, but now he had nothing to show for the months of fitful training and the twenty-one-round clobbering he had received. Although it was nice to be honored in song and story, such as the popular jingle "John L. Sullivan and Jim Corbett" ("These two men shook hands in the ring, and Sullivan he led out./But Jimmy was too smart for him, and nimbly dodged about"), he was broke again. With Johnston and Wakely, he arrived in New York on September 11. About two hundred of the faithful cheered him as he made his way from Grand Central Station to Matt Clune's Vanderbilt Hotel. There he entertained friends and steadfastly told reporters that he had no excuses.[44]

Corbett arrived the following day and sparred that evening before an elegant crowd, including Richard Harding Davis, Stanford White, and Charles Frohman. He was in town to take part in a benefit for John L., which everyone knew Sullivan badly needed. So, on September 17, a Saturday evening, over ten thousand people gathered in Madison Square Garden. Among the throng were politicians, aldermen, police officials, judges, and gamblers, the same loyal cross-section of American manhood that had followed John L. all along. Billy Madden was there, along with an old nemesis of John L.'s, Clubber Williams; so was One-Eyed Connolly, the self-styled "King of the Gate Crashers." Reserved seats went for as high as six dollars.

The audience was treated to several boxing exhibitions until, a few minutes before 10 P.M., Sullivan emerged from his dressing room at the Fourth Avenue end of the Garden, attired in green shirt and black trunks. As he climbed through the ropes, he was given a basket of flowers. Corbett then appeared, and as the two men stood side by side in the ring, the hall rang with cheering for a solid three minutes. No one in attendance doubted that most of the applause was for John L. At last, Sullivan, the marks of his beating still visible on his face, raised his hand for quiet. Then, his deep, rumbling bass echoed to the farthest reaches of the Garden: "Ladies and gentlemen . . . thank you . . . I was defeated and have no excuses, [I am] glad Corbett is an American. . . . When a defeated man begins to make excuses, he makes the mistake of his life."

Gentlemen Jim followed with another short speech; fans noted his voice was weaker and reedier than John L.'s and could not fill the hall. Three rounds of gentle sparring followed, with Corbett's agility being obvious; in fact, it was as if two different generations were meeting in the ring. The crowd departed well pleased, and for John L. it had been a sorely needed payday. Frank Moran received $6,030.37 on his friend's behalf as Sullivan's share of the benefit.[45]

## VI

In the years that followed it became common to mark the Sullivan-Corbett fight as a cultural event of significance, a kind of way station along the route of American progress. Skill and balance, it was held, came to dominate over sheer brute strength. An Army surgeon, Lieutenant Colonel A. A. Woodhull, argued that the fight had proved that speed and agility were superior qualities. Mere primitive force, exemplified by John L., was not enough; it must be made efficient through intelligence. "John L. Sullivan was the last champion of the world who gained and held his position solely through strength, ferocity, and physical force," wrote one commentator a decade later. Against Corbett, "brute strength was for the last time to be pitted against skill and scientific cleverness for a championship." When John L. was beaten, "ring craft had proved its superiority to mere muscular strength and activity."[46]

The usual argument has been that Sullivan was "caught in a period of transition," that Corbett was a new breed of fighter—as alien to John L.'s bare-knuckle generation as a man from Mars.[47] Thus, for many sports fans the fight cast a curtain over all that went before. Before 1892 there was Sullivan—ill-trained, self-taught, pure flaming instinct in the prize ring. After 1892 there was Corbett—educated in ring "science," cool, calculating, an "intelligent" fighter. With their bout as a watershed, John L. and the Dude have taken their place as milestones in the maturation of American culture.

These analyses, which are still common in sporting and cultural histories, are vastly overblown and unfair to both boxers. In Corbett's case, they overlook the Dude's considerable strength and punching power and also ignore the fact that he did something John L. had longed to do and never accomplished: in 1894 Corbett kayoed Mitchell in three rounds. Also, when Corbett himself was further along in ring years, he was knocked out twice (1900 and 1903) by another plodding fighter of exceptional strength, Jim Jeffries.

In Sullivan's case, the charge that his style was primitive, relying on bull-like rushes and sheer physical force, was true. But there would be other champions with the same qualities well after Sullivan—Jeffries, Jess Willard, Primo Carnera (to name three), and, at least in part, Jack Dempsey. Indeed, the heavyweight division has always featured boxers with the qualities of both Sullivan and Corbett. The men who combine the two—like Joe Louis and Muhammad Ali—have been, in their prime, unstoppable. Moreover, Sullivan preferred gloved fights, fought most of his bouts with gloves, and saw nothing wrong with gloves in the Corbett match. To see him as the last of the bare-knuckle breed and Corbett as the harbinger of a new era of "scientific" boxing simply overstates the argument.

John L. Sullivan was beaten because boxing, beyond almost all other athletic endeavors, is a sport for young men in the very prime of physical condition. With Corbett, John L. gave away eight years and countless boxing lessons. He gave away speed, conditioning, and the real desire to win. Nobody knows how much he gave away with his riotous life-style. The amazing aspect of his fight with Corbett is not that the Dude won. It is that a prematurely aged, overweight, short-winded man, who had been out of the prize ring for three years, stood in for one solid hour of battle with a man in his physical prime. If there was ever such a thing as "fighting heart," John L. had it in spades in New Orleans. Let the last word be his, a candid reflection on the fight written eighteen years later: "Although the muscle was there, the machinery inside had given out."[48]

The machinery inside had given out. Now what was there for him, a man whose being had been so tightly bound up with his physical prowess? In the back of his mind John L. had probably known this moment would come, and now, at long last, it was here. With crushing finality he realized that in New Orleans he had been stripped of a crucial part of himself—that come what may, he was no longer champion.

# PART III   EX-CHAMPION

# CHAPTER THIRTEEN

# Downhill:
# The Anatomy of a Has-been
# (1892—1905)

From the summit of fame and the glories of the championship throne, there now seemed to be only one direction for Sullivan to travel: down. No one before in American sporting life had risen so high from such beginnings, and John L.'s many enemies and detractors confidently expected him to return from whence he came, vanishing into dismal, drunken obscurity. Certainly this had been the general pattern of prize-fighters before him.

In the years following his defeat at the hands of Corbett, Sullivan again broke the mold. Indeed, he did not plummet far, first because he had always lived hand to mouth and continued to do so, and second because his amazing popularity continued, propelled now not by his pile-driver fists but by the nostalgia and respect his name evoked. Crowds came to see him in the theater and on the vaudeville stage, and he was still, outside the ring, a "drawing card." All things being equal, a comfortable prosperity in retirement should have been his.

All things were not equal. John L.'s freewheeling life-style, released from the physical regimen of pugilism, rapidly sped out of control, his or anybody else's. At the root of the problem was his alcoholism, now unleashed in fullest force. His drinking led to splintered friendships, more public brawls, assaults, and even jail. It contributed to several financial failures and eventually produced bankruptcy. The psychological costs were heavy, as well. He eventually grew to loathe his image as a drunkard and a brutal menace to polite society, but he remained wedded to the bottle more firmly than ever.

Thus, as during his ring career, he became a contradiction in terms, loved, pitied, and despised at the same time. Fame never left him, nor did the public attention. Slowly, of course, his generation passed on and with it the direct memories of his ring career. But he strove to be as "public" a man as ever. Never had the self-inflicted wounds of a prominent cultural figure been so open to scrutiny. And John L. went to pieces not once, but over and over again. He became, to a certain degree, a national joke. But it should be remembered that he was attempting something no other American had: to live out his days in the shadow of sporting fame that could never be renewed. Like so many athletes and celebrities who followed, he did it poorly.

## I

More than a few not only applauded Corbett's victory but also were ecstatic in proclaiming the ring demise of John L. In a vitriolic editorial entitled "Exit Sullivan," the *Brooklyn Eagle* spoke for all those who had suffered the champion's public outrages for years. John L. had been beaten, said the editors, "as a brawler, a bully, an unconscionable ruffian deserves to be beaten":

> For a decade Sullivan had blustered everywhere. A more pretentious person never vexed the gaze of men. A more consummate egoist never faced the light of day. A more shallow reprobate never gathered an army of sycophants in his train. His conspicuousness, for years, rivaled or surpassed that of statesmen, of scholars, of scientists, of philanthropists, of philosophers. Beside him a Cleveland, a Carlisle, a Harrison, a Blaine, a Bryce, an Eliot, an Edison, a Curtis, a Spencer, a Lowell or a Whittier shrunk into insignificance. A multitude of contriving knaves and silly fools cheered him on and boomed him as if he were a benefactor of his race. His movements were minutely reported. Portraits of him were strewn broadcast. Photographers reveled in opportunities to portray his figure, his surroundings, his attendants, even his sleeping apartments. For the time, he was monarch of all he surveyed. All that is ended now.[1]

Sullivan's generation had provided the first true sporting professionals in the nation's history. The postboxing careers of later leading pugilists have generally shown a precipitous descent, both economically and socially, from the standards of their high-living, free-spending years as champions or contenders. In fact, the broken-down, washed-up pug has become a hardy stereotype, one with a considerable degree of truth. One study has found that of ninety-five pugilists once at or near the top of their profession, eighty-three later worked in blue-collar occupations or worse. And as for the celebrity, he "cannot, like luckier folk, drop out of sight when he is ripened with age," wrote Ben Hecht, who saw more than his share of the breed. "He must stay on the vine and rot—for all to see and disdain."[2]

But these are twentieth-century statistics and impressions. John L. had been the first of his kind to "ascend," after a fashion, to shake hands with a president and chat with a prince. Would his later life be different as well? His critics confidently expected him to vanish into the inchoate urban ethnic mix from which he had come. After all, the professional athlete was, by necessity, a slave to what his body could do, and with the inevitable advance of age came disaster. Professional athletes were the worst evil in all of ancient Greece, fumed the dramatist Euripides. "In youth they strut about in splendor, the idols of the city, but when bitter old age comes upon them, they are cast aside like worn-out cloaks." Later, the medical philosopher Galen would say that the souls of professionals "are stifled as in a sea of mud." As they age, these veterans lack both health and beauty. "Even those who are naturally well proportioned become fat and bloated; their faces are often shapeless and unsightly owing to the wounds received in boxing and in the *pankration*. They lose their eyes and teeth, and their limbs are strained." The decay of the professional athlete, particularly the boxer, was a shibboleth with over two millenia of Western culture behind it. Even Oliver Wendell Holmes's urbane Autocrat knew of it:

> As for the muscular powers, they pass their maximum long before the time when the true decline of life begins, if we may judge by the experience of the ring. A man is "stale," I think, in their language, soon after thirty,— often, no doubt, much earlier, as gentlemen of the pugilistic profession are exceedingly apt to keep their vital fire burning *with the blower up*.[3]

John L. had been living with his "blower up" for more than fifteen years, and his entire adult life had been but an embellishment of the traditional stereotype. The amateur athletic ideal, by contrast, was enshrined with poignant beauty, given verse by the poet A. E. Housman in *To an Athlete Dying Young* (1896):

> Today, the roads all runners come,
> Shoulder-high, we bring you home,
> And set you at your threshold down,
> Townsman of a stiller town.[4]

John L., though, was not yet a "townsman of a stiller town." Far from being a universal ideal of athletic perfection, cut down in full bloom, he was decidedly imperfect, and, more to the point, he refused to retire quietly into obscurity. He saw himself as a "public man," and a public man he chose to remain. He and everyone else knew that his prime had come and gone; now he had to deal with that fact as best he could.

Freed from any demands of training whatsoever, his body rapidly mushroomed in size. The ring of fat around his middle quickly became a paunch and, then, a stomach of such commanding proportions that it advanced before him like the prow of a ship. For most of the rest of his life his weight oscillated between 270 and 320 pounds. Within months of his bout with Corbett his hair and mustache turned completely gray. Still in his thirties, he looked a good fifteen years older. To the press he became "Old John L.," and so he remained.

The ex-champion passed from his prime to "old age" in the public eye without missing a beat. In a real sense he had no middle age. He himself helped furbish this image by constantly looking back at his ring career. Once he had been young and had conquered men for money—now he was "old." Always, to the press, he would be an "old-timer." In 1900, not yet forty-two, he was described as an "old war-horse"; five years later he was a "famous old gladiator" and a "great old war horse." Usually, he identified with this image, although he balked at being called washed-up. Once, in Bridgeport, Connecticut, he and a big telephone lineman got into a fracas and had to be separated. John L. had attacked on hearing himself called a "has-been." Later, he was less than diplomatically introduced at a Madison Square Garden fight as "that greatest fighter of all time, the greatest has-been of any time," to which he snarled: "It's a damn sight better to be a has-been than a neverwas!" Still, it rankled. Jack McAuliffe would later tell a story of sitting with Sullivan after the Corbett fight. Battered and despondent, John L. said "Everyone gets his sometime. Do what I'm telling you now, Jack, and retire with the glory of a world's championship and avoid the disgrace of a knockout." (McAuliffe did; although he came back later, within months of seconding John L. he had turned over his lightweight title to Kid Lavigne.)[5]

The loss to Corbett was thus a turning point, in every sense, for Sullivan. It stripped him of his title, severely bruised his ego, cost him any more big paydays in the ring, and ushered him into a premature old age. Adding to this series of shocks, as the 1890s progressed, was the fact that many men of John L.'s prizefighting generation died.

Jack Ashton went first. This "genial, sociable man" had sparred hundreds of rounds with John L., even incongruously playing a jockey to set up the final match in *Honest Hearts and Willing Hands*. He had loyally trooped along to Australia and patiently served as the butt of Sullivan's crude practical jokes. Early in 1893, delirious, he was admitted to New York's Bellevue Hospital, where he soon died of erysipelas, "aggravated by other causes." He was twenty-nine.

Within months Mike Cleary was dead. Little Mike, who had given exhibitions with Sullivan as far back as 1883, had had a foot amputated a few years before after an accident. His body shrunk to a shadow from consumption, he died at William Muldoon's Belfast farm at the age of thirty-six.[6]

Late in 1893 Pete McCoy, who had barnstormed the Grand Tour with John L., was crossing Long Island Sound on his brother-in-law's tugboat, *Scranton*. Close to forty, Pete had been ill for some months. About four miles east of the lightship, he either slipped overboard or jumped. His brother-in-law thought it was a suicide, because Pete made no attempt to grasp a rope and ladder extended to him. Some months later news came that Alf Greenfield, whose running and falling tactics so enraged Sullivan back in 1884 and 1885, had died in an asylum in Birmingham, England. Alf had spent his last years running a saloon.[7]

In 1895 John L. lost his only brother. Mike Sullivan, after an illness of three weeks, died of Bright's disease at the age of twenty-nine in the Boston Highlands, with John L. and his sister, Ann, at his bedside. Mike, as slight and wiry as his father had been, had suffered several heart attacks the year before. He had lived constantly in his famous brother's shadow and had never held any employment separate from the living provided by John L. There was no wife, no family—only a sad epitaph of "social clubs" to which he had belonged. His body, encased in a broadcloth-covered coffin, was interred beside his parents in Mount Calvary.[8] John L. felt the loss keenly.

The following year was Harry Hill's turn. The man who had once run the most popular saloon in New York City was now in his seventies, so destitute that Richard Kyle Fox started a subscription for him, contributing one hundred dollars. Cronies of many years' standing chipped in to help keep the wolf from the door (Billy Madden gave five dollars), but John L. was not among them. Sullivan did appear with Hill, arm-and-arm, at the latter's successful benefit in May 1894 and told the cheering crowd of the esteem he had for Hill, but this was Harry's last fling. He died in September 1896, almost forgotten. That same month Ann Livingston, who had remarried after her prolonged affair with Sullivan, died in Bellevue Hospital after a lingering illness.[9]

Jack Burke, "the Irish Lad," who had lasted five fruitless rounds against Sullivan in Chicago in 1885, died in 1897 in Cheltenham, England, at the age of thirty-five. Steve Taylor, the New Jersey coroner whose real name was John Maher, died of pneumonia late in 1899. Taylor had met Sullivan in the ring on John L.'s first visit to New York, way back in 1881, and had later taken part in the Grand Tour. He was forty-seven. A year later Paddy Ryan, after an illness of six weeks, died at his simple home on Albany Avenue in Green Island, New York. This hard-luck fighter, who as champion had beaten no one, was to be remembered only as Sullivan's punching bag. He had lived from odd job to odd job in nearby Albany after returning east from San Francisco, but he had never made a go of anything. Dead at the age of forty-seven, he left a wife, son, and daughter.[10]

Sullivan may never have heard the details of Peter Jackson's grim end in Australia the following year, but the death of the once-great black fighter followed the dreary pattern. Certainly John L. knew of the demise of one of his oldest foes, John Flood. The Bull's Head Terror, who had never risen out of his spawning ground of Five Points, died in March 1904, and Sullivan attended the funeral. Later that year

John L.'s friend George Rooke, who as an elderly fighter had met John L. in Boston back in 1880, died at the age of sixty-two in Newark, New Jersey. Two years later Jere Dunn, onetime Chicago gambling man and ardent Sullivan backer, died of cancer of the esophagus in Elizabeth, New Jersey, at sixty-three. Dunn had gunned down Jim Elliott, another Sullivan opponent, in a barroom brawl in 1883. For this he had served two years, eight months for manslaughter in Sing Sing.[11]

And so, one by one, they passed into the shades. Most of them died fairly young, and almost all died destitute. Sullivan grieved for some, truly mourned for one (his brother), and probably knew of several more losses not recorded here. The importance of this parade of death is not in its occurrence, for this Sullivan shared with everyone, but in the fact that news of each funeral set John L. further apart from the ensuing generation. He survived while most of his pugilistic contemporaries were following the classic pattern of early decay and death.

Adding to his image (and self-image) of rapid aging, Sullivan was living now in the midst of an America in the full whirl of industrialization and urbanization. The cities were becoming electrified, and communication in the urban world had become almost instantaneous through the miracle of the telephone; by the end of the century the first long-distance lines were in place. During the 1890s a few daring souls, attired in duster, cap, and goggles, brought forth strange machines onto city streets, where they served mostly to frighten horses. The Gibson Girl—slender, athletic, poised—was the latest feminine ideal. A new, more active urban generation was on the scene.

Everywhere the pace of life seemed accelerated, speeded up; inventions conquered space and time. Indeed, the nation was in one of its periodic frenzies of self-confidence. The first part of the decade saw severe labor strife, and hard times down on the farm produced the Populist movement. There was intense political dissension, and in 1896 came the emotional spectacle of William Jennings Bryan's run for the presidency. But overall, as the turn of the century approached, the tone of Sullivan's America was forward-looking, aggressive, bubbling over with the future. The acquisition of empire, sudden and not without its opponents, still added to the confident mood. The past, even the recent past, had for many Americans little relevance whatsoever.

And there was John L., in the midst of this dynamism but somehow a man apart. He was now an "ex-champion": obese, gray-haired, with friends and prizefight comrades dead and dying all around him. If he was to live up (or down) to the tradition of his calling, he should now retreat into the wings, to moulder away as his fellows had done. What else was there for him, now that he had become an instant relic?

## II

Stubbornly, he refused to leave public life, and most of his fans remained eager for news of his doings, even though they felt he would never fight again. No longer "young," in any sense of the word, he nevertheless remained active. In a wide variety of ways—some of them positive, some of them markedly less so—he kept his name before the public. It was still good to hear the applause, and as the years passed, he was increasingly content to stand on his "record," warts and all.

He was never far from the fight game, following the common pattern of his fellow pugilists in attending fights, acting as a second, or serving as a referee. His friendship with Jake Kilrain, oddly established in the hours of broiling combat on Charles Rich's estate, deepened. Whenever he was in Baltimore, he stopped off in Jake's saloon, where the two would spend hours chatting amiably. He seconded Kilrain in the latter's fight with Steve O'Donnell in 1895, showing up intoxicated and badgering O'Donnell and his corner throughout the contest, which ended in an eight-round draw. While visiting Saint Louis, he reconciled with Charlie Mitchell, and he supported Mitchell against Corbett. Much later, when both he and Mitchell were on their uppers, they tried to stage an exhibition in New York City, only to be denied a permit, and tried again in Buffalo and Tacoma. (For the Buffalo fight Sullivan announced he would "trim" himself from 305 to 270.)[12]

The one man to whom he could never offer the hand of friendship was Corbett. His forthright speech from the ring on the night of his defeat was heartfelt enough, but as the months passed and the emotional trauma of his loss sank in, John L. grew increasingly bitter toward the Dude. Although there was some talk of a rematch, Sullivan's quick lapse into obesity clearly precluded this. Instead, he confined himself to sniping at the new champion through the press, even suggesting that Corbett had won because he, Sullivan, had been drugged before the fight. John L. always admitted that his conqueror was a "clever sparrer," but he called Corbett "that duffer" and predicted confidently that Mitchell would beat him. When the Dude knocked out the aging Charlie, John L. made noises about challenging Corbett, admitting that "I did not see how Corbett could lose at any stage of the game." At last, in April 1894, Sullivan bowed to the inevitable and announced that he had given up hope of fighting for the title again. Later that year he talked loosely of meeting the winner of a Corbett-Fitzsimmons match, but everyone knew by now it was only hot air. One boxing writer dismissed this as "akin to the raving of a shattered mind."[13]

Sullivan simply could not bring himself to concede admiration for Corbett, even after Jim generously staged two benefits for the ex-champion, the one shortly after New Orleans and another in 1895. Sullivan publicly stated that he was not Corbett's friend. From time to time, drunk or sober, he would lash out at the champion, obviously smarting at his whipping for years after the fact. Over and over, to whoever would listen, John L. growled that the Dude was slandering him in the press and that Corbett was no gentleman.[14] Sadly, the two Irish-American fighters, so alike in their temperaments, would never become close. The fault lay largely with Sullivan; in his mind the Dude had embarrassed him before the entire world.

Beyond contacts with other pugilists, Sullivan was the recipient of benefit after benefit during the years of his retirement. In part this series of exhibitions was good for his ego, since it brought him back into the ring to the applause of his admirers. But the benefits were also a frank admission of his impecunious ways, and as they continued, for over ten years after the Corbett fight, they became a constant reminder to the public that the ex-champion was continuing his profligate habits. The profitable evening with Corbett in New York shortly after the New Orleans match was only the first of many.

In May 1894 John L. was feted in Boston before about five thousand people. The crowd cheered wildly as Sullivan and Paddy Ryan, each weighing about 240 pounds, wallowed through three one-minute rounds. Afterward, John L. politely thanked them for coming "to aid me and also the sufferers in the recent fire." A month later he returned the favor at a benefit for Paddy. The two men did the same thing a year later in Jersey City, and again in 1897 in Philadelphia.[15]

By far his biggest benefit came in Madison Square Garden in the summer of 1895. Over seven thousand thronged to the arena, largely because Corbett had agreed to spar with the ex-champion. Many in the crowd were appalled at Sullivan's condition; he was a mound of blubber, swathed in black tights from waist to heel. His hair was gray, and he featured a filed-down, bristly mustache. Still, his popularity was undiminished. As he walked toward the ring, hands grasped his own or clapped his shoulders. Cries of "Hallo, John!" and "Good old John!" (he was thirty-six) rang out through the Garden.

Before the exhibition John L. made a brief thank-you speech twice, from opposite sides of the ring, and then went three brief rounds with the Dude, tapping and pawing. Overall, it was a good show; in addition to the headliners, fans such as the comedian De Wolf Hopper, the actor Maurice Barrymore, and William K. Vanderbilt himself got to see fighters like Peter Maher, George Dixon, and Joe Choynski. The gate was a healthy one; John L. took away over five thousand dollars as his share. For the next six years New York loosened its restrictions against prizefighting. In 1896 a state law declared boxing legal (nonsensically allowing decisions but no knockouts), so long as the fights were connected with established athletic clubs, and in this somewhat freer climate most of the rest of Sullivan's exhibitions were conducted.[16]

Thus John L. received over ten thousand dollars from the two Corbett benefits alone, which should have been enough to carry him for quite some while. But, for two reasons, it was not. First, he was Sullivan, and the money left his hands almost before it entered them. Second, promoters stripped off much of the profit of his benefits, usually leaving him with far less money than reported in the press. For example, during the second Corbett exhibition a deputy sheriff visited the Garden, bearing a writ of attachment against the receipts that had been secured by a job printing company, which alleged that John L. owed it twenty-four hundred dollars for lithographs. Parson Davies, the promoter, claimed that Sullivan had sold the "rights" to the exhibition to him. The Parson therefore walked away with most of John L.'s share of his "benefit," after paying off the writ.[17]

A year later Sullivan was back in the Garden for another exhibition, with "Sailor Tom" Sharkey. John L., "the grand old man," was cheered roundly. Sharkey, too, was popular with the crowd; in a real prizefight he was a tough heavyweight, but musclebound and never in the class of Corbett, Fitzsimmons, or Maher. John L. envied both the Sailor's youth—Sharkey was twenty-four—and his muscularity. Charley Johnston noted that John L., himself, had once been in his prime. Yes, Sullivan sadly agreed, "I was at my best when I went at Flood." The crowd of about five thousand was shocked at Sullivan's appearance. A great roll of stomach flab hung over his belt. "He was old, he was gray," wrote one observer, "and it was no more proper that he should be in the ring than that he should assay skirt dancing." The ponderous body could no longer move, although the arms could still flash out with an occasional blow. "Fat, slow, and far from vigorous," Sullivan tapped and clinched his way through three brief rounds, still managing to land more punches than his muscular opponent, on whose chest was tattooed a full-rigged brig with a blue star above it. In the third round, an already exhausted Sullivan tripped and nearly fell. He straightforwardly told the audience, "I have had my day and am now almost too fat to fight."[18]

In March 1897 John L. journeyed to Carson City, Nevada, to take in Corbett's championship match with Bob Fitzsimmons. Loudly he offered to post $5,000 to fight the winner, but no one was listening. Sullivan had a contract with the *New York World* to report the fight, but the actual writing was done by a young *World* reporter and great admirer of John L., William Inglis. The paper paid all Sullivan's expenses to Nevada and back, as well as a handsome sum for his byline. Sullivan wrote nothing at all but was much in evidence as the Dude and "Ruby Robert" made their final preparations. The result—Fitzsimmons won by a knockout in the fourteenth—must have satisfied John L. inordinately. Now he was not the *only* "ex-champion." Once back in New York, he had the cheek to dun the *World* a further $250 for "extra expenses." He made such a fuss that the paper paid, in two $100 bills and five tens, and within minutes Sullivan was back at a favorite haunt, the bar of the Vanderbilt Hotel, buying for the house.[19]

That summer he attempted to capitalize on the new champion's fame. He and Fitzsimmons arranged to go "six friendly rounds" at Ambrose Park in Brooklyn. Over twelve hundred people were waiting, but among them were seventy-five policemen. When the two men attempted to enter the ring, Police Inspector McLaughlin stopped them, saying they would be arrested if they so much as threatened a punch. Sullivan was forced to tell the crowd it would have to leave.[20]

He was back-page news now. The next year, 1898, was given over to the excitement of the Spanish-American War. The *New York Journal*, afire with patriotic enthusiasm, proposed the formation of a regiment of great athletes to whip the damned Dons. The paper suggested Corbett, Fitzsimmons, the baseball star Cap Anson, and the footballer Red Waters. "Think of a regiment composed of magnificent men of this ilk! They would overawe any Spanish regiment by their mere appearance."[21] John L. was not mentioned.

As the century turned, he was still receiving benefits. In 1900 he was in the Garden again, the headliner of a boxing bill that included the newest rising star in the heavyweight ranks, Jim Jeffries. There were several new twists this time. A committee, chaired by New York Senator Timothy D. Sullivan, handled the whole thing. The management of the Garden agreed not to bill for the use of the hall, and the receipts were to be held in trust for Sullivan. His friends realized he had no fixed income (indeed, he had *never*, since his days as an apprentice tradesman, had a fixed income), and sought to provide him one through an interest-bearing account. Over five thousand showed up to watch John L. spar three quiet rounds with Jeffries, an ex-boilermaker of exceptional size and strength. The crowd was satisfied with their "very fat and gray" warhorse, and the fifteen thousand dollars in receipts provided Sullivan a small income for the rest of his life.[22]

His final benefit came in 1904, in Boston. Through it he received over three thousand dollars, but the precautions taken in New York were not repeated, and he ran through the money quickly.[23] By now interest in seeing a middle-aged man waddle about the ring for less than three minutes had flagged, even if his name was John L. Sullivan.

The other connection he had with his former craft was as a boxing referee, in which capacity he was unusual, to say the least. When refereeing fighters of lighter weight, he was still strong enough to hurl them apart from the clinches, and he was known to "carry" a losing fighter well beyond the point at which most referees would have stopped the bout, wanting, like the crowd, to see a decisive knockout. Thus he helped lightweight Lew Curley last eight rounds against Kid Herman in Saint Louis in 1904, before Curley finally won by a TKO. Crowds loved his thundering bass voice as he lumbered about the ring, yelling advice and admonitions at the fighters.[24]

But all of this—hobnobbing with boxing buddies, appearing at sporadic and somewhat humiliating benefits, occasional stints as a referee—was not a "living." Had this been all there was to his life, John L., despite his enormous continuing popularity, would have been no different from his fellows, simply another "broken-down fighter." But throughout it all he had another career, one that had been previewed in the years before the Corbett match. Sullivan was now, come what may, a creature of the "theater."

## III

Within days of his loss to Corbett, John L. was back on the stage, and for five of the next six theatrical seasons, until 1898, he would tour with a theatrical troupe. His initial vehicle was the play he had been rehearsing even as he prepared to meet the Dude. Entitled *The Man from Boston*, it had been written specially for Sullivan by a New York lawyer named Edmund E. Price. On September 19, 1892, John L. opened in Providence, playing a character named Captain Harcourt in a mishmash every bit as melodramatic as *Honest Hearts and Willing Hands* had been. The Rhode Islanders gave him deafening cheers and would not let the play go on until he made a short speech. The fourth act featured a boxing match with Jack Ashton. The audience loved it, and Sullivan took three encores. New Yorkers were more skeptical when the piece opened a month later at the Columbus Theater. One critic called it a "pretty poor play—Sullivan was all there was to it." The rich timbre of Sullivan's voice charmed the audience, although his clothes were the same strange mélange that had distinguished his blacksmith's outfit in the earlier play.[25]

*The Man from Boston* toured the East for the entire 1892–93 season. Sullivan at first proved a good draw, and the play was successful enough for him to tour with it a second time during the following theatrical year. He proclaimed that comedy rather than melodrama was his forte and that a comedy was being written for him. This turned out to be *The True American*, also written by Price, and in this presentation John L. toured during the 1894–95 season. Playing the hero, John Desmond, he had a love scene but admitted that he was "no good in that line." Corbett was also on tour during part of this period, starring in a play called *Gentleman Jack* written expressly for him (at the urging of William A. Brady) by a competent hack named Charles T. Vincent. *Gentleman Jack* was a smash throughout the United States, and the Dude, while no Barrymore, proved more sure of himself onstage than John L.[26]

*The True American*, perhaps because of a decline in Sullivan's drawing power, had a rocky financial road. The cast disbanded on January 3, 1895, in Paris, Illinois, but Sullivan got the wherewithal from somewhere, and they staggered on through the Midwest, playing Nebraska and Kansas. Despite his problems John L. was still outgoing, engaging in a railroad conversation with ex-Senator J. J. Ingalls of Kansas and leaving Ingalls a picture of himself. At last, late in February, the troupe ground to a halt in Jacksonville, Florida, completely out of funds. In fact, the Jacksonville stopover was a consummate disaster.[27]

John L. arrived in Jacksonville on February 21 with his brother, Mike, and the manager of the company, John J. Howard. That night, before a packed and noisy crowd, he appeared in *The True American* at the Opera House. After the performance he showed up at the Crystal Saloon, from which he departed several hours later—on roller skates. The next day his cast quit, wholesale. The members claimed they had not been paid for six weeks and griped that the star had stayed at the best hotels while they were put up in seedy boarding houses. A comedian, Bobby Mack, said that Sullivan was drinking every night. "John L. takes all the money that comes in and blows it." The cast members, men, women, and children alike, had had enough. They had done very poor business since the beginning of the year, and the ladies in particular declared themselves fed up with Sullivan's foul language and his lavish generosity with his drinking buddies. One, Viola Armstrong, had John L.'s two baggage trunks attached in lieu of the $130 she asserted was due her.[28]

In the midst of this disintegration, Sullivan took off for Saint Augustine, Florida, tracked by the headlines: "BOSTON BOY STILL BOOZES" and "SULLIVAN IS STILL DRUNK." There, he mournfully confessed to a loss of six thousand dollars with the play. E. D. Chandler, an enthusiastic Florida temperance leader, pleaded for John L. to tour with him; the bleary-eyed Sullivan said he would consider it. Back in Jacksonville he tried to get his trunks back, with no luck. Desperate, he wired Charley Johnston in New York City for money and got two hundred dollars. It was the first time, said Johnston, that John L. had borrowed from him.[29]

The shipwreck of *The True American* did not deter Sullivan from continuing on stage, but it made the Corbett benefit that summer doubly welcome. For the 1895–96 season John L. signed on with a play called *The Wicklow Postman*, but he appeared only in an exhibition sparring match after the final act. This play also was not without its problems. The authorities in both Philadelphia and Cleveland refused to give Sullivan permission to spar on stage, and John L. left the cast from time to time to go to benefits for other fighters. There was even one rumor that he would move to Chicago and run a big café.[30]

Whether because of lack of backing or of interest, Sullivan had no play for the 1896–97 season. The following year, however, he put together a group called the John L. Sullivan Comedy and Big Vaudeville Company. It was a variety troupe that included in its repertoire a one-act playlet, "A Trip across the Ocean," in which John L. played the leading role. Later, in 1901–2, like so many before him he had a brief fling with an *Uncle Tom's Cabin* company. In Sullivan's version Simon Legree (John L.) was the hero, beating up Tom in the climactic sequence. ("'Who owns your black body?' says I, sockin' him again.") Like *The True American*, this enterprise foundered on the financial rocks, but it was not helped much by John L.'s refusal to increase the salary of the hapless white actor who played Uncle Tom in blackface.[31]

His career in the theater at a standstill, Sullivan turned to vaudeville. These years before World War I were the golden age of American vaudeville, which had developed from its beginnings in the immediate post-Civil War period into an infinitely varied form of entertainment. The industry was knit together by numerous circuits, from the Great White Way to the tiniest tank town. Vaudeville bills offered a true theater of democracy. If patrons only waited long enough, they were bound to see something they had never seen before. Moreover, some vaudeville routines became so beloved they were performed, virtually without change, for decades. The only prerequisite for a vaudeville act, it seemed, was that it draw a crowd. Indeed some acts, like the notorious Cherry Sisters, were so bad that people paid to watch in stunned amazement.

But if one act was a bomb, never fear; in vaudeville there was something new every few minutes. A typical bill contained eight to twelve acts, and the stage was usually a whirligig of activity. Should Sullivan be able to put together an act of his own, his name alone might ensure an audience, and he would be freed of the onus of managing his own company, an enterprise for which he was, to put it mildly, not well-suited.

Sullivan first showed an interest in vaudeville in 1897. It was announced that he would join a company to tour the British Isles, the capital being furnished by an entrepreneur named Frank Dunn. The ex-champion was to appear in a scene from *The Man from Boston* and also, as in 1885, do some *poses plastiques*. Before leaving for Carson City for the Corbett-Fitzsimmons fight, he actually appeared at Miner's

Bowery Theater in Hoboken, posing as Greek and Roman statuary, but the group, at least with John L., never went overseas.[32]

After this nibble and the failure of his own company, he moved from Boston to New York, where he was living as the nation exploded in the nationalistic frenzy of the Spanish-American War. For the next four years he was in and out of the city, trying his hand at a welter of occupations. In 1899 he ran a saloon at 608 Sixth Avenue, just off Broadway at Herald Square Plaza. The opening rivaled that of his Washington Street place in Boston years before. People thronged the bar, everyone shaking his hand and calling him "John" or "John L." Paddy Ryan and Jim Corbett both showed up (John L.'s saloon was within two blocks of Corbett's). "Sullivan's waistcoat buttons fairly creaked," wrote one sardonic observer. The saloon was lush, decorated with oil paintings, mirrors, and frescoes, all cast in dazzling "incandescent lights." The huge oval mirror behind the mahogany bar was twenty-five feet long and five feet high. In the rear of the establishment, which also served meals, was a small garden covered by a portable canopy. Here John L. held court, spinning tales of Ireland, his father, and his adventures both in and out of the prize ring.[33]

This venture lasted only a few months; then the ex-champion began to "manage" another saloon. Sullivan, of course, was a front; he had no money to start such an enterprise. His name was all he provided, in addition to the Championship Belt, which was prominently exhibited. His partner, Thomas Allen, paid an artist named E. C. Danton $125 for a painting of the ex-champion to adorn the bar. Danton's likeness pleased neither Allen nor John L. Payment was not forthcoming, the artist sued, and the whole thing wound up in court. There, Sullivan grumbled that "I could paint a better portrait of myself with my feet than that fellow did." The upshot was that the place reserved for Sullivan's portrait was incongruously taken over by a picture of Saint Francis of Assisi. Sullivan remarked that if Saint Francis ever saw *his* picture, he would feel the same way John L. felt about Danton's effort.[34]

After this, he opened a third New York saloon, which also went under very quickly, and then he tried his hand as a whiskey drummer. In 1901 he could be found driving the streets of New York in a small green automobile, peddling barrels to saloons. Selling the stuff was not half the hard work of drinking it, he said. Later that year he worked as a bookmaker for a few days at the Sheepshead Bay race track but apparently took major losses. Besides, he had never cottoned to gambling and did not like being jostled by the crowd.[35]

During these years, when he was not glad-handing in his saloons, selling whiskey, or placing bets, he was on the road as a vaudeville performer. At first, he offered a sparring act. During the 1898–99 season, he conducted a forty-four-week national tour, which, he claimed, brought him about eight hundred dollars a week. If so, he spent it in his usual style. He still lived in the fast lane, and in Astoria, Oregon, some church people got a warrant for his arrest for boxing on Sunday. A forewarned Sullivan fled Fisher's Opera House, hid in the engine of his departing train, and was last seen at the throttle as the train pulled out for British Columbia. From the coast, he wrote a friend in Chicago that the tour was going fine, but "the trouble is, I am so lame with rheumatism that I can't get around to spend it." He must have conquered the rheumatism by the time the tour ended in Youngstown, Ohio. When his company split up, Sullivan owed most of them money; he himself had but $126 to his name—$126 at the end of a forty-four-week season! He gamely offered to split the sum with his fellow performers, but only two of them took him up on the offer.[36]

In 1902, after the demise of his *Uncle Tom* company, he returned to vaudeville full time, leaving his days of whiskey drumming and bookmaking behind him for good. He would still joyfully umpire baseball games, but beginning in that year most of his public appearances were on the vaudeville stage. This time, however, he resolved to use his natural talents as a raconteur and worked up a monologue. He opened on November 17 at the Empire in the national capital, giving a fifteen-minute talk on his ring experiences. John L. had a touch of stage fright, compensating by telling a number of stories in a "wheezy bellow." He had two gestures: tapping his chest when referring to himself, and shifting from one foot to the other. So hard did he concentrate in his early routines that even his admirers admitted their idol seemed "parrot-like." Still, he won the audience immediately with his opening line: "The rent falls due the first of every month, and the landlord won't wait."

So, there he stood, his ponderous bulk encased in a tuxedo, telling Irish jokes, jokes about his weight, and stories of his drinking. He swore he had been on the water wagon for two weeks (he would fall off, with a resounding crash, that very night) and offered what became a staple of his act, "A Toast to Women":

> There is no time, no place, no power,
> No land serene, no roseate bower,
> No heaven, no secret place of bliss,
> No baby's cheek, nor baby's kiss,
> That's grander, sweeter, purer than
> A Woman's love for thoughtless man!
> Then take your feet and raise your glass
> And drink to woman as a class,
> And know the worst that's gone astray
> Is better than he that paved the way.[37]

The response of the woman who still was his wife and still living in Providence, if indeed Annie Bates Bailey Sullivan ever heard "A Toast to Women," was not recorded.

For the next five years the monologue was his bread and butter. As the months passed, he gained confidence on the stage and proved a considerable attraction. He was often billed as the headliner, his picture prominent on the advertising posters. By now he resembled nothing so much as an overstuffed walrus; his weight at times reached 350 pounds. Yet on stage he developed into a physically imposing if not commanding figure. While he was never completely comfortable with the spoken word, he found he could entertain audiences. Early in 1905 he began to bill himself as a "lecturer," but the act was much the same.[38]

At his best, John L. would slowly walk from the wings to center stage, where he would plant both feet and not budge for the remainder of his routine. Clad in a full dress suit, replete with black tie, bat-wing collar, and cummerbund set off by a dazzling expense of ruffed white shirt, he would slip his left hand into a trouser pocket and use the once-lethal right for gestures. His hair was almost white now; this and his full mustache lent him an air of solid distinction. He spoke in a rapid-fire bass monotone, but had trouble with inflections; when he attempted Irish or Jewish dialect jokes, the results often were ludicrous. His standardized opening was:

> Ladies and gentlemen: If you will give me your attention for awhile, I will show you what I can do with a monologue. Monologue, according to Hoyle, I mean Shakespeare, means soliloquy, and soliloquy means talking to yourself. Now, as a rule, this is a very bad habit. They say that most monologists are bad, but I will try and prove myself the exception to the rule.

And off he would ramble, story after story, some of them stale but many, especially those connected with the bare-knuckle days, real crowd-pleasers. At the end, usually, he would depart to tremendous applause. With this simple act he played the nation—New England, the Midwest, the Far West and the South—into 1907.[39]

As he grew more relaxed on the stage, he became more personal and opinionated. In addition to the boxing stores and the jokes, audiences who heard Sullivan, occasional garbled syntax and all, would find out that smoking cigarettes was bad and football was dangerous. They would listen to John L.'s nostalgic tales of his youth, including specious accounts of his years as a "bricklayer." Sometimes he would offer up his version of Patrick Henry's "Give Me Liberty or Give Me Death" speech. On one occasion, a combined monologue-benefit for himself in Chicago, he spoke for more than two hours all told.[40]

Many critics panned his sometimes clumsy delivery and his frequent lapses of taste. But his hide by now was elephant-thick, both literally

26. John L. as a monologist (about 1905) (William Schutte Collection)

and metaphorically. Year after year he would spin his stories, enjoying the contact with people, the travel, the memories suddenly evoked with the news that John L. Sullivan was in town. Drunk or sober, he was seldom a disappointment for the confirmed fan, and on his good nights he could be positively enchanting.

## IV

Alas, not all his nights were good, or his days either. He lived recklessly, and his health varied accordingly. John L. often suffered from colds, and at times these veered dangerously close to pneumonia. In 1896 he had a malignant "cancer" (melanoma) in his right hand removed at Emergency Hospital in Boston. His doctor advised him to cut out his "bibulous habits," and for a time he was scared, sticking to cigars only.[41]

Four years later he was hospitalized again, this time in Polyclinic Hospital in New York for an operation on a strangulated hernia, still a somewhat dangerous procedure at the time. His doctors universally agreed that his condition was congenital but had been aggravated by drinking and carousing. Operating without either chloroform or ether, they opened an incision fifteen inches long and eleven inches deep, cured the problem, and found their patient's heart beating as strongly as ever. John L. ended up with 120 stitches, weeks of hospitalization, and a loss of twenty pounds. He blamed his ailment on his having eaten seven chickens inside of four hours and made his condition part of his vaudeville routine; he claimed that he now had part of a kangaroo's tail and some fiddle strings sewn into him.[42]

In 1904 Sullivan was stricken with eye problems. For a while he was confined to his sister's home in Roxbury and reduced to wearing green goggles. The specific nature of the illness is unknown, but his doctors temporarily feared for his sight, and in the process of recovery he sloughed off fifty pounds of fat. "The doctors," said John L., "say some sort of germs poisoned the optic nerves."[43]

Through it all his exceptional constitution enabled him to rebound time and again, and his natural good humor was his most important ally. As open and gregarious as always, he could be captivating if he so chose. Theodore Dreiser, then working as a young reporter for the *St. Louis Globe*, interviewed him shortly after the Corbett fight:

And then John L. Sullivan, raw, red-faced, big-fisted, broad-shouldered, drunken, with gaudy waistcoat and tie, and rings and pins set with enormous diamonds and rubies—what an impression he made! Surrounded by local sports and politicians of the most rubicund and degraded character (he was a great favorite with them), he seemed to me, sitting in his suite at the Lindell, to be the apotheosis of the humorously gross and vigorous and material. Cigar boxes, champagne buckets, decanters, beer bottles, overcoats, collars and shirts littered the floor, and lolling back in the midst of it all in ease and splendor his very great self, a sort of prizefighting J. P. Morgan.

He remained an easy and colorful interview ("Write any damned thing yuh please, young fella, and say that John L. Sullivan said so," he yelled to Dreiser), and many a young reporter overlooked his obvious flaws to marvel at his energy and obvious lust for life. "I adored him," Dreiser confessed, and "would have written anything he asked me to write."[44]

Of course, even he could not keep up such a pace—drinking, traveling, performing—indefinitely. He often made noises about retiring to a bucolic existence. In 1894 he negotiated for farmland in Massachusetts, dreaming of using it as a training site for boxers. Sometimes he gave out that his next tour would be his last, that he would pay off his debts and buy a farm. The Populist movement effected him strongly. He was incensed at the hardships he saw as he traveled through rural America and combined this with what he knew of urban poverty. Those with wealth were to blame: "millionaire is only another name for a dishonest man." If he had the money, he said, he would buy small farms and stock them with the poor from the cities, not establish libraries like Andrew Carnegie or endow universities like John D. Rockefeller. "Poor people can't eat libraries and universities." His vision of America as the nation entered the twentieth century was from the ground floor and class-based: "God made the country for poor people. Man made the towns for the rich." Eventually he would concede that things were getting better for farmers and workingmen, but he always resented the better sort and hated them for their neglect of the little guy.[45]

His concern for the underprivileged and dispossessed was as real and unfeigned as it had been during his freewheeling years of championship glory. He could be incredibly obstinate and selfish, as with his disgusted group of actors in Jacksonville, but more often he gave what he could, when he could. After his loss to Corbett he heard of a man in Providence who had wagered everything he had, including his house, on a Sullivan victory. John L. supposedly saved the poor devil's mortgage and, in the bargain, redeemed the man's wedding rings, watch, and his wife's jewelry from a pawnshop.[46] He was still the softest touch in town.

In turn he expected favors, and he shamelessly asked them of anyone he thought could help him. Sometimes these were for himself; he would scribble a promotional notice of his play or vaudeville act and mail it to an agent he thought could do him some good. More often, though, his requests were for others, some of these perhaps less than deserving. In 1900 he sought a pardon for his friend Eddie Wise, who had been convicted for the murder of a man named Beasley. Sullivan's strategy was to drink all day in a saloon opposite New York's Criminal Court Building with a lawyer named Abe Levy, whom John L. hoped would introduce him to an assistant district attorney, John McIntyre. During the marathon drinking bout Levy failed to convince Sullivan that DA's did not grant pardons. An increasingly sodden John L. kept sending off messengers for all the assistant DA's in turn. Ultimately Sullivan carried his crusade to City Hall, loudly demanding to see the mayor, before he was unceremoniously ushered out. Here was a part of the cult of masculinity that would not respond, and Eddie Wise remained firmly within the grip of the law. "I can see that there ain't no consideration for a public man in this town," Sullivan groused.[47]

Back in 1889 some of the Boston faithful had made noises about running Sullivan for the Fourth District's seat in Congress, and in 1897 Frank Dunn, who was promoting the ex-champion's initial vaudeville tour, announced that John L. would be an independent Democratic candidate for mayor of Boston. Dunn said he would present Sullivan's name to the ward caucuses, but this was complete hyperbole.[48] John L.'s pattern of friendships was woven into the lower levels of ward politics in both Boston and New York, but he had no real interest in a politician's life for himself.

He did, however, make one true friend among the heavyweights in the political arena during these years. Sullivan may have met Theodore Roosevelt in the mid-1890s, when the exuberant patrician was prowling the streets of New York as police commissioner, hunting for miscreant patrolmen. Certainly the two came to know and admire each other after TR triumphantly (and noisily) returned from Cuba and embarked on his two-year term as governor of New York. They had much in common: each worshipped at the shrine of masculinity and had, in his different way, been a missionary of the strenuous life; each was his own brass band. TR cultivated friendships with the likes of Mike Donovan, Battling Nelson, and Bob Fitzsimmons and would continue sparring for exercise in the White House even after an eye injury should have slowed him down. Sullivan, in later years, would become a frequent guest at Sagamore Hill, and Roosevelt, a bit of a prude in his private life, would excuse his pal's ruder habits because of John L.'s ingenuous good nature. For his part Sullivan made an exception in his lifelong rule of supporting the Democracy. He often trumpeted TR's virtues to whoever would listen and may even have voted for Roosevelt in 1904. There were some boundaries, however, that even TR could not cross. When, as president, he issued his controversial invitation to the black leader Booker T. Washington for dinner at the White House, Sullivan commented that the two men would better have dined together at some restaurant.[49]

Undercutting many of his friendships and contributing to his physical ailments was the booze, always the booze. His alcoholism was in full stride now; after each spree he would swear he was giving it up, but he always returned to the bottle. It was an old pattern, noticed by an English boxing writer almost a century before:

> No men are subject more to the caprice or changes of fortune than the pugilists; *victory* brings them fame, riches, and patrons; their bruises are not heeded in the smiles of success; and basking in the sun-shine of prosperity, their lives pass on pleasantly, till *defeat* comes and reverses the scene: covered with aches and pains, distressed in mind and body, assailed by poverty, wretchedness, and misery,—friends forsake them—their towering fame expired—their characters suspected by losing—and no longer the "*plaything of fashion!*" they fly to inebriation for relief, and a premature end puts a period to their misfortunes.[50]

In his "retirement" Sullivan was doing better than any prizefighter had done before him. His fame persisted, he could still make respectable amounts of money, and he was, if he could curb his habits, reasonably assured of a placid, comfortable old age. But he was never far from a saloon, and his drunkenness was as public as it had ever been. There is a story, uncorroborated, of the famous temperance crusader Carry Nation's descending on New York at the height of her fame, at a time when Sullivan and Allen's saloon was going full bore. "If that old woman ever comes around to my place," John L. boasted, "I'll throw her down the sewer." The story that the formidable Mrs. Nation, accompanied by an army of reporters, went to the saloon, sent in her card, and was refused admittance by Sullivan was probably untrue. She mentioned nothing of such an incident in her autobiography, although such a duel of the titans would have made interesting reading. The two unlikely foes did, however, appear in a New York vaudeville theater only a week apart—truly a theater of democracy![51]

It was the natural right of everyone, declared Sullivan, to take a drink, yet he often vacillated on the temperance issue. During his hangovers he usually and shamefacedly maintained that he was dry, once bragging that he had not had a drink in five months. At times he blamed alcohol for his defeat by Corbett, and he sometimes even granted that he was a slave to drink. He might ostentatiously devote himself to seltzer water for a while, but always he started again. It was obvious to all, when he showed up stewed to the gills for the Kilrain-O'Donnell fight, that his alcoholism had not vanished with the championship. On that occasion he continued his loud behavior in the dining room of a nearby hotel after the bout, leading a witness to remark that the ex-champion was "a fit applicant for a bed in an inebriate's home."

This behavior was repeated, over and over, for years. As his true friends dwindled in number, either dead or driven away by his excesses, John L. moved through rapid cycles of despair and self-pity, each aggravated by drink. At last it came to the point where only glad-handers were willing to hoist a glass with him. On one New York binge he almost tore the nose off an unoffensive guest at the Vanderbilt Hotel and then moved on to the Metropole, where he was so boisterous he had to be ejected. These escapades prompted a once-friendly sports-writer to say that "he is simply a big foul mouthed, ignorant loafer, who works at nothing but making himself a nuisance. He *prefers to be* a miserable hulk and should be put away. He's no good and he has hurt pugilism irreparably."[52]

Because his drinking was done mostly in public, the reports of his latest rampage graced the press wires every few months or so. On occasion, his carousing even landed him on the front page, as it did in Detroit late in 1902. In that instance he was in town as part of a vaudeville tour. John L. appeared on the bill at the Avenue Theater with the actor Charles Dickson, the cartoonist Thomas Nast, Jr. (son of the famous Nast), "Little Elsie," an acrobatic act called the Five St. Leons, and a Japanese juggler named Satauma. At the Tuesday matinee, "looking very much like a fat man in a dime museum," he came out dead drunk to do his monologue. Slurring his words, he almost fell through the curtained backdrop. He called himself a sucker and made as if to throw money to the crowd. Stage hands grabbed him and tried to lead him from the stage. He fought them off but was eventually coaxed by Ben Harris, the manager of the tour, to go back to the Oriental Hotel. There he embarked on a monumental jag that ended with the police dragging him from the Russell House Café on Wednesday afternoon. Jailed for eight hours, he emerged chastened and contrite, promising to sign the pledge and carry out the remaining twenty-five weeks of the tour as booked. Harris, who was paying John L. three hundred dollars weekly, was understandably upset. As for the management of the Avenue Theater, it acted quickly and replaced Sullivan on the bill with "Mlle. Belle Monroso-Sigourney," a violinist.[53]

He knew that he was continually disgracing himself, of course. The incident in Detroit indicated his self-contempt and loathing at having to buy his popularity with drinks for other people. His was the common treadmill of the alcoholic, but it was compounded by the publicity and by his undoubted talent for involving himself in scrapes that inevitably caught the attention of the press. In addition, the temperance tide was rolling strongly again. Across the Midwest states were beginning to go dry, the first signs of the mighty moral wave that would eventually produce nationwide Prohibition. The issue of booze was thus more and more newsworthy, and Sullivan remained temperance enemy number one. In fact, he had become a highly convenient exemplar— the National Souse.

## V

Sullivan's alcoholism led him into disaster after disaster, financially, physically, and in what today would be called "public relations." Indeed, in this last category he displayed a negative talent that was almost as extraordinary as his prize-ring career itself. A few illustrations must suffice.

In May 1893 John L. and a few buddies in *The Man from Boston* company were railroading through Maine. A local lawyer, Max L. Lizotte, was traveling in the same sleeping car and somehow aroused Sullivan's wrath. John L. kicked him in the groin, the two men grappled, and as they separated, one of the ex-champion's cronies smashed the lawyer in the face, cutting his lip and giving him a bloody nose. Not satisfied at this, John L. lunged at Lizotte again, choking him hard enough to leave fingerprints on his throat. Two days later a grand jury in Alfred, Maine, indicted Sullivan for assault and battery, and Lizotte sued for $5,000. John L. settled for a lesser sum, $500, in time to catch the evening train for Portland, but the incident was national news: Max Lizotte had only one arm, and the spectacle of the ex-champion pummeling a one-armed man was scarcely edifying. Beating up Lizotte, with the settlement and legal fees, cost Sullivan $1,200.[54]

The next year John L. slugged a cabbie outside the Coleman House on Broadway, after which he fell to the sidewalk himself in a drunken stupor. Friends had to cart him to his hotel. Two years later, in Boston, he was out walking a large mastiff belonging to his brother-in-law, James Lennon. Always fond of animals, Sullivan sought to board a Meeting House Hill streetcar with the dog in tow. When the conductor, William Humphrey, told him to get off, John L. knocked him down. The rumpus took place right in front of Police Station Number Nine, in which Sullivan was immediately booked. The upshot was a fine of twenty-five dollars for assaulting a public official in the performance of his duty.[55]

One-armed lawyers, cabmen, and streetcar conductors were bad enough, but Sullivan also had the capacity to inflict injury on himself when no one else was around. The most spectacular instance occurred early in 1896 as he was touring through Illinois with the cast of *The Wicklow Postman*. As his Rock Island and Pacific train rambled along at forty miles an hour between the hamlets of Lafayette and Galva, John L. felt the urge to urinate. Finding the toilet occupied, he lurched onto the rear platform of his car to relieve himself; in the process he tumbled off the train. It was near midnight. He was not missed for several minutes, after which the train was backed up for four miles. At last they came across his 270-pound bulk, face-down and unconscious, covered with blood and ground-in gravel. As an added touch, his clothes were on fire, caused by the ignition of matches in his vest pocket. He had an eight-inch gash in the back of the head, and his face was a mess. All in all, he was lucky to be alive.

Sullivan was carried to the Palace Hotel in Springfield, where the lobby quickly filled with admirers and well-wishers. In his room he recuperated for a week, tended by a woman in the cast whom he fobbed off on reporters as "Mrs. Sullivan." Paddy Ryan, his sparring partner in the play, also stayed for a time, but eventually the play went on its way. John L., fighting off erysipelas, eventually rejoined the cast in Texas in early February, stitches out and none the worse for wear.[56]

In each of these incidents Sullivan was drunk or had been drinking heavily. Not surprisingly, alcoholism speeded up the flow of money through his hands. Despite the benefits and the theatrical appearances, he was usually in one of two conditions, in debt or bankrupt. Late in 1896 he appeared in debtor's court in Boston, having run up a bill of $318 with a local florist. An officer had gone to Sullivan's Roxbury home with a writ of attachment, but he had not found enough property to satisfy even this small claim, only, he said, a poker chip. Where had all the money gone? the lawyers asked John L. Neatly dressed and smooth-shaven, the ex-champion frankly answered that he did not know, but he promised to make restitution.[57]

It was a harbinger of things to come. Creditors hounded him constantly, and in 1897 he barely escaped the public ignominy of taking the poor debtor's oath in Boston, having come to an agreement with his pursuers to settle a mass of cases out of court. But nothing changed his spendthrift ways. Following his move to New York, the Anheuser-Busch Brewing Company hauled him into court for nonpayment of a sixteen-hundred-dollar beer bill for his first saloon. On the witness stand he claimed he had been double-crossed by the brewer's agent and blamed everyone, in fact, but himself. And, he said, he was broke.[58]

Forced by bankruptcy to close his Sixth Avenue saloon in New York, John L. moved over to Thomas Allen's establishment at 1177 Broadway. His duties, his lawyer later said, were to "sit around, drink with those who asked him and give them a friendly greeting." Early in 1900 he contracted with Allen's oddly named Dante's Inferno Exhibition Company to manage the saloon for 50 percent of the net earnings. In April he donated his prized possession, the Championship Belt, to Allen for exhibit in the saloon, and the owner faithfully secured the treasure in the safe every night. Inevitably, the two men quarreled, to the extent that Sullivan was locked up for a day for disturbing the peace. Allen argued that John L. owed thirty-one hundred dollars to Dante's Inferno and kept the belt as surety, vowing that Sullivan had given it to him.

They ended up in court. Sullivan's lawyer, James F. Mack, wanted the belt back, and Allen reluctantly surrendered it. Sullivan immediately opened a new (and short-lived) saloon on West Forty-second Street, where the prize was exhibited. But this was not the end. The two struggled for months, John L. asserting that his presence in Allen's establishment had raised receipts from $2,000 to $6,000 a month. He claimed that during his time at Allen's the place made $48,000, of which he had received nothing. Allen sold the business in October 1900 for $14,000, and John L. sued for $7,000.[59] Apparently, apart from the belt, he received nothing.

The West Forty-second Street saloon was a partnership with "Brooklyn Jimmy" Carroll, the man who had taken him to Polyclinic Hospital for the hernia operation. In the summer of 1901 this enterprise was attached for debt. In the process, the Championship Belt was lost. John L. managed to reclaim his prize, still studded with diamonds and rubies, but two years later he was forced to pawn it for $1,800. Late in the year the belt was sold at a pawnbroker's auction for $2,900. It was Sullivan, not the belt, whom the *National Police Gazette* now called a "pitiful relic."[60]

A pitiful relic, indeed. In November 1902 his attorney, Mack, filed a petition of bankruptcy in New York's District Court on behalf of his client. The ex-champion owed $450 on five notes in Boston, but Mack did not file in Massachusetts because that state had a law on the books that said a nonresident debtor could be imprisoned until the debt was paid, if the commonwealth could but get its hands on him. Sullivan was still earning money (his theatrical troupe was playing Washington, D.C., and Pittsburgh), but he owed too much. There was the still-outstanding debt to Anheuser-Busch; over $500 to Julius Palmer and Company, and $150 to a Park Avenue resident named Charles H. Stevens—a grand total of $2,658.78. Sullivan claimed as assets "wearing apparel valued at $60": the shirt on his back. The petition, humiliating as it might seem, actually was a device to allow John L. to perform in Boston. With a certified copy of the order of adjudication in bankruptcy in hand, his Boston creditor, J. H. Lewis, could not touch him, nor could the law. "It is the last straw that breaks the camel's back," sniffed one editor. "Popular adulation of the great can't stand everything."[61]

So now he was a bankrupt before the public. Even though his case eventually was discharged in February 1903 (his creditors receiving very little), he had reached financial bottom. One source estimated, with a suspicious amount of precision, that John L. had made, to 1903, the sum of $783,350 all told.[62] Whatever the amount, he lived from pillar to post, using legal strategems to avoid creditors while boozing and brawling his way around the nation, just as he had done in his youth. Nothing, it seemed, could change him or force him to mend his ways.

## VI

In the late winter of 1905 he found himself in Grand Rapids, Michigan, almost broke, friendless in the midst of "friends," suspicious, alienated, and alone. John L. was talking wildly of challenging Corbett (he was forty-six now, the Dude thirty-eight) or gathering a ten-thousand-dollar purse to fight the now-dethroned Fitzsimmons, this last a weird match that momentarily interested, as sponsors, the proprietors of the Arcade Hotel in Guthrie, Oklahoma. In the midst of the rodomontade, someone (perhaps Sullivan) wired money to Hot Springs, Arkansas, summoning a young fighter named Jim McCormick to come north and box with John L.

McCormick was from Galveston and no patsy. After turning pro he had produced a victorious ring record. Usually fighting at just under 200 pounds, he had been training in Hot Springs for a match with Kid McCoy. The news that Sullivan, unbelievably, would enter the ring again in earnest created a local sensation. On the night of March 1 the two met for a scheduled four-round "exhibition" at Smith's Opera House. The contrast was absurd; McCormick, in his mid-twenties, was a reasonably conditioned fighter, while John L., almost twice his age, was whale-fat at 273 pounds, his age exaggerated not only by his girth but also by his gray hair and heavy jowls.

Several exchanges marked the first round, at the end of which both men were breathing heavily. John L. had no tactics but to slog toward his smaller opponent, swinging ponderous haymakers right and left. At 1:23 of the second round one of them landed on McCormick's jaw, blasting him down in a neutral corner and rendering him unconscious for five minutes. The spectators responded as if watching some phoenix arise from the dead. They broke into wild, sustained applause, breaking chairs and furniture in the orchestra pit in an effort to congratulate Sullivan. John L. responded with one of his short, graceful speeches, making his old offer of one hundred dollars to anyone who could stay four rounds with him, and as a coda he challenged Jeffries, Fitzsimmons, and the entire world.

The next day a local pugilist named Kid Jackson challenged John L. As the Kid weighed only 115 pounds, Sullivan refused. Instead, he and McCormick later embarked on a short sparring tour. Many across the nation thought that their fight had been a put-up job, but Mc-

Cormick, for one, never did. Jim admitted that Sullivan was definitely "out of shape" (which he had been, spectacularly, for almost thirteen years) but said that he had been knocked out by a heavy hitter.[63]

What caused this sudden spate of ring activity—Sullivan had planned to fight a Canadian boxer named John W. Phillips and had substituted McCormick at the last minute—is anyone's guess. At any rate, it was the old bull's final bellow. For one moment, one last time, he had felt the exultation of triumph and heard the cheers of fight fans. It may have been a farce to some, but for John L. his night with young Jim McCormick became a fondly remembered Indian summer.

# CHAPTER FOURTEEN

# Rebirth: "I Have Seen It All"
# (1905—1918)

Sudden conversions in life-style or belief are rare, Saint Paul to the contrary, and for the historian the ability to precisely date such changes is rarer still. But in the late winter of 1905 John L. Sullivan underwent such a conversion, and it altered his life.

In later years John L. was quite specific about what had happened, and while he was never one to forgo the trappings on a good story, the outlines are clear. Immediately following his bout with Jim McCormick in Grand Rapids, he headed down to Terre Haute, Indiana. As usual, he was drinking incessantly, and in fact he had been forced to cancel several scheduled appearances in Michigan because of the bottle. At his second performance in Terre Haute he had to be helped onto the stage, where he mumbled his way incoherently through his monologue until the curtain was mercifully lowered. Bundled back to his hotel, he slept until noon the next day.

It was Saturday, March 5, 1905. Sullivan strolled into the hotel bar and ordered champagne. While he was waiting, as he later told the yarn, he ruminated on the amount of money he had spent on booze and high living, coming up with the astronomical figure of $500,000 "to pay for the privilege of being known around saloons as a good fellow." The champagne arrived. John L., while not regretting a dime of the money thus spent, took his glass and dramatically emptied it into a spittoon, proclaiming (so he said), "If I ever take another drink as long as I live I hope to God I choke!"[1]

Thus the convert's tale. However it happened, he had reached a momentous decision. He had gone dry before, literally dozens of times, but in this instance he kept his promise. Although his motives remain a matter of speculation, two events probably played a part. First, as ludicrous as the McCormick fight had seemed to many, in his own mind it had done much to erase the heartache of his thumping at the hands of Corbett. Grand Rapids had been a suitable envoi; it gave him the chance to go out a winner. Second, John L.'s particular road to Damascus coincided exactly with the inauguration of his friend Theodore Roosevelt as president in his own right. It seemed time for a fresh start.[2]

What this vow cost him only he knew, but he kept to it for the remaining years of his life. He may have sneaked a drink now and then, but from this point on, the brawls, assaults, and arrests vanish from the record. In the very best sense of the term he mellowed, in the process recapturing much of the charm and innocence that had characterized his occasional moments of sobriety. Like so many reclaimed sinners, he became a proselyte, adding yet another arrow to his quiver. In the autumn of his days he was, among other things, a temperance lecturer.

# I

About the time he made the second crucial decision of his life (the first had been to become a prizefighter), John L. acquired a new manager, Frank Hall. Hall, a Chicagoan, was an experienced entrepreneur. He had owned or managed three prosperous enterprises: the Mystic Maze, the Winter Circus, and the Eden Musée and Minstrel Show. Sullivan's record with his business associates, ever since he and Billy Madden had gone to New York in 1881, had been an abysmal one, marked on John L.'s part by suspicions, recriminations, and bitter partings. Hall, however, profited by his partner's newfound teetotalism. The two men got along splendidly and would be together for eight years. Hall skillfully managed the ex-champion's bookings, and John L. was seldom idle. In the winter he played vaudeville dates, alternating his old fight-game monologue with a temperance speech that featured vivid examples of his own tippling and carousing. In the summer he appeared at fairs, circuses, carnivals, and civic promotions.[3]

For the summer tours Sullivan and Hall added Jake Kilrain, and the two aging bare-knucklers sparred their way across the tank towns of the land in an endless diptych of their legendary fight on the Mississippi plain. Sullivan was not loath to drum up business for himself. "Undoubtedly," he wrote one showman, "our exhibition is the best Box Office attraction in America." He and Kilrain were willing to box anywhere, open air or enclosed, stage or gymnasium. The sight of the two grizzled gladiators would draw a crowd. Then John L. would deliver his monologue, usually for ten to fifty cents a head. Sometimes they would close by showing still-novel fight films, charging admission to them, as well. Sullivan now displayed a sharp interest in profits, and he made money—nothing near the fifty thousand dollars a year that was credited to Hall and him by one source, but a comfortable living, usually in the vicinity of one hundred dollars a week. Jake did not make as much ("It costs money to carry Kilrain," John L. once grumbled), but it was a living.[4]

One example of the milieu of their act will suffice. In the fall of 1909 they bobbed up in Pierre, South Dakota, drawn by something called the Third Gas Belt Exhibition. Pierre, like so many new western towns, was awash in self-confidence and civic pride, but this little community nestled on the banks of the Missouri River was, unlike so many of its compatriots, a success story. It had enticed the Chicago and North-western as a railhead years before. Only recently it had begun the erection of a neoclassical capital building, symbol of victory in another bitter struggle with other South Dakota towns. The local boosters and promoters, flush with these triumphs, were now convinced that they were sitting atop a huge deposit of natural gas—hence, their "exhibition."

Sullivan and Kilrain performed twice daily for a week, before men and women alike, in a tent set up on Pierre Street. They were not the entire program (they seldom were), but they drew large crowds. After each performance people stayed on the main thoroughfare to watch a Wild West show and a reproduction of Custer's Last Stand featuring Sioux Indians carted in from the Lower Brule Reservation. Folks in Pierre seldom thought small.[5]

And so it went, a peregrination through the American hinterland that lasted for years. John L. loved it. He was still a celebrity, a "public man." In the cities and the sticks alike his autograph was still sought, and the bold, slashing "Yours truly, John L. Sullivan" adorned greeting cards, envelopes, programs, and school notebooks across the country. Hotels remained his homes, but now he consciously and loudly avoided saloons, with more than a trace of self-satisfaction.

Sullivan's connection with the world of pugilism grew more tenuous, although he was always called on for comment whenever a key heavy-weight match was in the offing. In the year of John L.'s conversion, 1905, Jim Jeffries relinquished the title he had won from Bob Fitzsim-mons in 1899, tired of the ring and unable to find an opponent of his caliber. The crown passed to a Kentuckian named Marvin Hart, who defeated Jack Root in Reno with Jeffries refereeing. Within a year the lackluster Hart was decisioned by the French-Canadian Tommy Burns (Noah Brusso), who then embarked on a worldwide flight of almost three years to keep out of the range of the clear class of the heavy-weights, Jack Johnson. The man from Galveston finally caught up with the diminutive Burns in Sydney, Australia, and there, on December 26, 1908, he demolished the champion in fourteen rounds to win the title.

That a black man was now champion was a fact not lost on Sullivan. He had refused to fight Peter Jackson, and despite later disclaimers by his friend Jimmy Wakely that John L. was no racist, he was steadfast in holding to the color line he had first drawn back in the 1880s. In fact, Sullivan played a major role in the race baiting that accompanied the search for a Great White Hope to rid the boxing world of the sassy, talented Johnson. John L. criticized Burns (who, after all, had fled about as far as he could) for even stepping into the ring with a black fighter, calling Tommy money-mad and a "man who upsets good American precedents." Sullivan was far from the only sporting figure trumpeting racial purity in the wake of Johnson's triumph (Corbett also said he would favor a white man over a Negro), but he certainly was in the vanguard.[6]

In early 1909 John L. announced that he was the front man for a syndicate willing to put up seventy-five thousand dollars for a Jeffries-Johnson fight. Despite having been on the shelf for four years, the big boilermaker seemed the best bet against the agile, powerful champion. The only problem was Jeffries himself, grossly overweight and living contentedly on his California farm. If Jeffries would not re-enter the ring, said John L., "I will find somebody." After much coaxing and appeals to his white manhood, Jim at last consented to be the latest Great White Hope (Johnson by now had defended his title once, against scrappy Stanley Ketchel, whom he knocked out in twelve rounds). The ultimate contract had no connection with Sullivan.

John L. quickly signed a contract of his own with the *New York Times* to report on the coming battle. To him, the match was emblematic of race war. As he saw it, Johnson's symbolic importance served to drive the races further apart. "I know that when Stanley Ketchel fought Jack Johnson all the negroes in the South absolutely refused to work and tied up the steamboats, and the colored freemen refused to run the trains in several of the Southern States." The mixing of races in the ring was unnatural: "I do believe the negroes should fight in a class by themselves." However, he knew it would take an exceptionally strong effort to beat Johnson, who was far and away the best big fighter of his era. "Of course we shall all like to see the white man win," said John L., "but wishes can never fill a sack."[7]

The *Times* puffed its agreement with the ex-champion, defensively noting that his English was as fluent as the average man's, if not a bit better. In mid-June 1910 Sullivan and some pals headed west on the Pacific Coast Express. Of course, the paper had taken the precaution of sending some *real* reporters along, and they were kept busy filing dispatches as the chartered car rolled toward Reno, which had been selected as the fight locale after much acrimonious debate on all sides. John L. got a big welcome in Chicago and delivered opinions on Jeffries, the boxer Joe Gans (too bad about his consumption), and a pilot named Hamilton, who recently had made a daredevil round trip flight from New York to Philadelphia and back ("My hat's off to him, but terra firma for yours truly, John L.").[8]

He was not writing a word, but by the time the train rolled into Reno, the reporters had hit on the expedient of listening to his numerous remarks, writing them up in his bluff, hurry-on style and wiring them back under his byline. Thus readers of the *Times* were treated to a barrage of Sullivan "writings" from the scene. The brouhaha surrounding the fight was exceptional, even for a heavyweight championship bout, and John L. stepped right into the middle of it, slinging unsolicited opinions right and left. When the contest appeared in doubt, he was quoted as saying that "it does seem that with the enlightenment of civilization . . . there ought to be some more definite purpose about affairs of this sort." The only problem with the fight, he joked, was that "there is a 'nigger in the woodpile somewhere.' " Back in New York the editors of the *Times* felt obliged to defend their "reporter" against readers who charged that John L. had been employed to report on a "criminal proceeding." Somewhat lamely, they claimed the hiring of Sullivan "was merely the getting of a particularly competent man to do the work from the standpoint of an acknowledged expert. What he writes is having and will have both evidential and psychological value."[9]

Sullivan was not merely racist; he believed that Johnson, as champion, had inaugurated a decline in public appreciation of his beloved sport. Johnson, for his part, took John L. lightly enough, noting later only that Sullivan, "whose name stands out boldly in world fight records," had attended the Reno fight. As the day of the match drew near, John L., with little to do but deliver himself of pronouncements, became a bit of a nuisance. Articles appeared under his byline belittling Jeffries (who was indeed overweight and sluggish) and hinting that Johnson was about to take a dive. Corbett, in Jeffries's camp, told Sullivan that he was not welcome there, and the two former antagonists almost came to blows before William Muldoon smoothed it over.[10]

John L. was near the ring on July 4, 1910, part of a sun-drenched throng of twenty thousand people who had come from all over the nation to see the most widely ballyhooed fight since Sullivan and Corbett. Sullivan, hoping for flashes of the old Jeffries, saw only a sad image of himself back in 1892, a man who should never have entered the ring against a boxer at the height of his powers. Only three years in age separated the two, but Johnson was the master from the start, smiling at his lumbering, quickly exhausted opponent and taunting him throughout. It lasted fifteen one-sided rounds before Jeffries's seconds threw in the sponge.

Sullivan's byline was given page one of the *Times* the next day. The fight articles were completely ghostwritten, but the reporters took time to get the ex-champion's opinions. John L. freely admitted his "well-known antipathy to his [Johnson's] race." Still, he (unlike many other Americans) gave Johnson his due. The champion spoke in a fistic language Sullivan understood. Johnson, indeed, was one of the great heavyweights, a man who, if he had been able to discipline his own life-style and had not been hounded by white authorities, might have been even greater. In his capacity for excess, as well as his dominance of his boxing generation, Jack Johnson evoked memories of the young John L. To his credit, Sullivan at least glimpsed the similarity, and after Reno he disappeared from the forefront of the race baiting surrounding Johnson. John L., reluctantly to be sure, had been convinced on his own terms.[11]

All in all the trip to Reno was a grand outing, once again bringing Sullivan into the reflected sunlight of the boxing world. For weeks he had matched stories with old friends and had once more blustered away against ancient enemies. An excellent national newspaper had given him the chance to "comment" on the cultural importance of the fight itself. And, during the journey to Reno, everyone had had an opportunity to inspect yet another major change in his life, the second Mrs. John L. Sullivan.

## II

To describe a man such as Sullivan, with his myriad friends and acquaintances, as "lonely" during his years of "retirement" seems implausible. He was usually seen in groups or crowds, making it difficult to visualize him alone. Most Americans forgot that John L. had, to all intents, been a bachelor for most of his life.

But more and more the inevitable isolation of the traveling life was taking its toll. Never a religious man in practice, he had always tried to honor (mostly in the breach) the precepts of his church. Now he talked with priests and prelates more frequently than ever, including the eminent James Cardinal Gibbons of Baltimore, with whom he shared Irish stories for half an hour (the cardinal proved a little shaky on his sports, telling John L. that there was a local man named Jake Kilrain who had once been a boxer and asking if Sullivan knew him). And John L. began to pay more attention to the idea of family.[12]

For his own extended family, he would go the distance. He proved this in 1907 with John L. Lennon, the son of his sister, Ann. Young Lennon had enlisted in the Marine Corps and gone AWOL; he was convicted by court-martial of desertion and sentenced to a dishonorable discharge and one year's hard labor. Sullivan went right to the top. On April 2 he dashed off a letter to TR pleading his nephew's case, and the president promised to look into it. John L. also wrote the secretary of war, William Howard Taft, and visited the White House at least twice in early May to press the issue. As Roosevelt remembered it, Sullivan was greatly ashamed and hoped no disgrace would befall the family; the deserter should get "all that was coming to him." He had never understood the boy, said John L. "He was my sister's favorite son. . . . But there was just nothing to be done with him. His tastes were naturally low. He took to music!"[13]

TR stood by his "old and valued friend." John L. insisted that Private Lennon had merely overstayed his leave by three days, and the president agreed that the punishment was too severe. On May 16 he ordered Lennon pardoned, on condition that he reenlist and serve out his term. Press comment was sardonic, on two points. First, while no one questioned the executive's power to pardon Lennon, there was doubt over the legality of reenlisting a man who had been dishonorably discharged. Critics charged this could be done only by an act of Congress. Second, the Lennon pardon occurred in the wake of the notorious Brownsville Incident, in which Roosevelt had supported the dishonorable discharge of 167 black soldiers of the Twenty-fifth Infantry under conditions that were grossly unfair to the men. Yet here was a young scapegrace, obviously guilty, who was being readmitted to the full privileges of the uniform.[14]

John L. had made an end run around the system. But in his America this was how things were done: cut a deal, or get support from the man best placed to do so. On Roosevelt's part, the Lennon case was a minor favor for a friend. Sullivan was not the only boxer the president helped, and some of the pugilists, like Mike Donovan, would eventually follow him into Progressivism. Friends helped friends, did they not?[15]

The pardon fracas passed quickly, and Sullivan could feel that his family honor was intact. The incident sealed his friendship with Roosevelt. From this time onward John L. would fire off letters to TR on the spur of the moment, sending along clippings, songs, and, in one instance, a lucky rabbit's foot that TR carried along on his postpresidential African expedition. It was not a one-sided correspondence; Roosevelt always replied, his letters posting off to hotels in Philadelphia, New York, San Diego, and Hot Springs, Arkansas. TR, while somewhat bemused, was consistently friendly and issued many invitations to the White House and, later, Sagamore Hill. For Sullivan it became the one firm male bond of his later years. "I am your guard of honor in every country," he wrote TR after the failure of the Bull Moose campaign in 1912. "No one can say aught against you and get away with it when I am around. Just keep that part of my friendship sealed-up in your inside vest pocket."[16]

Clearly, the need for close human companionship was more and more paramount with him as the years passed. Possibly, some of his conversations with churchmen concerned the problem of divorce. He and his wife had lived apart for almost a quarter of a century when, in 1908, he at last took the step forbidden by his religion. In December he sued for divorce in Chicago on the ground of desertion. Annie Bates Bailey Sullivan, still living quietly in Rhode Island, did not contest the suit, although she was concerned over the unfounded rumor that her husband would charge infidelity. It was the legal end of a marriage that had long since been dead.[17]

This ultimate step was propelled by his increasingly close friendship with a longtime acquaintance, Katherine Harkins of Roxbury. The two had known each other since childhood, although stories of an early romance were grossly inflated. Kate, a tall, striking brunette, was six years younger than John L. She was the daughter of Dennis Harkins and Mary Doherty, both natives of County Derry in Ireland. Unlike Sullivan's father, Dennis had done fairly well in the New World, leaving his daughter real estate holdings in Sharon, Massachusetts. Kate, who had never married, lived comfortably on this income, although she was far from the wealthy spinster some of the press made her out to be.

Sullivan had been "keeping company" with Kate ever since his sobriety, whenever his schedule allowed. At last she was convinced that he had mended his ways, and with the divorce issue settled, the two were married in a civil ceremony at the bride's sister's home in Boston on February 7, 1910. John L. listed his occupation as "lecturer," and Kate gave none. Frank Hall stood in as best man. Sullivan, faultlessly attired in a new, well-fitting suit, carried his second nuptials off beautifully. The Boston papers all covered the simple service, except for the *Evening Transcript*, which was given to publishing an entire page of blue-blooded genealogical items every Monday and Wednesday. John L. had never really cracked the pages of this stiff-lipped sheet, and he never would.[18]

Kate was attired in traveling clothes for her wedding; within hours the newlyweds were off to England aboard the Cunard liner *Ivernia*. Frank Hall and Jake Kilrain went along as well. It was to be a combination honeymoon and money-making tour of the British Isles. For three months they toured England and Scotland with their act, a period saddened by the death of John L.'s old admirer, the Prince of Wales— Edward VII for the past nine years. The final week of their trip was passed in Ireland. It was Sullivan's second and final trip to the land of his forefathers. Despite the national mourning occasioned by the

27. John L. and Kate as they departed for Europe (1910) (William Schutte Collection)

king's death, they played two-a-days to thousands of people a week. John L. was still a draw.[19]

In late May they were home again, Sullivan making only a short theatrical engagement before he and Kate were off to Reno for the Jeffries-Johnson fight. By now the pattern of their lives together was established. An imposing yet friendly woman, Kate was wise enough to give her convivial husband leeway when he was with his cronies. But she accompanied him on many of his trips, and for the six years of their life together she watched steadily over his finances. More importantly, she gave him a home of his own and the dependable companionship he had wanted for so long. After years alone in the storm, John L. at last had reached safe haven.

## III

The Sullivans set up house in a small but comfortable clapboard and brick cottage situated on a speck of farmland in West Abington, about twenty miles south of Boston. There they settled in, and John L., after fulfilling his contracts for the next season, announced his retirement from the stage in 1911 There was enough money to allow for hired hands to work the seventy acres, which was just as well, because Sullivan was far too fat for the exertions of farming. He busied himself by overseeing the cutting of hay, buying farming tools, and ordering milk and meat. The little property was charming, bisected by a small stream called Mill Meadows Brook, and John L. laid plans to tear down the old house and build a stone bungalow.[20]

The role of country squire suited him well. From time to time he and Kilrain would take off on short tours arranged by Hall, but the old days, of months at a time spent hopping from hotel to hotel, were gone for good. The Sullivans named their little kingdom Donlee-Ross Farm, for Kate's birthplace in Donegal; Tralee, whence Mike Sullivan had come; and Roscommon, where John L.'s mother had been born. There they raised fruit, vegetables, and chickens, all the while holding open house for battalions of Sullivan's friends. He was as open-hearted and generous as always, but now he had no more to prove within the cult of masculinity. He rested content, placid enough to accept membership in something called the New England Fat Men's Club.[21]

John L. supported Roosevelt down the line in 1912 as TR jumped the Republican Party and stood at Armageddon. He advised the ex-president that neither of them was a "has-been," told TR to keep up the fight for a strong navy, and tried to get him to give some political preferment to his cousin, Lawrence Sullivan, who lived in Los Angeles and whom John L. touted as a "good Progressive." Although he was shameless in his importunities ("Now, I want you to do a favor for

28. The squire of Donlee-Ross (about 1916) (William Schutte Collection)

me without committing yourself in any manner whatsoever," he wrote TR), much could be forgiven a man who could write, "Well, my friend, I never tire talking about you. I am your champion at all times."[22]

In 1914 Hall lured him into one last lecture tour, this time through Nova Scotia and the other Maritime provinces. Joe Dorney, a reporter on the *Newark News*, went along. A Canadian lecture bureau picked up the tab, offering 75 percent of the gross receipts. Dorney was struck by the amazing popularity of the old lion. His lectures were crowded with graybeards and youngsters alike, and the crowds still followed him through the streets and into hotel lobbies. John L. took all this in his accustomed stride. Two years before, his autograph had gone for seventy-five cents at a New York auction house, compared with fifty cents for that of ex-President Eliot of Harvard; Sullivan thought this just, an example of the law of supply and demand. The two men were in a little town on Cape Breton Island when the Germans attacked through neutral Belgium to commence the war that would change Sullivan's America once and for all.[23]

John L. followed the lead of his friend and idol Roosevelt, becoming a staunch advocate of preparedness. In his public appearances during the uneasy years of American neutrality, however, he most often appeared in the guise of a temperance advocate. In fact, the boxing stories and the Irish jokes became diminuendo in his stage appearances. He was now a total "dry," using himself as the prime example of how demon rum could wreck a man and of how swearing off could return a former inebriate to his prime. Sullivan was against national or state prohibition, and thus he did not march in step with most of the temperance lecturers fighting the good fight throughout the Union. He believed the best way to promote temperance was by appealing to individual intelligence rather than through taking omnibus political action.

Sullivan did, however, support antisaloon legislation. He believed there would be comparatively little drunkenness if there were no saloons in which men could treat one another. In his talks he downplayed religious and moral issues, emphasizing what booze could do to the body and the pocketbook. At last he was harvesting his years of experience, and he meant what he said:

If I had not quit drinking when I did and gone to farming with my good wife, there would be somewhere in a Boston suburb a modest tombstone with the inscription on it, "Sacred to the memory of John L. Sullivan." That is why I am . . . [having] a go with a bigger champion than I ever was—the champion of champions—John Barleycorn. There is only one way to get the best of John Barleycorn, and that is to run away from him. There are men who say about liquor that they can take it or leave it, but those are the ones who always take it. And in the end it gets them. I . . . say to the young men of the United States: "Leave liquor alone. Liquor leads to bad companions, bad companions lead to evil places, evil places lead to disease, and disease destroys the home and the Nation."[24]

No American in public life was more familiar with liquor, bad companions, and evil places, and his very conviction enhanced his appeal as a lecturer. Roosevelt was among those who urged him on, correctly perceiving that John L.'s honesty and candor would appeal especially to young men. TR knew when to draw the line between friendship and politics, however. When Sullivan importuned the ex-president to introduce him at a big temperance rally scheduled for Atlantic City, in 1915, Roosevelt adroitly refused.[25]

The National Anti-Saloon League was planning a four-day extravaganza on Million-Dollar Pier over the Fourth of July break, after which Sullivan would tour the country under contract to the league, preaching temperance. The presiding officer of the convention was Nelson A. Miles, a retired general who had won his spurs in the Civil War, chased Indians around the western prairies and mountains, and eventually risen to command the army, "perhaps the least qualified man since the inception of the post." Miles was an important man (not least in his own mind), but he was haughty, cantankerous, and at one time had been badly bitten with the presidential bug. When Miles heard of John L.'s scheduled participation, he pompously declared that he would refuse to appear if the Irish Mephistopheles was coming. The decision between the two heroes, one self-proclaimed and the other authentic, was dumped in the laps of the league's Board of Directors.[26]

In the interim Sullivan fired off a telegram to the chairman of the convention:

> I have no desire to address a convention, if bigotry and narrowmindedness hold sway, with a pretense of doing good, and which is presided over by an arrogant, prejudiced, self-centered, strutting old peacock. I have never been jealous of any fighter; why should Miles be jealous of me? Yours for temperance.
>
> John L. Sullivan

The board compromised by scheduling Miles early and Sullivan late. The general duly delivered his address, on the evils of drink in the army, then packed his tent and left town. Then came a second wire from John L.:

> I refuse to appear on any platform where General Nelson A. Miles has strutted. The referee's decision is with me. Let us call it quits.
>
> John L. Sullivan

And he did *not* speak. The ashes may have been banked, but the old fire still smoldered.[27]

After this flap he went off on his lecture tour as scheduled, the leitmotif of his message being that he had lost at least $500,000 through drink. He opened in Asbury Park, New Jersey, where five hundred people paid fifty cents each to listen and cheer him heartily.[28] He was committed to his new calling in a way Nelson Miles could never be.

For the most part these were sunny autumn years. Sullivan resolved one nagging problem in 1915, when he reclaimed his beloved Championship Belt from a Chicago pawnshop. John L. had long since stripped the prize of its most valuable jewelry, but the belt itself was still a coveted icon. In 1903 it had been bought at a pawnbroker's auction by John Donahue, a New York saloon keeper, and three years later Donahue passed it on to a certain Bowery resident named Michael Rosenthal. Somehow the belt got to Chicago, where Sullivan reportedly paid fifty-three hundred dollars to get it out of hock.[29]

There was a last hurrah in the ring, too. Jack Johnson, in what was probably a setup, surrendered his crown to the hulking Kansas giant, Jess Willard, in Havana in 1915. On March 25, 1916, Willard was scheduled to defend his title for the first time against Frank Moran, a rugged ex-sailor from Pittsburgh. Over twelve thousand people packed Madison Square Garden for the affair. Boxing was big business now, and Sullivan had helped make it so. The promotion fees for the bout topped $100,000. Willard received a purse of $47,500, and Moran half that amount. The motion picture rights alone produced $10,000. At ringside sat a glittering battery of the elite: From the world of finance came the younger J. P. Morgan, Reginald Vanderbilt, Henry Payne Whitney, August Belmont, and Joseph W. Harriman. The opera stars Enrico Caruso, Geraldine Farrar, and John McCormack were there. So too were George M. Cohan and David Belasco from Broadway, not to mention such eccentrics as John Philip Sousa, the detective Allan Pinkerton, and Diamond Jim Brady.

John L. Sullivan had been the first to bring people such as these to the arena. Without really intending it, he had helped make boxing, and indeed American sport, both a cultural spectacle and a commercial enterprise. Unknowingly, he had become a grandfather to the modern sporting tradition in America. And the fans sitting in the Garden that night, waiting for the fight to start, knew it. Now, suddenly, there he stood under the electric glare as the announcer, Joe Humphries, boomed out, "Pree-senting—John L. Sullivan!" Waves of applause cascaded down on the old man as he stood squarely in the center of the ring, blocky as a slab of granite. His jowls were heavy, his hair and mustache completely white, but he was still *the* champion, still "Our John." From somewhere Humphries had dredged up the belt of colors Sullivan wore against Charlie Mitchell during the struggle in the thunderstorm at Chantilly over a quarter of a century before. This he presented to John

L. as the cheering rolled on. Sullivan's eyes were moist as he kissed
the silk flag and tenderly put it in a vest pocket.[30]

It was a memorable moment, made more so in a lithograph by
George Bellows that was transferred seven years later to an oil sketch.
The fight that followed did not share this description, being ten dull
rounds ending in no decision, as required by the state boxing law.
Observers were hard pressed to say who had won.[31] But if there was
a winner that night, it was neither of the two principals but the obese
old man who stood, for the last time in his life, in the center of a prize
ring. He, after all, had begun the whole thing.


# IV


After triumph came tragedy. Kate had been ill for some months with
cancer and was in bed at Donlee-Ross even as her husband took the
cheers in New York. The exact nature of her illness was not made
public, but it was debilitating and must have been a strain on a woman
who was known locally for her charitable work and her labors as an
unpaid visiting nurse. John L. kept vigil for weeks, but to no avail;
his wife died early in the afternoon of May 25, 1916.[32] In addition to
her sturdy companionship, Kate had helped provide their home. Sullivan's debt to her was great, and he was never slow in acknowledging
it.

He mitigated his sorrow by turning to the preparedness issue. As
the war in Europe entered its third inconclusive year, presidential
politics produced a national debate over potential American involve-
ment in the struggle. Many Irish Americans, hating England more than
they feared Germany, opted for an uneasy neutrality. Others stood
solidly behind the Union Jack. Sullivan had no difficulties in making
up his mind. He had never been a professional "Irishman," and now
he was four-square behind Theodore Roosevelt, who was preaching
preparedness to any audience that would give him a hearing. TR's
following, despite his defalcation in the campaign of 1916, was still
considerable.[33] Nationally, the pressure helped shift Woodrow Wilson's stance in the direction of preparedness, and this, in turn, probably
provided the president's narrow victory margin in November.

Wilson's various peace strategems at last played out early the next
year in the face of the German decision to once again wage unrestricted
submarine warfare. In early April the nation went to war, with John
L. Sullivan a fervent supporter of the American cause. In particular,
Sullivan supported TR's oft-stated request to be allowed to go to France
at the head of a division. This was a minor headache for Wilson (whom
TR had come to despise) but a real one. Roosevelt seemed to think,

despite his age, that the deadlock in the trenches could be broken by some kind of replay of San Juan Hill.

This sort of thinking—the quick, decisive thrust—was bound to appeal to Roosevelt's exact contemporary, rusticating on his tiny farm. John L. gave no thought to the fine distinction TR had drawn between sport and war; the first shaped character, the second destroyed it. The old Roughrider knew that sport offered little advantage in preparing young men for the practical aspects of war, but to John L., who had never smelled the smoke of battle, it seemed the same thing. "Colonel Roosevelt is the only man in America the Kaiser is afraid of," he proclaimed. "The presence of Colonel Roosevelt in the trenches would be sufficient to ensure a proper American representation."[34]

Roosevelt was never to get to the trenches, but it was not for lack of trying, either on his part or Sullivan's. As TR humiliated himself by continually beseeching his enemy in the White House for permission to go to France as a division commander, John L. headed a mass meeting at Boston's Faneuil Hall in May, with the object of getting his hero onto the battlefield. There, amid a potpourri of vaudeville routines, singing, and patriotic effusions, Sullivan urged support of TR's dream. He praised Roosevelt to the skies, in the process declaring that military training should be taught in schools, so that young people could go into manhood knowing the importance of being part of a military machine. He added that the same indoctrination should be given in workshops and factories. Always a political innocent, he had no idea of the darker side of the hyper-patriotism he preached that night, but then neither did millions of his fellow Americans.

After Sullivan finished his remarks, a majority of the crowd of around eight hundred people passed a resolution supporting his stand. But shortly thereafter a ruckus started. Two men, John F. Mallory and Frank M. Carpenter, sought to raise the interests of Ireland, in the process referring to socialists in a neutral fashion rather than in the expected style of condemnation. The audience began to scream oaths and insults, and for a moment the hallowed old building was on the brink of riot. John L., seated at the rear of the platform with an unlit cigar clenched between his teeth, advanced quickly to the front of the stage. In a booming voice, with arms uplifted, he shouted for order and got it. Still grumbling, the patriots filed out into the night, having given themselves a brief preview of the wartime hysteria to come.[35]

Sullivan, unlike so many of his countrymen, did not wallow in blood lust. He saw the cataclysm in Europe as a "horrible, murderous war," but it had to be won. "I would like to see one great drive consisting of a land and sea battle," he scrawled to TR, "and aeroplanes in the air belting (H) out of this Prussianism and autocracy so that they could talk gibberish in (H). . . . We are in this war and we have a lot to win;

that is the only answer to the situation." Reverie, however, was upon him; he dreamed of accompanying Roosevelt to France or, barring that, inaugurating a "United World League" that would negotiate peace. Interest in the war consumed his time throughout much of 1917, and it was a major blow when TR at last told him that the new version of the Roughriders was not to be. TR also had to contend with a proposal from Bat Masterson, now reporting sports for the *New York Morning Telegraph*. Bat wanted an appointment for himself and Tex Rickard, the flamboyant promoter of the Willard-Moran fight. "We want to tell you how to organize your European expedition and how to win your battles when you get there." At least John L. never went *that* far.[36]

So Sullivan's fondest wartime dream ended in futility. He had had his "rousing rally," though, and still fantasized of talking about "Colonel Roosevelt and temperance in every city, hamlet and town." To him, it was war on the most personal level: "Just as soon as this country consents to send Colonel Roosevelt to the front, Bill Hohenzollern will learn he has a real fight on his hands." Despite following the war news avidly, Sullivan had little notion of the nature of the remorseless, grinding struggle on the Western Front. He salved his disappointment by appearing in a few Liberty Loan campaigns.[37]

Mostly, though, he clung close to Donlee-Ross and his memories. He puttered with his small numbers of stock, feeding and grooming the horses, seeing that the cows and pigs were satisfied. He took particular pleasure in several collies, his favorite being the inquisitive Queenie. Time passed. Word came from Rhode Island that Annie Bates Bailey Sullivan had died, on March 7, 1917. Since Kate's death an old sparring partner, George Bush, had come to live with him and do odd jobs about the place. He and Bush spent hours listening to scratchy phonograph records and telling each other lies about the old days. John L. also took in a young man named William Kelly, put him to work around the farm, and began to have thoughts of adopting him.[38]

Kate had left him around four thousand dollars, and this was dissipating rapidly with nothing coming in. Sullivan's lawyer, Clarence W. Rowley, tried to keep the estate in shape, but John L. had other concerns. Children were much on his mind; he spent hours playing with the Rowleys' child. Back in 1894, there had been unfounded rumors that he had had himself appointed guardian of an orphan bootblack in Iowa, the boy even appearing with him in *The Man from Boston* billed as "Master Charles Nixon, the wonderful boy soprano." Whatever the truth of this, with Kate's death he felt, despite the support of Bush and the Rowleys, alone and isolated again. Late in 1917 he probably adopted young Kelly.[39]

Rowley was after him to make a will, but John L. offhandedly said he was good for twenty more years. At fifty-nine he was having more and more trouble breathing, though, and he began to use an electric vibrator to stimulate circulation. Still, he planned ahead. There would be more tours: the war effort had to be supported, and young Kelly's schooling needed attention. He negotiated with Ringling Brothers concerning a circus routine for the summer of 1918, in which he was to receive one thousand dollars a week for appearing in an "old Irish jaunting car act."[40]

But mostly he simply whiled away the time as winter set in. The Yanks were in France now, but the tide of battle had yet to turn. War news clogged the daily press. Old John L., at last, had become what many considered him to be back in 1892, a relic of a vanished era. Few took the trouble to remember him, now that the earth was shuddering with the birth of the modern age. One man did. Vachel Lindsay would write these lines on John L. Sullivan, tinted with the gauze of time—the last poem about him, and the best:

> When I was nine years old, in 1889
> I sent my love a lacy Valentine.
> Suffering boys were dressed like Fauntleroys,
> While Judge and Puck in giant humor vied,
> The Gibson Girl came shining like a bride
> To spoil the cult of Tennyson's Elaine.
> Louise May Alcott was my gentle guide. . . .
> Then . . .
> I heard a battle trumpet sound.
> Nigh New Orleans
> Upon an emerald plain
> John L. Sullivan
> The strong boy
> Of Boston
> Fought seventy-five red rounds with Jake Kilrain. . . .[41]

# V

January 1918: New England struggled against an exceptionally frigid winter. Sullivan heard of a coal shortage in Brockton and some neighboring towns; on the last day of the month he offered five hundred cords of wood from his farm to any who would cut it and take it away. The weather had done little to slow him down; he had climbed six flights of stairs in Boston's Old South Building with no difficulty only the week before, and then (somehow) he had touched his toes without bending his knees to show friends his agility. At a recent banquet in his honor at the United States Hotel, he had said: "If the good Lord shall call me right now, I may say that I have seen it all. I know the game of life from A to Z, from soda to hock."[42]

John L. had felt pains in his chest for three weeks but had ignored them. On Friday, February 1, he journeyed up to Boston and back. That night he sat up late, fiddling with another hobby, solitaire. He was up the next morning at eight, had breakfast, and returned to his room. Moments later Bush heard him fall to the floor. Running to the bedroom, he found Sullivan struggling to reach the bed. "Never mind," John L. groaned, "I'll be all right in a few minutes. Funny; that was the first attack I ever had in my life, George." He knew it was his heart.

Young Kelly sped off to fetch a doctor as Sullivan lay quietly in bed. The boy returned with Dr. R. B. Rand, who was not John L.'s regular physician. Rand administered a heart stimulant, advised rest, and departed. Around eleven o'clock came a second attack; Bush worked frantically, sponging his friend's face with cold water. By now Sullivan, he who had had a broken wrist reset without ether in 1887 and undergone major surgery the same way in 1900, was complaining of a terrific pain in the heart. "And then," Bush recalled, "I don't know just what happened. He closed his eyes, mumbled something I could not understand, and just slipped away, so quietly I didn't realize for a moment that he was dead." His regular physician, who had been treating him for three weeks under a diagnosis of fatty degeneration of the heart, arrived minutes later.[43]

The body was taken to a Boston undertaker, Timothy J. Mahoney, who had to send to New York for a larger casket. Reporters who arrived at Donlee-Ross too late to see Sullivan found only Queenie, disconsolately sniffing through its rooms searching for a trace of her master. The wake was held on Monday at Sullivan's sister's home in Roxbury, only blocks from where his adventures had begun years before. John L.'s body, in full evening dress, lay in state in the darkened parlor, malletlike right hand symbolically clenched over his broad chest. The New York casket (the Boston-New York connection again) was lined with white satin and bore a simple nameplate: "John L. Sullivan."

Now, despite the war and the weather, he was remembered. An unbroken line of mourners passed before his bier for hours. Some came in limousines; others left their trucks or wagon teams at the corner and took their place in line. Four hundred schoolchildren filed silently by. Ann Lennon sat throughout at the head of her brother's coffin, quiet and composed.[44]

The Lennons' sitting room, dining room, and kitchen were jammed with people telling Sullivan stories, most of them dealing with John L.'s big-hearted charity. William Muldoon came; so did Jake Kilrain, with his wife, daughter, and two sons. Telegrams flowed in by the bushel from all over the country: from sporting men, bankers, lawyers, doctors, politicians. Boston's own James Curley, for whom John L. had campaigned in the last mayoralty election, paid a call, and so did old Dan Dwyer, now seventy-six, who had been Sullivan's first real ring opponent, back in 1879.[45]

It was a grand wake, riddled with memories. Jim Corbett sent a floral horseshoe, but the old rancor still was there; he pleaded a theatrical engagement and said he would not attend the funeral. Frank Hall, out in West Baden, Indiana, wired regrets; so did Jim Jeffries. Charlie Mitchell, seriously ill for weeks in London, said of the man he had tormented for so long: "He had the heart of a lion." Some of the talk held that John L. had died broke, and a few of the sob sisters put forth the story that a ten-dollar bill folded inside a five-dollar bill had been found beneath the pillow on his deathbed, "the last of his fortune." In fact he died solvent. Donlee-Ross was in his name, and worth at least ten thousand dollars. There were also a few securities. It was not much to show from a million-dollar career, but it was far better than most prizefighters had done before him and many would do after him.[46]

The funeral took place at Saint Paul's Church on February 6. Police had had to keep order in front of the Lennon home the previous two days, and they were on hand again. In death as in life, John L. drew a crowd. The Reverend Peter A. Quinn was present but did not participate, perhaps due to the divorce stigma, and mass was celebrated by an assistant. The pallbearers were composed of Boston's Irish, to a man, and the ushers, including Kilrain, were all drawn from Sullivan's friends. Corbett had had a change of heart; he filed by the bier at the last moment and now, along with Muldoon, was an honorary pallbearer. The one man John L. would most have wanted there was not: Theodore Roosevelt, less than a year from death himself, was recovering from surgery and also pleaded a previous engagement. "I had a genuine regard for my old friend John L. Sullivan," TR said. "He was an old and valued friend, and I mourn his death." Few people noticed the slender, sour-faced man who was attending as a duty. Within a year Lieutenant Governor Calvin Coolidge would be catapulted to national fame during a Boston labor dispute, then on to the vice-presidency and the White House.[47]

Sullivan was interred in the family plot at Mount Calvary Cemetery that he had purchased for Mike and Catherine back in the 1880s. Kate was buried there as well. It was a bitterly cold day; the line of march from the church to the cemetery had been carefully sanded. En route, the cortege passed fire companies standing bare-headed before their machines, which were draped in black crepe. The engine-house bells tolled farewell. They buried him on the side of a little knoll. Jake

Kilrain, stooped a bit and with gray gathering at his temples, whispered, "It was just as John would have had it."

At the very end, John L. could not go without a bit more commotion. The frozen earth had to be dynamited away to make his grave.[48]

# An American Legend

## I

The place is called Old Calvary Cemetery now, swallowed up in suburbia. Crowded with tombstones, many of them huge edifices of granite and marble, its permanent population is overwhelmingly Irish-Catholic. The imposing Sullivan monument, a tall granite obelisk, was placed years later, marking the graves of thirteen members of the family; of John L.'s intimate relations, only two—his first wife and his son—are buried elsewhere, in Rhode Island. The plot is large by Old Calvary standards, a trapezoidal lot about twenty feet on a side, and is sheltered by enormous shade trees and pines. Situated on a gentle slope, it is a most restful spot, even though busy Cummins Highway cuts by only a few feet away.

Very few of Sullivan's generation survived him long. Within days of John L.'s death Billy Madden, staunch friend of his youth, died in a hospital in White Plains, New York. On March 24, 1918, Mike Donovan, who had made himself paramount among the nation's boxing instructors, passed away at St. Francis Hospital in New York City. A little more than a week later Charlie Mitchell was dead, at the age of fifty-seven. John L.'s sister, Ann, who had overseen his wake, perished in the raging influenza epidemic the next winter. And, on January 15, 1919, her husband James Lennon was killed in an explosion at work.[1] Thus, within a year everyone in John L.'s immediate family, as well as many of his friends, were gone.

Only three major participants in Sullivan's story lasted the twenties and lived on into the depression years. James J. Corbett resided quietly in his little stucco house in Queens with his second wife. He appeared in vaudeville, traveled the lecture circuit, and dabbled in radio and motion pictures. At times he was ridiculed for his gift of invariably picking the wrong fighter to win a championship bout. In early 1933, his once-powerful body wasted to 140 pounds, the Dude died from cancer of the liver. He was sixty-six. His estate, left entirely to his wife in a simple will of about 100 words, was evaluated at $100,000. A few months later William Muldoon, rich in years and honors, reluctantly expired at the age of eighty-eight on the old farm in Belfast where he had trained Sullivan. The apostle had served a stint as New York State Athletic Commissioner and consistently had lived his creed, keeping himself marvelously fit right to the end. The best his physician could do in describing the cause of death was "old age."[2]

The last of the bareknucklers lived on, scraping along from job to job. His Baltimore bar burned down; he found employment in the Parks Department in Somerville, a suburb of Boston. In 1930 his wife died, and then he became too old for the depression-shrunken city payroll. As hard times settled over the land, he eked out a living as a night watchman for a Quincy shipyard. Through it all, his memories of that boiling day on the Mississippi plain remained evergreen, and so did his recollections of his antagonist and friend; "I liked John L. Sullivan," he often said. At last, just before Christmas in 1937, Jake Kilrain died of diabetes at the age of seventy-eight.[3]

Not only the men were gone; many of the artifacts vanished as well. Most of the thousands of pieces of Sullivaniana—cards, statuettes, posters, engravings, lithographs, tickets, and ring paraphernalia—have crumbled into dust or lie forgotten in attic trunks. None of the scenes of Sullivan's matches survives, in any form. Madison Square Garden, for example, went through several transfigurations, and the building where John L. had so often performed (and misbehaved) has long since given way to a skyscraper:

> Jiminy, what a change! . . .
> In office 157, first floor,
> Where a bald little man
> Sits dozing over "Flitcraft's
>     Manual
> Of Insurance Rates" scribbling
> Figures and yawning
> And taking pills out of a
> Round box for his dyspepsia,
> Stood the very ring where
> John L. Sullivan battered
> Down Slade, "The Maori,"
> Dominick McCaffery and
> Charlie Mitchell. . . .
> A skyscraper twenty-eight
> Stories high and with 1,000
> Offices!

\* \* \*

Well, what of it?
There isn't a kick in
A whole block of 'em.[4]

The greatest artifact of Sullivan's life had as fantastic a career as its sometime owner. In the twenties it was rumored that the Championship Belt, long since denuded of gems, had been melted down in the Philadelphia Mint for its gold value. Sportswriter Grantland Rice claimed to have seen it in 1925 in the possession of the sons of a horsedealer, James King, in Baltimore.[5] The descendants of James and Anne Lennon had no idea what had become of it.

Indeed, the belt probably vanished in the smelter of the mint, bringing about six hundred dollars worth of gold. In 1901 a jewelry manufacturer named Mann had designed a facsimile for the Buffalo World's Fair, remembered since as the location of President William McKinley's assassination. A work of art in its own right, the facsimile had little intrinsic value. After Sullivan's death it passed into the hands of a man named Charles West. When West's estate was settled, the imitation belt was purchased by Melvin Herman, a sign painter in Hammond, Indiana. Just before Herman died in 1957, he sold what he believed to be the original icon to the publisher of the *Hammond Times*, James S. Delaurier. The publisher traveled the Midwest for years, using the belt as an exhibition piece for a talk on salesmanship. When he died, his daughter donated it to the National Museum of American History in the Smithsonian Institution. The facsimile Championship Belt resides there today, where it properly belongs—in the custody of the American people.[6]

The copy of the Championship Belt is the last tangible public memory of John L. Sullivan. No one presently alive ever saw him fight in his prime, although perhaps a scattered few recall him from the stage. He seems, when remembered at all, to belong irrevocably to another century, frozen in the ice of the past. "From the point of view of manners and tastes," wrote John P. Marquand, a novelist who paid a lot of attention to manners and tastes, "he is as extinct as the mustache cups that went with [his age]."[7]

## II

—Not quite. Manners and tastes change, of course, but the public phenomenon of Sullivan comprises much more than a mere recital of a ring career or a faded daguerreotype of a time thought obsolete. His America was largely inarticulate, and thus in the individual sense difficult to recapture historically. Therefore the public response to John L., both in and out of the ring, seems a useful litmus test with which to gauge the tensions and pressures within a rapidly industrializing and urbanizing nation. It was a time of whirl and grab, even more so than in most epochs of our history, and John L. was one of its centerpieces. Sullivan had *not* "seen it all," of course; who does? But he had seen, and experienced, more than his share.

He was far from a role model for young boys, but there were those who ignored his flagrant violations of propriety and remembered the gregarious champion, invincible and omnipotent. There is no way to judge how many youngsters actually tried to model themselves on Sullivan; probably not many, for the life of the prize ring (if followed properly) is one of the most arduous and self-sacrificing callings in American life. But perhaps some were like the Pennsylvania boy, Newton Bitzer, whose father took him to see a Sullivan exhibition against Herbert Slade. From a seat near the stage, young Bitzer beheld the champion with awe; even years later, when he had become a respected physician, he remembered the experience clearly. In at least one case, John L. was directly influential. Out in Manassa, Colorado, a tough, wiry little woman named Celia Dempsey lived on the edge of poverty. Pregnant, she bought Sullivan's autobiography from an itinerant peddler and, as she waited for delivery, passed away the time by reading and rereading the story of John L.'s career. When William Harrison Dempsey was born in 1895, she was sure he was going to grow up strong, "just like him."[8] She was right.

Without doubt, Sullivan was a hero-figure to many boys and adult males as well. Like legendary heroes, he was characterized by extraordinary power which was encapsulated in super-human feats. Like them, he performed alone, but before usually admiring audiences who could be counted on to both tell and embellish the tale. As with mythic figures, John L. proved himself superior in contest after contest, and like them he was acclaimed throughout the land as "champion." His Irish descent helped; the history of Ireland since medieval times is replete with the celebration of the warrior-hero in epic literature. He was at the very core of the stereotype of the "fighting Irish," and his popularity within his own ethnic group, while never complete, was strong and enduring.[9]

The hero-worship transcended all boundaries but the masculine, however. Sullivan's triumphs were unique, and seemed to require a different measure than that applied to ordinary people. "Do not think of John L. Sullivan as human," enthused one biographer. "Go ahead and call the man a brute, if it pleases you; but admit that a brute built on such a scale is as different from the rest of us as any pallid prince of old reared in the serene belief that God had done something special to himself and all his ancestors and that he had been born for the purpose of expressing God's will on earth. . . . Essentially this lad was a king, and adulation was his by divine right." The figure of 200 victories (over four times the actual total) came to be the accepted standard of his fame. "The wonder is that he never killed anyone," wrote one boxing authority, "for he had such a terrible punch."[10]

Over and over again, Sullivan was a hymn to raw power and the crude but vital energies of an expanding nation. His fist, said a sporting journalist, "seemed like the clapper of some great bell that had boomed the brazen message of America's glory as a fighting nation from one end of the earth to the other." John L. knew nothing about boxing, reckoned Mike Donovan, "but he was the most savage fighter and hardest hitter that ever lived." He was strong enough, savage enough, powerful enough, in a sense, to transcend death. When Celia Dempsey's son slashed his way to a Pier Six victory over Louis Angel Firpo in 1923, Tex Rickard was heard to murmur at ringside, " the ghost of Sullivan was in there just now."[11]

We live today in an age of media overexposure. We still worship our sports heroes and envy the astronomical salaries they receive, but we also insist, whenever possible, that their personal lives be laid bare for our inspection—just as Sullivan's was for more than a generation. The public interest in Sullivan set the pattern that is still followed; the media simultaneously inflate and deflate our athletic gods, rendering them superhuman and all too human at the same time. At the ends of their careers, they are placed in pantheons, or "Halls of Fame," just as John L. was when he became a charter member of the Boxing Hall of Fame in 1954. Perhaps modern sports have become, as one authority insists, a "secular faith " but if so it is a curious religion, for it concurrently ballyhoos and debunks its totems.[12]

Should such a thing as an "American consciousness" exist (and this is a highly debatable point), the phenomenon of Sullivan lies deep within it. There were other, and contrasting, definitions of masculinity than those exemplified by John L., of course. But manhood in his day, whatever its components, largely was defined in public—through one's actions, or by one's standing in a specific community, or by personal relations with others. The male world extended from the ideal of the patriarchal family into the areas of business, work, and the professions. Always, the individual was expected to assume personal responsibility for his acts. Sullivan's America was not yet a collective society.

So far, so good. Yet a man's duty lay first with his family; Sullivan, until late in life, was spectacularly unsuccessful in his relationships with women and as conspicuous an example of a raucous "bachelor" as could be found in public. A man was to secure a living wage; while John L. did this (and more), his many and significant profits dribbled away with a regularity probably unique in his time. And, a man should be active in the building of his community, a political participant.

Despite his occasional flirtations with the electorate, Sullivan usually gave every indication that he was wrecking rather than building his society.[13]

Many American men, like Socialist Eugene Debs, flatly rejected physical prowess as a definition of manhood ("it is . . . well-known that mules are hard hitters"). Yet many, perhaps a majority, did not. Particularly among the young, where education and the necessities of making a living have yet to take hold, the theme is a preponderant one in our culture. Those who celebrate Sullivan praise him first as the "Napoleon of the fistic brigade," a standard-bearer of "the fighting spirit which had always remained dominant in the human race." His "reputation and ferocity of aspect in the ring tried the courage of any man," wrote one celebrant of that spirit, Theodore Roosevelt. Hyperbole was unavoidable; John L.'s achievements, said one admirer, "elevated pugilism into the realm of epic poetry." At this pinnacle he remains, a veritable Hercules, "probably the most perfect piece of superfighting machinery the ages have ever beheld."[14]

Even those less florid in their praise measured Sullivan in terms appropriate to the dimensions of manhood. Arthur Brisbane, who had reported on the bizarre Sullivan-Mitchell match at Chantilly, continued to follow boxing all his life and was personally acquainted with many prominent prizefighters. He often compared Sullivan favorably with more modern pugilists. So did Mike Donovan, and so did a host of others not so familiar with the ring. The comparisons were commensurate with individualism and the cult of masculinity, as with Donovan: Sullivan "scorned to study the methods or copy the style of anyone. He had a natural genius for fighting. He never stepped back." Such a force could only be defeated by age and time, not by anyone his equal. A plaster cast of Corbett's right hand sold handsomely for several years, advertised as the hand that knocked out John L. Sullivan.[15]

John L. was a city counterpart of the likes of Davy Crockett, Paul Bunyan, and Mike Fink. In fact, it is appropriate to call him America's first real-life urban folk-hero. The tall tales surrounding him, half reality and half myth, are legion, and, as in all lasting legends, only grow with the telling. Many of the men he beat were supposedly "giants" (in fact, he outweighed most of his victims by a considerable margin, sometimes by as much as sixty or seventy pounds). He battled wild animals with his bare hands, drank rivers of liquor, and fornicated his way through regiments of women—all stories cast in the mold of masculine wish-fulfillment. A fictional tale that appeared in that window into middle-class America, the *Saturday Evening Post*, had Sullivan toiling in Quincy granite quarries, knocking heads together in a saloon, prying apart two scrapping bloodhounds with his bare hands and fling-

ing them twenty feet in opposite directions, guzzling beer from a favorite stein labelled "*Der erste Zug nie lang genug*" ("the first swig
never satisfies"), and slugging a horse and killing it. "Like Bernhardt,
he was only beautiful when he was wicked, and he was only wicked
when in action."[16]

Some of the whoppers had roots in reality, for unlike Bunyan and
Fink, John L. was all too tangible. In 1883 an Albany sport reported
that some New Yorkers wanted to bet $1,000 that Sullivan, given four
blows, could not fell an ox. Supposedly an effort was made to secure
Madison Square Garden for this extraordinary "contest." Coupled with
the later, and documented, stories of the champion's mistreatment of
horses, this passed into legend as the time John L. knocked out a horse
and an ox with a single punch. In 1904, a story was told of Sullivan's
visit to the training camp of featherweight Terry McGovern. "Terrible
Terry" kept a pet wildcat, and John L., ever curious around animals,
walked over and playfully rattled its cage. When ring announcer Joe
Humphries, years later, came to write his reminiscences, his version
offered a drunken Sullivan trying to pry open the cage to fight the
wildcat, finally giving up and chucking the cage with its screeching
feline out of a window.[17]

All of this was simply too good to pass up, and John L. entered the
twentieth century so weighted with apocrypha that the truth of most
of his shenanigans may never be discerned. But even so, the praise,
adulation, and legends do not address his essential importance. William Muldoon was more muscular and probably stronger, yet no tall
tales clung to him. Many in the fight game, like Paddy Ryan and Jake
Kilrain, had a notable love for the bottle, yet it is Sullivan's thirst that
drains whole distilleries. Numerous Americans carried on both public
and private *amours*, and Sullivan's heyday was the golden age of the
whorehouse, yet John L., like many athletes today, is credited with
"scoring" far more than his share of pliable females. Other fighters,
such as Rocky Marciano, had better records in the ring, and several
others, in their own time, were as dominant as Sullivan was in his.
Yet John L. lives on, enshrouded in myth, unquiet symbol of a vanished world. Why?

# III

The explanation of the Sullivan phenomenon lies as much in what he
was as in what he did. Certainly he climbed higher on fame's fickle
ladder than any ethnic American before him. One adulator judged him
"as rare in his chosen field as a Michelangelo or a Rembrandt in the
world of art. In his day, no man on earth was more widely known."
Another admirer felt that tales of Sullivan would be passed from father

to son, just like the stories of James Figg still being relayed in English fighting clubs and taverns almost two centuries later. After all, here was a man who dwarfed the temporarily famous, such as the Prince of Wales:

> Ho! Britons, raise a joyous shout.
>   Give voice in thrilling tones,
> Accompanying your song throughout
>   With banjo, harp, and bones.
> The olive branch floats on the breeze,
>   Peace marches in the van;
> The Prince's hand has had a squeeze
>   From John L. Sullivan.
>
> Perhaps some day the Prince will king
>   Become, when value much
> Enhanced to that same hand shall cling
>   Which Sullivan did touch.
> The loyal throng, as on they pass,
>   Shall step with more elan
> To kiss the hand which got the squeeze
>   From John L. Sullivan.[18]

His fame, however, was only the surface crust on a much more meaningful relationship. It was no accident that Americans measured Sullivan in heroic and legendary terms when they did; his was a symbiotic relationship with his era, which was one of "brutal but tremendously vital achievement." It was not the norm for the Gilded Age to describe its celebrities in hyperbole—the "greatest" this or that.[19] But Sullivan *was* so described; he was instant history, a living epic.

He was made so by word of mouth within the cult of masculinity, and by the press. Good, bad, or indifferent, he was news, and he was news because for whatever reason people wanted to read about him. In this sense, the reporters who dogged his heels were Boswells to Sullivan's Johnson, and since journalistic ethics (if they existed) were in their infancy, the scribes were not reluctant to embroider, distort, or lie. As one book reviewer wryly put it, "they knew how to bring out his best sayings."[20]

In part he was the product of journalistic fiction, and once he realized this he spent much of his life trying to live up (or down) to what in a later time would be called his "media image." Sullivan was a creature of print, and both positive and negative hyperbole about him saturated the popular culture with little or no check on it, save by the man himself. John L. was shrewd enough and spontaneous enough to cultivate his positive side, and he was also drunkard enough to ensure that the negatives kept appearing as well. Without doubt, the one-dimensional media attention contributed greatly to his status. The relationship between Sullivan, the press, and his fans became an un-broken loop, each element passing into another without a break and feeding off the others. John L. was far from a "symbol for an age," but he was a most useful symbol, or more probably, a caricature—a living embodiment of the aspirations and fears of his countrymen.

In the century since Sullivan's heyday he has appeared in other media, always as the drunken bullyboy with heart of gold. John L. has been in some unlikely places: short stories; novels (he pops up in Marquand's *The Late George Apley*, appears as an ardent but unre-quited lover in Mathias Harpin's *Trumpets in Jericho*, and does his boozy routine in Harry Stein's *Hoopla*); and even a children's book, where modern kids learn that Sullivan whipped over 200 men, hoisted a policeman over his head, and "could hardly read or write."[21]

Other fighters appeared on film—Corbett, Jack Dempsey, and Gene Tunney all made motion picture serials—but Sullivan, as a boxer, never did. Snippets of film exist showing him fooling around at the Jeffries-Johnson match in 1910, but that is all. One motion picture has been made about him, *The Great John L.* (1945). This B-grade Bing Crosby production starred an unknown hunk named Greg McClure and fea-tured Linda Darnell as Sullivan's "true love," Ann Livingston. Here we find that the champion was handsome, dashing, and competing for Ann's hand with "Richard Martin," a jealous newspaper publisher who behaves suspiciously like Richard Kyle Fox. Most movie fans remem-ber Sullivan from Ward Bond's performance, complete with broad Irish brogue, in the Errol Flynn vehicle *Gentleman Jim* (1942). This version of John L. swills champagne while training for the Corbett fight and later sheepishly says, as he hands the Dude his Championship Belt (something he never did): "Maybe you're bringin' somethin' new to the fight game, somethin' it needs, and never got from fellers like me."[22]

There remains a final judgment on his impact. One way of assessing him has it that he was the last of his kind—coarse, brutal, bestial. Corbett, the White Knight, "yanked boxing out of the beef-brine pot" and made it a respectable part of America's sporting culture. Another approach is to see Sullivan as still the "champion of champions." Of course, "he was undoubtedly the wickedest man of his time," but he also "cleaned up boxing, made it respectable, and placed it within the law." (When boxing became "respectable" is impossible to say—some would argue "not yet"—but the sport was featured in soap ads for women as early as 1900).[23]

In fact neither view is completely true. Sullivan was a transitional figure, a cultural hero who reflected many of the strains and uncer-tainties of an America in the throes of "modernization." He was a bare-knuckler who fought forty-four of his forty-seven prizefights with some form of gloves and pleaded for a "scientific" slant to a sport for which he seldom trained. An ethnic, and proud of it, he refused to keep his social place, instead associating when he could with princes and presidents. Child of the city, he was an object of both curiousity and concern to a countryside which well knew it was sliding into a secondary position in the nation's economy, society, and political life. A complete failure as a businessman, he inadvertently laid the groundwork for boxing and commercial sport as both a business and a spectacle.

The contradictions continue. A consummate racist, he endlessly appealed to the prize ring as an arena of democratic achievement. Preaching the uplifting qualities of sport, he was perceived as one of the greatest exemplars of unrestrained vice the nation had to offer. For years he careened drunkenly through an industrializing society which was struggling for social control, efficiency, and regimentation in the workplace. And always, he was a most problematic model of manhood. Undeniably, he was courageous, generous, and honest; as undeniably he was temperamental, suspicious, and violent. By his own lights he was a "square-shooter" in the world of men, yet he had trouble sustaining real friendships, both male and female, for most of his life.

He was the best in us, and the worst, too. Love him or hate him, at his apogee it was difficult to ignore him, so full was he of the relentless energy, combativeness, and raw power of his America.

## IV

A checkered legacy to be sure, but one fully consonant with the times in which he lived. The tumult and the shouting have long since died away, and Honeysuckle Path in Old Calvary Cemetery is a peaceful site, an island of tranquillity amid the bustle of the surrounding megalopolis. Perhaps half a dozen people come every year, specifically asking to see the grave of John L. Sullivan.[24]

If you are one of these, you might stand before the burial ground reflecting on the incredible life memorialized there. And as you think, you notice something both curious and ironic: on the great granite obelisk which marks the grave, there is no inscription—not a single one—to indicate that the man who lies beneath was once heavyweight champion of the world.

# APPENDIX A

# The Prizefight Record of John L. Sullivan

Sullivan gave hundreds of exhibitions during his career. Some of these are listed in the *Ring Record Book*, but more are presented in this book. A "prizefight," in contrast, is defined as a boxing match in which money is directly at stake for one or both of the contestants. Thus John L.'s bouts on his tours in 1883–84 and 1886–87 are included, as he made his standard offer of one thousand dollars for four rounds during these trips.

*KEY:*    LPR:   fight under the London Prize Ring Rules, with bare knuckles
          MQ:   fight under the Marquis of Queensberry Rules, with gloves (varying in size from skintight to eight ounces)
            K:   kid gloves
          W:   win
          D:   draw
        KO:   knockout
        (*):   not listed in the *Ring Record Book*

| Date | Location | Rules | Opponent | Results |
|---|---|---|---|---|
| April 6, 1880 | Boston | MQ | Joe Goss | W3 |
| June 28, 1880 | Boston | MQ | George Rooke | KO3 |
| December 24, 1880 | Cincinnati | LPR:K | John Donaldson | KO10 |
| January 3, 1881 | Boston | MQ | Jack Stewart | KO2 |
| March 31, 1881 | New York | MQ | Steve Taylor | W2 |
| May 16, 1881 | New York | LPR:K | John Flood | W8 |
| July 11, 1881 | Philadelphia | MQ | Fred Crossley | KO1 |
| July 21, 1881* | Philadelphia | MQ | Dan McCarthy | KO1 |
| August 13, 1881 | Chicago | MQ | James Dalton | KO4 |
| September 3, 1881 | Chicago | MQ | Jack Burns | KO1 |
| February 7, 1882 | Mississippi City | LPR | Paddy Ryan | KO9 |
| April 20, 1882 | Rochester, N.Y. | MQ | John McDermott | KO3 |
| July 4, 1882 | Brooklyn | MQ | James Elliott | KO3 |
| July 17, 1882 | New York | MQ | Tug Wilson | W4 |
| September 23, 1882* | Buffalo | MQ | Hen Higgins | KO3 |

| Date | Location | Rules | Opponent | Results |
|------|----------|-------|----------|---------|
| October 16, 1882* | Fort Wayne, Ind. | MQ | S. P. Stockton | KO2 |
| October 30, 1882* | Chicago | MQ | Charley O'Donnell | KO1 |
| November 17, 1882* | Washington, D.C. | MQ | P. J. Rentzler | KO1 |
| January 25, 1883* | Toronto | MQ | Harry Gilman | KO3 |
| May 14, 1883 | New York | MQ | Charlie Mitchell | W3 |
| August 6, 1883 | New York | MQ | Herbert Slade | KO3 |
| October 17, 1883* | McKeesport, Pa. | MQ | James McCoy | KO1 |
| November 3, 1883* | East St. Louis, Ill. | MQ | James Miles | KO1 |
| November 25, 1883* | St. Paul | MQ | Morris Hefey | KO1 |
| December 4, 1883* | Davenport, Iowa | MQ | Michael Sheehan | KO1 |
| January 14, 1884 | Butte, Mont. | MQ | Fred Robinson | KO2 |
| February 1, 1884* | Astoria, Ore. | MQ | Sylvester Le Gouriff | KO1 |
| February 6, 1884* | Seattle | MQ | James Lang | KO1 |
| March 6, 1884 | San Francisco | MQ | George Robinson | W4 |
| April 10, 1884 | Galveston, Tex. | MQ | Al Marx | KO1 |
| April 29, 1884 | Hot Springs, Ark. | MQ | Dan Henry | KO1 |
| May 1, 1884 | Memphis | MQ | William Fleming | KO1 |
| May 2, 1884 | Nashville | MQ | Enos Phillips | W4 |
| November 10, 1884 | New York | MQ | John Laflin | W4 |
| November 18, 1884 | New York | MQ | Alf Greenfield | W2 |
| January 12, 1885 | Boston | MQ | Alf Greenfield | W4 |
| January 19, 1885 | New York | MQ | Paddy Ryan | W1 |
| June 13, 1885 | Chicago | MQ | Jack Burke | W5 |
| August 29, 1885 | Cincinnati | MQ | Dominick McCaffery | W6 |
| September 18, 1886 | Allegheny, Pa. | MQ | Frank Herald | W2 |
| November 13, 1886 | San Francisco | MQ | Paddy Ryan | KO3 |
| December 28, 1886 | Denver | MQ | Duncan McDonald | D4 |
| January 18, 1887 | Minneapolis | MQ | Patsy Cardiff | D6 |
| March 10, 1888 | Chantilly, France | LPR | Charlie Mitchell | D39 |
| July 8, 1889 | Richburg, Miss. | LPR | Jake Kilrain | KO75 |
| September 7, 1892 | New Orleans | MQ | James Corbett | KO BY 21 |
| March 1, 1905 | Grand Rapids, Mich. | MQ | Jim McCormick | KO2 |

*Total prize bouts:* 47
*Won by knockout:* 29
*Won by decision:* 14
*Drew:* 3
*Lost by knockout:* 1

# Estimates of the Career Earnings
# of John L. Sullivan

Four estimates of John L.'s earnings exist. The first, and most inaccurate, appeared in *The Modern Gladiator* in 1889. Ten years later a young reporter from the *Brooklyn Eagle* visited Sullivan and asked him about his earnings. Puffing on a cigar, John L. looked over his personal records with the reporter and came up with some figures. In 1912 Richard Barry included a list of Sullivan's earnings in an article on John L. in *Pearson's Magazine*. His sum, $996,400, was $95,000 short of the actual amount of his figures. Finally, after Sullivan's death the *New York Herald* printed a table of his estimated earnings through 1898, which was reprinted in the *Literary Digest*. Obviously, the *Herald* drew mostly on Barry's article.

These estimates tabulate in dollars as follows:

| Event | Modern Gladiator | Brooklyn Eagle | Barry | New York Herald |
|---|---|---|---|---|
| | (1889) | (1899) | (1912) | (1918) |
| John Donaldson (1880) | | $    78 | | |
| John Flood (1881) | $  1,000 | | $     750 | $     750 |
| Paddy Ryan (1882) | 3,200 | 4,500 | 5,000 | 5,000 |
| Exhibitions (1882) | | 24,900 | | |
| James Elliott (1882) | | 2,600 | 1,100 | 1,100 |
| Tug Wilson (1882) | | 10,000 | 12,000 | 12,000 |
| Show business (1883) | | 16,000 | | |
| Tour (1882–83) | | | 105,000 | 105,000 |
| Boston benefit (1883) | 11,565 | | 3,700 | 3,700 |
| Charlie Mitchell (1883) | 6,745 | 12,000 | 11,000 | 11,000 |
| Herbert Slade (1883) | 6,485 | 12,000 | 13,000 | 13,000 |
| Grand Tour (1883–84) | 50,000 | | 195,000 | 195,000 |
| New York tour (1884) | 10,000 | | | |
| Boston saloon (1883–84) | 25,000 | 50,000 | | |

| Event | Modern Gladiator | Brooklyn Eagle | Barry | New York Herald |
|---|---|---|---|---|
| | (1889) | (1899) | (1912) | (1918) |
| Charlie Mitchell (1884) | 1,250 | | 5,000 | 5,000 |
| McCaffery exhibition (1884) | | | 1,800 | 1,800 |
| Laflin and Greenfield (1884) | 11,500 | 33,000 | 16,000 | 16,000 |
| Alf Greenfield (1885) | | | 5,500 | 5,500 |
| Statuary (1885) | | 35,000 | | |
| Paddy Ryan (1885) | 2,500 | 8,000 | 7,000 | 7,000 |
| "Pitching ball" | 6,800 | | | |
| "New Brunswick tour" | 1,000 | | | |
| Jack Burke (1885) | 4,855 | | 4,300 | 4,300 |
| Dominick McCaffery (1885) | 5,680 | | 8,500 | 8,500 |
| Frank Herald (1885) | | 8,000 | 2,300 | 2,300 |
| Paddy Ryan (1886) | | 15,000 | 6,500 | 6,500 |
| Duncan McDonald (1886) | | | 2,800 | 2,800 |
| Patsy Cardiff (1887) | | 10,000 | 3,750 | 3,750 |
| Tour (1886–87) | | 40,000 | 60,000 | 60,000 |
| Championship Belt (1887) | | | 3,000 | 3,000 |
| European tour (1887–18) | | 28,000 | 97,000 | 97,000 |
| Charlie Mitchell (1888) | | | 4,000 | 4,000 |
| Boston benefit (1888) | | 5,000 | 4,000 | 4,000 |
| New York benefit (1888) | | | 6,900 | 6,900 |
| Jake Kilrain (1889) | 24,600 | 26,000 | 10,000 | 10,000 |
| Corbett exhibition (1891) | | | 2,000 | 2,000 |
| Australian tour (1891) | | | 58,000 | 58,000 |
| *Honest Hearts and Willing Hands* (1891–92) | | 30,000 | 85,000 | 85,000 |
| New York benefit (1892) | | 17,000 | | |
| *The Man from Boston* (1892–94) | | 120,000 | 45,000 | 45,000 |
| *The True American* (1894–95) | | 30,000 | 85,000 | 85,000 |
| Tour (1896) | | | 90,000 | 90,000 |
| Sharkey exhibition (1896) | | | 1,500 | 1,500 |
| Tour (1897) | | | 40,000 | 40,000 |
| Tour (1898) | | | 25,000 | 25,000 |
| New York saloons (1898–1902) | | 15,000 | | |
| Vaudeville engagements (1898–1908) | | | 65,000 | |
| Totals | $172,180 | $552,078 | $1,091,400 | $1,026,400 |

Such widely scattered and fragmentary evidence cannot be conclusive. However, when Sullivan's twentieth-century earnings in the theater and vaudeville, on the lecture circuit, and on tour with Kilrain are considered, the totals mount even more.

Although he was never a millionaire, there is a strong indication that John L. Sullivan, in his several occupations, was the first American nonentrepreneur from the popular culture to earn over a million dollars in his lifetime.

# Acknowledgments

John L. Sullivan's life could not have been examined without the generous help of many people and institutions. I am particularly grateful to those descendants of John L.'s sister, Ann Lennon, who took the time to write, look for correspondence, and research family artifacts and Bibles on my behalf. My thanks go to Eileen Jennings (grandniece), Maureen J. Sawyers (great-grandniece), Charles Westwater (grandnephew), and Richard Westwater (grandnephew). I owe a special debt to William C. Brick, whose genealogical research into another branch of the Sullivan family turned up much useful information on John L.'s antecedents and on the Boston of his childhood.

The staffs of the following libraries have been most helpful with their assistance: Duke University Library; Library of Congress; Milner Library, Illinois State University; University of Nebraska Library, Lincoln; Nimitz Library, United States Naval Academy; and L. E. Phillips Memorial Public Library, Eau Claire, Wisconsin. I also owe much to the help of the following institutions: Genealogical Society of Utah, Salt Lake City; Office of the Registrar, Boston College; Massachusetts Historical Society, Boston; Registry Division, city of Boston; Chancery Office, Archdiocese of Boston; Supreme Judicial Court, Suffolk County, Massachusetts; Superior Court of Cook County, Illinois; and the Executive Office of Public Safety, commonwealth of Massachusetts.

A number of people were kind enough to correspond concerning their stories about John L. I thank all of them for proving that, for some of us, his name is still alive: Charles D. Brown, Ronald C. Butler, James R. Castleberry, Ray Cohan, Edward R. Cuniffe, Joseph DeGrace, John R. Dempsey, John B. Drisko, J. F. Hopkins, Orval Hopkins, Dorothy H. Johnson, A. L. Johnston, John R. Kelly, Edward J. Keyes, William F. McOsker, Virginia T. Mosley, Gardner Moyer, Doris Nicholas, Larry A. Nickel, Leonard J. Panaggio (who was particularly helpful on material from Rhode Island), John Pyle, Frank R. Ramos, Steven A. Riess, Hy Rosenberg, Harold Rosenthal (a true sports fan), Frederick A. Ryan, Coraell C. Stage, Ben Weinstock, Elizabeth Bailey Willis, and Karolyn Wrightson.

Many friends and colleagues have generously given time to critique all or parts of the manuscript, most of them having the same suggestion: "Cut it down." I am most grateful to all for their trenchant comments and advice: Richard P. Abels, Thomas Brennan, Phyllis Culham, Thomas J. Cutler, Jan

Dejnozka, Nancy W. Ellenberger, Elliott Gorn, Kenneth J. Hagan, Frederick S. Harrod, Andrew Koczon, Charles R. Middleton, David Peeler, Anne T. Quartararo, Benjamin Rader, Randy Roberts, William R. Roberts, Jack Sweetman, Craig L. Symonds, Larry V. Thompson, Philip W. Warken, and Roger T. Zeimet. I have acted on many of their suggestions. Some, however, I have resisted, as I find I have at least two traits in common with John L.: an inordinate love of beer and a certain stubbornness. Much of whatever credit this book deserves is the work of these friends and colleagues; mistakes in both fact and interpretation are mine alone.

On a chill winter's day Carl H. Scheele, the curator of the Division of Community Life in the National Museum of American History, Smithsonian Institution, gave amply of his time to guide me through his treasure trove of artifacts from the world of American sport. In the process I examined the facsimile of the Championship Belt, which eventually may be on display. I am grateful for Mr. Scheele's generosity and interest in my topic. The chance to swing Jim Thorpe's bat and hold the ball that gave Bill Russell his ten thousandth rebound provided a treasured memory for one who was once a so-so first baseman and the slowest guard who ever played basketball.

The manuscript for this book has gone through many revisions. I am highly indebted to Bernadette Coates, Judy Waltz, Tara Gray, and, above all, Connie Grigor, for their patience and good humor while typing and retyping so many times that they have become specialists on John L.

At the University of Illinois Press, Larry Malley has lived with this book for several years, and he, his wife Maggie, and the indefatigable Bastille Malley have been kindness itself. My copy editor, William Waller, proved himself both a discerning wordsmith and an exceptional judge of analytical detail; he deserves much credit for whatever is positive in this book. Most of the pictures come from the indispensable collection of Bill Schutte, and Bill was also generous in sharing his encyclopedic knowledge of nineteenth-century American boxing with me.

Finally, I owe much to members of my family. Nugget, Ginger, Nutmeg, and Sage were considerate with their attention during the process of writing and rewriting. Most importantly, my mother, Maxine Isenberg, consistently displayed those two conspicuous traits of a parent cursed with an author for a child: she has been at once my most biased critic and my strongest booster.

# Notes

## PROLOGUE

[1]*Historical Statistics of the United States, Colonial Times to 1857* (Washington, D.C.: U.S. Bureau of Commerce, 1960), 14.

[2]Sam Bass Warner, Jr., *The Urban Wilderness: A History of the American City* (New York: Harper and Row, 1972), 70; Kermit Vanderbilt, *The Achievement of William Dean Howells: A Reinterpretation* (Princeton: Princeton University Press, 1968), 154.

[3]*New York Herald*, May 17, 1881, 12.

[4]James D. McCabe, Jr., *Lights and Shadows of New York Life; or, The Sights and Sensations of the Great City* (Philadelphia: National Publishing Co., 1872), 603. McCabe was a bit of a sensationmonger and a moralist, but his description of Harry Hill's in its prime (600–604) is the best we have. I have drawn on McCabe heavily here, filtering out some of the prudery, but see also Edward Van Every, *Sins of New York as "Exposed" by the Police Gazette* (Detroit: Gale Research Co., 1976 [1930]), 203–5. Harry Hill went out of business in 1886, a victim of Democratic Mayor Abraham Hewitt's wave of reform.

[5]*New York Clipper*, November 13, 1880, 266.

[6]Parker Morell, *Diamond Jim: The Life and Times of James Buchanan Brady* (New York: Simon and Schuster, 1934), 34–35. This book is partially apochryphal, contains direct quotes that are impossible to attribute, and must be used with extreme care.

[7]*The Modern Gladiator, Being an Account of the Exploits and Experiences of the World's Greatest Fighter, John Lawrence Sullivan* (St. Louis: Athletic Publishing Co., 1889), 18–20; John L. Sullivan, *Life and Reminiscences of a 19th Century Gladiator* (Boston: Jas. A. Hearn & Co., 1892), 43–44; *Boston Daily Globe*, November 27, 1879; Van Every, *Sins of New York*, 161–62. Flood's nickname probably was taken from a popular New York tavern.

[8]*New York Clipper*, May 7, 1881, 106; Sullivan, *Reminiscences*, 44–45.

[9]Mark D. Hirsch, *William C. Whitney: Modern Warwick* (New York: Dodd, Mead, 1948), 94. Five Points is now Chatham Square; it became "Six Points" when Worth Street cut through.

[10]William Leach, *True Love and Perfect Union: The Feminist Reform of Sex and Society* (New York: Basic Books, 1980), 311–12.

[11]Joe Dorney and Sid Sutherland, "John L. Sullivan," *Liberty*, April 11, 1925, 21. Dorney advertised himself as Sullivan's friend, employee, and business counselor for many years, an exaggeration. This article, part of a sprawling twelve-part series running from March to June 1925, is typical of the secondary literature on Sullivan. It is loaded with imaginary quotes and invented scenes, unsupportable allusions, and a melodramatic air that gives it an excellent fictional quality.

[12]*New York Daily Tribune*, May 17, 1881.

[13]*Boston Daily Globe*, May 17, 1881.

[14]Sullivan, *Reminiscences*, 45.

[15]The fullest account of the Sullivan-Flood fight is in the *Boston Daily Globe*, May 17, 1881, from an eyewitness; I have used primarily this recapitulation. See also the *New York Clipper*, May 21, 1881, 135, and the *National Police Gazette*, June 4, 1881, 6.

[16]*New York Herald*, May 17, 1881.

[17]*New York Clipper*, May 21, 1881, 135; *ibid.*, June 4, 1881, 171.

[18]*Ibid.*, June 18, 1881, 203; Sullivan, *Reminiscences*, 46–48.

[19]Sullivan, *Reminiscences*, 47.

[20]For those interested in analyzing "fame," how many political and military leaders of the past could be recognized immediately, given only their first names and middle initials?

[21]The phrase is borrowed from the excellent book by John William Ward, *Andrew Jackson: Symbol for an Age* (New York: Oxford University Press, 1962).

## CHAPTER ONE

[1]Oscar Handlin, *Boston's Immigrants, 1790–1880: A Study in Acculturation*, rev. ed. (New York: Atheneum, 1974), 50–51.

[2]Frederick A. Bushee, *Ethnic Factors in the Population of Boston* (New York: Macmillan, 1903), 2–3.

[3]*Ibid.*, 3; Peter R. Knights, *The Plain People of Boston, 1830–1860: A Study in City Growth* (New York: Oxford University Press, 1971), 33.

[4]Mike Sullivan seems to have told different reporters different stories of his youth and immigration, or the reporters got it wrong. I have chosen the consensus dates. See *Boston Daily Globe*, September 8, 1890; *Boston Herald*, July 9, 1889; *ibid.*, September 8, 1890; *National Police Gazette*, August 19, 1899, 11; *ibid.*, June 9, 1883, 14; *Boston Pilot*, September, 1890, *passim*. In fairness the *Pilot* was given over during this period to eulogizing one of Irish Boston's best, the editor-athlete John Boyle O'Reilly. Regardless, however, the Irish nationalism, Anglophobia, and militant Catholicism of the *Pilot* produced middle–class pretension that had little place for Mike Sullivan or "his kind." *The Modern Gladiator: Being an Account of the Exploits and Experiences of the World's Greatest Fighter, John Lawrence Sullivan* (St. Louis: Athletic Publishing Co., 1889), 12–13, placed Mike's birthdate in 1828.

[5]*Boston Herald*, August 31, 1889; *Boston Daily Globe*, August 31, 1889; the *Boston Evening Transcript*, September 1, 1889, placed Catherine's birth in 1834, as did the *Boston Pilot*, September 7, 1889, 8. Certificate of Marriage,

Archdiocese of Boston, Brighton, Massachusetts; letter, Mrs. Eileen Jennings to author, February 3, 1985. Mrs. Jennings, a grandniece of John L. Sullivan, has custody of the family Bible. Letter, William C. Brick to author, September 29, 1985.

⁶*Boston Pilot*, September 7, 1889, 8; *Modern Gladiator*, 80; letter, William C. Brick to author, September 29, 1985.

⁷A birthdate of October 15, 1858, is given by Sullivan himself in *Life and Reminiscences of a 19th Century Gladiator* (Boston: Jas. A. Hearn & Co., 1892), 21, and is repeated by every secondary source. The Sullivan family Bible also gives October 15. Sullivan's birth certificate, however, on file in the Registry Division of Boston, gives the date as October 12, 1858. It is possible that the parents celebrated their new firstborn's baptismal date as his birthday, although a Certificate of Baptism, Archdiocese of Boston, Brighton, Massachusetts, records his baptism on October 13, 1858. Ann followed on May 28, 1861, and young Michael Francis on November 30, 1866. Letter, Mrs. Eileen Jennings to author, February 3, 1985; Birth Records, Registry Division, City of Boston.

⁸Bushee, *Ethnic Factors*, 44.

⁹*Modern Gladiator*, 12–14.

¹⁰*New York Times*, September 5, 1892, 2:3; Sullivan, *Reminiscences*, 21–22.

¹¹Joe Dorney and Sid Sutherland, "John L. Sullivan," *Liberty*, March 21, 1925, 8–11, 13. The account, suspect for reasons mentioned in the Prologue, is valuable for two reasons. First, Dorney worked with materials gained from Sullivan's surviving sister, Ann Lennon, after the fighter's death, and second, he published many rare pictures, including boyhood photos of Sullivan. As to the famous eyes, Dorney says they looked black and photographed black but were actually "the dead, remorseless gray of slate."

¹²*Boston Herald*, July 9, 1889; *New York Times*, November 21, 1883, 1:6; *National Police Gazette*, October 31, 1885, 10.

¹³*Modern Gladiator*, 184–185.

¹⁴Page Smith, *The Nation Comes of Age: A People's History of the Ante-Bellum Years* (New York: McGraw-Hill, 1981), 4:533.

¹⁵Carl F. Kaestle, *Pillars of the Republic: Common Schools and American Society, 1780–1860* (New York: Hill and Wang, 1983), 88; Thomas Colley Grattan, *Civilized America* (London: Bradbury and Evans, 1859), 2:41.

¹⁶For an interesting cross-section, provided by an Irishman evaluating the habits of his countrymen, in this case a list of approbation, the reader is referred to Jeremiah O'Donovan's bookselling attempts among the Boston Irish in his *A Brief Account of the Author's Interview with His Countrymen, and of the Parts of the Emerald Isle Whence They Emigrated, Together with a Direct Reference to Their Present Location in the Land of Their Adoption, Among His Travels Through Various States of the Union in 1854 and 1855* (Pittsburgh: Author, 1864), 184–93. O'Donovan's compendious catalog of prospective Irish book-readers in Boston includes neither Mike Sullivan's nor Catherine Kelly's family.

¹⁷Stephen Thernstrom, *The Other Bostonians: Poverty and Progress in the American Metropolis, 1880–1970* (Cambridge: Harvard University Press, 1973), 24–25; Knights, *The Plain People of Boston*, 47.

¹⁸Handlin, *Boston's Immigrants*, 131.

[19]Dennis P. Ryan, *Beyond the Ballot Box: A Social History of the Boston Irish, 1845–1917* (Rutherford, N.J.: Fairleigh Dickinson University Press, 1983), 21, 23; Bushee, *Ethnic Factors*, 84.

[20]Richard Stivers, *A Hair of the Dog: Irish Drinking and American Stereotype* (University Park: Pennsylvania State University Press, 1976), 138–139; Thernstrom, *The Other Bostonians*, 34, 36, 100–103, 131; E. P. Hutchinson, *Immigrants and Their Children, 1850–1950* (New York: Russell and Russell, 1976 [1956]), 88–89, 95, 132, 178.

[21]Handlin, *Boston's Immigrants*, 62; Barbara Miller Solomon, *Ancestors and Immigrants: A Changing New England Tradition* (Chicago: University of Chicago Press, 1972 [1956]), 45; Charles Phillips Huse, *The Financial History of Boston From May 1, 1822, to January 31, 1909* (New York: Russell and Russell, 1916), 17; John K. Mahon, *History of the Militia and the National Guard* (New York: Macmillan, 1983), 86.

[22]Martin E. Marty, *Righteous Empire: The Protestant Experience in America* (New York: Harper and Row, 1977), 128, 156.

[23]Solomon, *Ancestors and Immigrants*, 2; Marty, *Righteous Empire*, 159–160.

[24]Marty, *Righteous Empire*, 22–23; Arthur Mann, *Yankee Reformers in the Urban Age: Social Reform in Boston, 1880–1900* (Chicago: University of Chicago Press, 1974 [1954]), 42; Solomon, *Ancestors and Immigrants*, 46; *Boston Pilot*, July 9, 1887. The phrase "Rum, Romanism, and Rebellion" refers to the sermon delivered by a Protestant minister on the eve of the 1884 election, which was popularly believed to have cost "the Plumed Knight," James G. Blaine of Maine, the presidency.

[25]Alexis de Tocqueville, *Democracy in America* (New York: Knopf, 1980), 1:300–303.

[26]Justin Winsor, ed., *The Memorial History of Boston, Including Suffolk County, Massachusetts, 1630–1880*, 4 vols. (Boston: James R. Osgood and Co., 1880–81). Winsor was the librarian of Harvard; the reference to Irish famine relief occurs in 4:667. James Bernard Cullen, ed., *The Story of the Irish in Boston, Together with Biographical Sketches of Representative Men and Noted Women* (Boston: James B. Cullen and Co., 1889); Donald Barr Chidsey, *John the Great: The Times and Life of a Remarkable American, John L. Sullivan* (Garden City, N.Y.: Doubleday, 1942), 3.

[27]Cullen, ed., *The Story of the Irish in Boston*, 255–56, 425–28.

[28]*Ibid.*, 428–29.

[29]Mann, *Yankee Reformers in the Urban Age*, 46; Solomon, *Ancestors and Immigrants*, 153–55; Nathaniel S. Shaler, "The Scotch Element in the American People," *Atlantic Monthly* 77 (1896): 516.

[30]Thernstrom, *The Other Bostonians*, 160.

[31]Edward Dicey, *Six Months in the Federal States* (London: Macmillan, 1863), 2:171–81.

[32]George Wingate Chase, *Abstract of the Census of Massachusetts, 1860* (Boston: Wright and Potter, 1863); Handlin, *Boston's Immigrants*, 214.

[33]Sullivan, *Reminiscences*, 21–24; *Boston Herald*, February 3, 1918; *Boston City Directory* (1882), Library of Congress. The impression of Sullivan's grad-

uation date from Dwight Grammar School is reflected in his autobiography. In dating, I am using the common age of fourteen for boys of his generation.

³⁴Sullivan, *Reminiscences*, 24.

³⁵*Boston Herald*, February 3, 1918; Sullivan, *Reminiscences*, 25; Huse, *Financial History of Boston*, 117.

³⁶*Boston City Directory* (1858), Library of Congress.

³⁷Handlin, *Boston's Immigrants*, 169; Ryan, *Beyond the Ballot Box*, 73–74; Joseph F. Dineen, *Ward Eight* (New York: Harper and Brothers, 1936), 113. The Chestnut Hill locale for Boston College was established in 1913. *Ward Eight* is a fictional account of Irish life in Boston in the nineteenth century.

³⁸*New York Times*, October 21, 1883, 2:5; *National Police Gazette*, November 24, 1883, 2; *ibid.*, April 26, 1884, 7; Sullivan, *Reminiscences*, 25; John Lardner, "The Big Man with the Biggest Punch," *New York Times Magazine*, August 26, 1956, 34; *Modern Gladiator*, 11.

³⁹Letter, Angelina C. Graham (Archives of Boston College) to author, July 29, 1983. I am grateful to Ms. Graham for examining these registers on my behalf.

⁴⁰Sullivan, *Reminiscences*, 25–29; *Modern Gladiator*, 12.

⁴¹Sullivan, *Reminiscences*, 27–28; Dorney and Sutherland, "John L. Sullivan," *Liberty*, March 28, 1925, 32, 34. The Scannell fight was not reported in the Boston press and cannot be dated with any precision. William Inglis, *Champions off Guard* (New York: Vanguard Press, 1932), 23–24, says the fight was for five dollars.

⁴²Huse, *Financial History of Boston*, 195–97. John Sullivan himself may have worked for a short time alongside his father on sewer projects. *National Police Gazette*, April 26, 1884, 7.

⁴³R. Terry Furst, "Boxing Stereotypes versus the Culture of the Professional Boxer: A Sociological 'Decision,'" *Sport Sociology Bulletin* 3, no. 2 (Spring 1974): 14, 18, 20, 23, 25, 36; S. Kirson Weinberg and Henry Arond, "The Occupational Culture of the Boxer," *American Journal of Sociology* 57, no. 5 (March 1952), 461, 465.

⁴⁴*National Police Gazette*, February 26, 1887, 10, reprinted in *Modern Gladiator*, 11–12.

⁴⁵William E. Harding, *The Champions of the American Prize Ring: A Complete History of the Heavy-weight Champions of America, with Their Battles and Portraits* (New York: Police Gazette, 1881), 32–34; Alexander Johnston, *Ten . . . and Out!: The Complete Story of the Prize Ring in America*, 3rd rev. ed. (New York: Ives Washburn, 1947), 47–49; *Boston Daily Globe*, October 14, 1878.

⁴⁶Harding, *Champions of the American Prize Ring*, 34–35.

⁴⁷*Boston Daily Globe*, November 24, 1878; *ibid.*, November 29, 1878; *ibid.*, December 24, 1878; *ibid.*, January 21, 1879; *ibid.*, February 4, 1879.

⁴⁸Sullivan, *Reminiscences*, 30–31; *Boston Daily Globe*, March 15, 1879. Sullivan erroneously dates the Woods fight in 1878 and gets the location wrong; so do Dorney and Sutherland, "John L. Sullivan," 2:33, who have it occurring in Cockerill Hall on March 6, 1878. Dorney's account of the Woods fight (33–34) exceeds his usual talent for creative fiction.

⁴⁹Harding, *Champions of the American Prize Ring,* 10–20; Alan Lloyd, *The Great Prize Fight* (New York: Coward, McCann and Geohegan, 1977), 162–63; Mark O. Hirsch, *William C. Whitney: Modern Warwick* (New York: Dodd, Mead, 1948), 149–50.

⁵⁰O'Donovan, *A Brief Account,* 146. O'Donovan is here lyrically describing a local Philadelphia pug named Dominick Bradley.

## CHAPTER TWO

¹Stephen Thernstrom, *The Other Bostonians: Poverty and Progress in the American Metropolis, 1880–1970* (Cambridge: Harvard University Press, 1973), 5, 13; Peter R. Knights, *The Plain People of Boston, 1830–1860: A Study in City Growth* (New York: Oxford University Press, 1971), 20.

²David McCullough, *Mornings on Horseback* (New York: Touchstone, 1981), 199, 204.

³Arthur Mann, *Yankee Reformers in the Urban Age: Social Reform in Boston, 1880–1900* (Chicago: University of Chicago Press, 1974 [1954]), 3.

⁴Edward L. Ayers, *Vengeance and Justice: Crime and Punishment in the 19th-Century American South* (New York: Oxford University Press, 1986 [1984]), 82; Robert A. Woods, ed., *Americans in Process: A Settlement Study* (Boston: Houghton Mifflin, 1903), 157; Kathleen Neils Conzen, "Immigrants, Immigrant Neighborhoods, and Ethnic Identity: Historical Issues," *Journal of American History* 66, no. 3 (December 1979), 607, 613.

⁵Thernstrom, *The Other Bostonians,* 41, 10; Conzen, "Immigrants," 605.

⁶Merle Curti, *Roots of American Loyalty* (New York: Columbia University Press, 1946), viii; Michael B. Katz, *People of Hamilton, Canada West: Family and Class in a Mid-Nineteenth Century City* (Cambridge: Harvard University Press, 1976), 61–62; Newman Smyth, *Social Problems: Sermons to Workingmen* (Boston: Houghton Mifflin, 1885), 29, 34–36.

⁷Woods, *Americans in Process,* 250.

⁸Martin E. Marty, *Righteous Empire: The Protestant Experience in America* (New York: Harper and Row, 1977 [1970]), 110; Thomas Colley Grattan, *Civilized America* (London: Bradley and Evans, 1859), 2:318.

⁹Gunther Barth, *City People: The Rise of Modern City Culture in Nineteenth Century America* (New York: Oxford University Press, 1980), 19; Thernstrom, *The Other Bostonians,* 132.

¹⁰Curti, *Roots of American Loyalty,* 42, 100; Sam Bass Warner, Jr., "Preface" (1st ed.) to Robert A. Woods and Albert J. Kennedy, *The Zone of Emergence: Observations of the Lower Middle and Upper Working Class Communities of Boston, 1905–1914,* 2nd ed. (Cambridge: M.I.T. Press, 1962), 17.

¹¹Page Smith, *The Nation Comes of Age: A People's History of the Antebellum Years* (New York: McGraw-Hill, 1981), 4:894.

¹²Johan Huizinga, *Homo Ludens: A Study of the Play Element in Culture* (Boston: Beacon Press, 1955), 192; Mann, *Yankee Reformers in the Urban Age,* 20.

¹³Huizinga, *Homo Ludens,* 46, 13, 8.

¹⁴John Dizikes, *Sportsmen and Gamesmen: From the Years that Shaped American Ideas about Winning and Losing and How to Play the Game* (Boston: Houghton Mifflin, 1981), 25–30.

¹⁵Barth, *City People*, 63–64, 154, 24.

¹⁶Warner, in *The Zone of Emergence*, 27.

¹⁷Barth, *City People*, 224, 149.

¹⁸*Ibid.*, 39; Dizikes, *Sportsmen and Gamesmen*, 4.

¹⁹Andrew Sinclair, *The Emancipation of the American Woman* (New York: Harper and Row, 1966 [1965]), 242–44.

²⁰Richard Stivers, *A Hair of the Dog: Irish Drinking and American Stereotype* (University Park: Pennsylvania State University Press, 1976), 109; Hasia R. Diner, *Erin's Daughters in America: Irish Immigrant Women in the Nineteenth Century* (Baltimore: Johns Hopkins University Press, 1983), xiv.

²¹*National Police Gazette*, October 6, 1883, 14; William Leach, *True Love and Perfect Union: The Feminist Reform of Sex and Society* (New York: Basic Books, 1980), 205–06; Dennis P. Ryan, *Beyond the Ballot Box: A Social History of the Boston Irish, 1845–1917* (Rutherford, N.J.: Fairleigh Dickinson University Press, 1983), 41, 47.

²²Peter Gay, *Education of the Senses*, vol. 1 of *The Bourgeois Experience: Victoria to Freud* (New York: Oxford University Press, 1984), 208–9; *National Police Gazette*, December 15, 1900, 10; Peter N. Stearns, *Be a Man!: Males in Modern Society* (New York: Holmes & Meier, 1979), 59–60; Diner, *Erin's Daughters*, 21.

²³Stivers, *A Hair of the Dog*, 80.

²⁴J. Hector St. John de Crèvecoeur, *Letters from an American Farmer and Sketches of 18th-Century America*, ed. Albert E. Stone (New York: Penguin, 1981), 78, 85.

²⁵Justin Kaplan, *Walt Whitman: A Life* (New York: Bantam Books, 1980), 58; F. O. Matthiessen, *The James Family: A Group Biography, Together with Selections from the Writings of Henry James Senior, William, Henry, and Alice James* (New York: Vintage Press, 1980), 47; Smith, *The Nation Comes of Age*, 688.

²⁶McCullough, *Mornings on Horseback*, 202; Lyman Abbott, *Henry Ward Beecher* (New York: Chelsea House, 1980 [1903]), 7, 21.

²⁷Marty, *Righteous Empire*, 96; Woods and Kennedy, *The Zone of Emergence*, 129; Herbert W. Schneider, *A History of American Philosophy*, 2d ed. (New York: Columbia University Press, 1963 [1946]), 228.

²⁸Grattan, *Civilized America*, 2:100; W. J. Rorabough, *The Alcoholic Republic: An American Tradition* (New York: Oxford University Press, 1979), 143–44.

²⁹William I. Cole, "Criminal Tendencies," in Robert A. Woods, ed., *The City Wilderness: A Settlement Study* (Boston: Houghton Mifflin, 1898), 172; Perry R. Duis, *The Saloon: Public Drinking in Chicago and Boston, 1880–1920* (Urbana: University of Illinois Press, 1983), 16.

³⁰Oscar Handlin, *Boston's Immigrants: A Study in Acculturation, 1790–1880*, rev. ed. (New York: Atheneum, 1974 [1959]), 121; Stivers, *A Hair of the Dog*, 16.

³¹Herbert Asbury, *The Gangs of New York: An Informal History of the Underworld* (Garden City, N.Y.: Garden City Publishing Co., 1928), 27; Cole, "Criminal Tendencies," 157–58.

³²Stivers, *A Hair of the Dog*, 22–23; Duis, *The Saloon*, 152, 165.

[33]Duis, *The Saloon*, 102.

[34]Stephen Hardy, *How Boston Played: Sport, Recreation and Community, 1865–1915* (Boston: Northeastern University Press, 1982), 54–55, 58; Stivers, *A Hair of the Dog*, 129.

[35]Stivers, *A Hair of the Dog*, 87.

[36]*Ibid.*, 30–31; Cole, "Criminal Tendencies," 157–58; "The Roots of Political Power," in Woods, *The City Wilderness*, 118.

[37]Duis, *The Saloon*, 106, 2–3.

[38]Stivers, *A Hair of the Dog*, 48–49; Duis, *The Saloon*, 12, 29, 31.

[39]Benjamin G. Rader, *American Sports: From the Age of Folk Games to the Age of Spectators* (Englewood Cliffs, N.J.: Prentice-Hall, 1983), 17–18, 32.

[40]Roger Lane, *Violent Death in the City: Suicide, Accident and Murder in 19th-Century Philadelphia* (Cambridge: Harvard University Press, 1979), 59; unfortunately, no comparable study exists for nineteenth-century Boston. Stivers, *A Hair of the Dog*, 7.

[41]Reuben Fine, *A History of Psychoanalysis* (New York: Columbia University Press, 1979), 226–29; Konrad Lorenz, *On Aggression* (New York: Harcourt, 1963).

[42]Robert R. Dykstra, *The Cattle Towns* (New York: Knopf, 1971), 142–48.

[43]Dickson D. Bruce, Jr., *Violence and Culture in the Antebellum South* (Austin: University of Texas Press, 1979), 4; Bertram Wyatt-Brown, *Southern Honor: Ethics and Behavior in the Old South* (New York: Oxford University Press, 1982), 350–52.

[44]Wyatt-Brown, *Southern Honor*, 165; Elliott J. Gorn, " 'Gouge and Bite, Pull Hair and Scratch:' The Social Significance of Fighting in the Southern Backcountry," *American Historical Review* 90, no. 1 (February 1985): 42, 23.

[45]Lane, *Violent Death in the City*, 124, 34; but see p. 76 for a decline in these statistics. See also Theodore N. Ferdinand, "The Criminal Patterns of Boston since 1849," *American Journal of Sociology* 73, no. 1 (July 1967): 84–99, and Roger Lane, "Urbanization and Criminal Violence in the 19th Century: Massachusetts as a Test Case," in Hugh Davis Graham and Ted Robert Gurr, eds., *The History of Violence in America: Historical and Comparative Perspectives* (New York: Praeger, 1969), 468–84.

[46]Huizinga, *Homo Ludens*, 101; Christopher Hibbert, *The Roots of Evil: A Social History of Crime and Punishment* (Boston: Little, Brown, 1963), 46.

[47]Hibbert, *The Roots of Evil*, 72.

[48]Gorn, " 'Gouge and Bite,' " 34, 42, 36.

[49]John Keegan, *The Face of Battle: A Study of Agincourt, Waterloo and the Somme* (New York: Vintage Books, 1977), 314.

## CHAPTER THREE

[1]For ancient boxing, see Joan F. Loubet, "Bare Knuckles: A Forgotten Era in Boxing," *Ring Magazine*, March 1979, 63; Edward McNall Burns, Robert E. Lerner, and Standish Meacham, *Western Civilizations: Their History and Culture*, 9th ed. (New York: Norton, 1980), 96; Věra Olivová, *Sports and Games in the Ancient World* (New York: St. Martin's Press, 1984), 52, 71, 85, 90, 140, 143–44, 153, 182; K. T. Frost, "Greek Boxing," *Journal of Hellenic*

*Studies* 26 (1906): 213–25; Richard Lattimore, ed. and trans., *The Odyssey of Homer* (New York: Harper and Row, 1968), 124–25, 176; Richard D. Mandell, *The First Modern Olympics* (Berkeley: University of California Press, 1976), 7, 12, 24; Jerome Carcopino, *Daily Life in Ancient Rome: The People of the City at the Height of the Empire,* ed. Henry T. Rowell, trans. E. O. Larimer (New Haven: Yale University Press, 1960 [1940]), 237–38, 264–79, 297; *The Modern Gladiator, Being an Account of the Exploits and Experiences of the World's Greatest Fighter, John Lawrence Sullivan* (Saint Louis: Athletic Publishing Co., 1889), 346–49; Suetonius, *The Twelve Caesars,* trans. Robert Graves (New York: Penguin, 1957), 162; Jacob Burckhardt, *The Age of Constantine the Great,* trans. Moses Hadas (Berkeley: University of California Press, 1983), 23; Peter Arnott, *The Romans and Their World* (New York: St. Martin's Press, 1970), 168; C. Day Lewis, trans., *The Aeneid of Virgil* (Garden City, N.Y.: Doubleday, 1953), 114–18; and John Durant, *The Heavyweight Champions,* 6th ed. (New York: Hastings House, 1976), 1.

²For English boxing, see Randy Roberts, "Eighteenth Century Boxing," *Journal of Sport History* 4, no. 3 (Fall 1977): 247–48; Peter Burke, *Popular Culture in Early Modern Europe* (New York: Harper and Row, 1978), 248–49; "Boxiana, or, Sketches of Pugilism," nos. 1–8 (July 1819–October 1820), *Blackwood's Edinburgh Magazine*; Lawrence Hulton, "Prize-fighting in the Olden Times," *Harper's Weekly,* August 31, 1895, 825; Bohun Lynch [John Gilbert], *The Prize Ring* (London: Country Life, 1925); Frank Butler, *A History of Boxing in Britain: A Survey of the Noble Art from its Origins to the Present-Day* (London: Arthur Barker, 1972); *Modern Gladiator,* 286–98; Thomas S. Henricks, "The Democratization of Sport in Eighteenth-Century England," *Journal of Popular Culture* 18, no. 3 (Winter 1984): 11–14; Pierce Egan, *Boxiana: Sketches of Ancient and Modern Pugilism* (London: G. Smeeton, 1812); Daniel Mendoza, *The Memoirs of the Life of Daniel Mendoza* (New York: Arno Press, 1975); John Ford, *Prizefighting: The Age of Regency Boximania* (New York: Great Albion Books, 1971); James E. Marlow, "Popular Culture, Pugilism, and Pickwick," *Journal of Popular Culture* 15, no. 4 (Spring 1982): 19–20; Austen Pember, "Patrician Pugilism," *The National Review* (London), December 1889, 479–90; Alan Lloyd, *The Great Prize Fight* (New York: Coward, McCann, and Geoghegan, 1977; and "R.," "The Crime of Prizefighters— Addressed to Viscount Duncannon," *The New Monthly Magazine and Literary Journal* (London) 42 (1834): 326–36.

³John R. Betts, "Mind and Body in Early American Thought," *Journal of American History* 54, no. 4 (March 1968): 805.

⁴Allen Guttmann, *From Ritual to Record: The Nature of Modern Sports* (New York: Columbia University Press, 1978), 16, 82.

⁵Thorstein Veblen, *The Theory of the Leisure Class: An Economic Study of Institutions* (New York: Mentor Books, 1953 [1899]), 170.

⁶Guttmann, *From Ritual to Record,* 151; James O. Robertson, *American Myth, American Reality* (New York: Hill and Wang, 1980), 198, 290.

⁷Donald J. Mrozek, *Sport and American Mentality, 1880–1910* (Knoxville: University of Tennessee Press, 1983), 30; Benjamin G. Rader, "Modern Sports: In Search of Interpretations," *Journal of Social History* 13, no. 2 (Winter 1979): 308; Alexander Johnston, *Ten . . . and Out! The Complete Story of the Prize*

*Ring in America*, 3rd rev. ed. (New York: Ives Washburn, 1947), 1; Robert Edgren, "Fighters by Nature," *Outing*, December 1903, 343.

[8]*National Police Gazette*, January 28, 1888, 7; Duffield Osborne, "A Defense of Pugilism," *North American Review*, April 1888, 434–35; Johnston, *Ten . . . and Out!* 12.

[9]Denis Mack Smith, *Mussolini: A Biography* (New York: Knopf, 1982), 114; Adolf Hitler, *Mein Kampf*, trans. Ralph Manheim (Boston: Houghton Mifflin, 1943), 410.

[10]Frederick L. Paxson, "The Rise of Sport," *Mississippi Valley Historical Review* 4, no. 2 (September 1917): 145, 167; Rader, "Modern Sports," 318. Rader's interesting attempt to develop a "countercultural" argument for boxing falls short, however, as prizefighting sought to emulate many of the sporting ethics of Paxson's "honest sport."

[11]Guttmann, *From Ritual to Record*, 84; Robertson, *American Myth, American Reality*, 250–57; Benjamin G. Rader, *American Sports: From the Age of Folk Games to the Age of Spectators* (Englewood Cliffs, N.J.: Prentice-Hall, 1983), 358; Grantland Rice, "Boxing for a Million Dollars," *American Review of Reviews*, October 1926, 416–20. The claim of Al-Tony Gilmore, *Bad Nigger! The National Impact of Jack Johnson* (Port Washington, N.Y.: Kennikat Press, 1975), 54, n. 3a, that from 1892 to 1900 boxing ranked slightly ahead of baseball as America's most popular sport is unsubstantiated and most unlikely.

[12]John Dizikes, *Sportsmen and Gamesmen: From the Years that Shaped American Ideas About Winning and Losing and How to Play the Game* (Boston: Houghton Mifflin, 1981), 71, accents the moral issue but downplays commercialism in the early American rejection of prizefighting. Mrozek, *Sport and American Mentality*, xiii.

[13]Roberts, "Eighteenth Century Boxing," 249–50; Joseph Abbott Liebling, *The Sweet Science* (New York: Viking Press, 1956); *Modern Gladiator*, 265–85.

[14]Charles E. Clay, "A Bout with the Gloves," *Outing*, April 1887, 26–31; A. Austen, "Theory and Practice of Boxing," *Outing*, March 1890, 419; Daniel L. Dawson, "With the Gloves," *Lippincott's Magazine*, January 1892, 97.

[15]Dawson, "With the Gloves," 96, 103; *Spirit of the Times*, December 29, 1877, 582.

[16]Charles E. Clay, "A Bout with the Gloves," *Outing*, January 1887, 359–67; *National Police Gazette*, October 21, 1882, 11; John Boyle O'Reilly, *Athletics and Manly Sport* (Boston: Pilot Publishing Co., 1890), 5; *National Police Gazette*, January 28, 1888, 7; John Boyle O'Reilly, *Ethics of Boxing and Manly Sport* (Boston: Ticknor and Co., 1888), 82, 87; Barbara Miller Solomon, *Ancestors and Immigrants: A Changing New England Tradition* (Chicago: University of Chicago Press, 1972 [1956]), 59.

[17]A. Austen, "A Bout with the Gloves," *Outing*, March 1891, 449–50; Charles E. Clay, "A Bout with the Gloves," *Outing*, February 1887, 473; Johnston, *Ten . . . and Out!* 10; *National Police Gazette*, March 3, 1883, 11; *New York Clipper*, February 17, 1883, 771.

[18]Lyman Abbott, *Henry Ward Beecher* (New York: Chelsea House, 1980 [1903]), 406; Robert W. Johannsen, *Stephen A. Douglas* (New York: Oxford University Press, 1973), viii, 4, 132; Robert Edgren, "The Modern Gladiator:

Why the American Succeeds—Brute Strength Superceded by Cleverness," *Outing*, March 1903, 737–38.

[19]Betts, "Mind and Body," 795–96, 803; Arthur C. Cole, *The Irrepressible Conflict, 1850–1865*, vol. 7 of *A History of American Life*, ed. Arthur Meier Schlesinger and Dixon Ryan Fox (Chicago: Quadrangle Books, 1971 [1934]), 188; Oliver Wendell Holmes, *The Autocrat of the Breakfast-Table: Every Man His Own Boswell* (Boston: Houghton Mifflin, 1842), 35, 171; Mark D. Hirsch, *William C. Whitney: Modern Warwick* (New York: Archon Books, 1969 [1948]), 17; Mandell, *The First Modern Olympics*, 53; Harvey Green, *Fit for America: Health, Fitness, Sport and American Society* (New York: Pantheon Books, 1986), 208.

[20]David McCullough, *Mornings on Horseback* (New York: Touchstone, 1982), 210–11; Theodore Roosevelt, *An Autobiography* (New York: Macmillan, 1913), 47–51.

[21]Mrozek, *Sport and American Mentality*, 49; R. W. Stallman, *Stephen Crane: A Biography* (New York: Braziller, 1968), 12–13, 25; G. Stanley Hall, *Life and Confessions of a Psychologist* (New York: D. Appleton and Co., 1924), 578–79.

[22]John L. Sullivan, *Life and Reminiscences of a 19th Century Gladiator* (Boston: Jas A. Hearn Co., 1892), 273; McCullough, *Mornings on Horseback*, 153; Thomas C. Reeves, *Gentleman Boss: The Life of Chester Alan Arthur* (New York: Knopf, 1975), 152. See also Donald Barr Chidsey, *The Gentleman from New York: A Life of Roscoe Conkling* (New Haven: Yale University Press, 1935), and David M. Jordan, *Roscoe Conkling of New York: Voice in the Senate* (Ithaca: Cornell University Press, 1971).

[23]The London Prize Ring Rules are reprinted in *The Modern Gladiator*, 299–304, and the *National Police Gazette*, January 21, 1883, 11. See also Egan, *Boxiana*, 229, 237.

[24]*National Police Gazette*, December 1, 1888, 3; Ted Morgan, *Maugham: A Biography* (New York: Touchstone, 1980), 37; Durant, *The Heavyweight Champions*, 20; *Modern Gladiator*, 305–7; Dawson, "With the Gloves," 101.

[25]The claim of James Corbett's manager, William A. Brady, *The Fighting Man* (Indianapolis: Bobbs-Merrill, 1916), 66, that Sullivan won all his fights under the London Prize Ring Rules, is false. Sullivan, *Life and Reminiscences*, 240–51; *Modern Gladiator*, 350–51. For a description of a fight with skintight gloves, in this case between the lightweights Mike Coburn and "Spring Heel Dick" Goodwin at the Masonic Hall on Thirteenth Street in New York, see the *National Police Gazette*, March 8, 1879, 7.

[26]*New York Daily Tribune*, August 8, 1882; O'Reilly, *Athletics and Manly Sport*, 5; Sullivan, *Life and Reminiscences*, 281.

[27]Paxson, "The Rise of Sport," 143–44; Solomon, *Ancestors and Immigrants*, 24; Marcus Cunliffe, *George Washington: Man and Monument* (New York: Mentor Books, 1958), 18.

[28]William H. Adams, "New Orleans as the National Center of Boxing," *Louisiana Historical Quarterly* 39 (January 1956): 92; George C. Bernard, *The Morality of Prizefighting* (Washington, D.C.: Catholic University of America Press, 1952), 160.

29Adams, "New Orleans as the National Center of Boxing," 110; Austen, "A Bout with the Gloves," 447; "Prizefighters as Swindlers," *Outlook*, December 3, 1898, 801–2; Herbert Asbury, *Sucker's Progress: An Informal History of Gambling in America from the Colonies to Canfield* (New York: Dodd, Mead, 1938), 180–81.

30John Rickards Betts, "Sporting Journalism in Nineteenth-Century America," *American Quarterly* 5 (Spring 1953): 44; Paxton Hibben, *Henry Ward Beecher: An American Portrait* (New York: The Press of the Readers Club, 1942 [1927]), 142; Page Smith, *Trial by Fire: A People's History of the Civil War and Reconstruction* (New York: McGraw-Hill, 1982), 5:974; Rader, *American Sports*, 34.

31Martin E. Marty, *Righteous Empire: The Protestant Experience in America* (New York: Harper and Row, 1977 [1970]), 194–96; *National Police Gazette*, January 28, 1888, 7.

32*Boston Pilot*, February 18, 1882, 4; "A Point in Journalism," *Nation*, March 23, 1893, 209–10; *National Police Gazette*, June 26, 1889, 10; A. Austen, "A Plea for Style in Boxing," *Outing*, November 1891, 140; *Modern Gladiator*, 381–82.

33"The Renaissance of Pugilism," *Saturday Review* (London), January 10, 1885, 48–49; "Boxing and Sparring," *Saturday Review* (London), January 26, 1884, 107–9; "Presence at Prize-Fights," *Saturday Review* (London), March 25, 1882, 463–64; "The Future of the Prize-Ring," *Spectator* (London), April 8, 1882, 463–64; "The Barbarity of Glove-Fighting," *Saturday Review* (London), January 19, 1895, 86–88.

34*New York Times*, May 28, 1880, 4:6; Thomas M. Croak, "The Professionalization of Prizefighting: Pittsburgh at the Turn of the Century," *Western Pennsylvania Historical Magazine* 62, no. 4 (1979): 335; Lamar W. Bridges, "An Editor's Views on Anti-Cruelty: Eliza Jane Nicholson of the *Picayune*," *Journal of Mississippi History* 39, no. 4 (1977): 310–12; Clarence Greeley, "Public Opinion vs. Prize-Fighting," *Outlook*, November 1893, 888; John K. Mahon, *History of the Militia and the National Guard* (New York: Macmillan, 1983), 110–11.

35"The Evils of the Professional Tendency of Modern Athletics," *Outing*, February 1885, 379; Betts, "Sporting Journalism," 46; *New York Daily Tribune*, July 18, 1882, 2.

36R. C. McDonald, "Scientific Boxing under Boston A.A. Rules," *Outing*, October 1892, 23–24; Gunther Barth, *City People: The Rise of Modern City Culture in Nineteenth-Century America* (New York: Oxford University Press, 1980), 157–58.

37Asbury, *Sucker's Progress*, 178–79; Page Smith, *The Nation Comes of Age: A People's History of the Ante-Bellum Years* (New York: McGraw-Hill, 1981), 4:776; *National Police Gazette*, August 29, 1846, 429 (the first mention of boxing in the paper); Cole, *The Irrepressible Conflict*, 227.

38Theodore Roosevelt, "The Recent Prize Fight," *Outlook*, July 16, 1910, 550–51; David Noble, *Historians against History: The Frontier Thesis and the National Covenant in American Historical Writing Since 1830* (Minneapolis: University of Minnesota Press, 1965), 122–23; Susan P. Montague and W. Arens, eds., *The American Dimension: Cultural Myths and Social Realities*,

2d ed. (Sherman Oaks, Calif: Alfred Publishing Co., 1981), 4–5; James A. Michener, *Sports in America* (New York: Fawcett Crest, 1977), 344.

[39]Rader, *American Sports*, 25–26, 35–37; S. Kirson Weinberg and Henry Arond, "The Occupational Culture of the Boxer," *American Journal of Sociology* 57, no. 5 (March 1952): 460; *National Police Gazette*, November 22, 1903, 3.

[40]O'Reilly, *Athletics and Manly Sport*, 105.

[41]Barrett O'Hara, *From Figg to Johnson: A Complete History of the Heavyweight Championship* (Chicago: Blossom Book Bourse, 1909), 5, 164; Sullivan, *Life and Reminiscences*, 54–58.

[42]Dizikes, *Sportsmen and Gamesmen*, 199–201; John Allen Krout and Dixon Ryan Fox, *The Completion of Independence, 1790–1830*, vol. 5 of *A History of American Life*, ed. Arthur Meier Schlesinger and Dixon Ryan Fox (Chicago: Quadrangle Books, 1971 [1944]), 390–91; R. Carlyle Buley, *The Old Northwest: Pioneer Period, 1815–1840* (Bloomington: Indiana University Press, 1978 [1950]), 1:318; Elliott J. Gorn, " 'Gouge and Bite, Pull Hair and Scratch': The Social Significance of Fighting in the Southern Backcountry," *American Historical Review* 90, no. 1 (February 1985): 19.

[43]Betts, "Mind and Body," 788.

[44]Dale A. Somers, *The Rise of Sports in New Orleans, 1850–1900* (Baton Rouge: Louisiana State University Press, 1972), 53–59; Dizikes, *Sportsmen and Gamesmen*, 201–6.

[45]*Modern Gladiator*, 309–10; Kenneth W. Stampp, *The Imperiled Union: Essays on the Background of the Civil War* (New York: Oxford University Press, 1980), 141.

[46]*Modern Gladiator*, 310; John Durant, "Yours Truly, John L. Sullivan," *American Heritage*, August 1959, 56; Robert M. DeWitt, *The American Fistiana, Showing the Progress of Pugilism in the United States from 1816 to 1873* (New York: Robert M. DeWitt, 1873) 17–19; *National Police Gazette*, February 7, 1849, 2; *ibid.*, April 27, 1878, 6; John Rickards Betts, "The Technological Revolution and the Rise of Sport, 1850–1900," *Mississippi Valley Historical Review* 40, no. 2 (September 1953): 238.

[47]*Modern Gladiator*, 310–11; DeWitt, *The American Fistiana*, 19–22, 63.

[48]Cole, *The Irrepressible Conflict*, 190–91; Robert H. Bremner, *The Public Good: Philanthropy and Welfare in the Civil War Era* (New York: Knopf, 1980), 4; *Modern Gladiator*, 311; DeWitt, *The American Fistiana*, 58–61.

[49]Lloyd, *The Great Prize Fight*, 35–37; *Modern Gladiator*, 311–12.

[50]Melvin L. Adelman, *A Sporting Time: New York City and the Rise of Modern Athletics, 1820–1870* (Urbana: University of Illinois Press, 1986), 230, 235, 238; Henry Collins Brown, *In the Golden Nineties* (Hastings-on-Hudson, N.Y.: Valentine's Manual, 1928), 274–75; Dizikes, *Sportsmen and Gamesmen*, 129.

[51]Stephen Hardy, *How Boston Played: Sport, Recreation, and Community, 1865–1915* (Boston: Northeastern University Press, 1982), 4; Michener, *Sports in America*, 210–11; Dennis P. Ryan, *Beyond the Ballot Box: A Social History of the Boston Irish, 1845–1917* (Rutherford, N.J.: Fairleigh Dickinson University Press, 1983), 115; Rader, *American Sports*, 97–104.

[52]*Modern Gladiator*, 312–19; DeWitt, *American Fistiana*, 103–15.

⁵³DeWitt, *American Fistiana*, iv; Jack Kofoed, *Brandy for Heroes: A Biography of the Honorable John Morrissey, Champion Heavyweight of America and State Senator* (New York: Dutton, 1938) is an overwrought and highly colored biography. See Rader, *American Sports*, 98–99; Mark D. Hirsch, *William C. Whitney: Modern Warwick* (New York: Archon Books, 1969), 56, 149–50; James L. Ford, "New York of the Seventies," *Scribner's Magazine*, June, 1923, 745; Lately Thomas, *Sam Ward: "King of the Lobby"* (Boston: Houghton Mifflin, 1965), 190.

⁵⁴Edward Van Every, *Sins of New York As "Exposed" by the Police Gazette* (New York: Frederick A. Stokes Co., 1930), 72–90; *National Police Gazette*, May 24, 1879, 2, 5; *ibid.*, December 20, 1879, 15; *New York Daily Tribune*, March 2, 1883.

## CHAPTER FOUR

¹*Boston Daily Globe*, November 1, 1879.

²*Ibid.*, November 15, 1879; *ibid.*, December 29, 1879.

³*Ibid.*, February 4, 1879; Edward Van Every, *Sins of New York as "Exposed" by the Police Gazette* (New York: Frederick A. Stokes Co., 1930), 158–60.

⁴Joe Dorney and Sid Sutherland, "John L. Sullivan," *Liberty*, April 4, 1925, 23–24; Mike Donovan, *The Roosevelt That I Know: Ten Years of Boxing with the President—and Other Memories of Famous Fighting Men*, ed. F.H.N. (New York: B. W. Dodge and Co., 1909), 37–46; John L. Sullivan, *Life and Reminiscences of a 19th Century Gladiator* (Boston: Jas. A. Hearn and Co., 1892), 30–31; Marshall Stillman, *Mike Donovan: The Making of a Man* (New York: Moffat, Yard and Co., 1918), 20, 290; Robert Edgren, "Fighters by Nature," *Outing*, December 1903, 345. Sullivan remembered the Donovan exhibition as three rounds; Donovan's injuries make him the better witness for the four-round length of the bout.

⁵*New Yorker Clipper*, March 13, 1880, 402; Zander Hollander, ed., *Madison Square Garden: A Century of Sport and Spectacle on the World's Most Versatile Stage* (New York: Hawthorn Books, 1973), xviii, 2.

⁶J. W. Buel, *Metropolitan Life Unveiled; or, The Mysteries and Miseries of America's Great Cities, Embracing New York, Washington City, San Francisco, Salt Lake City, and New Orleans* (Saint Louis: Historical Publishing Co., 1882), 49–51.

⁷Herbert Asbury, *The Gangs of New York: An Informal History of the Underworld* (Garden City, N.Y.: Garden City Publishing Co., 1928), 49–51.

⁸*National Police Gazette*, May 22, 1880, 14–15; *ibid.*, June 12, 1880, 14; *ibid.*, June 26, 1880, 14.

⁹Edward Van Every, *Muldoon: The Solid Man of Sport* (New York: Frederick A. Stokes Co., 1929), 13–28.

¹⁰*Ibid.*, 31–62; William E. Harding, *Champions of the American Prize Ring, with their Battles and Portraits* (New York: Police Gazette, 1881), 32.

¹¹Van Every, *Muldoon*, 50–84, 91–127; W. O. McGeehan, "The Last Gladiator," *Saturday Evening Post*, September 28, 1929, 37, 149–50, 153.

¹²Dorney and Sutherland, "John L. Sullivan," 24; *Boston Daily Globe*, April 7, 1880; *The Modern Gladiator: Being an Account of the Exploits and Expe-*

*riences of the World's Greatest Fighter, John Lawrence Sullivan* (Saint Louis: Athletic Publishing Co., 1889), 12, 16–17; Sullivan, *Reminiscences,* 31–32.

[13]Sullivan, *Reminiscences,* 38; *New York Clipper,* July 10, 1880, 123; *Boston Daily Globe,* June 29, 1880; *National Police Gazette,* July 17, 1880, 15.

[14]*Modern Gladiator,* 18, 343–44; *Cincinnati Daily Gazette,* December 25, 1880; *Cincinnati Daily Enquirer,* December 25, 1880, 4; *New York Times,* December 26, 1880, 1:6; *New York Clipper,* January 1, 1881, 322; *National Police Gazette,* January 8, 1881, 14; Sullivan, *Reminiscences,* 38–42.

[15]*New York Clipper,* January 8, 1881, 330; *National Police Gazette,* January 29, 1881, 14; Sullivan, *Reminiscences,* 42.

[16]Sullivan, *Reminiscences,* 43; *Boston Herald,* January 4, 1881; *Boston Daily Globe,* January 4, 1881; *New York Clipper,* February 5, 1881, 362.

[17]*Boston Daily Globe,* March 22, 1881.

[18]John Dizikes, *Sportsman and Gamesmen: From the Years that Shaped American Ideas about Winning and Losing and How to Play the Game* (Boston: Houghton Mifflin, 1981), 213.

[19]Van Wyck Brooks, *The Times of Melville and Whitman* (New York: Dutton, 1947), 242; Michael Schudson, *Discovering the News: A Social History of American Newspapers* (New York: Basic Books, 1978), 116–17.

[20]Gunther Barth, *City People: The Rise of Modern City Culture in Nineteenth-Century America* (New York: Oxford University Press, 1980), 71–72; John Rickards Betts, "Sporting Journalism in Nineteenth-Century America," *American Quarterly* 5 (Spring 1953): 43.

[21]Barth, *City People,* 80, 61–62. Barth argues (58–59) that the press identified the pursuit of money as the common denominator of urban life—an overstatement.

[22]Schudson, *Discovering the News,* 60, 27, 65–66.

[23]John Rickards Betts, "The Technological Revolution and the Rise of Sport," *Mississippi Valley Historical Review* 40, no. 2 (September 1953): 234, 236–37.

[24]Dennis P. Ryan, *Beyond the Ballot Box: A Social History of the Boston Irish, 1845–1917* (Rutherford, N.J.: Fairleigh Dickinson University Press, 1983), 103–4.

[25]*Boston Daily Globe,* August 19, 1879, 1; *Boston Herald,* February 8, 1882.

[26]Barth, *City People,* 83.

[27]Betts, "Sporting Journalism," 41–42; Dizikes, *Sportsmen and Gamesmen,* 56, 62–63.

[28]Betts, "Sporting Journalism," 42–43; *New York Clipper,* June 4, 1881, 171.

[29]Van Every, *Sins of New York,* 10–11; Walter Davenport, "The Nickel Shocker," *Collier's,* March 10, 1928, 26, 28; Betts, "Sporting Journalism," 42.

[30]Davenport, "The Nickel Shocker," 28.

[31]*Ibid.,* 40; Van Every, *Sins of New York,* 25–28.

[32]Betts, "Sporting Journalism," 50–51; Walter Davenport, "The Dirt Disher," *Collier's,* March 24, 1928, 26, 30; *National Police Gazette,* June 1880–September 1, 1881, *seriatim.*

[33]Davenport, "The Dirt Disher," 30; Van Every, *Sins of New York,* 145–47.

[34]Simon Michael Bessie, *Jazz Journalism: The Story of the Tabloid Newspapers* (New York: Dutton, 1938), 61–65; David McCullough, *The Great Bridge:*

*The Epic Story of the Building of the Brooklyn Bridge* (New York: Touchstone Books, 1982), 527.

[35]Van Every, *Sins of New York*, 169–70.

[36]"A Point in Journalism," *Nation*, March 23, 1893, 209–10; *National Police Gazette*, January 10, 1880, 2; *ibid.*, February 8, 1902, 11; *ibid.*, February 1, 1890, 10; Theodore Roosevelt, *Ranch Life and the Hunting-Trail* (New York: Century Co., 1888), 126.

[37]*National Police Gazette*, October 30, 1880, 14; Nat Fleischer, *The Boston Strong Boy: The Story of John L. Sullivan, the Champion of Champions* (New York: Ring Magazine, 1941), 23–24; Davenport, "The Dirt Disher," 52; Van Every, *Sins of New York*, 261–62; Joe Dorney and Sid Sutherland, "John L. Sullivan," *Liberty*, April 11, 1925, 23–24; *New York Daily News*, March 28, 1881; John Durant, *The Heavy-weight Champions*, 6th ed. (New York: Hastings House, 1976), 22; *National Police Gazette*, May 13, 1882, 14.

[38]Asbury, *The Gangs of New York*, 184; Sullivan, *Reminiscences*, 44–47; *National Police Gazette*, April 30, 1881, 14; *ibid.*, May 14, 1881, 14; *ibid.*, May 21, 1881, 14; *ibid.*, June 4, 1881, 6; *ibid.*, July 2, 1881, 4.

[39]Sullivan, *Reminiscences*, 43; *National Police Gazette*, June 18, 1881, 14.

[40]*New York Clipper*, November 22, 1882, 582; *Boston Daily Globe*, February 4, 1918; W. W. Naughton, *Kings of the Queensberry Realm* (Chicago: Continental Publishing Co., 1902), picture of Madden opposite 269; *Indianapolis Sentinel*, October 19, 1882, 4–5; *National Police Gazette*, April 22, 1882, 11.

[41]*New York Clipper*, July 9, 1881, 250; *National Police Gazette*, July 23, 1881, 14.

[42]*Philadelphia Press*, July 12, 1881, 6; Dorney and Sutherland, "John L. Sullivan," April 11, 1925, 24–25; *Boston Daily Globe*, March 28, 1879; *National Police Gazette*, July 30, 1881, 14; *New York Clipper*, July 16, 1881, 267; Sullivan, *Reminiscences*, 49. The claims of Dorney (24–25) that Chambers "really wrote the modern boxing rules" and that he "exercised [a] strange dominance" over Sullivan for ten years are nonsense.

[43]*New York Clipper*, July 30, 1881, 295; Sullivan, *Reminiscences*, 49–50; *National Police Gazette*, August 13, 1881, 14.

[44]*Chicago Tribune*, August 14, 1881, 6:6; *Chicago Daily Inter Ocean*, August 15, 1881, 6:3; *New York Clipper*, August 20, 1881, 347; Sullivan, *Reminiscences*, 50–51; *National Police Gazette*, September 3, 1881, 14.

[45]*Chicago Tribune*, September 4, 1881, 8:2–3; *Chicago Daily Inter Ocean*, September 5, 1881, 6:3–4; *New York Clipper*, September 10, 1881, 899; Sullivan, *Reminiscences*, 51–52, remembered Burns as a 6-foot 6½-inch giant.

[46]*New York Clipper*, September 10, 1881, 899; *National Police Gazette*, August 27, 1881, 14; *ibid.*, October 1, 1881, 14.

[47]*National Police Gazette*, November 12, 1881, 14.

[48]*Ibid.*, August 27, 1881, 14; Harding, *Champions of the American Prize Ring*, 22–25; *National Police Gazette*, October 29, 1881, 14.

[49]*National Police Gazette*, February 26, 1881, 14; *New York Clipper*, June 11, 1881, 187; *ibid.*, June 25, 1881, 214; *National Police Gazette*, May 28, 1881, 14; *ibid.*, June 18, 1881, 14; *ibid.*, June 25, 1881, 2.

[50]*National Police Gazette*, June 25, 1881, 14; *ibid.*, September 3, 1881, 14; *ibid.*, September 17, 1881, 14.

[51]*Ibid.*, October 8, 1881, 14; *ibid.*, October 29, 1881, 11; *New York Times*, September 25, 1881, 5:5. Sullivan had been briefly mentioned in the *Times* in 1880.

[52]*National Police Gazette*, November 5, 1881, 10; *ibid.*, November 12, 1881, 14; *ibid.*, November 19, 1881, 14.

[53]*Ibid.*, November 26, 1881, 14; *ibid.*, December 17, 1881, 14; *ibid.*, December 31, 1881, 14; *ibid.*, December 10, 1881, 11.

[54]*Ibid.*, January 7, 1882, 14; *ibid.*, January 14, 1882, 4–5, 11; *ibid.*, January 21, 1882, 14; *ibid.*, January 28, 1882, 14; *ibid.*, February 11, 1882, 11; S. Kirson Weinberg and Henry Arond, "The Occupational Culture of the Boxer," *American Journal of Sociology* 57, no. 5 (March 1952): 465; *New York Clipper*, February 4, 1882, 751.

[55]*National Police Gazette*, February 4, 1882, 11; *New York Times*, February 7, 1882, 1:5; Van Every, *Sins of New York*, 263.

[56]*New York Clipper*, December 31, 1881, 675; *ibid.*, January 28, 1882, 735; Dale A. Somers, *The Rise of Sports in New Orleans, 1850–1900* (Baton Rouge: Louisiana State University Press, 1972), 165.

[57]Somers, *The Rise of Sports in New Orleans*, 165–66; *Modern Gladiator*, 23.

[58]Somers, *The Rise of Sports in New Orleans*, 165; *New York Clipper*, February 11, 1882, 772.

[59]Sullivan, *Reminiscences*, 78–80.

[60]*National Police Gazette*, February 18, 1882, 14.

[61]Sullivan, *Reminiscences*, 80–83; *Modern Gladiator*, 23–25; *National Police Gazette*, February 18, 1882, 2; *New York Clipper*, February 11, 1882, 772; *Boston Post*, February 8, 1882, 1; *Boston Daily Globe*, February 8, 1882, 1; *New York Times*, February 8, 1882, 1:7; *Natchez (Miss.) Daily Democrat*, February 8, 1882, 1.

[62]*National Police Gazette*, February 18, 1882, 2; *ibid.*, February 25, 1882, 11; Sullivan, *Reminiscences*, 82; *Modern Gladiator*, 26–33; *New York Times*, February 8, 1882, 1:7.

[63]*Boston Daily Globe*, February 8, 1882, 1; Lamar W. Bridges, "An Editor's Views on Anti-Cruelty: Eliza Jane Nicholson of the *Picayune*," *Journal of Mississippi History* 39, no. 4 (1977): 310; *New York Times*, February 8, 1882, 1:7; *ibid.*, February 9, 1882, 1:3.

[64]*New York Times*, February 10, 1882, 1:6; *ibid.*, February 12, 1882, 7:4; *National Police Gazette*, May 6, 1882, 11.

[65]*New York Clipper*, February 18, 1882, 787; *ibid.*, March 11, 1882, 839. James Keenan gave Sullivan a further $1,000 as a present following the fight, the amount representing Keenan's winnings. Sullivan also made over $1,300 on his share of the excursion fees. *National Police Gazette*, March 4, 1882, 14; *ibid.*, March 11, 1882, 11.

[66]*National Police Gazette*, March 11, 1882, 14; *ibid.*, March 18, 1882, 14.

[67]*Ibid.*, April 8, 1882, 11; *ibid.*, March 25, 1882, 11; *ibid.*, April 1, 1882, 11; *ibid.*, March 4, 1882, 11; Van Every, *Sins of New York*, 166.

[68]*Ibid.*, March 25, 1882, 11; *ibid.*, April 15, 1882, 11; *Boston Pilot*, February 18, 1882, 4.

[69]"The Moral of the Prize Fight," *Nation*, February 16, 1882, 137–38; Sullivan, *Reminiscences*, 92–93.

## CHAPTER FIVE

[1]John L. Sullivan, *Life and Reminiscences of a 19th Century Gladiator* (Boston: Jas. A. Hearn and Co., 1892), 95; *New York Clipper*, April 1, 1882, 27.

[2]*New York Times*, March 28, 1882, 2:7; *New York Clipper*, April 1, 1882, 27; Sullivan, *Reminiscences*, 96. Sullivan remembered his opponent as "Jack Douglass."

[3]*National Police Gazette*, April 15, 1882, 11; *Rochester Daily Union and Advertiser*, April 21, 1882.

[4]*Rochester Daily Union and Advertiser*, April 21, 1882; *Rochester Democrat and Chronicle*, April 21, 1882; *Boston Daily Globe*, April 21, 1882; *Boston Herald*, April 21, 1882; *National Police Gazette*, May 6, 1882, 11; *New York Clipper*, April 29, 1882, 95; Sullivan, *Reminiscences*, 96–97.

[5]*National Police Gazette*, March 11, 1882, 11; *ibid.*, May 13, 1882, 11; *New York Clipper*, May 6, 1882, 11.

[6]*National Police Gazette*, May 20, 1882, 2; *ibid.*, May 27, 1882, 14; *ibid.*, June 17, 1882, 11.

[7]William E. Harding, *Champions of the American Prize Ring: A Complete History of the Heavy-weight Champions of America, with Their Battles and Portraits* (New York: Police Gazette, 1881), 17–18; *Boston Daily Globe*, May 9, 1879.

[8]*National Police Gazette*, April 15, 1882, 11; *ibid.*, May 13, 1882, 11; *ibid.*, May 20, 1882, 11; *ibid.*, June 3, 1882, 14; *The Modern Gladiator: Being an Account of the Exploits and Experiences of the World's Greatest Fighter, John Lawrence Sullivan* (Saint Louis: Athletic Publishing Co., 1889), 34.

[9]*New York Clipper*, July 8, 1882, 251; *National Police Gazette*, July 22, 1882, 2; Sullivan, *Reminiscences*, 97–98; *Modern Gladiator*, 34–36; *New York Herald*, July 5, 1882; *New York Daily Tribune*, July 5, 1882; *New York Times*, July 5, 1882, 8:3.

[10]*National Police Gazette*, May 20, 1882, 2; *ibid.*, June 24, 1882, 11; *ibid.*, July 1, 1882, 14.

[11]*Ibid.*, July 8, 1882, 14; *ibid.*, July 15, 1882, 11; *New York Times*, June 29, 1882, 2:4.

[12]*National Police Gazette*, July 29, 1882, 2; *New York Herald*, July 18, 1882; *New York Daily Tribune*, July 18, 1882, 2; *New York Clipper*, July 22, 1882, 286; Edward Van Every, *Sins of New York As "Exposed" by the Police Gazette* (New York: Frederick A. Stokes Co., 1930), 265–66; Sullivan, *Reminiscences*, 99, 102; *Modern Gladiator*, 38–43; *New York Times*, July 19, 1882, 2:7; *ibid.*, July 28, 1882, 4:5.

[13]*National Police Gazette*, August 5, 1882, 10–11, 14; *New York Times*, July 20, 1882, 8:6; *ibid.*, July 21, 1882, 5:5; *ibid.*, July 22, 1882, 8:4.

[14]*National Police Gazette*, August 12, 1882, 2; *ibid.* August 19, 1882, 15; *ibid.*, August 26, 1882, 2, 11; *New York Clipper*, July 29, 1882, 302–3; *New York Times*, August 8, 1882, 2:6; *ibid.*, August 9, 1882, 8:3; *ibid.*, August 13, 1882, 5:5; Sean Dennis Cashman, *America in the Gilded Age: From the Death*

*of Lincoln to the Rise of Theodore Roosevelt* (New York: New York University Press, 1984), 115; James F. Richardson, *The New York Police: Colonial Times to 1901* (New York: Oxford University Press, 1970), 193, 204–7.

[15]*National Police Gazette*, September 16, 1882, 14; *ibid.*, October 28, 1882, 2; *Modern Gladiator*, 43.

[16]*Brooklyn Daily Eagle*, December 22, 1899, 11:5; *New York Clipper*, July 29, 1882, 302.

[17]Sullivan, *Reminiscences*, 103–4; *New York Clipper*, August 19, 1882, 351; *ibid.*, September 2, 1882, 385.

[18]*National Police Gazette*, December 16, 1882, 11; *ibid.*, August 19, 1882, 11; *New York Daily Tribune*, August 8, 1882.

[19]*National Police Gazette*, September 9, 1882, 14; *ibid.*, September 23, 1882, 14; *ibid.*, October 7, 1882, 14; *ibid.*, October 14, 1882, 14; *New York Clipper*, August 26, 1882, 367; *ibid.*, October 7, 1882, 471; Sullivan, *Reminiscences*, 104, 108–9. Sullivan misdates the Higgins fight as October 20.

[20]*National Police Gazette*, November 4, 1882, 14; Sullivan, *Reminiscences*, 104–8. Sullivan calls Stockton "Stockwell."

[21]*New York Clipper*, November 4, 1882, 531; *ibid.*, January 20, 1883, 707; *National Police Gazette*, November 11, 1882, 5; *ibid.*, November 18, 1882, 11; *ibid.*, December 9, 1882, 11; *ibid.*, December 23, 1882, 14; *ibid.*, January 13, 1883, 14.

[22]*Chicago Daily Inter Ocean*, October 31, 1882, 5:6; *National Police Gazette*, November 18, 1882, 14.

[23]*Washington Evening Star*, November 18, 1882, 8:5; *Washington Post*, November 18, 1882, 1:3, 4; *New York Clipper*, November 25, 1882, 582; Sullivan, *Reminiscences*, 109. Sullivan calls his opponent "Reintzel."

[24]Sullivan, *Reminiscences*, 109; *National Police Gazette*, January 20, 1883, 14; *New York Times*, November 3, 1882, 2:7; *ibid.*, November 12, 1882, 7:3; *ibid.*, November 21, 1882, 8:4; *ibid.*, November 28, 1882, 8:4; *New York Clipper*, December 2, 1882, 594.

[25]*New York Times*, December 15, 1882, 2:4; *National Police Gazette*, November 18, 1882, 11; *ibid.*, November 25, 1882, 11; *ibid.*, December 9, 1882, 11; *ibid.*, December 16, 1882, 11; *ibid.*, December 30, 1882, 11; *ibid.*, January 13, 1883, 14; *ibid.*, March 17, 1883, 10; *ibid.*, March 24, 1883, 10; *New York Clipper*, December 30, 1882, 661; *New York World*, March 2, 1883.

[26]*New York Clipper*, December 16, 1882, 631; Harding, *Champions of the American Prize Ring*, 14–16; *National Police Gazette*, December 23, 1882, 14.

[27]*National Police Gazette*, January 13, 1883, 14; *New York Times*, December 29, 1882, 3:3; *New York Clipper*, January 6, 1883, 674; *New York Sun*, December 29, 1882; *New York Herald*, December 29, 1882; Sullivan, *Reminiscences*, 110–12.

[28]*National Police Gazette*, February 10, 1883, 11; *ibid.*, February 17, 1883, 2.

[29]*New York World*, March 2, 1883; Joe Dorney and Sid Sutherland, "John L. Sullivan," *Liberty*, May 2, 1925, 33, 35; *New York Times*, March 2, 1883, 5:4.

[30]*New York Clipper*, February 17, 1883, 771; *ibid.*, March 24, 1883, 7; *Boston Daily Globe*, March 20, 1883, 1; *New York Times*, March 20, 1883, 2:5; Sullivan, *Reminiscences*, 113; *National Police Gazette*, April 7, 1883, 14.

[31]*Boston Herald*, March 20, 1883, 1; *New York Clipper*, March 24, 1883, 7; *Boston Daily Globe*, March 20, 1883, 1; *New York Times*, March 20, 1883, 2:5; Sullivan, *Reminiscences*, 113; *National Police Gazette*, April 7, 1883, 14.

[32]*New York Herald*, April 25, 1883; Sullivan, *Reminiscences*, 113.

[33]*National Police Gazette*, March 31, 1883, 11; *ibid.*, May 12, 1883, 14; *New York Herald*, April 25, 1883; *New York Sun*, April 26, 1883.

[34]*New York Daily Tribune*, April 26, 1883; *Boston Daily Globe*, April 25, 1883; *ibid.*, April 26, 1883; *New York Times*, April 26, 1883, 1:4, 5:5.

[35]*Boston City Directory*, 1878–83, Library of Congress. In 1881 there were thirty-two Michael Sullivans listed as laborers in the directory.

[36]Dorney and Sutherland, "John L. Sullivan," *Liberty*, March 28, 1925, 34; *ibid.*, May 2, 1925, 38, 39.

[37]*Boston Journal*, May 29, 1885, 3–4; *Boston Daily Globe*, May 29, 1885, 5:1–4.

[38]*Boston Daily Globe*, May 29, 1885, 5:1–4; Marriage Record, John Sullivan and Annie Bailey, Registry Division, city of Boston; *Boston Herald*, February 8, 1910; *Boston Post*, February 3, 1918, 1.

[39]*Providence Sunday Journal*, April 8, 1906. For a fictional account of the "romance" between John and Annie, see Mathias P. Harpin, *Trumpets in Jericho* (West Warwick, R.I.: Commercial Printing Publishing Co., 1961), 158–72, 228.

[40]Hasia R. Diner, *Erin's Daughters in America: Irish Immigrant Women in the Nineteenth Century* (Baltimore: Johns Hopkins University Press, 1983), 55; *Providence Journal*, June 9, 1883, 8:6; *ibid.*, June 12, 1883, 1:5; *ibid.*, June 13, 1883, 4:3, 4; *Providence Evening Bulletin*, June 11, 1883, 5:3; *Providence Evening Press*, June 11, 1883, 4:1.

[41]*New York Times*, June 12, 1883, 5:4; *New York Clipper*, June 16, 1883, 207; *National Police Gazette*, June 30, 1883, 14; *Providence Sunday Journal*, December 13, 1908, 9.

[42]*National Police Gazette*, July 14, 1883, 14.

[43]*Ibid.*, June 23, 1883, 14.

[44]*New York Daily Tribune*, May 29, 1883; *New York Herald*, May 29, 1883; *New York Times*, May 29, 1883, 2:3; *New York Sun*, May 29, 1883; *New York World*, May 29, 1883.

[45]W. W. Naughton, *Kings of the Queensberry Realm* (Chicago: Continental Publishing Co., 1902), 146–49; *National Police Gazette*, April 7, 1883, 14; *ibid.*, April 14, 1883, 11.

[46]*National Police Gazette*, April 21, 1883, 11; *ibid.*, April 28, 1883, 2; *ibid.*, May 5, 1883, 10; *ibid.*, May 12, 1883, 14; *ibid.*, May 19, 1883, 10; *New York Clipper*, May 5, 1883, 99.

[47]*New York Times*, May 15, 1883, 5:1; *New York Clipper*, May 19, 1883, 133; *New York Daily Tribune*, May 15, 1883.

[48]*New York Clipper*, May 19, 1883, 133; *Modern Gladiator*, 44–45; *New York Herald*, May 15, 1883; Van Every, *Sins of New York*, 266–68; Sullivan, *Reminiscences*, 113–16; *National Police Gazette*, May 26, 1883, 2.

[49]*National Police Gazette*, June 2, 1883, 14; *New York Daily Tribune*, May 15, 1883.

[50]Harding, *Champions of the American Prize Ring*, 30–32.

[51]*National Police Gazette*, December 2, 1882, 2; *ibid.*, January 13, 1883, 14; *ibid.*, January 20, 1883, 5, 14; *ibid.*, April 28, 1883, 2; *New York Clipper*, January 13, 1883, 692.

[52]*New York Times*, February 9, 1883, 3:2; *National Police Gazette*, January 27, 1883, 2; *ibid.*, February 10, 1883, 11; *ibid.*, February 17, 1883, 2, 11; *ibid.*, February 24, 1883, 10, 11; *ibid.*, March 10, 1883, 10.

[53]*National Police Gazette*, March 31, 1883, 11; *ibid.*, April 14, 1883, 11; *ibid.*, July 21, 1883, 14; *ibid.*, August 4, 1883, 14; *ibid.*, August 11, 1883, 14.

[54]John Rickards Betts, "The Technological Revolution and the Rise of Sport, 1850–1900," *Mississippi Valley Historical Review* 40, no. 2 (September 1953): 245–46; *New York Daily Tribune*, August 7, 1883.

[55]*National Police Gazette*, August 18, 1883, 2; *New York Clipper*, August 11, 1883, 330–31; *New York Times*, August 7, 1883, 1:5; *Modern Gladiator*, 47–49; Sullivan, *Reminiscences*, 119–22; Van Every, *Sins of New York*, 269–71.

[56]*New York Times*, August 7, 1883, 1:5; *National Police Gazette*, August 25, 1883, 10.

[57]*Brooklyn Daily Eagle*, December 22, 1899, 11:5.

[58]*New York Clipper*, May 19, 1883, 133; *ibid.*, August 18, 1883, 351; Perry R. Duis, *The Saloon: Public Drinking in Chicago and Boston, 1880–1920* (Urbana: University of Illinois Press, 1983), 138; *National Police Gazette*, May 19, 1883, 10.

[59]*New York Clipper*, August 18, 1883, 351; *New York Times*, August 9, 1883, 1:5; *Boston Daily Globe*, August 8, 1883; *National Police Gazette*, August 18, 1883, 14.

[60]*New York Times*, August 9, 1883, 1:5; *New York Clipper*, August 18, 1883, 351; *Boston Herald*, August 8, 1883; *New York Daily Tribune*, August 8, 1883.

[61]*Boston Herald*, August 8, 1883; *Boston Daily Globe*, August 8, 1883.

[62]*New York Clipper*, August 18, 1883, 351; *National Police Gazette*, January 19, 1884, 10; *Boston Daily Globe*, August 8, 1883.

[63]*New York Clipper*, August 18, 1883, 351; *Boston Daily Globe*, August 8, 1883.

[64]*New York Daily Tribune*, August 8, 1883; *Boston Daily Globe*, August 8, 1883; *New York Times*, August 9, 1883, 1:5; Duis, *The Saloon*, 69.

[65]*Boston Herald*, August 8, 1883; *New York Daily Tribune*, August 8, 1883.

[66]*Life*, October 11, 1883, 180.

## CHAPTER SIX

[1]Mike Donovan, *The Roosevelt That I Know: Ten Years of Boxing with the President—and Other Memories of Famous Fighting Men*, ed. F.H.N. (New York: B. W. Dodge and Co., 1909), 90–91.

[2]*Boston Daily Globe*, September 19, 1883; *New York Times*, September 19, 1883, 8:2; *New York Clipper*, September 22, 1883, 435; *National Police Gazette*, October 6, 1883, 14.

[3]*New York Times*, September 19, 1883, 8:2; John L. Sullivan, *Life and Reminiscences of a 19th Century Gladiator* (Boston: Jas. A. Hearn and Co., 1892), 126–28; *National Police Gazette*, October 6, 1883, 14.

[4]Lewis Atherton, *Main Street on the Middle Border* (New York: Quadrangle, 1966 [1954]), *passim*; see also Morton White and Lucia White, *The Intellectual versus the City: From Thomas Jefferson to Frank Lloyd Wright* (New York: Oxford University Press, 1977 [1962]).

[5]*National Police Gazette*, October 6, 1883, 14.

[6]*Richmond Daily Dispatch*, October 2, 1883, 1:5; (Columbus) *Ohio State Journal*, October 26, 1883, 4:2.

[7]*Washington Post*, October 7, 1883, 1:4; *Harrisburg Daily Patriot*, October 8, 1883, 1:5.

[8]*New York Clipper*, October 20, 1883, 507; *New York Times*, October 14, 1883, 1:4; *National Police Gazette*, November 3, 1883, 14.

[9]*New York Times*, October 21, 1883, 2:5; Sullivan, *Reminiscences*, 138–40.

[10]*Pittsburgh Dispatch*, October 20, 1883, 1:7, 5:1; *ibid.*, October 22, 1883, 3:2; *New York Times*, October 21, 1883, 2:5.

[11]*Wheeling Register*, October 22, 1883, 4:4; *ibid.*, October 23, 1883, 2, 4.

[12]Braathen Papers, Circus and Related Arts Collection, Milner Library, Illinois State University; *Ohio State Journal*, October 26, 1883, 4:2.

[13]*National Police Gazette*, November 17, 1883, 10; *Cincinnati Commercial Gazette*, October 28, 1883, 3; *ibid.*, October 29, 1883, 2:4.

[14]*Louisville Courier-Journal*, October 30, 1883, 6:6; *Indianapolis Sentinel*, October 31, 1883, 4:6.

[15]*Saint Louis Globe-Democrat*, November 4, 1883, 7:4; (Saint Louis) *Missouri Republican*, November 4, 1883, 16:4–6; *National Police Gazette*, November 24, 1883, 2; Sullivan, *Reminiscences*, 140–41.

[16]David Quentin Voigt, *American Baseball: From Gentleman's Sport to the Commissioner System* (Norman: University of Oklahoma Press, 1966), 130, 138–40; *Saint Louis Globe-Democrat*, November 5, 1883, 2:3; (Saint Louis) *Missouri Republican*, November 5, 1883, 5:4; Sullivan, *Reminiscences*, 141–42; *National Police Gazette*, December 1, 1883, 10.

[17]*New York Clipper*, November 17, 1883, 575; Sullivan, *Reminiscences*, 142; *National Police Gazette*, December 1, 1883, 10.

[18]*National Police Gazette*, November 24, 1883, 2; *ibid.*, December 1, 1883, 10.

[19]*Ibid.*, December 8, 1883, 10; Sullivan, *Reminiscences*, 142.

[20]*Saint Paul and Minneapolis Pioneer Press*, November 27, 1883, 2:6; Sullivan, *Reminiscences*, 146; (Minneapolis) *Daily Minnesota Tribune*, November 28, 1883, 7:2–4.

[21]Sullivan, *Reminiscences*, 146–47; *National Police Gazette*, December 29, 1883, 14.

[22](Des Moines) *Iowa State Register*, December 12, 1883, 3:3; *Omaha Daily Republican*, December 13, 1883, 5:3; *ibid.*, December 14, 1883, 4:2–4.

[23]*Atchison Globe*, December 17, 1883, 1:2; *ibid.*, December 18, 1883, 4:2–3; *Leavenworth Times*, December 18, 1883, 4:3; *ibid.*, December 19, 1883, 4:3; (Topeka) *Daily Kansas State Journal*, December 20, 1883, 1:2, 6; *ibid.*, December 21, 1883, 1:6.

[24]*New York Clipper*, December 1, 1883, 609.

[25]Rodman Wilson Paul, *Mining Frontiers of the Far West, 1848–1880* (Albuquerque: University of New Mexico Press, 1974), 121; Duane A. Smith,

*Rocky Mountain Mining Camps: The Urban Frontier* (Lincoln: University of Nebraska Press, 1974 [1967]), 136; (Denver) *Rocky Mountain News*, December 25, 1883, 8:1.

[26]Paul, *Mining Frontiers*, 126; *Rocky Mountain News*, December 26, 1883, 5:1–2.

[27]Sullivan, *Reminiscences*, 148; *National Police Gazette*, January 19, 1884, 10.

[28]*National Police Gazette*, January 19, 1884, 10; *ibid.*, January 26, 1884, 10; *ibid.*, February 9, 1884, 10; Smith, *Rocky Mountain Mining Camps*, 147; Paul, *Mining Frontiers*, 127–31.

[29]*National Police Gazette*, January 26, 1884, 10; (Pueblo) *Colorado Chieftain*, January 3, 1884, 2:1; Sullivan, *Reminiscences*, 149.

[30]*Rocky Mountain News*, January 2, 1884, 3:2.

[31](Salt Lake City) *Deseret Evening News*, January 5–16, 1884, *passim*; *Salt Lake City Daily Tribune*, January 5, 1884, 4:2; *ibid.*, January 6, 1884, 4:2; *National Police Gazette*, February 2, 1884, 14.

[32]Sullivan, *Reminiscences*, 149; *National Police Gazette*, February 9, 1884, 10; Paul, *Mining Frontiers*, 146–48; Smith, *Rocky Mountain Mining Camps*, 202.

[33]*Salt Lake City Daily Tribune*, January 15, 1884, 4:4; *ibid.*, January 16, 1884, 4:4; (Reno) *Daily Nevada State Journal*, January 18, 1884, 3:3; *Virginia City Daily Territorial Enterprise*, January 22, 1884, 3:1.

[34]*New York Clipper*, February 2, 1884, 783; *ibid.*, February 9, 1884, 799; *National Police Gazette*, February 16, 1884, 14; *ibid.*, February 23, 1884, 10; *ibid.*, March 1, 1884, 8–9.

[35]*New York Clipper*, February 16, 1884, 815; (Portland) *Morning Oregonian*, February 2, 1884, 1:4; Sullivan, *Reminiscences*, 149–50; *National Police Gazette*, March 1, 1884, 10.

[36]*Morning Oregonian*, February 3, 1884, 5:3.

[37]*Seattle Daily Post-Intelligencer*, February 7, 1884, 2:2–3; *ibid.*, February 10, 1884, 2:1–2; (Eugene) *Oregon State Journal*, February 9, 1884, 5:1; *New York Clipper*, February 23, 1884, 827.

[38]*National Police Gazette*, March 15, 1884, 10.

[39]*Ibid.*, March 22, 1884, 3, 7; *New York Clipper*, March 8, 1884, 859.

[40]*San Francisco Examiner*, March 7, 1884; *San Francisco Chronicle*, March 7, 1884; *New York Times*, March 8, 1884, 3:2; *New York Clipper*, March 15, 1884, 877; *National Police Gazette*, March 22, 1884, 3; Sullivan, *Reminiscences*, 150; *The Modern Gladiator, Being an Account of the Exploits and Experiences of the World's Greatest Fighter, John Lawrence Sullivan* (Saint Louis: Athletic Publishing Co., 1889), 50–51.

[41]*National Police Gazette*, March 22, 1884, 3, 15–16; *New York Clipper*, March 15, 1884, 877; *ibid.*, March 22, 1884, 5; *San Francisco Chronicle*, March 7, 1884.

[42]*National Police Gazette*, April 5, 1884, 10; *New York Clipper*, March 15, 1884, 877.

[43]Robert M. Utley, *Frontier Regulars: The United States Army and the Indian, 1866–1890* (New York: Macmillan, 1973), 380; (Tucson) *Arizona Weekly Citizen*, March 22, 1884, 3:1.

[44]*Arizona Weekly Citizen*, March 29, 1884, 2:5–8, 3:2; *National Police Gazette*, April 19, 1884, 15.

[45]*Galveston Daily News*, April 10, 1884, 4:3; *ibid.*, April 11, 1884, 4:2; *New York Clipper*, April 26, 1884, 88; Sullivan, *Reminiscences*, 150–52. Sullivan refers to his opponent as "Marks" and has the fight going three rounds.

[46]*New Orleans Daily Picayune*, April 12, 1884, 5:2; *ibid.*, April 13, 1884, 2:6; *New Orleans Times-Democrat*, April 12, 1884, 3:7; Donovan, *The Roosevelt That I Know*, 47.

[47]*New Orleans Daily Picayune*, April 14, 1884, 8:1; *ibid.*, April 15, 1884, 7:6; *New Orleans Times-Democrat*, April 14, 1884, 2:4; *ibid.*, April 15, 1884, 3:5.

[48]*Mobile Daily Register*, April 16, 1884, 4:2; *Savannah Morning News*, April 19, 1884, 4:3; *ibid.*, April 20, 1884, 8:6.

[49]*Charleston News and Courier*, April 21, 1884, 4:2; *ibid.*, April 22, 1884, 1:8.

[50]*Atlanta Constitution*, April 23, 1884, 5:2; *ibid.*, April 24, 1884, 7:3; *Atlanta Journal*, April 24, 1884, 4:1.

[51]Sullivan, *Reminiscences*, 154–55; *Nashville Daily American*, April 26, 1884, 5:1; *ibid.*, April 27, 1884, 1:7; *Memphis Daily Appeal*, April 29, 1884, 4:8; *National Police Gazette*, May 24, 1884, 10.

[52]Sullivan, *Reminiscences*, 155–56; *Little Rock Daily Arkansas Gazette*, April 29, 1884; *ibid.*, April 30, 1884, 13:1; *ibid.*, May 1, 1884, 5:1.

[53]*Memphis Daily Appeal*, May 2, 1884, 1; *New York Clipper*, May 10, 1884, 115; Sullivan, *Reminiscences*, 155; *National Police Gazette*, May 24, 1884, 10.

[54]*Nashville Daily American*, May 3, 1884; Sullivan, *Reminiscences*, 156.

[55]*Louisville Courier-Journal*, May 3, 1884, 6:3; *ibid.*, May 4, 1884, 7:6; Sullivan, *Reminiscences*, 156; *National Police Gazette*, May 31, 1884, 10.

[56]*Cincinnati Enquirer*, May 4, 1884, 10; *ibid.*, May 5, 1884, 8:1; *Missouri Republican*, May 7, 1884, 6:4; *ibid.*, May 8, 1884, 6:3; *ibid.*, May 9, 1884, 6:4; *New York Clipper*, May 10, 1884, 115; *National Police Gazette*, May 24, 1884, 14.

[57](Springfield) *Illinois State Journal*, May 10, 1884, 7:4; (Springfield) *Illinois State Register*, May 10, 1884, 3:4; *Detroit Evening News*, May 22, 1884, 4:3.

[58]*National Police Gazette*, June 14, 1884, 5, 10, 14.

[59]*Ibid.*, 14; *ibid.*, May 17, 1884, 10; *New York Times*, July 2, 1884, 8:1.

[60]Sullivan, *Reminiscences*, 128; *National Police Gazette*, July 5, 1884, 14.

[61]*National Police Gazette*, April 15, 1905, 6; Sullivan, *Reminiscences*, 156.

[62]Voigt, *American Baseball*, 111.

## CHAPTER SEVEN

[1]*National Police Gazette*, April 26, 1884, 7.

[2]*Ibid.*, June 28, 1884, 14; *New York Times*, July 2, 1884, 8:1; *New York Clipper*, June 28, 1884, 231.

[3]*New York Clipper*, July 5, 1884, 247; *National Police Gazette*, July 12, 1884, 2; *New York Sun*, July 1, 1884; *New York Times*, July 1, 1884, 1:7.

[4]*New York Times*, July 2, 1884, 8:1; *New York Sun*, July 1, 1884; *National Police Gazette*, July 19, 1884, 2.

[5]*National Police Gazette*, July 19, 1884, 10, 14; *ibid.*, July 26, 1884, 2; *New York Daily Tribune*, July 1, 1884; *New York Clipper*, July 26, 1884, 294.

[6]John L. Sullivan, *Life and Reminiscences of a 19th Century Gladiator* (Boston: Jas A. Hearn and Co., 1892), 157–59; *National Police Gazette*, August 30, 1884, 14; *Boston Herald*, August 14, 1884.

[7]*National Police Gazette*, October 25, 1884, 10; *ibid.*, November 1, 1884, 10; *Washington Post*, April 5, 1887; *Boston Daily Globe*, August 9, 1887.

[8]*National Police Gazette*, October 25, 1884, 10; *ibid.*, November 15, 1884, 10; *New York Times*, November 9, 1884, 2:7.

[9]*National Police Gazette*, November 29, 1884, 9–10; *New York Times*, November 11, 1884, 1:5; *New York Clipper*, November 15, 1884, 556; *New York Daily Tribune*, November 11, 1884; *The Modern Gladiator: Being an Account of the World's Greatest Fighter, John Lawrence Sullivan* (Saint Louis: Athletic Publishing Co., 1889), 51–54. Sullivan, *Reminiscences*, 159, and *Ring Record Book* say the Laflin fight lasted only three rounds, but all contemporary accounts agree it went the scheduled four, with the victory clearly Sullivan's.

[10]Sullivan, *Reminiscences*, 159–60.

[11]*National Police Gazette*, November 1, 1884, 10; *ibid.*, November 15, 1884, 10; *ibid.*, November 22, 1884, 7.

[12]Sullivan, *Reminiscences*, 161.

[13]*National Police Gazette*, December 6, 1884, 7; *New York Times*, November 23, 1884, 13:5; *New York Clipper*, November 22, 1884, 572.

[14]*National Police Gazette*, December 6, 1884, 7, 10; *New York Times*, November 16, 1884, 14:3; *ibid.*, November 18, 1884, 8:1; *ibid*; November 19, 1884, 1:5; *ibid.*, November 20, 1884, 8:1; Sullivan, *Reminiscences*, 163–66; Mike Donovan, *The Roosevelt That I Know: Ten Years of Boxing With the President—and Other Memories of Famous Fighting Men*, ed. F.H.N. (New York: B. W. Dodge and Co., 1909), 103–7; *New York Daily Tribune*, November 19, 1884; *Modern Gladiator*, 54–59.

[15]*National Police Gazette*, January 3, 1885, 2, 7; Edward Van Every, *Sins of New York as "Exposed" by the Police Gazette* (New York: Frederick A. Stokes Co., 1930), 271–74; *New York Daily Tribune*, December 17, 1884; *ibid.*, December 18, 1884; *New York Times*, December 17, 1884, 3:1; *ibid.*, December 18, 1884, 8:1; William Inglis, *Champions off Guard* (New York: Vanguard Press, 1932), 19; *New York Clipper*, December 27, 1884, 651; Sean Dennis Cashman, *America in the Gilded Age: From the Death of Lincoln To the Rise of Theodore Roosevelt* (New York: New York University Press, 1984), 127.

[16]*New York Daily Tribune*, December 18, 1884; *Frank Leslie's Illustrated Newspaper*, November 29, 1884, 227.

[17]*National Police Gazette*, January 24, 1885, 10; *New York Clipper*, January 10, 1885, 685.

[18]*New York Times*, January 17, 1885, 2:7; *National Police Gazette*, January 17, 1885, 10; *ibid.*, January 31, 1885, 13; *New York Clipper*, January 17, 1885, 701; *Boston Herald*, January 13, 1885, 1; *Boston Daily Globe*, January 13, 1885, 1; Sullivan, *Reminiscences*, 166–67.

[19]*National Police Gazette*, September 24, 1883, 14; *ibid.*, December 22, 1883, 15; *ibid.*, January 12, 1884, 10.

[20]*New York Times*, January 20, 1885, 5:4; *New York Daily Tribune,* January 20, 1885; *National Police Gazette,* February 7, 1885, 7; *New York Clipper,* January 24, 1885, 717; Sullivan, *Reminiscences,* 167–68.

[21]*New York Daily Tribune,* January 20, 1885.

[22]*New York Clipper,* January 31, 1885, 733; *ibid.,* February 7, 1885, 749; *Boston Post,* January 24, 1885, 1:3; *National Police Gazette,* February 14, 1885, 10; *ibid.,* February 21, 1885, 10.

[23]*New York Times,* March 23, 1885, 5:6; *ibid.,* April 9, 1885, 8:3; *New York Clipper,* March 14, 1885, 832; *ibid.,* March 28, 1885, 27; William E. Harding, *The Champions of the American Prize Ring, with Their Battles and Portraits* (New York: Police Gazette, 1881), 32–34; *Boston Post,* March 26, 1885, 1:7; *National Police Gazette,* April 18, 1885, 10; *ibid.,* April 25, 1885, 8–9; *ibid.,* May 2, 1885, 10.

[24]*New York Times,* April 3, 1885, 2:4; *Philadelphia Inquirer,* April 4, 1885; Sullivan, *Reminiscences,* 168; *National Police Gazette,* March 28, 1885, 14; *ibid.,* April 11, 1885, 6.

[25]*Boston Post,* February 25, 1885, 4:3; *New York Clipper,* February 28, 1885, 797; William L. O'Neill, *Divorce in the Progressive Era* (New York: New Viewpoints, 1973), 11.

[26]*Boston Journal,* May 28, 1885, 4:5; *Boston Post,* May 29, 1885, 1:3; *New York Clipper,* May 30, 1885, 174.

[27]*Boston Daily Globe,* May 27, 1885, 1:2; *ibid.,* May 29, 1885, 5:1, 2, 3, 4.

[28]*Ibid.,* May 27, 1885, 1:2; *ibid.,* May 30, 1885, 8:4; *Boston Journal,* May 29, 1885, 3:4; *New York Clipper,* June 6, 1885, 178. The Sullivan divorce proceedings can be found in the Supreme Judicial Court Records for Suffolk County, Commonwealth of Massachusetts, 1885.

[29]*Chicago Tribune,* June 13, 1885; *ibid.,* June 14, 1885; *National Police Gazette,* June 27, 1885, 4, 6; *New York Clipper,* June 20, 1885, 211; *ibid.,* June 27, 1885, 238; *New York Times,* June 14, 1885, 7:4; Sullivan, *Reminiscences,* 168.

[30]*New York Times,* August 26, 1885, 5:3; *National Police Gazette,* April 11, 1885, 6; *Cincinnati Enquirer,* August 25, 1885, 2; *ibid.,* August 26, 1885, 2; *ibid.,* August 29, 1885, 2.

[31]*National Police Gazette,* August 15, 1885, 10; *New York Times,* August 29, 1885, 2:6; *Cincinnati Enquirer,* August 28, 1885, 2.

[32]*Cincinnati Enquirer,* August 28, 1885, 2; *ibid.,* August 29, 1885, 2.

[33]*National Police Gazette,* September 12, 1885, 2; *Cincinnati Enquirer,* August 30, 1885, 1; *New York Clipper,* September 5, 1885, 395; *ibid.,* September 12, 1885, 414. The *New York Times,* August 30, 1885, 1:3, 4, called the McCaffery fight "tame and bloodless," a description belied by the eyewitness testimony. *Modern Gladiator,* 64–67; Sullivan, *Reminiscences,* 168–70.

[34]*National Police Gazette,* September 19, 1885, 10; *New York Times,* August 31, 1885, 1:6.

[35]*New York Times,* September 14, 1885, 1:4; *New York Clipper,* September 12, 1885, 414; *Cleveland Press,* September 2, 1885, 2:5; *ibid.,* September 14, 1885, 3:2.

[36]*National Police Gazette,* July 11, 1885, 10; *ibid.,* October 31, 1885, 10.

[37]*New York Clipper*, June 13, 1885, 206; *National Police Gazette*, June 20, 1885, 10; *ibid.*, July 11, 1885, 10; *ibid.*, August 22, 1885, 10; *ibid.*, September 12, 1885, 16.

[38]*National Police Gazette*, October 31, 1885, 10; *ibid.*, November 7, 1885, 10; *ibid.*, December 26, 1885, 10; *ibid.*, January 23, 1886, 10.

[39]*New York Herald*, December 22, 1885; *New York World*, December 22, 1885; *National Police Gazette*, January 2, 1886, 10; *New York Times*, December 22, 1885, 2:2.

[40]*National Police Gazette*, January 16, 1886, 10; *ibid.*, March 6, 1886, 10; *ibid.*, March 20, 1886, 10; *ibid.*, April 10, 1886, 10; Sullivan, *Reminiscences*, 171–72.

[41]*New York Times*, January 24, 1886, 8:1; *ibid.*, February 20, 1886, 2:7; *ibid.*, April 9, 1886, 8:3; *ibid.*, May 17, 1886, 1:7; *ibid.*, February 18, 1886, 5:6; *ibid.*, May 20, 1886, 5:3; *National Police Gazette*, March 6, 1886, 10.

[42]*Boston Daily Globe*, May 29, 1885, 5:4; *National Police Gazette*, June 26, 1886, 10.

[43]*New York Times*, May 17, 1886, 7:1; *National Police Gazette*, July 10, 1886, 10; *Boston Daily Globe*, June 26, 1886, 2:3; *ibid.*, June 27, 1886, 3:3; *New York Times*, June 27, 1886, 2:6.

[44]*New York Times*, July 2, 1886, 8:2; *ibid.*, July 3, 1886, 3:2, 4:5; *ibid.*, July 4, 1886, 5:5; *National Police Gazette*, July 24, 1886, 10; *New York Clipper*, July 10, 1886, 258.

[45]Sullivan, *Reminiscences*, 172–73.

[46]*New York Clipper*, September 4, 1886, 398; *ibid.*, September 25, 1886, 443; Sullivan, *Reminiscences*, 172–73; *Modern Gladiator*, 67–69; *Pittsburgh Dispatch*, September 19, 1886, 1; *National Police Gazette*, August 28, 1886, 10; *ibid.*, October 2, 1886, 2; *ibid.*, October 16, 1886, 10.

[47]Sullivan, *Reminiscences*, 173; *National Police Gazette*, October 9, 1886, 10; *ibid.*, November 20, 1886, 10; *ibid.*, October 30, 1886, 10; *ibid.*, November 6, 1886, 10; Henry Collins Brown, *In the Golden Nineties* (Hastings-on-Hudson, N.Y.: Valentine's Manual, 1928), 43–44; *New York Times*, September 28, 1886, 4:2.

[48]*Providence Evening Bulletin*, October 29, 1886, 3:6; *New York Clipper*, November 6, 1886, 537; *National Police Gazette*, November 13, 1886, 10; "When Dynamite Was Used to Blast John L.'s Grave," *Literary Digest*, May 19, 1928, 64.

[49]*New York Times*, January 10, 1886, 10:2; *San Francisco Chronicle*, November 14, 1886; *San Francisco Examiner*, November 14, 1886; *Modern Gladiator*, 61–63; *New York Clipper*, November 20, 1886, 570; *ibid.*, November 27, 1886, 586; Sullivan, *Reminiscences*, 173; *National Police Gazette*, November 27, 1886, 2, 16; *ibid.*, December 4, 1886, 10.

[50]*San Francisco Examiner*, November 14, 1886; (Denver) *Rocky Mountain News*, December 27, 1886, 2; *ibid.*, December 29, 1886, 3, 4, 6; *National Police Gazette*, January 1, 1887, 2.

[51]*Minneapolis Tribune*, January 19, 1887, 3; *Modern Gladiator*, 70–73; *New York Clipper*, January 29, 1887, 729; Sullivan, *Reminiscences*, 173–74; *National Police Gazette*, January 22, 1887, 10; *ibid.*, January 29, 1887, 2.

[52]*Minneapolis Tribune*, January 19, 1887, 3; *New York Clipper*, January 29, 1887, 729.

[53]*Modern Gladiator*, 74–76; *New York Clipper*, February 5, 1887, 745; *ibid.*, March 26, 1887, 26; *National Police Gazette*, February 12, 1887, 7.

[54]*New York Clipper*, April 2, 1887, 42; *Washington Star*, April 4, 1887; *ibid.*, April 5, 1887; Constance McLaughlin Green, *Washington: A History of the Capital, 1800–1950* (Princeton: Princeton University Press, 1976 [1962]), 2:39; *National Police Gazette*, March 26, 1887, 10; *ibid.*, April 2, 1887, 10; *ibid.*, April 16, 1887, 10.

[55]Allan Nevins, *Grover Cleveland: A Study in Courage* (New York: Dodd, Mead, 1933), 302–5, 214; *Washington Post*, April 5, 1887; *National Police Gazette*, April 23, 1887, 7.

[56]Sullivan, *Reminiscences*, 175–76; *New York Times*, April 21, 1887, 4:2; *ibid.*, May 17, 1887, 4:5; *ibid.*, May 19, 1887, 4:5; *ibid.*, May 22, 1887, 2:7; *ibid.*, May 23, 1887, 4:6; *ibid.*, May 24, 1887, 1:6; *ibid.*, May 26, 1887, 1:7; *Rochester Democrat and Chronicle*, May 18, 1887; *National Police Gazette*, May 21, 1887, 10.

[57]*New York Clipper*, June 18, 1887, 218; *National Police Gazette*, June 25, 1887, 2.

*New York Clipper*, July 23, 1887, 295; *ibid.*, August 13, 1887, 313; Sullivan, *Reminiscences*, 176–77.

[59]*Boston Daily Globe*, August 9, 1887; *Boston Herald*, August 9, 1887; *New York Times*, August 9, 1887, 2:3; *National Police Gazette*, August 20, 1887, 2.

[60]*Brooklyn Daily Eagle*, December 22, 1899, 11:5.

## CHAPTER EIGHT

[1]John Milton, *Samson Agonistes*, line 971.

[2] *National Police Gazette*, January 1, 1887, 1; *ibid.*, April 23, 1887, 7.

[3]Donald J. Mrozek, *Sport and American Mentality, 1880–1910* (Knoxville: University of Tennessee Press, 1983), 195–96.

[4]*National Police Gazette*, July 9, 1881, 12; Henry Collins Brown, *New York in the Elegant Eighties* (Hastings-on-Hudson, N.Y.: Valentine's Manual, 1927), 176–78; *New York Daily Tribune*, August 6, 1882.

[5]John L. Sullivan, *Life and Reminiscences of a 19th Century Gladiator* (Boston: Jas. A. Hearn and Co., 1892), 29–30.

[6]*National Police Gazette*, June 6, 1885, 10.

[7]*Ibid.*, March 19, 1887, 10; Robert H. Walker, *Life in the Age of Enterprise, 1865–1900* (New York: Capricorn Books, 1970), 165; Brown, *New York in the Elegant Eighties*, 223.

[8]Frederic L. Paxson, "The Rise of Sport," *Mississippi Valley Historical Review* 4, no. 2 (September 1917): 150; *The Modern Gladiator: Being an Account of the World's Greatest Fighter, John Lawrence Sullivan* (Saint Louis: Athletic Publishing Co., 1889), 104–5.

[9]*Brooklyn Daily Eagle*, July 3, 1892, 12:1; *National Police Gazette*, July 23, 1887, 10.

[10]Merle Curti, *The Roots of American Loyalty* (New York: Columbia University Press, 1946), 184–85; Thomas M. Croak, "The Professionalization of Prize Fighting: Pittsburgh at the Turn of the Century," *Western Pennsylvania Historical Magazine* 62, no. 4 (1979): 334, 343.

[11]*Modern Gladiator*, 383–84; Sullivan, *Reminiscences*, 117; Oliver Carlson, *Brisbane: A Candid Biography* (New York: Stackpole Sons, 1937), 88; *National Police Gazette*, February 19, 1887, 10.

[12]William Lyon Phelps, *Autobiography with Letters* (New York: Oxford University Press, 1939), 356; Herbert Asbury, *The Gangs of New York: An Informal History of the Underworld* (Garden City, N.Y.: Garden City Publishing Co., 1928), 319; Arthur Mann, *Yankee Reformers in the Urban Age: Social Reform in Boston, 1880–1900* (Chicago: University of Chicago Press, 1974 [1954]), 29.

[13]Sullivan, *Reminiscences*, 136; *National Police Gazette*, December 13, 1884, 10; Joe Dorney and Sid Sutherland, "John L. Sullivan," *Liberty*, May 16, 1925, 41–42.

[14]James J. Corbett, *The Roar of the Crowd: The True Tale of the Rise and Fall of a Champion* (New York: Grosset and Dunlap, 1925), 171–72; "Corbett to Tunney on 'How to Win the Mob,' " *Literary Digest*, January 14, 1928, 56.

[15]William A. Brady, *The Fighting Man* (Indianapolis: Bobbs-Merrill, 1916), 62–63.

[16]Page Smith, *The Nation Comes of Age: A People's History of the Antebellum Years* (New York: McGraw-Hill, 1981), 4:919. The traditional view of American heroes can be found in Dixon Wecter, *The Hero in America: A Chronicle of Hero-Worship* (New York: Scribner's, 1941), passim.

[17]Page Smith, *America Enters the World: A People's History of the Progressive Era and World War I* (New York: McGraw-Hill, 1985), 7:9–10; Arthur M. Schlesinger, Jr., and Morton White, eds., *Paths of American Thought: American Intellectual History from Colonial Times to the World of Today* (Boston: Houghton Mifflin, 1970 [1963]), 4.

[18]John Cawelti, *Apostles of the Self-made Man* (Chicago: University of Chicago Press, 1968), passim.

[19]Richard D. Mandell, *The First Modern Olympics* (Berkeley: University of California Press, 1976), 12; Mrozek, *Sport and American Mentality*, 226–27, 173.

[20]Croak, "The Professionalization of Prizefighting," 335; Mrozek, *Sport and American Mentality*, xx; Conal Furay, *The Grass-Roots Mind in America: The American Sense of Absolutes* (New York: New Viewpoints, 1977), 35–36.

[21]*National Police Gazette*, May 24, 1884, 14; *Modern Gladiator*, 99, 105, 364.

[22]*Modern Gladiator*, 8; John Boyle O'Reilly, *Athletics and Manly Sport* (Boston: Pilot Publishing Co., 1890), 77.

[23]*Modern Gladiator*, 5; William Inglis, "The Night 'the Big Fellow' Went Out," *Harper's Weekly*, December 3, 1910, 15; O'Reilly, *Athletics and Manly Sport*, 75; John Boyle O'Reilly, *Ethics of Boxing and Manly Sport* (Boston: Ticknor and Co., 1888), 79.

[24]*Modern Gladiator*, 379–80; *Pittsburgh Dispatch*, September 19, 1886; *National Police Gazette*, February 5, 1887, 10; Sullivan, *Reminiscences*, 130–31.

25Sullivan, *Reminiscences*, 254–65; *National Police Gazette*, February 26, 1887, 10; for extended discussion of the metaphor, see Leo Marx, *Machine in the Garden: Technology and the Pastoral Ideal in America* (New York: Oxford University Press, 1964), passim.

26John Durant, *The Heavyweight Champions*, 6th ed. (New York: Hastings House, 1976), 37; Paxson, "The Rise of Sport," 150–51; "Classics of a Ring Recollection, as Told to Charles Francis Coe," *Saturday Evening Post*, January 8, 1927, 26.

27Nat Fleischer, *The Boston Strong Boy: The Story of John L. Sullivan, the Champion of Champions* (New York: Ring Magazine, 1941), 46–47.

28Sullivan, *Reminiscences*, 237–40; *National Police Gazette*, December 2, 1899, 11; Carl Van Doren, *Benjamin Franklin* (New York: Viking Press, 1938), 630.

29Letter, John L. Sullivan to "Manager Ringling Brothers," October 31, 1908, in Braathen Papers, Circus and Related Arts Collection, Milner Library, Illinois State University.

30Orrin E. Klapp, "Hero Worship in America," *American Sociological Review* 14, no. 1 (February 1949): 54, 60, 57; Stephen Hardy, *How Boston Played: Sport, Recreation, and Community, 1865–1915* (Boston: Northeastern University Press, 1982), 168–75.

31Richard M. Dorson, *America in Legend: Folklore from the Colonial Period to the Present* (New York: Pantheon Books, 1973), 99–108; Orrin E. Klapp, "Heroes, Villains, and Fools as Agents of Social Control," *American Sociological Review* 19, no. 1 (February 1954): 59.

32Klapp, "Heroes, Villains, and Fools," 61, 59, 57.

33Stephen Jay Gould, *The Panda's Thumb: More Reflections in Natural History* (New York: Norton, 1982), 259; Sullivan, *Reminiscences*, 216; *New York Times*, January 15, 1885, 5:5.

34Tom S. Andrews, *Ring Battles of Centuries*, rev. ed. (n.p.: Tom Andrews Record Book Co., 1924), 16; " 'John L.,' Last of the Bare-fisted Fighters of the Ring," *Literary Digest*, February 23, 1918, 64; "John L. as a Literary Rival of Gene Tunney," *ibid.*, January 12, 1929, 70–71; *Modern Gladiator*, 3–4.

35*National Police Gazette*, October 18, 1884, 10; Inglis, "The Night 'the Big Fellow' Went Out," 15.

36" 'John L.,' Last of the Bare-fisted Fighters of the Ring," 64; *National Police Gazette*, September 4, 1886, 10; *ibid.*, January 15, 1887, 10; Parker Morell, *Diamond Jim: The Life and Times of James Buchanan Brady* (New York: Simon and Schuster, 1934), 88.

37*Atchison Globe*, December 17, 1883, 1:2; Joe Dorney and Sid Sutherland, "John L. Sullivan," *Liberty*, April 18, 1925, 36–37; *National Police Gazette*, May 29, 1886, 10; Ray Ginger, *Altgeld's America: The Lincoln Ideal versus Changing Realities* (Chicago: Quadrangle Books, 1965), 45–55; Richard Gambino, *Vendetta: A True Story of the Worst Lynching in America, the Mass Murder of Italian-Americans in New Orleans in 1891, the Vicious Motivations Behind It, and the Tragic Repercussions That Linger to This Day* (Garden City, N.Y.: Doubleday, 1977), 76. For the Gambino reference, I am indebted to Ben Weinstock.

[38]*New York Clipper*, September 1, 1888, 399; *ibid.*, May 7, 1887, 123; *National Police Gazette*, March 29, 1890, 10.

[39]*New York Times*, May 30, 1883, 4:5; *National Police Gazette*, May 23, 1885, 10; *ibid.*, June 11, 1887, 10.

[40]Jackson Lears, *No Place of Grace: Antimodernism and the Transformation of American Culture, 1880–1920* (New York: Pantheon Books, 1981), 13; Gunnar Myrdal, *An American Dilemma: The Negro Problem and Modern Democracy* (New York: Harper and Row, 1944), 22.

[41]*Modern Gladiator*, 362.

[42]Johan Huizinga, *Homo Ludens: A Study of the Play Element in Culture* (Boston: Beacon Press, 1955), 121; *Modern Gladiator*, 335–36.

[43]*New York Times*, September 13, 1885, 6:5; *Modern Gladiator*, 217.

[44]*Modern Gladiator*, 101.

[45]*National Police Gazette*, April 7, 1888, 7; *Brooklyn Daily Eagle*, February 17, 1892, 6:2; Herbert Asbury, *The Barbary Coast: An Informal History of the San Francisco Underworld* (New York: Capricorn Books, 1968 [1933]), 134–35.

[46]*Modern Gladiator*, 217, 51; Richard Barry, "John L. Sullivan, the Old Roman," *Pearson's Magazine*, September, 1912, 33.

[47]*Modern Gladiator*, 358; *National Police Gazette*, August 25, 1888, 10; "How John L. licked John Barleycorn," *Literary Digest*, May 2, 1925, 39–40, 45.

[48]*San Francisco Examiner*, June 27, 1891; John Durant, "Yours Truly, John L. Sullivan," *American Heritage*, August 1959, 58.

[49]*New York Times*, September 15, 1886, 8:2; *ibid.*, September 16, 1886, 2:4; Sullivan, *Reminiscences*, 251.

[50]Brown, *New York in the Elegant Eighties*, 236.

[51]Brady, *The Fighting Man*, 68; Alexander Gardiner, *Canfield: The True Story of the Greatest Gambler* (Garden City, N.Y.: Doubleday, Doran, and Co., 1930), 174.

[52]Brady, *The Fighting Man*, 82; *National Police Gazette*, December 27, 1890, 10; *ibid.*, January 14, 1883, 2.

[53]*National Police Gazette*, March 8, 1890, 11; *ibid.*, October 11, 1884, 10; *Modern Gladiator*, 338–42, 366; Mike Donovan, *The Roosevelt That I Know: Ten Years of Boxing with the President—and Other Memories of Famous Fighting Men*, ed. F.H.N. (New York: B. W. Dodge and Co., 1909), 47–51.

[54]Sullivan, *Reminiscences*, 170–71; *Modern Gladiator*, 84–85, 86–88.

[55]"The Death of a Notable American," *Outlook*, February 13, 1918, 235; *National Police Gazette*, September 27, 1884, 10; Sullivan, *Reminiscences*, 51.

[56]Walker, *Life in the Age of Enterprise*, 172; *New York Times*, October 21, 1883, 2:5.

[57]*Modern Gladiator*, 32; *San Francisco Examiner*, June 27, 1891; *National Police Gazette*, November 24, 1883, 2; *ibid.*, December 15, 1883, 14.

[58]Joe Dorney and Sid Sutherland, "John L. Sullivan," *Liberty*, March 21, 1925, 13.

[59]William Lyon Phelps, "I Wish I'd Met . . . ," *Good Housekeeping*, January 1942, 39; "The Great John L.," *Newsweek*, August 24, 1942, 64; Curt Gentry, *The Madams of San Francisco: A Hundred Years of the City's Secret History* (New York: Ballantine Books, 1964), 205.

[60]Mrozek, *Sport and American Mentality*, 15; John Dizickes, *Sportsmen and Gamesmen: From the Years that Shaped American Ideas about Winning and Losing and How to Play the Game* (Boston: Houghton Mifflin, 1981), 307; Furay, *The Grass-Roots Mind in America*, 41.

[61]*New York Herald*, September 8, 1889; *National Police Gazette*, October 2, 1886, 2; Lears, *No Place of Grace*, 35.

## CHAPTER NINE

[1]*New York Clipper*, September 17, 1887, 429; *ibid.*, September 24, 1887, 445; *ibid.*, October 8, 1887, 479; *National Police Gazette*, September 17, 1887, 2; *ibid.*, October 29, 1887, 10; *ibid.*, June 30, 1888, 10. The claim that Sheedy advised Sullivan to "resign" the championship before the champion went abroad is almost surely spurious; see *The Modern Gladiator: Being an Account of the World's Greatest Fighter, John Lawrence Sullivan* (Saint Louis: Athletic Publishing Co., 1889), 77.

[2]Quoted in *National Police Gazette*, August 27, 1887, 10.

[3]*Modern Gladiator*, 107; *National Police Gazette*, December 17, 1887, 6.

[4]John L. Sullivan, *Life and Reminiscences of a 19th Century Gladiator* (Boston: Jas. A. Hearn and Co., 1892), 177–78; *New York Times*, October 28, 1887, 1:6; *National Police Gazette*, November 12, 1887, 2; *ibid.*, November 19, 1887, 11.

[5]Sullivan, *Reminiscences*, 178–79; *New York Clipper*, November 12, 1887, 560; *Modern Gladiator*, 78–80.

[6]*National Police Gazette*, January 21, 1888, 16; *New York Clipper*, November 12, 1887, 560; Sullivan, *Reminiscences*, 179–80; *New York Times*, November 8, 1887, 1:3; *London Daily Telegraph*, November 8, 1887, 3:6; *Pall Mall Gazette* (London), November 8, 1887, 1.

[7]Elizabeth Longford, *Queen Victoria: Born to Succeed* (New York: Harper and Row, 1965), 498–503.

[8]Don Russell, *The Lives and Legends of Buffalo Bill* (Norman: University of Oklahoma Press, 1960), 330–34; Colonel W. F. Cody, *Buffalo Bill's Life Story: An Autobiography* (New York: Cosmopolitan Book Corp., 1920), 317–26; *Life*, November 24, 1887, 286.

[9]*New York Times*, November 10, 1887, 1:3; *London Daily Telegraph*, November 10, 1887, 2:5; *New York Clipper*, November 19, 1887, 574; *ibid.*, December 3, 1887, 608; *London Daily News*, November 10, 1887, 4:4; *London Times*, November 10, 1881; Sullivan, *Reminiscences*, 180–84.

[10]Sullivan, *Reminiscences*, 191, 193.

[11]*Ibid.*, 185–91; *New York Clipper*, December 17, 1887, 640; *Modern Gladiator*, 78, 80–82; Oliver Carlson, *Brisbane: A Candid Biography* (New York: Stackpole Sons, 1937), 263.

[12]Letter, Mrs. Maureen J. Sawyers (great-grandniece of John L. Sullivan) to author, February 15, 1985. The gift jewelry from the future Edward VII is still in the possession of Sullivan's indirect descendants. " 'John L.,' Last of the Bare-fisted Fighters of the Ring," *Literary Digest*, February 23, 1918, 60.

[13]Sullivan, *Reminiscences*, 193–95, 280.

[14]*Ibid.*, 196.

[15]*National Police Gazette*, November 26, 1887, 11; *New York Clipper*, December 10, 1887, 623; Sullivan, *Reminiscences*, 197–99.

[16]*National Police Gazette*, February 11, 1888, 10; *ibid.*, February 18, 1888, 10.

[17]*Ibid.*, March 3, 1888, 10; *New York Clipper*, February 25, 1888, 806.

[18]*National Police Gazette*, March 10, 1888, 10–11; *ibid.*, March 17, 1888, 7.

[19]Sullivan, *Reminiscences*, 198–99; *National Police Gazette*, March 17, 1888, 11.

[20]Stephen Bonsal, "Heyday in a Vanished World," *Scribner's Magazine*, June 1934, 454.

[21]*Ibid.*, 455.

[22]Frederic Morton, *The Rothschilds: A Family Portrait* (New York: Atheneum, 1962), 192–97; *New York Sun*, March 11, 1888.

[23]*New York Sun*, March 11, 1888; *New York Times*, March 11, 1888, 2:4; *National Police Gazette*, March 24, 1888, 2.

[24]*Modern Gladiator*, 89–91; *National Police Gazette*, March 24, 1888, 2.

[25]*Modern Gladiator*, 91–98; *New York Sun*, March 11, 1888; Sullivan, *Reminiscences*, 199–201; *New York Clipper*, March 17, 1888, 13; *New York Times*, March 11, 1888, 2:4; Bonsal, "Heyday in Vanished World," 16–19; *National Police Gazette*, March 24, 1888, 2.

[26]*National Police Gazette*, March 24, 1888, 2; *ibid.*, March 31, 1888, 2; Carlson, *Brisbane*, 91–92; *New York Sun*, March 11, 1888; Sullivan, *Reminiscences*, 201–4; *New York Clipper*, March 24, 1888, 30.

[27]*National Police Gazette*, March 31, 1888, 6; *ibid.*, April 7, 1888, 7; *ibid.*, May 19, 1888, 7.

[28]*Ibid.*, April 7, 1888, 7; John Boyle O'Reilly, *Athletics and Manly Sport* (Boston: Pilot Publishing Co., 1890), 6–7; Joe Dorney and Sid Sutherland, "John L. Sullivan," *Liberty*, May 9, 1925, 47.

[29]Sullivan, *Reminiscences*, 204; *New York Clipper*, April 28, 1888, 111; *National Police Gazette*, April 21, 1888, 10; *ibid.*, May 12, 1888, 11.

[30]*National Police Gazette*, May 5, 1888, 10; James Bernard Cullen, ed., *The Story of the Irish in Boston, Together with Biographical Sketches of Representative Men and Noted Women* (Boston: James B. Cullen and Company, 1889), 334, 336.

[31]Sullivan, *Reminiscences*, 195–96; *Brooklyn Daily Eagle*, December 22, 1899, 11:5.

[32]*New York Clipper*, May 26, 1888, 171; Sullivan, *Reminiscences*, 204.

[33]*National Police Gazette*, June 23, 1888, 11; *ibid.*, September 1, 1888, 10.

## CHAPTER TEN

[1]*Boston Daily Globe*, May 16, 1888; *Boston Herald*, May 16, 1888; *New York Herald*, June 5, 1888.

[2]*New York Clipper*, March 24, 1888, 30.

[3]*National Police Gazette*, June 9, 1888, 10; *ibid.*, August 1, 1888, 10.

[4]*Ibid.*, August 1, 1888, 10; John L. Sullivan, *Life and Reminiscences of a 19th Century Gladiator* (Boston: Jas. A. Hearn and Co., 1892), 204; *Boston Post*, August 17, 1885, 8:5; *New York Clipper*, August 25, 1888, 383.

[5]*National Police Gazette,* September 29, 1888, 7; *ibid.,* October 6, 1888, 7; *ibid.,* November 3, 1888, 10; *ibid.,* November 17, 1888, 10; *New York Clipper,* September 29, 1888, 470; *ibid.,* October 13, 1888, 499; *ibid.,* October 20, 1888, 518; *New York Sun,* September 21, 1888; *The Modern Gladiator, Being an Account of the Exploits and Experiences of the World's Greatest Gladiator, John Lawrence Sullivan* (Saint Louis: Athletic Publishing Co., 1889), 106, 328; *New York Times,* September 21, 1888, 1:3; Sullivan, *Reminiscences,* 204–5.

[6]Edward Van Every, *Sins of New York as "Exposed" by the Police Gazette* (New York: Frederick A. Stokes Co., 1930), 274–76; *National Police Gazette,* November 10, 1888, 7.

[7]William E. Harding, *Life and Battles of Jake Kilrain* (New York: Richard K. Fox, 1888), 1; *Modern Gladiator,* 110–12; *National Police Gazette,* June 15, 1889, 6.

[8]Harding, *Life and Battles of Jake Kilrain,* 2–13; *Boston Herald,* July 9, 1889; Oland D. Russell, "When Sullivan Kayoed Kilrain," *American Mercury,* January, 1938, 31; *National Police Gazette,* December 31, 1887, 2–3.

[9] *National Police Gazette,* February 23, 1889, 11; *Baltimore Sun,* July 5, 1889.

[10] *Modern Gladiator,* 107–8; *National Police Gazette,* May 7, 1887, 2, 10; *ibid.,* May 28, 1887, 2; *ibid.,* June 18, 1887, 2, 10; *ibid.,* May 25, 1889, 3; *New York Clipper,* May 14, 1887, 142.

[11]*National Police Gazette,* June 25, 1887, 2; *ibid.,* September 10, 1887, 10.

[12]*Ibid.,* December 22, 1888, 10; *ibid.,* January 5, 1889, 10; *New York Clipper,* December 29, 1888, 678; the facsimile of Sullivan's challenge is in *Modern Gladiator,* 109.

[13]*Modern Gladiator,* 112–15; *National Police Gazette,* January 19, 1889, 3; *ibid.,* January 26, 1889, 3; *New York Times,* January 8, 1889, 3:3.

[14]*National Police Gazette,* April 22, 1889, 3; *ibid.,* June 15, 1889, 6; *ibid.,* June 22, 1889, 10; *ibid.,* June 29, 1889, 3; *New York Times,* April 16, 1889, 8:3.

[15]*National Police Gazette,* February 23, 1889, 11; *ibid.,* March 23, 1889, 10.

[16]*New York Clipper,* May 4, 1889, 127; *ibid.,* May 18, 1889, 168.

[17]*Modern Gladiator,* 219–25, 236–62; *National Police Gazette,* June 8, 1889, 7, 9; Edward Van Every, *Muldoon: The Solid Man of Sport* (New York: Frederick A. Stokes Co., 1929), 131–44.

[18]*Modern Gladiator,* 226–29; *National Police Gazette,* June 19, 1889, 3, 10.

[19]*Modern Gladiator,* 6, 230, 233–34, 250–52; *New York Clipper,* June 15, 1889, 232; *ibid.,* June 19, 1889, 263.

[20]*New York Clipper,* June 8, 1889, 213; *National Police Gazette,* July 6, 1889, 3, 11; Van Every, *Muldoon,* 132–33; W. O. McGeehan, "The Last Gladiator," *Saturday Evening Post,* September 28, 1929, 37, 149, 151, 153; George Creel, "When Sullivan Fought Kilrain," *Collier's,* September 27, 1930, 26–27, 59–60; *Modern Gladiator,* 327; Sullivan, *Reminiscences,* 205–7.

[21]Herbert Asbury, *Sucker's Progress: An Informal History of Gambling in America from the Colonies to Canfield* (New York: Dodd, Mead, 1938), 398; Lamar W. Bridges, "An Editor's Views on Anti-Cruelty: Eliza Jane Nicholson of the *Picayune,*" *Journal of Mississippi History* 39, no. 4 (1977): 311; William H. Adams, "New Orleans as the National Center of Boxing," *Louisiana His-*

*torical Quarterly* 39 (January 1956): 92–94; *Boston Herald*, July 8, 1889; *New York Times*, July 2, 1889, 5:5; *ibid.*, July 3, 1889, 5:2.

²²*Modern Gladiator*, 191–93, 353.

²³ *Ibid.*, 116–25; *National Police Gazette*, July 13, 1889, 6–7; *ibid.*, July 20, 1889, 2–3, 6–7; *New York Clipper*, July 6, 1889, 282; *New York Times*, July 3, 1889, 5:2; *ibid.*, July 5, 1889, 2:5; *ibid.*, July 6, 1889, 2:3.

²⁴*Modern Gladiator*, 125–27; *New York Times*, July 4, 1889, 5:6; *ibid.*, July 5, 1889, 2:5; *ibid.*, July 7, 1889, 2:7; *Baltimore Sun*, July 5, 1889.

²⁵*New York Times*, July 6, 1889, 2:3; *ibid.*, July 7, 1889, 2:7; *ibid.*, July 8, 1889, 5:5.

²⁶Dale A. Smith, *The Rise of Sports in New Orleans, 1850–1900* (Baton Rouge: Louisiana State University Press, 1972), 171; *New York Times*, July 9, 1889, 1:5.

²⁷*New York Times*, July 9, 1889, 1:5; Somers, *Rise of Sports in New Orleans*, 172; *Modern Gladiator*, 129; *National Police Gazette*, July 29, 1889, 2–3; Sullivan, *Reminiscences*, 203.

²⁸*New York Times*, July 9, 1889, 1:5; *Modern Gladiator*, 129–30, 178–79; Robert K. De Arment, *Bat Masterson: The Man and the Legend* (Norman: University of Oklahoma Press, 1979), 218–19, 339–41, 353.

²⁹Mike Donovan, *The Roosevelt That I Know: Ten Years of Boxing with the President—and Other Memories of Famous Fighting Men*, ed. F.H.N. (New York: B. W. Dodge and Co., 1909), 120.

³⁰Joe Dorney and Sid Sutherland, "John L. Sullivan," *Liberty*, May 16, 1925, 29, 40; *Modern Gladiator*, 129–30.

³¹The accounts of the Sullivan-Kilrain match are many and varied. Eyewitness, round-by-round descriptions can be found in *Modern Gladiator*, 130–64; *New York Clipper*, July 13, 1889, 286–87; *National Police Gazette*, July 27, 1889, 2–3. See also *Modern Gladiator*, 172–84; Donovan, *The Roosevelt That I Know*, 120–28; Sullivan, *Reminiscences*, 208–12; *New York Daily Tribune*, July 9, 1889, 3; *Boston Herald*, July 9, 1889, 1. The Sullivan-Kilrain bout became the most famous of John L.'s fights, and it generated many untrustworthy secondary accounts. Among these are Richard Kyle Fox, *The Great Battle between John L. Sullivan and Jake Kilrain* (New York: R. K. Fox, 1889); Dorney and Sutherland, "John L. Sullivan," 39–40; George Creel, "When Sullivan Fought Kilrain," *Collier's*, September 27, 1930, 26–27, 59–60; Russell, "When Sullivan Kayoed Kilrain," 30–37; Arthell Kelley, "Sullivan-Kilrain Fight, Richburg, Mississippi, July 8, 1889," *Southern Quarterly* 8, no. 2 (January 1970): 135–44; Ossi Brucker, "Das 'Drama von Richburg,'" *Olympisches Feuer* 5 (September–October 1979), 32–35; and Sherwin D. Smith, "Duel in the Sun," *New York Times Magazine*, August 9, 1964, 72–73. Among the better secondary accounts are John Durant, "Yours Truly, John L. Sullivan," *American Heritage*, August 1959, 92–94; Somers, *Rise of Sports in New Orleans*, 170–74; and James A. Cox, "The Great Fight: 'Mr. Jake' vs. John L. Sullivan," *Smithsonian*, December 1984, 152–54, 156, 158, 160, 162, 164, 166, 168. My account is drawn from eyewitness sources at ringside.

³²*Modern Gladiator*, 356.

³³*New York Times*, July 9, 1889, 1:5; *Boston Pilot*, July 13, 1889, 5; *Boston Evening Transcript*, July 9, 1889; *New York Daily Tribune*, July 9, 1889, 3.

[34]*Boston Herald*, July 8, 1889, 1; *New York Daily Tribune*, July 9, 1889; *Modern Gladiator*, 186–90.

[35]Donovan, *The Roosevelt That I Know*, 128–30; *Modern Gladiator*, 165–67, 185; *National Police Gazette*, July 27, 1889, 6–7; *New York Times*, July 15, 1889, 5:3.; *Baltimore Sun*, July 9, 1889.

[36]*Modern Gladiator*, 182; Sullivan, *Reminiscences*, 212–13; *New York Times*, July 10, 1889, 1:4.

[37]Sullivan, *Reminiscences*, 213–17; *National Police Gazette*, July 27, 1889, 6–7; *ibid.*, August 3, 1889, 6–7, 11; *New York Clipper*, July 20, 1889, 313; *Modern Gladiator*, 194–95; *New York Times*, July 12, 1889, 1:5; *ibid.*, July 15, 1889, 5:3.

[38]*Modern Gladiator*, 205–15; *New York Clipper*, August 10, 1889, 357; *ibid.*, August 17, 1889, 375; *ibid.*, August 24, 1889, 393; *National Police Gazette*, August 17, 1889, 7; *ibid.*, August 31, 1889, 2; *ibid.*, September 14, 1889, 10; *New York Times*, August 1, 1889, 1:6; *ibid.*, August 2, 1889, 8:5; *ibid.*, August 17, 1889, 1:4; *ibid.*, August 18, 1889, 1:7; Sullivan, *Reminiscences*, 217–20.

[39] *New York Times*, July 19, 1889, 5:6; *ibid.*, July 24, 1889, 2:7; *ibid.*, August 5, 1889, 1:4; *Modern Gladiator*, 196; *New York Clipper*, August 31, 1889, 409; Van Every, *Muldoon*, 233–35.

[40]*New York Times*, August 15, 1889, 2:6; *Modern Gladiator*, 369–70.

[41]*New York Times*, December 15, 1889, 1:6; *ibid.*, March 25, 1890, 5:5; *New York Clipper*, March 29, 1890, 42.

[42]*New York Times*, March 18, 1890, 1:6; *67 Mississippi Reports 352*, 346–56; *New York Clipper*, June 28, 1890, 30.

[43]*New York Times*, June 25, 1890, 1:2; *Modern Gladiator*, 371–77; *New York Clipper*, June 28, 1890, 254; *ibid.*, July 5, 1890, 263.

[44]*Modern Gladiator*, 168–71, 216–17, 333–34.

[45]*Ibid.*, 321–24.

## CHAPTER ELEVEN

[1]*Boston Daily Globe*, August 31, 1889; *Boston Evening Transcript*, September 1, 1889; *Boston Herald*, August 31, 1889; *New York Clipper*, September 7, 1889, 427; *New York Times*, August 31, 1889, 2:5.

[2]*Boston Daily Globe*, August 31, 1889; *Boston Herald*, August 31, 1889; *Boston Pilot*, September 7, 1889, 8; *The Modern Gladiator: Being an Account of the World's Greatest Fighter, John Lawrence Sullivan* (Saint Louis: Athletic Publishing Co., 1889), 359.

[3]*National Police Gazette*, September 21, 1889, 10; *New York Clipper*, September 14, 1889, 446; *New York Herald*, September 8, 1889.

[4]*National Police Gazette*, October 12, 1889, 11; *ibid.*, January 4, 1890, 10; *ibid.*, January 11, 1890, 10; *ibid.*, February 8, 1890, 10; *ibid.*, July 19, 1890, 10; *New York Clipper*, September 28, 1889, 490.

[5]*New York Clipper*, September 21, 1889, 463; *ibid.*, February 15, 1890, 816; *New York Herald*, September 10, 1889.

[6]*National Police Gazette*, November 9, 1889, 11; *New York Clipper*, June 21, 1890, 231.

[7]*New York Herald*, September 8, 1889.

⁸*Boston Daily Globe,* September 30, 1889; Theodore Roosevelt to Henry Cabot Lodge, August 28, 1889, in Henry Cabot Lodge, ed., *Selections from the Correspondence of Theodore Roosevelt and Henry Cabot Lodge, 1884–1918* (New York: Scribner's, 1925), 90.

⁹*New York Times,* September 8, 1890, 1:4; *Boston Daily Globe,* September 8, 1890; *New York Clipper,* September 13, 1890, 430; ibid., September 20, 1890, 443; *Boston Herald,* September 8, 1890.

¹⁰*New York Clipper,* December 13, 1890, 632.

¹¹David Grinsted, *Melodrama Unveiled: American Theater and Culture, 1800–1850* (Chicago: University of Chicago Press, 1968), 171–203.

¹²Alan Woods, "James J. Corbett: Theatrical Star," *Journal of Sport History* 3, no. 20 (1976): 163, n. 4.

¹³John L. Sullivan, *Life and Reminiscences of a 19th Century Gladiator* (Boston: Jas. A. Hearn and Co., 1892), 220–21.

¹⁴*National Police Gazette,* September 13, 1890, 2.

¹⁵*New York Times,* August 29, 1890, 8:2.

¹⁶*Ibid.,* September 2, 1890, 4:6; *New York Herald,* September 2, 1890; *New York World,* September 2, 1890; *New York Daily Tribune,* September 2, 1890.

¹⁷Sullivan, *Reminiscences,* 220–25; *New York Clipper,* February 15, 1890, 816; ibid., May 24, 1890, 171; *National Police Gazette,* December 6, 1890, 11.

¹⁸*Brooklyn Daily Eagle,* December 22, 1889, 11:5.

¹⁹Benjamin G. Rader, *American Sports: From the Age of Folk Games to the Age of Spectators* (Englewood Cliffs, N.J.: Prentice-Hall, 1983), 94; David Quentin Voigt, *American Baseball: From Gentleman's Sport to the Commissioner System* (Norman: University of Oklahoma Press, 1966), 278–79.

²⁰Nat Fleischer, *John L. Sullivan: Champion of Champions* (New York: Putnam, 1951), 88. The claim of William A. Brady, *The Fighting Man* (Indianapolis: Bobbs-Merrill, 1916), 61, that Sullivan boxed with a black in San Bernardino, California, on one of his exhibition tours is possible but unsubstantiated by any evidence.

²¹Nat Fleischer, *Black Dynamite: The Story of the Negro in the Prize Ring from 1782 to 1938* (New York: Ring Athletic Library, 1938), 1:123–72; W. W. Naughton, *Kings of the Queensberry Realm* (Chicago: Continental Publishing Co., 1902), 156–71; W. J. Doherty, *In the Days of Giants: Memories of a Champion of the Prize-Ring* (London: George G. Harrap and Co., 1931), 47–55, 227–33.

²²*Boston Pilot,* August 31, 1889, 6.

²³Fleischer, *Black Dynamite,* 1:161–72; Naughton, *Kings of the Queensberry Realm,* 170–71.

²⁴*National Police Gazette,* September 15, 1894, 10; Jack Johnson, *In the Ring and Out* (London: Proteus Publishing, 1977), 41.

²⁵Al-Tony Gilmore, *Bad Nigger! The National Impact of Jack Johnson* (Port Washington, N.Y.: Kennikat Press, 1975), 26.

²⁶*New York Times,* January 10, 1891, 2:6; *New York Sun,* January 10, 1891.

²⁷*San Francisco Examiner,* June 26, 1891.

²⁸*Ibid.,* June 27, 1891.

²⁹Sullivan, *Reminiscences,* 229.

[30]*Ibid.*, 229–30; *Melbourne Australasian*, July 25, 1891, 167; Doherty, *In the Days of Giants*, 85–86.

[31]Sullivan, *Reminiscences*, 230–31; *Melbourne Australasian*, August 1, 1891, 241.

[32]*Melbourne Australasian*, August 1, 1891, 219; *ibid.*, August 8, 1891, 267.

[33]*Ibid.*, August 15, 1891, 338.

[34]Sullivan, *Reminiscences*, 231; *Melbourne Australasian*, August 15, 1891, 315; *ibid.*, August 22, 1891, 363; *ibid.*, August 29, 1891, 411; *ibid.*, September 5, 1891, 459.

[35]Sullivan, *Reminiscences*, 231–32; *Melbourne Australasian*, September 12, 1891, 507; *ibid.*, September 19, 1891, 555.

[36]*Melbourne Australasian*, October 3, 1891, 656; *ibid.*, October 10, 1891, 695; Doherty, *In the Days of Giants*, 85–86.

[37]Sullivan, *Reminiscences*, 232–33; *Brooklyn Daily Eagle*, January 24, 1892, 14:2; *New York Clipper*, November 7, 1891, 591.

[38]*San Francisco Examiner*, December 21, 1891.

[39]Sullivan, *Reminiscences*, 233–34.

[40]*Ibid.*, 234–37.

[41]*New York Times*, January 25, 1891, 2:4; *ibid.*, January 30, 1891, 4:6.

[42]*Brooklyn Daily Eagle*, December 11, 1891, 4:4.

[43]*Tacoma Daily News*, January 15, 1892; *New York Times*, January 15, 1892, 8:4.

[44]*New York Times*, January 15, 1892, 1:8; *Brooklyn Daily Eagle*, January 15, 1892, 1:8.

## CHAPTER TWELVE

[1]*Brooklyn Daily Eagle*, May 30, 1892, 4:2.

[2]John L. Sullivan, *Life and Reminiscences of a 19th Century Gladiator* (Boston: Jas. A. Hearn and Co., 1892), 272–73.

[3]R. F. Dibble, *John L. Sullivan: An Intimate Narrative* (Boston: Little, Brown, 1925), 96–98; James J. Corbett, *The Roar of the Crowd: The True Tale of the Rise and Fall of a Champion* (New York: Grosset and Dunlap, 1925), 164–66. I have provided paragraphing for Sullivan's challenge.

[4]"Boxiana; or, Sketches of Pugilism," *Blackwood's Edinburgh Magazine*, December 1819, 282.

[5]Corbett, *The Roar of the Crowd*, 166–69.

[6]John Durant, *The Heavyweight Champions*, 6th ed. (New York: Hastings House, 1976), 32–33; Corbett, *The Roar of the Crowd*, 18, 230; *San Francisco Examiner*, August 17, 1898, 16; *San Francisco Chronicle*, August 17, 1898, 9:1–5; *New York Clipper*, August 27, 1898, 429.

[7]Corbett, *The Roar of the Crowd*, 18–19; Durant, *The Heavyweight Champions*, 32.

[8]Corbett, *The Roar of the Crowd*, 9; Durant, *The Heavyweight Champions*, 32.

[9]Durant, *The Heavyweight Champions*, 33–34; Corbett, *The Roar of the Crowd*, 170; *National Police Gazette*, March 8, 1890, 10.

[10]Corbett, *The Roar of the Crowd*, 115–21.

[11]*Ibid.*, 147–51; Durant, *The Heavyweight Champions*, 34.

[12]*Ibid.*, 151, 325.

[13]*New York Times*, March 6, 1892, 2:5; *ibid.*, March 16, 1892, 3:3; *New York Clipper*, March 19, 1892, 27; *ibid.*, March 26, 1892, 42; Corbett, *The Roar of the Crowd*, 169–70.

[14]Dale A. Somers, *The Rise of Sports in New Orleans, 1850–1900* (Baton Rouge: Louisiana State University Press, 1972), 177–79.

[15] *New York Clipper*, May 28, 1892, 183; Sullivan, *Reminiscences*, 265–67.

[16]*Brooklyn Daily Eagle*, January 24, 1892, 14:2; *ibid.*, May 16, 1892, 1:4.

[17]*New York Clipper*, June 25, 1892, 249; *ibid.*, July 9, 1892, 285; *ibid.*, July 30, 1892, 329; *National Police Gazette*, September 3, 1892, 7; William Inglis, "On the Story: The Night 'The Big Fellow' Went Out," *Harper's Weekly*, December 3, 1910, 15.

[18]Corbett, *The Roar of the Crowd*, 170–73.

[19]*Ibid.*, 177–85. The training regimens of both Sullivan and Corbett may best be followed in *National Police Gazette*, September 10, 1892, 3; *ibid.*, September 17, 1892, 7; *New York Clipper*, August 20, 1892, 377; *ibid.*, August 27, 1892, 397; *ibid.*, September 3, 1892, 415; *ibid.*, September 10, 1892, 429–30.

[20]R. W. Stallman, *Stephen Crane: A Biography* (New York: Braziller, 1968), 49; *New York Times*, August 30, 1892, 2:5–7; *ibid.*, August 31, 1892, 2:6.

[21]Sullivan, *Reminiscences*, 276–81.

[22] *Ibid.*, 283–94.

[23]*Ibid.*, 280–81.

[24]William H. Adams, "New Orleans as the National Center of Boxing," *Louisiana Historical Quarterly* 39 (January 1956): 93, 101–2.

[25]*New York Times*, September 2, 1892, 3:4; *ibid.*, September 4, 1892, 3:4.

[26]Adams, "New Orleans as the National Center of Boxing," 101; Corbett, *The Roar of the Crowd*, 186.

[27]*New York Times*, August 27, 1892, 3:3; *ibid.*, September 1, 1892, 3:7; *Brooklyn Daily Eagle*, September 1, 1892, 2:7; Robert K. De Arment, *Bat Masterson: The Man and the Legend* (Norman: University of Oklahoma Press, 1979), 342; *National Police Gazette*, September 17, 1892, 10.

[28]*New Orleans Daily Picayune*, September 4, 1892; *ibid.*, September 6, 1892; *New Orleans Times Democrat*, September 6, 1892; Adams, "New Orleans as the National Center of Boxing," 102; *National Police Gazette*, September 17, 1892, 2; Somers, *The Rise of Sports in New Orleans*, 179–80.

[29]Somers, *The Rise of Sports in New Orleans*, 180; *New Orleans Daily Picayune*, September 6, 1892; *New Orleans Times Democrat*, September 6, 1892; *National Police Gazette*, September 17, 1892, 2; Adams, "New Orleans as the National Center of Boxing," 102.

[30]Somers, *The Rise of Sports in New Orleans*, 180–83; *Chicago Tribune*, September 7, 1892; *New Orleans Times Democrat*, September 7, 1892; *New Orleans Daily Picayune*, September 7, 1892; Adams, "New Orleans as the National Center of Boxing," 102–3; *New York Times*, September 7, 1892, 3:4.

[31]*New York Times*, September 3, 1892, 3:4; *New Orleans Daily Picayune*, September 8, 1892; Adams, "New Orleans as the National Center of Boxing," 103.

[32]John Rickard Betts, "The Technological Revolution and the Rise of Sport, 1850–1900," *Mississippi Valley Historical Review* 40, no. 2 (September 1953): 239–40.

[33]Corbett, *The Roar of the Crowd*, 187–88, 191–92; William A. Brady, *The Fighting Man* (Indianapolis: Bobbs-Merrill, 1916), 88.

[34]Mike Donovan, *The Roosevelt That I Know: Ten Years of Boxing with the President—and Other Memories of Famous Fighting Men*, ed. F.H.N. (New York: B. W. Dodge and Co., 1909), 144–50.

[35]Corbett, *The Roar of the Crowd*, 193–96; Brady, *The Fighting Man*, 89–91; Donovan, *The Roosevelt That I Know*, 175–78; Inglis, "On the Story," 16.

[36]The best eyewitness accounts of the Sullivan-Corbett match can be found in the following: Donovan, *The Roosevelt That I Know*, 178–87; Corbett, *The Roar of the Crowd*, 197–201; Inglis, "On the Story," 16; *New York Times*, September 8, 1892, 3:1; *National Police Gazette*, September 24, 1892, 2–3; *New York Clipper*, September 17, 1892, 445–46. See also Somers, *The Rise of Sports in New Orleans*, 183–84; Richard Kyle Fox, *Life and Battles of James J. Corbett: Champion of the World* (New York: National Police Gazette, 1894), 55; *New Orleans Times Democrat*, September 8, 1892; *New Orleans Daily Picayune*, September 8, 1892; Nat Fleischer, *The Heavyweight Championship: An Informal History of Boxing from 1719 to the Present Day* (New York: Ring Magazine, 1949), 102; Alexander Johnston, *Ten . . . and Out! The Complete Story of the Prize Ring in America*, 3rd rev. ed. (New York: Ives Washburn, 1947), 95–99; Durant, *The Heavyweight Champions*, 34–37; Bohun Lynch [John Gilbert], *Knuckles and Gloves* (London: W. Collins Sons and Co., 1922), 127–32; W. W. Naughton, *Kings of the Queensberry Realm* (Chicago: Continental Publishing Co., 1902), 173–204; Brady, *The Fighting Man*, 90–95; William A. Brady, *Showman* (New York: Dutton, 1937), 77–109.

[37]Somers, *The Rise of Sports in New Orleans*, 185; Adams, "New Orleans as the National Center of Boxing," 104–5; *New Orleans Daily Picayune*, September 9, 1892; William Manchester, *The Last Lion, Winston Spencer Churchill: Visions of Glory, 1874–1932* (Boston: Little, Brown, 1983), 196.

[38]*New York Times*, September 9, 1892, 3:1; Lamar W. Bridges, "An Editor's Views on Anti-Cruelty: Eliza Jane Nicholson of the *Picayune*," *Journal of Mississippi History* 39, no. 4 (1977): 313; Henry Collins Brown, *In the Golden Nineties* (Hastings-on-Hudson, N.Y.: Valentine's Manual, 1928), 382.

[39]*New York Times*, September 9, 1892, 3:1; *National Police Gazette*, September 24, 1892, 2–3.

[40]Corbett, *The Roar of the Crowd*, 201–5.

[41]*Ibid.*, 205–7; Somers, *The Rise of Sports in New Orleans*, 185–86. Brady, *The Fighting Man*, 99, avows that he and Corbett made at least $300,000, but the promoter was always fast and loose with the truth.

[42]*National Police Gazette*, September 24, 1892, 2–3; *ibid.*, October 1, 1892, 2–3.

[43]*Boston Pilot*, September 17, 1892, 4; *New York Clipper*, September 17, 1892, 446.

[44]Tristram Potter Coffin and Hennig Cohen, eds., *The Parade of Heroes: Legendary Figures in American Lore* (Garden City, N.Y.: Doubleday [Anchor], 1978), 70–72, 544; *National Police Gazette*, October 1, 1892, 2–3.

[45]*National Police Gazette*, October 1, 1892, 2–3; *ibid.*, October 8, 1892, 2–3; *New York Clipper*, September 24, 1892, 465; Donovan, *The Roosevelt That I Know*, 196–202; *New York Times*, September 13, 1892, 2:6; *ibid.*, September 18, 1892, 3:4. Brady, *The Fighting Man*, 100, claims Sullivan grossed $13,500 from his benefit.

[46]Donald J. Mrozek, *Sport and American Mentality, 1880–1910* (Knoxville: University of Tennessee Press, 1983), 56; Robert Edgren, "The Modern Gladiator," *Outing*, March, 1903, 738, 740.

[47]Robert H. Walker, *Life in the Age of Enterprise* (New York: Capricorn Books, 1971), 151–53.

[48]*New York Times*, May 1, 1910, part 4, 1:2.

CHAPTER THIRTEEN

[1]*Brooklyn Daily Eagle*, September 8, 1892, 4:2.

[2]S. Kirson Weinberg and Henry Arond, "The Occupational Culture of the Boxer," *American Journal of Sociology* 57, no. 5 (March 1952): 469; Ben Hecht, *A Child of the Century* (New York: Donald A. Fine, 1982 [1954]), 376.

[3]Allen Guttmann, *From Ritual to Record. The Nature of Modern Sports* (New York: Columbia University Press, 1978), 37; Oliver Wendell Holmes, *The Autocrat of the Breakfast Table* (New York: Macmillan, 1928), 172.

[4]Alfred E. Housman, *A Shropshire Lad*, XIX.

[5]*National Police Gazette*, September 1, 1900, 11; *ibid.*, August 19, 1905, 10; *ibid.*, May 31, 1902, 6; " 'John L.,' Last of the Bare-fisted Fighters of the Ring," *Literary Digest*, February 23, 1918, 63; Alexander Johnston, *Ten . . . and Out! The Complete Story of the Prize Ring in America*, 3rd rev. ed. (New York: Ives Washburn, 1947), 322.

[6]*New York Clipper*, January 14, 1893, 726; *Brooklyn Daily Eagle*, July 3, 1892; *National Police Gazette*, January 28, 1893, 11; *ibid.*, September 30, 1893, 10; *New York Clipper*, September 16, 1893, 449.

[7]*New York Clipper*, November 18, 1893, 598; *ibid.*, July 20, 1895, 311.

[8]*National Police Gazette*, August 31, 1895, 11; *Boston Post*, August 10, 1895, 6:2; *Boston Daily Globe*, August 10, 1895, 2:8.

[9]*National Police Gazette*, March 17, 1894, 3; *ibid.*, March 31, 1894, 10; *ibid.*, April 7, 1894, 6; *ibid.*, April 14, 1894, 10; *ibid.*, May 12, 1894, 7; *ibid.*, May 19, 1894, 10; *ibid.*, September 19, 1896, 10; Nat Fleischer, *The Boston Strong Boy: The Story of John L. Sullivan, the Champion of Champions* (New York: Ring Magazine, 1941), 57.

[10]*New York Clipper*, July 24, 1897, 341; *ibid.*, January 6, 1900, 944; *ibid.*, December 22, 1900, 955.

[11]*Ibid.*, August 17, 1901, 536; *National Police Gazette*, April 2, 1904, 10; *ibid.*, November 19, 1904, 3; *ibid.*, July 14, 1906, 10; *ibid.*, September 29, 1906, 6.

[12]*National Police Gazette* February 17, 1893, 10; *ibid.*, April 6, 1895, 10; *ibid.*, July 27, 1901, 10; *ibid.*, August 10, 1901, 10; *ibid.*, June 3, 1905, 10; *ibid.*, June 10, 1905, 10; William A. Brady, *Showman* (New York: Dutton, 1937), 162–63; *New York Clipper*, March 11, 1893, 8.

[13]*National Police Gazette*, January 14, 1893, 10; *ibid.*, March 18, 1893, 10; *ibid.*, September 30, 1893, 10; *ibid.*, October 7, 1893, 10; *ibid.*, January 27, 1894, 10; *ibid.*, February 17, 1894, 3; *ibid.*, April 14, 1894, 11; *ibid.*, November 3, 1894, 10; *ibid.*, August 31, 1895, 11.

[14]*Ibid.*, November 2, 1895, 11; *New York Clipper*, February 25, 1893, 824; *ibid.*, October 19, 1895, 525; *New York Times*, February 21, 1893, 3:7; *ibid.*, March 1, 1893, 3:3.

[15]*National Police Gazette*, June 9, 1894, 11; *ibid.*, June 9, 1894, 11; *ibid.*, July 14, 1894, 10; *New York Clipper*, October 19, 1895, 525; *ibid.*, February 27, 1897, 834.

[16]*National Police Gazette*, July 13, 1895, 10; *ibid.*, July 20, 1895, 11; *New York Clipper*, July 6, 1895, 279; *New York Herald*, June 28, 1895; *New York World*, June 28, 1895; *New York Times*, June 28, 1895, 7:3.

[17]*New York Clipper*, July 6, 1895, 279; *New York Herald*, June 28, 1895.

[18]*National Police Gazette*, September 12, 1896, 11; *New York World*, September 1, 1896; *New York Herald*, September 1, 1896.

[19]Johnston, *Ten ... and Out!*, 118; William Inglis, *Champions off Guard* (New York: Vanguard Press, 1932), 21; William Inglis, "John L. Sullivan Collects a Little Bill," *New Yorker*, July 9, 1933, 36–38.

[20]*New York Times*, July 6, 1897, 4:1.

[21]David F. Trask, *The War with Spain in 1898* (New York: Macmillan, 1981), 156.

[22]*National Police Gazette*, September 1, 1900, 11; *ibid.*, September 15, 1900, 7; *New York Clipper*, August 18, 1900, 552.

[23]*National Police Gazette*, May 21, 1904, 10; *ibid.*, June 4, 1904, 10.

[24] *Ibid.*, September 24, 1904, 7; *St. Louis Daily Globe Democrat*, September 9, 1904, 4:3.

[25]*National Police Gazette*, October 8, 1892, 3; *ibid.*, October 22, 1892, 2; *New York Clipper*, October 8, 1892, 493; Alan Woods, "James J. Corbett: Theatrical Star," *Journal of Sport History* 3, no. 20 (1976): 163.

[26]*National Police Gazette*, March 10, 1894, 10; *ibid.*, April 7, 1894, 10; *ibid.*, April 14, 1894, 11; *ibid.*, September 8, 1894, 11; *ibid.*, September 15, 1894, 10; Woods, "James J. Corbett," 163–75; *Brooklyn Daily Eagle*, January 30, 1895, 4:7.

[27]*National Police Gazette*, January 19, 1895, 10; *ibid.*, February 9, 1895, 10; (Lincoln) *Nebraska State Journal*, January 13, 1895, 8:4; *Kansas City Star*, January 26, 1895, 5:4.

[28](Jacksonville) *Florida Times-Union*, February 22, 1895, 3:1; *ibid.*, February 23, 1895, 8:1; *ibid.*, February 24, 1895, 7:1.

[29]*Ibid.*, February 25, 1895, 2:3; *ibid.*, February 26, 1895, 8:1; *ibid.*, February 27, 1895, 5:1; *Boston Post*, August 29, 1895, 5:1; *National Police Gazette*, March 16, 1895, 11.

[30]Woods, "James J. Corbett," 163; *National Police Gazette*, October 19, 1895, 11; *ibid.*, January 11, 1896, 10.

[31]Woods, "James J. Corbett," 163; "How John L. Broke Up the Show," *Literary Digest*, May 15, 1926, 81; Russel B. Nye, *The Unembarrassed Muse: The Popular Arts in America* (New York: Dial Press, 1970), 154–55; *Providence Sunday Journal*, June 5, 1898; *ibid.*, December 29, 1901.

[32]*National Police Gazette*, February 6, 1897, 11; *New York Clipper*, March 13, 1897, 28.

[33]*New York City Directory* (1898–1902), Library of Congress; *National Police Gazette*, August 19, 1899, 11; *ibid.*, August 26, 1899, 11; *New York World*, August 4, 1899; *New York Clipper*, August 12, 1899, 469.

[34]*National Police Gazette*, June 16, 1900, 7; *New York Times*, May 23, 1900, 14:1; *New York Clipper*, April 21, 1900, 181.

[35]*National Police Gazette*, March 16, 1901, 10; *ibid.*, October 5, 1901, 10.

[36]*Ibid.*, May 13, 1899, 11; *ibid.*, May 27, 1899, 11; *ibid.*, July 1, 1899, 11.

[37]*Providence Journal*, August 19, 1901; *Washington Evening Star*, November 18, 1902; *Washington Post*, November 19, 1902; letter, Mrs. Maureen J. Sawyers (great-grandniece of John L. Sullivan) to author, February 15, 1985; *National Police Gazette*, October 7, 1905, 6.

[38]*National Police Gazette*, March 12, 1904, 11; *ibid.*, February 4, 1905, 6, 2.

[39]*Ibid.*, May 27, 1905, 10; *ibid.*, August 19, 1905, 10; *ibid.*, September 30, 1905, 3; *ibid.*, November 24, 1906, 6.

[40]*Chicago Record-Herald*, January 18, 1905, 4:4; *Chicago Inter Ocean*, January 17, 1905, 4:1; *Chicago Daily News*, January 17, 1905, 6:2; *Chicago Daily Tribune*, January 17, 1905, 3:4.

[41]*National Police Gazette*, April 20, 1895, 10; *ibid.*, November 14, 1896, 10; *ibid.*, December 26, 1896, 10; *New York Clipper*, November 7, 1896, 575.

[42]*Ibid.*, November 17, 1900, 10; *ibid.*, December 22, 1900, 7, 11; *New York Clipper*, November 3, 1900, 797; *ibid.*, December 15, 1900, 932.

[43]*National Police Gazette*, April 9, 1904, 10.

[44]Theodore Dreiser, *A Book about Myself* (New York: Boni and Liveright, 1922), 150–51.

[45]*National Police Gazette*, November 3, 1894, 11; *ibid.*, December 15, 1894, 10; *ibid.*, October 5, 1895, 11; *ibid.*, October 7, 1905, 6; *ibid.*, October 20, 1906, 6.

[46]*Ibid.*, October 22, 1892, 2.

[47]*New York Times*, April 11, 1900, 5:1; *ibid.*, May 16, 1900, 2:3.

[48]*Ibid.*, October 1, 1889, 2:5; *ibid.*, August 20, 1897, 1:3.

[49]*Boston Herald*, February 4, 1918; Theodore Roosevelt, *An Autobiography* (New York: Macmillan, 1913), 47–51; *Chicago Daily Tribune*, January 17, 1905, 3:4.

[50]Pierce Egan, *Boxiana: Sketches of Ancient and Modern Pugilism* (London: G. Smeeton, 1812), 5–6.

[51]Herbert Asbury, *Carry Nation: The Woman with the Hatchet* (New York: Knopf, 1929), passim; Carry A. Nation, *The Use and Need of the Life of Carry A. Nation* (Topeka, Kan: F. M. Steves and Sons, 1909), 299–300.

[52]*Boston Post*, August 17, 1895, 5:1; *National Police Gazette*, November 11, 1893, 11; *ibid.*, December 30, 1893, 10; *ibid.*, September 15, 1894, 10; *ibid.*, December 22, 1894, 10; *ibid.*, April 6, 1895, 10; *ibid.*, April 13, 1895, 10; *ibid.*, March 28, 1903, 10.

[53]*National Police Gazette*, January 10, 1903, 10; *Detroit Free Press*, December 14, 1902, 4, 10; *ibid.*, December 18, 1902, 3; *ibid.*, December 19, 1902, 5; *Detroit Evening News*, December 17, 1902, 1:7–8, 5:2.

[54]*New York Times*, May 16, 1893, 1:3; *ibid.*, May 17, 1893, 3:2; (Portland, Maine) *Daily Eastern Argus*, May 16, 1893, 1:5; *ibid.*, May 17, 1893, 1:1; *ibid.*, May 18, 1893, 1:6.

[55]*Brooklyn Daily Eagle*, August 17, 1894, 1:6; *ibid.*, September 22, 1896, 12:4; *Boston Post*, September 22, 1896, 3:4; *Boston Herald*, September 22, 1896, 7; *Boston Daily Globe*, September 22, 1896, 5:4; *New York Clipper*, October 10, 1896, 511.

[56](Springfield) *Illinois State Journal*, January 30, 1896, 6:3; *ibid.*, January 31, 1896, 5:3; *ibid.*, February 1, 1896, 6:3; *ibid.*, February 2, 1896, 5:5; *ibid.*, February 3, 1896, 6:2; *ibid.*, February 6, 1896, 6:3; (Springfield) *Illinois State Register*, January 30, 1896, 6:4; *ibid.*, February 1, 1896, 5:4; *ibid.*, February 4, 1896, 6:4; *New York Times*, January 30, 1896, 1:2; *ibid.*, January 31, 1896, 8:4; *National Police Gazette*, February 15, 1896, 11.

[57]*Boston Daily Globe*, December 23, 1896; *New York Times*, December 23, 1896, 1:4.

[58]*New York Clipper*, January 23, 1897, 752; *New York Times*, December 21, 1899, 4:6.

[59]*New York Sun*, July 21, 1900; *ibid.*, July 31, 1900; *ibid.*, December 20, 1900; *New York Times*, July 21, 1900, 7:1; *ibid.*, December 20, 1900, 6:4; *New York Daily Tribune*, July 21, 1900; *ibid.*, July 31, 1900.

[60]*National Police Gazette*, August 24, 1901, 7; *ibid.*, July 18, 1903, 10; *ibid.*, November 14, 1903, 10; *ibid.*, December 12, 1903, 10.

[61]*New York Herald*, November 29, 1902; *New York Times*, November 29, 1902, 16:2; *New York Daily Tribune*, November 29, 1902; *Brooklyn Daily Eagle*, December 9, 1902, 4:4.

[62]R. F. Dibble, *John L. Sullivan: An Intimate Narrative* (Boston: Little, Brown, 1925), 143-44; *National Police Gazette*, February 28, 1903, 6. There was a second McCormick, Jack, who fought out of Philadelphia as a heavyweight and who is often confused with Jim. Like the McAuliffes—heavyweight Joe and lightweight champion Jack, who also were unrelated—the two McCormicks were often mixed up by the press, including the *Grand Rapids Herald*. I am indebted to Bill Schutte for this information.

[63]*Grand Rapids Herald*, February 27, 1905; *ibid.*, March 2, 1905; *ibid.*, March 3, 1905; *National Police Gazette*, March 18, 1905, 3.

## CHAPTER FOURTEEN

[1]Joe Dorney and Sid Sutherland, "John L. Sullivan," *Liberty*, May 30, 1925, 31-32; " 'John L.,' Last of the Bare-fisted Fighters of the Ring," *Literary Digest*, February 23, 1918, 63-64.

[2]"John L.'s Best Fight," *Literary Digest*, September 7, 1912, 400-401; *Boston Herald*, February 4, 1918.

[3]Dorney and Sutherland, "John L. Sullivan," 31.

[4]John L. Sullivan to advertising manager, Ringling Brothers, November 17, 1908; Charles Ringling to John L. Sullivan, November 4, 1908; John L. Sullivan to Charles Ringling, November 20, 1908; all in Braathen Papers, Circus and Related Arts Collection, Illinois State University.

⁵*Pierre* (South Dakota) *Daily Capital-Journal*, October 4, 1909; *ibid.*, October 5, 1909; *ibid.*, October 8, 1909; John L. Sullivan to advertising manager, Ringling Brothers, November 17, 1908, in Braathen Papers.

⁶Joe Dorney and Sid Sutherland, "John L. Sullivan," *Liberty*, May 16, 1925, 40–41; Al-Tony Gilmore, *Bad Nigger! The National Impact of Jack Johnson* (Port Washington, N.Y.: Kennikat Press, 1975), 27–28.

⁷ *New York Times*, January 21, 1909, 7:4; *ibid.*, May 1, 1910, part 4, 1:2; *ibid.*, April 17, 1910, part 2, 1:4.

⁸*Ibid.*, June 5, 1910, part 4, 3:12; *ibid.*, June 16, 1910, 2:2; *ibid.*, June 15, 1910, 10:1.

⁹*Ibid.*, June 21, 1910, 4:2–3; *ibid.*, June 24, 1910, 1:2; *ibid.*, June 23, 1910, 6:4.

¹⁰Gilmore, *Bad Nigger!*, 30; Jack Johnson, *In the Ring and Out* (London: Proteus Publishing, 1977), 145; Edward Van Every, *Muldoon: The Solid Man of Sport* (New York: Frederick A. Stokes Co., 1929), 300–301.

¹¹John Durant, *The Heavyweight Champions*, 6th rev. ed. (New York: Hastings House, 1976), 59–60; *New York Times*, July 5, 1910, 1:7, 3, 4.

¹²*Ibid.*, February 22, 1907, 1:2; *ibid.*, March 1, 1907, 1:4.

¹³*Washington Evening Star*, May 17, 1907; Theodore Roosevelt to John L. Sullivan, April 4, 1907, in Theodore Roosevelt Papers, Library of Congress; *ibid.*, May 9, 1907; C. C. Wagner (acting private secretary to William Howard Taft) to John L. Sullivan, April 9, 1907, in William Howard Taft Papers, Library of Congress; Theodore Roosevelt, *An Autobiography* (New York: Macmillan, 1913), 51.

¹⁴Roosevelt, *An Autobiography*, 51; *Washington Evening Star*, May 17, 1907; Jack D. Foner, *Blacks and the Military in American History: A New Perspective* (New York: Praeger, 1974), 95–103; *New York Times*, May 17, 1907, 1:6. For the president's pardoning power, see Edward S. Corwin, with Randall W. Bland, Theodore T. Hindson, and Jack W. Peltason, *The President: Office and Powers, 1787–1984*, 5th rev. ed. (New York: New York University Press, 1984), 180–91.

¹⁵Mike Donovan to Theodore Roosevelt, May 22, 1912, in Theodore Roosevelt Papers, Library of Congress; *The Report of the Attorney General* (1907), 62, 76, lists Lennon as confined at Fort Leavenworth, which was probably originally intended as his destination.

¹⁶Theodore Roosevelt to John L. Sullivan, February 27, 1908, in Theodore Roosevelt Papers, Library of Congress; *ibid.*, April 17, 1908; *ibid.*, October 30, 1908; John L. Sullivan to Theodore Roosevelt, April 24, 1913, in the same papers.

¹⁷*New York Times*, December 13, 1908, part 3, 6:3; *Chicago Record-Herald*, December 13, 1908; *Chicago Inter Ocean*, December 13, 1908; *Providence Sunday Journal*, December 13, 1908, 9; Sullivan divorce, court record, Superior Court of Cook County, Illinois.

¹⁸*Boston Daily Globe*, February 8, 1910; *Boston Herald*, February 8, 1910; *New York Times*, February 8, 1910, 1:6; *Variety*, February 12, 1910, called Kate a "widow."

¹⁹*Boston Daily Globe*, February 8, 1910; *New York Times*, May 24, 1910, 4:3; *ibid.*, May 28, 1910, 11:1; *ibid.*, May 1, 1910, Part 4, 1:2.

[20]William Inglis, *Champions off Guard* (New York: Vanguard Press, 1932), 106; *New York Times*, June 27, 1911, 5:2; *ibid.*, July 17, 1911, 2:4.

[21]Joe Dorney and Sid Sutherland, "John L. Sullivan," *Liberty*, June 6, 1925, 32; *New York Times*, January 1, 1912, 7:3.

[22]Theodore Roosevelt to John L. Sullivan, May 2, 1913, in Theodore Roosevelt Papers, Library of Congress; *ibid.*, May 19, 1913; John L. Sullivan to Theodore Roosevelt, May 9, 1913, in the same papers; *ibid.*, May 19, 1913; *ibid.*, May 8, 1913.

[23]Joe Dorney and Sid Sutherland, "John L. Sullivan," *Liberty*, March 21, 1925, 9; Dorney and Sutherland, "John L. Sullivan," June 6, 1925, 32–33; *New York Times*, January 8, 1912, 3:6.

[24]"John L. Sullivan, Temperance Advocate," *Outlook*, October 27, 1915, 454–56.

[25]Theodore Roosevelt to John L. Sullivan, August 26, 1915, in Elting E. Morison, ed., *The Letters of Theodore Roosevelt* (Cambridge: Harvard University Press, 1954), 8:962; Same to Same, August 26, 1915, in Theodore Roosevelt Papers, Library of Congress.

[26]*New York Times*, June 24, 1915, 6:7; *ibid.*, July 3, 1915, 16:6; Russell F. Weigley, *History of the United States Army* (New York: Macmillan, 1967), 289–90.

[27]*New York Times*, July 7, 1915, 7:1; *ibid.*, July 9, 1915, 20:1; *ibid.*, July 10, 1915, 16:5; *Boston Evening Transcript*, July 7, 1915.

[28]*New York Times*, August 2, 1915, 4:7; *ibid.*, August 9, 1915, 5:3.

[29]*Ibid.*, August 11, 1906, 2:5; *ibid.*, October 8, 1915, 8:6; *Boston Evening Transcript*, October 7, 1915. The *Boston Post*, February 5, 1918, reported that Sullivan gave the Championship Belt to James King, a Baltimore horse dealer, "about ten years ago." But John L. probably died in possession of his prize.

[30]Durant, *The Heavyweight Champions*, 65; Joe Humphries, "A Thousand and One Fights," *Collier's*, July 14, 1928, 49; *New York Sun*, March 26, 1916.

[31]E. A. Carmeau, Jr., John Wilmerding, Linda Ayres, and Deborah Chotner, *Bellows: The Boxing Pictures* (Washington, D.C.: National Gallery of Art, 1982), 36–37; Durant, *The Heavyweight Champions*, 65.

[32]*Boston Globe*, May 26, 1916; *New York Times*, May 27, 1916, 11:4.

[33]John L. Sullivan to Theodore Roosevelt, March 25, 1916, in Theodore Roosevelt Papers, Library of Congress.

[34]Donald J. Mrozek, *Sport and American Mentality, 1880–1910* (Knoxville: University of Tennessee Press, 1983), 35; *New York Times*, May 12, 1917, 13:1.

[35]*Boston Post*, May 15, 1917; *Boston Globe*, May 15, 1917, 16; *Boston Herald*, May 15, 1917, 1.

[36]John L. Sullivan to Theodore Roosevelt, June 27, 1917, in Theodore Roosevelt Papers, Library of Congress; Theodore Roosevelt to John L. Sullivan, April 28, 1917, in the same papers; *ibid.*, May 17, 1917; *ibid.*, May 22, 1917; W. B. Masterson to Theodore Roosevelt, May 14, 1917, in the same papers.

[37]John L. Sullivan to Theodore Roosevelt, May 14, 1917, in the same papers; *ibid.*, May 19, 1917; *New York Sun*, May 12, 1917; Inglis, *Champions off Guard*, 107.

[38]*Boston Herald*, February 3, 1918, 1; *Boston Post*, February 3, 1918. Kelly's age in 1917 is variously given as twelve or fourteen.

[39]*Boston Post*, February 4, 1918; *Brooklyn Daily Eagle*, February 19, 1894, 8:2. William Kelly's adoption is called "probable" only because no adoption papers have been found. Suffolk County adoption records are "segregated" and unavailable. All newspaper accounts call him Sullivan's "adopted son."

[40]*Boston Post*, February 3, 1918; *ibid.*, February 4, 1918; *New York Times*, February 3, 1918, 2, 7:1.

[41]Vachel Lindsay, "John L. Sullivan, The Strong Boy of Boston," *New Republic*, July 16, 1919, 357–58.

[42]*Boston Post*, February 3, 1918, 1; *Boston Herald*, February 3, 1918, 1; *Boston Sunday Globe*, February 3, 1918, 1.

[43]Dorney and Sutherland, "John L. Sullivan," June 6, 1925, 35; *Boston Sunday Globe*, February 3, 1918, 1; *New York Times*, February 3, 1918, 2, 7:1; *Variety*, February 8, 1918, 10.

[44]*Boston Herald*, February 4, 1918; *ibid.*, February 5, 1918; *Boston Daily Globe*, February 4, 1918; *ibid.*, February 6, 1918; *New York Times*, February 4, 1918, 10:4; *ibid.*, February 5, 1918, 10:4.

[45]*Boston Post*, February 3, 1918; *ibid.*, February 4, 1918; *Boston Daily Globe*, February 5, 1918; *ibid.*, February 6, 1918; Van Every, *Muldoon*, 321–24.

[46]Inglis, *Champions off Guard*, 107; *New York Times*, February 5, 1918, 10:4; *ibid.*, February 6, 1918, 10:3; *Boston Daily Globe*, February 5, 1918.

[47]*Boston Daily Globe*, February 7, 1918; *Boston Herald*, February 6, 1918; *ibid.*, February 7, 1918; *New York Times*, February 5, 1918, 10:4; *ibid.*, February 7, 1918, 12:6; *ibid.*, February 10, 1918, part 3, 4:1; *ibid.*, February 11, 1918, 10:3; *Boston Post*, February 7, 1918.

[48]*Boston Pilot*, February 9, 1918, 8; "When Dynamite Was Used to Blast John L.'s Grave," *Literary Digest*, May 19, 1928, 65.

## EPILOGUE

[1]Edward Van Every, *Muldoon: The Solid Man of Sport* (New York: Frederick A. Stokes Co., 1929), 324; Marshall Stillman, *Mike Donovan: The Making of a Man* (New York: Moffat, Yard and Company, 1918), 282; Alexander Johnston, *Ten . . . and Out! The Complete Story of the Prize Ring in America* (New York: Ives Washburn, 1947), 204; Eileen Jennings (grandniece of Sullivan) to author, February 3, 1985.

[2]*New York Times*, February 19, 1933, 1:2, 32:1–8; *ibid.*, March 22, 1933, 15:4; *ibid.*, June 4, 1933, 32:1.

[3]*Ibid.*, December 23, 1937, 21:1–2.

[4]Henry Collins Brown, *New York in the Elegant Eighties* (Hastings-on-Hudson, N.Y.: Valentine's Manual, Inc., 1927), 364–65.

[5]Nat Fleischer, *John L. Sullivan: Champion of Champions* ((New York: G.P. Putnam's Sons, 1951), 197; "How John L. Broke Up the Show," *Literary Digest*, May 15, 1926, 81; Grantland Rice, "The Sportlight," New York *Tribune*, May 8, 1925.

[6]*Chicago Tribune*, November 9, 1957; Arthur Daley, "The Lost Belt of John L. Sullivan," *New York Times*, December 3, 1959, 50; *Hammond* (Ind.) *Times*,

November 5, 1957, p. 573. For citation of these sources I am grateful to Carl H. Scheele, Curator, Division of Community Life, National Museum of American History, Smithsonian Institution.

7John P. Marquand, Introduction to Donald Barr Chidsey, *John the Great: The Times and Life of a Remarkable American, John L. Sullivan* (Garden City, N.Y.: Doubleday, Doran and Company, Inc., 1942), xi.

8Johnny Hauck, "World's Famous Pugilists Box at the Fulton Opera House," *Journal of the Lancaster County Historical Society*, 79, No. 3 (1975), 147; Jack Dempsey, with Barbara Piatelli Dempsey, *Dempsey* (New York: Harper & Row, 1977), 7–8.

9Orrin E. Klapp, "The Folk Hero," *Journal of American Folklore*, 62, No. 243 (January–March, 1949), 19; Karl S. Bottigheimer, *Ireland and the Irish: A Short History* (New York: Columbia University Press, 1982), 47, 262.

10Chidsey, *John the Great*, 6, 50–51; John Durant, *The Heavyweight Champions* (6th Rev. ed.)(New York: Hastings House, 1976), 24; "The Death of a Notable American," *Outlook*, February 13, 1918, 236.

11"When Dynamite Was Used to Blast John L.'s Grave," *Literary Digest*, May 19, 1928, 64; " 'John L.,' Last of the Bare-fisted Fighters of the Ring," *ibid.*, February 23, 1918, 65; Joe Humphreys, "A Thousand and One Fights," *Collier's*, July 21, 1928, 41.

12Marjorie Smeltsor and Carol Billman, "Ballyhoo and Debunk: The Unmaking of American Political and Sports Heroes," *North Dakota Quarterly* 46, No. 3 (Summer, 1978), 5; Allen Guttmann, *From Ritual to Record: The Nature of Modern Sports* (New York: Columbia University Press, 1978), 25.

13Nick Salvatore, *Eugene V. Debs: Citizen and Socialist* (Urbana: University of Illinois Press, 1982), 19, 23.

14 *Ibid.*, 64; Nat Fleischer, *The Boston Strong Boy: The Story of John L. Sullivan, The Champion of Champions* (New York: Ring Magazine, 1941), 29; Theodore Roosevelt to Admiral French Ensor Chadwick, July 1, 1908, in Elting E. Morison, ed., *The Letters of Theodore Roosevelt* (Cambridge: Harvard University Press, 1952), 6:1103; R.F. Dibble, "Champion of Champions," *American Mercury*, July, 1924, 267; Joe Dorney and Sid Sutherland, "John L. Sullivan: The Life Story of 'The Most Popular Man Who Ever Lived,'" *Liberty*, April 18, 1925, 37.

15Oliver Carlson, *Brisbane: A Candid Biography* (New York: Stackpole Sons, 1937), 263; Mike Donovan, *The Roosevelt That I Know: Ten Years of Boxing with the President—and Other Memories of Famous Fighting Men*, ed. F.H.N. (New York: B.W. Dodge and Co., Inc., 1909), 231–34; Alan Woods, "James J. Corbett: Theatrical Star," *Journal of Sport History*, 3, no. 20 (1976), 173.

16Robert Edgren, "The Modern Gladiator," *Outing*, March 1903, 738–40; Richard Matthews Halley, "Throw Him Down, McCloskey," *Saturday Evening Post*, January 21, 1933, 10–11, 41–45.

17*New York Times*, December 2, 1883, 7:2; *National Police Gazette*, October 22, 1904, 3; Joe Humphries, "A Thousand and One Fights," *Collier's*, July 14, 1928, 18–19, 46.

18Fleischer, *The Boston Strong Boy*, 2; Edgren, "The Modern Gladiator," 736; Fleischer, *John L. Sullivan*, 104–5.

[19]Cameron Rogers, "Two Vivid Americans," *World's Work*, June, 1925, 198; Henry Collins Brown, *In the Golden Nineties* (Hastings-on-Hudson, N.Y.: Valentine's Manual, Inc.,) 332–33.

[20]Edmund Lester Pearson, "The Sometimes Noble Art," *Outlook*, July 1, 1925, 340.

[21]Millicent Bell, *Marquand: An American Life* (Boston: Little, Brown, 1979), 228; John P. Marquand, *The Late George Apley: A Novel in the Form of a Memoir* (Boston: Little, Brown, 1937); Mathias P. Harpin, *Trumpets in Jericho* (West Warwick, R.I.: Commercial Printing Publisher's Co., 1961); Harry Stein, *Hoopla* (New York: Alfred A. Knopf, 1983); Syd Hoff, *Gentleman Jim and the Great John L.* (New York: Coward, McCann, and Geohegan, 1977).

[22]Carlton C. Lahue, *Continued Next Week: A History of the Moving Picture Serial* (Norman: University of Oklahoma Press, 1964), 70, 77, 131–32; *The Great John L.* (United Artists, 1945); James Edward Grant, *The Great John L.* (Cleveland: World Publishing Company, 1945) (a "novelization" of the United Artists screenplay); *Gentleman Jim* (Warner Brothers, 1942).

[23]"Corbett to Tunney on 'How to Win the Mob,' " *Literary Digest*, January 14, 1928, 55; Fleischer, *John L. Sullivan*, ix, xii–xiii; Susan Strasser, *Never Done: A History of American Housework* (New York: Pantheon Books, 1982), 91.

[24]Interview with Mrs. Mary K. Collins, Old Calvary Cemetery, September 4, 1984.

# Bibliographic Essay

This essay is by no means exhaustive. In particular, I omit specific accounts of John L. Sullivan's prizefights, which are covered in detail in the notes. My purpose is to indicate those materials that were most helpful in forming a sense of Sullivan and his times.

* * * *

"Scrape the country over," John L. once said, " and you probably wouldn't round up more than a hundred letters written and signed by John L. Sullivan" (*New York Times*, January 8, 1912, 3:6). He was certainly right; today fugitive bits of correspondence, mostly from late in his life, can be found in the Theodore Roosevelt Papers, Library of Congress; Elting Morison, ed., *The Letters of Theodore Roosevelt*, 8 vols. (Cambridge: Harvard University Press, 1954); William Howard Taft Papers, Library of Congress; and Braathen Papers, Circus and Related Arts Collection, Milner Library, Illinois State University.

Therefore this book is a (deliberate) exercise in examining the life of a man who left tantalizingly little of direct historical value. Biographers love reams of intimate letters, diaries, memorandums, and published writings, the kinds of things usually produced by cultural elites. Sullivan left nothing of the sort. Apart from the correspondence mentioned above, the only personal written material that survives is mostly in the form of letters to sporting papers and the press. These are cited in the notes. As pertinent as a "psychobiography" of a character like John L. might be, the material for such an effort, even if one agreed with the general approach, does not exist.

The place to begin is the ghostwritten autobiography, *John L. Sullivan: Life and Reminiscences of a 19th Century Gladiator* (Boston: Jas. A. Hearn and Co., 1892). Inaccurate in spots and carrying the story only down to the Corbett fight, this source is nevertheless indispensable for understanding Sullivan's early years, his travels, and part of the essence of his extraordinary ego.

The biographers had at Sullivan almost immediately. In order of dates of publication, accounts of his life are: R. K. Fox, *Life and Battles of John L. Sullivan* (New York: Police Gazette, 1883, 1891); *The Modern Gladiator, Being an Account of the World's Greatest Fighter, John Lawrence Sullivan* (Saint Louis: Athletic Publishing Co., 1889), mostly a collection of press clippings; *Life and Fights of John L. Sullivan* (London: Health and Strength, 1909); R. F.

Dibble, *John L. Sullivan: An Intimate Narrative* (Boston: Little, Brown, 1925); Nat Fleischer, *The Boston Strong Boy: The Story of John L. Sullivan, the Champion of Champions* (New York: Ring Magazine, 1941); Donald Barr Chidsey, *John the Great: The Times and Life of a Remarkable American, John L. Sullivan* (Garden City, N.Y.: Doubleday, Doran and Co., 1942); Nat Fleischer, *John L. Sullivan: Champion of Champions* (New York: Putnam, 1951); and Gilbert Odd, *I Can Lick Any S.O.B. in the House* (London: Proteus Publishing Co., 1980). None of these is a scholarly biography; Chidsey's perhaps comes the closest.

In article form, Sullivan's life is covered extensively by Joe Dorney and Sid Sutherland, "John L. Sullivan: The Life Story of 'The Most Popular Man Who Ever Lived,' " 12 installments, *Liberty*, March 21–June 26, 1925. Wildly inaccurate and even fictitious in places, this series is valuable for its numerous rare photographs and becomes more reliable as it reaches Sullivan's later life. An interesting early assessment is Richard Barry, "John L. Sullivan, the Old Roman," *Pearson's Magazine*, September, 1912, 32–38; R. F. Dibble, "Champion of Champions," *American Mercury*, July 1924, 267–73, is catch-as-catch-can. The best of the modern accounts is John Durant, "Yours Truly, John L. Sullivan," *American Heritage*, August 1959, 55–59, 91–95.

Vignettes on Sullivan's life are far too numerous to list here. Some of my favorites occur in the *Literary Digest*, which could not resist Sullivan stories. A few of these are "John L.'s Best Fight," September 7, 1912, 400–401; " 'John L.,' Last of the Bare-fisted Fighters of the Ring," February 23, 1918, 60, 63–66; "How John L. Licked John Barleycorn," May 2, 1925, 39–40, 45; "How John L. Broke Up the Show," May 15, 1926, 81–82; "When Dynamite Was Used to Blast John L.'s Grave," May 19, 1928, 62, 64–65; and "John L. as a Literary Rival of Gene Tunney," January 12, 1929, 70–71. See also William Inglis, "The Night 'the Big Fellow' Went Out," *Harper's Weekly*, December 3, 1910, 15–16; "John L. Sullivan, Temperance Advocate," *Outlook*, October 27, 1915, 454–56; "The Death of a Notable American," *Outlook*, February 13, 1918, 235–36; Joe Humphries, "A Thousand and One Fights," 2 installments, *Collier's*, July 14, 1928, 18, 46–50, and July 21, 1928, 10, 40–41; and, most importantly, Stephen Bonsal, "Heyday in a Vanished World," *Scribner's Magazine*, June 1934, 412–16, 453–56, 15–20.

Very few men in Sullivan's world left their memoirs. Of these, by far the most important are Mike Donovan, *The Roosevelt That I Know: Ten Years of Boxing with the President—and Other Memories of Famous Fighting Men*, ed. F.H.N. (New York: B. W. Dodge and Co., 1909), and James J. Corbett, *The Roar of the Crowd: The True Tale of the Rise and Fall of a Champion* (New York: Grosset and Dunlap, 1925). Theodore Roosevelt, *An Autobiography* (New York: Macmillan, 1913), and Jack Johnson, *In the Ring and Out* (London: Proteus Publishing, 1977) are tangentially useful. W. J. Doherty, *In the Days of Giants: Memories of a Champion of the Prize-Ring* (London: George G. Harrap and Co., 1931) contains some bits of information.

Biographies of Sullivan's peers are likewise rare. These include Jack Kofoed, *Brandy for Heroes: A Biography of the Honorable John Morrissey, Champion Heavyweight of America and State Senator* (New York: Dutton, 1938); Marshall Stillman, *Mike Donovan: The Making of a Man* (New York: Moffat, Yard and Co., 1918); Edward Van Every, *Muldoon: The Solid Man of Sport* (New York: Frederick A. Stokes Co., 1929); W. O. McGeehan, "The Last Gladiator" (Muldoon), *Saturday Evening Post*, September 28, 1929, 37, 149–50, 153; William A. Harding, *Life and Battles of Jake Kilrain* (New York: Richard K. Fox, 1888); Richard Kyle Fox, *Life and Battles of James J. Corbett: Champion of the World* (New York: National Police Gazette, 1894); and Al-Tony Gilmore, *Bad Nigger! The National Impact of Jack Johnson* (Port Washington, N.Y.: Kennikat Press, 1975). All of these, including Gilmore's scholarly but slanted work, must be used with care.

Corbett's manager, William A. Brady, left two extremely biased memoirs, *The Fighting Man* (Indianapolis: Bobbs-Merrill, 1916), and *Showman* (New York: Dutton, 1937). For biographies that offer occasional insights into Sullivan's America, I prefer David McCullough, *Mornings on Horseback* (TR) (New York: Touchstone Books, 1981); Mark D. Hirsch, *William Whitney: Modern Warwick* (New York: Dodd, Mead, 1948); Oliver Carlson, *Brisbane: A Candid Biography* (New York: Stackpole Sons, 1937); Robert K. De Arment, *Bat Masterson: The Man and the Legend* (Norman: University of Oklahoma Press, 1979); and Parker Morell, *Diamond Jim: The Life and Times of James Buchanan Brady* (New York: Simon and Schuster, 1934).

The *Ring Record Book*, while incomplete on Sullivan's career, is indispensable for any student of boxing. For the numbers concerning John L.'s early life in Boston, I relied on *Historical Statistics of the United States, Colonial Times to 1857* (Washington, D.C.: U.S. Bureau of Commerce, 1960), and George Wingate Chase, *Abstract of the Census of Massachusetts, 1860* (Boston: Wright and Potter, 1863). The *Boston City Directory* and the *New York City Directory*, both in the Library of Congress, are useful in understanding the milieu of the two cities in which Sullivan spent most of his life. One special legal citation is of interest: *67 Mississippi Reports 352*, which deals with the appellate process following the Sullivan-Kilrain fight.

There are many modern studies of the cultural context of American sport, some of which are highly critical. Benjamin G. Rader, *American Sports: From the Age of Folk Games to the Age of Spectators* (Englewood Cliffs, N.J.: Prentice-Hall, 1983) is the best, while James A. Michener, *Sports in America* (New York: Fawcett Crest, 1977) is the most readable. Interpretative studies include Johan Huizinga, *Homo Ludens: A Study of the Play Element in Culture* (Boston: Beacon Press, 1955); John Dizikes, *Sportsmen and Gamesmen: From the Years that Shaped American Ideas about Winning and Losing and How to Play the Game* (Boston: Houghton Mifflin, 1981); Allen Guttmann, *From Ritual to Record: The Nature of Modern Sports* (New York: Columbia University Press, 1978); Donald J. Mrozek, *Sport and American Mentality, 1880–1910* (Knoxville: University of Tennessee Press, 1983); Harvey Green, *Fit for America: Health, Fitness, Sport and American Society* (New York: Pantheon Books, 1986); Frederick L. Paxson, "The Rise of Sport," *Mississippi Valley Historical Review* 4, no. 2 (September 1917): 143–68 (an older but still useful view); and John Rickards Betts, "The Technological Revolution and the Rise of Sport, 1850–1900," *Mississippi Valley Historical Review* 40, no. 2 (September 1953): 231–56. The recent approaches are nicely summed up by Benjamin G. Rader,

"Modern Sports: In Search of Interpretations," *Journal of Social History* 13, no. 2 (Winter 1979): 307–21.

For the English ancestry of American boxing, see Pierce Egan, *Boxiana: Sketches of Ancient and Modern Pugilism* (London: G. Smeeton, 1812); Bohun Lynch [John Gilbert], *The Prize Ring* (London: Country Life, 1925); and John Ford, *Prizefighting: The Age of Regency Boximania* (New York: Great Albion Books, 1971). General treatments of American boxing vary widely in quality; I have found the following helpful: Robert M. DeWitt, *The American Fistiana, Showing the Progress of Pugilism in the United States from 1816 to 1873* (New York: Robert M. DeWitt, 1873); W. W. Naughton, *Kings of the Queensberry Realm* (Chicago: Continental Publishing Co., 1902); Tom S. Andrews, *Ring Battles of Centuries*, rev. ed. (n.p.: Tom Andrews Record Book Co., 1924); William Inglis, *Champions off Guard* (New York: Vanguard Press, 1932); Nat Fleischer, *Black Dynamite: The Story of the Negro in the Prize Ring from 1782 to 1938*, 4 vols. (New York: Ring Athletic Library, 1938); Alexander Johnston, *Ten . . . and Out! The Complete Story of the Prize Ring in America*, 3rd rev. ed. (New York: Ives Washburn, 1947); Joseph Abbott Liebling, *The Sweet Science* (New York: Viking Press, 1956); Rex Lardner, *The Legendary Champions* (New York: American Heritage Press, 1972); and John V. Grombach, *The Saga of the Fist: The 9,000 Year Story of Boxing in Text and Pictures* (New York: A. A. Barnes and Co., 1977).

The heavyweights have their particular chroniclers, also varying widely in quality. I have relied on William E. Harding, *The Champions of the American Prize Ring: A Complete History of the Heavy-weight Champions of America with Their Battles and Portraits* (New York: Police Gazette, 1881); Barrett O'Hara, *From Figg to Johnson: A Complete History of the Heavyweight Championship* (Chicago: Blossom Book Bourse, 1909); Nat Fleischer, *The Heavyweight Championship: An Informal History of Boxing from 1719 to the Present Day* (New York: Ring Magazine, 1949); John Lardner, "The Big Man with the Biggest Punch," *New York Times Magazine*, August 26, 1956, 16, 34, 38; Stanley Weston, *The Heavyweight Champions* (New York: Ace Books, 1970); and John Durant, *The Heavyweight Champions*, 6th ed. (New York: Hastings House, 1976).

The bare-knucklers can best be followed in Randy Roberts, "Eighteenth Century Boxing," *Journal of Sport History* 4, no. 3 (Fall 1977): 246–59; Lawrence Hulton, "Prize-fighting in the Olden Times," *Harper's Weekly*, August 31, 1895, 825–26; Joan F. Loubet, "Bare Knuckles: A Forgotten Era in Boxing," *Ring Magazine*, March 1979, 63–74; and, most importantly, in Elliott Gorn, *The Manly Art: Bare-Knuckle Prize Fighting in America* (Ithaca: Cornell University Press, 1986).

Special studies relating sport and boxing to specific localities include Stephen Hardy, *How Boston Played: Sport, Recreation and Community, 1865–1915* (Boston: Northeastern University Press, 1982); Melvin L. Adelman, *A Sporting Time: New York City and the Rise of Modern Athletics, 1820–1870* (Urbana: University of Illinois Press, 1986); William H. Adams, "New Orleans as the National Center of Boxing," *Louisiana Historical Quarterly* 39 (January 1956): 92–112; Dale A. Somers, *The Rise of Sports in New Orleans, 1850–1900* (Baton Rouge: Louisiana State University Press, 1972); Thomas M. Croak, "The Professionalization of Prizefighting: Pittsburgh at the Turn of the Century," *Western Pennsylvania Historical Magazine* 62, no. 4 (1979): 333–43; and Johnny Hauck, "World's Famous Pugilists Box at the Fulton Opera House," *Journal of the Lancaster County Historical Society* 79, no. 3 (1975): 142–49.

Very few scholarly studies exist that relate boxing to its social and intellectual background. I have profited from examining S. Kirson Weinberg and Henry Arond, "The Occupational Culture of the Boxer," *American Journal of Sociology* 57, no. 5 (March 1952): 460–69; John R. Betts, "Mind and Body in Early American Thought," *Journal of American History* 54, no. 4 (March 1968): 787–805; R. Terry Furst, "Boxing Stereotypes versus the Culture of the Professional Boxer: A Sociological 'Decision,' " *Sport Sociology Bulletin* 3, no. 2 (Spring 1974): 13–39; and James E. Marlow, "Popular Culture, Pugilism, and Pickwick," *Journal of Popular Culture* 15, no. 4 (Spring 1982): 16–30.

The contemporary debate over the value of boxing in Sullivan's era can best be followed in John Boyle O'Reilly, *Ethics of Boxing and Manly Sport* (Boston: Ticknor and Company, 1888); John Boyle O'Reilly, *Athletics and Manly Sport* (Boston: Pilot Publishing Co., 1890); "The Evils of the Professional Tendency of Modern Athletics," *Outing*, February 1885, 379; Duffield Osborne, "A Defense of Pugilism," *North American Review*, April 1888, 430–35; A. Austen, "A Bout with the Gloves," *Outing*, March 1891, 447–52; A. Austen, "A Plea for Style in Boxing," *Outing*, November 1891, 140–43; Clarence Greeley, "Public Opinion vs. Prize-fighting," *Outlook*, November 18, 1893, 888–89; Robert Edgren, "The Modern Gladiator: Why the American Succeeds—Brute Strength Superseded by Scientific Cleverness," *Outing*, March 1903, 735–47; Robert Edgren, "Fighters by Nature," *Outing*, December 1903, 343–46; and Lamar W. Bridges, "An Editor's Views on Anti-Cruelty: Eliza Jane Nicholson of the *Picayune*," *Journal of Mississippi History* 39, no. 4 (1977): 303–16. The moralist's position is put most strongly by George C. Bernard, *The Morality of Prizefighting* (Washington, D.C.: Catholic University of America Press, 1952).

There are many treatments of the Gilded Age. Useful introductions are Robert H. Walker, Jr., *Life in the Age of Enterprise, 1865–1900* (New York: Capricorn Books, 1970), and Sean Dennis Cashman, *America in the Gilded Age: From the Death of Lincoln to the Rise of Theodore Roosevelt* (New York: New York University Press, 1984). The best introductions to the urbanization process are Sam Bass Warner, Jr., *The Urban Wilderness: A History of the American City* (New York: Harper and Row, 1972), and Gunther Barth, *City People: The Rise of Modern City Culture in Nineteenth-Century America* (New York: Oxford University Press, 1980). Of particular intellectual interest is Jackson Lears, *No Place of Grace: Antimodernism and the Transformation of American Culture, 1880–1920* (New York: Pantheon Books, 1981).

Sullivan, when not traveling, spent most of his life in either Boston or New York. For Boston, I relied heavily on Walter Muir Whitehill, *Boston: A Topographical History*, 2nd ed. (Cambridge: Harvard University Press, 1968); Arthur Wellington Brayley, *Schools and Schoolboys of Old Boston: An Historical Chronicle of the Public Schools of Boston from 1636 to 1844, to Which Is Added a Series of Biographical Sketches, with Portraits of Some of the Old Schoolboys of Boston* (Boston: Louis P. Hager, 1844); Edward H. Savage, *Police*

*Records and Recollections; or, Boston by Daylight and Gaslight for Two Hundred and Forty Years* (Montclair, N.J.: Patterson Smith, 1971 [1873]); Justin Winsor, ed., *The Memorial History of Boston, Including Suffolk County, Massachusetts, 1630–1880*, 4 vols. (Boston: James R. Osgood and Co., 1880–81); Charles Phillips Huse, *The Financial History of Boston from May 1, 1822, to January 31, 1909* (New York: Russell and Russell, 1916); Peter R. Knights, *The Plain People of Boston, 1830–1860: A Study in City Growth* (New York: Oxford University Press, 1971); and, of crucial importance for this study, Stephen Thernstrom, *The Other Bostonians: Poverty and Progress in the American Metropolis, 1880–1970* (Cambridge: Harvard University Press, 1973).

For New York, particularly juicy evidence of Sullivan's urban world can be lifted from James D. McCabe, Jr., *Lights and Shadows of New York Life; or, the Sights and Sensations of the Great City* (Philadelphia: National Publishing Company, 1872); J. W. Buel, *Metropolitan Life Unveiled; or the Mysteries and Miseries of America's Great Cities, Embracing New York, Washington City, San Francisco, Salt Lake City, and New Orleans* (Saint Louis: Historical Publishing Co., 1882); Herbert Asbury, *The Gangs of New York: An Informal History of the Underworld* (Garden City, N.Y.: Garden City Publishing Co., 1928); Edward Van Every, *Sins of New York as "Exposed" by the Police Gazette* (Detroit: Gale Research Co., 1976 [1930]); Zander Hollander, ed., *Madison Square Garden: A Century of Sport and Spectacle on the World's Most Versatile Stage* (New York: Hawthorn Books, 1973); and James F. Richardson, *The New York Police: Colonial Times to 1901* (New York: Oxford University Press, 1970). Interesting comparative studies include Michael B. Katz, *People of Hamilton, Canada West: Family and Class in a Mid-Nineteenth Century City* (Cambridge: Harvard University Press, 1976), and Paul E. Johnson, *A Shopkeeper's Millenium: Society and Revivals in Rochester, New York, 1815–1837* (New York: Hill and Wang, 1978).

The problems of ethnic acculturation in the urban wilderness are treated in Robert A. Woods, ed., *The City Wilderness: A Settlement Study* (Boston: Houghton Mifflin, 1898); Robert A. Woods, ed., *Americans in Process: A Settlement Study* (Boston: Houghton Mifflin, 1903); Robert A. Woods and Albert J. Kennedy, *The Zone of Emergence: Observations of the Lower Middle and Upper Working Class Communities of Boston, 1905–1914*, 2nd ed. (Cambridge: M.I.T. Press, 1962); E. P. Hutchinson, *Immigrants and Their Children, 1850–1950* (New York: Russell and Russell, 1976 [1956]); Stanley Lieberson, *Ethnic Patterns in American Cities* (New York: Free Press of Glencoe, 1963); and Katherine Neils Conzen, "Immigrants, Immigrant Neighborhoods, and Ethnic Identity: Historical Issues," *Journal of American History* 66, no. 3 (December 1979): 603–15.

The Irish experience in America was central to Sullivan's life. A good general background introduction is Karl S. Bottigheimer, *Ireland and the Irish: A Short History* (New York: Columbia University Press, 1982). Excellent modern studies include Carl Wittke, *The Irish in America* (Baton Rouge: Louisiana State University Press, 1956); George W. Potter, *To the Golden Door* (Boston: Little, Brown, 1960); William Shannon, *The American Irish* (New York: Macmillan, 1963); and Thomas Brown, *Irish-American Nationalism* (Philadelphia: J. B. Lippincott, 1966). Genealogy can be unraveled through John Rooney, *A Ge-*

*nealogical History of Irish Families, with Their Crests and Armorial Bearing* (Washington, D.C.: Library of Congress, 1895). Classic contemporary accounts that include views of the Irish situation in the New World are J. Hector St. John de Crèvecoeur, *Letters from an American Farmer and Sketches of 18th-Century America*, ed. Albert E. Stone (New York: Penguin, 1981); Alexis de Tocqueville, *Democracy in America*, 2 vols. (New York: Knopf, 1980); Thomas Colley Grattan, *Civilized America*, vol. 2 (London: Bradbury and Evans, 1859); and Edward Dicey, *Six Months in the Federal States*, vol. 2 (London: Macmillan, 1863). The religious dimension in the response to the wave of Irish Catholics is covered in Martin E. Marty, *Righteous Empire: The Protestant Experience in America* (New York: Harper and Row, 1977).

For the Boston Irish, I was greatly aided by the following: Jeremiah O'Donovan, *A Brief Account of the Author's Interview with His Countrymen, and of the Parts of the Emerald Isle Whence They Emigrated, Together with a Direct Reference to Their Present Location in the Land of Their Adoption, Among His Travels Through Various States of the Union in 1854 and 1855* (Pittsburgh: Jeremiah O'Donovan, 1854); James Bernard Cullen, ed., *The Story of the Irish in Boston, Together with Biographical Sketches of Representative Men and Noted Women* (Boston: James B. Cullen and Co., 1889); Frederick A. Bushee, *Ethnic Factors in the Population of Boston* (New York: Macmillan, 1903); Oscar Handlin, *Boston's Immigrants, 1790–1880: A Study in Acculturation*, rev. ed. (New York: Atheneum, 1974) (of great importance); and Dennis P. Ryan, *Beyond the Ballot Box: A Social History of the Boston Irish* (Rutherford, N.J.: Fairleigh Dickinson University Press, 1983). The response to the Irish influx can be followed in Arthur Mann, *Yankee Reformers in the Urban Age: Social Reform in Boston, 1880–1900* (Chicago: University of Chicago Press, 1974 [1954]), and Barbara Miller Solomon, *Ancestors and Immigrants: A Changing New England Tradition* (Chicago: University of Chicago Press, 1972 [1956]).

Sullivan provided a new dimension of the American hero. For the traditional view, see Dixon Wecter, *The Hero in America: A Chronicle of Hero-Worship* (New York: Scribner's, 1941). I have also been influenced by John Cawelti, *Apostles of the Self-made Man* (Chicago: University of Chicago Press, 1968); Conal Furay, *The Grass-Roots Mind in America: The American Sense of Absolutes* (New York: New Viewpoints, 1977); and three articles by Orrin E. Klapp: "Hero Worship in America," *American Sociological Review* 14, no. 1 (February 1949): 53–62; "The Folk Hero," *Journal of American Folklore* 62, no. 243 (January–March 1949): 17–25; and "Heroes, Villains, and Fools, as Agents of Social Control," *American Sociological Review* 19, no. 1 (February 1954): 56–62. Of special interest is Marjorie Smeltsor and Carol Billman, "Ballyhoo and Debunk: The Unmaking of American Political and Sports Heroes," *North Dakota Quarterly* 46, no. 3 (Summer 1978): 4–11.

The beginning point for the study of the mythic aspects of Sullivan is Richard M. Dorson, *America in Legend: Folklore from the Colonial Period to the Present* (New York: Pantheon Books, 1973); supplements are James O. Robertson, *American Myth, American Reality* (New York: Hill and Wang, 1980); Susan P. Montague and W. Arens, eds., *The American Dimension: Cultural Myths and Social Realities*, 2nd ed. (Sherman Oaks, Calif.: Alfred Publishing

Co., 1981); and Tristram Potter Coffin and Hennig Cohen, eds., *The Parade of Heroes: Legendary Figures in American Lore* (Garden City, N.Y.: Doubleday [Anchor], 1978).

My ideas on the cult of masculinity were shaped most by Peter N. Stearns, *Be a Man! Males in Modern Society* (New York: Holmes and Meier Publishers, 1979); Andrew Sinclair, *The Emancipation of the American Woman* (New York: Harper and Row, 1966 [1965]); William Leach, *True Love and Perfect Union: The Feminist Reform of Sex and Society* (New York: Basic Books, 1980); Hasia R. Diner, *Erin's Daughters in America: Irish Immigrant Women in the Nineteenth Century* (Baltimore: Johns Hopkins University Press, 1983); William O'Neill, *Divorce in the Progressive Era* (New York: New Viewpoints, 1973 [1967]); Carl F. Kaestle, *Pillars of the Republic: Common Schools and American Society, 1780–1860* (New York: Hill and Wang, 1983); and, for an early reformer's view, Newman Smyth, *Social Problems: Sermons to Workingmen* (Boston: Houghton Mifflin, 1885).

Much of Sullivan's life revolved around his alcoholism, and here I have been fortunate in having three excellent works on which to draw: W. J. Rorabaugh, *The Alcoholic Republic: An American Tradition* (New York: Oxford University Press, 1979); Richard Stivers, *A Hair of the Dog: Irish Drinking and American Stereotype* (University Park: Pennsylvania State University Press, 1976); and Perry R. Duis, *The Saloon: Public Drinking in Chicago and Boston, 1880–1920* (Urbana: University of Illinois Press, 1983).

The question of comparative rates of violence in different areas of America during the Gilded Age is an extremely difficult one. The following were for me the most suggestive: Roger Lane, *Violent Death in the City: Suicide, Accident and Murder in 19th Century Philadelphia* (Cambridge: Harvard University Press, 1979); Robert R. Dykstra, *The Cattle Towns* (New York: Knopf, 1971); Dickson D. Bruce, Jr., *Violence and Culture in the Antebellum South* (Austin: University of Texas Press, 1979); Bertram Wyatt-Brown, *Southern Honor: Ethics and Behavior in the Old South* (New York: Oxford University Press, 1982); Edward L. Ayers, *Vengeance and Justice: Crime and Punishment in the 19th-Century American South* (New York: Oxford University Press, 1986 [1984]); Elliott J. Gorn, " 'Gouge and Bite, Pull Hair and Scratch:' The Social Significance of Fighting in the Southern Backcountry," *American Historical Review* 90, no. 1 (February 1985): 18–43; Theodore N. Ferdinand, "The Criminal Patterns of Boston since 1849," *American Journal of Sociology* 73, no. 1 (July 1967): 84–99; and Roger Lane, "Urbanization and Criminal Violence in the 19th Century: Massachusetts as a Test Case," in Hugh Davis Graham and Ted Robert Gurr, eds., *The History of Violence in America: Historical and Comparative Perspectives* (New York: Praeger, 1969), 468–84.

Much of this work is built on the record of the press. The popular press, which tied Sullivan's America together, can be approached through John Rickards Betts, "Sporting Journalism in Nineteenth-Century America," *American Quarterly* 5 (Spring 1953): 39–56; Simon Michael Bessie, *Jazz Journalism: The Story of the Tabloid Newspapers* (New York: Dutton, 1938); Michael Schudson, *Discovering the News: A Social History of American Newspapers* (New York: Basic Books, 1978); and two articles by Walter Davenport in *Collier's*: "The

Nickel Shocker," March 10, 1928, 26, 28, 38, 40, and "The Dirt Disher," March 24, 1928, 26, 30, 52–53.

Of the Big Three of sporting journalism, the *New York Clipper* is of considerable assistance, although after the turn of the century it cut down its sports coverage and turned to the theater, vaudeville, and the circus. *The Spirit of the Times* covered "amateur" sports—everything from lacrosse to billiards, with the accent on the turf. Its coverage of boxing, particularly prizefighting, is extremely limited. The bulk of the evidence from the sporting press comes from that most unreliable of sheets, Richard Kyle Fox's outrageous *National Police Gazette*. Since this is probably one of the few scholarly books ever printed to place Fox's pink-tinted rag so squarely on the witness stand, a word or two—not of apology for him, but of explanation—is in order. First, Fox was publishing for an audience eager for the sporting "records" of the industrial age, and the *Gazette*, despite its decidedly low tone, usually tried to get the basic facts straight—names, dates, places. This paper is often the only place to go for the more arcane details of Sullivan's career, and one of the tasks of the historian is to go where the evidence is. Second, the *Gazette* is so patently obvious when its bias is present (as it almost always is) that the historian has little difficulty in sorting out the badly needed fact from the extraneous or trivial opinion. I owe a great debt to Fox, and would have loved to see him in action; he certainly deserves a biography.

Of the other specialized papers and periodicals, *Variety* has bits on Sullivan's stage career, but not much. I also drew on the files of *Frank Leslie's Illustrated Newspaper*, the *Nation*, and the old *Life*. The *Melbourne Australasian* is a helpful source for the Australian tour.

John L. can best be followed through his numerous travels around the country and overseas in the pages of the local press. Pieces of Sullivan's story are doubtless squirreled away in the newspaper morgues of virtually every city and town through which he passed. I have tried to hit the major ones: *Atchison* (Kansas) *Globe, Atlanta Constitution, Atlanta Journal, Baltimore Sun, Boston (Daily) Globe, Boston Evening Transcript, Boston Herald, Boston Journal, Boston Pilot, Boston Post, Brooklyn Daily Eagle, Charleston News and Courier, Chicago Daily News, Chicago Inter Ocean, Chicago Record-Herald, Chicago Tribune, Cincinnati Commercial Gazette, Cincinnati (Daily) Enquirer, Cincinnati Daily Gazette, Cleveland Press,* (Columbus) *Ohio State Journal,* (Denver) *Rocky Mountain News,* (Des Moines) *Iowa State Register, Detroit Evening News, Detroit Free Press,* (Eugene) *Oregon State Journal, Galveston Daily News, Grand Rapids* (Michigan) *Herald, Hammond* (Indiana) *Times, Harrisburg* (Pennsylvania) *(Daily) Patriot, Indianapolis Sentinel,* (Jacksonville) *Florida Times-Union, Kansas City Star, Leavenworth* (Kansas) *Times,* (Little Rock) *Daily Arkansas Gazette,* (Lincoln) *Nebraska State Journal, London Daily News, London Daily Telegraph, Louisville Courier-Journal, Memphis Daily Appeal, Minneapolis (Daily Minnesota) Tribune, Mobile Daily Register, Nashville Daily American, Natchez* (Mississippi) *Daily Democrat, New Orleans Daily Picayune, New Orleans Times-Democrat, New York Daily News, New York Daily Tribune, New York Herald, New York Sun, New York Times, New York World, Omaha Daily Republican, Pall Mall Gazette* (London), *Philadelphia Inquirer, Philadelphia Press, Pierre* (South Dakota) *Daily Capital-Journal, Pittsburgh Dis-*

*patch*, (Portland, Maine) *Daily Eastern Argus*, (Portland) *Morning Oregonian*, *Providence Evening Bulletin*, *Providence Evening Press*, *Providence Journal*, (Pueblo) *Colorado Chieftain*, (Reno) *Daily Nevada State Journal*, *Richmond Daily Dispatch*, *Rochester* (New York) *Daily Union and Advertiser*, *Rochester* (New York) *Democrat and Chronicle*, *Saint Louis Globe-Democrat*, Saint Louis *Missouri Republican*, *Saint Paul and Minneapolis Pioneer Press*, *Salt Lake City Daily Tribune*, (Salt Lake City) *Deseret Evening News*, *San Francisco Chronicle*, *San Francisco Examiner*, *Savannah Morning News*, *Seattle Daily Post-Intelligencer*, (Springfield) *Illinois State Journal*, (Springfield) *Illinois State Register*, *Tacoma Daily News*, (Topeka) *Daily Kansas State Journal*, (Tucson) *Arizona Weekly Citizen*, *Virginia City* (Nevada) *Daily Territorial Enterprise*, *Washington* (D.C.) *(Evening) Star*, *Washington* (D.C.) *Post*, and *Wheeling* (West Virginia) *Register*.

John L. has made occasional appearances in works of art, fiction, and film. The George Bellows paintings are in E. A. Carmeau, Jr., John Wilmerding, Linda Ayres, and Deborah Chotner, *Bellows: The Boxing Pictures* (Washington, D.C.: National Gallery of Art, 1982). Vachel Lindsay's nostalgic paean to Sullivan was first printed as "John L. Sullivan, The Strong Boy of Boston," *New Republic*, July 16, 1919, 357–58.

Good fictional introductions to nineteenth- and early-twentieth-century Irish life in Boston are, for the lighter side, Aloan F. Sanborn, *Meg McIntyre's Raffle and Other Stories* (Boston: Copeland and Day, 1896); and, more seriously, Joseph F. Dineen, *Ward Eight* (New York: Harper and Brothers, 1936). For John L.'s appearances in fiction, see Richard Matthews Healy, "Throw Him Down, McCloskey," *Saturday Evening Post*, January 21, 1933, 10–11, 41–45; John P. Marquand, *The Late George Apley: A Novel in the Form of a Memoir* (Boston: Little, Brown, 1937); Syd Hoff, *Gentleman Jim and the Great John L.* (New York: Coward, McCann, and Geohegan, 1977) (children's book); and Harry Stein, *Hoopla* (New York: Knopf, 1983).

Motion pictures featuring Sullivan include *Gentleman Jim* (Warner Brothers, 1942), and *The Great John L.* (United Artists, 1945). James Edward Grant, *The Great John L.* (Cleveland: World Publishing Co., 1945) is a "novelization" of the United Artists screenplay.

\* \* \* \*

Like my subject, I have tried to be "always on the level." But Sullivan's life is so filled with apochrypha and hyperbole that patent untruths and downright lies have doubtless crept into this biographical study. I welcome, in what I hope is the best tradition of historical research, any corrections of fact or notices of error. The interpretations herein, of course, are my own.

# Index

# Note on the Author

Michael T. Isenberg is assistant professor of history at the United States Naval Academy. He is the author of *The Puzzles of the Past: An Introduction to Thinking About History* and *War on Film: The American Cinema and World War I, 1914–1941.*

University of Illinois Press
1325 South Oak Street
Champaign, Illinois 61820-6903
www.press.uillinois.edu